REASONABLE DOUBT

Also by Henry Hurt
Shadrin: The Spy Who Never Came Back

·HENRY HURT·

REASONABLE DOUBT

An Investigation into
the Assassination of
John F. Kennedy

HOLT, RINEHART AND WINSTON • NEW YORK

Copyright © 1985 by Henry Hurt
All rights reserved, including the right to reproduce
this book or portions thereof in any form.
First published in January 1986 by Holt, Rinehart and Winston,
383 Madison Avenue, New York, New York 10017.
Published simultaneously in Canada by Holt, Rinehart
and Winston of Canada, Limited.

Library of Congress Cataloging in Publication Data
Hurt, Henry.
Reasonable doubt.
Bibliography: p.
Includes index.
1. Kennedy, John F. (John Fitzgerald), 1917–1963—
Assassination. I. Title.
E842.9.H84 1985   973.922'092'4   85–7571
ISBN 0-03-004059-0

First Edition

Designer: Victoria Hartman
Printed in the United States of America
10 9 8 7 6 5 4 3 2 1

ISBN 0-03-004059-0

For
Fulton Oursler, Jr., and Edward T. Thompson

• • •

Vision, Courage, Integrity

Contents

32 pages of photographs follow pages 132 and 262

Acknowledgments

It is clear throughout these pages that the greatest contribution lies in the massive work of the independent critics and researchers who have so meticulously investigated every aspect of the Kennedy assassination. It has been no small undertaking to draw from their diverse work a coherent and cohesive presentation of the salient points. It is important to note, nonetheless, that no assertion by these critics has been taken for granted. Whenever possible, and with few exceptions, every fact has been checked against the original source.

Of all the professional guidance, none has been more important than the wisdom and genius of Fulton Oursler, Jr. As my editor, he has worked with me at every step, from the book's conception to its completion. As my friend, too, his support and counsel have been essential. Edward T. Thompson approved the book project, and it is his confidence and support that made it go forward. The book is dedicated to Mr. Thompson and Mr. Oursler, a small reflection of the enormous esteem I have for them as editors and as men.

Caroline Sissi Maleki is responsible for coordinating all the research checking. She has persisted in documenting every factual assertion. In cases where the documentary support could not be found, Miss Maleki has prevailed in seeing that the material was deleted from the text. In other cases, her dogged pursuit of an elusive fact has bolstered the integrity of the book. Her persistence also has served to strip minor imperfections from certain assertions so that they can contribute fully to the thrust of the work. My debt to Sissi Maleki is enormous.

Steven Frimmer's incisive pencil is responsible for the original editing of the manuscript. Not only am I grateful for his adroitness as an editor, but I feel much gratitude for his good humor and patient guidance. David O. Fuller's wise legal counsel has been a mainstay from the very inception of the book.

Others who have contributed mightily include Mary Lyn Maiscott, who copy-edited the manuscript and worked diligently on the footnotes, Joanne Frasene, Susan Bernstein, and Nancy Tafoya. Those who helped in other ways are Rose Mermer and Dorothy Kavanaugh.

A considerable portion of the original research pertains to the confession of Robert W. Easterling. Thomas K. Noonan, a private researcher, was intimately involved in the development of many aspects of the Easterling story. Several of the significant breakthroughs are the direct result of Mr. Noonan's work. He is a superb field investigator with an uncanny ability to locate people who long ago faded into obscurity. His contributions are found throughout the book. I am grateful for his work as well as his friendship.

The specific contributions of various assassination critics are described in the book. However, many of those critics have been particularly helpful, several spending hundreds of hours volunteering their skills in the pursuit of facts and documents. I owe special gratitude to Mary Ferrell of Dallas, one of the most brilliant of the critics, who has amassed a fabulous store of documents on the assassination. She has spent hundreds of hours assisting this project.

I also owe particular appreciation to Harold Weisberg, who critiqued large portions of the manuscript. Though Mr. Weisberg often expressed sharp disagreement with my approach to certain aspects of the case, he remained unfailingly willing to assist. Sylvia Meagher has given generously of her time and intellectual resources in reviewing the manuscript and offering criticism.

In any undertaking of this magnitude, special relationships develop. Ways of understanding each other arise that enormously enhance the whole process of writing a book like this. In this respect, I owe special thanks to J. Gary Shaw and Paul L. Hoch, who have spent countless hours of consultation and guidance as I sorted through the morass of the Kennedy case. Their frank and often contrasting perspectives—as well as their friendship—have helped me find balance in areas where, at times, it seemed impossible to attain.

Others who have been of considerable help in reviewing the manuscript, as well as digging out obscure books and documents, include Bernard Fensterwald, Jr., James H. Lesar, Arch P. Kimbrough, and

Dan O'Keefe. Others who have been helpful include Gary Mack, Mark Allen, Robert Groden, Peter Dale Scott, David S. Lifton, Seth Kantor, Earl Golz, Larry Harris, Jack Swike, Edgar Tatro, and Fred Newcomb.

And there are many others, including Professor G. Robert Blakey of Notre Dame University, Ray and Marjorie Cline of the Center for Strategic and International Studies, William Johnson of the JFK Library in Boston, Marion Johnson of the National Archives, Aaron Kohn, Buck Ferrell, Jim Ewell, Gaeton Fonzi, the Dallas County Historical Commission, Professor Jorge Dominguez of Harvard University, and Professor Herbert S. Parmet of The City University of New York.

I am particularly indebted to the Rockefeller Foundation, which played a significant role in launching my career as a writer. In the same vein, I express deepest appreciation to Robert Penn Warren, Peter Taylor, Evans B. Harrington, and Granville Smith.

I am also grateful to Richard Seaver, president of Holt, Rinehart and Winston, and to David Stanford, for their confidence and encouragement. Others at Holt, Rinehart and Winston who were of enormous value in preparing the book for publication include Sally Smith and Trent Duffy.

Most of the book was written at Redeye, Virginia, where I keep an office. The friendliness of my neighbors there has meant a great deal. I also am indebted to the administration of Chatham Hall, a private boarding school in Chatham, Virginia, that allowed me the use of the Gatewood House during the early stages of writing the book.

In a massive undertaking such as this, the work unavoidably becomes a part of the author's life and the lives of his family. I owe a great debt to Frances Hallam Hurt, my mother, who lives nearby and has consistently offered the harshest, most constructive criticism of early drafts of each chapter. Her support and counsel have been invaluable.

My greatest gratitude goes to my wife, Margaret Williams Hurt. As the first reader of each chapter, her editorial contribution has been immense. However, it is her affection and support through the tumultuous course of writing the book—as well as the topsy-turvy events preceding its publication—that constitute her unparalleled contribution.

An accounting such as this would be incomplete without an expression of my devotion and appreciation to our children, Charles, Robert, and Elizabeth. Each knows far more about the JFK assassination than any minor should.

—Henry Hurt
March 19, 1985
Chatham, Virginia

REASONABLE DOUBT

INTRODUCTION

The death of President John F. Kennedy, regarded today as the most popular president in American history, profoundly affected a whole generation. His murder, at the prime age of forty-six, evoked haunting despair and impassioned rage in the hearts of those who admired him. It generated bitter resentment as well as sadness among most of those who opposed him. To this day, the terrible episode festers like a wound in the national spirit.

The deepest concern of most Americans over the years has been that, no matter where blame for the assassination is finally placed, they were forced to face the barbaric reality that their country's electoral process was ravaged by gunfire. Citizens were denied the orderliness and civility of an election to change the course of their government. In general, Americans seemed to believe that this sort of catastrophe could happen only in less civilized countries.

The most haunting question was whether the assassination could have been prevented. During the nine months prior to Kennedy's death, the Secret Service received more than four hundred threats on the President's life. A good case can be made that at least one of Kennedy's trips was canceled only a few weeks prior to the assassination because of the gravity of information received by the Secret Service. In another case, in Miami only a few days before the assassination, Kennedy's ground-transportation plans were switched at the last minute, after information was received concerning an assassination threat.[1]

The reported Miami plot, according to documents disclosed years later, had eerie similarities to what came to pass in Dallas several days later.[2] There was every reason to suspect that President Kennedy faced special danger that bright fall day as Air Force One landed in Dallas, yet no special security measures were taken. The extent of that danger, in retrospect, is all too evident. What is not evident is the full truth about what happened that day—and if there was a conspiracy, the identities of those who were responsible.

• 1

Twenty years after his death, John F. Kennedy has attained a popularity among Americans bordering on adulation. Each year, 3½ million people pay their respects at his grave in Arlington National Cemetery. Thousands make the pilgrimage to Dealey Plaza. Polls indicate that 30 percent of all Americans wish that John F. Kennedy were in the White House today.[3]

What is the key to such unprecedented popularity on the part of a man who was elected to his high office by the thinnest margin in modern history? What did John Kennedy touch in Americans during his thousand days in the White House? What did this man possess in addition to his charm, wealth, wit, and good looks? Did he offer Americans a bright promise of what might be, and then, in his death, leave a lingering national frustration? Is it a longing for that fulfillment that accounts for the extraordinary popular yearning for John Kennedy?

Even the most adoring of the pro-Kennedy historians do not claim that the specific achievements of his presidency were extraordinary. The major programs Kennedy envisioned were not embraced by Congress, and few believe that all of them would have been enacted through his efforts, had he lived. However, JFK's presidency seems to have stimulated a deep and vibrant hope among millions of Americans who for a variety of reasons had become jaded in their perception of the political experience.

John Kennedy was the first national politician to grasp the power of television and to use it with skill and force. But more than that, Kennedy was an orator of considerable gifts. Much was made during his lifetime of his unusual style, speech patterns, and accents. This focus sometimes overshadowed what was more important—his innate understanding of delivery and timing. His speech writers were gifted in the use of rousing ideas and colorful language. Whether one liked him or not, the man could move even his detractors.

Is it possible that some of the factors perceived as negatives were, in truth, political strengths that struck latent chords in the American psyche? Was it, possibly, to Kennedy's great advantage that his family—the ties to Ireland kept fresh—had prospered in ways that nearly all second-generation immigrant families would wish to? That prosperity, compounded with the President's immensely attractive family and his own well-known personal shortcomings, seemed to create a powerful blending of virtue and vice that millions could understand.

What Americans seem most to remember about John Kennedy is an image, a dream—what has been called by his admirers a brief shining moment in America. This illusion—sustained, to be sure, by at least some reality—was battered, but not permanently tarnished, by the revelations over the years concerning President Kennedy's weaknesses with women, his lapses in judgment, and his almost certain acquiescence in the murder plots against Cuban Premier Fidel Castro. Part of the American indifference to these exposures may be that Kennedy never lied to the public about them. It is the lying by two of his successors that so agitated the press and public.

Perhaps John Kennedy's greatest contribution was that he opened the mind of America to the possibilities of what might be. Haynes Johnson, a veteran chronicler of events during the Kennedy years, wrote on one of the anniversaries of Kennedy's death: "[Kennedy] made it seem possible to believe we could be better; . . . he inspired a sense of confidence, trust, and purpose; . . . to millions, he represented the pursuit of excellence in national life. . . . That was the real Kennedy promise."[4]

Anthony Lewis, a columnist for *The New York Times*, put it this way: "The explanation of Kennedy's human appeal is straightforward. . . . He *was* human, in the best sense. He responded to experience and emotion. He made mistakes, and he learned from them. He did not accept the conditions of life as unchangeable; he looked deeper into them, and into himself. People sensed all that, and it gave them hope."[5]

This intangible asset was, it seems, something of the mind, of the heart, of the spirit. One of the few certainties is that there is not now—nor will there ever be—unanimity on the explanation of Kennedy's popularity. Perhaps his brother, Senator Edward M. Kennedy, speaking with unabashed adulation, came close to an explanation in his tribute on November 22, 1983, when he stated: "The qualities that made us love him were the same human qualities that attracted so many millions who never met him at all. He knew historians would write of him but his truest history is written in the hearts of people everywhere. They forgave him his shortcomings because he gave us a sense of what human beings, despite their imperfections, can aspire to do."[6]

It is improbable that this image could have been sustained and nourished if JFK had lived. In death he garnered the sympathy even of many of his enemies, or if not quite that, their voices were somewhat neutralized out of respect.

Without understanding fully the reasons for JFK's lasting enchantment, it is not unfair to say that it is based more on illusion than reality. And in this country too often it is the illusion that counts. There was an unprecedented outpouring of sentiment on the occasion of the twentieth anniversary of JFK's death. Special books were published, television movies were created, old film clips were aired again, network news programs assessed his life and work. It was a time of national adulation.

In a sense, the twentieth anniversary observance of President Kennedy's death was a merging of the myth and the reality, a recognition that the two perceptions are forever wedded in the public mind. No matter how history ultimately judges Kennedy's brief presidency, those who lived through it are inclined not to deny him his extraordinary popularity, his nearly universal appeal. His greatest political value to the country was not what he accomplished so much as what he promised to do, what he held out, the youthfulness that set him in such clear contrast to the aging figures of Western Europe and the Soviet Union—men who, ironically, would live longer and come to see perhaps better what his gifts and values were.

In Europe, following Kennedy's death, there was a significant change in how America was perceived. Arthur F. Burns, U.S. ambassador to West Germany, has explained that following World War II, in the eyes of Europeans, "America became a country whose institutions merited unbounded admiration." But there came a turning point, Burns says, and that was perhaps

> the violent death of President John F. Kennedy, who was immensely popular in Europe. . . . His assassination . . . came as a terrible shock and it changed the image of the United States drastically. Many Europeans wondered how a country that brought forth such senseless violence could ever have served as their ideal. Then came the terrible assassinations of Robert F. Kennedy and Dr. Martin Luther King, Jr., the Vietnam War, the civil rights turbulence, Watergate—with the result that the golden image of America was shattered.[7]

Certainly John Kennedy and his brief presidency stand as a watershed in American history. Up until and through the years of the

Eisenhower administration, there was a historical cohesiveness to our power brokers and institutions. The government, the press, the prominent politicians, the large corporations, the wealthy, the powerful secret services like the FBI and the CIA, all were controlled by men who perceived common goals for America and who worked together, usually in an informal fashion, to achieve these goals. It was not a formal agreement that required any written rules, but an *understanding*. It was a loosely knit brotherhood—one cemented by a perception of common decency and goodwill—that felt no guilt or hesitation about these bonds of perceived patriotism. It was all seen in a richly paternalistic fashion as being good for America—and that, after all, was considered far more important than the preservation of those rancorous rights of dissent and contradiction that caused such bedlam through the sixties.

John Kennedy was a part of this traditional structure of influence—albeit, a somewhat tentative, connective link between what had always been and what, after his death, would come to be. Clearly, he was not comfortable as a part of this brotherhood of men like his rich and powerful father, but his political intuition dictated that he must use these men if he hoped to prevail.

But he bridled against it, as he jawboned Big Steel into rolling back a price increase, as he fought the CIA on matters that had always been their preserve. Kennedy may have been the last president to persuade a publication to tone down a sensational breaking news story (the Bay of Pigs invasion) on the grounds of national security.[8]

In this manner, Kennedy was an odd president, a man with one foot in the past ways of politics, the other in the future. Rooted in the past, he aspired to what he believed was a better way of doing things, and in that vision lay his strength and his enduring popularity. It can be seen now that his presidency—and the terrible disappointment and doubt that sprang from his death—became a genesis for the distrust and skepticism about all institutions, both public and private.

While there was nothing simple about the life of John Kennedy, his death stands as one of the great mysteries of modern times. The earliest official investigation—the report of the Warren Commission issued in September 1964—concluded that a lone assassin, Lee Harvey Oswald, shot and killed President Kennedy. After a brief period of acceptance of this conclusion, public skepticism began to grow as people learned more about the work of the Warren Commission, the shambles of the official autopsy, and the investigative approach taken by the FBI.

Rarely in the United States had the government—in theory a responsive political institution—been at such loggerheads with its people over so emotional an issue. As a political reality, it was inevitable that eventually the Kennedy case would be reopened. Seeming to realize this, the FBI became acutely vigilant in spotting and attempting to neutralize criticism and dissent. Among the hundreds of thousands of now disclosed FBI reports and memoranda on the case, there are numerous examples in which FBI Director J. Edgar Hoover personally directed his agents on how to handle some minor dissenter. In his own handwriting, Hoover's notes often instructed his staff on how to respond to the most obscure criticisms. This furious blizzard of paper, much of it now available to the public, stands as mute evidence of the frenzied efforts of Hoover and his men to protect the perilously hasty position, taken on that November day so many years earlier, that Oswald alone was the assassin.

Twelve years after the Warren Report, with a massive erosion of public confidence in those official findings, it became politically expedient to reopen the assassination case in the form of a Congressional investigation. The House Select Committee on Assassinations came up with a conclusion that was, on its surface, startlingly different from the Warren Commission—that Kennedy probably died at the hands of conspirators. The Select Committee did not have time to develop its leads but asked the Justice Department and the FBI to pursue them.

The public reaction seemed blasé toward this official conclusion of conspiracy. A majority of Americans already believed in some conspiracy theory prior to the Congressional conclusion, and polls show these figures to be about the same after that finding. The conclusion was what the public believed all along. What is more astonishing is that in 1983, despite the immense popularity of JFK *and* the common belief that he was killed by a conspiracy, 70 percent of those Americans saw no reason to reopen the case to learn the truth.[9] That seems in keeping with the feeling of the Kennedy family, not one of whom has ever expressed doubt in public about the official version. Nonetheless, the overwhelming belief of the public that JFK was killed by conspirators cries out for resolution.

Did Oswald, alone, really kill John Kennedy? That basic question, one that has gripped the public's attention for nearly a generation, is the central focus of this book.

The genesis of this work is as improbable as many of the events chronicled in its pages. It all started in the fall of 1981, when I received a telephone call from a man who stated that he had participated in a conspiracy to assassinate President Kennedy. At the very least, he was the first fully identifiable person ever known to have offered a detailed confession to participation in the Kennedy assassination—a fact that alone demanded the sharpest attention. That conversation lasted about an hour and might have been the last except for one factor: I did not have sufficient knowledge of the Kennedy assassination to make a fair assessment of the man's account. I decided to see the man and get his complete story. A few weeks later, having met with him, there seemed no responsible alternative but to investigate his extraordinary claims. To weigh those claims, it was necessary to charge headlong into the murk of the Kennedy assassination.

Thus began my odyssey to the people who had spent so many years trying to sort out the truth about the crime of the century. The most apt description of that odyssey is found in the words of Gaeton Fonzi, a Congressional investigator of the case, who once wrote: "It was a journey into a maze that had grown, over the years, to bewildering proportions. Yet what emerged were similar images along many of the pathways, an indication—often only gossamer— of a concealed thread emanating from a common spool."[10]

In my quest to understand the case, I was not burdened by any preconceived notion, beyond a general feeling that the official version seemed illogically simplistic, that it seemed virtually impossible that Lee Harvey Oswald had done what the government said that he had done. In that sense, I was one of the 80 percent of Americans who doubted the official version. Beyond that, the only special knowledge I had of the case derived from research work I had done in connection with *Legend: The Secret World of Lee Harvey Oswald*, by Edward J. Epstein, published in 1978. However, my work on that book did not go beyond locating and interviewing Marines who had served with Oswald and then finding and interviewing some witnesses in the Dallas area.

During the early months of work, I fully expected that at any moment I would encounter that single, unalterable piece of evidence that left no question that Oswald was the man who killed Kennedy. The case had been wrapped up by the Warren Commission and the FBI as being so simple, so clear-cut, that around each turn I expected to find the fact that would, once and for all, settle the matter to my satisfaction. That discovery never came. Instead, the evidence continued to point in a different direction, nurturing an ever mounting feeling of doubt about the government's open-and-shut case.

Take this basic question: is it *possible* that Lee Harvey Oswald killed President Kennedy? The search for the answer to that question drives one on into the case. After the thousands of hours of debate on this point, one basic fact stands as a monument to doubt: the United States government, in its massive efforts to shore up the official guilt of Oswald, has never conducted a test in which Oswald's shooting ability has been matched. The country's top experts can work the ancient Mannlicher-Carcano rifle bolt with sufficient speed. Those experts can hit a similarly moving target. But no official expert has ever been able to do both at the same time. That feat belongs to Oswald alone—a man of questionable shooting skills who had not engaged in regular firing practice in any documentable instance after leaving the military service more than four years earlier.

Another point of maddening simplicity is this: If Lee Harvey Oswald, acting alone, killed John Kennedy, why is there not a *single* clean, indisputable piece of evidence firmly linking him to the actual murder? Why is it all so grindingly confusing and contradictory? To be sure, many murder cases are successfully prosecuted in the absence of a smoking gun, but in a case that the government has claimed is as open and shut as this one, a layman would expect at least one clean link of overwhelming persuasiveness. All sorts of evidence was immediately seized that strongly implicated Oswald—but there is not a single piece of it that cannot be reasonably and rationally challenged, not a piece that can stand alone unplagued by reasonable doubt. That deficiency in the case against Oswald is at the heart of the enduring skepticism.

A powerful case can be made that Oswald did *not* kill Kennedy. The answer to who *did* is as beclouded as ever.

In the end, the claims of the confessor whose telephone call set me on this course could not be substantiated to the point that no doubts about the veracity of his confession remained. However, the investigation of his claims had led inexorably to a review of the whole JFK case. After eight investigations by various government bodies, there is no clear resolution of the greatest crime of modern times. As time passes, evidence vanishes and witnesses die. The chance of a resolution seems remote.

What is numbing to contemplate is the failure of the government to handle a case of this magnitude. If, in spite of all the contradictions, the original government version is correct, then there is something abysmally wrong with the manner of its presentation. Defenders of the official version often blame the critics for having fomented the broad dissent—attributing to these critics a power in falsehood that eludes the government in its perceived truth. There are few, if any, examples in modern history of occasions in which such topsy-turvy logic prevails.

The FBI's failure, from the earliest moments following Kennedy's death, to push for a wide-ranging investigation is well documented. In the end, the FBI and the Justice Department failed in their roles. The executive branch, with its presidentially created Warren Commission, failed in its purpose—either to find the truth or to allay the fears and concerns of the public. Subsequently, the legislative branch, with its investigations that deepened the muddle, failed to resolve the case.

But of all the failures in the investigation of JFK's murder, none is more disappointing than the performance of the press. Generally, magazines and newspapers, as well as television networks, were supportive of the official version. This was during those mellow days before Vietnam and Watergate turned the press into such a ferocious watchdog of morality. In 1963 and 1964, instead of challenging the fuzzy, weak points of the case as they emerged, the press lent credence to those points by its embrace and reassurances to its public.

Despite these failures, it is encouraging that it was the very resiliency of the American system that prevented the JFK case from being stifled. A band of people—lawyers, homemakers, a goose farmer, businessmen, a mathematician, an architect, scholars, secretaries, doctors, professors, a weekly-newspaper editor, photographers, even former government agents—would not swallow the official line. They began, each in his or her own way, their diverse work to get at the truth. Known as the critics, these people have managed, through sheer diligence and persistence, to keep the case alive and to inch it toward some plausible resolution.

They have been denounced from some of the most prestigious podiums in the land—called blood-sucking scavengers, accused of personal greed. (There is probably but one example of a critic who has made a livelihood out of the assassination, while there are hundreds of examples of men and women who have given years of their spare time—and often generously from their personal resources—in the pursuit of answers.) It is they who have kept alive the search for truth. Without their work, the evidence uncovered and the legitimate leads developed would likely have been lost many years ago. Without their work, this book—and the continuing quest for truth about the JFK assassination—would simply be impossible.

Monuments to the life of John F. Kennedy are found all over the world. Great stone buildings stand as testaments to how he was viewed by the rich and the powerful. The tallest memorial named in his honor is Mount Kennedy, a mountain peak in Canada. JFK's name was given to America's premier international airport—and to the nation's major space center. The eternal flame at Kennedy's grave, inspired by his family, is the only one at Arlington National Cemetery. But the greatest of all tributes to JFK is seen and felt in the vibrancy of those millions who believe that he was the country's greatest President. There is pathos in the fact that they no longer hope to know the truth about his murder. Their calloused reaction, to be sure, is realistic, caught as they are between stonewalling and confusion. Such an impasse poorly serves the memory of the man so many millions revere.

There is no way of knowing how John Kennedy would view the mystery surrounding his death. Would he want the intractable questions resolved? Or would he not want to disrupt the blue-ribbon façade that holds that the lone assassin was Lee Harvey Oswald? Would JFK want the persistent interest in the case to evaporate, for America to get on with the business of the future? Whatever President Kennedy's wishes would be, it is clear that among his virtues seemed to be a respect for the public trust. Of his well-known shortcomings, lying to the public is not one.

A clue to how he might have viewed these matters is found in a speech he made in February of 1962. The occasion was the twentieth anniversary of the Voice of America. President Kennedy told the employees of America's voice to the world:

> You are obliged to tell our story in a truthful way, to tell it, as Oliver Cromwell said about his portrait, "Paint us with all our blemishes and warts, all those things about us that may not be so immediately attractive."
>
> We compete with . . . those who are our adversaries who tell only the good stories. But the things that go bad in America, you must tell that also. And we hope that the bad and the good is sifted together by people of judgment and discretion and taste and discrimination, that they will realize what we are trying to do here. . . .
>
> We seek a free flow of information. . . . We are not afraid to entrust the American people with unpleasant facts, foreign ideas, alien philosophies, and competitive values. For a nation that is afraid to let its people judge the truth and falsehood in an open market is a nation that is afraid of its people.[11]

And President Kennedy spoke of the heavy burden that can accompany truth: "The barrage upon truth will grow more constant, and some people cannot bear the responsibility of a free choice which goes with self-government. And finally, shrinking from choice, they turn to those who prevent them from choosing, and thus find in a kind of prison, a kind of security."[12]

There is, to be sure, a certain security in the insistence that Lee Harvey Oswald, alone, murdered John F. Kennedy. But, if that proposition happens not to be true, then there is an infection coursing through our moral fiber as a nation that will not, of its own and by itself, ever go away. It demands, if not the attention of the government powers, then at least the continued vigilance of a concerned public.

The assassination of John F. Kennedy set into motion a pervasive transfer of power, one that shifted the basic thrusts of American policy—both domestic and foreign. If the purpose of the assassination by whatever hands was to bring about such profound changes, then the killing of President Kennedy was a shattering success. Indeed, the political impact of Kennedy's death is why the question of his assassination is as important today as it was two decades ago—

and as it will be twenty years hence, and for all the years of this republic. If the atrocity was the result of a conspiracy, the country and its government even at this hour are subtly threatened by a cunning, invisible enemy as politically potent as the most menacing superpower. Moreover, the historical integrity of the whole country remains fractured until the questions are answered.

1 · THE STAGE

Dallas, Texas

The verdant spot at the southwest corner of Elm and Houston streets in Dallas, pastoral during the quiet hours, has become one of the great stages in world history. It is sobering that a place of violent death should attract the thousands who flock there each year to retrace the minute details of one of the most shocking episodes in this country's history. People come from around the world to feel the haunting reality that on this spot a body was shattered, a human life destroyed. Not just an ordinary human life expired here, but that of a man revered by millions. It is here at Dealey Plaza, at a spot just down from the long reflecting pool, that the curious join the faithful to ponder and reflect, to tell impatient children what probably happened, to snap pictures, to point to certain buildings overlooking the area, to stare at the proximate spot where John F. Kennedy drew his last conscious breath.

A few blocks away stands a memorial to President Kennedy, a high-walled cavernous cenotaph. In the center is a single slab of black granite bearing only the name of the slain President. People saunter over to inspect the memorial, but after a quick look most of them return to the actual assassination site to muse and to wonder. It is here that one can come the closest to grasping the reality of the terrible event. The buildings surrounding Dealey Plaza along Elm and Houston—representing an unorthodox assortment of architecture—are still there, overlooking the graceful pergolas, the same configuration of highways, overpasses, railroad tracks, open areas, and, of course, the famous grassy knoll. Physically, little has changed. Psychically, not much has changed either, since the controversy spawned on that dreadful day persists more than two decades later.

November 22, 1963

It was 12:30 P.M., Central Standard Time, when the first gunfire
burst upon the President's motor procession as it moved slowly down
Elm Street, having just turned off Houston Street. President Kennedy's hands reached for his neck. The moment marked the start
of one of the most intensely studied few seconds in history, a tiny
span of time frozen forever by film. The Secret Service agents immediately responsible for the President's protection looked around,
puzzlement glued to their faces. At that point, Kennedy's wound
was one that, with proper medical attention, he could be expected
to survive.[1]

But the presidential limousine, which had been moving at about
eleven miles an hour, slowed perceptibly. More gunfire was heard.
Several seconds had ticked away since the first shot, but the limousine seemed nearly immobilized. Five seconds after Kennedy first
clutched at his neck, the limousine still seemed to be in its stultifying
pause, the driver looking over his shoulder into the back seat. Then
came the fatal shot. The right side of President Kennedy's head
exploded, ringing him with a bright pink nimbus of blood and bone
and brain tissue. It was only then that the powerful limousine was
stirred from its doldrums to race toward Parkland Hospital four miles
away.[2]

At the hospital, President Kennedy was rushed into a trauma room
on the ground floor, where physicians found lingering vital signs,
despite the massive and readily visible destruction of brain tissue.
Fighting against all odds and knowing it was hopeless, the doctors
struggled to preserve the President's life. They observed a small
hole in his throat that they believed to be a wound of entry. A
tracheotomy was performed at this spot. External cardiac massage
was administered. The doctors had no reason to turn the President's
body over, so they never saw the wound in his back.[3]

Texas Governor John B. Connally, who had been a passenger in
Kennedy's car, had also been shot during the ambush. He lay gravely
wounded in a second trauma room a few yards away. Within minutes,
Vice-President Lyndon B. Johnson, who had been in the motorcade,
arrived at Parkland Hospital and was engulfed by Secret Service
agents, who believed that Kennedy was fatally wounded. Johnson
was hustled into a small room in the emergency area where he could

be best protected. The wives of President Kennedy and Governor Connally also were at the hospital. The corridors were filled with medical personnel, Secret Service agents, at least one CIA agent, FBI agents, people associated with the President's entourage, and others. Outside, the milling crowd increased by the second.[4]

Around 1:00 P.M., thirty minutes after the attack, President Kennedy received the last rites of the Roman Catholic Church. The President's wife, Jacqueline, was at his side. She kissed her husband, slipped a ring from her finger, and placed it on one of his.[5]

While Secret Service Agent Richard E. Johnsen was still posted at the entrance to Kennedy's trauma room, Parkland Hospital's director of security approached him with the slug of a bullet found after it was jarred out from under the padding of a stretcher that had been left down the hall from the trauma room. There was a possibility that the stretcher had been used to transport Governor Connally when he was moved from the trauma room to an operating room on a higher floor. This slug, in nearly pristine condition when handed to Agent Johnsen, would become the cornerstone of the investigation into the events that occurred in Dallas that day. In the press of other official duties, Agent Johnsen slipped the slug into his pocket.[6]

At the time of Kennedy's death there was no federal statute covering the assassination of the President. In the eyes of the law, such an act was no different from any other murder. Moreover, under Texas law as it was invoked that afternoon, an autopsy should have been performed in Dallas. But at Parkland Hospital, President Kennedy's loyal aides insisted upon immediately removing his body and rushing it to Washington. When Texas officials notified them that legally an autopsy was required, the Kennedy men became adamant. A coffin and hearse were summoned from a local mortuary, and Kennedy's body was whisked to the airfield where the presidential airplane waited. Minutes after Lyndon B. Johnson was sworn in aboard Air Force One, the plane took off for Washington carrying the new President as well as the body of John F. Kennedy. The decision about where to conduct an autopsy on Kennedy's body was left up to his widow, who selected the Naval Medical Center at Bethesda, Maryland.[7]

By four o'clock the following morning, Washington time, less than sixteen hours after he began his rousing cavalcade through Dallas,

President Kennedy's body was on its way to the East Room of the White House, where it would lie in state for an anguished nation. Later, when the body was moved to the Rotunda of the U.S. Capitol, 250,000 people filed past it to pay their last respects. On Monday, November 25, John Kennedy was buried. Of all the searing impressions of those haunting days, few who watched would ever forget the sight of the prancing riderless horse, the stoic faces of the Kennedy family, or the brave salute by toddler John F. Kennedy, Jr., as horses pulled his father's funeral bier through the streets of Washington to Arlington National Cemetery. It was the boy's third birthday. There, in place at the gravesite, was a gas flame that was lighted by Mrs. Kennedy and designed to burn eternally.[8]

The only certainty that gripped the people in Dealey Plaza at 12:30 that ugly afternoon was the belief that President Kennedy and perhaps others in his party were hit by gunfire in an ambush. Among the 266 known witnesses to the attack, there would forever be disagreement over the number of shots and their source. Of the witnesses officially interviewed who expressed a firm opinion, 32 placed the origin of the shots at the Texas School Book Depository (TSBD), which was located on the northwest corner of Elm and Houston, above and behind President Kennedy's position. Fifty-one witnesses—including two Secret Service agents and a variety of police officers—expressed the belief that the shots came from the area of a grassy knoll, above and in front of President Kennedy. Others believed the shots came from both directions.[9]

Initially, the disagreement was as strong among officials and police as it was among spectators at large. Photographs show policemen and civilians running toward various spots, depending upon where each thought the shots came from. Some scrambled up the grassy knoll while others raced toward the TSBD Building. Several witnesses who had been standing on the grassy knoll—including Abraham Zapruder, whose home movies of the event became the most important record—related hair-raising accounts of hearing gunfire behind them. Some of these people, who were directly in front of and below the grassy knoll, flattened themselves on the ground and covered their children in attempts to escape being hit.[10]

Three employees of the Book Depository, watching the procession from the fifth floor of the TSBD Building, reported hearing the shots directly above their position, adding that they could hear ejected cartridge shells striking the floor. Six of the witnesses who were on the steps of the Depository Building testified that they heard the shots come from in front of and to the right side of Kennedy's car, from the grassy knoll.[11]

These are but a few of the dozens of accounts that bolster the proposition that eyewitness evidence could not possibly be used to substantiate the existence of a single assassin's lair in Dealey Plaza that day. For establishing what really happened, material evidence was needed.

Immediately after the shooting, Dallas police seized and detained at least a dozen men for questioning. After being held briefly, all of them were released. In many cases, no record was made of the names of those taken into custody.[12]

Less than fifteen minutes after Kennedy was shot, radio dispatchers at the Dallas Police Department broadcast the description of a man wanted for questioning in connection with the shooting. The source for this description has never been clear, but it may have been based on information provided by a witness on the ground who said he saw a man with a rifle in a sixth-floor window of the TSBD Building. Broadcast just before 12:45 P.M., the description was for "an unknown white male, approximately thirty, slender build, height five feet ten inches, weight one hundred sixty-five pounds, reported to be armed with what is believed to be a .30-caliber rifle."[13]

Forty-five minutes after Kennedy was struck by bullets, police dispatchers received a frantic call from a civilian using the radio of a police car. The citizen reported that a police officer had just been shot and was lying dead in the street in the Oak Cliff section of Dallas. Oak Cliff was across the Trinity River, several miles from Dealey Plaza. This report was received at approximately 1:16 P.M., thirty-one minutes after the description of the suspect in the Kennedy killing had been broadcast. At 1:22 P.M., police officers at the scene of the Oak Cliff shooting broadcast the following description of the assailant as given by several witnesses: "a white male, about thirty, five feet eight inches, black hair, slender, wearing a white jacket, white shirt, and dark slacks."[14]

About twenty minutes later, Johnny Calvin Brewer, a manager of a shoe store six blocks from the Oak Cliff shooting, heard a radio report that a policeman had been shot a short distance away. Brewer then heard police sirens and looked to the front of his store. Just at that moment, Brewer saw a man who had stepped into his entrance from the sidewalk and stood with his back toward the street as the patrol car passed. As soon as the police were gone, the man departed.[15]

Suspicious, Brewer followed him for about twenty yards and watched him duck into the Texas Theatre without buying a ticket. Brewer alerted the theater cashier to the man's presence. The cashier called the police, who broadcast an alarm at 1:45 P.M. From all over, police converged on the Texas Theatre. The house lights were turned up, and Johnny Brewer pointed out the man he had followed into the theater.[16]

Six minutes later, at 1:51 P.M., officers in Oak Cliff radioed headquarters that they had seized the man who had entered the Texas Theatre and that they believed him to be the killer of the police officer. The suspect had put up a brief struggle, during which he had pulled a pistol. He was then disarmed and taken into custody. The police drove to headquarters with the suspect. Around 2:00 P.M., Sergeant Gerald L. Hill was about to process his prisoner when Captain J. Will Fritz, chief of the Dallas Homicide Division, entered the room. Captain Fritz had just returned from the TSBD Building, where he had been informed that one of the employees was missing. Captain Fritz ordered some detectives to drive out to a Dallas suburb to pick up the missing employee, a man named Lee Oswald. He was wanted for questioning. Sergeant Hill informed Captain Fritz that the trip would not be necessary, that Lee Oswald was already in custody.[17]

Until that moment, Lee Harvey Oswald had been a nondescript pseudointellectual, a high school dropout who drifted from job to job, maintaining contacts that would forever be a puzzle. Suddenly he was cast into a roiling cauldron of world attention as the prime suspect in the assassination of the President of the United States.

A little after 7:00 P.M., five hours after his arrest at the Texas Theatre, Oswald was formally charged with murdering Police Officer J. D. Tippit. Around 1:30 on Saturday morning, Oswald was formally charged with murdering John F. Kennedy. Even before Oswald was charged with anything, FBI Director J. Edgar Hoover issued an internal memo stating that police "very probably" had Kennedy's killer in custody. In the memo, which was sent at 5:15 P.M. on the day of the assassination, Hoover described Oswald as being "in the category of a nut and the extremist pro-Castro crowd . . . an extreme radical of the left." In Dallas, a prosecutor emerged from seeing Oswald and told the press: "I detest him. He's the most arrogant person I ever met." The tone characterized the atmosphere.[18]

During most of the nearly twelve hours between his arrest and his being charged in the Kennedy murder, Oswald was interrogated by a variety of federal, state, and local officials. Although no stenographic record or tape recording was kept of these periods of questioning, interrogators have said Oswald made repeated denials of his guilt. For the rest of that Saturday and most of the following morning, Oswald's time was filled chiefly with additional unrecorded interviews with police officials. He was also permitted brief visits from members of his family.[19]

Oswald's last visit to Captain Fritz's office was on Sunday morning, November 24, prior to his transfer to the Dallas County Jail. The transfer party left Fritz's office at 11:15 A.M. Six minutes later, in the basement of the Police and Courts Building, Oswald was gunned down by Jack Ruby. Unlike the murder of John F. Kennedy, with no reliable eyewitness to the actual pulling of a trigger, millions looked at their television screens in stark horror as Lee Oswald crumpled into the arms of his custodians. He was declared dead at 1:07 P.M. at Parkland Hospital, where President Kennedy had been declared dead almost exactly forty-eight hours earlier.[20]

From the time of his arrest until his death, Oswald absolutely denied that he shot Kennedy or Tippit. "I'm just a patsy!" he once yelled to reporters.[21]

Less than two hours after Oswald's death, FBI Director J. Edgar Hoover telephoned the White House with the following message for President Johnson: "The thing I am most concerned about . . . is having something issued so we can convince the public that Oswald is the real assassin." Indeed, a Senate Select Committee issued a report in 1976 stating: "Almost immediately after the assassination, Director Hoover, the Justice Department and the White House 'exerted pressure' on senior Bureau officials to complete their investigation and issue a factual report supporting the conclusion that Oswald was the lone assassin."[22]

In Dallas, the pressure also was on. In a press conference a few hours after Oswald's death, Dallas District Attorney Henry M. Wade told the world that there was no question that Oswald was the killer of President Kennedy.[23]

It is clear today that even before Kennedy's burial on the day following Oswald's murder, any open-minded investigation into his assassination either was unnecessary or undesirable—at least in the eyes of the Dallas police, the leadership of the FBI, and even in the minds of the highest officials in the United States. It was reported that the White House had sent word to Dallas that it was important to quell any speculation about a conspiracy behind the assassination. Almost immediately, the new chief executive began to make plans for a blue-ribbon panel of distinguished leaders to investigate the assassination and assure the public that the ship of state had not faltered.[24]

The silencing of Oswald sealed forever the prospect of an open trial in which evidence could be aired and weighed, motivation considered. There would be no chance for the tried and true adversary process to work its remarkable balancing influence. For answers, a surrogate of justice was chosen. A presidential commission was created to slip into the secret corridors of government agencies and plumb records controlled by people and agencies that were aghast at such a prospect under any circumstances. It would be arbitrary to say that the establishment of truth is impossible under such conditions. It is now certain, though, that truth—even if established under such conditions—is forever suspect in the minds of millions.

2 · BLUE-RIBBON WHITEWASH

On September 24, 1964, the President's Commission on the Assassination of President Kennedy, popularly called the Warren Commission, presented its final report to President Lyndon B. Johnson.[1] The work of the commission was remarkable for many reasons, not the least of which was the speed with which its conclusions were reached. A mere ten months had passed since the murder of President Kennedy. The press and public keenly awaited the commission's findings. The assassination case itself was strenuously complex and further complicated by two related murders the commission was obligated to examine—those of Lee Harvey Oswald and Dallas Police Officer J. D. Tippit. Illusions to the contrary, there was by no measure anything clear-cut about either of these murders.

The Warren Report ran to nearly 900 pages and included 6,710 footnotes. Along with twenty-six supporting volumes of evidence released several months later, the Warren Commission presented the American public with a staggering 20,000 pages of material, containing more than 10 million words. The commission reported that the FBI conducted 25,000 interviews which were handed over to the commission and that the Secret Service provided reports on 1,550 interviews that it conducted. Much of this was included in the twenty-six volumes—all presented with no comprehensive index, a factor that would make it necessary for researchers to spend years just trying to correlate the testimony and evidence.[2]

Out of this massive spectacle of paperwork came the following conclusions:

- Lee Harvey Oswald, acting alone, killed President Kennedy;[3]
- Lee Harvey Oswald, acting alone, killed Officer Tippit;[4]
- Jack Ruby, acting alone, killed Lee Harvey Oswald;[5]
- There was no credible evidence of a conspiracy, foreign or domestic;[6]

• All the shooting in the Kennedy assassination was done from a sixth-floor window of the Texas School Book Depository Building, where a rifle owned by Oswald was discovered;[7]

• Only three shots were fired at President Kennedy's procession, one of which passed through Kennedy's neck and then probably through the chest and wrist of Governor Connally. Another shot hit Kennedy's head. Another shot missed.[8]

With this, the Warren Commission made clear to President Johnson and to the American people that the whole terrible business should be dismissed, that the case should be closed. That was precisely what J. Edgar Hoover and the FBI had urged from the beginning. And it was just what President Johnson and most government officials wanted to believe and what they apparently felt was best at the time for the country.[9]

The initial press reception of the Warren Commission Report was one of glowing enthusiasm and almost fawning admiration. Repeatedly, the sheer mass of material was cited as evidence of the towering rectitude of the commission, the report, and its conclusions. It is unlikely that any government report has ever been given the promotional boosterism enjoyed by the Warren Report. There was hardly a word of dissent in the establishment press as high government officials and politicians commented on the superlative job that had been done. The most prestigious of America's media joined the thunderous chorus of assent.[10]

Though a considerable segment of the American public and the foreign press were skeptical,[11] praise for the work of the commission came from every corner of the American establishment. None was more eloquently expressed than that of Louis Nizer, one of the country's most famous lawyers. In an introduction to Doubleday's edition of the Warren Report, published soon after its release, Nizer was aggressively supportive in his analysis of the commission's work. Among his observations were the following general comments:

> Unprecedented public grief, and the raging volatile passions which flowed beneath it, did not deter the Commission from assuming that the accused was innocent until proved guilty. . . . The report will be of inestimable value in helping to restore our national reputation as an enlightened people who

even in their most trying hour acted rationally, soberly and justly to seek the truth. . . .

In the final analysis, it is not the banked lights on the outside of the edifice which will stir and persuade us, but the inner glow emanating from the report itself. . . .

Will the report's conclusions be accepted by the public? . . . The reader who matches the report in dispassionate approach and objective quest for truth will be overwhelmed by the exhaustive scientific and documentary evidence which support the main theses of the report. I believe that all but a few will bring to the report minds open to light, and therefore that the report will ultimately receive the widest acceptance.

There will be some who will resist persuasion. . . . They will persist in theories which exploit rumors and inconsistent statements made in the early turmoil. . . . They will insist that the failure to explain everything perfectly taints all that is explained. They will put the minor factors of the unknown or unknowable against major revelations. They will not joust fairly, by offering facts to be tested against facts, but will utilize a question or a doubt as if it were equivalent to disproof.

In this sense the report will not end all speculation. But in the historic sense, now that all the facts available have been quarried and justly evaluated, the report will dispose convincingly of the major questions.

This is the incalculable service rendered by the Commission. This is its achievement in effectuating domestic tranquility and overcoming foreign skepticism. This is its contribution to history.[12]

The tone of Nizer's statements seems clearly one of assuaging the national psyche, ameliorating the cancerous doubt that already had begun its festering within a segment of the public. This, of course, was a malignancy all members of the government seemed to want to dispel. According to Arthur Schlesinger, the Kennedy advisor, "All the pressures in Washington were toward a quick and uncomplicated verdict."[13] A prime purpose for the appointment of the Warren Commission appeared to be the very accomplishment noted by Nizer: "effectuating domestic tranquility."

In the days immediately following the release of the report, there seemed to be a national sense of relief that a solitary, peculiar young man, who claimed to be an avowed Marxist, had taken it solely upon himself to assassinate John F. Kennedy. His apparent lack of motive encouraged the official stance that he was "a lone nut." It was much more comforting to accept this than to wait for the other shoe to drop, to contemplate the potential turmoil and repercussions if the killing were shown to be part of a conspiracy.[14]

But this illusion was fleeting. The "inner glow" that Louis Nizer sensed in the Warren Report was not apparent to the general populace. No matter how neat the impressive wrappings of the Warren Commission, the fancy paper and ribbons began to become undone. Once started, the spreading skepticism knew no politics as liberals and conservatives looked with consternation at what they saw as a tangled web of contradictory and self-serving evidence.[15]

Soon enough the critics began their discordant symphony of protest against the manner in which the commission had conducted its investigation and the procedures it had pursued to reach its conclusions. One critic wrote: "The enormous numbers of printed pages [were] entirely wasted except as intellectual quicksand in which the casual reader or serious researcher is engulfed by the sheer volume and disorganization. . . . There was . . . no logical way of following the testimony, comparing it with the Report that ostensibly comes from it or with the many but inadequate exhibits that are entirely chaotic and unclassified, unindexed and incomplete."[16]

In a multitude of instances, the critics charged, the commission overlooked evidence that would impede its basic thesis, and it embraced evidence and witnesses that streamlined its march toward preconceived conclusions.[17] Commissioners as well as staff lawyers vigorously disputed these charges from the beginning, and some of them continue to do so until this day.[18]

The initial suspicions of a broad concealment of truth came from some of the foreign press, where there seemed to be a more conspiratorialist mentality and a feeling that the Warren Commission had left too many important questions unanswered. In the United States, the first general assault came primarily from books and magazine articles, while most newspapers—especially the establishment ones—expressed confidence in the report. One of the earliest critics, and certainly the most persistent one, was Harold Weisberg, a former Senate investigator, who wrote and privately published a series on the Warren Commission called *Whitewash*. Since the assassination, Weisberg has directed all his energies toward exposing what he sees as duplicity and deceit in the government's handling of the investigation. Other early books published in the United States that raised serious questions about the commission's work were *Rush to Judgment* by Mark Lane, *Inquest* by Edward J. Epstein, Sylvia Meagher's *Accessories After the Fact*, and Sylvan Fox's *The Unanswered Questions About President Kennedy's Assassination.*[19]

In the beginning, these critics were generally scorned by the establishment press. A few magazines, such as *Commentary*, carried early articles that broached important and reasonable questions. In most cases, publications presented such information standoffishly as sort of an aberration—interesting but not to be taken all that seriously. *The New York Times*, for example, stood reverentially by the Warren Commission until the end of 1966, sniffing loftily at those who dared to be critical of the massive report. Finally, though, the *Times* became curious about the burgeoning conflicts and contradictions in the report and launched its own investigation.[20]

During this period, *Life* magazine, which had been a stalwart (and some critics said *conniving*) supporter of the commission, began to question essential supportive points in the report, particularly the single-bullet theory. This powerful voice was soon followed by *The Saturday Evening Post*. By the middle of 1967, the deluge of published skepticism had begun. But public-opinion polls suggest that generally newspapers and magazines were lagging behind the public in the timing and intensity of their skepticism. Most politicians and government officials lagged behind even further.[21]

The range of questions raised by critics in the early debate was extraordinary, although much of the criticism was diffuse, its thrust poorly formed. But the larger public discontent was generated by a belief that somehow the commission's findings had been manipulated. A good example was the propitiousness of settling the whole matter just six weeks before the 1964 elections.[22]

Critics insist that a primary reason for the speed with which the commission finished its work was the tremendous pressure from President Johnson to issue satisfactory conclusions prior to the November elections. It would have been politically disastrous for Johnson to face his first presidential election with the verdict still out on the Kennedy assassination. It would be even worse for him if the commission's conclusions were to contain hints of a conspiracy. Such a finding, if unresolved, might well dominate the election and burst open all the political and national wounds Johnson and the government were trying so desperately to keep stitched together.[23]

At the time of the report's release in September, indications were that the commission had reached its conclusions, which were reported as unanimous, with a minimum of disagreement. There seemed, on the surface, to be no hedging. But a careful reading shows that the report meticulously states, in many instances, that its conclusions are based on the *evidence available.* In a subtle way, this shoved responsibility onto the FBI, which had been largely responsible for gathering evidence for the panel. In truth, though, some commission members knew certain evidence was being withheld and shirked their duty to demand full revelation.[24]

Years later, Congressional committees would conclude that the FBI as well as the CIA had been seriously derelict—and in some cases devious—in withholding key evidence from the Warren Commission that might have stimulated different findings. In some cases the committees found that certain evidence was altered or destroyed, further depriving the commission of the basic building blocks for its work.[25] An unofficial analysis of Warren Commission documents showed that at least sixty witnesses claimed that the FBI in some way altered what the witnesses had reported.

Documents released years after the Warren Commission completed its business show the FBI was not alone in altering testimony. The President's widow, Jacqueline Kennedy, was not questioned by the Warren Commission, but rather was deposed by Chief Justice Earl Warren at her house. The official account of this reported that Mrs. Kennedy said that if she had pulled the President down after the first shot, the second shot "would not have hit him." Actually, disclosed documents reveal, Mrs. Kennedy stated that the second shot "would have got Governor Connally." Someone on the Warren Commission thought such words were inappropriate, so they were simply changed.[26]

However, it is arguable that none of these alterations and deprivations of evidence made any essential difference. A persuasive case can be made that the conclusions rendered ten months after Kennedy's assassination were largely foregone from the moment of the panel's inception. Established a week after the assassination—over the objections of FBI Director Hoover, who wanted the case closed—the Warren Commission had in its hands by December 9,

1963, a full report by the FBI purporting to document the guilt of Lee Harvey Oswald. That report, which boldly brandished the massive investigatory resources of the FBI, stated categorically that the bureau could find no evidence that anyone other than Oswald was involved in the assassination. And this initial report was only the beginning of a great mustering of detail to support the FBI conclusion. More evidence poured in each day to bolster the FBI position, and as the evidence arrived, Hoover's men supposedly took it directly to the Warren Commission.[27]

Fifteen years later, the House Select Committee on Assassinations reviewed the whole case and stated in its report: "The FBI generally exhausted its resources in confirming the case against Lee Harvey Oswald as the lone assassin, a case that Director J. Edgar Hoover, at least, seemed determined to make within 24 hours of the assassination."[28]

In some ways, the FBI reporting was more significant for what it failed to tell the commission than for what it revealed. Evidence indicating the need to pursue new or onerous leads often did not reach the commission. There was, to be sure, a great deal of circumstantial evidence pointing to Oswald as the gunman, and—guilty or not—he was a supremely convenient target for blame. Some critics have made the point that if Oswald could be painted as a lone nut, the FBI was absolved of responsibility, since no one expected the bureau to foresee the actions of lone nuts.[29]

Arthur Schlesinger has made this point in describing the thorny problems the Warren Commission faced in its task:

> The Chief Justice and his colleagues had perforce to depend greatly on the intelligence agencies. They did not know that the agencies had their own secret reasons to fear a thorough inquiry. If it came out that the putative killer might have had intelligence connections, domestic or foreign, that FBI agents should have had him under close surveillance, that CIA assassins might have provoked him to the terrible deed, the agencies would be in the deepest trouble. But if Lee Harvey Oswald could be portrayed as a crazed loner acting on some solitary impulse of his own, they would be in the clear.[30]

While busy shoring up the evidence against Oswald, Hoover also made sure no outsiders knew that he had discovered disturbing irregularities in the performance of the FBI in Dallas prior to the assassination. In fact, he had censured seventeen agents, suspending pay in one case, and transferred those who had provoked his greatest wrath to less important locations. Hoover kept these actions a closely held secret for years.[31]

Hoover's initial efforts to influence the conclusions of the Warren Commission were highly effective. As early as January 11, 1964, General Counsel J. Lee Rankin apprised the commission of the staff's progress to date. In a document released after the Warren Report was issued, there is strong evidence that even at that early date the commission had no serious question about Oswald's guilt. The procedural outline for investigation offered to the commission by Rankin is based on an assumption that Oswald alone killed Kennedy. The most elaborate section is entitled "Lee Harvey Oswald as the Assassin of President Kennedy." A subsection of that category is called "Evidence Identifying Oswald as the Assassin of President Kennedy." Within *this* section, diminished almost beyond consideration, there is the title "Evidence Implicating Others in Assassination or Suggesting Accomplices," which includes nothing of substance. There is no investigative category for developing angles beyond building the case against Oswald, unless one argues that such a category is present in a part called "Refutation of Allegations."[32]

Clearly, short shrift is given to the possibility that anyone other than Oswald was involved in the assassination.

In the course of its business, the Warren Commission considered the accounts of 522 witnesses, 94 of whom actually appeared before one or more members of the panel. In any jury-trial proceeding, the absence of a juror during deliberations is viewed as such a grave matter that the whole trial is disrupted and either abandoned or started over again. The Warren Commission—which of course was not such a proceeding but was charged with finding the truth—disregarded the importance of the consistent presence of the commissioners. Never once during the testimony of the 94 witnesses were all seven commission members present at the same time. Congressman Gerald R. Ford of Michigan, who apparently acted as an FBI informant regarding some of the secret proceedings of the commission, had the best record, with his presence to hear 70 witnesses. On the other hand, Senator Richard B. Russell, who was spearheading a civil-rights filibuster during that period, managed to be on hand for only 6 witnesses. Hale Boggs and John J. McCloy also heard fewer than one-half of the witnesses. The other commission members were Senator John Sherman Cooper and former CIA Director Allen W. Dulles.[33]

Since the primary figure in the Warren Commission investigation, Lee Harvey Oswald, was dead, it is hardly fair to criticize the commission for not conducting its proceedings as if Oswald were on trial. It simply was not possible in any practical sense. And there are ample precedents for the sort of procedure the commission followed, notably the approach traditionally taken by Congressional investigating committees. The practical purpose of such committees is usually to develop an accumulation of evidence aimed at a particular conclusion and then to issue findings and recommendations for possible legislation. In the highest sense, the conclusions are not preconceived, but few Congressional investigators would claim any absolute purity of purpose in this regard.[34]

The Warren Commission adopted the general format of a Congressional committee, even structuring its hearings along those lines, with one major exception. The distinct difference was that Congressional investigative hearings are generally open to the public, with the press on hand to report developments as each witness testifies. Such an approach ensures complete freedom for the flow and interpretation of information as the inquiry proceeds, with the press and public every bit as entitled as the panel members and staff to draw their own conclusions. To be sure, there are executive sessions of such Congressional hearings from which the public is excluded, but that is the exception rather than the rule.[35]

On the other hand, the Warren Commission operated almost entirely in secret, although under its rules any single witness could demand that his testimony be given in public. Only one did.[36] While the more open approach encourages trust and understanding, the secretive approach spawns suspicion, cynicism, and distrust.

It is an almost peerless irony that the Warren Commission, quite unwittingly, managed to establish the Kennedy assassination as one of the most enduring controversies of the twentieth century. Two decades later it still nags relentlessly at the public conscience, demanding explanation and resolution. Whatever the reasons behind the findings of the Warren Commission, the aftermath of its report signaled one appalling certainty: the government seemed ineffective in responding to the murder of its President. If there was a conspiracy, then the conspirators had won and America had lost—a hideous prospect from any perspective. If, on the other hand, the commission was correct that Oswald was a nut acting alone, the government had failed abysmally in presenting a case the people could accept. Either way, the credibility of government and its institutions suffered greatly in the public's perception.[37]

Meanwhile, in areas where the government, the Warren Commission, and the American press were reluctant to tread, American students, scholars, and skeptics of all stripes continued their resolute quest. Their march was long and frustrating as it wound through a maze of government deceit, manipulation, and even the wholesale destruction of official records.

The work of these dissenters was bolstered in early 1970 when Senator Richard Russell, a member of the Warren Commission, stated in a television interview that he never believed Oswald acted alone. He said that he felt a conspiracy was behind the assassination. Senator Russell described the minute alterations in the wording of the report that he had insisted upon to make it possible for him to sign it. In addition to this extraordinary revelation, Senator Russell confirmed the long-standing suspicion that a majority of the commission members *wanted* to show that Oswald acted alone.[38]

Senator Russell's reasoning for believing a conspiracy existed was startlingly similar to the suspicions that had fueled the massive public dissent from the beginning. In that interview, Senator Russell stated:

> I have never believed that Oswald planned that altogether by himself. There were too many things, the fact when he was at Minsk, and that was the principal center for educating Cuban students. There were six hundred or seven hundred there. He was very close to some of them and the trip that he made to Mexico City and a number of discrepancies in the evidence as to, or conflicts in the evidence as to his means of transportation, the luggage he had, and whether or not anyone was with him, caused me to have doubts that he planned it all by himself. I think someone else worked with him.[39]

An even more stunning defector from the ranks of the Warren Commission supporters was the very creator of it: President Lyndon B. Johnson. In an interview with CBS News broadcast after his death, President Johnson revealed to Walter Cronkite that he had never been convinced Oswald acted alone. President Johnson's own feeling, which he discussed at the time with aides and friends, was that Kennedy probably was killed as the result of a conspiracy involving Cuban President Fidel Castro. Johnson told of his astonishment upon succeeding to the presidency to discover the intense efforts by the American government to assassinate Castro. "We had been operating a damned Murder Inc. in the Caribbean," he told one of his aides. Johnson believed that Castro might have moved against Kennedy in retaliation.[40]

Such a revelation was electrifying. The very man who conceived the Warren Commission and who encouraged and supported its conclusions had bared an innermost secret: a concession that from the very start he doubted the basic conclusion of the commission and believed that, in truth, a conspiracy lay behind the assassination of John F. Kennedy.

Another figure connected to the Warren Commission investigation who has expressed reservations about the findings is Lewis F. Powell, Jr., associate justice of the United States Supreme Court. In 1964 he was president-elect of the American Bar Association. In that capacity, Powell was asked by Walter E. Craig, then the president of the American Bar Association, to serve with him and several other distinguished lawyers as sort of an informal oversight committee to judge the fairness of the procedures followed by the commission.[41]

In a letter to the author in 1982, Justice Powell noted that he had never been completely certain that Oswald acted alone. He wrote:

> The only reservation I had at the time was an intuitive feeling that Oswald may have been an agent of, or encouraged by, an enemy country. I have no doubt that he was the triggerman. Nor have I ever credited the speculation that he was a hitman for some domestic conspiracy. But Oswald's stay in the Soviet Union, his interest in communism, and his otherwise curious movements (e.g., Mexico City), were enough to create suspicion. I was aware, however, of no hard evidence that linked the crime with a foreign power or its agents.[42]

Justice Powell was far from alone in his "intuitive feeling."

On the other hand, there are staunch loyalists among the Warren Commission members, such as former President Gerald R. Ford. In a 1982 letter to the author, President Ford expressed his vehement support for the commission. He wrote:

In my opinion, the conclusions of the Warren Commission are more valid today than at any time. For the past eighteen years, critics, skeptics, cynics and demagogues have sought to undermine the conclusions of the Warren Commission. No new credible evidence has been found. Several new theories have arisen, but were either "blown out of the water" by the facts included in the Warren Commission Report or by subsequent authorities or investigations.[43]

It is ironic that Gerald Ford, certainly one of the most resolute defenders of the Warren panel, should be the one commissioner who violated the top secret classification of certain commission proceedings. The breach, which is a violation of federal laws, occurred in 1965, when he published his book called *Portrait of the Assassin.* Ford, who earned at least $15,000 for his literary efforts, was asked about this by the Senate Rules and Administration Committee in 1973, during his confirmation hearings after Richard Nixon appointed him to the position of Vice-President. Ford told the Senate committee: "We did not use in that book any material other than the material that was in the 26 volumes of testimony and exhibits that were subsequently made public. . . ."[44]

President Ford's word prevailed until six months after his confirmation, when a top secret transcript of an executive session of the Warren Commission was released under pressure from Harold Weisberg's legal efforts. One of the transcripts showed indisputably that in his 1965 book Ford had directly used material that, until its release in 1974, was classified top secret. Contrary to President Ford's sworn testimony, the material had never been available to the public and had even been denied to writers who requested it.[45]

During his tenure on the Warren Commission, Congressman Ford played an extracurricular and highly sensitive role that remained a closely guarded secret for more than a dozen years. Within days of his appointment to the commission, Ford summoned a top FBI official, Cartha D. "Deke" DeLoach, to his office. According to a disclosed memo from DeLoach to his superiors, "Ford indicated he would keep me thoroughly advised as to the activities of the Commission." Since the commission activities were supposed to be secret, Ford explained that his briefings would have to be in the strictest of confidence.[46]

When President Ford appeared before the House Select Committee on Assassinations (HSCA) in 1978, he was asked about the DeLoach memoranda that described his relationship with the FBI. Ford acknowledged the accuracy of the DeLoach statements but asserted that the relationship described by DeLoach "did not continue during the investigation period of the Commission." He explained, "In the organizational phase, we had a lot of questions, and, frankly, I think it was very proper to do what I did."[47]

President Ford's loyalty to the commission conclusions has remained so strong that even today he denounces any effort to review the assassination investigation. In his letter to the author, he stated: "The most inexcusable waste of taxpayers' money was the $6 million spent by the House Committee to Investigate the Assassination of John F. Kennedy."[48]

In contrast to President Ford's denunciation, the establishment of the HSCA stirred great hope in some quarters that at last there would be a respectable investigation. There were promising new scientific testing techniques that might unlock old riddles. There was at least superficial reason to believe that, given the new cast of characters at the FBI and the CIA, an unfettered review of the case might be possible. And the investigative staff assembled by the HSCA had no links with the original investigation.[49]

In early 1979 the committee issued a report with the following general conclusions:

- Lee Harvey Oswald fired three shots at President Kennedy from the sixth floor of the Book Depository. The first shot missed. The second shot wounded both Kennedy and Governor Connally. The third shot blasted Kennedy's head apart, killing him.[50]
- Scientific acoustical evidence established a "high probability" that a second gunman was firing from the front, but missed Kennedy.[51]
- On the basis of available evidence, Kennedy "was probably" assassinated as the result of a conspiracy, the extent of which the committee could not determine.[52]

The findings of "probable conspiracy" caused a brief firestorm in Washington, and there were strong dissents by some of the committee members. Most of the criticism was heaped on the acoustics evidence, and the Justice Department had a panel of experts named to examine the HSCA acoustics findings. That panel decided the HSCA was flatly wrong, which really settled nothing. It simply returned the acoustics evidence to the arena of technical debate and attendant uncertainty.[53]

In the end there was a feeling among critics and much of the public that the committee never ventured beyond certain hallowed perimeters which guarded areas so sacrosanct that, to protect them, the government and its intelligence agencies could only erect a barrier of silence.[54] Whether there is truth to these suspicions cannot be known with certainty. What can be known is that provocative evidence, convincing to any open mind, continues to become available to suggest that there was far more to the Kennedy assassination than the simplistic version presented by the Warren Commission. And this same evidence continues to underscore the fact that the HSCA managed to avoid opening some of the most tantalizing doors that have been locked for two decades.

The people who have pursued and developed this evidence are not government officials with expansive budgets and subpoena power. To the contrary, they have been ordinary citizens who are encouraged by the same sort of reasoning noted by Senator Russell and President Johnson—originally stalwart public supporters of the Warren Report. The public doubt was not diminished in the least by the reassurances from the HSCA that—despite its findings of probable conspiracy—Lee Harvey Oswald did fire the shot that killed John F. Kennedy.[55]

Soon after President Ronald Reagan was shot in an assassination attempt on March 30, 1981, a public-opinion poll was conducted concerning Americans' feelings about violence and assassinations. Their country is, after all, one of the most violent in the industrial world—one where one out of four presidents has been attacked by would-be assassins. It is a country where one of ten presidents has been murdered in office. The 1981 poll showed that still only about one-fifth of the American people believe that Lee Harvey Oswald acted alone in killing John F. Kennedy.[56] To put it another way, the Warren Commission's basic conclusion is not embraced by a staggering 80 percent of the American people. This alone is legitimate reason for examining the evidence that has developed in recent years and for reviewing some of the astonishing inconsistencies offered by official investigators.

3 · AUTOPSY OF THE CENTURY

The tragic, tragic thing is that a relatively simple case was horribly botched from the very beginning, and then the errors were compounded at almost every other step along the way. Here is a historic event that will be discussed and written about for the next century, and gnawing doubts will remain in many minds, no matter what is done or said to dispel them.[1]

> —Dr. Milton H. Helpern,
> Medical Examiner for New York City

There is every reason to believe that we did get a comprehensive, thorough, professional autopsy report from trained, skilled experts.[2]

> —U.S. Senator Arlen Specter,
> Former Assistant Counsel
> to the Warren Commission

In the bleak waning hours of the day of President Kennedy's death, a team of military doctors at Bethesda Naval Hospital outside Washington rushed to complete the physical work of the autopsy. Their duty was mightily complicated by the presence of the many luminaries crowded into the autopsy room—among them the personal physician to President Kennedy, the surgeon general of the Navy and the commanding officer of the Naval Medical Center—along with agents from the Secret Service and the FBI. In all, there were more than two dozen people in the autopsy room. Unfortunately for the sake of history, there was not a single practicing forensic pathologist present—no one with any special expertise in examining bullet wounds.[3]

Adding to the pressure on the three clinical pathologists conducting the autopsy was the fact that the President's widow and his brother Robert, attorney general of the United States, remained in the building. They had arrived there after Mrs. Kennedy selected that hospital for the site of the autopsy. A Kennedy aide relentlessly pressured the doctors to complete their work, since the Kennedy family would not leave the hospital until the autopsy was completed and the body prepared to be taken to lie in state at the White House. Attorney General Robert Kennedy had signed an authorization for a complete autopsy, even though there had been initial resistance to this by the family. Under these circumstances, the confidence shown by the military pathologists seemed tentative at best. Later, they would claim to have felt hindered during their pursuit of a full examination.[4]

It was a damning measure of official ineptitude that the blue-ribbon autopsy team, recognized for their ability as hospital techni-cians and administrators, had virtually no experience in day-to-day forensic pathology.[5] In charge of the autopsy for the most important gunshot murder of the century was Commander James J. Humes, the director of laboratories at the Naval Medical School. By his own account, Commander Humes's experience in such matters was lim-ited to "several occasions . . . where . . . I have had to deal with violent death, accidents, suicides, and so forth."[6] There is no evi-dence that Commander Humes had ever before performed even one autopsy on a gunshot victim.[7]

Assisting Commander Humes was Commander J. Thornton Bos-well, chief of pathology at the Naval Medical School, and Lieutenant Colonel Pierre Finck, chief of the Wounds Ballistics Section of the Armed Forces Institute of Pathology. (Colonel Finck was more ex-perienced than his two colleagues, but he was called in by Com-mander Humes only after the autopsy was begun.) Of the three doctors, only Dr. Finck was a member of the American Academy of Forensic Sciences.[8]

Among the drawbacks faced by these doctors was that of trying to perform in a hospital facility that did not, as a primary routine, conduct postmortems into gunshot deaths. Ironically, the staff at Parkland Hospital, where Kennedy was pronounced dead, was well accustomed to conducting autopsies on gunshot victims. Indeed, had Texas law been observed and the autopsy conducted in Dallas, the country might have been spared the enduring confusion spawned by the events at Bethesda.[9]

The trouble at the Naval Hospital did not begin immediately.

Preparations were in place, and preliminary X rays and photographs were made of the President's body as soon as it was received at 7:35 P.M. X-ray pictures were taken of the front, back, and side of the head and also of the torso. Photographs were made showing the full face of the President as well as the massive head wound. This was all standard procedure to create a complete photographic record of the wounds.[10]

Once the actual dissection and examination were under way around 8:15 P.M., additional X rays and photographs were made as the work progressed. The hospital developed the X rays that night, but the photographic film was immediately turned over to the Secret Service. According to FBI documents that logged the transfer that night to the Secret Service, there were a total of forty-five exposures along with eleven X rays. (It is impossible to assess the accuracy of these figures except to note that they were the first ones recorded. Virtually every time the photographic material has been transferred and logged over the years, there appears to be a different count.)[11]

The existence of such an impressive photographic record of the President's wounds and autopsy should have provided a historical assurance that any confusion over details of the wounds might quickly be settled. There has been confusion, to be sure, but the actual photographs have not helped. Those photographs that have not vanished remain under seal at the National Archives.[12]

From the start, for a combination of reasons, it was clear this would be no ordinary autopsy proceeding. When Colonel Finck, who was more experienced than the others in forensic pathology, requested the clothing for examination, the request was refused. Experts in forensic pathology insist that clothing examination—the testing for bullet traces, the examination of bullet holes—is essential to the performance of a proper autopsy. In this case, the FBI was handling the examination of the clothing—not the autopsy doctors.[13]

There were four wounds in the President's body that were readily obvious. Each of these, in its own fashion, has stirred tremendous controversy in the ensuing two decades. The only agreement was that the massive hole in President Kennedy's head was the cause of death. It was a horrible wound that left part of the President's brain protruding and chunks of his skull in the limousine and on the street in Dallas. Pieces of the skull were brought in while the autopsy was in progress.[14]

The debate over the President's wounds continues in some quarters to this day. The first official description of these wounds was made by the Warren Commission, even though among the members and staff, only Earl Warren so much as glimpsed the autopsy photographs. While the Warren Commission *could* have reviewed the pictures, it decided to rely on schematic drawings. Incredibly, these drawings were not based on the photographs themselves but on the autopsy doctors' oral recollections of the wounds.[15]

In its report, the commission located the President's wounds, in addition to the massive head wound, as follows:

• A wound "about an inch . . . to the right and slightly above the large bony protrusion . . . [at] the back of the skull."
• A "wound . . . near the base of the back of President Kennedy's neck slightly to the right of his spine. . . ."
• A wound in the front portion of the President's neck.[16]

There was nothing simple about how the Warren Commission arrived at these seemingly clear-cut findings. But the commission's performance was strictly humdrum compared to the imaginative machinations of the military men who persisted in revising the autopsy report until it fit the clearly preconceived version of events created by the FBI and promulgated by the commission. Few would dispute that such manipulation lies at the root of most public doubt that persists today.

Some of the greatest controversy over these wounds swirls about the wound described by the commission as being near "the base of the back of the President's neck."[17] Since the Warren Commission believed the assassin was shooting downward from a sixth-floor window—and since one bullet had to enter the rear of Kennedy's body and exit the front—it was essential that the rear-entry wound be high enough on the President's back to accommodate the bullet exiting from the lower neck in the front. If the rear-entry wound was at the same level as, or lower than, the frontal exit wound, the fundamental commission thesis was knocked asunder.[18]

All of this was further complicated by the fact that the autopsy pathologists did not track a bullet path from the back to the front—a situation that could mightily disrupt the theory that the bullet passed through Kennedy.[19] Thus, it was vital to establish the rear-entry wound in the back as high as possible and to come up with a way to state with certainty that there *was* a bullet path through Kennedy's body.

The only known contemporaneous account of what happened during the autopsy procedure is a report made by the two FBI agents who observed the activities of the doctors and recorded what they saw. That report, which was not released with the Warren Report, has since been disclosed. The account takes note of the discovery of the wound in the back, which the Warren Commission said was at the "base of the . . . neck," and describes what happened next: "This opening was probed by Dr. Humes with the finger, at which time it was determined that the trajectory of the missile entering at this point had entered at a downward position of 45 to 60 degrees. Further probing determined that the distance traveled by this missile was a short distance inasmuch as the end of the opening could be felt with the finger."[20]

Three years later, a researcher for *Life* named Josiah Thompson sought out Commander Humes's assistant, Dr. Boswell, and asked about this probing. Thompson reported: "Boswell told me that this was correct and that, in fact, all three doctors had probed this wound with their fingers up to the first or second knuckle—a penetration of one to two inches. Boswell also indicated that the back wound had been examined with a metal probe—a thin piece of stiff wire some eight inches long with a knob on the end."[21]

Another eyewitness to the probing was Secret Service Agent Roy H. Kellerman, who had been riding in the presidential limousine at the time of the attack. Kellerman testified to the Warren Commission that there was consternation over the absence of a "shell" that might have been responsible for "the hole in the President's shoulder." He described the scene this way: "There were three gentlemen who were performing this autopsy. A Colonel Finck—during the examination of the President, from the hole that was in his shoulder, and with a probe, and we were standing right alongside of him, he is probing inside the shoulder with his instrument and I said, 'Colonel, where did it go?' He said, 'There are no lanes for an outlet of this entry in this man's shoulder.' "[22]

Dr. Finck, of course, was the lone pathologist present with some experience in examining bullet wounds.[23]

Commander Humes later told the Warren Commission that "attempts to probe in the vicinity of this wound were unsuccessful without fear of making a false passage." Dr. Humes added, "We were unable, however, to take probes and have them satisfactorily fall through any definite path at this point."[24]

Adding to the doctors' confusion was their failure to find any bullets in the body. After all, if there was no exit wound, they reasoned, a bullet should have been found. In the search for an answer, a call was made to the FBI laboratory. Only then did the doctors learn of the discovery of an unscratched bullet slug on a hospital stretcher in the Parkland emergency area.[25]

According to the eyewitness FBI report, Commander Humes told his colleagues that discovery of the Parkland bullet accounted for the fact that no bullet was found at Bethesda to explain the bullet wound in the back that failed to traverse the body. He explained that since external cardiac massage had been administered at Parkland, "it was entirely possible that through such movement the bullet had worked its way back out of the point of entry and had fallen on the stretcher."[26]

This news allowed Commander Humes and his associates to march toward certain conclusions, even though they made no effort to communicate with the doctors in Dallas who had tried to save the President.[27] Around 11:00 P.M., when the President's body was turned over to the morticians, the autopsy team had come to the following summations:

1. One missile entered the rear of the skull and exited from the front of the skull.

2. One missile entered the back of the President and was apparently dislodged during cardiac massage at Parkland Hospital.[28]

On the next morning, with his autopsy report already in mind, Commander Humes made his first contact with the medical team who had cared for President Kennedy at Parkland Hospital. During the course of his telephone conversation with Dr. Malcolm O. Perry, Dr. Humes learned that the Parkland doctors had observed a bullet wound in the front of the President's neck, just below the Adam's apple. Dr. Perry explained that he had made a lateral incision across the opening of the wound, creating the opening for the tracheotomy.[29]

Commander Humes was astonished to learn of this other bullet wound—one the autopsy team had completely overlooked. Humes and his associates had assumed that the tracheotomy in Kennedy's neck was only that—and never noticed that it had been fashioned over a bullet wound. (However, in 1968 a panel convened to review the autopsy found that indeed the tracheotomy did *not* obscure the original wound, even to the naked eye.) By this time, the President's body was lying in state at the White House. There was no chance for further examination. The autopsy report would have to be written to include a gunshot wound that the official pathologists had not examined.[30]

More than a decade later, Dr. Humes explained to the House Select Committee the details of his conversation with the Dallas doctor who had performed the emergency tracheotomy incision over the neck wound. Stating that the Dallas doctor had obscured the wound "very gorgeously for us," he added that the minute Dr. Perry told him of the neck wound, "lights went on, and we said, ah, we have some place for our missile to have gone." In a dramatic contradiction of earlier positions, Dr. Humes for the first time expressed his belief that the bullet wound in the back exited through the wound in the throat.[31]

Commander Humes left the hospital soon after learning about the neck wound. Carrying with him the blood-stained autopsy notes, he went to the quiet of his home to compose the official report. To account for the "new" bullet wound in the throat, Humes and his colleagues had already agreed that common sense indicated strongly that the throat wound must be the exit wound for the bullet entry in Kennedy's back. It was to be a report written largely from memory—memory surely beclouded by the last-minute introduction of a bullet wound not even seen during the actual autopsy.[32]

But in the end, everything was made to fit. The bullet wound in the throat could be explained as an exit wound, chiefly because in Humes's eyes it could be nothing else. This proposition also could conveniently account for the back wound, even though all three autopsy doctors had agreed—in front of numerous witnesses—that this track could be palpated no more than two inches into the body. The back wound that had no exit and the front wound that suddenly needed to be accounted for could be explained in a mutually useful way. One could take care of the other. Moreover, the new bullet that had turned up at Parkland could be credited with the damage.[33]

All that was needed was a way logically to discover a path through the body that might connect the two wounds. The purported entry wound was caused by a bullet fired downward into Kennedy's back from a point high behind him. But it somehow was to have exited from below his Adam's apple.[34] To any layman, this would seem impossible. It appeared to be a pure case of shoehorning irreconcilable pieces of evidence into a forced pattern and in the process bending the pieces to fit.

It was deep in the night when Commander Humes concluded his draft of the autopsy report. What happened next has been told so many different ways by Humes under oath that the truth may be lost forever. By Humes's own account, he walked to his fireplace and burned certain autopsy evidence. Exactly what he destroyed is not known, for Humes has vacillated each time he has described the incident. He has alternately claimed he burned the original autopsy notes, or an early draft, or various notes not specifically described. He has noted that he did not want the pieces of paper splotched with the blood of the President to get into the hands of the public.[35]

Whatever he burned, such an outrageous act shows irrefutably that Commander Humes possessed little knowledge of the basic standards for conducting a forensic autopsy. His behavior calls into question whether such an attitude guided him in other aspects of performing the autopsy and reporting the results. On the other hand, if Humes had been *ordered* to burn certain documents—as some respected critics believe—this would cast him in a different light.[36]

On Sunday Commander Humes met with the other autopsy doctors to go over his draft of the report. As they were working, word came that Oswald had been murdered in Dallas. Years later Humes told the Select Committee: "We interrupted our work to try and figure out what that meant to us."[37] How Oswald's death could conceivably have any bearing on a supposedly dispassionate autopsy report being written twelve hundred miles away challenges the imagination.

But one thing is clear: the autopsy doctors suddenly were relieved of the burdensome possibility that whatever they wrote in the report would be examined and challenged in a court by defense lawyers for the accused assassin. It is not known whether or not news of Oswald's death was the impetus for any specific revision, but the pathologists continued writing the autopsy report—one designed to provide answers for the most troublesome points hindering an easy case for the lone-assassin theory.[38]

By Sunday night, when Commander Humes officially finished the report, the conclusions were markedly different from the observations recorded earlier by the FBI in the contemporaneous report. Now there was the flat statement: "One missile entered the back of the President and exited in the front of the neck."[39]

Among the factors that weigh against this conclusion is that nearly every person who saw the neck wound at Parkland Hospital thought it to be an entry wound, or described it as having the typical characteristics of an entry wound. The doctors at Bethesda, who claimed they never paid any special attention to what they assumed was a tracheotomy, concluded the neck wound was one of exit. Then there is the agreement of all three autopsy doctors that they could not probe the back wound but a short distance; they even concluded at the finish of the autopsy that the missile that caused the damage must have fallen out of the back. They believed there was no bullet path, based on their examination of the back wound.[40]

If these matters seem puzzling twenty-two years later, it is interesting to consider that members of the Warren Commission initially had the same reaction. In a mid-December meeting, Commissioner John J. McCloy stated that the evidence concerning bullets "is looming up as the most confusing thing that we've got."[41]

In 1974 the transcript of an executive session of the Warren Commission for January 27, 1964, was disclosed. The transcript shows that the commission's general counsel, J. Lee Rankin, was every bit as confused by the evidence as millions of Americans to follow him. Considering the autopsy report, Rankin stated:

> There is a great range of material in regard to the wounds, and the autopsy and this point of exit or entrance of the bullet in front of the neck, and that all has to be developed much more than we have at the present time.
>
> We have an explanation there in the autopsy that probably a fragment came out the front of the neck, but with the elevation the shot must have come from, and the angle, it seems quite apparent now, since we have the picture of where the bullet entered in the back, that the bullet entered below the shoulder blade to the right of the backbone, which is below the place where the picture shows the bullet came out in the neckband of

the shirt in front, and the bullet, according to the autopsy, didn't strike any bone at all, that particular bullet, and go through—

COMMISSIONER BOGGS: I thought I read that bullet just went in a finger's length—

COUNSEL RANKIN: That is what they first said. They reached in and they could feel where it came, it didn't go any further than that . . . and then they proceeded to reconstruct where they thought the bullet went, the path of it, and, which is [why] we have to go into considerable items and try to find out how they could reconstruct that when they first said that they couldn't even feel the path beyond the first part of a finger.

And then how it could become elevated; even so it raised rather than coming out at a sharp angle that it entered, all of that, we have to go into, too, and we are asking for help from the ballistic experts on that.

We will have to probably get help from the doctors about it, and find out, we have asked for the original notes of the autopsy on that question, too.[42]

Some of the autopsy material, of course, had gone up in flames in Commander Humes's fireplace. But the suggested trajectory of the bullet Rankin speaks of—along with the necessity of this trajectory in explaining the extraordinary feats of what has come to be known as the Magic Bullet—would confound and perplex forensic pathologists and the general public perhaps for the rest of time.[43] (See Chapter 4 on the Magic Bullet.)

The 1974 disclosure of the top secret transcript of the January 27, 1964, commission executive session raised other curious questions. General Counsel Rankin refers to an autopsy report as indicating that a fragment might have come out of the front of Kennedy's neck, causing that wound. But there is no such reference in the official autopsy report published later that year by the commission. This is what raised the possibility that the January reference to an autopsy report was actually to an earlier autopsy report—one never seen by the public and later revised to reflect the official findings.*[44]

But the Warren Commission was, in the words of Commissioner

*Paul L. Hoch, one of the most meticulous and respected of the critics, disagrees with this assessment. Hoch told the author: "Rankin's language in that session was very informal and sloppy. Many things he said could not be taken literally. Based on the documents we now have which evidently formed the basis for what he was telling the commission, he simply wasn't being precise."

McCloy at an executive session, "set up to lay the dust . . . not only in the United States but all over the world."[45] Language would be preeminently important in efforts to achieve such a lofty goal. The commission faced a particularly thorny problem in accounting for the acute confusion that preceded the final autopsy findings. What the Warren Report finally stated was: "The autopsy also disclosed a wound near the base of the back of President Kennedy's neck slightly to the right of his spine. The doctors traced the course of the bullet through the body and, as information was received from Parkland Hospital, concluded that the bullet had emerged from the front portion of the President's neck that had been cut away by the tracheotomy at Parkland."[46]

Given the hundreds of hours of consideration of these very difficult contradictions, it is clear that the commission struggled to compress so much confusion into so neat a package of words. The confusion might have been reduced by the commission's examination of the photographs and X rays. This logical step was never taken, even though strongly recommended by some commission staff members.[47]

Commander Humes and his associates already had shown an impressive proclivity to use language—and in some cases omission—to shade reality. The holograph of the autopsy report, no doubt the most important one of this century, bears no date. Perhaps this is an oversight, or perhaps it is because the conclusions of the autopsy doctors were undergoing frequent revision to adapt to fresh information. Strong evidence of this possibility was uncovered with the release of the January 27 session transcript.[48]

In writing his report, Commander Humes faced quite a challenge in accounting for the fact that three doctors found it impossible to probe the back bullet wound more than about two inches—a bullet wound that *had* to traverse the President's body if the overall account was to make any sense.[49] Getting around this worrisome detail, Commander Humes told it this way in his final autopsy report: "The missile path through the fascia and musculature cannot be easily probed."[50]

Considering what is widely perceived as the gross incompetence of the presidential autopsy, Commander Humes and his associates may have welcomed a stern order from Admiral Edward C. Kenney, the surgeon general of the Navy, that they "discuss with no one events connected with your official duties on the evening of 22

November–23 November." Presumably such an order was aimed at making certain the autopsy report itself—a distillation of so much conjecture, blundering, and contradiction—stood as the final word. Indeed, it was a document that could withstand little questioning.[51]

Despite the order from the surgeon general of the Navy, Commander Humes and his two colleagues have been asked over the years to cooperate in official efforts to unravel the mysteries that still plague the original autopsy. One of the most persistent questions has been why the autopsy team failed to report on the condition of President Kennedy's adrenal glands. For years some critics have speculated that President Kennedy suffered from Addison's disease, and that this would be confirmed by the examination of his adrenal glands.[52]

In 1977 Commander Humes appeared before the Forensic Pathology Panel of the House Select Committee on Assassinations. It seems absurdly out of character for any investigation, but the committee staff explained that it was not going to ask any questions of Dr. Humes and Dr. Boswell inasmuch as they "have come voluntarily." Panel member Dr. Charles S. Petty, however, opened the session with Dr. Humes by asking "the question . . . on the lips of everyone here. . . . Did you or didn't you look at the adrenals?"

DR. HUMES: I would ask you—did that bear, or does that bear, on your investigation of the event that took place that night?

DR. PETTY: No; all we were wondering was—we noticed that that was noticeably absent from the autopsy report.

DR. HUMES: Since I don't think it bore directly on the death of the President, I'd prefer not to discuss it with you, doctor.

DR. PETTY: All right. Fine. If you prefer not to, that's fine with me. We were just curious because normally we examine adrenals in the general course that the autopsy, as we undertake it. Okay, so—

DR. HUMES: I'd only comment for you that I have strong personal reasons and certain other obligations that suggest to me that it might not be preferable.[53]

Dr. Humes obviously is correct in his opinion that President Kennedy's adrenal glands were irrelevant to his death and the autopsy.[54] And Dr. Humes cannot really be faulted for the fact that the committee staff decided to let him get away with avoiding whatever questions he pleased. What matters is that Dr. Humes's state-

ments make it clear that he was under "certain other obligations."
If Dr. Humes was referring simply to the privacy of the family, he
might have said so. It is essential that the nature of these obligations
be understood if the public is to accept any aspect of the committee's
autopsy findings. It is curious, to say the least, that the committee
did not see fit to press Commander Humes about these "certain
other obligations" he was under.

In spite of what might appear today to be irregularities in the
performance of Dr. Humes, indications are that he continued to
enjoy the high esteem of the Warren Commission staff.[55] In March
1964 consideration was being given to exhuming the body of Lee
Harvey Oswald in order to examine a scar on his wrist. An internal
Warren Commission staff memo suggests that Dr. Humes would be
a good man to call on to perform the examination. The memo described Humes as "competent and trustworthy."[56] In 1965 he was
promoted to the rank of captain.[57]

Of all the confusion and controversy spawned by the autopsy, no
aspect has caused more difficulty than the furious argument over
the location of the back wound. If the Warren Commission version
of Kennedy's death is to make any sense, then the bullet wound in
the back had to exit from the front of Kennedy's neck. Thus, it was
acutely important that the back wound be in a position high enough
to allow for the physical possibility of having it exit from Kennedy's
neck—taking into account that the bullet had been fired from a spot
above and behind the President. If the bullet that went into Kennedy's back did not exit from his neck, then there is no ordinary
way to explain the neck wound except as a wound of entry. This, of
course, would mean there was a shooter in the front of Kennedy as
well as one behind, thus leading to the indisputable conclusion of
a conspiracy.[58]

In the accounts of the witnesses to the autopsy, there is not a
single instance of anyone describing the wound in back as being in
Kennedy's neck. The FBI and Secret Service agents all described
the wound as being either in the back or the shoulder.[59] One Secret
Service agent even used the neck as a reference point in describing
the location of the wound. Clinton Hill testified that he observed
the wound "about six inches down from the neckline on the back
just to the right of the spinal column."[60]

It was only later, in the preparation of the revised autopsy report, that the wound began to be described as higher on the body. In the final analysis, the Warren Commission placed the rear wound at "the back of his neck," which allowed it to be aligned with the neck wound in the front. If the location of the wound had not been moved up, the basic thesis of the Warren Commission would have appeared even more ludicrous.[61]

In a less extraordinary autopsy, one would expect the location of the back wound to be described with anatomical precision in the autopsy report. However, Dr. Humes used as his reference points parts of the body that vary from person to person, as well as according to the position of the body. (Dr. Humes used the acromion and the mastoid process as his points of reference.)[62]

One of the original pieces of autopsy evidence that survived Dr. Humes's fireplace was the actual body chart of the President's wounds prepared by Commander Boswell. The diagram is compelling evidence that the back wound was precisely where the various autopsy witnesses said it was. Commander Boswell has casually dismissed what he claims is an error on his part, explaining that the diagram was only a rough sketch. Nonetheless, the other wounds pinpointed in Commander Boswell's diagram all appear almost precisely correct. It is significant that the back wound in Commander Boswell's diagram is not really even near the neck, but clearly down the back and to the right.[63]

In the course of events, Commander Boswell's diagram became a part of the Warren Commission evidence, showing the wound well down Kennedy's back. However, in 1966 Dr. Boswell explained in an interview that he had erred in pinpointing the back wound and that really the wound was at the base of the back of Kennedy's neck. That location for the wound had become one of the linchpins to the Warren Commission's thesis.[64]

It was not until 1975 that new light was shed upon the diagram. For nine years, assassination researcher Harold Weisberg had been pressuring the government for a variety of documents. Much to his surprise, misfiled with some other material he had acquired under legal pressure, Weisberg discovered copies of the original holograph of the autopsy as well as Boswell's original diagram. In the lower left-hand corner of Dr. Boswell's diagram, which he had disavowed, there is an extraordinary handwritten notation—one that had been omitted in the version passed on to the public by the Warren Commission. Admiral George Burkley, President Kennedy's personal physician, who had been present at the autopsy, had examined Dr. Boswell's diagram of the wounds and written "verified" and signed his name.[65]

It is significant that Dr. Burkley had been with the President in Dallas, with him in the Parkland Hospital emergency room, with his body as it was flown east, and present during the autopsy. It is also significant that even though he was the only doctor present both at Parkland and at Bethesda, Dr. Burkley's testimony was never taken by the Warren Commission, nor was it taken later by the House Select Committee.[66]

In 1982 Dr. Burkley told the author in a telephone conversation that he believed that President Kennedy's assassination was the result of a conspiracy.[67] This startling statement, after so long a silence, amplified an obscure exchange Dr. Burkley had in an oral-history interview on file at the Kennedy Library in Boston. The interviewer asks Dr. Burkley if he agrees with the Warren Report "on the number of bullets that entered the President's body."

"I would not care to be quoted on that," states Dr. Burkley.*[68]

Although the autopsy doctors were denied access to the President's clothing, the FBI laboratory examined it and pinpointed to the Warren Commission the exact location of the bullet holes in the back of Kennedy's jacket and shirt. In each instance, the bullet hole was between five and six inches from the top of the back of the collar and between one and two inches to the right of the midline of the clothing. This location, of course, was precisely where so many autopsy witnesses, including the President's personal physician, agreed that they were.[69]

Undaunted by this evidence from the FBI laboratory, the Warren Commission reported the findings and described the location of the holes in the clothing as being "in the vicinity of his lower neck."[70]

In light of the preposterous handling of evidence by officials and the commission's nearly incomprehensible interpretation of it, there is no difficulty in understanding the massive skepticism of the Amer-

---

*When he originally telephoned the author, Dr. Burkley expressed his willingness to discuss various matters concerning the assassination. He asked for a letter detailing the areas the author wished to discuss. Dr. Burkley acknowledged receipt of the letter with a letter of his own. Two months later, the author proposed a meeting with Dr. Burkley to discuss the points. The doctor responded with an abrupt refusal to discuss any aspect of the case.

ican public. It was this issue more than any other that propelled the early critics—primarily Epstein, Lane, Weisberg, and Meagher—to expose the incompetence and duplicity that were integral to the most important autopsy of the century.

As the debate over the autopsy persists in certain quarters, it is useful to listen to how one of this country's most eminent forensic pathologists, Dr. Milton Helpern, now deceased, described the autopsy of the President. For twenty years the chief medical examiner for New York City, Dr. Helpern supervised or performed 60,000 autopsies during his career, including some 10,000 involving bullet wounds.[71]

In the book *Where Death Delights*, by Marshall Houts, Dr. Helpern stated in an interview:

> The Warren Commission had an opportunity to settle once and for all a great many confusing doubts about the assassination. Yet because none of its members or its legal staff had any training in forensic medicine, those opportunities fell by the wayside. . . . [The Warren Commission] failed tragically because it did not have sufficient knowledge in the field of forensic medicine even to appreciate the need to call in an expert with experience in bullet wounds.[72]

Finally, in 1966, the original autopsy doctors were allowed for the first time to view the photographs made of the autopsy—at least the evidence that had not vanished. Those doctors believed the evidence supported their findings concerning the wounds.[73] In 1968 Attorney General Ramsey Clark convened a panel of experts to review the same material, and this group reported that the entry wound in the back of the President's *head* was actually four inches higher than described by the autopsy doctors. This represented the advent of yet a second floating wound, one that would cause consternation for years to come. In 1975 the Rockefeller Commission, impaneled by President Ford to investigate CIA activities within the United States, agreed with the findings of the Clark panel.[74]

The deepening confusion created by such contradiction among qualified medical authorities was a prime reason that, in 1976, the House of Representatives voted to reopen the Kennedy case.[75]

The creation of the House Select Committee on Assassinations was aimed primarily at settling, once and for all, the nagging questions surrounding the Kennedy case. G. Robert Blakey, chief counsel and staff director of the HSCA, was forthright in stating that events surrounding the autopsy—and the autopsy itself—had created more questions and doubt than any other aspect of the case. Blakey and his staff set out, once again, to settle the dust. One of the first steps was to convene a nine-man panel of forensic experts to be chaired by Dr. Michael Baden, then the medical examiner of New York City. The members of the panel collectively had participated in 100,000 autopsies.[76]

There was never any disagreement among the doctors that the original autopsy was disastrous in the way it was performed and in many of the specific findings.[77] While most of the doctors seemed restrained as they made their criticisms of the original autopsy, Dr. Cyril H. Wecht was not. A former president of the American Academy of Forensic Medicine, Dr. Wecht had been one of the earliest and most outspoken critics of the President's autopsy. His analytical articles describing his reservations had appeared in medical journals for years.[78] Dr. Wecht described the original autopsy as "extremely superficial and sloppy, inept, incomplete, incompetent in many respects, not only on the part of the pathologists who did this horribly inadequate medical-legal autopsy but on the part of many other people. This is the kind of examination that would not be tolerated in a routine murder case by a good crew of homicide detectives in most major cities of America."[79]

Dr. Baden himself may have pinpointed one of the most serious problems when he testified that the

> experience of each and every panel member is that in a homicide situation the last person to have control and tell the medical examiner how to proceed . . . is the family. . . . The very concept of the family having control of the body . . . [causes] great concern for forensic pathologists because of its implications in other homicides where the family . . . is not permitted . . . to have control over what happens to the bullet that killed Uncle Louie. The district attorney handles that and not the family.[80]

The HSCA's forensic panel agreed with earlier medical panels that disputed the original autopsy doctors in their location of the wound in Kennedy's head. (This dispute is different from the argument over the location of the back wound.) The committee decided, on the basis of photograph examinations, that the skull entry wound was four inches higher than the point specified by Humes and the Warren Commission. Dr. Humes was given a chance to modify his original findings, but he refused each opening offered by the committee's panel. He insisted that there had been no wound at that location, that he had examined the area himself and would not be swayed by the autopsy photographs being reviewed by the committee.[81]

The controversy over the President's head wound was far more onerous to resolve than the confusion over the back wound. That, at least, seemed explainable in terms of the misrepresentation of facts and shoehorning of evidence that marks other aspects of the Warren Commission investigation. With the head wound, however, there are discrepancies that can only be called suspicious. It seems significant that even Dr. Humes, who had been nothing if not amiable and "trustworthy," was adamant in his refusal to agree that the head wound was four inches *higher* than he and his colleagues had originally designated on their autopsy chart.[82]

In addition to the bewildering switch in the location of the head wound, the contradiction about the size of that wound was even more astounding. First, there is the tremendous difference in the size of the head wound as described by doctors in Dallas and the autopsy doctors in Bethesda. No one in Dallas actually measured the head wound, but the difference is so enormous that the point that no actual measurement was made is academic. Dallas doctors observed the head wound to be about 35 square centimeters. The autopsy doctors a few hours later put the size at a minimum of 130 square centimeters—nearly four times larger. (Author David S. Lifton has made an impressive study of these discrepancies which, along with his sensational theories concerning the conspiratorial alteration of the President's body, is examined in a later chapter.[83])

Even more disturbing is the intense contradiction over the location of the skull wound. Six of the doctors who examined the President in Dallas argue that there was a massive exit wound on the rear of the head.[84] "I was in such a position that I could clearly examine the head wound," stated Dr. Robert N. McClelland in testimony to the Warren Commission. "I noted that the right posterior portion of the skull had been blasted."[85]

This considered observation, supported by the five other doctors who first examined the President, was ignored in favor of the autopsy report, which describes a massive exit wound in the *right front* of the head and a small entry wound in the back of the head.[86] If the Dallas doctors are to be believed (and there is not the slightest reason to doubt their integrity), the rear area officially pinpointed for the entry wound had been blown away by the time the President's body reached Parkland. The skeletal area was not even there!

Three items would be of incalculable value in sifting through this morass. The original autopsy notes would provide a contemporaneous description of the wound, but those notes were apparently burned by Commander Humes in his fireplace. The brain itself could reveal striking details about the path of the bullet, but it has vanished from the National Archives, along with the slides of sectioned brain tissue, which could be similarly revealing.[87]

In the late 1970s, when the HSCA's medical panel went over the autopsy photographs with the autopsy doctors, the three doctors were absolutely positive that the photographs did *not* reflect what they had seen as the small entry wound in the back of the head.[88] Examining the wound in the cowlick area, four inches higher than the original autopsy placed it, Dr. Humes said, "I just don't know what it is, but it certainly was not any wound of entrance."[89]

During the exhaustive debate over this point, one panel doctor had such strenuous objections to the on-record discussion that he cautioned his colleagues: "We have no business recording this. This is for us to decide between ourselves; I don't think this belongs in this record. . . . You guys are nuts writing this stuff. It doesn't belong in this damn record."[90]

In the end, after enormous coaxing, Dr. Humes finally agreed that the head-wound location was where the Select Committee said it was, four inches higher than Humes and his colleagues originally agreed.[91] Drs. Finck and Boswell, however, stood firm in their contention that the bullet wound they saw was four inches lower than the HSCA medical panel claimed it was. What all this means is one of the most tantalizing mysteries that grip the case.

The committee's forensic panel also concluded that the entry wound in the back was two inches *lower* than stated by the Warren Commission. This was based on a scientific examination of the autopsy photographs, or at least those photographs that had not disappeared or been destroyed. So, after the struggle by the earlier doctors to raise the wound from the back to the posterior base of the neck, the latest panel moved its location from the neck to the back. Even in view of this, the original autopsy team stuck by its untenable contemporaneous measurements that were based on flexible anatomical points. And they, of course, were the only doctors who ever actually saw that wound. It remains nearly incomprehensible that there could be so much dispute and confusion over what a layman would guess should be a fairly routine description of medical conditions by trained professionals.*[92]

Another point established clearly by the HSCA was that the Parkland doctors believed initially and so stated publicly that the wound to the President's neck was probably one of entry—an impression the Warren Commission had encouraged the Parkland doctors to abandon. While the latest experts all agreed the anterior neck wound was one of exit, it remained utterly confusing that the initial opinions of the dozen or so witnesses from Parkland Hospital could be overruled by the opinions of the twenty-six witnesses at Bethesda who did not know the bullet wound existed. And, of course, none of the doctors on the HSCA panel even saw the President's body.[93]

As for the mysterious floating back wound, the Select Committee agreed that it was the entry wound for the exit wound on the front of the neck.[94] However, Dr. Baden was forthright about the deficiencies of evidence: "The track wasn't dissected out. We have to speculate from other sources of information."[95]

In the end, after all this contradictory evidence, the HSCA agreed that the general conclusions of the original autopsy doctors had been correct in terms of the number and direction of bullets that hit the President. Even the committee's forensic pathology panel was nearly unanimous in its agreement, with the lone and strong dissent of Dr. Wecht. The committee found these conclusions bolstered by its own discovery of certain subtle twists of the President's body, seconds before he was hit, that could explain what appeared to be so extraordinary a trajectory by the bullet that supposedly passed through his upper torso.[96]

---

* The Select Committee employed a medical artist, Ida Dox, to draw exact replicas of several of the autopsy photographs. Three of the Dox drawings were published by the committee. They are widely accepted as accurate depictions of the autopsy photographs of the wounds to President Kennedy's back, neck, and head.

However meritorious these conclusions, there was something darkly ironic about the fact that the HSCA seemed to feel that though the original autopsy team had done nearly everything wrong, it had still reached the right conclusions.

Inevitably, this begged the very charge heard so often from the critics—that the official conclusion concerning the number and direction of shots was mandated by the lone-assassin theory. If the shooting did not happen the way the Warren Commission and the Select Committee agreed it happened, then there had to have been two people shooting and hitting the President. The greatest irony is that throughout the intensely detailed evidence and testimony, an occasional supporter will point out that, after all, it must have happened this way since there was but one assassin. By the same token, the argument is offered that even though no track is ever established between the back wound and the neck wound, it must be there because no bullet came from the front. Such logic, of course, is based on a predetermined premise.[97]

Of all the lingering anomalies, nothing is more outrageous than the disappearance of extremely important evidence. The most dramatic missing item is the President's brain, but in addition there are brain sections as well as sections from the skin around the wounds that were prepared for microscopic examination. They are all missing from the National Archives, along with supplemental photographs that were taken of the interior of the President's chest.[98]

While experts can—and *do*—argue endlessly over the importance of this missing evidence, the certainty is that this particular evidence pertains directly to the very points that are in the greatest dispute. Examination of the interior chest photographs could diminish the debate over whether or not the back-entry wound traversed the body. The brain itself, which was never fully sectioned, could settle the question of an apparently foreign object that can be seen in some of the photographs of the head that show the brain. The object could be a tumor, or it could be a fragment of a bullet or any of a number of other things. But if it were a bullet fragment, there would suddenly be an entirely new set of conditions to consider.[99]

The first nongovernment pathologist to have access to the autopsy materials in the National Archives was Dr. Cyril Wecht, who examined the evidence in the summer of 1972. From the beginning and almost alone in the medical profession, Dr. Wecht had been preaching the horrors of the Kennedy autopsy and had reported widely that crucial pieces of the autopsy materials had vanished from the National Archives. Naturally, it was Dr. Wecht who later persisted as a member of the Select Committee's forensic pathology panel in urging the committee to track down the missing evidence. An analysis was made of the movements of the evidence, but in the end the committee was not successful.[100]

Following the autopsy in 1963, all materials were turned over to the Secret Service and kept at the White House under the official custody of Dr. Burkley, the White House physician. In April 1965 Robert F. Kennedy authorized that the materials be turned over to Evelyn Lincoln, the President's former secretary; she had an office at the National Archives, where she was working on the transfer of President Kennedy's papers to the Kennedy Library, which is under the control of the Archives. Among the materials inventoried in the transfer from the White House to Evelyn Lincoln was a stainless steel container, measuring seven inches in diameter and eight inches high, which it is believed contained the President's preserved brain.[101]

On Halloween of 1966, Burke Marshall, a lawyer representing the Kennedy estate, ordered the transfer of the evidence to the official custody of the National Archives. It is at that point, according to the HSCA, that the steel container and certain other materials were found missing. More than thirty people were interviewed by the Select Committee staff in order to find out what happened to the steel container and the other missing items. Among those questioned were Burke Marshall, Dr. Burkley, Dr. Humes, Ramsey Clark, and Evelyn Lincoln. Chief Counsel Blakey explained that while some of the people were merely interviewed, "the closer they came to the chain of evidence, they were deposed." He did not say who was deposed. In any event, according to Blakey, they all professed ignorance about the missing autopsy materials.[102]

In his report to the HSCA, Blakey speculated that possibly Robert Kennedy had destroyed the evidence. Blakey stated that a Kennedy family representative had indicated to the committee staff that the President's brother "expressed concerns that these materials could conceivably be placed on public display many years from now and he wanted to prevent that."[103] In its conclusion, the committee found that "circumstantial evidence tends to show that Robert Kennedy either destroyed these materials or otherwise rendered them inaccessible."[104]

If there is any validity to this speculation, it is curious that Robert Kennedy would select these particular pieces of evidence to make off with. In addition to the brain, there are photographs of the President's chest laid open. And there are laboratory slides of tissue sections of the skin surrounding the wounds on Kennedy's body. All of this could have been of tremendous value to forensic pathologists in determining how the President died.[105]

The trouble with Blakey's speculation is that if Robert Kennedy stole these items to prevent sensational display of them, he picked the wrong material. The open-chest photographs presumably show the innards of a chest much like that of any forty-six-year-old man. The tissue sections would be indistinguishable from those taken from an animal's carcass. And certainly the appearance of the brain was no different from any other brain. The materials that have not vanished have far greater value in terms of ghoulish sensationalism than those that are missing. The missing items would have minimal value to anyone sick enough to want to display them—and surely those who came to see them would have no way of knowing that they were genuine.

If Robert Kennedy was truly concerned about the possibilities mentioned by Blakey, it seems logical that he would have removed certain other pieces of evidence. Much more gruesome are the photographs of John F. Kennedy's familiar face, his eyes open in a death stare, the side of his head blown away. That, it would seem, is the sort of photograph the Kennedy family might want destroyed. Instead, they gave it to the National Archives. And Robert Kennedy did not try to stop his brother's bloody clothing from being displayed to the commission and photographs of it published in the Warren Commission exhibits.[106]

One of the most peculiar aspects of the entire mystery surrounding the missing brain of the President is why it was never coronally sectioned in the first place. That is a procedure in which the brain is sliced at precise anatomic points into thin sections. This permits the tracking of bullet paths as well as possible discovery of additional bullet fragments or even other damage. Commander Humes testified that he and his colleagues removed the brain and "fixed" or solidified it in a formaldehyde solution, which is essential prior to sectioning. Also in keeping with normal practice, Commander Humes and his associates convened two weeks later to examine the brain. But instead of slicing the brain apart, Commander Humes sliced gingerly around the edges of the brain. He explained in his report that a full sectioning was not done "in the interest of preserving the specimen."[107]

No one has ever explained why the doctors wanted to "preserve the specimen" (Kennedy's brain), especially at the expense of failing to perform one of the most important procedures in the autopsy. The brain represented a highly valuable piece of forensic evidence that was not buried in President Kennedy's grave. Even today, experts believe, a proper examination of the preserved brain could yield new clues on the question of whether more than one bullet passed through the President's head.[108]

It is a shocking breach of this country's expressed standards of judicial procedure that this evidence could be stolen or destroyed after being ignored in the official investigation. It is one of the many aspects of the case that continue to fan the flames of doubt.

Among the legions of doubters is Dr. Wecht, who does not believe that Commander Humes and his associates were simply blundering in their failure to examine the brain properly. Dr. Wecht states: "To voluntarily omit such an examination is to be incompetent or a fool, and I do not believe the autopsy pathologists were either. I believe that they were *instructed* not to do a complete examination of the brain. The decision was not theirs."[109]

Dr. Wecht's charges raise the terrible specter of a conspiracy involving a cover-up by respectable American citizens. To laymen— those four out of five Americans whose doubts persist—Dr. Wecht's comments make far more sense than does the Select Committee's endorsement of the Warren Commission findings. It is ironic that perhaps the most powerful ally Dr. Wecht has in his argument is Commander Humes himself, who swore to the HSCA that he could not discuss another omitted aspect of the autopsy—the report on Kennedy's adrenal glands—because of "certain other obligations." The HSCA may have been the last forum in history where Dr. Humes could be questioned about his "certain other obligations." As awesome in its implication as Dr. Wecht's charges is the fact that that question was never asked.[110]

One of the most fragile underpinnings of the official version of President Kennedy's murder is the proposition that a bullet entered his back, passed through his body, exited from his lower neck, and went on to pass through Governor Connally. Official medical experts largely agree that this is what happened. If it did not happen this way, it is generally agreed, then there was a second assassin, and thus a conspiracy. The whole flimsy case becomes unglued. Enormous official effort has gone into trying to prove this particular point. Comedy has flashed through the outrageousness as doctors arbitrarily moved the location of the back wound several inches upward so that it could be high enough to manage a logical exit from the front of the neck—even though the bullet, which the Warren Commission said hit no bones in Kennedy, was supposedly moving at a sharply downward angle when it entered Kennedy's back. It was a tough case to make, and few people ever believed the government's feeble account. Still, though, it is the official version.[111]

Government officials and their supporters have worked over the years to maintain this legend. Some apparently perjured themselves in service to their cause. Meanwhile, a lone citizen was pursuing the question from quite a different angle. Of the millions of Americans who believed the official version to be a lie, Harold Weisberg set out to prove it so. Alone, he has come far closer to making his case on this point than the whole United States government has in defending its.[112]

Weisberg did not focus on the location of the back wound. He accepted that the body chart drawn and later disavowed by Commander Boswell was correct in showing the back wound to be between five and six inches below President Kennedy's collar line. (The HSCA finally agreed that the wound was much lower than previously concluded by the Warren Commission.) Weisberg was far more interested in the wound in the front of the neck that was supposed to be the exit for the bullet in the back. The autopsy report, which was embraced by the Warren Commission, described this wound as being in the "low anterior neck."[113]

That front neck wound, of course, was largely believed to have been one of entry by those experienced observers at Parkland Hospital. That was the thrust of their initial impressions and was stated several times at a press briefing conducted at the hospital by a White House official. But the official version ruled that it was a wound of exit and suggested that the exiting bullet caused the nick on the side of the knot of the President's tie. The government version also suggested that the slits through the front of the neckband of the President's shirt were caused by an exiting bullet.[114]

The initial difficulty with the government's case was that the FBI laboratory—after spectrographic analysis—could find no metal traces on the tie or the neckband of the collar, traces that should have been there if a bullet had caused the damage.[115]

The second major problem was one that often plagued the commission: a highly credible witness who saw and said things that contradicted the larger picture. Dr. Charles Carrico, the doctor who examined Kennedy in the emergency room *before* his shirt and tie were removed, testified to the Warren Commission (and later confirmed in an interview) that the anterior neck wound was *above the knot of his tie.*[116] A wound location this high in the front would render fatuous the whole teetering premise of the Warren Commission. (The commission ignored Dr. Carrico's testimony on this point, even though he was the doctor in the best position to have any direct knowledge.)

Weisberg pressed his case in court to have the National Archives release clear photographs of the President's shirt and tie, because the pictures that had been provided by the FBI to the Warren Commission were unclear and virtually worthless. The photographs finally disclosed to Weisberg show that the suggested bullet holes in the shirt's front neckband are not bullet holes at all. They are slits made by scalpels used by nurses to cut off the President's necktie. One nurse who cut off the clothing confirmed this, adding impressive credence to Weisberg's observations. The other astonishing confirmation is that the bullet hole in the back of the shirt is precisely where the first body chart placed it. That chart had been ignored by the commission and disavowed by the doctor who prepared it.[117]

The testimony of Dr. Carrico, combined with the revelations in the photographs, shows with absolute certainty to almost any layman that the bullet that entered Kennedy's back nearly six inches below his collar at a sharply downward angle *could not possibly* have exited from Kennedy's neck, above the collar, where Dr. Carrico saw the wound.

Where, then, did the frontal neck wound come from? That is a question never pursued by the commission. The answer is one the government seems not to want to know.

4 · THE MYSTERY OF
THE MAGIC BULLET

There is no more vital buttress for the official version of the assassination than the viability of the single-bullet theory. If that proposition fails, every finding of the Warren Commission and essential findings of the House Select Committee on Assassinations (HSCA) become unglued. Collapse of the theory means there must have been at least two gunmen who hit President Kennedy in Dealey Plaza. For the single-bullet theory to stand, a lone bullet must be credited with feats that are bewildering in scope. One must accept that in wounding President Kennedy and Governor Connally, this remarkable bullet traversed seven layers of skin, pierced through muscle tissue, and smashed bones. The bullet then emerged practically unscathed. If this super-bullet did not accomplish all of these nonfatal wounds, then there had to be a second bullet—and a second deadly accurate shooter. The possibility of a second shooter, which would seem to be a logical consideration in such an investigation, was hardly discussed by the Warren Commission and given highly esoteric treatment by the HSCA.[1]

Over the years this remarkable bullet has assumed a mystique of its own in the minds of critics and much of the public. Despite dozens of tests by officials aimed at showing that the feats of the bullet are at least *possible*, no test—regardless of how tilted in favor of the official outcome—has managed to duplicate such a stunning performance. Officials refer to the bullet by the number originally assigned it by the Warren Commission, Commission Exhibit (CE) 399. Popularly, CE 399 has earned a more descriptive and fitting sobriquet of its own: the Magic Bullet.[2]

At the center of the furious debate over the actual shooting is the fact that there is no proof of how many shots were fired. Testimony from witnesses and experts was conflicting from the start. Three, four, or even five shots were believed by various people to have wrought the carnage that terrible afternoon. In the end, the Warren Commission concluded that there had been three shots, strongly citing as evidence the fact that only three spent cartridges were found in what the commission concluded was the lair of the lone assassin, Lee Harvey Oswald, above and behind President Kennedy's position.[3] (Fourteen years later, citing modern analysis of acoustics evidence, the HSCA concluded that a fourth shot was fired from the grassy knoll in front of the President—but the Select Committee declared that this shot missed its target.[4])

In 1964, however, as the Warren Commission worked toward its conclusions, it found itself laboring under the harsh discipline of an excruciatingly accurate built-in timing device. This was part and parcel of the famous home movie taken that day by Abraham Zapruder, a motion picture that provides a nearly complete record of the assassination in gruesome color. Early on, the FBI laboratory determined how many frames moved through the camera per second, thus establishing an indelible constant to which the official version had to adhere. Indeed, this possibly was one of the few stern constraints that guided the commission as it reached its conclusions regarding the actual shooting.[5]

Of the three shots, the Warren Commission credits one with shattering Kennedy's head. A second shot was believed by the commission to have missed the car. The remaining shot would, ipso facto, have to account for all other bullet damage that occurred during the given moments. If this was not true, an additional hit would be necessary, a shot that would spell conspiracy. These factors placed a terrible strain on the potential of this bullet, the Magic Bullet, as well as on the basic credibility of the single-bullet theory.[6]

There were, of course, bullet fragments that were left in the wake of the shooting. The largest of these were found nearly twelve hours after the assassination in the presidential limousine, which had been transported to Washington after having sat unattended among the milling crowd at Parkland Hospital. The smallest fragments were recovered from the bodies of the victims.[7]

Despite mutilation so severe that the FBI could not tell if they were from one or two bullets, the limousine fragments were ballistically linked to the rifle found on the sixth floor of the Texas School

Book Depository, the gun believed by the Warren Commission to have fired all of the shots. However, star billing for ballistics linkage to the Oswald rifle quickly went to the Magic Bullet, that nearly pristine bullet discovered in Parkland Hospital after President Kennedy was declared dead.[8]

In addition to the seemingly convincing presence of the Magic Bullet as evidence, investigators had to rely on eyewitness testimony along with the well-timed sequence provided by the Zapruder film. At first glance it was only logical to assume that President Kennedy and Governor Connally were wounded by separate shots. That is the way it looks to nearly anyone who views the Zapruder film. That possibility was pursued briefly by the Warren Commission, but it was soon abandoned upon the realization that it meant that two shots would have to have been fired less than two seconds apart. It was impossible for Kennedy and Connally to have been hit by two separate shots from Oswald's ancient, bolt-action rifle, given the time span between the apparent reaction to hits of the two men in the Zapruder film. Even the FBI's top rifle experts were not able to fire the rifle twice in that period of time.[9]

Therefore, the Warren Commission decided—and the Select Committee later agreed—that the body and limb wounds of Kennedy and Connally must have been caused by the same bullet.[10] One of the Warren Commission lawyers, Norman Redlich, told an interviewer in 1965 that "to say that they were hit with separate bullets is synonymous with saying that there were two assassins."*[11]

Thus arose the necessity for a single bullet of this type to exhibit feats of penetrating power, trajectory, and toughness unseen since—despite the dozens of official tests aimed at proving that the bullet's feats were really not unique. It is an unsurpassed irony that each test seemed to strengthen the arguments of the critics. In the end, it was hardly surprising that this remarkable bullet, still in nearly perfect condition following its amazing achievements, came to be known as the Magic Bullet.[12]

The accomplishments of the Magic Bullet can be viewed on several levels—all of them highly impressive. At a muzzle velocity of 2,000 feet per second—and having been fired from about two hundred

---

*When contacted in 1983, Norman Redlich said he could not recall having stated this, although he was aware of the quote's being widely attributed to him over the years. He conceded that he had never made any attempt to publicly disavow the quotation.

feet above and behind the President—CE 399 entered Kennedy's back two inches to the right of his spine and more than five inches below his collar line. The FBI agents at the autopsy reported that the missile entered the body at a downward angle of forty-five to sixty degrees. Then, having moved along a slightly upward line and from right to left, the bullet exited at the front of the neck just to the right of Kennedy's Adam's apple. (See Chapter 3 for an account of the fact that no bullet track was ever found from the back to the front of his body. The presumed track was based on speculation, according to the autopsy doctors.)[13]

Though in the commission's account the bullet allegedly struck no bones that might have caused a deflection in course as it passed through Kennedy, it then entered Connally's body at the rear of his right armpit. Since Connally was seated in front of Kennedy, it is difficult to grasp how the bullet (while going to the left) got from the front of Kennedy's neck far enough to the right to begin its leftward path through Connally. The bullet then moved downward more steeply through the governor's chest, at an angle of twenty-five degrees, where it "literally shattered" his fifth rib, leaving five inches of it "pulverized." The bullet then exited Connally's chest below the right nipple.[14]

The bullet continued downward and struck Connally's right wrist, which gripped his white Stetson hat. The bullet shattered the radius bone at the largest point. The bullet then exited the wrist and entered Connally's left thigh. Then, according to the official version, the bullet stopped and some time later fell out of the thigh wound— still later to be discovered in nearly perfect condition in a hospital corridor. There was no visible blood or tissue on the bullet. Later, it was made a part of the official evidence.[15]

This is the version put forth by the Warren Commission. Astonishingly, fourteen years later, it was certified by the HSCA. Dr. Cyril Wecht, a member of the Select Committee's forensic pathology panel, voiced his incredulous dissent when he told the committee: "The vertical and horizontal trajectory of this bullet . . . under the single-bullet theory is absolutely unfathomable, indefensible and incredible."[16]

Though few seem to know it, Dr. Wecht had impressive company in his strong dissent. Records disclosed after the Warren Report was published reveal that the FBI and the Secret Service from the earliest time believed that Governor Connally was struck by the second bullet from the Oswald rifle, one that did not hit the President. However, in keeping with their supportive roles to the commission, the FBI and the Secret Service never went beyond the simple statement of belief that it was the second bullet, not the first, that hit Connally. The Warren Commission did not make public these dissents.*[17]

Dr. Wecht, however, did not show the reserve of the Secret Service and the FBI in offering his thundering dissent—a dissent that echoed years of doubt in the public's mind. In fact, it is hard to find *any* persuasive discourse in support of the single-bullet theory in the testimony of the Warren Commission or the Select Committee.

One of the most cogent observations about the single-bullet theory comes from William F. Alexander, Dallas County assistant district attorney at the time of the assassination. In 1983 Alexander told the author, "The Magic Bullet is like the Immaculate Conception. You either accept it or you don't."[18]

One significant reason for the irreconcilable debate over the matter of CE 399 is that the bullet's exact original weight is not known. The average weight of a 6.5-millimeter slug, according to the FBI laboratory, is about 161 grains. CE 399 was weighed by the FBI as 158.6 grains. The FBI then removed two samples for testing. A sample of copper alloy was removed from the nose of the slug, and a cone of lead alloy was removed from the base. These samples were to be used for spectrographic analysis. Assuming the figure of 161 grains for the original weight of CE 399, only 2.4 grains—or 1.5 percent—is missing.[19]

Dr. Robert R. Shaw, a surgeon who operated on Governor Connally, expressed his own reservations on this important point. He told the Warren Commission that he doubted CE 399 could have passed through Connally—not to mention Kennedy also—and not have lost more particles of lead than it apparently did. He based his judgment strictly on the number of metal fragments left by the bullet in Connally's wrist, expressing the opinion that more than three grains were in the wrist alone. (More than thirteen years later, Dr.

*Another major dissenter from the official version, whose account will be discussed later, was Governor Connally himself, who to this day is certain that he and the President were hit by separate shots.

Shaw was quoted by an HSCA investigator as saying that he was "not qualified to speculate" about the size of the fragments—a mild recantation with shades of the manner in which Warren Commission witnesses were encouraged to revise opinions in order to be supportive of the official conclusions.)[20]

Dr. Charles Gregory, an orthopedic surgeon who worked on Connally's wrist, testified that he believed he retrieved two metal fragments from the wrist. Dr. Gregory was able to show the Warren Commission the fragments in X rays made prior to the surgery—and that subsequent X rays showed they were gone. In addition, a fragment remains in Connally's chest that commonly is ignored in accounts of the governor's wounds.[21]

Moreover, no one has ever explained satisfactorily what happened to the metal fragments from Connally's operating room that were handed to Texas State Trooper Charles Harbison, a veteran of thirty-one years on the force. Harbison was standing guard at the door to the operating room when a nurse, who has supported Harbison's account, handed him the fragments. Harbison told the author, "I immediately turned around and handed them to somebody else. And who that somebody else was, I'll never know." The operating room nurse, Audrey Bell, is explicit in stating that those fragments were not dustlike particles, as defenders of the Warren Commission insist. She told an interviewer that there were four or five fragments "anywhere from three to four millimeters in length by a couple of millimeters wide."[22]

In any event, the weight loss to CE 399 was so minimal that Robert Frazier, a ballistics expert from the FBI laboratory, testified that his examination of the slug convinced him that there "did not necessarily have to be any weight loss to the bullet." He added that there possibly was "a slight amount of lead missing from the base of the bullet." Frazier thought that no more than three or four grains could be missing at the most.[23]

Considering how much metal was removed from Connally after the shooting—and the indeterminate amounts left in his body—it becomes virtually impossible in the layman's mind for the nearly perfect CE 399 to be responsible for all of the damage. But that is what the Warren Commission concluded and the HSCA endorsed.[24]

To understand how crucial the lone-bullet theory is to the official version of the assassination, the timing of the whole event must be considered. Based primarily on the Zapruder film, it is largely agreed that all of the shooting occurred during a span of 5.6 seconds. Master marksmen—the highest rifle-expert rating of the National Rifle Association—and top FBI experts tried to match this firing time with the Oswald rifle in shooting tests. The rickety rifle had been overhauled, yet the experts found that getting off three shots was extremely difficult for them, even though, unlike Oswald, they could take their time aiming the first shot. Even the shots they could fire in that time span did not match Oswald's supposedly superlative accuracy.[25]

Assuming, for the sake of the commission argument, that Oswald *could* shoot better than the country's best experts, there still remain serious problems with the single-bullet account. Analysis of the Zapruder film shows Kennedy already reacting to the first hit at what the Warren Commission designated as frame Z225, just as he emerged from behind a highway sign. This suggested that he was hit while behind the sign and out of view of the camera. In that same frame, Governor Connally shows no indication of distress. He is still firmly holding his big white Stetson, using the wrist that was supposed to have been shattered within the last second.[26]

It is nearly a full second after emerging from behind the sign that Connally shows the first indications of reacting to a hit. This means either that Oswald got off a second shot within 1.7 seconds after the first one or that there was another shooter who hit Connally. The third possibility—the one officially accepted—is that the bullet that struck Connally had already passed through Kennedy.[27]

Governor Connally, a man experienced in hunting and using rifles, has strong feelings about what happened at that moment—feelings that have persisted for twenty-two years. At the first sound, Governor Connally knew instantly that he heard rifle fire: "I instinctively turned to my right because the sound seemed to come from over my right shoulder . . . but I did not catch the President in the corner of my eye. . . . Failing to see him, I was turning to look back over my left shoulder into the back seat, but I never got that far in my turn."[28]

Hit, Connally slumped to the side and was pulled by his wife into her lap. A few moments later, Connally heard the final shot slap into the President. The governor was splattered with blood and brain tissue. There is not the slightest doubt in Connally's and Mrs. Connally's minds that they distinctly heard a rifle shot and were wondering about it at the moment the governor was hit. Governor Connally, who reaffirmed his belief to the author in 1982, knew that a bullet—moving faster than the speed of sound—reaches its target well before the sound of the shot. Since he clearly heard the first shot, Governor Connally is absolutely certain he was not hit by the same bullet that struck Kennedy in the back.[29]

In 1966 Governor Connally told *Life*: "They talk about the 'one-bullet or two-bullet theory,' but as far as I'm concerned, there is no 'theory.' There is my absolute knowledge . . . that one bullet caused the President's first wound, and that an entirely separate shot struck me. . . . It's a certainty. I'll never change my mind."[30]

When Governor Connally testified before the HSCA in 1978, he stated that his opinion remained "very, very strong" on that point: "I do not believe, nor will I ever believe, that I was hit with the first bullet. . . . I heard the first shot. I reacted to the first shot and I was not hit with that bullet."*[31]

Another original dissenter who agrees with Governor Connally is Secret Service Agent Roy Kellerman, who was in charge of the detail at the time of the shooting. Kellerman flatly told the Warren Commission: "If President Kennedy had from all reports four wounds, Governor Connally three, there have got to be more than three shots, gentlemen."[32]

In the end, the perceptions of Governor Connally, the testimony of eyewitnesses, the evidence seen in the Zapruder film, the reservations of nearly all of the on-scene doctors, were cast aside in favor of the single-bullet theory. This theory, of course, was conceived in the minds of men who had no firsthand knowledge of the events. Only one explanation was offered by the Warren Commission for discarding Governor Connally's powerfully persuasive testimony: he must have suffered a delayed reaction to his wounds. Years later, the HSCA concurred. Again, the conclusions appeared to rule the evidence.[33]

Dr. Milton H. Helpern, who supervised more than 10,000 gunshot autopsies during his four decades of examining bodies in New York City, was scathing in his assessment of the feats attributed to the Magic Bullet. Stated Dr. Helpern:

---

*FBI Agent J. Doyle Williams, who played Connally's role in the Warren Commission reenactment of the shooting, told the author in 1983 that he believed he was "hit" by a separate "bullet" from the first shot that hit Kennedy.

This bullet wasn't distorted in any way. I cannot accept the premise that this bullet thrashed around in all that bony tissue and lost only 1.4 to 2.4 grains. . . . I cannot believe either that this bullet is going to emerge miraculously unscathed, without any deformity. . . .

The energy of the bullet is sometimes so spent that it can't quite get out through the final layer of skin, and it comes to rest just beneath the outside layer of skin. If it does get through the skin, it may not have enough energy to penetrate even an undershirt or a light cotton blouse. It has exhausted itself, and just more or less plops to a stop.[34]

Whatever the truth about which wounds were caused by the Magic Bullet, it is troubling that CE 399 ever found its way into the annals of acceptable evidence. It is unlikely that any piece of evidence of such pivotal significance has ever had such a sullied past. Indeed, there isn't even the faintest, most informal evidentiary chain to link the bullet to the wounds of Kennedy and Connally—*save one.* *

The bullet *was* fired from the rifle found on the sixth floor of the Book Depository. That rifle's purchase was traced to Lee Harvey Oswald. Since the Warren Commission and the Select Committee were convinced for other reasons that Oswald did the shooting, they *assumed* that he must have fired CE 399 at the victims. Once more, an unproved premise governed the conclusion. Given the circumstances of the discovery and handling of CE 399, its acceptance as a persuasive piece of evidence is highly debatable.[35]

The official conclusion states that CE 399 was found on a stretcher used to transport Governor Connally at Parkland Hospital in Dallas. An examination of the testimony and evidence shows, however, that there is absolutely no support for this proposition. Indeed, Parkland Hospital senior engineer Darrell C. Tomlinson, the man who discovered the bullet, was excruciatingly precise in his Warren Commission testimony that he did not know which stretcher it had been. The commission counsel, Arlen Specter, repeatedly led Tomlinson through the testimony, seeming to try to confuse him by suggesting what he *might* have said in earlier interviews with the FBI and the

---

*Neutron activation analysis was performed on bullet fragments as well as on the Magic Bullet by the HSCA. For several reasons the results remain questionable. They are examined later in this chapter.[36]

Secret Service. But Tomlinson was resolute in his refusal to be pinned down about whose stretcher the bullet was found on.[37]

The significant point that emerges clearly from the testimony of Tomlinson and other hospital-staff personnel is that the stretcher in question was parked unattended for more than thirty minutes in a busy corridor where dozens of people were milling about—many of whom had barged in from the streets without any sort of credentials.[38]

In the end, not a whit of proof can be found to support the claim that CE 399 came from Connally's stretcher. Nonetheless, the Warren Commission stated: "A nearly whole bullet was found on Governor Connally's stretcher at Parkland Hospital after the assassination." If that bullet was not linked somehow to Governor Connally, then the single-bullet theory would evaporate.[39]

Putting aside the point that there is no evidence to support the allegation that CE 399 was found on Connally's stretcher, it is equally astonishing to consider that the people who discovered and first handled the bullet declined later to positively identify it as the one discovered on the stretcher. Even the agents from the Secret Service were unable to identify the bullet, presumably because no one bothered to mark it until it reached the FBI laboratory.[40]

Tomlinson had given the bullet he found to the hospital's security director, O. P. Wright, who in turn handed it over to the Secret Service. However, after the Warren Report was issued, Wright insisted to a consultant for *Life* that the bullet he turned in to the Secret Service had a sharply pointed nose. This was quite different from the blunt, rounded nose of the Magic Bullet. But, of course, the records show that the bullet turned in by Tomlinson that afternoon was passed from hand to hand without receipt, until a bullet purported to be the stretcher bullet was officially given to the FBI laboratory 1,200 miles away, late on the night of November 22.[41]

And that bullet, after ballistics analysis, was determined without dispute to have been fired from the rifle traced to Lee Harvey Oswald.[42]

There is hardly a hint of evidence to suggest that any official consideration was given to the possibility that CE 399 or the limousine fragments could be planted evidence. Nevertheless, there is no evidence that these bullets were fired from the Oswald rifle on the day of the assassination—or that the fragments ever passed through a human body. It would seem that any open-minded investigation would consider whether these bullets were fired from the Mannlicher-Carcano at an earlier time and planted on the stretcher and in the limousine to enhance the case against the ready-made suspect. Even in released transcripts of the Warren Commission executive sessions, there is no indication that such an obvious possibility was considered. Ironically, the very tests conducted by the FBI, for the Warren Commission, to try to duplicate the feats of the Magic Bullet amply demonstrate the ease with which bullets can be fired into various substances and recovered in a variety of conditions, some quite similar to the condition of the limousine fragments and the Magic Bullet itself.[43]

For years there has been speculation that the appearance of the Magic Bullet on the stretcher might be related to a bizarre confrontation that took place just outside the trauma room where President Kennedy lay. Until now, the incident has never been fully explained. Students of the assassination have long puzzled over documents from the Warren Commission about an unidentified man who tried to barge into the trauma room. The documents indicated that when the man refused orders to halt from the Secret Service agents guarding the door, one of the agents slugged the man, who then retreated to the end of the corridor. That was basically all that was known, leading some to believe that the unidentified man's presence could have been related to the appearance shortly after that of the Magic Bullet in the hospital corridor.[44]

In pursuing this angle in 1983, the author tracked down the "unidentified man," whose name had become known in a recent release of documents. It was Special Agent J. Doyle Williams, now retired from the FBI, who gave a different and even more dramatic account of the incident—and revealed, for the first time, an interesting encounter with Jacqueline Kennedy. Williams, a large man who looks strikingly like John Connally, was the FBI agent who wore Connally's clothes and took the governor's position in the limousine during the reenactment of the assassination for the Warren Commission.[45]

Williams, who was assigned to the Dallas FBI office in 1963, explained to the author that at the moment of the assassination he was a few blocks from Dealey Plaza. Upon hearing the news, he ran the three blocks to the FBI office, where he found J. Gordon Shanklin, special agent in charge, in the process of telephoning FBI Director J. Edgar Hoover in Washington to convey the news. Shanklin immediately ordered Williams to go to Parkland Hospital, locate the Secret Service agent in charge there, and inform him that Hoover had ordered all bureau resources to be at the ready to assist the Secret Service. Agent Williams sped to the hospital, where he contacted the Secret Service agent in charge, Roy Kellerman, and conveyed Hoover's message.[46]

Williams's next move was to offer Jacqueline Kennedy the condolences of J. Edgar Hoover. Williams states: "Mrs. Kennedy was quiet, sitting alone, somewhat erect, looking straight ahead and not apparently noticing activities of nurses, doctors and others in the immediate small area. I approached Mrs. Kennedy and knelt down by her right side to extend Mr. Hoover's sympathies and to offer any assistance she might request of the FBI. Gracious in the tense moment, Mrs. Kennedy thanked me for Mr. Hoover's message."[47]

Following that, Williams asked one of the nurses to help him find a telephone so that he could report to his superiors. This involved leaving the area of the trauma room and going to a different part of the hospital, since all the phones in the immediate area were tied up. Some minutes later, when Williams returned, still in the company of the nurse, this is what he says happened: "As she and I entered the emergency-room door, two Secret Service agents, without challenging me, grabbed me from behind and wrestled me to the hall floor. . . . I really hit the deck, and my gun fell out right there, and it's a wonder I didn't just pick it up and shoot, but I didn't."[48]

Williams explained that with his gun out—and the fact that the Secret Service agents, who "were so hyped up," also had guns—"a bunch of other people in that hall" could have been shot.[49]

Moments later, according to Williams, the Secret Service agent in charge, Roy Kellerman, to whom Williams had originally identified himself, approached the scene and asked Williams to leave. "I was never so proud of training in my life, that I kept control of myself and just kept my mouth shut," Williams said. "I just got out, and that's the best thing I ever did." Williams left the hospital and returned to the FBI office.[50]

As basically innocuous as this incident was, considering the tense circumstances, one would expect that the Warren Commission would have explained the bizarre report. There is no evidence that the commission considered it.

The curious absence of interest in the possibility of planted evidence becomes even more peculiar when one realizes that the commissioners who had access to the compiled evidence knew that at least two witnesses placed Oswald killer Jack Ruby at Parkland Hospital during the general period when the stretcher was unattended in the milling corridor. One of these witnesses was Seth Kantor, an experienced and reliable national reporter who was acquainted with Ruby and talked to him at Parkland that day.[51]

Only one clear conclusion can be drawn from the testimony offered about the assassination bullets: rarely have so many witnesses and experts differed so profoundly. There is no universally convincing, unchallenged evidence to show which or how many bullets did what. The reports from pathologists, the examinations of drawings and photographs, the study of X rays, and all the scientific techniques brought to bear yield not clarity but more contradiction and confusion. At times it appears impossible that the doctors and scientists in conflict are even talking about the same evidence.

Yet, based on the selected testimony of certain eyewitnesses, the Warren Commission—and the Select Committee fourteen years later—concluded that bullets fired solely by Lee Harvey Oswald killed President Kennedy and wounded Governor Connally. A significant linchpin in that conclusion is the existence of the Magic Bullet and the official acceptance of its tortuous travels.[52]

But as the Warren Commission considered such conflicting evidence, the commissioners surely must have asked themselves: where can truth be found?

Most of the early contradictions and conflicts arose from human observation and interpretation. But it was hoped that objective scientific testing and analysis could once and for all settle the mystery of the Magic Bullet and clarify the vagaries of the single-bullet theory. (A later chapter will examine other aspects of the scientific assessment of the ballistics evidence.) And so the commission ordered a number of tests.

From the start, the most logical tests were those that sought to approximate the feats of the Magic Bullet by firing similar cartridges into substances closely resembling the tissues and bones through which CE 399 passed. Even though the exact approximations and circumstances could never be duplicated, it was not unreasonable to expect a fair approximation of factors to produce somewhat similar results. That, at least, is what the Warren Commission and its staff thought as they set about conducting such tests.[53]

The thrust of the Warren Commission testing efforts was aimed at fortifying the credibility of the single-bullet theory. This, of course, depended on the validity of the proposition that the Magic Bullet, CE 399, could go through seven layers of skin of two well-muscled mature adults, smash bones, and emerge in such near perfect condition that an FBI expert would testify that virtually no visible damage had been done to the bullet. Indeed, one ballistics expert testified later to the HSCA that he was not sure the bullet had lost *any* of its original weight.[54]

There was much fanfare surrounding the testing conditions implemented by the Warren Commission. This included the use of human cadavers, goats, and gelatin blocks that were supposed to simulate the tissues traversed by the Magic Bullet. If anything, the test results did more to bolster the position of the commission's critics and detractors than they did to enhance the commission's version of events. In the end it seemed virtually certain that the Magic Bullet's impressive reputation was false, that such shenanigans by this 6.5-millimeter bullet could not be duplicated in official tests.[55]

The most dramatic illustration of the test results is seen by simply lining up certain bullets that became commission exhibits after they underwent official testing. This was done by Dr. Wecht in his dissent before the Select Committee in 1978. There is CE 399, which is as close to perfect to the layman's eye as any expended bullet could be. The only damage to the bullet's nose is the small sliver removed by the FBI for testing. There is a slight flattening of the base of the bullet, and that is the only observable deformity.[56]

Next to CE 399 are two bullets known as CE 572, identical ammunition to that fired from the Oswald rifle. Under Warren Commission testing, these two bullets were fired into cotton wadding and never struck anything of substance. Incredibly, to the eye, the deformity to one of these bullets is greater than to CE 399, which purportedly pierced through seven layers of skin, through muscle tissue and two bones.[57]

Next in Dr. Wecht's exhibit is an expended bullet, CE 853, which was fired through the carcass of a goat, breaking one of the goat's ribs. Even though the goat and its rib are far smaller than Governor

Connally and his rib, CE 853 is swollen and somewhat truncated, with a significant extrusion of lead from its copper jacket. The deformity is clearly greater than that seen in CE 399.[58]

The last item in Dr. Wecht's exhibit is CE 856, a bullet fired through the wrist of a human cadaver, breaking the radius bone as in the case of Governor Connally's wound. This slug shows the most extreme deformation of all, particularly in its nose, which is smashed flat.[59]

Each of these exhibits—one of the slugs fired into the cotton, the slug fired through the goat rib, the slug fired through the cadaver wrist—shows greater deformity than that seen in CE 399, even though the Magic Bullet *alone* did all of its ascribed damage. It is not surprising that first the Warren Commission and later the HSCA sought to diminish the significance of these tests, for they would make far more sense to the general public than all of the technical explanations from experts.[60]

And, indeed, the explanations came like a blizzard. Warren Commission experts—later bolstered by experts testifying before the HSCA—were ready with highly convoluted reasons why the logical conclusions could not be drawn from the tests. They argued that, believe it or not, the results of these tests, which seemed to make a mockery of the ascribed feats of CE 399, were not at all inconsistent with the miraculous condition of the Magic Bullet.[61]

In the case of the wrist test, for example, the official experts claimed that the fact that the Magic Bullet passed undamaged through Connally's wrist as it shattered the largest bone was prime evidence that the bullet had lost a great deal of its velocity from its arduous travels through the bodies of Kennedy and Connally. This, of course, would seem to make it even more remarkable that the undamaged bullet could go on to penetrate Connally's thigh and leave a metal fragment embedded at his thighbone.[62]

Dr. Michael Baden, the pathologist who headed the forensic pathology panel of the Select Committee, went to great lengths in his testimony to explain why such tests were meaningless. Dr. Baden stated:

> I don't want to belabor the point, but the panel majority . . . does feel that the injuries sustained by Governor Connally and President Kennedy, and the trajectory and the ballistics

could not be precisely duplicated . . . there were myriads and myriads of ways the experiment could be done wrong and only one way it could be done right—and if by chance it were done right once we wouldn't know it or be able to prove it. There would still be room for argument.[63]

This led to a question from Congressman Richardson Preyer, who served as chairman of the JFK Subcommittee of the Select Committee. Stating that the behavior of the Magic Bullet seemed "to fly in the face of common sense," Congressman Preyer asked Dr. Baden if he had "ever seen a bullet that has done this much damage as the bullet CE 399 did and still emerge in as good condition as this bullet is in?"[64]

"Yes, sir," Dr. Baden replied. "Absolutely, but with qualification." Dr. Baden proceeded to explain that really the Magic Bullet was not in "pristine" condition, that the rib it smashed was actually a very thin bone, that the radius of the wrist "is not a very hard bone. It can damage some bullets, and not others."[65]

However correct Dr. Baden and his colleagues might be, their reasoning was accepted by strikingly few of the critics and members of the general public who later considered it.

Chief Counsel G. Robert Blakey of the Select Committee told the committee that "under the best possible circumstances, the experiments could only yield a statement about probability." He reported that a private company told the committee staff that "the number of shots required to produce the chance result of Commission Exhibit 399 could range from one up to infinity." This was the reason given for the HSCA's refusal to be lured into conducting more tests that, it seems in all likelihood, would have strengthened the position of those who scorn the Magic Bullet and the single-bullet theory.[66]

Dr. Wecht, in his dissent to the HSCA, made a simple plea regarding the Magic Bullet. Citing his dozen years of work on the matter of the Magic Bullet, he stated:

I have repeatedly . . . implored, beseeched, urged, in writing, orally, privately, collectively, my colleagues; to come up with one bullet, that has done this. I am not talking about fifty percent of the time plus one, [or] five percent or one percent—just one bullet that has done this.

I . . . heard reference today by Dr. Baden that, yes, we have seen such bullets . . . in civilian life. I can only say to you as a member of the panel, at no time did any of my colleagues ever bring in a bullet . . . and say here is a bullet in a documented case . . . [that] broke two bones in some human being, and look at . . . its condition, it is pristine.[67]

Dr. Wecht was scathing in his denunciation of his colleagues' motives in refusing to conduct tests that might duplicate the feats of the Magic Bullet. "It is clear to me," stated Dr. Wecht, "that their reluctance was based upon their knowledge that such studies would further destroy the single-bullet theory."[68]

Indeed, there is no official evidence yet shown that any other similar-type bullet in the world has ever accomplished the feats of CE 399. It alone rightly retains its claim as the Magic Bullet.

The Warren Commission lawyer generally credited with originating the single-bullet theory is Arlen Specter, today a U.S. senator from Pennsylvania. That theory—and its embrace of the Magic Bullet's phenomenal feats—has emerged as one of the most controversial aspects of the Warren Commission's legacy. It is interesting that following the dissolution of the Warren Commission, Specter, in replying to a question from a colleague about the single-bullet theory, stated, "I don't think people are going to believe this . . . this year, next year, or a hundred years from now . . . this thing will be challenged today, tomorrow and forever."[69]

Today, Senator Specter remains firmly convinced of the validity of the single-bullet theory.[70]

After all was said and done with the Warren Commission testing, the report offered the following statement concerning the Magic Bullet: "The results of the wound ballistics tests support the conclusions of Governor Connally's doctors that all of his wounds were caused by one bullet. . . . In addition, the wounds ballistics tests indicated that it was most probable that the same bullet passed through the President's neck and then proceeded to inflict all the wounds on the Governor."[71]

Despite thousands of words from witnesses and experts, along with dozens of tests and photographs hashing over the Magic Bullet, there is not a shred of solid, undisputed evidence to show that the bullet had anything at all to do with the shooting of President Kennedy. Based on Warren Commission evidence, all that could be said with certainty was that CE 399 was fired from the rifle found on the sixth floor of the TSBD Building, overlooking Dealey Plaza. No one could say when the bullet was fired or who was holding the rifle when it was actually fired. Moreover, no one could say on whose hospital stretcher CE 399 was found or how it got there. There is evidence to show that any number of people, including Jack Ruby, had the opportunity to plant it. At the conclusion of the Warren Commission, no firm evidence confirmed that the almost perfect bullet struck Kennedy or Connally even once.[72]

Since efforts to duplicate the assassin's timing and accuracy had failed, and since there was no hope for establishing the chain of possession of CE 399 after the hospital muddle, the FBI turned in 1963 and 1964 to a highly technical scientific analysis of bullet fragments called emission spectrography. These tests held the potential for showing that various fragments of metal associated with the shooting either could or could not come from the same missile.[73]

It is unlikely that any aspect of the Warren Commission's effort is more contradictory and confusing than the spectrographic examination of the recovered bullet fragments. While it is simple under such testing to establish that two fragments are *not* from the same source, proving that they *are* from the same source is not so easily achieved. What is important to show is the percentage of elemental composition of particular fragments. When two fragments have nearly identical percentages of certain components—such as lead, copper, antimony—then it is probable that they share a common origin. If, on the other hand, the percentages of composition are dissimilar beyond a certain range, it becomes virtually certain that the source is different.[74]

The presentation of findings of the FBI's spectrographic analyses of fragments was, as it appeared in the Warren Report, incomprehensibly vague. Years later it would become clear that the handling of the matter bordered on the duplicitous. The commission staff lightly interrogated an FBI ballistics expert about the spectrographic tests, but his references to what had been done by his colleagues in spectrographic analysis were little more than hearsay evidence. When the commission swore in the actual spectrographic expert—and he was called as the very last witness in the commission's history—not a single question was asked of him relating to the spectrographic analysis of the bullet fragments. (Questions to him were confined to those concerning the paraffin tests.) A key question would have dealt with the results of spectrographic testing on the bullet fragments to determine for once and for all if fragments of the Magic Bullet were found in both Kennedy and Connally. That question was never asked.[75]

In its report, the Warren Commission noted that several of the fragments were "similar in metallic composition," a description commonly considered meaningless. Thus, there was established no firm evidentiary link between the Magic Bullet and the fragments taken from Connally's body.[76]

For seventeen years, Harold Weisberg sought the test data of the FBI's original spectrographic analysis. Weisberg, along with his volunteer lawyer James H. Lesar, argued ceaselessly that it made no sense for the government to conceal this information. In the first place, Weisberg argued, the material was supposed to represent an objective scientific analysis of historical significance, and secondly, it was supposed to weigh in favor of the official findings.[77]

There were several peculiar rulings as Weisberg's case moved slowly through the courts, but none more so than Judge John Sirica's agreement with what the Justice Department claimed was the attorney general's position that it was not in the "national interest" to divulge the test results of the spectrographic analyses. The government was never required to explain how release of such a standard scientific analysis could threaten the national interest. Earlier, the government argued that release of the then six-year-old test results could lead to the "exposure of confidential informants . . . possible blackmail and, in general, do irreparable damage." (Much later, James H. Lesar determined that the attorney general had not actually said what the Justice Department claimed that he said.)[78]

One of the most astonishing facts learned by Weisberg was that the FBI testing never attempted to determine the percentages of the elemental composition of the fragments. Even more peculiar was that no effort was made to compare any of the fragments with the unspent bullet found in the chamber of the Oswald rifle.[79]

As Weisberg's case plodded on, a break came in early 1973, when a volume of Warren Commission correspondence was released by the National Archives. The material was not classified, and it is not known why it was withheld from the public for nearly a decade.

Among the materials were letters from FBI Director Hoover in which he makes reference to the pertinent spectrographic analysis.[80]

Hoover's comments were disappointingly vague, even more so since there were no indications that any effort was made in the analysis to determine whether the fragments from Connally's wrist could be positively matched to CE 399. While Hoover avoided making any statement about a comparison between the Connally fragments and CE 399, he did state rather ambiguously that "no significant differences were found within the sensitivity of the spectrographic method." There is another statement that the fragment from Connally's wrist is "similar in composition" to one of the fragments found in the limousine.[81]

It is significant that the evidence on spectrographic analysis should come tiptoeing to the fore, out of channels, merely hinting that it was supportive of the Warren Commission. There is virtually no doubt that if the tests had been clearly supportive of the commission conclusions, the commission would have trumpeted the news and the proof to the world. Such support would be the only evidentiary link between CE 399 and any bullet that struck anyone in the presidential limousine on November 22, 1963. It was a support critically absent.

The most stunning news to emerge from the long obscured Hoover correspondence was that the Warren Commission went beyond the science of spectrography in its quest for support. In 1964 the FBI had apparently agreed to conduct neutron activation analyses on the bullet fragments—a process that, according to *Scientific American* magazine, utilizes radiation "to measure the concentration of trace elements often in amounts less than a billionth of a gram." (It was through neutron activation analysis, for example, that scientists in 1961 began to suspect that Napoleon died in 1821 from arsenic poisoning—a determination made by submitting bits of his preserved hair to neutron activation analysis.) The application of this technique is virtually boundless.[82]

Again, chances are excellent that if the results of neutron activation testing had yielded support for the basic Warren Commission findings, the commission would have also heralded these results in its report. But not a word about these tests appears in the report or in the twenty-six volumes of supporting testimony and exhibits. Indeed, there is little reason to believe that the commission ever received the complete results of the neutron activation testing. The first indication that the Magic Bullet and the fragments were subjected to neutron activation analysis came years later in the surprise appearance of the letters between the Warren Commission and FBI Director Hoover.

As conveyed from Hoover to the commission, the news was muted to say the least. In his letter written in July 1964, Hoover first mentions the spectrographic tests and that "no significant differences were found" among the fragments. Then, almost in passing, Hoover continues: "Because of the higher sensitivity of the neutron activation analysis, certain of the small lead fragments were then subjected to neutron activation analyses and comparison with larger bullet fragments." Hoover then notes that the stretcher bullet (CE 399) was analyzed, along with a fragment from Connally, fragments from Kennedy's head, and fragments found in different parts of the car.[83]

Hoover concludes: "While minor variations in composition were found by this method, these were not considered sufficient to permit positively differentiating among the larger bullet fragments and thus positively determining from which of the larger bullet fragments any given small lead fragment may have come."[84]

At best, Hoover seemed to be saying, the neutron activation analyses were inconclusive.

Confusion deepened as the Justice Department, representing the FBI, continued to stonewall legal efforts on the part of Harold Weisberg to force release of all the spectrographic and neutron activation analysis test results. At times, the legal battle became ludicrous, as the government struggled against all logic to keep secret the results. In the spring of 1975, for example, FBI Laboratory Agent John W. Kilty swore in an affidavit: "Neutron activation analysis and emission spectroscopy were used to determine the elemental composition of the borders and edges of holes in clothing and metallic smears present on a windshield and curbstone."[85]

But Weisberg had never been given the results from the neutron activation analysis of these items. About one month later, after Weisberg had begun pressing for them, Agent Kilty provided a second affidavit, in which he swore to a direct contradiction by stating: "NAA (neutron activation analysis) was not used in examining the clothing, windshield or curbing."[86]

This sort of performance has not been unusual in the government's desperate efforts to keep the testing and its results from reaching the public. Finally, the FBI yielded to Weisberg what it claimed was all of its test data. Given the direct contradictions in Kilty's affidavits, Weisberg remained skeptical about the completeness of the FBI's disclosures.[87]

In April 1983 a federal court of appeals ruled against Weisberg and found that the FBI had fulfilled its obligations in responding to Weisberg's requests. With hostility reminiscent of some earlier decisions against Weisberg, the court effectively closed the case forever.[88]

New hope for conclusive neutron activation analysis arose in 1977 with the convening of the House Select Committee on Assassinations. The committee engaged the services of Dr. Vincent P. Guinn, a respected scientist and chemist in the field. According to Chief Counsel Blakey, Guinn had no relation to the Warren Commission. However, Guinn himself agreed in 1983 that he has acted as an informal consultant on such matters to the FBI since even prior to the Kennedy assassination.[89]

Using newer equipment—more advanced than what was available in 1963 and 1964—Guinn was able to report to the HSCA in great detail just how the tests were done and how he arrived at his conclusion that it is "highly probable," if not conclusive, that the fragments taken from Governor Connally's wrist came from CE 399, the famous Magic Bullet found on the stretcher. Guinn also reported that, on testing, the fragments found in the limousine could be linked to the fragments allegedly removed from Kennedy's head. And he stated conclusively that he found evidence of no more than two bullets among all the fragments he tested.[90]

This, it would appear, offered strong (if rather late) support for the Warren Commission's original finding that only two bullets struck Kennedy and Connally. This evidence also represented the first link ever made between the Oswald rifle and a bullet fragment supposedly taken from a victim's body. That, certainly, is the conclusion embraced by the Select Committee.[91]

There were, however, terrible evidentiary deficiencies in all this— much like the original difficulties in connecting the Magic Bullet to the wounding of Kennedy and Connally. While these deficiencies were discounted by the HSCA, they are worth a close examination.

By Dr. Guinn's own admission, the wrist fragments that were originally tested in 1964 had vanished by the time Guinn began his work for the HSCA. The trouble with this, as critics were quick to point out, is that there is no way to be certain just *what* Guinn was testing. He did have several containers of metal fragments from the National Archives, and some of the fragments could be matched to the Magic Bullet by neutron activation analysis.[92]

Guinn explained to the Select Committee that the Archives had assured him that he had been given "the only bullet-lead fragments from this case still present in the Archives." Guinn stated: "Presumably those [missing fragments] are in existence somewhere . . . but where they are, I have no idea." He also told the committee that the original fragments would not have been destroyed by the 1964 testing. It has never been clear what happened to the original specimens.[93]

In view of such unnerving capriciousness in the handling of vital evidence, it was difficult to take seriously Guinn's findings of support for the official version of the assassination. It was perfectly obvious that Guinn could have been provided with fragments from the Magic Bullet and that tests would show such fragments to have a common origin.

Following his testimony before the HSCA, Guinn explained to the reporters and critics who swarmed about him in the corridor that it was only after he received the evidence from the Archives that he discovered that he was testing fragments different from those originally tested. When he weighed the particles, he found that none of the individual weights corresponded with those noted when the FBI attempted the tests in 1964. According to a tape recording of the hallway interview, Guinn was refreshingly candid in describing a hypothetical case: "Possibly they would take a bullet, take out a few little pieces and put it in the container, and say, 'This is what came out of Connally's wrist.' And naturally if you compare it with [CE] 399, it will look alike. . . . I have no control over these things."[94]

The situation with the comparison of the Kennedy brain fragments to the limousine fragments was similarly tainted, calling into question the legitimacy of the fragments said to have come from the President's car. On March 31, 1964, an FBI expert testified to the Warren Commission that the FBI laboratory had established a ballistics link between the limousine fragments and the Oswald rifle.

The testimony of the expert was unequivocal in its certainty of the connection—despite the gross deformation of the fragments.[95]

It is interesting and perhaps significant that this testimony came at the time the Warren Commission informed the FBI that it wanted the firearms evidence submitted to an outside laboratory for "reexamination." That suggestion, not disclosed until years later, was met with rage on the part of J. Edgar Hoover. The FBI director wrote: "It is obvious the Commission does not have confidence in our laboratory." The exact issues behind this argument are not clear.[96]

In spite of this dispute, the FBI expert's ballistics testimony a few days later was readily accepted by the Warren Commission. There was, however, a rather serious deficiency in the evidentiary status of the fragments in question. There was no firm indication, even at that relatively early stage, that the fragments had come from the limousine. It is unlikely that any court in the land would have accepted such evidence without serious challenge. Not only were the fragments unidentified, but they were also said to have been discovered nearly twelve hours after the crime, after the limousine had been parked in a milling crowd at the hospital in Dallas and then flown to Washington.*[97]

Eight weeks after this expert testimony, an FBI agent took the tiny fragments to the two men who had been credited with discovering them. Up until that point, the fragments had not been marked for even the simplest identification purposes. Despite the passage of more than six months, each man—one a Secret Service agent and the other a White House staffer—identified a crumpled, unmarked fragment as the very one he had found in the limousine. How such identification was possible has never been explained.[98]

As for the legitimacy of the fragments said to have been recovered from the President's brain during the autopsy, one has only to review the shocking manipulation of medical evidence, as described in Chapter

*New questions about the evidence from the limousine were raised when, on the twentieth anniversary of the assassination, *Life* published a photograph from its files that had never appeared. The picture is described simply as being of the limousine being cleaned, following the assassination, at Parkland Hospital. In the foreground of the picture is a metal bucket. There is no indication as to whether things were removed from the car and placed in the bucket, nor is there any way of telling whether the bucket might have been filled with soap and water for cleaning purposes. The point is that the photograph provides the first concrete evidence that the car was gone over by a variety of security people—including Dallas policemen, who can be seen in the picture—before it was returned to Washington and examined officially late that night.

3. That manipulation, along with the proven destruction and disappearance of vital medical evidence while in the hands of authorities, stirs little confidence in the legitimacy of the two fragments said to have come from President Kennedy's brain.[99]

The most astounding deficiency in the Select Committee's neutron activation analyses is one that has remained undisclosed until now. In his testimony explaining his testing procedures, Dr. Guinn went to elaborate lengths to establish the basis for his testing of the fragments. He pointed to certain unusual characteristics of this particular batch of Mannlicher-Carcano ammunition that permitted him to conduct effective tests and analysis of the material. Basically, the most significant unique characteristic of the ammunition is "that there seems to be no uniformity within a production lot" of certain elements, such as antimony. This characteristic appears to a layman to permit enormous ranges in the presence of certain elements in the metal, but ranges that Guinn insisted are normal.[100]

Guinn described the particular batch of Mannlicher-Carcano ammunition upon which he based his tests: "The Western Cartridge Co. reportedly made 1 million rounds of each of 4 production runs. . . . They were made at different times in 1954, and reportedly those are the only lots they ever produced, and we had boxes from each of those lots."[101]

If these bullets really were "the only . . . ever produced" by Western Cartridge, Guinn's test basis might have been legitimate in that single respect. However, there is a strong indication that, on this count, Guinn's presumption is flatly wrong. While Guinn's source for his information is not clear, it is obvious that he was not aware of pertinent FBI information, buried in the published Warren Commission papers, that states quite the opposite.

The FBI document, which is a memorandum over the name of J. Edgar Hoover, reports an interview with a Western Cartridge Company representative, who explained the source of the Mannlicher-Carcano ammunition in the United States: "The Western Cartridge Company . . . manufactured a quantity of 6.5 . . . Mannlicher-Carcano ammunition for the Italian Government during World War II. At the end of the war the Italian Carcano rifle, and no telling how much of this type of ammunition, was sold to United States gun brokers and dealers and subsequently was distributed by direct sales to wholesalers, retailers and individual purchasers."[102]

If in fact the cartridges believed to have belonged to Oswald came from *this*, earlier, batch of Western ammunition, then Dr. Guinn had based his whole testing procedure on the wrong bullets. It is, of course, Dr. Guinn who made so much of the importance of having precisely the correct batch of ammunition upon which to base his neutron activation analysis.

Whatever the truth, there is little reason for confidence in the Select Committee's scientific work on the elemental composition of the bullet fragments.

Despite such preposterous difficulties with the evidence—difficulties having nothing to do with Guinn's professional performance—the committee accepted Guinn's scientific findings in support of certain essential aspects of its own position as well as those of the Warren Commission.[103]

Ironically, this evidentiary conclusion was in perfect harmony with the nearly hopeless quagmire that has distinguished the history of the Magic Bullet. Nearly two decades after President Kennedy's death, the best experts in the land produced conclusions which, valid or not, were presented so unconvincingly that there was little evidence of a shift in the public's perception of the case. And however valid the conclusions in the eyes of the government experts and some critics, the revelation of yet new tainted basic evidence—in this case the disappearance of some of the bullet fragments—so sullies the whole atmosphere that the findings seem unlikely ever to be accepted by more than a tiny handful of American citizens.

5 · OSWALD AND THE

SNIPER'S PERCH

As turmoil and terror engulfed Dealey Plaza at 12:32 P.M., Dallas Police Officer Marrion Baker, brandishing his pistol, challenged a young man he encountered on the second floor of the Texas School Book Depository Building. The man was calm and collected as he eyed the policeman. The superintendent of the building, who was leading Officer Baker to the upper floors, quickly confirmed that he knew the young man, that he worked in the building. His name: Lee Harvey Oswald. Baker and the superintendent rushed on up the stairway. Oswald, who showed no apprehension when faced with the revolver, sauntered on his way and left the building.[1]

The elapsed time between the sound of the shots in Dealey Plaza at 12:30 and the encounter with Oswald was remarkable for its brevity: no more than ninety seconds by Warren Commission calculations. The Warren Report concluded that Baker reached the second floor within three seconds of Oswald's arrival there.[2]

Four floors above the spot where Oswald was encountered, investigators soon discovered what appeared to be an assassin's lair in the southeast corner of the sixth floor, overlooking Dealey Plaza and providing a sweeping view of the whole area. In this cavernous, warehouselike room, filled with cartons of textbooks, boxes stacked near the southeast window formed a partition that might allow someone to crouch there unobserved. Three expended cartridge shells were found on the floor, under the window, scattered near one another. A little later, a rifle subsequently identified as a 6.5-caliber Mannlicher-Carcano was found stashed behind some boxes in another part of the room. The rifle contained a single unexpended cartridge. And heavy wrapping paper, shaped like a bag, was found. Investigators suspected it might have been used to bring the rifle into the building.[3]

Soon the accumulation of evidence began to pay off. Perhaps the most persuasive development was that the Mannlicher-Carcano proved to have been ordered through a mail-order gun house and sent to the postal box in Dallas rented by Lee Harvey Oswald. However, the rifle was ordered in a name other than Oswald's—A. Hidell. That inconsistency was quickly cleared up. When he was arrested, Oswald was carrying a forged identification card made out to Alek J. Hidell. Moreover, the writing on the order for the rifle was established to be Oswald's.[4]

As the evidence against Oswald mounted, the FBI made an absolute ballistics determination that a bullet slug found in a corridor at Parkland Hospital, where Kennedy was pronounced dead, had been positively identified as having been fired from the Mannlicher-Carcano found in the Book Depository. Then there was the FBI's determination that the cloth fibers found in the stock of the rifle could have come from the shirt Oswald was wearing on the day of the assassination. However, the police failed to make a test to determine whether the rifle had been fired that day or even since the last time it was cleaned.[5]

There was initial difficulty in finding Oswald's prints on the rifle. The Dallas police laboratory was the first to make an effort, but the results were inconclusive. The rifle was delivered to the FBI laboratory in Washington, where attempts were equally disappointing. This was curious, for Oswald otherwise appeared to have been extremely sloppy, leaving a great abundance of apparent evidence against himself.[6]

Finally, a few days later, after Oswald's death, the Dallas police laboratory reported that actually their technicians *had* been able to come up with Oswald's palm print, a curious revelation that will be discussed later. Before sending the rifle to Washington, officials said, the print was lifted from an area of the gun that normally was covered except when it was dismantled. Earlier, police had found Oswald's fingerprint and palm print near the window. With this latest discovery, of the palm print on the rifle, the case against Oswald tightened.[7]

All of this represented a compelling accumulation of material evidence. It is endlessly arguable whether it would have yielded a conviction at trial, for there were severe difficulties in the case against Oswald when it came to witnesses. Howard Brennan, a steamfitter who was sitting on a low wall across Elm Street, 120 feet from the sniper's perch, claimed to be facing the Book Depository when the shooting started. Brennan was the closest the authorities could come to an eyewitness. While he claimed to have seen a man shooting from the window, at that night's police lineup he failed to positively identify Oswald. In repeatedly contradictory testimony, Brennan then decided he was sure it was Oswald whom he had seen. Later, he switched again and told the FBI he was no longer certain.[8]

By the time Brennan testified before the Warren Commission, he was again able to offer a positive identification of Oswald as the sniper he saw in the window. It was snapped up by the commission. However flimsy his testimony, Brennan was the only witness the panel could find to place Oswald at the window.[9] Years later, when the HSCA considered evidence on this point, it did not use Brennan's testimony.

And there were other difficulties in the eyewitness testimony, particularly in the area of timing Oswald's movements immediately before and after the shooting. The crucial time sequence pertains to the fact that Oswald was encountered by Officer Baker on the second floor less than ninety seconds after the last shot was heard.[10]

If it was Oswald in the window after the last shot, he was a very busy man. Two witnesses (one of them Brennan) reported that the gunman seemed to be in no hurry, slowly withdrawing his rifle from the window after the last shot. Oswald would first have to slowly squeeze through the rather tight opening into the lair, presumably wipe his prints from the rifle and then stash it with some meticulousness in another part of the room. He would then have to dash down four floors to the second floor, where he would appear calm and collected when confronted by the policeman with a drawn weapon. (It was initially reported that Oswald was drinking a soda when he encountered Baker, which would make his celerity even more remarkable.) It is also noteworthy that Oswald's demeanor when challenged was certainly different from the struggle he put up when confronted by police about an hour later.[11]

The other crucial time consideration is what could be the earliest possible moment Oswald was at the window on the sixth floor before the shooting. This point provides an excellent example of the Warren Commission's acceptance of witnesses whose testimony contributed to the case against Oswald while discounting those whose versions might exonerate him.

When the other workers went downstairs for their lunch break at

11:45 A.M., Oswald remained where he had been working on the fifth floor. Two employees testified that as they left, Oswald asked them to send an elevator back up so he could go down to the lunchroom. The commission found a witness who said he saw Oswald on the sixth floor at 11:55. But there is direct and indirect testimony from four witnesses that Oswald was downstairs at noon and even later.[12]

These accounts are bolstered by the fact that one employee, Bonnie Ray Williams, returned to the sixth floor around noon to eat his lunch alone. His lunch scraps—at first believed to be those of the assassin—were later found where he said he left them. Williams testified that he remained there until about 12:20 P.M. (The FBI agents who interviewed Williams reported that he told them he left the sixth floor after about three minutes. Williams denied to the commission that he ever made such a statement. He could hardly have eaten his sandwich and drunk his pop in three minutes.) Williams has testified that despite his proximity to the sniper's nest, he was aware of no other person on the sixth floor. The Warren Commission was, of course, aware of Williams's testimony but stuck with its version that Oswald was on the sixth floor from 11:55 A.M. until the final shot was fired about 12:30.[13]

The most damning indictment of the commission's version was revealed in an FBI report of an interview in 1963 with Carolyn Arnold. At that time she was secretary to the vice-president of the Book Depository. According to the FBI report, which Mrs. Arnold did not see until years later, she told an agent that while standing in front of the Book Depository at about 12:15, "she thought she caught a fleeting glimpse of Lee Harvey Oswald standing in the hallway."[14]

When presented with this account of seeing Oswald, Mrs. Arnold expressed surprise and stated that she never made such a statement. She said that her recollections of that traumatic day were perfectly clear, and she repeated what she had actually told the FBI. Though Oswald had not worked there long, he had the habit of dropping into Mrs. Arnold's office for change. She was certain of her ability to recognize him.[15]

Mrs. Arnold explained that she was pregnant at that time and recalled experiencing a craving for a glass of water just after noon. She stated: "About a quarter of an hour before the assassination, I went into the lunch room on the second floor for a moment. . . . Oswald was sitting in one of the booth seats. . . . He was alone as usual and appeared to be having lunch. I did not speak to him but I recognized him clearly."[16]

Carolyn Arnold's account would put Oswald downstairs as late as 12:15 P.M., which coincides with Bonnie Ray Williams's testimony that the sixth floor was apparently vacant when he left it around 12:20. And there is other testimony, which is corroborated by what Oswald himself told the police, that places him on the first floor shortly before the assassination. (Oswald himself claimed that he was in the lunchroom.)[17]

Would it be physically possible for Oswald to speed from the first or second floor to the sixth floor, make his way in between boxes into the sniper's perch, assemble the rifle, fire on his target with stunning accuracy, squeeze through piles of boxes (leaving not a single fingerprint) to hide his rifle, and already be sauntering about on the second floor ninety seconds after the last shot?[18]

Some skeptics believe that Oswald was indeed in the lunchroom between 12:15 and 12:32, as he claimed. The Warren Commission had no doubt as to its position. Managing to overlook most of this evidence, the report concluded that Oswald was in the sniper's nest and killed the President. The HSCA agreed, without presenting Carolyn Arnold as a witness. Such treatment of evidence has surely contributed to the lack of confidence in the two reports.[19]

In addition to the difficulty of accepting Oswald's truly spectacular feats of speed and efficiency, there are impressive witnesses who believe that there were two men visible in the sixth-floor sniper's perch. Another gave credible testimony that a rifleman was in another sixth-floor window. Some of these witnesses were heard by the Warren Commission and ignored. Others, ignored or misrepresented by the FBI when they tried to give their stories in 1963 and 1964, have provided their accounts in recent years.

There were at least eight witnesses, including the wife of the mayor of Dallas, who provided the Warren Commission with sufficient information to allow the commission's theory of a single sniper in the southeast window. The Warren Commission was eager to hear these witnesses, and their accounts were embraced.[20]

But short shrift was given to the testimony of Arnold Rowland, who was standing with his wife on the street across from the Book Depository. Just after the shooting, he reported to a deputy sheriff that he had seen a man with a rifle in the sixth-floor window to the far *left*, on the end opposite that of the location traditionally referred to as the sniper's nest. Rowland later told the commission that about fifteen minutes prior to the shooting, he had seen a dark-haired man, perhaps a Caucasian or a light Latin, standing back from that window and looking down at the crowd. The man was holding a rifle. Rowland assumed him to be a Secret Service agent.[21]

In the end, Rowland's testimony was not only disregarded by the commission, but a remarkable effort was made to discredit him as a witness. What happened provides an excellent example of the Warren Commission's manipulation of the credibility of a witness. While the commission struggled to accept—and finally embraced— Howard Brennan's self-contradictory testimony (without ever questioning his credibility), it applied diligence in seeking to discredit Rowland. The commission even asked the FBI to investigate Rowland's credibility, while, judging by the commission's own records, no such investigation was made of Brennan. (If one had been made and Brennan passed muster, it can be certain the commission would have heralded the news. Brennan himself claimed that his contradictions were due in part to a great fear he felt that someone might retaliate against him as a result of his testimony.)[22]

The commission discovered, in its investigation of Rowland, that he occasionally exaggerated such matters as his academic grades. His wife acknowledged that she had known her husband to make such exaggerations. With this, the commission tossed aside Rowland's testimony.[23]

On the other hand, Howard Brennan's contradictions were overlooked and parts of his testimony accepted as prime evidence. The point is not whether Rowland could be considered a simon-pure witness; the point is that at the very least, he was as good a witness as Brennan—yet the commission ignored his evidence, while Brennan was elevated to the status of a star witness to assert that Oswald was shooting from the sniper's perch.[24]

Inasmuch as Rowland was the only known witness to see a rifleman in the westernmost sixth-floor window, it is most significant to consider the neglected witnesses who happened to be looking at the upper windows near the sixth-floor window identified by the commission as the sniper's perch. For example, Carolyn Walther told the FBI about watching two men in an open corner window on the upper floors. The man who was holding a rifle had lightish hair and was wearing a white shirt. The second man was wearing a brown suit coat.[25]

"He [the gunman] was very casual," Mrs. Walther told a newspaper reporter many years later. "That's why it didn't scare me." Mrs. Walther gave her story to the FBI in 1963, but it was a typical example of the sort of report that was not followed up. "They [the FBI] tried to make me think that what I saw were boxes," Mrs. Walther said. "I never read their report. I talked to them, and it seemed like they weren't very interested. They were going to set out to prove me a liar, and I had no intention of arguing with them and being harassed."[26]

The Warren Commission ignored Carolyn Walther.

Another person who saw two men, one with a dark complexion, in an upper window of the TSBD Building, was Ruby Henderson, who gave her information to the FBI in 1963. She said that she watched the men before the arrival of the motorcade and that they were standing back from the window and seemed to be working and yet looking out in anticipation of the motorcade. She did not see a gun. Mrs. Henderson also was ignored by the Warren Commission.[27]

One of the more interesting witnesses to emerge was tracked down by Dallas reporter Earl Golz, who is among the most consistent chroniclers of assassination developments over the years. Golz located one of the forty prisoners who were being housed in the Dallas County Jail in a sixth-floor cell in direct sight of the infamous sniper's nest. The Warren Commission was urged at least once to interview these potentially excellent eyewitnesses, but there is no record that even one was ever contacted.[28]

In 1978 Golz located one of the former prisoners; he was seventeen at the time of the assassination and being held in the jail for three days on minor charges. He had never sought to publicize his story. According to this man, five or six minutes before the arrival of the motorcade he and several other inmates noticed two men in the sixth-floor window across from them. They were adjusting the scope on a rifle.[29]

"Quite a few of us saw them," he said, describing the men as having dark complexions. Apparently, the young inmate was watching the motorcade when the shooting took place and did not look back at the Book Depository until it was over. The men were gone. These prime witnesses were all ignored by the FBI, the Secret Service, and the Warren Commission.[30]

The accounts of two men in the window of the sniper's perch got a convincing boost in 1978 with the disclosure of a 1963 FBI memo concerning a motion picture and still film that the FBI disregarded soon after the assassination. The FBI report indicated that the FBI agents dismissed the importance of the film after viewing it, asserting that the Book Depository could not be seen.[31]

In 1978 Earl Golz and Gary Mack, another Dallas area researcher, tracked down Charles Bronson, the man who had made the film and still had it. A screening *did* show the TSBD Building, including eighty-seven individual frames showing the alleged sniper's perch and nearby windows. Viewers at that initial screening were astonished to realize that they could see what appeared to be two figures moving about in the pairs of windows around the sniper's nest minutes before the assassination.[32]

The electrifying discovery was made in the closing days of the work of the House Select Committee. However, Robert J. Groden, one of that panel's consultants on the photographic evidence and long a critic of the Warren Commission, enhanced and analyzed the film. His conclusions were startling: "The fact there is movement in two [pairs of] windows that are separated by a good eight feet indicates beyond question that there was more than one person up there."[33]

After a study of the Bronson film, Groden sent the following memorandum to the committee:

> Close inspection and optical enhancement reveals definite movement in at least two and probably three of the windows in question. . . . The man in window No. 1 is moving rapidly back and forth, and the man in No. 3 seems to be crouched down at the window and rocking on his toes in much the manner of a baseball catcher.
>
> The shape in window No. 2 is slightly less distinct than the other two. I originally felt that this "man" was actually the man in window No. 1 leaning back and forth, probably moving boxes around to construct what would be called "the sniper's nest."

I now feel that this is a distinctly different person who is probably handing boxes to man No. 1.[34]

The film was made a few minutes prior to the assassination, based on an examination of what is going on in the streets.[35]

One of the most mysterious pieces of evidence discovered in the sniper's lair was a large, homemade brown paper bag found lying on the floor near the window. It was 38 inches in length, large enough to transport the Mannlicher-Carcano when it was dismantled. The Warren Commission devoted considerable time to this bag, for it represented the most feasible way to account for Oswald's taking the rifle into the building. Investigators determined that its surface offered Oswald's fingerprint and palm print. Adhering to the bag were several fibers that, according to the FBI laboratory, matched fibers of a blanket in which the rifle may have been wrapped while purportedly in Oswald's possession. A major inconsistency in the evidence was that the rifle was in a well-oiled condition when discovered, but no oil traces were found on the paper bag.[36]

The Warren Commission concluded that this bag was used by Oswald to transport the rifle from the Dallas suburb of Irving, where he spent the night prior to the assassination.[37]

Wesley Frazier, who also worked at the Book Depository and who lived in Irving, gave Oswald a ride to work that morning. He told investigators that Oswald had with him a large brown bag that Oswald said contained curtain rods for his rented room in Dallas. Frazier's sister, Linnie Mae Randle, with whom he lived in Irving, also stated that she saw a brown bag in Oswald's hand that morning.[38]

Frazier last saw Oswald with the bag as he walked away from Frazier's car toward the TSBD Building. But the only person who saw Oswald as he entered the building that morning testified to the Warren Commission positively that nothing was in his hands. In fact, there are no other known witnesses who saw Oswald with the bag after he left Frazier, although presumably he was seen by other employees as he went to the sixth floor, where he worked.[39]

The FBI laboratory reported that the paper of the bag in question and the paper used for wrapping books at the Book Depository appeared to be similar. The Warren Commission concluded that

Oswald took the heavy wrapping paper from the TSBD prior to the assassination and fashioned the bag for the rifle. But Frazier, who had driven Oswald to Irving the previous evening, testified that Oswald had carried nothing with him. Investigation by the FBI indicated that it was highly unlikely that Oswald had access to the particular paper used for the bag if he had fabricated it at a much earlier period. This was true, the FBI reasoned, because the exact paper had become available in Oswald's area of the TSBD only a few days before the assassination.[40]

The only two people who ever testified that they saw the bag in Oswald's possession were Frazier and his sister, Mrs. Randle. Her initial impression was that the bag was about 28 inches in length and that "it almost touched the ground" as Oswald stood holding it by the top. (The police interrogators said that Oswald told them that he had his lunch in the bag.)[41]

What Frazier definitely recalled was the manner in which Oswald carried the bag as he walked away from the car toward the building. Oswald cupped one end of the bag in his hand and tucked the other in his armpit. Given Oswald's height, it would be impossible for him to carry something 35 inches long—the length of the dismantled Mannlicher-Carcano—in that manner. (One has only to imagine trying to cup one end of a yardstick in the palm of his hand and insert the other end in his armpit.)[42]

The testimony of Mrs. Randle and Frazier—both highly consistent and credible witnesses—provides one of the best illustrations of commission attempts to lead witnesses into statements that conveniently dovetail with foregone conclusions. But these two witnesses would not be swayed.

In the end, it was obvious from the evidence each of the witnesses gave on the brown-bag point that Oswald could not have carried the rifle that day, that he did not take it into the Book Depository, that he did not take any materials to Irving for manufacturing the bag. In the face of this, the Warren Commission was left with no alternative but to conclude that *all* the witnesses were "mistaken" in what they saw.[43]

The commission could not accept such persuasive testimony, simply because the brown bag was the only way it could find for Oswald to slip the purported assassination rifle into the TSBD.

Many critics believe the brown bag was not Oswald's—that it

somehow was planted to add legitimacy to the presence of the Mannlicher-Carcano and to the case for Oswald's guilt. And, indeed, in the commission's version, it did tighten the evidentiary noose around Oswald's neck.

In his book called *The Second Oswald*, Richard Popkin presents an intriguing suggestion for an added reason to place the brown bag at the scene. If the bag recalled by Frazier and Mrs. Randle is different from the bag found near the sniper's perch, then the rifle must have been taken into the building in a different fashion, perhaps at a different time. However, the commission's conclusion that Oswald used the bag as a means for getting the rifle into the building closed off any further search for another explanation.[44]

It was possibly foreseen that the paper bag, along with the Mannlicher-Carcano—both oozing evidence against Oswald—would most likely stifle any serious search for another murder weapon. And, in fact, there is no firm indication that any search of the Book Depository was made once evidence began to point squarely at Lee Harvey Oswald.

If there were conspirators who killed Kennedy and framed Oswald, the ploy of the brown paper bag was one of their most ingenious connivances.

There are two postscripts to the mystery of the brown paper bag. About two weeks after the assassination, according to a Warren Commission document discovered later, an undeliverable package came to rest at the dead-letter section of a post office near Dallas. It was addressed to Lee Oswald, but the street address was incorrect. There was no return address. The package contained a bag made of fairly heavy brown paper, and it was open on both ends. It is likely, given the time involved, that the package was mailed before the assassination. If Oswald was part of a conspiracy, it is possible that *this* was the bag that was supposed to play some role in the events. The Warren Commission knew about this strange bag but made no reference to it.[45]

The second tantalizing postscript came to light in 1980 as a result of the vigilance of two Texas researchers, Mary Ferrell and Gary Shaw. In 1968 there had been a disclosure of commission documents by the National Archives. Included was an FBI report on the laboratory tests done on the paper of the brown bag discovered in the TSBD Building. FBI Agent Vincent E. Drain reported that the laboratory found that the bag's paper "had the same observable characteristics" as the paper used for wrapping books at the TSBD. This, of course, was an important point accepted by the Warren Commission in building its case against Oswald.[46]

Twelve years later, Gary Shaw was going through thousands of pages of material at the National Archives. Mixed in with this great miscellany of material was a single page that looked identical to Agent Drain's one-page report on the testing of the brown paper bag. The wording and appearance of the two pages are initially indistinguishable—up to the key point of whether the paper in question is identical or not.[47]

In the version discovered in 1980, the word *not* appears, thus saying that the laboratory found that the paper bag was not made from the paper from the Book Depository. This finding is precisely contrary to the report accepted and used by the Warren Commission.[48]

It's anyone's guess what this means. Many critics are convinced that the FBI's first version was rewritten to make it appear that the paper *did* come from the TSBD but that the later version is the original. They feel it was a bureaucratic glitch that permitted the original to be released *after* the doctored version had become part of the record. Contacted in 1984, Agent Drain expressed bafflement over the two reports; "I am certainly as perplexed as you are," Drain told the author. However, he said that he believed the correct report to be the one that stated that the paper was the same. Drain's handwritten initials appear on the document he thinks is legitimate, while only his typed name appears on the other.[49]

Of all the debate surrounding the actual shooting, nothing has caused more argument than whether or not Oswald could have executed the spectacularly fast and accurate firing basic to the official conclusions. Both the Warren Commission and the House Select Committee agreed that he could. But from the first those findings have met with massive skepticism from the millions who scoff at the official findings.[50]

The Warren Commission, having committed itself to the proposition that Oswald was in the sniper's perch, had to produce evidence that he was capable of such superlative performance. Thus, the commission turned to Oswald's Marine records for a stamp of approval. It was a weak stamp, indeed.

During Oswald's first days in the Marine Corps in 1956, after a "very intensive" preliminary training period, he fired on the level of "sharpshooter," the middle range in Marine expertise. But in 1959 Oswald took another test on the firing range and scored only one point over the lowest possible level of qualification.[51]

What this means, the Marine Corps told the Warren Commission, is that when Oswald took his 1956 firing test, he was "a fairly good shot." But by the time he was about to leave the Marine Corps, according to a Marine Corps official interpretation, he had become "a rather poor shot." There is no evidence to suggest that Oswald's marksmanship improved after he left the Marines. But it seems unlikely it got any better, since there is no evidence of regular practice, which is necessary for any marksman to maintain his skill. In fact, judging from Oswald's movements and from the evidence available, he did not use the Mannlicher-Carcano for a period of nearly two months prior to the assassination.[52]

The Warren Commission heard testimony from one former Marine, Nelson Delgado, who stated that Oswald's marksmanship was "a joke," that he could hardly qualify on the range. This was not included in the Warren Report, but Delgado's comments about Oswald's shooting ability may explain why so few Marines were interviewed.[53]

In 1977 the author located and interviewed more than fifty of Oswald's Marine Corps colleagues, who had never been questioned by officials or journalists. (This was done in connection with research for *Legend*, by Edward J. Epstein.) On the subject of Oswald's shooting ability, there was virtually no exception to Delgado's opinion that it was laughable.[54]

Sherman Cooley, an expert hunter who grew up in rural Louisiana, knew Oswald well during their Marine Corps service. Cooley's comment capsulizes what several dozen Marines had to say about Oswald's ability as a marksman: "If I had to pick one man in the whole United States to shoot me, I'd pick Oswald. I saw that man shoot, and there's no way he could have ever learned to shoot well enough to do what they accused him of. Take me, I'm one of the best shots around, and I couldn't have done it."[55]

Many of the Marines mentioned that Oswald had a certain lack of coordination that, they felt, was responsible for the fact that he had difficulty learning to shoot. They believed it was the same deficiency in coordination responsible for his reported inability to drive a car. Repeatedly, as an illustration of his ineptitude, the former Marines harked back to the time Oswald managed to shoot himself in the arm while fooling with an unauthorized pistol he had stashed in his locker.[56]

In any discussion of Oswald's Marine marksmanship, there is a presumption that the rifle being used is one of acceptable quality. The ancient, bolt-action Mannlicher-Carcano—built around 1940—represents the opposite extreme. One handbook on rifles has called it "an odd choice" for the assassination, since it "has no great reputation for accuracy." This type of weapon also has "a good deal of recoil," making rapid shooting "notoriously difficult" considering the cheap telescope used.[57]

Mechanix Illustrated, one of this country's most respected journals of popular technology and gadgetry, carried an article in 1964 on the best way to find bargains in purchasing surplus military weapons. The article had nothing to do with the assassination rifle and did not even mention the connection. In advising its readers about various characteristics of more than a dozen rifles, *Mechanix Illustrated* dismissed the Mannlicher-Carcano as being "crudely made, poorly designed, dangerous, inaccurate . . . unreliable on repeat shots." The Oswald rifle was further handicapped by the fact that, according to the FBI, the scope was mounted off center, so that a shooter would have to compensate for the error.[58]

This is the rifle that Lee Harvey Oswald, "a rather poor shot" at last testing, was supposed to have used in his spectacular shooting exhibition at Dealey Plaza—a feat of marksmanship that remains unmatched in official tests.

Oswald's poor rifle ability and his grossly inferior weapon presented a considerable challenge to the Warren Commission. The challenge was heightened when expert sharpshooters failed in their efforts to duplicate Oswald's marksmanship. The three experts—rated as master marksmen by the National Rifle Association—each made two attempts to duplicate Oswald's performance and found it extremely difficult to do so, even with the conditions sharply tilted in their favor. They had corrected the scope on the Mannlicher-

Carcano and were shooting at fixed targets on a shooting range. Oswald, using a defective and off-center scope, was allegedly shooting at a target moving away from him and downhill at eleven miles an hour.[59]

Less than two months before the Warren Report was issued, Allen W. Dulles asked the commission's general counsel, "Where have we dealt with the evidence as to Oswald's ability to handle a rifle?" There was precious little time left for any additional consideration. But still the commission concluded that Oswald had the necessary ability.[60]

Years later, staff members of the House Select Committee on Assassinations undertook to settle once and for all the question of whether the Mannlicher-Carcano could have done the job. At a firing range outside Washington, HSCA Chief Counsel G. Robert Blakey met with four of the top rifle marksmen from the District of Columbia Police Department. All had prior military experience.[61]

A representative from the National Archives was present with the infamous Oswald rifle. After some testing, it was clear its condition was too poor to permit firing. A similar weapon was produced, one that had been used in earlier tests in Dealey Plaza.[62]

The specific purpose of the test, according to Blakey, was to see if it was possible for Oswald to fire two shots in less than 1.7 seconds. (The HSCA acoustics studies had determined this as the amount of time between the two closest shots.)[63]

The results were, at best, mixed. Blakey reported to the committee that such shooting *could* be done. He went on to explain: "It is apparently difficult but not impossible . . . to fire three shots, at least two of which score 'kills,' with an elapsed time of 1.7 seconds or less between any two shots, even though, *in the limited testing conducted, no shooter achieved this degree of proficiency* [italics added]."[64]

Echoes of the Warren Commission? What Blakey is saying is that while it is not *impossible* to duplicate Oswald's feat, none of the experts was able to do it. Moreover, the HSCA expert marksmen, like the experts in 1964, used stationary targets and were given unlimited time to prepare for their first shot. The fact remains that, to this day, no expert marksman has ever duplicated Oswald's shooting skills in any official test or demonstration.[65]

In the end, the HSCA agreed with the Warren Commission that

only Oswald and his Mannlicher-Carcano were responsible for all the bloodshed in Dealey Plaza.[66]

It is not surprising that there should be a strong dissent from the HSCA conclusion. Senator Christopher J. Dodd, then in the House and a member of the committee, declined to affirm the proposition that Oswald could have fired the first two shots with such speed. Addressing that particular point, Senator Dodd stated: "To believe that this option is correct, one must accept that Oswald was more proficient with a rifle than any of the committee's four expert marksmen. . . . Despite the fact that Oswald may have been more familiar with the Mannlicher-Carcano than any of the committee's expert marksmen, his record as a rifleman makes it hard for me to accept that he was able to fire faster than the experts and still hit both President Kennedy and Governor Connally."[67]

One of the most perplexing bits of evidence discounted by the official version was an assertion by one of the investigators who found the weapon hidden on the sixth floor. He identified it as a 7.65-millimeter Mauser, a far better rifle than the Mannlicher-Carcano.[68]

The investigator was Seymour Weitzman, a former Air Force pilot, who holds a degree in engineering. He also had been in the sporting-goods business and had some familiarity with guns. Weitzman's testimony clearly illustrates just how carefully the rifle had been concealed. In describing the discovery of the rifle to the Warren Commission, Weitzman first explained how it was deeply hidden among cartons of books: "It was covered with boxes. It was well protected as far as the naked eye because I would venture to say eight or nine of us stumbled over that gun a couple of times before we thoroughly searched the building."[69]

Weitzman was not the only one who thought the rifle was a Mauser. Deputy Sheriff Eugene Boone supported this view in an affidavit. Deputy Sheriff Roger D. Craig later even said the rifle had "Mauser" stamped on the barrel. All saw the rifle before it was removed.[70]

This description was repeated as late as midnight by Dallas District Attorney Henry Wade, who confirmed to reporters this identification of the rifle. Indeed, the perception that the rifle was a Mauser persisted for at least twelve hours and was repeated by high officials. Three days after the assassination, an internal CIA memorandum—

disclosed in 1976—noted that the murder weapon was a Mauser.[71]

This significant discrepancy in the description of the purported murder weapon was considered by the HSCA and dismissed as a simple error in the early confusion.[72] Asked about it in 1983, Chief Counsel G. Robert Blakey said he was not even aware of the report of a Mauser at the Book Depository Building.

No aspect of the physical evidence discovered in the sniper's nest is more bizarre than that which pertains to the rifle itself. The serial number of that rifle is C2766, which is the serial number of the rifle shipped to A. Hidell from the mail-order gun house—a point the Warren Commission considered very important in its linkage of evidence against Oswald. The Warren Report confidently states: "Information received from the Italian Armed Forces Intelligence Service has established that this particular rifle was the only one of its type bearing serial number C2766."[73]

This conclusion, bolstered by a variety of expert testimony on the point, manages to overlook a startling assertion contained in a report to the Warren Commission from FBI Director J. Edgar Hoover. The information is devastating to the commission's conclusion on the serial number: "The Mannlicher-Carcano rifle was manufactured in Italy from 1891 until 1941; however, in the 1930s Mussolini ordered all arms factories to manufacture the Mannlicher-Carcano rifle. Since many concerns were manufacturing the same weapon, the same serial number appears on weapons manufactured by more than one concern."[74]

Clearly, then, the tracing of the serial number does not have the evidentiary significance implied in the Warren Report. Other Mannlicher-Carcano rifles with the same serial number could be in existence in the United States. That such a clear contradiction could be glossed over is additional evidence of the familiar manipulation of facts to build the case against Oswald.

A point of critical importance to Oswald's reported shooting performance is the ammunition clip—the small, metallic device designed to feed cartridges into the rifle's firing chamber. Without a clip, the cartridges must be hand-loaded, one by one, making rapid shooting flatly impossible.[75]

There is not a shred of positive evidence that such a clip was found with the Mannlicher-Carcano in the sniper's nest. No reference to it is found in the original inventories of evidence. In her incisive analysis of this point, critic Sylvia Meagher dissects the Warren Commission testimony and arrives at this statement: "It was only when the Warren Report was issued in September 1964 that we learned that 'when the rifle was found in the Texas School Book Depository Building it contained a clip.' "[76]

Despite the voluminous and minute official analysis of what was found in the sniper's nest—including myriad details about the rifle itself—there is not one word of direct testimony that an ammunition clip was found.[77]

While there is no direct accounting of the clip, *references* to it begin to slip into commentary on other points, such as the testimony that no fingerprints were found on the clip. Once the presence of the clip came into acceptance, the Warren Commission went on to conclude, rather standoffishly, that "the rifle probably was sold without a clip; however, the clip is commonly available."*[78]

The exhaustive investigation into seemingly minor points that marked so many of the efforts of the Warren Commission did not extend to finding out where the clip came from or how Oswald acquired it. Beyond the *assumption* of the presence of the clip, there is nothing. As Sylvia Meagher writes: "No link between the clip and Oswald has been established—by purchase, possession, fingerprints or other methods."[79]

Nothing was more critically important to the Warren Report's picture of Oswald than the claim that an ammunition clip was found with his rifle. Without it, even the Warren Commission would not have had the gall to portray its lone assassin as hand-loading his cartridges as he carried off shooting skills never matched by the country's best shooting experts.

One of the enduring oddities of the Warren Commission's portrait of Lee Harvey Oswald concerns his peculiar preparation for his momentous deed. To carry off the crime of the century, Oswald possessed only four cartridges for the purported assassination rifle. Exhaustive FBI investigations have never turned up the source for Oswald's modest supply of ammunition. Not a single extra cartridge was found in his possessions, despite the massive dissection of his

---

*The author purchased a similar Mannlicher-Carcano in 1983 from a mail-order gun house. The ammunition clip was not included with the rifle and had to be purchased separately.

personal belongings.[80] (If it is true that Oswald took a shot at General Edwin Walker—a point examined in Chapter 9—then he supposedly had one other cartridge.)

A story in *The New York Times* two days after the assassination noted the enthusiasm of investigators as they began to track down the source of Oswald's ammunition: "The assassination, they said, involved excellent marksmanship that could only have come from regular practice recently, and this in turn would have required sizable quantities of the special ammunition."[81]

The quest was in vain, for the intense FBI search for the source of Oswald's four cartridges turned up nothing. In addition, there is no ordinary situation in which less than a full box of cartridges would be sold, any more than a person would buy only *four* cigarettes from a package of twenty. (Oswald's widow has provided directly contradictory testimony on the point of whether she ever saw ammunition in his possession.)[82]

If Oswald bought a box of cartridges from a source that was never discovered, it remains a mystery as to what he did with the bullets never used, since officials could find no concrete evidence of his engaging in target practice. If he did not buy a box of cartridges, there is an even greater mystery as to where—and from whom— he got his four cartridges, if, indeed, he did at all.

Instead of noting the mystery of Oswald's source for his four cartridges, the Warren Commission took the general approach of describing the ready availability and the high quality of the ammunition: "The ammunition used in the rifle was American ammunition recently made by the Western Cartridge Co., which manufactures such ammunition currently. . . . The cartridge is readily available for purchase from mail-order houses, as well as a few gun shops; some 2 million rounds have been placed on sale in the United States."[83]

This account suggests that not only was the ammunition easily available, it also was freshly made and doubtlessly reliable. Nothing could be further from the truth—as even Warren Commission documents demonstrated. An FBI report describes an interview with a representative of the Western Cartridge Company, who explained the origin of the ammunition in the United States: "The Western Cartridge Company . . . manufactured a quantity of 6.5 . . . Mannlicher-Carcano ammunition for the Italian Government during World

War II. At the end of the war the Italian Carcano rifle, and no telling how much of this type of ammunition, was sold to United States gun brokers and dealers and subsequently was distributed by direct sales to wholesalers, retailers and individual purchasers."[84]

Thus, it seems clear that the ammunition was around twenty years old and not a current item in any gun dealer's inventory. Other FBI reports show that only two dealers in the entire Dallas–Fort Worth area even stocked the odd ammunition. Both dealers were certain they had never sold to Oswald.[85]

Fourteen years after the assassination, new and peculiar information about the ammunition began to seep out of the FBI's store of secrets. One memorandum seized on by researchers concerned the manufacture, by Western Cartridge, of 6.5-caliber Mannlicher-Carcano ammunition for the Marine Corps in 1954. Dated December 2, 1963, the FBI memorandum points out that such ammunition "does not fit and cannot be fired in any of the [Marine Corps] weapons. This gives rise to the obvious speculation that it is a contract for ammunition placed by the CIA with Western under a [Marine Corps] cover for concealment purposes."[86]

How this bears on the case is not clear. The possible CIA connection simply raises more questions than are answered. It is also interesting, as researcher Edgar F. Tatro discovered, that the Select Committee permitted two documents pertaining to the Western Cartridge Company to be locked away in the National Archives for a fifty-year period. There is no solid clue as to what those documents contain—or what they might mean to the case.[87]

Crucial questions remain concerning the legitimacy of Oswald's print on the Mannlicher-Carcano. The Warren Report cited this palm print confidently as evidence linking Oswald to what it considered the assassination rifle. The curious history of this print is worth consideration.[88]

Before removing the rifle from the Book Depository, Lieutenant Carl Day of the Dallas police crime laboratory dusted the rifle and tried to bring out some vague prints he perceived in the vicinity of the trigger housing. Nothing emerged that was clear enough to be of any forensic value. Lieutenant Day took the rifle to the laboratory to continue his efforts. Later, he told the Warren Commission of the results of his work on the trigger housing prints on the day of the assassination: "I could not make positive identification of these prints."[89]

It was nearly midnight on November 22 when FBI Agent Vincent E. Drain picked up the Mannlicher-Carcano at the Dallas laboratory and carried it to Washington aboard an Air Force plane. In the early hours of November 23, the rifle was turned over to the FBI laboratory in Washington. Later that morning, Police Chief Jesse Curry told an NBC reporter that the partial fingerprints found on the rifle could not be identified as Oswald's.[90]

In Washington, the FBI laboratory examined the rifle for prints and found nothing. The next day, November 24, an FBI agent returned the rifle to the Dallas police. On that same day, Lee Harvey Oswald was murdered by Jack Ruby. After an autopsy, Oswald's body was taken to Miller's Funeral Home in Fort Worth to be prepared for burial.[91]

At the funeral home, teams of dogs fortified the police who stood guard that night. But no one attempted to molest the body. The only visitors reported were a team of FBI agents, who spent more than an hour with Oswald's body.[92]

The local paper reported the visit to the morgue by the FBI agents with a crime lab kit, stating that they "spent a long time in the morgue." Years later, Paul Groody, the funeral director, recalled the visit in an interview: "I was not in the room . . . but I had to clean up his fingers after they got through fingerprinting him. They put black gook on his fingers, and they can't get it off. . . . It was a complete mess of his entire hand, which would lead me to believe that they did take prints of his palms."[93]

In 1983 FBI Agent Drain, who was closely involved in the investigation, stated in an interview that he could not think of any logical reason that the FBI would want further prints from Oswald, since they had already taken sufficient ones for the case. What was even more puzzling to Drain was the report that the agents went to the funeral home, when there had been ample earlier opportunities.*[94]

About thirty miles away in Dallas that same night (November 24), there was a startling revelation by District Attorney Henry Wade.

*Some observers have speculated that perhaps the FBI needed prints from Oswald's body following his death for legitimate reasons. However, Oswald's fingerprints and palm prints were taken on the day of his arrest.

It had turned out, Wade said, that Oswald's print actually *was* found on the Mannlicher-Carcano. The news emerged from Wade in a most casual manner, as he said to reporters, "Let's see . . . his fingerprints were found on the gun. Have I said that?"[95]

Excitement swept through the ranks of reporters, who pressed Wade for details, assuring him that this was his first mention of such information. Wade explained that it was really a palm print. The presence of Oswald's print on the rifle was, of course, tremendously important in strengthening the case against him. Until then, there had been no absolute evidence that actually placed the rifle in Oswald's hands.[96]

On November 26, the rifle was again taken to the FBI laboratory in Washington. This time, the FBI was able to confirm a "lift" of a palm print as being that of Lee Harvey Oswald. Lieutenant Day stated that he had made the "lift" on the night of the assassination, prior to sending the rifle to Washington the first time. Lieutenant Day later explained that he failed to provide the print earlier because he was promptly ordered to turn over the rifle. In his rush to do so, he explained, he did not complete his work on the "lift" of the palm print.[97]

The Warren Report failed to address the significance of these peculiarities in the emergence of the palm print. It merely accepted the print as evidence against Oswald.[98] However, in 1978 a document was released by the FBI that showed the Warren Commission to be highly doubtful about the legitimacy of the palm print. Dated August 28, 1964, less than one month from the release of the Warren Report, the internal FBI memo stated: "[Warren Commission General Counsel] Rankin advised because of the circumstances that now exist there was a serious question in the minds of the Commission as to whether or not the palm impression that has been obtained from the Dallas Police Department is a legitimate latent palm impression removed from the rifle barrel or whether it was obtained from some other source and that for this reason this matter needs to be resolved."*[99]

The resolution, apparently, was simply to overlook the reasons

---

*On September 9, 1964, after the Warren Commission had finished its investigation, the FBI reported that it approached Lieutenant Day for further information about the Oswald print. Day refused to sign a statement about the print, saying that he would stand by his original written report.

that weighed against the legitimacy of the print and to embrace it as yet further evidence of the guilt of Lee Harvey Oswald.

In 1984, the author interviewed both Lieutenant Day and Agent Drain about the mysterious print. Day remains adamant that the Oswald print was on the rifle when he first examined it a few hours after the shooting. Moreover, Day stated that when he gave the rifle to Agent Drain, he pointed out to the FBI man both the area where the print could be seen and the fingerprint dust used to bring it out. Lieutenant Day states that he cautioned Drain to be sure the area was not disturbed while the rifle was in transit to the FBI laboratory.

Drain flatly disputes this, claiming that Day never showed him such a print. "I just don't believe there was ever a print," said Drain. He noted that there was increasing pressure on the Dallas police to build evidence in the case.

Asked to explain what might have happened, Agent Drain stated, "All I can figure is that it [Oswald's print] was some sort of cushion, because they were getting a lot of heat by Sunday night. You could take the print off Oswald's card and put it on the rifle. Something like that happened."[100]

Brash inconsistencies persist between the official account of Oswald's alleged activities at the Texas School Book Depository that day and a realistic assessment of the evidence. The official conclusion is that he could shoot well enough to do the job with an inferior weapon; yet there is a preponderance of commonsense reasoning to suggest that this is not possible. There is the conclusion that the creaky old Mannlicher-Carcano, showing "wear and rust" and bearing evidence allegedly linking it to Oswald,[101] was capable of the confounding performance at Dealey Plaza. To almost any layman, the evidence all points in the other direction.

Perhaps some might assume that Oswald was simply lucky that day—extraordinarily lucky. But given the limitations of that rifle and what is known of Oswald's life and his abilities, that does not seem likely. There is almost no doubt that Lee Harvey Oswald was somehow involved in the assassination, but just how and with whom is one of the great mysteries of the century.

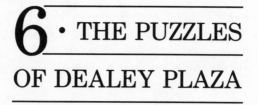

6 · THE PUZZLES
OF DEALEY PLAZA

Dallas Police Officer Joe Marshall Smith was standing in the middle of Elm Street at its intersection with Houston Street, bordering the Texas School Book Depository Building and away from the grassy knoll area. His assignment was to stop the flow of traffic into Dealey Plaza as the presidential procession approached. It was only a few seconds after President Kennedy's car had passed Officer Smith and started down Elm Street that the shooting began.[1]

"I heard the shots and thought they were coming from the bushes or the overpass," Smith later testified. "This woman came up to me and she was just in hysterics . . . [and] told me, 'They're shooting the President from the bushes.'"[2]

Officer Smith drew his pistol and went past the Book Depository and directly down the slope toward the grassy knoll area. While checking the bushes and cars in the adjacent parking lot, he encountered a man behind the stockade fence that separated the grassy area from the parking lot. Upon seeing Smith, the stranger at once produced Secret Service credentials. Smith allowed him to go on his way.[3]

Minutes later, up the hill, Sergeant D. V. Harkness went to the rear of the Book Depository to assist in sealing off the area. There he encountered several "well-armed" men dressed in suits. They told Sergeant Harkness they were with the Secret Service.[4]

The presence of Secret Service agents did not seem illogical to these two veteran police officers.[5] And no one has suggested that it was unreasonable on their part to accept them as such. But it is firmly established that, of the twenty-eight Secret Service agents present in Dallas that day, not a single man was ever in the grassy knoll area or the parking area behind it. No agent was on foot in the area before or after the shooting. The lone Secret Service agent who did go to the Book Depository later that afternoon did not do so until well after the encounters described by Sergeant Harkness and Officer Smith.[6]

Of the people present in Dealey Plaza, a large majority of those who have expressed an opinion believe the shots came from the area of the grassy knoll. Eleven law enforcement officers who were watching the parade from near the corner of Main and Houston streets believe the shots came from the knoll area. The two highest police officials in Dallas—Chief Jesse Curry and Sheriff Bill Decker—were in the motorcade when the shooting broke out. Each man immediately radioed orders to send officers to the grassy knoll area to see what had happened.[7]

Twelve of the people either inside the Book Depository or just outside it placed the shots in the area of the grassy knoll.[8] Two of the three men who were watching the parade from the fifth-floor window, just under the sniper's nest, reported that they heard shots directly above them. One of these witnesses underscored his certainty by noting that the ejected shells could be heard striking the floor over his head. Despite this testimony, the men immediately dashed to the other end of the building in order to have a prime view of the grassy knoll area. They stated that since so many others were headed for that area, they believed something might be going on there.[9]

Of the witnesses who were actually standing in the grassy knoll area watching the motorcade, many were certain the shots came from above and behind them—placing the shooting behind the bushes and the stockade fence, possibly in the parking lot that overlooked Dealey Plaza. They expressed terror for their very lives in recounting their experiences that afternoon.[10]

Cheryl McKinnon, a journalism student who was standing on the grassy knoll, recalls her shock as three shots rang out from behind her. Today a newspaper reporter in California, she has written: "[We] turned in horror toward the back of the grassy knoll where it seemed the sounds had originated. Puffs of white smoke still hung in the air in small patches. But no one was visible."[11]

One of the most convincing of these grassy-knoll witnesses is Gordon Arnold, who for fifteen years was believed by assassination experts to be a lump on the ground—perhaps a pile of earth. That is how he appeared to many of those who made intense studies of the photographs of the scene. That was precisely Arnold's desire as he felt the powerful reverberations of a bullet zing just past his left ear that afternoon.[12]

Home from basic training in the Army, Arnold had only recently spent time on the infiltration course, where he had been required to crawl along with bullets whizzing inches above his head. He knew the sound and the sensation, and he knew what he had been trained to do. He flattened himself on the ground and stayed there until the shooting stopped.[13]

Arnold had planned to take motion pictures of the motorcade from the railroad tracks on top of the triple underpass, overlooking Dealey Plaza. Wearing his Army uniform, he had gone up the grassy knoll toward the tracks over the underpass only a few minutes before the presidential procession arrived. Just as he got behind the stockade fence and headed toward the underpass, according to Arnold, a man in a civilian suit wearing a side arm approached him and told him no one was allowed up there.[14]

Arnold challenged the man's authority and indicated that he was going onto the overpass anyway. It was then, according to Arnold, that the man pulled out a large identification badge, held it toward the soldier and said that he was with the Secret Service and that he didn't want anyone up there.[15]

This seemed logical to Arnold. He retreated and went back to the front of the stockade fence. He took a position about three feet in front of the fence and began filming the approaching motorcade. That's when he felt the first shot nearly graze his left ear: "I thought they were shooting at me," Arnold told the author in 1982. "You don't really hear the whiz of a bullet; you feel it. You feel something go by, and then you hear a report just behind it. I automatically hit the ground. If I could have dug a hole and crawled in, I would have, because there was more than one shot fired. It was like a crack, just like I was standing there under the muzzle. One shot went past my ear, and the other went over me.[16]

"The next thing I knew, a police officer was standing there over top of me asking me what the hell I was doing, and I told him I was staying down so I wouldn't get hit."[17] The policeman then demanded the film from Arnold's camera, which he quickly turned over. A second policeman, whose face was streaked with tears, was waving a long gun. Arnold then went straight home. Two days later he was on his way to report for military duty in Alaska. No one asked his name, and he has never again seen the film he turned over.[18]

It is perhaps significant that Arnold never intended for his identity to be associated with the story. He sought no publicity, he says, for he was fearful of being connected with the incident.[19] He agreed in 1978 to talk with Earl Golz, then of the *Dallas Morning News*. According to Arnold, Golz agreed not to identify him. However, when the story was published, Arnold was fully identified, even in terms of his job with the consumer-affairs department in Dallas. Golz has confirmed this to the author, explaining that at the last minute his editor refused to run the story without giving Arnold's identity.[20]

Support for Arnold's claim to have been on the grassy knoll came from a surprising source. After the story appeared in the *Morning News*, former U.S. Senator Ralph Yarborough, who was riding with Vice-President Lyndon B. Johnson two cars back from the President at the time of the ambush, got in touch with the newspaper to say that he had observed just such an incident: "Immediately on the firing of the first shot," Senator Yarborough told the reporter, "I saw the man you interviewed throw himself onto the ground. He was down within a second of the time the shot was fired, and I thought to myself, 'There's a combat veteran who knows how to act when weapons start firing.' "[21]

The reports by Arnold and two police officers of Secret Service imposters in the immediate area of the assassination are chilling in their implications. But, many critics feel, it is no less shocking to consider other patterns of evidence, mostly disregarded or hidden by officials, that strongly suggest the presence of a conspiracy to murder the President. To be sure, much of it is circumstantial, but all of it is, at the least, more persuasive than the evidence used to build the final case against Lee Harvey Oswald.

Eyewitness accounts of what was going on in Dealey Plaza that day can roughly be divided into three segments: the period before the assassination, the moments surrounding the actual shooting, and the aftermath. There are accounts from seemingly credible witnesses—accounts that often independently corroborate one another—of sinister occurrences that morning that have never been explained satisfactorily. Then there is a plethora of puzzling evidence following the shooting that has never been explained—evidence heavy with design, not coincidence. These events have contributed substantially to the two decades of festering doubt, suspicion, and cynicism.

Were it not for other examples of the FBI's manipulation of evidence apparently to suit its own purposes, the story of Julia Ann Mercer might have to be tossed out as preposterous. But what happened to Miss Mercer during those terrible days in Dallas is not basically different from the experiences of others.

There are significant variations in the official reports of what happened to Miss Mercer. She was not called by the Warren Commission, and her account was ignored in its report. The House Select Committee was interested in her story but was not able to find her. [22] Miss Mercer was located in the course of investigation and research for this book and, in return for a promise not to reveal her current name or location, granted an interview to the author in 1983. She provided the following account of the events of November 1963:

A little before 11:00 A.M., on the day of the assassination, Miss Mercer, who was twenty-three years old, was driving west on Elm Street, just beyond the spot where the President would be killed in less than two hours. A few yards beyond the triple underpass, Miss Mercer brought her car to a stop. A green truck was blocking her lane, sitting partly on the curb. [23]

As Miss Mercer waited—perhaps as long as three minutes—a young man got out of the passenger's side of the truck and went around to the rear. He opened the long tool compartment on the side of the truck. According to Miss Mercer, he removed a package that she believed was a rifle wrapped in paper. The young man walked up the embankment in the direction of the grassy knoll area with the package. That was the last time Miss Mercer saw him. [24]

However, as she waited and then tried to move her car around the truck, Miss Mercer's eyes locked with those of the man behind the wheel. She was able to look at him clearly. He was heavily built with a round face. Miss Mercer edged her car by the truck and continued toward Fort Worth, where she was employed. [25] (A Warren Commission document, disclosed later, showed that a police officer on the scene had observed apparently the same truck and believed it to be a legitimate breakdown. [26])

Miss Mercer said that she stopped to have breakfast at a Howard

Johnson's restaurant on the toll road to Fort Worth. She often stopped there and was casually acquainted with the employees and regular customers, including policemen who regularly used the restaurant. When she entered the restaurant that day, she commented openly to several people that "the Secret Service is not very secret." She mentioned seeing the man with the rifle going up the embankment.[27]

Soon after Miss Mercer left the restaurant, two police officers who had heard her comments pursued her car and pulled her over. They stated that it was necessary for them to take her back to Dallas. Once in the police car, Miss Mercer learned that the President had been shot at Dealey Plaza, the location where she had seen the man with the rifle.[28]

Once back in Dallas, Miss Mercer was taken to the sheriff's office, where, for the next four or five hours, she was interrogated off and on by policemen and men in civilian clothes whom she believed to be federal investigators. She states that she was never shown a badge or any sort of identification by any of the men. She repeated her story many times before finally being driven home.[29]

At four o'clock the following morning, men came to her apartment and showed FBI identification. She accompanied them back to the sheriff's office, where they showed her a dozen or so photographs, asking her to pick out any she thought might be of the men she saw Friday morning. She selected two pictures. Miss Mercer had no idea of the men's identities.[30]

On Sunday morning, the day after Miss Mercer made the identification, she was watching the assassination coverage on television with friends and saw Ruby shoot Oswald. Instantly, she shouted that they were the two men she had seen on Friday and had identified for the FBI. Ruby, she said, was the driver and Oswald the man with the rifle.[31]

If true, Julia Mercer's identification of Jack Ruby *preceding* his murder of Oswald would have introduced a new twist to the official FBI version of the assassination. The revelation not only would have suggested a rifleman on the grassy knoll, but would have shown an FBI interest in Ruby in connection with the killing of Kennedy.*

It is not surprising that Miss Mercer's claim is not backed up by any official reports of the incident.

Some years later, when Miss Mercer saw the official reports, she

---

*Oswald's mother, Marguerite, insisted that the FBI showed her a photograph of Ruby and asked her if she had ever seen him—*prior* to Ruby's murder of her son.[32]

was aghast. The FBI, in its report of the Mercer interview, omitted her asserted identification of Jack Ruby as the driver of the truck. It also reported that even though Miss Mercer was shown pictures of Oswald, she was unable to identify him. The sheriff's department report included a statement attributed to Miss Mercer to the effect that she did not see the driver clearly enough to be able to identify him. Miss Mercer adamantly denounces the reports as corruptions and fabrications by the FBI and the sheriff's department of her actual experiences. Miss Mercer is one of many other witnesses who claim discrepancies between what was told to the authorities and what later appeared in the official reports.[33]

The key to any assessment of Miss Mercer's tremendously significant claim is, obviously, her own credibility. Nonetheless, the nature of her claims is not unprecedented. Indeed, there are proved examples of fact-fiddling in FBI reports that are far more blatant than this.[34] There are perhaps no examples concerning a more significant issue than this one. At this late date, it seems highly unlikely that the complete truth will ever be known about the experience of Julia Ann Mercer.

Another witness who reported men with long guns in the area that morning is Julius Hardie. As he drove along, Hardie saw three men on top of the triple underpass between 9:30 and 10:00 A.M. In a newspaper interview years later, Hardie stated that two of the men he saw were carrying long guns. Hardie could not be certain from his position whether they were rifles or shotguns. Hardie claimed that he made a report to the FBI.[35] No record of that report has surfaced.

The most often-cited witness to what was going on behind the stockade fence was Lee E. Bowers, Jr., a railroad employee, who on the day of the assassination was perched in a fourteen-foot railroad switching tower overlooking the parking lot behind the stockade fence. Bowers had worked in the tower for ten years, and he knew fellow railway employees. He also knew the faces of other people who worked nearby.[36]

A few minutes before noon that day, Bowers noticed an unfamiliar Oldsmobile station wagon enter the parking lot, which was almost full. The driver, according to Bowers, was a middle-aged white man with partially gray hair. He drove slowly about the lot and then left. The vehicle had out-of-state license plates.[37]

Around 12:15, a black 1957 Ford entered the lot. Bowers observed that the man was steering with one hand and seemed to be holding something in the other. Bowers believed it to be the microphone for a radio, or perhaps a mobile telephone. This car left the lot around 12:20, just as another unfamiliar vehicle—a 1961 Chevrolet—entered the lot. It was driven by a white man, who appeared to be between twenty-five and thirty years old, with long blond hair. The Chevrolet circled around and then left at about 12:25.[38]

In addition to the strange cars, Bowers noticed two men he did not know standing behind the stockade fence: "They were facing and looking up toward Main and Houston, and following the caravan as it came down," Bowers told the Warren Commission. At the very moment the shots rang out, Bowers noticed some "commotion" in precisely the area where he had seen the two men.[39]

Later, in an interview with Warren Commission critic Mark Lane which was recorded and filmed, Bowers said that while he could not be absolutely certain as to what had caught his attention, he believed "there was a flash of light . . . or something which caused me to feel like something out of the ordinary had occurred there."[40]

In addition to Bowers's precise testimony, at least five other witnesses independently reported seeing smoke rising from the grassy knoll area.[41]

For years some officials discounted this possibility, contending that modern gunpowder does not emit smoke when fired. However, the Select Committee concluded from studies by its experts that indeed even the "smokeless" gunpowder *does* release smoke that can be seen by the naked eye.[42]

And, in a surprising corroboration of the reports of smoke, at least seven witnesses—some of whom were dignitaries riding in the presidential motorcade—reported smelling the odor of exploded gunpowder in Dealey Plaza. Critics have pointed out that it is unlikely these witnesses could have smelled gunpowder at street level if it was coming from a sixth-floor window.[43]

Among the people who were standing on the grassy knoll watching the motorcade when the shooting broke out, the reaction was one of terror. Many believed that shots were being fired from directly behind them, just over their heads. Several of the witnesses, like Gordon Arnold, threw themselves onto the ground for protection.[44] Photographs of the grassy knoll show William and Gayle Newman, for example, frantically trying to cover their children to protect them from the gunfire.[45] In 1966 William Newman told author Josiah Thompson, "I thought the shots were coming from right off the tops of our heads . . . I thought the shot was fired from directly behind where we were standing. And that's what scared us, because I thought we were right in the direct path of gunfire."[46]

The Newmans' account is echoed with slight variations by other witnesses who were in the immediate vicinity of the grassy knoll at the time of the ambush. Even more significant is that dozens of witnesses—some even on the far side of the Book Depository—also believed the shots were fired from the grassy knoll area, possibly from the parking lot behind the stockade fence.[47]

Photographs show that as soon as the shooting was over, people began swarming toward the grassy knoll from all over Dealey Plaza. There is testimony that people surged toward the grassy knoll from various directions and that one policeman jumped off his motorcycle and raced up the hill toward the perceived source of the shots.[48]

S. M. Holland, a railroad worker who was standing on the railroad overpass watching the President's procession below him, heard the gunfire from just to his left. Holland and the two men he was standing with dashed toward the spot where they thought they heard shots, a spot in the parking lot just behind the stockade fence. Because of the congestion of parked cars in the lot, it took the men more than a minute to reach the spot.[49]

Others who had run from more distant spots joined the railroad workers behind the fence.[50] In the earth, still damp from a morning rain, the men discovered "numerous . . . footprints that did not make any sense because they were going [in] different directions."[51] Holland, who described his observations to Josiah Thompson, pointed out that all of the footprints were contained in a small area no wider than the length of a car bumper. "You could've counted four or five hundred [foot]prints," Holland said. "It looked like a lion pacing a cage."[52]

A superbly placed witness to the terrible events of that afternoon is Jean Lollis Hill, who was watching the procession from a spot on Elm Street directly across from the grassy knoll. The President's head exploded in front of her just as the limousine passed. At that precise moment, when nearly everyone else seemed stunned by the events of the last few seconds, Mrs. Hill saw a man in a brown overcoat sprinting toward the railroad tracks behind the grassy knoll. "He was the only thing moving up there," Mrs. Hill later testified. Her immediate impression was that the man was responsible for the shooting. She gave chase, dashing across the street and up the knoll. She was in pursuit when a man in a business suit stopped her in the parking lot behind the fence and showed her his Secret Service identification. Mrs. Hill heard someone yell that it appeared her quarry had escaped. The last Mrs. Hill saw of the man in the brown overcoat, he was running toward the railroad tracks just as they connected with the triple underpass.[53]

(Another witness, Jesse C. Price, who was on the roof of a building on the south side of Dealey Plaza, reported seeing a man fleeing across the railroad yard with something in his hand at just this time. But Price's description did not match that given by Mrs. Hill of the man she pursued. Price, of course, was a far greater distance away than was Mrs. Hill.)[54]

An impressive variety of independent, corroborative reports describe the movements in Dealey Plaza, following the shooting, of a gray Nash Rambler station wagon with a luggage rack on top. Several witnesses, from various vantage points, have provided descriptions, and there are even photographs of Dealey Plaza in which the Rambler can be seen moving along with the traffic.[55]

Richard Randolph Carr, a steelworker who was on an upper floor of a building under construction near Dealey Plaza, went down to the street when he heard the gunfire. In Carr's initial account, he reported seeing a man in the street whom he identified as the person he had seen on an upper floor of the Book Depository just prior to the shooting. Carr followed him for about a block and watched him get into a Nash Rambler. Carr later stated that the man at the wheel was "real dark complected" and appeared to be Spanish or Cuban.[56]

(It should be noted that over the years Carr's testimony has been somewhat inconsistent. And, for whatever reason, he has been seriously intimidated since originally offering his account to officials. He has been shot at and has found sticks of dynamite wired to his automobile's ignition switch. Still, Carr's earliest reports to officials are consistent on his sighting of the Nash Rambler.[57])

Soon after the shooting, Marvin C. Robinson was driving west along Elm Street in heavy traffic. According to an FBI report dated the next day, just as Robinson crossed the Elm and Houston intersection, he saw a "light-colored Nash station wagon" stop in front of the Book Depository. A white man walked down the grassy incline from the building, got into the Nash, and the car moved off in the direction of Oak Cliff. Robinson was unable to provide any additional information.[58]

Robinson's account—alone as innocent as any one of hundreds that were published—was omitted from the twenty-six volumes of Warren Commission exhibits. It finally was discovered years later in documents housed in the National Archives.[59]

The accounts of the Nash Rambler were also corroborated in highly convincing fashion by one persistent witness the Warren Commission was unable to avoid—Deputy Sheriff Roger D. Craig. In 1960 Craig had been named first-place winner of a meritorious award for his professional conduct, and his superiors strongly vouched for his veracity and integrity. When Deputy Sheriff Craig was first challenged about his reports of activities in Dealey Plaza, Dallas County Sheriff Bill Decker assured the FBI that Craig was "completely honest."[60]

The report that brought Roger Craig into his greatest difficulty was his statement that in the aftermath of the shooting, as he moved about Dealey Plaza on foot, he observed the following incident:

> I heard a shrill whistle and I turned around and saw a white male running down the hill from the direction of the Texas School Book Depository Building, and I saw what I think was a light-colored Rambler station wagon with [a] luggage rack on top pull over to the curb and this subject who had come running down the hill get into this car. The man driving this station wagon was a dark-complected white male. I tried to get across Elm Street to stop the car and talk with [the] subjects, but the traffic was so heavy I could not make it.[61]

Then, in another curious note, Craig stated that at the time he provided this information "to a secret service officer whose name I do not know."[62] Of course, there were no genuine Secret Service agents anywhere near the area at that time. Photographs of the scene—not available until after Craig's report—clearly show Craig looking toward the spot where he said he saw the running man.[63]

Later, after Oswald's arrest, Craig claimed that it was Oswald, or a man who looked strikingly like Oswald, whom he saw running down the incline and getting into the Rambler.[64] The fact that Craig never wavered from his basic testimony was, no doubt, a contributing factor in his gradual loss of credibility with the sheriff's office.[65] While Craig may not have seen the real Lee Harvey Oswald running down the slope, there is impressive evidence that there was a second man involved in the assassination who looked strikingly like Oswald. (The possibility of an Oswald imposter will be examined in a later chapter.)

By late afternoon on the day of the assassination, there was little official doubt in either Washington or Dallas that the assassin was Lee Harvey Oswald. The frantic media assured an anxious world that the case was virtually resolved.[66] New leads were hardly pursued after that time. Still, this does not explain the lackadaisical attitude shown by Dallas police officials immediately after the shots were fired, even before Oswald was in custody.

Nearly a dozen people were taken into custody in and around Dealey Plaza within minutes of the shooting. In some cases the suspects were taken in for questioning, and in other cases they were released on the spot. It is forever perplexing that in most of these instances, no records were kept of the identities of those detained.*[67]

The most famous of those taken into custody have come to be known as the Dallas tramps, three bedraggled-looking men rounded up in the railroad yards near the area of the grassy knoll. They were discovered in a boxcar and, many critics believe, had been in a prime location to have something to do with the assassination. Even if they had nothing to do with the killing, the argument goes, they should have been regarded as potential witnesses. They had been in a potentially good location to see activities that could have helped in an investigation. However, no record exists of what any of them said. There is no record even of their names or where they came from or what they were doing in the boxcar behind the grassy knoll. To this day, there is unending speculation about who these men were.[68]

It is ironic that while no official record exists of the detention of the Dallas tramps, their seizure is one of the best-photographed

*In 1975, the House Subcommittee on Government Information and Individual Rights discovered that the arrest records for November 22, 1963, prepared for the Warren Commission by the Dallas Police Department, were missing.

events in Dealey Plaza. Indeed, the number of photographs provide a solid basis for identification—a point that has contributed immensely to the intense interest in the tramps. Some critics point out that the photographs show clearly that two of the three tramps seem to be tramps *only in their dress*. Careful inspection shows that their hair is closely and neatly cropped, obviously by a competent barber. And their shoes are thick-soled and in good repair. They are freshly shaven and wearing clothing that appears raggedy but, on close inspection, is merely wrinkled.[69]

It was more than two weeks after the assassination that the *Dallas Times Herald* reported that a thirty-one-year-old Dallas man, arrested the day of the assassination, remained in jail even though he had been cleared of original suspicion of involvement in the Kennedy killing. The newspaper reported that the man was arrested in the railroad yards.[70]

The newspaper described the arrest: "The suspect was unarmed when arrested but booked, along with others arrested in the hectic hours following the assassination, on charges of 'investigation of conspiracy to commit murder.'" The newspaper report added that once these charges were dropped, the man continued to be held on "city charges."[71]

To this day, the man's identity has not been released. There is no record indicating that any federal or state officers ever questioned the man about what he had seen in the lot behind the stockade fence at the time the shooting started. It is fair to assume that if he had seen nothing suspicious from that vantage point, his testimony would have been used to bolster the official version that nothing unusual was going on behind the stockade fence.

Another arrest chronicled by the *Times Herald* was that of a young man on the street who was pointed out to police by spectators standing at a third-floor window of the Book Depository. The newspaper reported that workers were "pecking on a window . . . and pointing to a man wearing horn-rimmed glasses, a plaid coat and rain coat."[72]

A Dallas police officer arrested the young man and took him to Sheriff Bill Decker's office nearby, according to the newspaper, which added: "With the young man protesting, the crowd all along the way jeered at him as he was escorted across the street. . . . Officers on the case would not explain what connection the man might have with the shooting, nor would they identify him."[73]

There is no other record of this incident.

Deputy Sheriff Roger Craig, the police officer who had been cited for his superior work, revealed one of the most astonishing arrests. Craig made his statements in a taped interview in 1971 with assassination researcher and author Gary Shaw. Craig stated that minutes after the shooting, Dallas police detained a Latin man whom they had seized on Elm Street. Craig, who witnessed the arrest, stated that this was the same man he later saw driving the Rambler station wagon that picked up a man in front of the Book Depository.[74]

According to Craig, the Latin man was released when he indicated he could not speak English.[75]

While the three tramps, along with the Dallas man, were taken into custody in the general area behind the grassy knoll, other arrests were made on the upper side of Dealey Plaza, near the Book Depository. Directly across Houston Street from the Depository Building is the Dal-Tex Building, which affords a straight view down Elm Street directly to the point where the President and Governor Connally were hit. Some critics and researchers have long believed that this building is the most logical location for a second gunman to the rear of the President. Indeed, if a shot fired from that position nearly coincided with one fired from the sixth floor of the Depository, two things could be accomplished: first, it could at last explain how two shots could be fired in 1.66 seconds; second, the bullet—by striking Connally an instant after Kennedy was hit—could relieve the Magic Bullet of its miraculous performance.

In any event, at least three people who were in the Dal-Tex Building were detained by the authorities. Photographs show police searching one young man, who claimed to have wandered into the Dal-Tex Building in search of a telephone. When he found that all of the lines were tied up, he left the building, outside of which he encountered police. He was taken to the sheriff's office and then released.[76]

Another young man was led from the Dal-Tex Building by police, according to witnesses. He was described as wearing a black leather jacket and gloves. There is no record of his statement.[77]

Of all the activity at the Dal-Tex Building, nothing is more astonishing than the arrest of a shadowy figure with a pocketful of aliases. On that day, he used the identity of Jim Braden. Dallas police took him into custody after an elevator operator pointed out that his passenger did not have a familiar face.[78]

Braden, who then had an FBI rap sheet with about three dozen arrests, was in Dallas on the day of the assassination because of a meeting on the previous day with one of H. L. Hunt's sons to discuss some oil-leasing business. It so happened that Oswald's killer, Jack Ruby, was also in the Hunt offices that day, but there is no record indicating that there was a common meeting of Braden, Ruby, and one of the Hunts.[79]

Braden claimed that he had been walking along the streets near Dealey Plaza when the shooting started. He tried to flag down a taxi but had no luck. As he was walking past the Dal-Tex Building, according to Braden, he inquired of someone standing out front if a public telephone was available inside. He was told he might find one on the third floor. Braden claims he went to the third floor, found the phone was out of order, and immediately returned to street level by the elevator.[80]

Deputy Sheriff C. L. Lewis, tipped off by the elevator operator, took Braden into custody and escorted him to the sheriff's office for questioning. Braden, apparently, was well prepared. A few months earlier, he had started using the name Jim Braden; in reality, he was Eugene Hale Brading. If Dallas police had been given that name, they might have readily identified him as a man with serious felony convictions around the country, including burglary, embezzlement, mail fraud, and conspiracy.[81]

Braden was released about an hour later. The sheriff's office accepted his story that he was simply in town on oil business.[82]

Much has been written about the intimidation of witnesses to events that day. Always, though, these stories seemed to lie in that tantalizing netherworld between coincidence and design. The experiences of Deputy Sheriff Roger Craig may be more pronounced than those of some other dissenting witnesses, but in some ways they are typical. Under normal circumstances, Roger Craig would be any prosecutor's idea of an ideal witness. Gary Shaw, one of the most diligent researchers into the Kennedy case, spent much time with Craig developing the story of just what happened to him in the aftermath of his refusal to bend his story to fit the official version.[83]

Handsome and well-liked in 1963, Craig at twenty-seven had already earned four promotions in the Dallas Sheriff's Department. It should have been accepted as highly significant that such a reputable police officer reported an encounter with a purported Secret

Service agent in Dealey Plaza and later believed that he saw Lee Harvey Oswald run from the Book Depository and get into the Nash Rambler station wagon. However, Craig's testimony, though corroborated by others, was aggressively discredited.[84]

Perhaps the earliest dispute arose when Craig stated that he was in the office of Homicide Chief J. Will Fritz while Oswald was being questioned. Craig claimed to have identified Oswald as the one who got into the Rambler. He also recalled that the suspect—with whom he had a fleeting exchange of words—indicated some familiarity concerning the Nash Rambler. (There was, of course, no verbatim record of what Oswald said during these sessions. Captain Fritz told the author in 1983 that rumors of a secret recording of the interrogation are unfounded.)[85]

Captain Fritz, himself one of the most respected police officials in Dallas, at once disputed Craig's claim that he was in Fritz's office with Oswald. In fact, Fritz later swore to the Warren Commission that Craig absolutely was not in his office while Oswald was there, thus making a liar out of Craig.[86]

It was years later that Roger Craig was vindicated of Fritz's charge that he had lied about being in the office. It came when Dallas Police Chief Jesse Curry published his memoirs of the investigation. The book contains a photograph taken through the door of Captain Fritz's office to show the interrogation of Oswald. There, in plain view, is Roger Craig.[87]

In July 1967 Craig was dismissed from his job for supposedly talking to New Orleans District Attorney Jim Garrison. He then went to New Orleans, where he tried to assist in the Garrison investigation. Upon his return to Dallas, he was shot at as he walked to a parking lot; the bullet grazed his head. In 1973, while Craig was driving in the hills of West Texas, his car was forced off the road. Craig seriously injured his back. A few months later his car was bombed.[88]

His wife left him soon after that, saying she was unable to live with the violent attempts against his life. On May 15, 1975, Roger Craig was killed with a rifle, reportedly by his own hand. He was thirty-nine years old.[89]

Outside Dallas on the day of the assassination, police proved to be more efficient in recording the names of people arrested in connection with President Kennedy's death. In Fort Worth, twenty-

eight miles from Dallas, police picked up a young man who somewhat resembled Oswald. The arrest came as the result of a telephone
tip from a woman, in another town not far from Dallas, who reported
cryptically that the car the suspect was driving (she gave the license
number) had been involved in the assassination. There was no known
effort made to question the caller about why she had this idea, but
the young man's story is interesting.[90]

When interviewed by the FBI, the suspect explained that he had
driven the one hundred miles from his home at Ranger, Texas, to
Dallas hoping to visit an old friend, though he had not told the friend
that he was coming. He reached Dallas in midmorning and tried to
telephone his friend. When he was unsuccessful, he decided that
since he was downtown and traffic was heavy, he would stay there
and see the presidential parade. He parked his car on Commerce
Street.[91]

Following the assassination, the young man left downtown Dallas
in his green and white 1957 Ford. At 1:35 P.M., the police, having
received the tip indirectly from the out-of-town caller, broadcast a
description of the man's car and the license number. A few minutes
later Fort Worth police picked him up, took him to jail and kept
him there until FBI agents arrived. When Oswald's arrest was announced, the young man was released.[92]

A bit after this, Dallas police received a report that a man in a
residential section of Dallas was seen removing a rifle from a light
green, two-tone car. Investigation by the police showed that the car
in question was registered to a man of the same last name as the
"friend" the suspect had tried unsuccessfully to telephone.[93]

Gary Shaw has tried to interview the young man about these
matters and has been "met with extreme hostility." Shaw and others
wonder, in light of evidence that Oswald was set up as a patsy, if
other patsies were in the making that day. Indeed, the suspect in
this case does resemble Oswald, and the manner in which police
were led to him is no more muddled than the way in which police
found themselves on Oswald's trail. To this day, no one has recon-
structed with assuredness the origin of the description of Oswald
broadcast by police. Even more obscure is the origin of the tip
leading to the arrest of this individual.[94]

Another unheralded arrest in Dallas that afternoon was that of an
ardent right-wing speaker who, according to some witnesses, had
been seen in Jack Ruby's nightclubs. According to information

pieced together by assassination researcher and author Bernard Fensterwald, Jr., this man arrived in Dallas in October and applied for a job at the Downtown Lincoln-Mercury dealership, which is only two blocks west of Dealey Plaza. He presented favorable references from a New Orleans automobile dealership—references that later proved to be fabricated. He was hired as a car salesman.[95]

The day before the assassination, the new salesman was given permission to borrow one of the company cars. He is supposed to have told his boss that he needed it because he had a "heavy date" that evening. The next morning, the individual failed to show up for work. His superiors became worried about the car he had borrowed.[96]

Thirty minutes after the assassination, only a couple of blocks away, the salesman appeared at the showroom. According to Gary Shaw's *Cover-up*, in an account Shaw says is based on Fensterwald's work, this is what happened next: "[He] came hurrying through the showroom with mud on his clothes, pale and sweating profusely; he ran to the restroom and threw up. He told co-workers that he had been ill that morning, tried to drive the car back to the dealership and finally parked it because traffic was so heavy. Two employees went to get the car . . . [and found it] parked . . . behind the wooden fence on the knoll, overlooking the assassination site." The young man had also been an expert marksman in the Air Force.[97]

All of this caused great suspicion among the new salesman's associates. He was arrested but soon released. He left Dallas immediately. He was never questioned by the Warren Commission.[98]

Another unusual figure who may have been at Dealey Plaza during the assassination is the late Joseph Milteer, an ultra-right-wing Georgia businessman who seems to appear in one of the crowd photographs of Dealey Plaza. Milteer had demonstrated strikingly accurate knowledge of an assassination plot against President Kennedy during the President's visit to Miami only two weeks before the Dallas trip. Even Milteer himself later reportedly claimed to have been in Dallas when Kennedy was killed. However, the Select Committee concluded that the photograph was not that of Milteer, basing its finding on an expert's analysis of the picture.[99] (Milteer will be discussed in detail in a later chapter.)

The most important evidence about what happened in Dealey Plaza is, with little dispute, the famous home movie made by Abraham Zapruder. This film was shot from the President's right, as the limousine moved along Elm Street. It shows almost the entire period of the shooting, with the exception of a few moments a street sign obscures the image of the limousine.[100]

A viewer can see the instant the President's head is blown apart, a force that appears to slam the President violently leftward and to the rear. One can see Mrs. Kennedy as she scrambles onto the rear of the open car, seeming to try to retrieve a part of the skull that appears to have come to rest on the left rear of the car. In color, the film is a gruesomely shocking few moments to watch. It is the only motion picture in existence that shows what happened.[101]

Within the first twenty-four hours of the assassination, *Life* magazine had acquired the film from Zapruder, eventually paying him $150,000. More than a decade passed before the public was allowed to see the Zapruder film. No one had access to the film other than *Life* personnel, although the film was made available for all official investigative purposes. The Warren Commission recognized the tremendous value of the film and used it as a time clock in efforts to describe what happened at Dealey Plaza. The commission also published many of the individual frames of the film.[102]

From the earliest days, there is evidence that the custodians of the Zapruder film seemed sure the public would never view the horrifying sequence. A prime example of this is seen in how *Life* described the bullet wound in the President's throat. At first, there were the reported impressions of the Dallas doctors who almost unanimously believed they had observed a bullet wound of *entry* in the President's throat. This was obviously in conflict with the almost instantaneous official version that Oswald, alone and behind Kennedy, did all the shooting. The front throat wound posed a stark contradiction. How could the President have been hit in the throat by a rifleman shooting from behind him?[103]

Life, the only news organization with access to the Zapruder film, explained the anomaly in its issue of December 6, 1963. After describing the medical report about the front-entry wound, *Life* explained: "But the 8 mm [Zapruder] film shows the President turning his body far around to the right as he waves to someone in the crowd. His throat is exposed—toward the sniper's nest—just before he clutches it."[104]

That account is flatly wrong. Any viewer of the film would agree that at no time does the President make such a turn. Moreover, of course, the official version held that actually the throat wound was one of *exit*. No explanation for this blatantly false description of the Zapruder film has surfaced. It is not known whether the *Life* writer, Paul Mandel, viewed the film himself, or whether he based his account on what others told him. Mandel died in 1965.[105]

The most electrifying aspect of the Zapruder film is the moment the President's head is blown apart. The impact clearly seems to cause the President's body to be slammed rearward and to his left. Tissue and bone can be seen moving in that direction. A motorcycle policeman riding to the left rear of the limousine was splattered with blood and tissue, and later a large piece of the President's skull was found to the left rear of the car's position.[106]

No layman can watch these frames and avoid the clear impression that the shot came from the right front of the President, the grassy knoll area. Nothing in the Zapruder film is more compelling than this violent backward, leftward motion of the President's head and body. Moreover, there is probably nothing in the film that deserved more attention and official analysis.[107]

The Warren Commission handled the matter of the left rearward head-snap by not mentioning it in its report or in any of its volumes of evidence. The commission did publish these frames from the Zapruder film but, in one of the most shocking examples of "mistakes," the key frames showing the impact of the head shot were transposed. With the frames so reversed, the certain perception of a front-to-rear shot is removed. The FBI took responsibility for the faulty sequence, and in 1965 Director J. Edgar Hoover called the transposition "a printing error."[108]

By 1975, when a copy of the Zapruder film was shown on national television, the violent rearward head-snap at last had to be given some official explanation. The HSCA addressed the question and heard expert testimony that the motion of Kennedy's body could have been a neurological spasm. According to the Select Committee report, the expert concluded that "nerve damage from a bullet entering the President's head could have caused his back muscles to tighten which, in turn, could have caused his head to move toward the rear." A motion picture was shown of a goat being shot in the head, causing *all* the goat's muscles to go into a violent, involuntary spasm. Clearly, this does not appear to be what happened to Kennedy, whose whole body appears to go limp as he is thrown backward. There is no splaying of his limbs, as in the shooting of the goat.[109]

The HSCA also turned to its medical panel for an explanation, but the answer there was far from satisfactory. The doctors even suggested the fallacy of the goat experiments, stating, "It would be reasonable to expect that all [the President's] muscles would be similarly stimulated." It is obvious to any viewer that the President's muscles were not in any state of spasmodic stimulation.[110]

In the end, the HSCA could not offer any sure explanation for the violent backward head-snap. The committee's report stated that "the rearward movement of the President's head would not be fundamentally inconsistent with a bullet striking from the rear."[111]

A weaker statement of explanation is hard to imagine.

Dealey Plaza on that Friday was a jungle of perplexities and contradictions. Such a multitude of witnesses, of course, could never yield anywhere near a totally cohesive account of what happened. Few critics would demand that official investigators resolve every conflict in evidence. And given the nature of any broad investigation, it is hardly surprising that there are so many examples of officials apparently sifting and shifting the evidence to find material to bolster their theories and conclusions.

But in this miasma of confusion, there is one mind-bending mystery in the handling of evidence that remains as bewildering today as ever. It has received virtually no publicity. In its most sinister interpretation, the puzzle suggests overt acts by federal officials—particularly the FBI—to conceal solid evidence that could prove a conspiracy in the assassination. At their most benign, the events are simply inexplicable. Either way, in 1983 the U.S. Department of Justice remained as determined as it was twenty years earlier not to allow a resolution of the mystery by disclosing certain specified scientific materials.

James T. Tague, a twenty-seven-year-old Dallas automobile salesman, was standing near the concrete abutment of the triple underpass, about 260 feet downhill from the President's position. As Tague was straining to get a glimpse of the President, he heard a "cannon-type sound" and looked around to try to identify it. When he heard subsequent gunfire, he ducked behind a concrete post.[112]

Moments later a police officer jumped from his motorcycle in front of Tague and drew his pistol. He rushed up the embankment, apparently in search of the shooter. A few minutes later, Tague recalled that just when the shooting broke out he had felt a sting on his cheek, which he had forgotten in the excitement. He mentioned this to a nearby deputy sheriff who confirmed that Tague, indeed, had blood on his cheek. Tague reached up and found a few drops of blood.[113]

The officer asked where he had been standing. Tague led him to the spot. They inspected the concrete curbing along the street and discovered a fresh mark they believed had been made by a bullet. It was 23 feet, 4 inches east of the abutment of the triple underpass.[114]

A patrolman immediately radioed that a man had been "possibly hit by a ricochet from the bullet off the concrete."[115] Soon the press was there to make news photographs, including close-ups showing where the bullet had hit the concrete, leaving a distinct pockmark. Such a picture appeared in newspapers that weekend.[116]

All this information was available to the FBI, which had been ordered by President Johnson to lead the investigation. Two weeks later, when the Warren Commission received the FBI's five-volume report on its investigation, there was not a word about the Tague incident.[117]

Although some parts of the report—a damning indictment of Lee Harvey Oswald—were leaked to the press immediately,[118] no one had reason to suspect that the Tague curbstone shot had been completely ignored. It was reasonable to assume that the Tague shot would be covered in the 372-page document. (That report, Commission Document 1, was not released to the public until 1965.)

The official indifference to the Tague curb shot is instantly puzzling, even suspicious. One would expect the investigators to be interested in *any* shot fired in Dealey Plaza at that time. In this case spectrographic analysis might have yielded enormously pertinent information. If it were possible to match the metal traces from the Tague curb shot with the bullet and fragments associated with the assassination, the case against Oswald as the lone gunman would be strengthened.

On the other hand, if the metal traces from the curb shot were inconsistent with the alleged assassination bullet and fragments, the whole lone-assassin theory would be seriously jeopardized. As desperate as the FBI was for evidence to shore up its lone-assassin theory, its apparent decision to ignore that the shot hit the curbing was perplexing to say the least. And since the FBI was the Warren Commission's chief investigative arm, the commission had no other direct, formal source for the information. (There are indications, however, that the Warren Commission members knew of the shot months before they finally gave it their attention. Initial accounts of it are included in the transcripts of the police radio broadcasts made by the Dallas police for the commission.)[119]

There are several possible reasons for the FBI's initially overlooking the Tague curb shot. First, though improbable, is that the FBI field agents in Dallas did not know about the shot, even though thousands of citizens learned about it from the news media and saw pictures of the bullet nick in the curb.[120]

A second possibility is that the FBI was aware of the commonsense likelihood that there *was* another shooter in Dealey Plaza and believed the bullet that caused the curb shot was from his gun. If so, presentation of scientific evidence confirming a second gun would be devastating to the lone-assassin theory. Acknowledgment of the shot would wreak havoc with the FBI/Secret Service conclusion that all shots hit within the limousine.[121]

A third possibility is that with so much eyewitness evidence of shots coming from places other than the Book Depository, the FBI simply did not *want* to know the origin of the Tague shot—or what it meant. An immediate spectrographic analysis could have yielded support for the FBI position—or could have spelled doom to it. Ever cautious, for whatever reasons, Hoover's agents took no known action to investigate the Tague shot. Months later, when a news story appeared on Tague, the Dallas FBI clumsily portrayed him to FBI headquarters as a publicity seeker.[122]

It was not until the following April 1 that the Warren Commission counsel took testimony from two assassination witnesses, Tom Dillard and James Underwood. These witnesses also happened to be the two newsmen who had seen and photographed the Tague curb shot months earlier.[123] However, no questions were asked them about the curb shot. (It was revealed during the questioning of Dillard that he was interviewed by the FBI on November 25. The report of that interview, released in 1965, clearly shows that the Tague curb shot was not mentioned, despite the wide publicity it had received by that point.)[124]

About a week later, the Tague curb shot was dragged past the nose of Warren Commission Counsel David Belin, who ignored it. This was the first time it is known with certainty that the commission was told that a bystander was slightly injured by a ricocheting bullet or fragment. Belin was taking the testimony of Police Officer Clyde Haygood, who mentioned speaking to a witness who had been hit "by a piece of concrete or something." Belin clarified the victim's location and then said: "Talk to anyone else?"[125]

Officer Haygood, who began to tell of another witness who had heard shots from the Book Depository, again mentioned the witness who had been "hit by a piece of concrete from the ricochet." Belin again ignored what would seem to be extraordinary information and began an intense pursuit of everything Haygood could tell him— which was nothing new—about the Book Depository.[126] That line of questioning was supportive of the commission's preconceived findings.

In May 1964 leaks began to appear in the press indicating that the Warren Commission was moving toward the conclusion that one bullet caused all the nonfatal wounds in both Kennedy and Connally. This, of course, was the famed single-bullet theory that had as its buttress the exceptional performance of the Magic Bullet. The single-bullet theory emerged as the only way to explain various certainties while clinging to the basic proposition of Oswald as a lone assassin.[127]

But adoption of the single-bullet theory also meant the rejection of the findings of the Secret Service and the FBI that Kennedy and Connally were hit by separate bullets. If the first shot was responsible for all these nonfatal injuries, the clear indication was that the second shot missed entirely. Suddenly, one can presume, there was a legitimate way to explain the long-ignored Tague shot. He could have been hit by a fragment of concrete splintered off by a bullet that completely missed the presidential limousine.[128]

Around the end of May, James Tague returned to Dealey Plaza to take some motion pictures. He was about to travel to Indiana to visit his family, and he wanted to show them where he had been and what he had seen on that infamous day.[129] When Tague went to take a close-up shot of the bullet defect in the curbing, he was astounded.

It was no longer visible.[130]

On June 11, in tentative language and for unclear reasons, Commission Counsel Arlen Specter, the creator of the single-bullet theory, suggested in a memo that "if any additional depositions are taken in Dallas," James Tague be deposed to determine his knowledge of "where the missing bullet struck."[131] The reference to *the missing bullet* suggests that Specter's single-bullet theory was destined for acceptance over the belief of the Secret Service and the FBI that all three bullets hit the presidential limousine.

Soon after Specter's indifferent request for a deposition from Tague, the U.S. attorney's office in Dallas learned that there were photographs of the damaged curbstone. The photographer, Tom Dillard, provided glossy photographs of it. The U.S. attorney sent the information to Washington, urging that the curb shot not be overlooked. Almost immediately, the Warren Commission formally requested the FBI to look into the matter. By this time, of course, the prime evidence had disappeared.[132]

Prodded by the Warren Commission, the FBI swung into action right away and took the two Dallas newsmen to the scene of the curb shot in an attempt to locate the bullet-pocked section of concrete. The effort was fruitless. In its report for the Warren Commission, the FBI concluded: "No nick or break in the concrete was observed . . . nor was there any mark similar to the one in the photographs taken [in November 1963]."[133]

The FBI report then offered some bureau speculation about what might have happened: "It should be noted that, since this mark was observed on November 23, 1963, there have been numerous rains, which could have possibly washed away such a mark and also that the area is cleaned by a street cleaning machine about once a week, which would also wash away any such mark." The report did not explain how rains might wash away an indentation in the concrete and leave a smooth surface.[134]

The finding that the bullet's pockmark in the curb had vanished was almost as amazing as the feats of the Magic Bullet. The Warren Commission responded by sending Wesley Liebeler, an assistant counsel, back to Dallas for a hasty deposition of James Tague, who until then had had no contact with the Warren Commission. The

FBI laboratory dispatched its laboratory photographic expert, Lyndal L. Shaneyfelt, from Washington to inspect the Dallas curb. At last, it seemed, there was to be action.[135]

On July 23, more than a month after the Warren Commission was supposed to have finished its investigation, James Tague was at last deposed. The account he gave was unwavering as he related just what he had heard and felt and then seen when he examined the curb with the deputy sheriff and others. There was not a hint of contradiction or uncertainty in his basic points.[136]

Tague's account was fully supported by a second witness deposed by Liebeler that day, Deputy Sheriff Eddy Walthers, one of the officers who inspected the curb just after the shooting. Walthers noted that he had been in the sheriff's office for nine years and testified: "It was a fresh ricochet mark. I have seen them and I noticed it for the next two or three days as it got grayer and grayer and grayer as it aged."[137] That aging process, of course, would do nothing to fill the obvious indentation that can be seen in the original photographs of the bullet mark.

The truly astounding aspect of Tague's testimony occurred when Commission Counsel Liebeler stated, "Now I understand that you went back there subsequently and took some pictures of the area, isn't that right?"

Perplexed and believing that no one knew he had done this, Tague asked Liebeler to repeat his question. Liebeler repeated the question, and when Tague answered affirmatively, Liebeler added, "With a motion picture camera?"

"Yes," Tague replied. "I didn't know anybody knew about that."[138]

Liebeler did not respond. Clearly, though, Liebeler's knowledge had to represent information given to him by some investigatory agency—presumably the FBI. (In any event, some years later Tague discovered that his movie had vanished from his home.) But Liebeler brushed past this oddity concerning his knowledge of Tague's film to ask if he had been able to find the damaged curb section when he looked for it. Tague stated that he had not been able to find it.[139]

With it established that even Tague agreed the scar or nick was no longer there, the FBI's Lyndal Shaneyfelt went to the scene. Sighting from the original photographs, he was able to pinpoint the precise location of the spot in question. He had the curb section sawed out and flown to Washington for technical analysis.[140]

It is obvious that at this point officials *knew* the curb section was not in its original state. In the synopsis page of a long FBI report pertaining to various angles of the assassination, the case agent, Robert P. Gemberling, makes the following reference: "Additional investigation . . . concerning mark on curb . . . near triple underpass, which it is alleged was possibly caused by bullet fired during assassination. *No evidence of mark or nick on curb now visible. Photographs taken of location where mark once appeared.* [italics added]."[141]

Gemberling's reference to "where mark once appeared" is a compelling addition to the accumulated evidence on the point. On the very date of Gemberling's report, the altered curb section was on its way to Washington to undergo sophisticated testing.[142]

Even though the nick in the curbing had vanished, the FBI laboratory did find some "metal smears." This was done by submitting the "smears" to spectrographic analysis. The FBI laboratory reported the smears to be essentially of lead composition with a trace of antimony. It states that no traces of copper were found. The report made no reference to any other ingredients of bullets.[143]

In a report to the commission, FBI Director Hoover stated: "The lead could have originated from the lead core of a mutilated metal-jacketed bullet such as the type of bullet loaded into 6.5 millimeter Mannlicher-Carcano cartridges or from some other source having the same composition."[144]

After this perhaps calculated reference to the type of rifle believed by officials to have been used by Oswald, Hoover went on to state that because of the composition of the "smear" and the minor damage to the curbing, "this mark could not have been made by the first impact of a high-velocity rifle bullet."[145]

Presumably the "metal smears" could have been from almost anything containing lead and antimony. The possibilities ranged from paint to a wheel-balancing weight spinning off a moving vehicle some time earlier.[146] These could not, however, have caused bleeding to James Tague's face. The essential point is that the specimen tested was not the defect observed in the curb by experienced police officers, the injured James Tague, and the two news photographers.

For more than a dozen years, Harold Weisberg tried through the courts to force the FBI to disclose its basic scientific records on this matter, as well as on other similar tests of material related to evidence in the Kennedy assassination. He finally lost his case in 1983, but the twists and turns of the case make it certainly one of the most significant of its kind.[147]

Some of the statements elicited by Weisberg from FBI agents turned out to be contradictory and inconsistent—hence raising the question as to whether there was false swearing by officials.[148] But the most maddening element, according to Weisberg, has been the almost completely cavalier manner of the FBI and the Department of Justice in their misrepresentations under oath.[149]

Weisberg felt that none of his assertions were rebutted by the FBI or the Justice Department.[150] One of the oddest twists came when the Justice Department found it convenient to cite Weisberg's expertise. In a motion, the Justice Department stated: "[Weisberg] alleges the existence of certain documents which he claims have not been provided by the FBI. In a sense, [Weisberg] could make such claims ad infinitum since he is perhaps more familiar with events surrounding the investigation of President Kennedy's assassination than anyone now employed by the FBI."[151]

As for the particular spectrographic evidence on the curbstone, it was supposed to be housed in a section of the laboratory reserved for cases of historical significance.[152] The prime piece of test evidence is a thin strip of film that was exposed during the actual spectrographic test. That film strip, or plate, contains the basic information needed for an interpretation of the results. Of all the pieces of thin film in this cabinet, the FBI finally claimed that the one of the curbstone test—and that one alone—had been "destroyed" or "discarded" in "routine housecleaning."[153] That single piece of evidence was the key to the truth behind the Tague curbstone.

As for the case in general, Weisberg flatly charges that the records "have not been produced because they would show that the FBI knowingly covered up evidence of a conspiracy to assassinate the President."[154] He believes that the revelations of the shenanigans of the FBI in terms of the curbstone would have destroyed the lone-assassin, no-conspiracy conclusion of both the FBI and the Warren Commission—thus giving it an "exceptionally powerful motive" for its continuing resistance.[155]

A crucial point established in the court battle was the assertion by an FBI expert that it is possible to determine through scientific testing whether the Tague curbstone—now housed at the National

Archives—was or was not actually patched.[156] Weisberg repeatedly alleged that it *was* patched, and there was no denial by the FBI.[157] A scientific determination of whether the curbstone was patched— along with modern testing of the material beneath such a patch— could have historic ramifications.

In 1983, a firm with expertise in the analysis of concrete was commissioned to examine the curbstone. The report stated: "The dark spot shows visual characteristics which are significantly different from those of the surrounding concrete surface. While any one of the differences could be easily explained in terms other than a patch, the simultaneous occurrence of those differences would amount to a rather curious coincidence. But a surface patch would also be consistent with and explain all of the observed differences."[158]

The public may never know what happened to the original evidence held by the bullet-pocked curbstone. It is known, though, that reliable witnesses examined and photographed the curbstone showing the bullet mark. And it appears certain to nearly any layman that *something* was done to alter the evidence. However the curbstone was altered and the evidence destroyed, there is one absolute certainty:

It was not done by Lee Harvey Oswald acting alone.

President Kennedy speaks to an early-morning crowd in Fort Worth on November 22, several hours before his assassination. Behind JFK, on the left, is Texas Governor John Connally. On the right is Vice-President Lyndon B. Johnson, who would become president a few hours later.

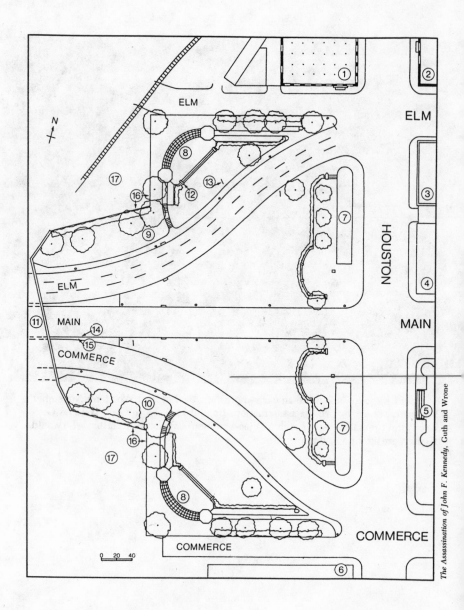

ELM

N

17

8

16
13
12

9

ELM

11 MAIN

14
15
COMMERCE

10

16

17

8

COMMERCE

0 20 40

ELM

1

2

ELM

3

7

HOUSTON

4

MAIN

5

7

COMMERCE

6

The Assassination of John F. Kennedy, Guth and Wrone

Squire Haskins

Dealey Plaza

1 Texas School Book Depository. Alleged assassin's lair on the sixth floor, easternmost window.
2 Dal-Tex building
3 Dallas County Records building
4 Dallas County Criminal Courts building
5 Old Court House
6 United States Post Office building
7 Peristyles and reflecting pools
8 Pergolas

9 Grassy knoll north
10 Grassy knoll south
11 Triple underpass
12 Position of Abraham Zapruder
13 Stemmons Road sign
14 Approximate location of curbstone hit
15 Position of James T. Tague
16 Stockade fences
17 Parking lots

President Kennedy's son, John, Jr., gives his father's caisson a last salute. With him is his sister, Caroline. Behind the children are Senator Edward Kennedy, Jacqueline Kennedy, and Senator Robert Kennedy.

Lee Harvey Oswald, accused assassin of the President, gives a defiant gesture to the press. At one point he yelled, "I'm just a patsy!" There are no records of Oswald's interrogation during the hours before he was silenced by Jack Ruby, although he denied that he shot anyone.

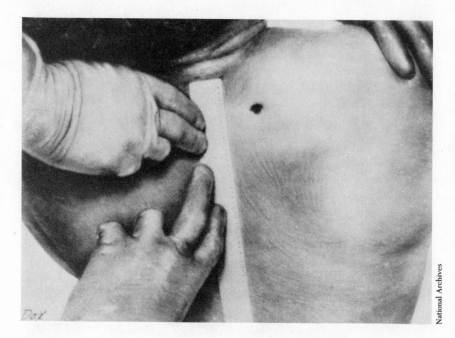

The medical artist's drawing above, based on the autopsy photographs and released by the House Select Committee on Assassinations, shows that the shot did not enter the neck, as the Warren Commission claimed. Actually, the shot that passed through the President's body entered in his back, below and to the right of the neck. The bullet hole in the President's suit jacket was six inches below the collar line. The Warren Commission drawing, opposite above, illustrates the original official version that the bullet entered the neck. This drawing also shows a bullet entering the lower rear of the President's head and exiting the right front. The drawing of the actual autopsy photograph of the head wound (opposite below) shows that, in reality, the bullet entered four inches higher than the Warren Commission version claimed.

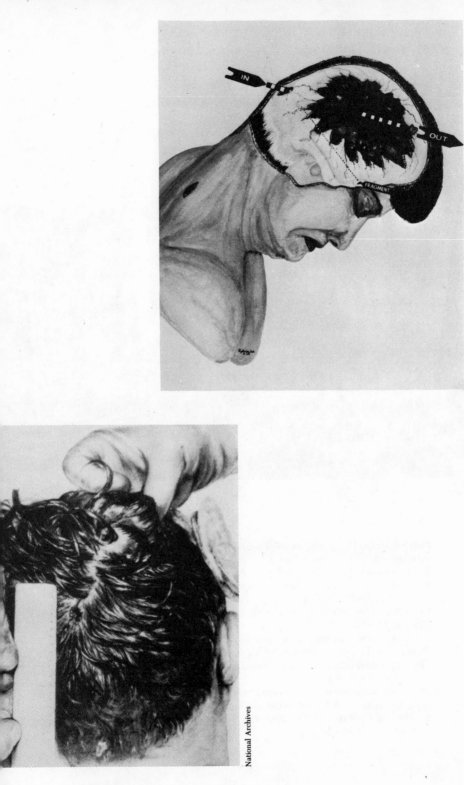

Roger Craig, a highly respected member of the Dallas Sheriff's Department, swore that he watched a man he later believed to be Oswald run from the area of the Book Depository Building and get into a Rambler station wagon driven by a man with dark complexion, perhaps a Latin. Craig claimed that later that day, while in Homicide Chief Will Fritz's office, he identified Oswald as the man he had seen. Craig was denounced as a liar. Officials said that Craig was never in Will Fritz's office and that he had no opportunity to identify Oswald. However, the photograph above, taken ten minutes after the shooting according to the clock atop the Book Depository, indeed shows a Rambler station wagon on the right, just behind a bus. Five years later, a document emerged revealing that the FBI interviewed a second witness who saw the white male entering the Rambler station wagon. Six years after the assassination, when Dallas Police Chief Jesse Curry published his memoirs of the case, his book included the photograph on the opposite page. Taken through the door of Captain Fritz's office, the picture clearly shows that Roger Craig was present (note arrow).

The Dallas home of General Edwin Walker, at whom Oswald was accused of firing a shot in the spring of 1963. The slug recovered from Walker's home was never ballistically linked to Oswald's Mannlicher-Carcano rifle. This picture was taken by the author in 1977. Note the sign erected by Walker in his front yard.

Nov. 8, 1963

Dear Mr. Hunt,

I would like information
concerning my position.
I am asking only for information.
I am suggesting that we discuss the
matter fully before any steps are
taken by me or anyone else.

Thank You,
Lee Harvey Oswald

Bearing Oswald's name, this note to "Mr. Hunt," dated November 8, 1963, was mailed anonymously to a Texas assassination researcher in 1975. Handwriting experts have differed over whether the writing is really Oswald's. No definite answer could be reached by experts empaneled by the House Select Committee on Assassinations. However, there are striking similarities to Oswald's erratic style and handwriting. The identity of the "Mr. Hunt" is unknown.

Oswald, in foreground of photograph, with his Marine colleagues in the Philippines. Over the past eight years, the author has interviewed more than fifty of the Marines who served with Oswald. Only several of the men had been interviewed by officials. Nearly all of them recalled their fascination with watching the activities of the ultra-secret U2 spy planes housed near their unit in Japan as well as in the Philippines.

Sherman Cooley, who went through boot camp with Oswald, remembers that he could hardly qualify on the rifle range. "I saw that man shoot," says Cooley. "There's no way he could have ever learned to shoot well enough to do what they accused him of doing in Dallas."

Henry Hurt

Sgt. Miguel Rodriguez (left), a career Marine, was at the Blue Bird Bar near Atsugi, Japan, when Oswald provoked a confrontation by throwing a drink in his face. The action was completely uncharacteristic of the normally mild-mannered Oswald. However, as a result of the incident, Oswald was court-martialed and served time in the brig. This continued an odd Oswald pattern of having himself removed from routine activities of his associates.

Henry Hurt

James R. Persons (left), today a bank president
calls Oswald as a quiet, polite young man who ra
had much to say. However, Persons did observe
Oswald enjoyed the company of girls in Japan.
also remembers that Oswald possessed a lack of
ordination that contributed to his being very poc
rifle marksmanship.

Jerome Daniels (right), a large man who gained the
nickname of "Gator" for his alligator-wrestling ex-
ploits, liked Oswald and tried to teach him to play
poker. Daniels even worked at finding a girl for Oswald. When Daniels was short of cash, he could count
on Oswald to lend him money until payday.

Pete Connor (left), who served with Oswald in Japan, recalls that some of the men tormented Oswald because of his bookishness. "The kid was a jerk, always mouthing off. If he went into a bar, somebody would nail him," Connor says. Connor was present in Oswald's cubicle when Oswald fired an unauthorized pistol. Oswald was treated for a flesh wound in his upper arm and punished for having the illegal weapon.

e Cassisi (right), who served with Oswald apan, recalls that Oswald had an aloof at-de that sometimes got him into trouble with other Marines. Cassisi enjoyed picking on vald, adding, "He would walk away from any ence. You could hit him, and he'd never hit back."

Henry Hurt

FEDERAL BUREAU OF INVESTIGATION

1   Date ___11/30/63___

       Lt. CARL DAY, Dallas Police Department, stated he
found the brown paper bag shaped like a gun case near the
scene of the shooting on the sixth floor of the Texas School
Book Depository Building. He stated the manager, Mr. TRULY,
saw this bag at the time it was taken into possession by Lt.
DAY. TRULY, according to DAY, had not seen this bag before.
No one else viewed it. TRULY furnished similar brown paper
from the roll that was used in packing books by the Texas
School Book Depository. This paper was examined by the FBI
→ Laboratory and found to have the same observable characteristics
as the brown paper bag shaped like a gun case which was found
near the scene of the shooting on the sixth floor of the Texas
School Book Depository Building. The Dallas police have not
exhibited this to anyone else. It was immediately locked up
by DAY, kept in his possession until it was turned over to FBI
Agent DRAIN for transmittal to the Laboratory. It was examined
by the Laboratory, returned to the Dallas Police Department
November 24, 1963, locked up in the Crime Laboratory. This bag
was returned to Agent DRAIN on November 26, 1963, and taken back to
the FBI Laboratory.

       Lt. DAY stated no one has identified this bag to the
Dallas Police Department.

FD-302 (Rev. 3-3-59)

FEDERAL BUREAU OF INVESTIGATION

Date ___11/30/63___

1   NOV 30 1963

       Lt. CARL DAY, Dallas Police Department, stated he
found the brown paper bag shaped like a gun case near the
scene of the shooting on the sixth floor of the Texas School
Book Depository Building. He stated the manager, Mr. TRULY,
saw this bag at the time it was taken into possession by Lt.
DAY. TRULY, according to DAY, had not seen this bag before.
No one else viewed it. TRULY furnished similar brown paper
from the roll that was used in packing books by the Texas
School Book Depository. This paper was examined by the FBI
→ Laboratory and found not to be identical with the paper gun
case found at the scene of the shooting. The Dallas police
have not exhibited this to anyone else. It was immediately
locked up by DAY, kept in his possession until it was turned
over to FBI Agent DRAIN for transmittal to the Laboratory.
It was examined by the Laboratory, returned to the Dallas Police
Department November 24, 1963, locked up in the Crime Laboratory.
This bag was returned to Agent DRAIN on November 26, 1963, and
taken back to the FBI Laboratory.

       Lt. DAY stated no one has identified this bag to the
Dallas Police Department.

A key problem in the government's case against Oswald was how he got the rifle into the Book Depository. It was concluded, finally, based on an FBI laboratory analysis, that Oswald used paper from the Book Depository to fashion a bag in which he carried his dismantled rifle. The document (upper left, see arrow) indicates a positive identification of the paper. However, many years later, the apparently identical report turned up in a release of documents from the National Archives (lower left). In *that* document, the word "not" appears, indicating the opposite conclusion about the paper used to make the bag. The discrepancy has never been explained. Above is the bag in question.

Committee plans to examine the double murder. Even Texas wasn't. The state's attorney general has ordered an inquiry. The public especially wasn't satisfied and, accordingly, it was a week of breathless rumors: that Oswald had been a hired killer; that Oswald had used an accomplice; that Oswald had not killed the President at all; that Oswald had been framed and then shot to silence him. The rumors grew because the best evidence which could dissolve them, the contents of Oswald's mind, was now irretrievable. But even though the investigations were just under way, there was already enough other evidence on hand to answer some of the hard questions.

Was it really Oswald who shot the President?

Yes. The evidence against him is circumstantial and it received an incredibly bush-league battering around by the Dallas police, but it appears to be positive.

Three shots were fired. Two struck the President, one Governor Connally. All three bullets have been recovered—one, deformed, from the floor of the limousine; one from the stretcher that carried the President; one that entered the President's body. All were fired from the 6.5mm Carcano carbine which Lee Oswald bought by mail last March.

The murder weapon, although subsequently manhandled for the benefit of TV, still showed Oswald's palm print. His own carbine was missing from its usual place. A witness had seen him bring a long, gun-sized package to work. And threads from Oswald's clothing were found in the warehouse sniper's nest.

Many rumors have grown out of the presumed difficulty of firing three accurate shots in the time Oswald had

Oswald was an ex-Marine sharpshooter, and he was firing from a perfect sniper's position. He had piled some boxes to prevent being seen from an adjoining building. He had put another box off in a corner so he could sit on it and look out the window—again so as not to be seen. Finally, in front of the window he had stacked three boxes as a rest for his carbine. Two big pipes ran vertically along a wall near his window, natural braces for a shoulder. His position while shooting at a car going away to his right would have been comfortable and rock-steady, and Oswald had both the time and the ability to zero in three times.

The description of the President's two wounds by a Dallas doctor who tried to save him have added to the rumors. The doctor said one bullet passed from back to front on the right side of the President's head. But the other, the doctor reported, entered the President's throat from the front and then lodged in his body.

Since by this time the limousine was 50 yards past Oswald and the President's back was turned almost directly to the sniper, it has been hard to understand how the bullet could enter the front of his throat. Hence the recurring guess that there was a second sniper somewhere else. But the 8mm film shows the President turning his body far around to the right as he waves to someone in the crowd. His throat is exposed—toward the sniper's nest—just before he clutches it.

Had authorities been watching Oswald?

They had—but not when it mattered. Oswald first came to the FBI's attention when he tried to defect to Russia in October 1959. On Aug. 10 this year the FBI interviewed him again,

Despite pre
evidently did n
never been in
seems to have I
about his acti
about his ass
police officers
the shooting,
had a gun, she
to the place
kept his carbir
did, to find th
that she had I
her husband.

There still a
Oswald's asso
he nevertheles
ey to travel te
no previous pa
an alias whil
Dallas roomii
out that Osw
ated with secr
ing subversive
think he plot
last, most o
act absolutely

How did

Jack Ruby e
casual fashior
enabled him t
walking towai
"I saw a poli
and I guess t
walked on do
Oswald was b
This story
for the investi
jury trial—to
tually was in
quently after
On the very
sination, whe
and snapping
in the city he
already there
"Jack, what t
here?" He wa

Early points of confusion surrounding the shooting of the President were reports from attending physicians that JFK suffered an entry wound in his throat, which would suggest a gunman in the front as well as the rear. The December 6, 1963, issue of *Life* sought to explain this anomaly. Citing the Zapruder film, which *Life* owned and which the public was not allowed to see until 1975, the article reported that the film showed JFK turned completely around so that he was *facing* the sniper's nest—thus explaining the entry wound in the throat. As any viewer of the Zapruder film can instantly discern, no such turn was made by the President.

7 · TIPPIT'S MURDER:

ROSETTA STONE

OR RED HERRING?

The Rosetta Stone to the solution of President Kennedy's murder is the murder of Officer J. D. Tippit. . . . Once the "hypothesis is admitted" that Oswald killed Patrolman J.D. Tippit, there can be no doubt that the overall evidence shows that Lee Harvey Oswald was the assassin of John F. Kennedy.[1]

> —David W. Belin
> Assistant Counsel to
> the Warren Commission

Earlene Roberts fiddled quickly with the knobs on the television set, trying to bring into focus a picture to accompany the numbing words of the newscaster telling her that President Kennedy had been shot a few miles away in downtown Dallas. A friend had called to alert her to the unfolding horror. As Mrs. Roberts adjusted the set, a young man who roomed in the house, known to her as O. H. Lee, came hurrying through the front door. Mrs. Roberts spoke to Lee, but he rushed silently past her and across the room. He entered his tiny bedroom and shut the door behind him.[2]

It was just then, a minute or so past one o'clock, that Mrs. Roberts heard an automobile horn honk twice. The sound came from the street in front of the house, which was located at 1026 North Beckley Street in the Oak Cliff section of Dallas. Mrs. Roberts, who was the housekeeper at the rooming house, looked out the window and saw a Dallas Police Department patrol car stopped on the street in front. Two uniformed officers were seated in it. Mrs. Roberts tried for a moment to make out the number marked on the car to see if it was familiar. This was her usual manner of recognizing the patrol car driven by police officers for whose wives she occasionally did housework. But it was not that car. Mrs. Roberts returned her attention to the television set.[3]

Shortly afterward, the man known to her as O. H. Lee came bustling out of the door to his room, zipping up a light jacket. He went out of the house, and Mrs. Roberts saw him walk toward the bus stop nearby. When Mrs. Roberts last glanced out the window, she could see Lee waiting at the bus stop, which served northbound bus routes. It was several minutes past 1:00 P.M.[4]

When Earlene Roberts next saw O. H. Lee, his picture was being flashed on the television screen as Lee Harvey Oswald, the prime suspect in the assassination of John F. Kennedy.[5]

Perhaps it is because Earlene Roberts is a lone witness that her account of Oswald's presence at his rooming house has remained essentially unchallenged, a benchmark for the spectacular events that were to develop within the hour. But, to be sure, no one ever found a shred of serious reason to doubt the veracity and credibility of Mrs. Roberts.

In contrast, the testimony of witnesses used to chronicle Oswald's movements from Dealey Plaza to the rooming house prior to 12:48 P.M. is hopelessly contradictory. Nonetheless, the Warren Commission picked through what was offered and came up with an account that seemed reasonable enough at first glance, though it was soon to become primary grist for the researchers and critics beginning their dissection of the official version of events.

Though no one testified to seeing Oswald leave the Book Depository, the Warren Commission concluded that he departed about 12:33 P.M. This assumption was based on the knowledge that Officer Marrion Baker stopped a man believed to be Oswald a minute or so before this. The commission decided—without benefit of eyewitnesses—that Oswald walked from the Book Depository seven blocks to the east on Elm Street, in a direction that took him directly away from his rooming house in Oak Cliff. In doing so, he walked past five bus stops.[6]

At 12:40, according to the commission reconstruction, Oswald, having walked the seven blocks to the east to catch it, boarded a westbound bus. A few blocks later, at about 12:44, as the bus approached the congestion of Dealey Plaza, Oswald is supposed to have gotten off and walked south to the Greyhound bus station in search of a taxicab.[7]

At about 12:48, according to the first reasonably consistent testimony concerning his movements, Oswald entered a cab parked outside the bus station and—after courteously offering the cab to a woman—asked to be driven to Oak Cliff. He directed the driver to drop him off several blocks beyond his rooming house and, if the commission reconstruction is correct, emerged from the cab at 12:54. He then reached the rooming house around 1:00 P.M., which coincides with the independent account of the housekeeper, Earlene Roberts.[8]

The testimony from eyewitnesses concerning Oswald's boarding and leaving the bus on Elm Street is so contradictory that it seems virtually useless. The single sliver of concrete evidence was a bus-transfer slip supposedly in Oswald's possession when he was arrested. However, it seems indisputable that Oswald did get a cab at the bus station and arrived at his rooming house around 1:00 P.M. And the evidence is persuasive that he departed the rooming house several minutes past one o'clock, at the earliest.[9]

It is intriguing, to say the least, that Oswald's departure from the rooming house occurred only moments after the strange appearance and horn-blowing of the patrol car from the Dallas Police Department. Exhaustive investigations have virtually established that the only police car officially in the vicinity was that of Officer J. D. Tippit. Less than fifteen minutes after this incident, Officer Tippit was savagely murdered and left dead in the street about a mile from Oswald's rooming house.[10]

The fact of Tippit's death is one of the few sure things about the entire incident. Even the number of times he was shot at remains in some dispute, and the autopsy performed on his body was not made a part of the published Warren Commission records. In fact, accounts of Tippit's murder and the descriptions of his assailant are as contradictory as any aspect of the whole assassination story.[11]

Such contradictions notwithstanding, the Warren Commission arrived at a simple and straightforward version of the murder of Officer Tippit. The official account is shaded by the same myopia and questionable logic that typified so much of the commission's work. According to the official version of events, Officer Tippit was in the Oak Cliff area of Dallas, about four miles from Dealey Plaza. At 12:45 P.M., Tippit is presumed to have heard the broadcast of a physical description of the suspect wanted for questioning in the Dealey Plaza shooting. The description broadcast included no outstanding features of clothing or physique; indeed, it would have fit nearly any white man of normal appearance.[12]

Thirty minutes after the description was broadcast, according to the commission account, Tippit spotted a man walking east along Tenth Street who seemed to fit this description of the suspected assailant in Dealey Plaza. In a move that would seem utterly uncharacteristic of a veteran police officer facing a potential presidential assassin, Tippit supposedly stopped and called the man over to his car. The man walked to the car, leaned down, and spoke to the policeman through the window on the passenger's side. There is no indication that Tippit was at all concerned about the possibility of danger.[13]

Then, according to the Warren Report, "Tippit got out and started to walk around the front of the car. As Tippit reached the left front wheel, the man pulled out a revolver and fired several shots. Four bullets hit Tippit and killed him instantly. The gunman started back toward Patton Avenue, ejecting the empty cartridge cases before reloading with fresh bullets."[14]

Domingo Benavides, one of the witnesses driving by, watched as the gunman emptied his revolver, reloaded, and moved from the scene. Benavides waited "a few minutes" until the gunman was gone and then ran to Tippit's car. Unfamiliar with the police radio, Benavides fumbled with the microphone unsuccessfully. At that moment, another passerby, T. F. Bowley, ran up, grabbed the microphone from Benavides and radioed the dispatcher that an officer had been shot. That transmission was logged around 1:16 P.M.[15]

The commission's account of Tippit's and Oswald's movements leading up to the policeman's murder is as speculative as anything the commission produced. All of it is squarely aimed at one conclusion: that the brutal deed was done by Lee Harvey Oswald. Before that day, there is no corroborated evidence that this mild-mannered young man had ever committed an act of serious violence—much less murder. The evidence suggesting his capacity for violence is as tenuous today as it was two decades ago.*

---

*Oswald was posthumously accused of having taken a shot at Maj. Gen. Edwin Walker in April 1963. However, the evidence the Warren Commission produced was, again, of the flimsiest kind.[16]

But Lee Harvey Oswald was to be charged with the savage execution of a police officer and the supremely efficient assassination of the President of the United States. The two acts neatly complemented each other. Responsibility for the assassination could explain why Oswald might be driven to the brutal murder of Tippit; and the murder of Tippit was offered as irrefutable proof of Oswald's capacity for violence. Blaming Oswald for the murder of Tippit provided a powerful psychological foundation for the acceptance of Oswald as the lone killer of John F. Kennedy. And such a foundation was sorely needed.[17]

The evidence allegedly linking Oswald to Tippit's murder was oddly similar to that which linked him to the sniper's perch from which President Kennedy was supposedly assassinated. The cartridge shells curiously tossed at the scene by the fleeing murderer were indeed fired from the revolver reportedly found on Oswald when he was arrested a short while after Tippit's death. However, the bullets in Tippit's body were never linked ballistically to Oswald's revolver.*[18]

Thus, for Oswald to be accepted as Tippit's murderer, it was vital that he be placed at the scene. To do this, there were several crucial factors to be considered:

• Could Oswald have gotten from his rooming house to the scene a mile away in time to commit the murder?
• Could witnesses be found who could place Oswald along the routes he might have walked between the rooming house and the murder scene?
• Could witnesses identify Oswald as the murderer?

To consider these points, it is necessary first to examine the probable time of Tippit's murder, as well as the length of time it would

---

*Because of alterations that had been done on the revolver, a routine ballistics matching was impossible. The revolver had been fitted with chambers that would accommodate cartridges minutely smaller than the diameter of the revolver's barrel. Hence, when a cartridge was fired through the barrel, there was a slight slippage of the missile in the barrel that prevented the normal ballistics markings from occurring on the slug. Thus, a ballistics determination was not possible. This was the explanation offered by the Warren Report. In 1984 Dr. William J. Bruchey, Jr., a research physicist and ballistics expert, was asked by the author to conduct an independent examination. In his conclusions, Dr. Bruchey concurred with the Warren Report.

take for Oswald to reach the murder scene traveling by foot from his rooming house.

The Warren Commission heard the testimony from Earlene Roberts that she last saw Oswald at 1:03 or 1:04 P.M. standing at a bus stop providing service in a direction precisely opposite that of the location where Tippit was murdered. About twelve minutes later, almost one mile away, Tippit was reported shot. Benavides, the man who attempted to report the shooting by police radio, testified that he waited "a few minutes" after the shooting before contacting the police—a report which was officially logged at 1:16 P.M. Thus, if the Warren Commission version is accepted, Oswald managed to walk nearly a mile, encounter Tippit and murder him, reload his pistol, and be on his way in a little more than ten minutes. By most any standards, this was extraordinary if not impossible.[19]

But the Warren Commission, ignoring compelling evidence to the contrary, concluded that this is what happened. The familiar logic again seemed to prevail: since Oswald was presumed to have committed the murder, he must have been there in time to do it.

As in other aspects of its investigation, the Warren Commission found itself using as key witnesses those whose accounts must have been distressing in the formulation of the official version. For the Tippit murder, Helen Markham emerged as the star of the commission's presentation, even though she claimed she saw Tippit being shot no later than 1:07 P.M.—significantly earlier than the murder could have happened if it was committed by Oswald. (Mrs. Markham, while highly inconsistent in other areas, seems credible on the matter of the timing because she was on her way to catch a bus at 1:15 to go to her regular job.)[20]

Other eyewitnesses also plagued the commission. The only person who claimed he actually checked the time was T. F. Bowley, who stated that his watch indicated that it was 1:10 P.M. And Bowley came upon the murder scene after Tippit was shot, while he was still lying in the street. Bowley's report gives credence to the 1:07 time Helen Markham gave for the actual shooting. Four other witnesses put the time even earlier, stating that it occurred around one o'clock. On the other hand, there were a few witnesses who said they thought the murder occurred later, two stating that it happened as late as 1:30.[21]

In the end, however, a majority of the eyewitnesses who were asked about the time of the murder believed it happened closer to 1:00 P.M. than to 1:15. Even if the shooting happened as late as 1:15, it is virtually impossible for Oswald to have walked nearly a mile in twelve minutes, murdered Tippit, and lingered long enough to reload his pistol before leaving the murder scene.[22]

It is conceivable that Oswald ran the distance or caught a ride. But the former possibility, in those days before runners were common, would have created a spectacle, and the latter would be probative evidence of a conspiracy of some sort. In any event, no witness has emerged who saw Oswald walking the route assumed by the commission.[23]

The commission was undaunted by these glaring discrepancies in timing. Not only did the commission have cartridge shells fired from a revolver linked to Oswald, it also had at least two eyewitnesses who claimed in some fashion that they watched Oswald shoot Tippit. Seven eyewitnesses said that Oswald was the man they saw running from the murder scene. However, Benavides, who was perhaps in the best location, could not identify Oswald as the gunman.*[24]

This left the commission with its star witness, Helen Markham. Consider her testimony when she was asked by Assistant Counsel Joseph Ball to tell the panel about picking Oswald from the police lineup about three hours after Tippit's murder. Ball had already carefully elicited from Mrs. Markham her assurances that no one at the police station coached her prior to her identification of Oswald as the man she saw murder Tippit.[25]

Following is the exchange that took place as Mrs. Markham gave her testimony in the presence of Commissioners Earl Warren, Gerald Ford, and Allen Dulles—testimony that seems fragile at best:[26]

MR. BALL: Now when you went into the room you looked these people over, these four men?

MRS. MARKHAM: Yes, sir.

MR. BALL: Did you recognize anyone in the lineup?

MRS. MARKHAM: No, sir.

MR. BALL: You did not? Did you see anybody—I have asked you that question before—did you recognize anybody from their face?

MRS. MARKHAM: From their face, no.

MR. BALL: Did you identify anybody in these four people?

*As time passed, Benavides's memory apparently improved. *Three years later*, he identified Oswald as the gunman to CBS News.

MRS. MARKHAM: I didn't know nobody.

MR. BALL: I know you didn't know anybody, but did anybody in that lineup look like anybody you had seen before?

MRS. MARKHAM: No. I had never seen none of them, none of these men.

MR. BALL: No one of the four?

MRS. MARKHAM: No one of them.

MR. BALL: No one of all four?

MRS. MARKHAM: No, sir.

MR. BALL: Was there a number two man in there?

MRS. MARKHAM: Number two is the one I picked.

MR. BALL: Well, I thought you just told me that you hadn't—

MRS. MARKHAM: I thought you wanted me to describe their clothing.

MR. BALL: No. I wanted to know if that day when you were in there if you saw anyone in there—

MRS. MARKHAM: Number two.

MR. BALL: What did you say when you saw number two?

MRS. MARKHAM: Well, let me tell you. I said the second man, and they kept asking me which one, which one. I said number two. When I said number two, I just got weak.

MR. BALL: What about number two, what did you mean when you said number two?

MRS. MARKHAM: Number two was the man I saw shoot the policeman.

MR. BALL: You recognized him from his appearance?

MRS. MARKHAM: I asked—I looked at him. When I saw this man I wasn't sure, but I had cold chills just run all over me.[27]

The man designated in the lineup as "number two" was, of course, Lee Harvey Oswald, thus constituting the commission's prime eyewitness identification of him as the man who murdered Officer Tippit. Later, in her testimony, Helen Markham confirmed her earlier impression that the man she saw shooting Tippit had black hair—which could hardly be used to describe Oswald's brownish hair.[28]

Despite Mrs. Markham's obvious difficulties in describing the police lineup and her identification of Oswald, she emerged as the commission's star witness on the Tippit murder.[29]

Other eyewitness testimony concerning Oswald and the Tippit

murder also seemed shaky at best, calling into question the whole lineup procedure used that afternoon and evening by the Dallas Police Department. One witness taken to view the lineup told the Warren Commission that one reason he was able to pick out the prime suspect was that Oswald was complaining loudly that he was being framed by the procedure. In fact, he was the only one in the lineup with a bruised and swollen face, the results of the scuffle at the time of his arrest. He certainly was the only one who, when questioned so that the witness could hear his voice, stated that he worked at the Texas School Book Depository—by then heralded to the world as the almost certain site of the assassin's lair.[30]

Five of the witnesses who identified Oswald as the man fleeing the scene picked him out of the lineup under the dubious conditions described. Others were asked two months later to look at a photograph of Oswald and to say whether he was the man observed running from the murder scene. (These witnesses were not asked to pick the person they saw from among several photographs— only to say whether Oswald was the man they had seen.) Several witnesses made positive identifications in this fashion, while others did not.[31]

One of the witnesses handled in this manner, Warren Reynolds, is significant not only for what he saw and *could* have testified to, but also because of what happened to him. Reynolds's office at a used-car dealership was one block from the site of the Tippit murder. When Reynolds heard the shots, he went out onto a porch and looked in that direction. He saw a man running toward him, stuffing a pistol under his belt. Hoping to be of assistance to the police, Reynolds rushed down to the street and followed the gunman. He lost him after about a block, when the gunman ducked behind a building.[32]

Reynolds did not at the time know what the shooting was about. He assumed it was a marital dispute. His aim was to be able to help the police. Later, when it turned out that the shooting was linked to the assassination of President Kennedy, Reynolds's Oak Cliff section of town was invaded by the press. Reynolds openly gave interviews and made no secret of what he had seen. Indeed, he might have been the best available witness for identifying the fleeing gunman.[33]

However, two months passed before any official investigative agency asked him a single question.[34]

It was January 21 when FBI agents finally went to see him, showed him a photograph of Lee Harvey Oswald, and asked if Oswald was the fleeing gunman. The FBI reported that while Reynolds was "of the opinion" the man was Oswald, he stated that he could not "definitely identify Oswald as the individual."[35]

Two days later Reynolds was shot in the temple, the bullet passing through much of his head. Miraculously, he survived and was able to testify before the Warren Commission six months later. With the passage of time, his memory had "improved." He was certain beyond the slightest doubt that the man he saw fleeing the Tippit scene was Lee Harvey Oswald. Whether Reynolds's earlier testimony was connected to the attempt on his life is not known. Reynolds believes that it surely was. The case has never been solved.*[36]

To grasp the true flimsiness of the eyewitness evidence against Oswald in Tippit's murder, one must consider it the way it might look to a defense attorney. By almost any standards, Helen Markham, the commission's star witness, would be an unmitigated calamity under the gentlest of cross-examination. Even the friendly commission examiner could hardly stuff the right answers in her mouth.

No better example of her incompetence as a witness is seen than in her insistence that she spent twenty minutes talking to the dying Tippit before he was placed in an ambulance. Unchallenged records show that the ambulance reached Tippit within no more than five minutes of the shooting, and every indication is that he had died instantly from a head wound.[37]

In any event, the commission accepted Helen Markham as its star witness to the exclusion of others who had far more comprehensible and consistent testimony about the events.†

Consider, for example, the Frank Wrights, who were only half a block away. Mrs. Wright was the person among all others who had the presence of mind to ring the operator and request an ambulance. Her husband was sitting by the door of their ground-floor apartment

---

*In 1983 the author sought out Reynolds, who simply smiled and refused to discuss any aspect of the matter.

†Commenting on the case against Oswald as the killer of Tippit, Joseph Ball, the Warren Commission lawyer who examined Helen Markham, stated: "In all of my courtroom experience, I have never seen a more 'open-and-shut case.' "[38]

when he heard the shots; he immediately ran outside to see what had happened. His account of what he saw differs drastically from the official version. Though ignored by the Warren Commission and the FBI, the Wrights were sought out and interviewed in 1964 by researchers from Columbia University.[39] This is Frank Wright's account of what he saw when he ran from his house upon hearing the shots:

> The police car was headed toward me. . . . I saw a person right by the car. . . . He had just fallen down. . . . Part of him was under the left front fender of the car. . . .
> I saw a man standing right in front of the car. He was looking toward the man on the ground. . . . [He] was about medium height [and] . . . had on a long coat. It ended just above his hands. I didn't see any gun. He ran around on the passenger side of the police car . . . and he got into his car . . . a gray, little old coupe . . . about a 1950–1951, maybe a Plymouth. . . . He got in that car and he drove away as quick as you could see.
> I've seen what came out on television and in the papers but I know that's not what happened. I know a man drove off in a gray car. I know what I saw.[40]

Other ignored witnesses included the ambulance drivers, who were on the scene almost immediately. They presumably would be more accustomed to such a traumatic event and might have provided crucial testimony about just what was going on when they reached Tippit. (In contrast, Helen Markham, the commission's star witness, said later in an interview that she had "fainted three or four times" after the arrival of police, who "treated me like a queen.")[41]

Acquilla Clemmons has told independent researchers consistently that from her vantage point, across the street and about six houses from the murder scene, she watched *two* men—one with a gun—beside Tippit's car at the time of the shooting. These were lucid accounts. Officials preferred the testimony of poor Helen Markham.[42]

One of the most glaring discrepancies of all is seen in the accounts of the direction in which Tippit's killer was walking just before Tippit stopped. William Scoggins, a cab driver who was an eyewitness, testified that the gunman was walking west toward Tippit's car prior to the shooting. Another witness reported similarly. Reports from the Dallas police as well as the first reports of the Secret Service reflect the same impression. Despite the preponderance of evidence that the killer and Tippit's car were moving *toward* each other, the Warren Report concluded that the killer was walking in the opposite direction. The commission version held that Tippit's car overtook the pedestrian killer.[43]

This was necessary for the Warren Commission's tenuous version to work at all. If he was Oswald, the killer had to be walking *east*, in the same direction as the police car was moving when it overtook the killer. Otherwise, Oswald, on his exceedingly tight time schedule, would have had to move from the rooming house to a point *beyond* the scene of the shooting and then to have turned and been heading *back* to reach the location of the murder. Because of time considerations, that was preposterous even by commission standards, so the commission ignored the testimony.[44]

Of the potential leads ignored, none is more astonishing than that concerning the clipboard in Tippit's patrol car. Its contents might have helped to determine *why* Tippit stopped alongside his killer.

According to testimony to the Warren Commission, the clipboard was "installed on the dash of all squad cars for the officers to take notes on and to keep their wanted persons' names on." This clipboard, which can be seen in a photograph of the interior of Tippit's car after the murder, might have contained clues to the case, even including Tippit's notes of the description of the man being sought as the assassin of President Kennedy.[45]

David Belin, one of the Warren Commission lawyers closely involved in the Tippit aspect of the JFK investigation, examined W. E. Barnes of the Dallas crime laboratory on this point. "Were there any notes on there that you saw that had been made on his clipboard?" Belin asked.

"I couldn't tell you what was on the clipboard," Barnes responded. "We never read his clipboard."[46]

There is no evidence that any effort was ever made to examine Tippit's clipboard or its contents.

One of the most promising pieces of material evidence police had in hand soon after Tippit's murder was a light jacket reportedly discarded by the killer a few blocks from the scene. Even before Oswald's arrest, a patrolman examined the jacket and radioed his colleagues: "The jacket the suspect was wearing . . . bears a laundry tag with the letter B 9738. See if there is any way you can check this laundry tag."[47]

Such evidence—and a second laundry mark was later found— would quicken the pulse of any reader of mysteries or of the lore of the famed FBI laboratory. With a laundry tag, the avenues spread into several promising directions, including the ultimate possibility of positive identification of the owner.[48]

The FBI garnered its forces to check cleaning establishments in an effort to locate even one of the two identifying marks in the jacket. Every laundry and dry-cleaning establishment in the Dallas– Fort Worth area was checked—424 of them in all—with no success. Knowing that Oswald had lived in New Orleans, the FBI checked 293 establishments in that area with similarly negative results.[49]

In the end, after checking more than 700 establishments, the FBI and the Warren Commission were left with the testimony of Oswald's wife, Marina, that while she believed the jacket to be her husband's, she never knew him to take any jacket to a laundry or dry-cleaning establishment. Indeed, the FBI's examination of all of Oswald's clothing showed not a single laundry or dry-cleaning mark. The FBI also learned that while the jacket was size medium, all of Oswald's other clothing was size small.[50]

The Warren Report contains no reference to this massive and futile effort to trace the laundry mark—an effort that virtually established that the jacket did not belong to Lee Harvey Oswald.[51]

There is no indication that the FBI checked the jacket's manufacturer to see where it might have been bought. A designer's label in the jacket stated that it was "created in California." During the period in question, the manufacturer sold the jacket almost exclusively on the West Coast, an exception being one large department store in Philadelphia. Oswald is never known to have been in Philadelphia or to have lived on the West Coast as a civilian.[52]

To a layman, this exhaustive and unsuccessful effort to link the killer's jacket to Oswald indicates that the jacket belonged to someone else. However, in the face of all of this contradictory evidence, the Warren Commission concluded that the jacket belonged to Lee Harvey Oswald.

These peculiar developments, at the least, would seem to cast doubt on the strength of the basic case against Oswald. They did not. Undeterred, the Warren Commission overlooked the evidence and testimony that was in the way and marched to what it perceived to be an area of strength in the Tippit case—the ballistics evidence.

It is indisputable that the four cartridge cases said to have been pitched at the murder scene by the fleeing gunman were fired from the revolver found on Oswald at the time of his arrest some thirty minutes later. (However, no one could say *when* the bullets had been fired from Oswald's revolver.) According to the FBI laboratory, the ballistics markings on the bullets taken from Tippit's body were too erratic to allow ballistics testing to see if they were fired from that pistol. Had it been established that they were, there would be an irrefutable link between Tippit's death and the pistol found on Oswald.[53]

In the absence of this, all that is left of a ballistics nature to nurture the case against Oswald are the four expended cartridge cases tossed at the scene by the killer. The manufacturer of these cases was simple to determine. And one of the few certain factors about the bullets removed from Tippit's body was their origin of manufacture. One might expect the bullets to correspond in this one respect with the cartridge cases tossed at the scene.[54]

They do not.

On the contrary, *two* of the cases were made by Winchester-Western, and *two* were made by Remington-Peters. Of the four bullets that struck Tippit, *one* came from Remington-Peters and *three* from Winchester-Western.[55]

The Warren Commission expert tried to explain away its "slight problem"—as this astounding development was called by counsel—with some imaginative suggestions, including the possibility of a lost case and an extra shot that missed. That would put the total number of shots at five, while most witnesses recalled fewer shots. The wildest suggestion was that the parsimonious Oswald might have hand-loaded the bullets, an exercise requiring him to possess special equipment never found. An FBI examination later ruled this out. The conflict concerning the bullets fired and the cartridge cases tossed at the scene has never been resolved in any commonsense manner.[56]

One of the most astonishing inconsistencies concerns the cartridge hulls that stand as the only solid evidence linking Oswald's pistol to the slaying of Officer Tippit. At the scene of the Tippit murder,

Dallas Police Officer J. M. Poe was ordered by a superior to place his identifying mark on the cartridge hulls—a routine matter in the proper handling of evidence. Poe, who has an excellent reputation as a homicide detective, marked the cartridges with his initials, scratching them on the inside lip of the open end of the hull. Later, he stated to the FBI that he was certain he had done this.[57]

However, when Poe appeared before the Warren Commission, he waffled in his testimony on this point. When asked by counsel if he had marked the hulls, Poe stated, "I can't swear to it." Pressed by counsel, who noted that the hulls *had* been marked, Poe added, "There is a mark. I believe I put on them, but I couldn't swear to it. I couldn't make them out anymore."[58]

In 1984, Poe explained to the author that he was absolutely certain that he marked the hulls. Indeed, he could not be certain of a single other instance during his twenty-eight years of police work when he had failed to properly mark evidence. He indicated that he became aware that he could not find his markings prior to his Warren Commission testimony when "the FBI came down and interviewed us. . . . We were down in the [FBI] office, and I just could not be absolutely positive that my mark was in there." While Poe did not specifically say that he was pressured to "find" his marks in the hulls, he volunteered this comment about his experience: "I wasn't going to lie to the man and say I saw my mark when I didn't. I still wouldn't do that."

Officer Poe insisted to the author that even though he could not find his identifying marks, he felt certain that the hulls were the ones he had taken into evidence at the scene of the Tippit murder. Poe recalled one explanation that he had not mentioned to the Warren Commission two decades earlier. He stated that the reason he was not able to find his markings might have been that so many other identifying marks had been placed in the cartridge hulls, actually on top of his identifying marks, thus obscuring his markings in the thicket of marks from other officials through whose hands the evidence passed. Stated Poe: "When it came to [my] looking at them again, there were so many marks in there that I couldn't find mine. . . . In a better light, or [with] a magnifying glass, I might be able to pick it out."[59]

Soon after Poe made this statement, the author examined the cartridge hulls at the National Archives with a lighted magnifying glass. Only Officer Poe can state whether his identifying mark is on the hulls, and he has stated that he cannot find it because it appears lost among so many other marks. What is readily apparent to anyone who examines the hulls is that while there are several identification marks scratched in them, in no case is a marking obliterating another marking. Moreover, in each hull at least 50 percent of the surface area around the inside rim has no marking at all, leaving ample space for even additional identifying marks. There is no conceivable reason for any marking to be placed over another marking.

The markings in the hulls are distinctive and clearly seen—even with the naked eye. It seems impossible that if Poe's marks were actually *there*, he could not find them. Confronted with this, Officer Poe flatly stated, "I [have] talked to you all I'm going to talk to you. You already got your mind made up about what you're going to say. I know what the truth is." He then hung up the telephone, refusing to discuss the matter further.[60]

Dallas Police Sergeant Gerald Hill, a key figure in the arrest of Oswald, was one of the first policemen to arrive at the scene of the Tippit slaying. He had sped there from the Book Depository with Assistant District Attorney William Alexander the moment word had come over the police radio about the shooting in Oak Cliff. At the scene, Sergeant Hill inspected the cartridge hulls and ordered Officer Poe to mark them as evidence and turn them over to the crime lab.

In 1984 the author interviewed Hill, who rose to the rank of lieutenant before his retirement from the police force. Today, Hill owns and operates an extensive used paperback bookstore near Dallas and claims a personal collection of 7,000 first-edition paperbacks at his home. Hill is a strong supporter of the official version of the assassination. When asked if he believed the official version on Tippit's death, he dismissed the question with bombast, stating that the cartridge hulls from the scene, proved to have been fired in Oswald's pistol, sealed the case.

The author referred to the grave inconsistencies concerning Poe's identification of the hulls, suggesting the possibility that they might have been replaced by hulls *not* discovered at the scene and marked by Poe. The implication, of course, is that when the hulls marked by Poe were tested in the lab and were found *not* to have been fired from Oswald's pistol, they were replaced by hulls that *had* been fired from Oswald's pistol—*after* it came into the custody of the police. (Ironically, Hill also is the officer who physically marked Oswald's pistol as evidence and turned it over when he brought Oswald in after his arrest.)

Hill dismissed this suggestion with the following statement: "If they did that [replaced the cartridge hulls], they would also have forged Poe's marks."

It was pointed out to Hill that, as the facts prove, it made no difference that Poe's marks could not be found. The evidence still became the cornerstone of the case against Oswald in the killing of Tippit. Hill acknowledged that the circumstances concerning the apparent disappearance of Poe's marks made it *appear* that something like this might have been done. Then, Hill added, "If it were any other police department in the United States, I would say that that is possible. But this department is so clean that it scares me."[61]

The two technicians in the Dallas police laboratory who actually worked with the physical evidence could not be interviewed. Both are reported to be dead.

Suspicion about the cartridge cases is further whetted by the bizarre absence of any reference to the cases in the lists of evidence compiled by the police on the day of Officer Tippit's murder. Various pieces of evidence—all inventoried—were turned over to the FBI regularly during the days immediately following the murder. However, *six days* passed before the cartridge cases were turned over to the FBI, much longer than the time taken for other evidence to be turned over.[62]

Another oddity concerns the bullets and their examination by the FBI laboratory. On the day of Tippit's murder, Dallas police turned over one bullet that struck Tippit. According to the FBI, the Dallas police claimed that it was the only bullet recovered in the Tippit killing. It was not until March that this peculiarity was addressed by the Warren Commission, which asked the FBI to see what happened to the other bullets. An inquiry disclosed that they were housed in the files of the Dallas Police Department.[63]

Another inexplicable aspect of the initial police accounts from the crime scene are the reports that the killer was using an *automatic* weapon. Oswald's pistol was a revolver. The reliability of these early reports was fortified when a policeman at the scene examined a discarded cartridge case. Even before Oswald's arrest, the police officer radioed that the case appeared to have come from an automatic weapon. Sergeant Hill, the man who actually brought Oswald in a few minutes later, was explicit in making the distinction: "The shell at the scene indicates that the subject is armed with an automatic .38 rather than a pistol."[64]

Accounts differ sharply about the events leading to Oswald's actual arrest. The certainty is that he was seized as he sat in the Texas Theatre during a showing of *Cry of Battle*, starring Van Heflin.[65] While movie theaters have traditionally been choice spots for clandestine meetings, there is no hint that this possibility was considered. From the start, there was an official presumption that Oswald fled there after murdering Tippit.

According to the official version, Oswald's trail was picked up a short distance from the Texas Theatre—six blocks from the Tippit murder—by an alert manager of a shoe store. Johnny Calvin Brewer, who could hear police sirens nearby, observed a man who stepped into the recessed area in front of the shoe store and remained there with his back to the street until a patrol car had passed. Brewer described the man this way: "His hair was sort of messed up and looked like he had been running, and he looked scared, and he looked funny."[66]

Based on this, Brewer decided to follow the stranger. He saw him duck into the Texas Theatre, slipping past Julia Postal, the ticket clerk who had left her post to go to the curbside to see what the police sirens were about. She had heard news of the shooting at Dealey Plaza. According to the Warren Commission, Mrs. Postal, who asked Johnny Brewer to pursue the gate-jumper, said to him, "I don't know if this is the man they want . . . but he is running from them for some reason."[67]

Julia Postal called the police, and an alarm was broadcast that "a suspect" had just entered the Texas Theatre. Minutes later police cars carrying fifteen officers converged on the theater. The house lights were turned up, and Brewer pointed out Oswald from among the dozen or so patrons scattered about the theater. (These patrons were never canvassed and questioned in any inclusive fashion by the FBI or the Warren Commission.) After a scuffle, during which Oswald pulled his pistol, he was arrested and hauled off to police headquarters.[68]

There is conflicting testimony among arresting officers about just what happened during the arrest, when the revolver was supposedly taken from Oswald. However, it is of potential significance that the rules of handling evidence were not followed. The revolver was not marked as evidence at the time it was seized. It was not until several hours after the officers and the gun reached headquarters in downtown Dallas that the gun was marked as being Oswald's. However, the revolver had been ordered under the same name (Hidell) and in the same fashion (by mail) as the Mannlicher-Carcano officially accepted as the Kennedy assassination rifle. But no evidence has ever emerged to show that Oswald fired the revolver even once prior to his alleged attack on Tippit.[69]

Such discrepancies in the evidence and blundering in the investigation have long encouraged public skepticism. Critics speculate that the irregularities in the case cast substantial doubt that Oswald was the killer of Tippit. Even William Alexander, the assistant district attorney of Dallas County who would have been Oswald's primary prosecutor in the Tippit murder, concedes that his office stopped developing evidence once it was decided to charge Oswald as the assassin of President Kennedy.[70]

"The Tippit case just went by the boards," Alexander told the author in an interview in 1983. Today an assistant U.S. attorney in Dallas, Alexander further stated that when Oswald was killed two days later, official interest in developing evidence in the Tippit case ceased altogether. There was never an indictment in the case or further investigation.[71]

The curious handling and status of this case calls attention to its origins. Again, William Alexander, a firm supporter of Oswald's guilt as the killer of both Kennedy and Tippit, offers ironic insight into just what led police to believe Oswald was Tippit's killer. Alexander was at Dealey Plaza when word came of the shooting of a police officer: "We all knew the same man who killed the President had killed Tippit," says Alexander, who rushed to the scene of the slaying in Oak Cliff. "We had made up our minds by the time we got there." Alexander explains that the two acts were so similarly drastic and unusual that it was virtually impossible that they were committed by separate killers.[72]

While the investigation of Tippit's murder was incomplete in Texas, the Warren Commission seemed determined to cast Oswald as Tippit's killer. Presumably, this determination was related to the clear fact that showing Oswald's capacity for violence added great strength to the case against him as Kennedy's killer. Then, too, there is ample room in the case for all sorts of manipulation of evidence by unscrupulous Dallas police officers who, for reasons not necessarily the same as the commission's, might have wanted to seal the case against Oswald in the slaying of Officer Tippit. That possibility was never investigated.[73]

If Lee Harvey Oswald did not murder Officer J. D. Tippit, then who did? And why?

These questions were not addressed in the Warren Report, and no public records indicate that any official investigators ever seriously considered the possibilities. Indeed, Tippit's murder was never accorded even a complete and routine homicide investigation. Given the pointed and provocative contradictions in the evidence, the questions are worth examining.

The possibilities for intrigue in the Tippit case are wide-ranging and for years have been the basis for conjecture among critics. Was Tippit a player in a plot that called for him to execute Oswald? Was Tippit's job thwarted when Oswald turned the tables and killed him first? Was Tippit to play a role in the Oswald getaway, only to change his mind at the last minute? Was Tippit a pawn in a plot, and was he supposed to be killed after he killed Oswald? Did Tippit have complex personal problems that might have led to his murder by someone completely unrelated to the assassination case? Or was it the simple, official version that Tippit, as an alert police officer, stopped the right suspect and was murdered by a desperate assassin?

Little is known officially about Officer Tippit—beyond the Warren Report description of him as a good policeman. Indeed, he served as a policeman for eleven years without promotion or official reprimand. Tippit's wife, Marie, was one of the last people to see him alive. Her account might have shed light on her husband's last thoughts, but she has never been called to testify.[74]

From the earliest hours after his death, Officer Tippit was portrayed in the press as a heroic victim in a murderous rampage by Lee Harvey Oswald. Americans responded with typical generosity—in this case to the tune of $650,000 in unsolicited contributions for Marie Tippit and her children.[75]

In the two decades since the murder of J. D. Tippit, there has emerged the picture of a man not quite so pure. The blemishes are not necessarily damning, but they must be considered along with the legions of other questions surrounding his death.

Consideration of Tippit must begin with the undisputed fact that he was highly regarded by his fellow police officers. All evidence suggests that he was considered to be dependable and friendly, the last man to create any difficulty for his fellow officers. He was, in all respects, a part of the rank-and-file fraternity that is such a powerful bond in a large metropolitan police department. Despite Tippit's good record, there did appear to be a problem with his activity on that fateful day. He was not in his assigned district at the time he was killed. In fact, he was more than three miles from where he was supposed to be.[76]

In light of Tippit's close association with other police officers, some credence must be given to a startling but persuasive possibility favored by some of the critics who have tried to sort out the Tippit morass. Several of the most curious aspects of Tippit's movements just prior to his death seem clearer in view of his associations with fellow police officers—and the bonds his survivors in the ranks might have felt for their dead comrade.

Put simply, the speculation goes, if Officer Tippit was in the wrong place when he got into such deadly trouble, why court disgrace to his name by revealing that he had done anything wrong? Would it not be better for Tippit—and better for his wife and children—to amend the record so that there would be an official reason for Tippit's actions, for his being where he had no business being? And, the reasoning might go, such an emendation could not hurt anyone else—even the dead man (Oswald) who was widely believed to be the murderer.

When Tippit was killed, he was at least three miles from the center of the patrol district to which he was assigned that day. He did not appear to be on his way to downtown Dallas, some four miles away. And no witness has suggested that just prior to the shooting Tippit was doing anything but moving slowly along a quiet street. One of the earliest questions was *why* Tippit was in central Oak Cliff and not in his regularly assigned area several districts away.[77]

Early in December, the Warren Commission received the first of three different transcripts of the Dallas police radio transmissions on the day of the assassination. In an excellent analysis of the anomalies arising from these transcripts, Sylvia Meagher in *Accessories After the Fact* explains that the first transcript was prepared by the Dallas police and was supposed to highlight communications pertinent to the murders of Officer Tippit and President Kennedy, excluding other police matters. The Warren Commission staff studied the transcript futilely in an attempt to find some radio dispatch that could explain why Tippit had moved from his assigned district into the area where he was killed. Nothing could be found. The puzzle persisted.[78]

The Warren Commission continued to struggle with the question throughout the spring. It heard testimony from three supervisors from the Dallas Police Department who tried to explain why Tippit was in the wrong place. The reasons were purely speculative, vaguely suggesting the demonstrably absurd possibility that Tippit was heading for Dealey Plaza four miles away to be of assistance there. During this testimony, there was never any reference to the possibility that Tippit might have been ordered to go to central Oak Cliff by the police radio dispatcher. And, of course, the three supervisors were quite aware of the intense effort being made to find an answer to this riddle.[79]

The mystery remained unresolved until finally, in the spring, the Warren Commission requested and received a *verbatim* transcript of the radio transmissions—not one edited to include only transmissions related to Kennedy and Tippit. The commission hoped that such a transcript might yield the elusive answer.[80]

It must have been a stunning revelation for the commission to discover that this new transcript contained, at last, the badly needed answer to the puzzle. According to the transcript—and supported by the actual tape—there was an order given to Tippit at 12:45 P.M. directing him to "move into central Oak Cliff." Not only was such an inexplicable instruction believed to be unique in the Dallas Police Department, it also had not been in the first transcript. Moreover, none of the police supervisors who testified earlier indicated that they knew anything about it.[81]

But there it was—an instruction to Tippit and another police officer to move into central Oak Cliff. It was logged at 12:45 P.M. Suddenly, one of the Warren Commission's stickiest problems was resolved. Tippit, according to the new evidence, had been *ordered* to go to central Oak Cliff. He was precisely where he was supposed to be. It must have been a great relief for the commission to have this anomaly out of the way. By the same token, the sudden appearance of the curious dispatch gave rise to speculation that it had been dubbed onto the tape by police friends of J. D. Tippit.[82]

From the beginning, there were peculiarities that surrounded not only the fortuitous emergence of the evidence but also the specific radio dispatch. As critic Meagher points out, the dispatch was made at the very height of the bedlam that engulfed the Dallas Police Department during the minutes following the assassination. No event in the city's history had created such frenzy. Not only was the police switchboard jammed, but police officers had difficulty getting through with crucially important radio messages concerning the state of emergency in the wake of the assassination of President Kennedy.[83]

Yet, there was time, at the height of this turbulence, for the dispatcher to order Tippit and one other officer—who, if he heard the order, did not obey it—to move into central Oak Cliff, where at that time there was not a single significant crime that needed police attention. Even more odd, of course, was that this transmission was omitted in the first transcript, even when police transcribers were searching strictly for dispatches related to the murders of Kennedy and Tippit.[84]

In any event, the Warren Commission immediately embraced the 12:45 order to Tippit as the explanation for his being in the wrong place. With this out of the way, Tippit's murder could be presented as gruesome evidence of Oswald's capacity for violence—as well as a strong indication that he was a man in desperate flight from some awful deed.

The peculiarity of the 12:45 order to Tippit cries out for closer examination. There is no doubt, of course, that Tippit *was* in the central Oak Cliff section a few minutes after the radio dispatch. It is perhaps instructive to consider how Patrolman R. C. Nelson, the other officer ordered into central Oak Cliff in the same dispatch, responded. Like Tippit, Officer Nelson never specifically acknowledged the order to move into central Oak Cliff. (In virtually all other instances that day, the officer did acknowledge his instructions from the dispatcher.) But the 12:45 order for Tippit and Nelson is without direct acknowledgment from either man.[85]

In response to the 12:45 dispatch, one would expect to find Officer

Nelson in central Oak Cliff. To the contrary, the next time he reports his position, it is at 1:22, just a few minutes after Tippit was shot in Oak Cliff. Nelson's location? He was at Elm and Houston, the site of the assassination. Nothing is said about his apparent disregard for the orders given him earlier to move into central Oak Cliff. Indeed, one would expect that had Officer Nelson been with Tippit in Oak Cliff, his presence might have prevented the gunman from murdering Tippit.[86]

In 1984, the author located R. C. Nelson, who stated that it was surprising to him that no official investigation had ever sought his account of what he knew about the day of the assassination and the murder of Oswald. Not only was Nelson at several key places during the immediate period of the assassination, he also was posted at one of the doorways in the basement of the Dallas County Jail at the moment Jack Ruby shot Oswald. Nelson had expected to be questioned by the Warren Commission and, later, by the House Select Committee on Assassinations. He was fully prepared to cooperate.

"I've been waiting a long time to tell my story," Nelson said. He explained that since his account of events had never become part of the public record, he felt his story had a monetary value. He wanted to come to some agreement before granting a full interview.

However, in the initial encounter with Nelson—standing in a parking lot in Corsicana, Texas, where Nelson is in private business—the author asked, "Did you get the call to go to central Oak Cliff? Did you hear the dispatcher's order telling you to go there?"

"I'm not sure what you mean," Nelson said. A little more of the circumstances were explained, and Nelson then said, "I had rather not talk about that." He said he considered that to be a part of the story he was willing to negotiate—a willingness that, despite several efforts, had not materialized as this book went to press.[87]

While Nelson might later recall that he *did* receive the controversial order to go to Oak Cliff, his initial response clearly suggested that he was puzzled over the question.

Murray Jackson, the dispatcher whose voice broadcast the order to Tippit and Nelson, was never questioned by the Warren Commission or the Select Committee. In 1984 Jackson, still a Dallas police officer, told the author that he gave the orders exactly as they are heard on the tapes. He explained that he had been a very close personal friend of Tippit and his family and that this close friendship may have been a subconscious reason why he singled Tippit out for an insignificant dispatch at a time when intense turmoil gripped the communications section of the police department. Jackson stoutly denied knowledge of any fraudulent manipulation of the tapes in order to provide an excuse for Tippit's being so far away from his assigned district at the time of his death. On the other hand, Jackson could offer no explanation as to why his odd dispatch to Nelson and Tippit could not be found, despite intense investigation, until seven months after the assassination.[88]

All these inconsistencies surrounding the Tippit shooting were known to the Warren Commission. None was investigated. The dispatcher who gave the order to Tippit and Nelson that day might have provided some answers, but he was never called to testify. And Officer Nelson was never called to testify. There is no public record that official investigators ever questioned either man on this matter.[89]

One of the oddest assumptions of the Warren Commission was that Officer Tippit stopped Oswald because he was able to identify him as the man described in the police broadcasts that started about 12:45 P.M. According to an FBI statement to the commission, the source of the original description was "an unidentified citizen." The description provided by this citizen (later assumed to be Howard Brennan) was for a man "running from the Texas School Book Depository immediately after the assassination."[90]

The description itself was of a "white male, approximately thirty, slender build, height five feet, ten inches, weight one hundred sixty-five pounds" and believed to be armed with a .30-caliber rifle. This description missed Oswald by six years and about fifteen pounds, yet the Warren Commission reasoning accepted as fact that based on this description Officer Tippit stopped Oswald.[91]

Still, the most persistent enigma pertains to Tippit's curious movements. In 1982 Earl Golz, the Dallas reporter, conducted separate interviews with two merchants who had fresh evidence concerning the Tippit case. On the day of Tippit's murder, the two men, who have long since gone their separate ways, were working together in a record shop about seven blocks from the place where Tippit was killed. The shop was about one block from the Texas Theatre. They were acquainted with Tippit because of his habit of stopping by the store to use the telephone.[92]

On this day, the two men independently recalled to Golz, Tippit entered the shop in an obvious hurry. He asked customers to step aside so he could reach the telephone. After dialing a number, Tippit let it ring for a minute or so. When he apparently failed to get an answer, he hung up and rushed from the store. About ten minutes later, the two storekeepers heard the first report that a policeman had been shot nearby.[93]

There are other accounts of odd movements by Tippit shortly before his death, including that of five witnesses who saw him sitting in his patrol car parked at a service station in the area. According to that account, he sat there for about ten minutes and then drove off at a high rate of speed. That was shortly before his death. Just as tantalizing is the report that Oswald and Tippit were seen together on at least one earlier occasion, but no known reports of such an association can be substantiated.[94]

It is almost impossible to make any sound assessment of such reports, beyond citing them as evidence to suggest that Tippit was involved in some activity that has never been understood. Second, the miscellaneous sightings of Tippit—all in the vicinity of the Oswald rooming house—have inevitably led to speculation that it was Tippit who stopped his police car out front and sounded the horn a few minutes past one o'clock, while Oswald was inside. What *that* could mean is anyone's guess. The possibilities have caused relentless speculation.

One point of intense dispute among critics is Tippit's possible connection to Oswald's killer, Jack Ruby. Tippit's associates and places of residence over his adult life have repeatedly raised the possibility that he knew Ruby, or certain of Ruby's organized-crime associates. There was one instance when Tippit lived near a nightclub owned by Ruby's sister. Later, Ruby himself came to operate that club.[95]

Then there was Tippit's friendship with fellow police officer Harry Olsen, who was working privately as a guard at an Oak Cliff home when Tippit was murdered nearby. Late that night, it is firmly established, Olsen spent about an hour talking with his friend Jack Ruby. Moreover, Olsen's location at the time of Tippit's murder, the location of the murder itself, and Jack Ruby's apartment were within a radius of a few blocks. (Some critics have long speculated that Oswald was on his way to Ruby's apartment when he encountered Tippit, murdered him, and fled.)[96]

But in spite of these alluring leads, no absolute connection has ever been made between Tippit and either Ruby or Oswald.

Due to the exceedingly sloppy investigation of the Tippit murder—at each official level—it is impossible to make any reasonable assessment of what it all means. Perhaps the propinquity of Tippit's residence to the Ruby club means something. Perhaps Tippit's and Ruby's common friendship with Olsen means something. The only certainty is that these elements will forever feed the speculation surrounding the case.

Of all the tantalizing connections drawn between Tippit, Ruby, and the underworld, none has excited more speculation than Tippit's part-time employment at a greasy-spoon restaurant in Oak Cliff called Austin's Barbecue. Tippit worked there as a security guard during his off-duty hours, usually late at night.[97]

Tippit's employer at the restaurant was the owner and operator, Austin Cook. One of Cook's friends happened to be Ralph Paul, a man with longtime links to organized crime in Dallas—including business ties to Jack Ruby. For many years, these connections have stirred the suspicions of critics. Again, though, no concrete connection between Tippit and the mob has been made, despite enormous efforts.[98]

But something far more significant emerges from Tippit's tenure at Austin's Barbecue. For fourteen years there was speculation that Tippit had been having a sexual relationship with a waitress at Austin's. The matter was finally confirmed when investigators from the House Select Committee interviewed the woman in 1977. She confirmed the relationship and stated that the affair had ended in the summer of 1963. The public record of the HSCA suggests that it probed no further, presumably concluding that Tippit's sexual dalliances had nothing to do with the issues at hand.[99]

However, the woman, her husband, and their several children lived in Oak Cliff, within a few minutes' drive of Tippit's strange activities just before he was murdered.[100] The woman's confirmation of the affair supported the original speculation that Tippit's presence far from his own patrol district, his peculiar movements and activities, even his murder, could all be laid to an intensely emotional and explosive set of personal circumstances.

Long before any of this was acknowledged officially, evidence for such a case was building.

In 1968, at the height of the publicity over Jim Garrison's investigation into the assassination, the New Orleans district attorney received an anonymous letter from a person who lived in Oak Cliff. It was well expressed and the tone sincere. It was in no sense malicious.[101]

"I have done a little soul-searching," the writer stated, "and should like to pass along some information which may or may not be helpful to you. . . . Quite by accident, I was told that Officer Tippets [sic] had gotten a married woman pregnant . . . a waitress who worked at Austin's Bar-B-Cue [sic]." From there, the writer went on to provide sketchy details that might help in identifying the woman.[102]

In 1970 assassination critic and writer Gary Shaw obtained the letter. In 1976 he suggested to Larry Harris, a young researcher with whom he had collaborated on a book, that he look into it. Harris's intense, longtime interest in the Tippit case had led him to take a job as a letter carrier in central Oak Cliff, in the hope that he could get to know people who might shed new light on the puzzle. (Harris's interest in the assassination case and his outrage at its handling were so intense, in fact, that he acquired a job at the Texas School Book Depository, so he could look into that aspect firsthand. People who did not work there were barred from the building.) Impressed with the details of the anonymous letter, Harris began pursuing the clues.[103]

Early on, Harris became satisfied that not only was there an affair going on but that the woman was possibly pregnant by Tippit at the time he was murdered. Indeed, her youngest child was born seven months after Tippit's murder.[104]

These matters would be irrelevant were it not for the fact that they bear significantly on whether Lee Harvey Oswald was really the killer of J. D. Tippit. The case against Oswald is so arrantly flimsy that one is compelled to consider other possibilities.

Certainly, Tippit's murder could have been a line-of-duty matter—a case of Tippit's finally catching up with a desperado who knew the police officer was out to apprehend him. However, it is no less likely, given the personal circumstances of Tippit's life on the day of his death, that other forces were at work.

Considering those general circumstances and their potential significance, the details become relevant. The child in question was born around the middle of June 1964. Given normal conditions, the child would have been conceived around the middle of September

1963. If so, the woman would have been about two months into her pregnancy in mid-November—commonly the earliest time such a state is medically confirmed.[105]

Although pure speculation, one cannot avoid the possibility that on November 22, 1963—while the country was gripped with its national nightmare—J. D. Tippit was in the throes of a personal trauma every bit as intense. He might have learned that very morning that his lover was pregnant. Could that explain his erratic behavior? Could it explain his curious and rather desperate effort to place a phone call? Already the father of three children with his own wife, Tippit could hardly have relished this new complication.[106]

An additional factor heated the entire situation. Court records show that Tippit's girlfriend and her husband, after a separation of some months and a brief divorce, had a reconciliation in September 1963. They resumed living together. The court records do not specify the day in September they were reconciled, so it is anyone's guess whether the woman became pregnant before or after the reconciliation. Uncertainty about so delicate a point would not have been a balm to the woman's husband.[107]

The major point is that the pregnancy could have been confirmed around the time of November's terrible events. It is possible that on that day Tippit, who had just come from seeing his own wife, arranged by a telephone call to meet either his lover or her husband on a quiet street, to sort out what should be done. If the official version is correct, such a meeting never took place because of Tippit's chance encounter with Lee Harvey Oswald.[108]

In a series of interviews in 1983 with the author, the woman readily conceded her illicit sexual relationship with Tippit. She also described the sequence of events in their affair during the months immediately preceding Tippit's murder. She explained that she began seeing Tippit in 1963, while they were both employed at Austin's Barbecue and following her divorce from her husband that spring. Despite that divorce, her estranged husband followed Tippit and the woman around Oak Cliff at night when they were together during the months of their affair.[109]

In September, according to court records, the woman and her husband resumed living together—establishing a common-law marriage. While conceding that she *believed* she was pregnant with Tippit's child at the time of this reconciliation, the woman insists that while living with this false impression she actually became pregnant by her husband.[110]

However, the husband today denies this, insisting that the child was fathered by Officer Tippit. The man and woman have long since been divorced again. Both deny any knowledge of Tippit's death other than what is in the official account.

Most Dallas policemen interviewed by the author either do not want to discuss the Tippit case or say that they have no reason to doubt the official version of their comrade's death. However, one officer, now retired, asserted flatly and without prompting that he believed Tippit was killed as a result of a volatile personal situation involving his lover and her estranged husband. He added, "It would look like hell for Tippit to have been murdered and have it look like he was screwing around with this woman. . . . Somebody had to change the tape. Somebody had to change the cartridge hulls. Somebody had to go to the property room and change those hulls and put some of Oswald's hulls in there—hulls that fit Oswald's gun."[111]

This retired police officer claims that others on the force share his beliefs about the Tippit murder—and that some of these policemen will be inclined to talk about it once they have retired and their pensions are secure.[112]

Even if this is true, there is not the slightest reason to believe that anyone directly involved in the possible fraud will ever reveal his or her role.

What does it mean if Lee Harvey Oswald did not kill J. D. Tippit? Among other things, it strongly suggests that material evidence (particularly the cartridge cases) linking Oswald to the Tippit murder— flimsy as it is—had to be planted. The evidence had been so conspicuously mishandled that there was ample opportunity for wholesale alteration or planting of evidence. The purpose, perhaps, would be twofold: to seal the case against Oswald by showing irrevocably his capacity for violence and to wrap up the case of Tippit's murder without disgracing him, his family, and the unborn child. And, of course, there would be an outpouring of grief for a police comrade slain by the presidential assassin.

Not a scintilla of evidence suggests that the Warren Commission had anything to do with the basic deceit of the Tippit case. Indeed, the commission asked some pertinent questions about some of the peculiarities that—if pursued vigorously—could have blown apart the whole corrupt package. That the commission did not pursue the questions relentlessly was typical of its standard operating procedure—a deficiency that marked so much of its work.

The Warren Commission sorely needed the Tippit case in just the form it came to them. It was burdensome enough that the panel was unable to establish a *motive* for Oswald as Kennedy's assassin; it would have been utterly devastating for the commission to fail even to show that its assassin had a capacity for violence. Remove these elements, powerful to any criminal case, and the Kennedy assassination might not have been closed so quickly.

8 · JACK RUBY:

PIMP FOR

ALL SEASONS

The Commission has found no evidence that Jack Ruby
acted with any other person in the killing of Lee Harvey
Oswald.[1]
—Warren Report, 1964

The murder of Oswald by Jack Ruby had all the earmarks
of an organized-crime hit, an action to silence the assassin,
so he could not reveal the conspiracy.[2]
—G. Robert Blakey, Chief Counsel
to the House Select Committee
on Assassinations, 1980

Jim Garrison, the New Orleans district attorney who launched his
own investigation into the Kennedy assassination, once referred to
the overall official investigation by saying: "In this case, white is
black and black is white."[3] That seemed to be the Warren Commission's tenet as it groped myopically to fit Jack Ruby into the
picture with no sinister overtones. That was not an easy task.

It was of paramount importance to establish Ruby's motives and
actions as being totally unrelated to Lee Harvey Oswald as the lone
assassin of President Kennedy. This was a major challenge, considering that Ruby—in nearly classic gangland fashion—had silenced
Oswald, the only known person who could fully explain his own
role, motive, and possible guilt or innocence.[4]

In addition to the obviousness of Ruby's act, there was the equally
stark obviousness of Ruby's noisome past. But the Warren Commission scarcely looked into it. The commission found that Ruby,
like Oswald, had danced onto the scene innocent of any conspira-

torial association.[5] He performed his bizarre act, then collapsed in center stage. It is unlikely that the fairy tale of a patriotic, Kennedy-loving Jack Ruby, consumed with grief, could have survived, even if critics had not begun at once to pick at the fragile veneer of the story. In the light of what is now established, the Warren Commission came up with an astonishing distortion of reality.[6]

In summary, the commission concluded that Ruby conspired with no one in the killing of Oswald and that he had nothing to do with the assassination of President Kennedy. Furthermore, the commission found that Ruby had no significant connection to Cuba or to any Castro elements. Most important—and certainly most dismaying—was the commission's finding that Ruby had no significant associations with organized crime.[7]

The commission, for the most part, accepted everything Ruby said. It embraced his claim that his only reason for murdering Oswald was out of personal devotion to the Kennedy family. By killing Oswald, he proclaimed, he spared Jacqueline Kennedy the agony of returning to Dallas to testify at Oswald's trial. Ruby also presented himself as a man consumed with pity for the Kennedy children.[8]

Two decades later, it is clear that almost none of the commission's conclusions regarding Ruby possess any significant merit. Perhaps the most revelatory work on Ruby's background, connections, and probable motives was published by the House Select Committee. In some cases, however, that work pursued leads established over the years by citizen-critics who specialized on the Ruby angle of the assassination.

Although the HSCA concluded that there was sufficient evidence pointing to a possible conspiracy involving Ruby, it could go no farther.[9] There was, after all, no absolute proof. But G. Robert Blakey, chief counsel to the HSCA and an expert on organized crime, and Richard Billings went the final step in their book, *The Plot to Kill the President.*

They concluded that Ruby's actions were clearly part of a mob-connected conspiracy in the larger assassination plot.[10]

It seems unfathomable today that the Warren Commission and the FBI—the nation's guardian against organized crime—were able to ignore the striking bits of evidence inculpating Ruby. Even more, it seems impossible that the commission could fail to see the *chains* and *patterns* of evidence showing Ruby to be a classic two-bit pawn in the hierarchy of organized crime. Jack Ruby probably was not strong enough or smart enough to survive in his native Chicago, but he was able to serve as an adequate gofer in handling syndicate interests in Dallas.

There is every reason to believe that the criminal ties Ruby established as a youthful street brawler in Chicago controlled him at the moment he murdered Oswald in 1963. It is equally likely that those same clawlike fingers kept their grip on him through thirty-seven months of custody. A force powerful enough to make him murder would certainly be strong enough to seal his lips. Except for the most minor slips, Ruby kept his silence until a blood clot and cancer took his last breath at Parkland Hospital on January 3, 1967.[11]

Jacob Rubenstein was born in 1911 to Polish immigrant parents on Chicago's West Side. With 50,000 people per square mile, it was one of the toughest Jewish neighborhoods spawned by the ethnic deprivations of the early twentieth century. Though his family ostensibly kept a conservative Jewish household, it is clear that the emotional and material amenities of a happy childhood were far removed from the Rubenstein home. There were eight children in all. Ruby's father, a carpenter and an alcoholic, fought constantly with his mother. They separated when Ruby was about ten years old. Jack grew up largely in the streets, learning there what it took to survive.[12]

Soon enough, because of his hot temper, young Jack earned the sobriquet of Sparky, a name he would still use many years later in Dallas, when harking back to old mob contacts from his Chicago days. One of his earliest heroes appears to have been Al Capone, the notorious murderer and gangster, whose wars with rival gangs contributed to the thousand corpses scattered about the streets of Chicago in gangland slayings during those years. Indeed, Ruby worked for Capone in a minor capacity as a runner during his teenage years. Even in 1963, when Ruby with all his tawdriness burst upon the world stage, he was wearing a gray fedora—the style of hat that characterized Capone.[13]

From his earliest days, Jack Ruby was no stranger to violence. He ran with a violent street gang in Chicago and then, in the mid-1930s, tried his skills on the streets of several California cities. In

1937, at twenty-five and back in Chicago, Ruby became associated with the mob-dominated Scrap Iron and Junk Handlers Union, which later was described by an AFL-CIO report as "largely a shake-down operation." During those days there was heavy violence, including the murder of some of Ruby's closest associates.[14]

In June 1947, after service in the Army Air Force, Ruby moved to Dallas, where his sister, Eva Grant, had opened a nightclub. From that point forward, Ruby's life was peppered with the fast-buck corruption of the sleazy underside of Dallas. As a pimp, Ruby lived in a world of striptease girls, prostitutes, dope dealers, gun smugglers, and, indeed, all the illegal operations that have traditionally characterized organized-crime activities. He was always looking for deals—no matter how illegal or immoral—that held promise for turning a dollar or aggrandizing himself.[15]

Ruby's arrival in booming Dallas coincided with the Chicago mob's efforts to gain control of the rackets that flourished there. Steve Guthrie, elected sheriff of Dallas County in 1946, told the FBI that even before he took office he was approached on a golf course by a man named Paul Rowland Jones from the Chicago syndicate. Jones explained to Guthrie that he could make a large amount of money by cooperating with the Chicago mob as they took over the Dallas territory from the home-grown racketeers. Sheriff Guthrie reported all of this to the proper authorities. The following year—the same year Ruby arrived in town—Jones was convicted of attempted bribery.[16]

In 1963, when the FBI interviewed former Sheriff Guthrie about the 1946 incident, he recalled that Jack Ruby's name came up several times. Guthrie stated that the man who tried to bribe him explained that Ruby would be moving into Dallas to open a "very fabulous restaurant" that would have an upstairs gambling facility. The club also would serve as a front operation for the Chicago mob's interests.[17]

While there is some question as to Guthrie's accuracy in his recollection about Ruby's connection at this early point, one thing seems certain: following the period of Jones's trial for attempted bribery, the Chicago crowd was hanging out at the Singapore Club in Dallas—the drinking establishment and dance hall operated by Ruby's sister.[18] When Ruby took over the place in 1947, he renamed it the Silver Spur, which Sheriff Guthrie recalls well: "Whenever I wanted to find anyone from the syndicate, I went to Ruby's Silver Spur."[19]

Ruby's business ventures in Dallas eventually turned out to be little more than erratic investment attempts, usually involving cheap nightclubs.[20] In 1953 he opened the Vegas Club. His partner was a fellow expatriate from Chicago named Joe Locurto, who used the name Joe Bonds.[21] Records indicate that Ruby and Bonds should have been quite comfortable in each other's company. According to a 1953 FBI report: "Ruby and Bonds always carried concealed pistols and were in constant association with . . . a well-known Dallas safecracker . . . [who] with other hoodlums and safecrackers . . . usually hung around Sue's Used Car Lot."[22]

But the Ruby-Bonds relationship, despite its promise, was short-lived. Bonds was convicted of engaging in sodomy with a fifteen-year-old girl—and sent to state prison for eight years.[23] To be sure, Bonds and Ruby had their differences. One FBI report stated that Ruby was seen chasing Bonds and firing a pistol at him. However, Bonds was not hit.[24]

With Bonds away in prison, Ruby still had the friendship of the man who had arrived in Dallas with Bonds, a New Yorker with a Russian Jewish background named Ralph Paul. Ruby and Paul would remain confidants for years, operating various nightclubs singly and in partnership. Most commonly, Ralph Paul found himself bank-rolling Ruby.[25]

Despite all the wheeling and dealing, success for Jack Ruby was elusive. Of his strip joint and numerous nightclubs, none enjoyed any long-term success. Most were hopelessly in debt.[26] A violent proprietor, Ruby did not hesitate to beat up drunks and women who angered him. The Warren Commission reported that normally the victims of the beatings were people who were "drunk, female, or otherwise incapable of successfully resisting Ruby's attack."[27] However, Ruby once pistol-whipped a Dallas police officer, and no charges were brought.[28] (Of his eight arrests in Dallas, Ruby paid but one fine, and that was for disturbing the peace.[29])

Ruby did not reserve his bullying violence strictly for customers. By most accounts he treated his employees with equal barbarism. However, some of his strippers recalled him as a man who would advance them money when they were down on their luck—stories that sounded all too much like the old company store. Perhaps the real miracle is that Ruby was able to remain in business at all.[30]

The best overall study of Jack Ruby is a book by Seth Kantor called *Who Was Jack Ruby?* Kantor reports persuasive evidence that Ruby was involved in narcotics smuggling; he cites a 1956 FBI report in which a narcotics runner claims to have gotten "the okay to operate through Jack Ruby of Dallas."[31] Kantor also dug up evidence that Ruby engaged in obtaining false identification for a minor who was one of his strippers and that he was heavily involved in illegal gambling operations in the area.[32] Ruby and a California con artist even set up large bets with wealthy Texans on sporting events; in the event of a significant loss, the Californian would "pay off" with a bad check and then skip town. One of these Texans was oil magnate H. L. Hunt.[33]

By 1963 Jack Ruby bore many marks of his life of crime and violence. By reputation, he was a hoodlum with mob connections. Physically, the first joint of his left forefinger was missing—having been bitten off during a brawl at one of his establishments.[34] Ruby, who did not smoke and rarely drank, was never married. According to ambiguous testimony, he may have been a homosexual—a charge hotly denied by his male roommate.[35] The most bizarre aspect of Ruby's personal life, however, was his sexual antics with dogs. Allegations about his behavior with the dogs troubled the American Society for the Prevention of Cruelty to Animals at the time. Ruby even referred to one of the dogs, Sheba, as his "wife" and referred to other of the dogs as his "children."[36]

In every respect, Jack Ruby was on the outside fringes of decency, if not sanity. His roots and his religion were alien to the mainstream of his adopted Dallas, and his personality and line of business served to keep him in a position of quasi-isolation from the more respectable elements. Assistant District Attorney William Alexander once put it this way: "Jack Ruby was about as handicapped as you can get in Dallas. First, he was a Yankee. Second, he was a Jew. Third, he was in the nightclub business."[37]

But there is much evidence of Ruby's urgent yearning for acceptance, for respect, if even from the people who surrounded him. All this, it would seem, made him an ideal pawn in the hands of the rich and flashy mobsters whose attention he craved, as he kept up his ties in Chicago, Miami, New Orleans, and Havana.

The picture that emerges of Ruby is one of a violent, bullying small-time hoodlum—a man who picked on women and helpless drunks, a man whose sexual perversions ran to animals. Could such a beastly human being have genuine connections with the under-world—ties to those glamorous chieftains so romanticized by movies and popular fiction?

The answer, two decades later, is an almost certain yes. Jack Ruby seems to have maintained business associations that kept him in touch with important mobsters of the sixties. He was linked to men who, in turn, were dealing with such diverse figures as Fidel Castro and President Kennedy, in addition to the crime syndicates of New Orleans, Chicago, and Havana. Indeed, some of the connections had links to the Central Intelligence Agency. Just how closely Jack Ruby was involved is debatable, but he clearly had contacts with elements of the mob that were dealing with these powerful entities.

Ruby's connections within the Chicago mob, going all the way back to his childhood on the streets, can be traced to a henchman of the infamous mobster Sam Giancana. Giancana was a gangster with an exquisitely unsavory relationship with the U.S. government, quite different from his warm and close personal relationship with Judith Campbell Exner,[38] who was then a sex partner of President Kennedy. Telephone logs reveal that during this period there were seventy telephone calls between the White House and Miss Campbell. The President's keen interest in Miss Campbell coincided with the frequent company she kept with Giancana and another mobster, John Roselli.[39]

Giancana's second most important connection with the U.S. government was his agreement in 1960—along with Roselli—to assist the CIA in its plots to assassinate Fidel Castro. It is firmly established that the two gangsters were recruited for this purpose, although full details of their recruitment and work will probably never be known. Both men were eventually murdered in particularly heinous fashion, creating speculation that they were silenced because of their knowledge.[40]

Since Jack Ruby dealt in women, he must have been enormously impressed if he knew that the mob supplied the President with a comely young woman. She once made herself available to the President for a quick twenty minutes in a Chicago hotel as he was on his way to speak at a fund-raiser.[41] Ruby, in a pathetic comparison, had attained power of sorts by supplying girls to Dallas policemen.[42] It would have been the ultimate power play in Ruby's mind for the mobsters he admired to be furnishing a girl to the most powerful man in the world.

As for Ruby's contacts with Cuba, the strongest evidence of his association with Cuban interests shows up during the period just after Castro took over the country on January 1, 1959. Castro had promised to wipe out the heavy organized-crime activities that were the staple of Havana nightlife—even though they were an important ingredient in the Cuban economy. The pervasive gambling and prostitution interests on the island were as profitable as any of the mob's similar enterprises in the United States. Castro's announced shutdown prompted the mob's interest in getting him out of the way—an interest that coincided precisely with that of the Central Intelligence Agency. It was a near-perfect confluence of interests.[43]

Shortly after Castro's march into Havana, Jack Ruby reportedly made two contacts with a Texas gunrunner named Robert McKeown. He had been one of Castro's principal suppliers of guns during the revolution. In the first incident, Ruby told McKeown that he represented someone in Las Vegas who wanted to get three prisoners out of Castro's jails and thus needed McKeown's help. On the second occasion, Ruby, who was rarely known to have large sums of extra cash, offered McKeown $25,000 in return for a special introduction to Castro.[44] (Castro had jailed a number of big-time mobsters, including Santos Trafficante.[45])

About a month after this, Ruby was approached by the FBI and agreed to work as a potential criminal informant. He was so listed in bureau files, a matter that has never been adequately explained. As far as is known, Ruby provided no information on his new Cuban connection, raising the possibility that he simply wanted a channel open with the FBI, just in case he got caught in some nefarious activity. He then could claim to the authorities that he was working to glean information for the bureau—not an uncommon ploy in those days.[46]

During this period when he was traveling to Cuba, an apparently innocuous instrument came into Ruby's life for the first time—a safe-deposit box. He used it fifteen times in two years. After that period, he never used it again. It was empty when opened under court order, following Ruby's murder of Oswald.[47]

Although no one has ever ascertained why Ruby was using the box, its existence clearly indicates that there are dimensions of Ruby's activities not yet uncovered. One rational belief is that Ruby used the box to keep cash or some sort of contraband that he then ferried into Cuba on his trips. There are no persuasive clues as to what Ruby might have been receiving in return.

None of these activities was acknowledged by the Warren Commission. When asked about Cuba, Ruby lied to the commission and said that he had been there only once, in August 1959. His purpose, he said, was to visit an old friend named Lewis McWillie, a former Dallas gambler and nightclub operator. McWillie had gone on to richer pastures as the manager of the famed Tropicana nightclub in Havana.[48]

The original investigative accounts of Ruby and McWillie regarding Ruby's visit to Cuba are Runyonesque in their innocence. The pair basically claimed that they wandered about Havana enjoying the sunshine and bright sights as they renewed their old friendship. McWillie said that he had "extended this invitation as one would to a brother." He said that he had sent Ruby travel tickets from Havana, explaining that his old friend had been "working hard" and "needed a rest."*[49]

McWillie himself possesses a background that might have stirred the interest of investigators. Born in 1908 in Kansas City, McWillie lived from 1941 to 1958 in Dallas, where he was well locked into the network of gangsters who controlled gambling in Texas. He then moved to Cuba. Though McWillie and Santos Trafficante deny they were associated with each other in Cuba, there is evidence to the contrary. The HSCA found reasons to suggest that McWillie and Ruby visited Trafficante in prison during Ruby's 1959 visit to Cuba. Suspicion about the relationship between Trafficante and McWillie was sharpened by Trafficante's denial of having any financial connection in either of the places McWillie worked in Havana—the Tropicana or the Capri. FBI records indicate that Trafficante owned part of the Capri.[50]

Although no absolute link was established between Trafficante and Jack Ruby, the link is strongly in place between McWillie and

*By the time he testified before the Select Committee, McWillie's account of the purpose for Ruby's trip had undergone a definite change: he said Ruby was supposed to have gone to Havana with a Dallas columnist to stimulate some publicity for the Tropicana. At the last moment, the columnist could not go. Ruby used his ticket without informing McWillie of the change in plans. McWillie's attitude toward Ruby had also changed. When asked about Ruby's activities, he said, "I don't remember a darn thing he did but bug me all week."

Ruby, with persuasive evidence of ties between McWillie and Trafficante.[51] Even if McWillie and Ruby had nothing to do with Trafficante, the circumstances still place Ruby in a sharply peculiar situation, considering that he would later silence Oswald. If there is any doubt about this, consider for a moment the implications if the investigation had *proved* a link between Ruby and Trafficante. Such a revelation might have been dramatic enough to force the Warren Commission into a full investigation.

Some respected critics believe there is persuasive evidence to indicate that Ruby was involved in Cuban gunrunning activities.[52] However, firm substantiation of these points is elusive.

The whole sweep of Ruby's Cuban connections hangs darkly over an understanding of any role of organized crime in Ruby's convenient silencing of Oswald. Whatever Ruby was doing in Cuba, he was likely operating under the auspices of organized crime. Until this connection is fully understood, Ruby's role must remain in question.*

While the HSCA did not solve Ruby's mysterious Cuban connection, it at least got on record the statements of McWillie, Trafficante, and various Cuban officials produced for the committee by Castro's government.[53] (Even Castro himself was interviewed by the committee.)[54] However, the Cuban government refused to permit the committee to talk to Manuel Piniero Losada, the member of the Directorate of Intelligence who interviewed Trafficante following his release from prison and gave him twenty-four hours to get out of the country. The least sinister explanation of the Cuban government's refusal is that Trafficante paid a bribe to Piniero and the government did not care to have that news bandied about. More somberly, Piniero may have had knowledge of Trafficante's activities that would have upset the stereotype of Ruby, pictured, oddly enough like Oswald, as a lone nut.[55]

In his book, Chief Counsel Blakey summed up the Select Committee's impression of the Cuba connection:

> The picture that was being formed by the pieces of the puzzle was coming into focus: Ruby's trips to Cuba were an important,

*While the gentle authors of the Warren Report stepped lightly around Cuba, it should be noted that two commission staff members—Leon D. Hubert, Jr., and Burt W. Griffin—tried desperately to prod the commission into examining it in full. This recommendation was turned down because, a top staffer told the HSCA in 1977, "these Cuban pursuits represented some kind of bottomless pit."[56]

if minor, part of an organized-crime operation, which may have had to do with Trafficante's detention. It was a conclusion radically at odds with the view of Ruby in 1964, since the Warren Commission found nothing "sinister" in his travels and determined he was not part of the "organized underworld." Had the Commission found otherwise, it is doubtful that its conclusion that Ruby was a lone gunman would have received such wide acceptance.[57]

This does little to dismiss questions about Ruby and Cuba—a point about which Ruby was understandably sensitive. In 1964, after he was convicted of murdering Oswald and sentenced to death, Ruby was talking in his jail cell with a former employee named Wally Weston. Later Weston told the HSCA: "[Ruby] was shook [and] he said, geez, . . . they're going to find out about Cuba, they're going to find out about the guns, find out about New Orleans, find out about everything."[58]

What did Jack Ruby fear the investigators might find out about New Orleans?

In 1963 Ruby spent—for him—an unusual amount of time dealing with people in New Orleans. Traditionally, Ruby had turned to Chicago for his strippers, but the spring of 1963 found him negotiating with Harold Tannenbaum of the Old French Opera House on Bourbon Street in New Orleans. Tannenbaum was a key man in running several sleazy operations for associates of New Orleans mob boss Carlos Marcello. Telephone records show that Ruby first contacted Tannenbaum on May 15, 1963.*[59]

Ostensibly, Ruby's reason for calling was that he was on the hunt for new nightclub acts. Two weeks later he was told about a hot act at Tannenbaum's strip joint performed by one Janet Mole Adams Conforto, whose stage name was Jada. Ruby drove to New Orleans around June 5, 1963, and remained there several days. His stated reason was to look over the girlie shows with an eye for recruiting fresh flesh for his Carousel Club in Dallas.[60]

On June 8, Ruby saw Jada perform. He liked what he saw and

---

*In 1978 the Select Committee, reporting Tannenbaum as dead, asserted that he had organized-crime connections. However, in 1983, alive and well, Tannenbaum denied to the author having ever had such associations.

presumably decided to recruit her. When Ruby got back to Dallas, he made a series of telephone calls through the remainder of the month—most placed to the Old French Opera House. On June 28, Jada opened at Ruby's place in Dallas, her act being a bit daring even by Ruby's standards. (She did not always maintain legal protocol regarding the placement of her G-string.)[61]

Although Ruby had presumably fulfilled his mission of locating hot talent in New Orleans, his calls to that city continued. (All known calls, of course, were made openly and charged to Ruby's account. It is not known whether other calls were made from coin-operated telephones.) There were about a half-dozen known calls between Ruby and Tannenbaum's club through July and early August, including some from Tannenbaum, who telephoned Ruby supposedly to ask for help in finding a job in Dallas. On September 6, Tannenbaum arrived in Dallas and stayed at Ruby's apartment. In October Tannenbaum was back in New Orleans and again called Ruby to ask about possible employment.[62]

There is no question that Ruby was having serious trouble with the entertainment union to which his strippers belonged (American Guild of Variety Artists), and it is entirely possible that his New Orleans activities were strictly related to trying to acquire strippers from outside his normal circuit.[63] On the other hand, it is not unreasonable to wonder if Ruby had reached out to New Orleans for some other reason.

As autumn settled over Dallas, there was one certainty about Jack Ruby's life: he was in terrible financial trouble. He owed tens of thousands of dollars in back taxes, and the pressures on him were tremendous.[64] Worst, perhaps, was that he remained a loser. As a man of violence—and as a man unconcerned with the laws of society—Ruby was a pawn aching for a master to move him on any chess board where there was money.

It is interesting to look at the volume of Ruby's long-distance telephone calls during the seven months preceding the assassination of President Kennedy. In March, Ruby made fewer than ten toll calls. From May until September, Ruby averaged twenty-five to thirty-five calls per month. But for October and November, the volume of calls escalated tremendously. In October, Ruby placed more than seventy toll calls. The number reached nearly one hundred during the first three weeks of November, before he was jailed for murdering Oswald.[65]

Among the calls never explained were three recorded on November 7 and November 8 to two of Jimmy Hoffa's top henchmen in Chicago and Miami. Two of the conversations were with Robert "Barney" Baker, whom Attorney General Robert Kennedy once called "Hoffa's ambassador of violence."[66]

Two weeks earlier, Ruby telephoned Irwin S. Weiner, a prominent bail bondsman associated with organized crime in Chicago. When the FBI contacted Weiner three days after Ruby's arrest to ask what he and Ruby talked about for twelve minutes, Weiner refused to reveal the nature of the conversation. Years later, the Select Committee noted that Weiner conducted his activities "at the highest levels of organized crime nationally and in Chicago." In 1983 Weiner was with Allen Dorfman, a top Chicago mobster, when Dorfman was shot eight times in the head at close range. Weiner was untouched.[67]

Also of particular interest was a call Ruby made on October 30 to Nofio Pecora in New Orleans. Pecora is an important figure in the crime syndicate of New Orleans mob boss Carlos Marcello. The call to Pecora, for whatever reason, placed Ruby in the heart of the Marcello organization.[68] Aaron Kohn, former managing director of the New Orleans Metropolitan Crime Commission, has described the Marcello-Pecora relationship this way: "Pecora and Marcello used to be street thugs together a long time ago when they both were in narcotics traffic. Both Mr. and Mrs. Pecora are still considered very active members of the Marcello organization."[69]

Pecora told the HSCA that he "did not recall" speaking to Ruby on the telephone. However, Harold Tannenbaum, the French Quarter strip-joint operator Ruby was in such close touch with during those days, lived in the Tropical Court Tourist Park, which was owned by Pecora.[70]

The real significance is Ruby's indisputable association with Harold Tannenbaum, who not only lived in Pecora's trailer court but worked for the Marcello interests on Bourbon Street. Aaron Kohn has pointed out that in 1963 Marcello's brother and some of his closest associates ran five of the most profitable strip joints in the French Quarter. Tannenbaum was a key employee in the operation of these establishments.[71]

Perhaps the sole connection between Ruby and Tannenbaum was their professional interest in swapping strippers. However, it is certain that the transactions placed Ruby into association with the Marcello organization—a group of legally sophisticated thugs who had a special hatred for the Kennedys—particularly Robert, who had waged a single-minded campaign to deport Marcello.[72] An FBI memorandum records information received about an alleged eyewitness account of a meeting at Marcello's 3,000-acre estate, just outside New Orleans: "Marcello was alleged to have said that in order to get Bobby Kennedy they would have to get the President, and they could not kill Bobby because the President would use the Army and the Marines to get them. The result of killing the President would cause Bobby to lose his power as Attorney General because of the new President."[73]

According to the witness to the meeting, which supposedly took place in September 1962, at the height of Robert Kennedy's war against Marcello, a plan was discussed in which an assassination would be blamed on a "nut." In explaining why it was important to murder the President instead of the attorney general, Marcello is supposed to have likened the two brothers to a dog—Robert being the tail and John being the head.[74] According to Chief Counsel Blakey's interpretation of the grim metaphor, Marcello reasoned: "If you cut off the tail the dog will keep biting; but if you chop off the head, the dog will die, tail and all."[75]

In 1978 Marcello appeared at an executive session of the HSCA and, not surprisingly, denied that he ever made such threats or that any meeting as described took place.[76] A similar denial was offered by Mafia kingpin Santos Trafficante, who had reportedly been heard predicting that President Kennedy was "going to be hit."[77]

Few aspects of the assassination have been officially examined more rigorously than the activities of Jack Ruby on November 22, 1963. After the murder of Oswald, numerous stories surfaced that placed Ruby and confederates in key places to participate in the killing of Kennedy. The silencing of Oswald seemed such a natural step in a conspiracy that millions of people assumed that Ruby was a player in the earlier acts as well. This assumption in place, reports flooded in that Ruby was everywhere.

Among the few certainties is that Jack Ruby was in the offices of the *Dallas Morning News* around the time of the assassination.[78] However, one reporter who knew Ruby told the FBI that Ruby was "missed for a period of about twenty to twenty-five minutes" before reappearing shortly after the assassination.[79] The newspaper building is situated about four blocks from Dealey Plaza. Ruby was seeing acquaintances at the newspaper to discuss his advertisement for the Carousel Club. Given Ruby's later claim of great devotion to President Kennedy, it seems odd that he did not walk the short distance to watch his idol pass.*[80] Ruby remained at the newspaper until 1:10 P.M. It has been speculated that Ruby wanted to be in a place and among people who could provide him with an ironclad alibi.[81] That purpose was served.

The next reliable report of Ruby places him at Parkland Hospital around 1:30. Seth Kantor, a respected Washington correspondent who as a Dallas reporter in earlier days had known Ruby, was approached by Ruby at Parkland. Kantor spoke to him and called him by name. Ruby asked Kantor if he thought he should close his strip joints out of respect for the late President.[82]

Ruby later denied he was at Parkland. The Warren Commission accepted Ruby's word, discounting the reports of Kantor and another witness. Years later the HSCA concluded that Kantor was right and Ruby had lied.[83] It is possibly significant that for some reason Ruby—after heralding his presence to Kantor at the hospital—would later deny that he was there.†

Only the wildest speculation has Jack Ruby pulling a trigger in Dealey Plaza. The important point is whether evidence indicates that Ruby began stalking Oswald on that day. If, as he claimed, Ruby acted out of the passion of the moment in killing Oswald, he could never let himself be perceived as stalking his prey.[84]

On the other hand, if Ruby was ordered to silence Oswald, Ruby's behavior between Friday afternoon and Sunday morning should give a clue. The Warren Commission did not look for clues and accepted Ruby's version of his motive. The HSCA did try to put the clues

*Ruby's excuse for this later was that he didn't "want to go where there is big crowds." However, the crowded conditions he encountered later that night at the police department failed to bother him.

†Ruby's presence at Parkland during this crucial period has led some critics to wonder if Ruby played a role in the planting of the Magic Bullet, which became the cornerstone of the Warren Report.

together and came up with a conclusion that was just the opposite.[85]

On the eve of President Kennedy's death, Ruby dined at the Egyptian Lounge with his old friend and financial backer Ralph Paul. The owners of the restaurant, Joseph and Sam Campisi, later confirmed to the FBI that the men had a late dinner there. Joe Campisi was an influential organized-crime figure in Dallas, and one 1967 FBI informant report indicated that he was due to take over as the city's mob boss. In 1978 Campisi acknowledged to the HSCA that he had known Ruby since 1947—but he changed his story in one interesting respect. He stated, in contradiction to what he told the FBI in 1963, that he did *not* see Ruby at the Egyptian Lounge on the eve of the assassination.[86] Campisi's denial of seeing Ruby that night is, if nothing else, another example of the mob distancing itself from the man who silenced Oswald.

In any event, Joe Campisi acknowledged that he was on very good terms with Carlos Marcello, noting that each Christmas he sends 260 pounds of Italian sausage to the New Orleans crime lord and his associates. Evidence of his close connection with New Orleans is cemented by Campisi's telephone records, which noted as many as twenty calls a day from his telephone to various telephone numbers in New Orleans.[87]

By 2:00 P.M. on the day of the assassination, Oswald was in custody on the third floor of the Police and Courts Building. There was bedlam, of course, and the press could be found in every public cranny. Practically no security was in force.[88]

Numerous reliable witnesses have placed Ruby on the third floor as early as 4:30 P.M. He spoke and shook hands with people he knew. Telephone records show that Ruby was back at his apartment by 9:00 P.M., and he was seen at a synagogue at about 10:00 P.M.[89]

After that, according to the version Ruby gave the Warren Commission, he decided to take some sandwiches up to the police, who were working overtime on the Oswald case. Ruby called first and was told the food was not needed. Then, Ruby later explained, he returned anyway to the third floor and mingled with the milling throng of reporters. It was after midnight when Ruby followed the reporters to the basement, where Oswald was presented to the press for a brief appearance. The purpose was to assure the press that Oswald had not been abused while in custody. News pictures show Ruby seeming to pose as a reporter.[90]

Ruby later told the FBI that he had a pistol in his pocket on this occasion—a claim he recanted in testimony before the Warren Commission. Descriptions of the tumultuous scene in the basement during the press conference suggest—as many critics have pointed out—that it was virtually impossible for Ruby to get off a clean shot.[91]

This midnight press conference nonetheless yielded one of the most tantalizing and baffling elements of the Ruby story. District Attorney Henry Wade, in briefing the newsmen about Oswald's background, noted that he had belonged to the Free Cuba Committee. Upon hearing this, Ruby spoke up and corrected Wade, stating that Oswald had actually belonged to the Fair Play for Cuba Committee (FPCC), a group with precisely the opposite goals.[92]

How Ruby, at that very early stage, could have been so well versed in Oswald's murky biography has never been explained or even officially investigated. Despite early press reports about the FPCC, it remains remarkable that Ruby would possess such precise knowledge of the political group Oswald claimed to represent in New Orleans some months earlier. The incident strongly suggests Ruby's prior knowledge of Oswald and his activities—which is not to say that the two were mutually acquainted.* It simply means that for some unexplained reason, Jack Ruby knew about Oswald's activities in New Orleans some months earlier, when Ruby was keeping the telephone wires hot. This was information virtually unknown in Dallas at that hour.

The next day, Saturday, Ruby was again busily engaged in activities that can be interpreted as stalking Oswald. He was seen again in the police building where Oswald was being held, and he telephoned a radio station and asked for any news about when Oswald would be transferred.[93]

Witnesses have testified that on Saturday Ruby demonstrated an acute interest in finding out just when Oswald was going to be transferred to the county jail. An NBC producer recalled that Ruby made a nuisance of himself as he tried to follow activities on the third floor by watching the television monitor in an NBC van parked on the street.[94]

On Sunday morning, minutes before Oswald's arrival, Ruby joined

---

*Earlier that November, Ruby and Oswald each rented a postal box at the Dallas Terminal Annex.[95]

the teeming crowd of more than one hundred policemen and reporters in the basement to see the suspect's transfer.*[96] As soon as Oswald came into sight, Ruby burst from the crowd and fired one bullet into Oswald's abdomen at point-blank range. The bullet ripped through the aorta, also striking the liver, spleen, pancreas, and kidney. It was a stunningly effective shot. Oswald made the famous grimace seen by millions on television and, without uttering another word, collapsed. He was declared dead at 1:07 P.M.[97]

The basic question of how Ruby got into the basement has never been resolved. Ruby's version—an on-again, off-again recitation— was that he simply walked down the ramp from the street and entered the basement just after the exit of a police car. The Warren Commission, despite the objection of some of its staff, accepted this account. It was readily accepted in all its simplicity by the Dallas police. Years later, however, the Select Committee realized that the eyewitness testimony clearly did not jibe with Ruby's explanation.[98]

Some critics have suggested connivance on the part of some Dallas police officers in letting Ruby into the basement.†[99] While that may be true, it may not have been necessary, given the ease with which Ruby had entered the building while Oswald was in custody.[100] The critical point is whether Ruby was stalking Oswald. HSCA Chief Counsel Blakey summed up the committee findings in this fashion:

> The only firm conclusion we could come to was that Ruby . . . and the . . . officers who questioned him probably did not tell the truth about how Ruby got into the basement. . . . Our conclusions about Ruby's entry into the basement were inconsistent with a conspiracy that called for Ruby to kill Oswald at the specific time he did, but they did not reduce the likelihood of a plot that called for Ruby to kill Oswald whenever he could get to him. The evidence of Ruby's repeated efforts to reach

*An odd message from Chicago for Jack Ruby reached Dallas about 9:00 A.M. on Sunday. The message was from an officer of the American Guild of Variety Artists, the mob-dominated union that normally provided Ruby with strippers. The message, never delivered, from the officer to Ruby was: "Tell Jack not to send the letter today, it would be awkward in Chicago." This was before Ruby's sudden infamy. The message has never been adequately explained.

†Sergeant Patrick Dean, a friend of Ruby's who was in charge of the security of the basement that Sunday morning, continued the friendship during Ruby's long months in jail. In 1983 Dean showed the author a copy of the Warren Report, personally inscribed by Ruby to Dean in this fashion: "Remember me as you have known me in the past. Sincerely hope you will always believe me and should never forget me."

Oswald on Friday and Saturday made it appear probable to us that Ruby was stalking him, ready to shoot him when the opportunity arose. Ironically, when the opportunity did arise, it was so sudden and so dependent on coincidence, that Ruby's act did not appear to be conspiratorial.[101]

Ruby's trial took place during twenty-seven days in March 1964. He was not allowed by his defense attorney, Melvin Belli, to take the stand. A jury found him guilty of premeditated murder and sentenced him to die in the electric chair. This verdict was overturned on technical grounds in late 1966 by the Texas Court of Criminal Appeals. Three months later, before there could be a new trial, Ruby was dead of cancer.[102]

The Warren Commission conducted its formal interviews with Ruby several months after his trial had ended. Even though he faced the death sentence, Ruby knew there was an excellent chance for a new trial. He had high hopes for getting a much more favorable disposition in a new trial—perhaps as little as a five-year sentence.[103]

Thus, Ruby was not necessarily filled with hopelessness as he sat down at a table with the Chief Justice of the Supreme Court, Earl Warren, and future President Gerald Ford.[104] Given the promise of a new trial, it seems logical that Ruby's compulsion to maintain a cover story—to protect others involved in the conspiracy—would not have been diminished by the death sentence he faced.

Ruby told the Warren Commission his familiar tale, including his fanciful motive that he wanted to spare the Kennedy family the agony of Oswald's trial.[105] (Melvin Belli later wrote that he was "sure the story was false because it didn't square with everything else we knew."[106]) The commission dutifully recorded Ruby's comments, swallowed most of them without serious question, and thereby became a convenient if unwitting partner in the promulgation of Ruby's story.[107]

Ruby recited his story to the Warren Commission, which took his testimony in a small, kitchenlike room in a Dallas courthouse.[108] But throughout his testimony, Ruby exuded signals—some subtle, some direct—that given the opportunity, there was a great deal he would like to tell the commission. Scattered through his testimony are statements that are a variation on one direct plea he made to Chief Justice Warren: "I want to tell the truth, and I can't tell it here."[109]

Ruby must have spent those months living in terror for his life. But, as always, Ruby seemed to toady to authority, to try to ingratiate himself as he had spent so many years doing with the Dallas Police Department. It was not really surprising that there were signs that under certain circumstances he would like to cooperate, after a fashion, with the commission. To what *degree* he might have cooperated is anyone's guess.

Before the commission completed its interviews with him in Dallas, Ruby was virtually begging to be taken to Washington, where, he said, he could talk freely. He argued repeatedly that he could not talk while in Dallas. In all, Ruby asked the commission *eight times* to allow him to testify in Washington.[110] Ruby was told that it could not be done.[111] Why it could not be done has never been convincingly explained. This denial of Ruby's simple request flies in the face of the fact that of the ninety-four witnesses who testified before the commission, only one—Jack Ruby— was not summoned to Washington.[112]

It is now clear, more than two decades after the events in Dallas, that Ruby himself believed that he was a pawn in a larger conspiracy. In a taped interview just after his trial—an interview discovered by assassination researchers in 1978—Ruby stated: "Everything pertaining to what's happened has never come to the surface. The world will never know the true facts of what occurred [or] my motive. . . . The people [who] have so much to gain and had such an ulterior motive to put me in the position I am in . . . will never let the true facts [be known] to the world."[113]

Far more to the point is the assessment of a psychiatrist who examined Ruby in 1965. That confidential medical report, which has remained virtually unknown until now, states: "[Ruby] considers himself a victim of a conspiracy and was 'framed' to kill Oswald, so that Oswald could never say who made him kill President Kennedy."[114]

The psychiatrist, who notes that Ruby's comments were "colored by marked fear," quotes him as stating, "I am doomed. I do not want to die, but I am not insane. I was framed to kill Oswald."[115]

The Warren Commission's ineptitude in pursuing fresh leads left the HSCA with little to work with beyond old evidence and foggy memories. Even those memories that might still be clear found an easy hiding spot behind the passage of fifteen years. Robert Blakey summed up the HSCA work on Ruby this way:

> We could not accept the Warren Commission's benign view of Ruby's background, character, associations, and conduct. . . . Ruby's violent character had been molded in a matrix of crime and corruption in Chicago, one of the nation's centers of organized crime. His business activities were an integral part of a system of criminal operations, even if they were not illegal as such. At least on his trip to Cuba, Ruby played an important, if minor, role in a sophisticated syndicate operation that involved one of the most powerful underworld leaders. Ruby's associates in Dallas for the years and months prior to the assassination included a number of prominent organized-crime figures. He was in serious financial difficulty in the period leading up to the assassination, and a number of organized-crime figures were aware of it. Those same figures, under heavy pressure from the Kennedy organized-crime program, had a strong motive to assassinate the President.[116]

The fundamental finding by the HSCA is that more than one person was probably involved in the President's assassination, and that both Oswald and Ruby were far from "loners."[117] But the loose ends left fluttering by the committee raise far more questions than were settled.

Take, for example, the lingering skepticism surrounding the Magic Bullet—skepticism that has been hardly abated by the finding of the HSCA's Forensic Panel that the bullet *could* have done the extraordinary damage attributed to it.[118] In view of the deep doubt that swirls about the issue, it becomes pertinent to ask what Jack Ruby was doing at Parkland Hospital following the assassination. Even more, why did he lie about it later, after seeking out a reputable acquaintance and speaking to him at the hospital? As long as there are those who wonder if the preposterously tainted Magic Bullet was planted, Ruby's presence in the immediate area just before the bullet was discovered will persist as solid grounds for suspicion.

The other astonishing aspect of the case is Ruby's entry into the basement. According to Ruby's story, the entry was so simple and so logical that not one other person could be implicated. Yet, if there were not other conspirators involved in his getting into the basement, why then did Ruby vacillate so erratically in his willingness to tell what happened? These questions, which seem critical to any solution of the mystery, are today shrouded in the murkiness of time as well as purposeful obfuscation by those whose shields the HSCA failed to penetrate.

Perhaps the most intriguing question—and one that has received the least attention by official investigators—concerns Ruby's activities in New Orleans. What did Ruby mean when he said that he feared officials would "find out about" New Orleans? Was Ruby fearful that investigators would learn that he had been scouting around Bourbon Street seeking new talent for his strip joints? Was he afraid of a criminal charge that could lead to a sentence more drastic than the death sentence he faced? Or was Ruby concerned about sullying his reputation by having it known he trafficked in women?

To believe that any of these reasons troubled Ruby is absurd. Harold Tannenbaum, the New Orleans man with whom Ruby was in such close touch, was, according to the House Select Committee on Assassinations, a prime—if low-level—operative in the Marcello crime syndicate.[119] (In fact, Ruby and Tannenbaum seem to have had similar responsibilities.) The Marcello organization, without question, had one of the most powerful motives of any criminal element for the elimination of President Kennedy and his brother Robert, the attorney general. While the national community of organized crime was seriously threatened by the Kennedy administration, it is significant that Robert Kennedy's threat to Marcello was every bit as personal as his efforts to imprison Jimmy Hoffa. By any gauge, the prosecutions in each instance turned into vendettas.[120]

There can be little doubt that Ruby was up to much more in New Orleans than simply finding fresh female flesh. For example, he demonstrated on the night of the assassination his familiarity with the Fair Play for Cuba Committee—and that it was a pro-Castro group in which Oswald purportedly was active. This is not information Ruby would have picked up routinely in Dallas.

How Ruby knew something like this—and what he was really doing in New Orleans—may never be known. The real pity is that all the leads—once so fresh and promising—lie marooned on the shoals of abandoned investigations. Truth, always elusive in this case, may in the matter of Jack Ruby's role be lost forever.

9 · FINGERPRINTS

OF INTELLIGENCE

Oswald was playing out an intelligence role. . . . All the
fingerprints . . . point to Oswald as being a product of . . . the
intelligence community.[1]

—Senator Richard Schweiker

A Veil of Confusion

At each murky plateau in the peripatetic life of Lee Harvey Oswald,
there are the shadowy signs of espionage. As he maneuvered about
the world, often with baffling purposefulness, Oswald left wide and
mysterious gaps in his personal history, gaps that persist despite
massive investigations. With no known close friends, Oswald managed to move across great distances and tight borders with astounding ease for one so young, so uneducated, so impoverished. And
with his movements there always seemed to be little helping fingers—never quite touching, just out of sight—that guided him, that
barely tipped the balance of his affairs by placing him in certain
locations, with particular people, in positions that, when taken all
together, reflect an intriguing continuity. It is a continuity dotted
with coincidences so tantalizing that even if viewed singly, they
would stir suspicions of espionage activities.

To be sure, there is no *hard* evidence of Oswald's intelligence
connections. But, it seems fair to say, such activities rarely leave
trails of hard evidence—rather, there are the whispers of faint clues,
the suspicions fostered by the unexplained coincidence. And, always, there is the maddening certainty that the negative position—
that Oswald was *not* an intelligence operative—can never be proved.
Such an absence of evidence is not surprising in an area as beclouded
by official deceit and manipulation as intelligence activities.

Given the quirkiness of Oswald's personality, the oddness of the associations he developed, one might expect that he himself had a hand in the insinuation of intelligence connections. But the evidence yields not a single example of Oswald's ever suggesting that he was a spy of any sort—unless his bizarre defection to the Soviet Union in 1959, accompanied by his blatant offer to reveal U.S. military secrets, can be considered a form of self-professed espionage activity.[2] It is an argument that not even the government has attempted. On the contrary, suspicions that Oswald served as an intelligence operative—and, in any such case, there is great disagreement over *whom* he might have been working for—arise from examinations of his activities by observers dedicated to the study of the world of spies.

In considering these possibilities, it is important to keep in mind that *all* the evidence suggesting Oswald's intelligence connections is circumstantial. Such a role by Oswald is denied by the FBI, the CIA, and various branches of U.S. military intelligence.[3] An equally implied denial comes from the other leading candidate for sponsorship of Oswald—the government of the Soviet Union. Such denials obviously do not take into account the possibility that Oswald might have worked for some branch of U.S. intelligence that, to this day, remains hidden from the public.

Still, many reasonable observers—both inside and outside the government—have agreed over the years that the fingerprints of intelligence seen everywhere in Oswald's adult life cannot be casually erased. It is ironic and persuasive that one of the strongest arguments in support of the valid significance of these fingerprints comes from a previously top secret exchange of comments among Chief Justice Earl Warren, commission member Hale Boggs, and Allen W. Dulles, a member of the Warren Commission and former Director of Central Intelligence. Dulles is widely considered to be the leading figure in the development of American intelligence enterprises. Among the earliest of those troubled by Oswald's "fingerprints" were the members of the Warren Commission. Their comments on the possibility that Oswald was a spy remained under a top secret classification until 1974.[4]

It was during an executive session on January 27, 1964, that General Counsel J. Lee Rankin broached what he called the "dirty rumor" that Oswald had been an informant for the FBI.[5] It was natural for commission members to turn to the man who knew more about U.S. intelligence practices than perhaps any other American—and certainly more than any other serving on the Warren Commission. The exchange:

ALLEN DULLES: [This] is a terribly hard thing to disprove, you know. How do you disprove a fellow was not your agent? How do you disprove it.

HALE BOGGS: You could disprove it, couldn't you?

DULLES: No. . . . I never knew how to disprove it.

BOGGS: . . . Did you have agents about whom you had no record whatsoever?

DULLES: The record might not be on paper. But on paper [you] would have hieroglyphics that only two people knew what they meant, and nobody outside of the agency would know and you could say this meant the agent and somebody else could say it meant another agent.

BOGGS: . . . The man who recruited [an operative] would know, wouldn't he?

DULLES: Yes, but he wouldn't tell.

EARL WARREN: Wouldn't tell it under oath?

DULLES: I wouldn't think he would tell it under oath, no. . . . He ought not tell it under oath. . . .

BOGGS: . . . What you do is . . . make our problem utterly impossible because you say this rumor can't be dissipated under any circumstances.[6]

So, from the earliest consideration of Oswald's possible intelligence connections, it was clear that if such connections existed, there was little reason to believe that anyone in the government would ever admit it—and that intelligence officials could be expected to lie about it, *even under oath.*

In view of this, persistent government denials of Oswald's intelligence links have been widely scorned. It is a reasonable presumption that no U.S. intelligence service will ever acknowledge any connection with Lee Harvey Oswald—no matter how innocent. (Most critics do not actually believe that Oswald killed President Kennedy as an official act of an intelligence agency. The belief is in the possibility that he was a part of some murky intelligence operation that went awry—or that Oswald himself went awry, if he was anything other than a patsy. Probably an even greater number of critics believe that Oswald had a simple informant relationship with one of the intelligence services—a relationship that had nothing to do with the assassination but was, all the same, vehemently denied in view of the disastrous actions blamed on Oswald.[7])

Nonetheless, it is interesting that suspicions of Oswald's connections have had currency at the highest reaches of the U.S. government. In April 1967, for example, the FBI's assistant director, Cartha "Deke" DeLoach, wrote a memo concerning White House suspicions, a memo that was released many years later. Reporting on a talk he had with a top White House aide, DeLoach wrote that President Johnson "was now convinced that there was a plot in connection with the assassination. . . . The President felt that CIA had had something to do with this plot."[8]

Such an involvement by the CIA would, given the official findings, necessarily include Lee Harvey Oswald in some sort of intelligence role.

To interpret the fingerprints of intelligence that marked Oswald's life, it is necessary to review in broad stroke the curious twists and turns of his brief and tumultuous passage through the world. Born in New Orleans in 1939, Oswald and his domineering, eccentric mother lived in various places, including New York City and Fort Worth. Oswald's father died before his birth, and his mother relied on various relatives in New Orleans, some of whom, many years later, were ascertained to have had certain tenuous, low-level connections with illegal gambling and organized crime.[9]

Although a voracious reader throughout his life and with an IQ of 118, Oswald was no student. He dropped out of school in New Orleans in the tenth grade. In October 1956 he entered the Marine Corps, where, showing no particular aptitude for military life, he managed to get through basic training. Though teased for his bookishness and his inexperience with girls and alcohol, Oswald got along with the other young men with whom he served.[10]

After eight months of training in the United States, Oswald was sent to the naval air station near Atsugi, Japan. Trained as an "aviation electronics operator," Oswald's primary job was to work in the radar huts identifying and controlling aircraft. Basically a radar operator, Oswald was present at two locations—Atsugi and Cubi Point in the Philippines—that served as bases for the super-secret reconnaissance missions by the U-2 spy planes. Dozens of his fellow Marines have provided detailed descriptions of their own knowledge of the U-2 during a period when the plane was still considered highly secret.[11]

In September 1959, after claiming he was needed at home to help take care of his mother, Oswald acquired an early discharge from the Marine Corps. Following three days with his mother in Fort Worth, Oswald went to New Orleans. From there he headed east by slow steamer to France, to England, and then on to Finland and finally the Soviet Union. Soon after his arrival there, he rejected his United States citizenship and announced his intention to offer the Soviets all his knowledge of U.S. military affairs—which would include details concerning the top secret U-2 reconnaissance flights. He remained in the Soviet Union for nearly three years. He married a young Soviet woman named Marina Prusakova, who bore him a daughter.[12]

In June 1962 Oswald and his family returned to the United States with a minimum of difficulty. They settled in Fort Worth, where Oswald's mother and brother were living. Oswald went to work at a small welding company within walking distance of the duplex where he and his wife and daughter lived. In October Oswald found a job more to his liking at a graphic-arts company in Dallas; the company happened to be doing classified work for the Department of Defense. He and his family moved to Dallas.[13]

In April 1963 Oswald was on the move again, after losing his job at the graphic-arts company. This time he returned to the city of his birth, New Orleans, where he found a job as an oiler at a coffee company. That city was smoldering in 1963 with the pressures of a volatile Cuban exile community anxious to reverse the galling disaster of their Bay of Pigs invasion failure in April 1961. The failure was blamed squarely on President Kennedy, who, because of this and his conciliatory stance at the end of the Cuban Missile Crisis in 1962, was generally considered a traitor to the exile cause. Both the CIA and the FBI had domestic operations headquartered in New Orleans. Informants of all stripes augmented the phalanx of federal agents working to keep tabs on the exile community.[14]

With all the possibilities for political action in New Orleans, Lee Oswald ostensibly went his own way. He became the founder and sole member of the local chapter of a pro-Castro group called the Fair Play for Cuba Committee (FPCC). His activities in this capacity led to a street scuffle that got Oswald and a couple of the militant anti-Castro exiles arrested and hauled to the police station.[15]

In September Oswald made his way to Mexico City, where he allegedly paid visits to the Soviet and Cuban embassies. He sup-posedly wanted to make plans to return to the Soviet Union.[16]

Oswald returned to Dallas in early October and soon after went to work at the Texas School Book Depository. During that period, which was immediately prior to the assassination, his wife lived with a friend in the Dallas suburb of Irving. Oswald lived in small rooming houses in the Oak Cliff section of Dallas and visited his family on weekends. Then came the black Friday of November 22, 1963. Two days later, Oswald was murdered by Jack Ruby. He was barely twenty-four years old.[17]

Thousands of hours have been spent analyzing the short, enigmatic life of Lee Harvey Oswald. Volumes have been published covering his relationship with his wife, with his mother, with the authorities who crossed his path. The only certain conclusion is that no clear or firm answers can be found in an examination of his inter-personal relationships. Firm answers, if they exist, must be found elsewhere.

Looking over the sweep of Oswald's life, one is struck not so much by what is known. Far more tantalizing is what is *not* known. Those areas remain obscure today in spite of the enormous efforts by both official and unofficial investigators and researchers. It is against this erratic background, pockmarked with intriguing and bewildering contradiction and coincidence, that the fingerprints of intelligence must be examined.

PFC Oswaldskowich: The Oddest Leatherneck

By nearly any standard, the Marine career of Lee Harvey Oswald is highly unusual, if not downright bizarre. There is a tendency, in any effort to fashion an honest portrayal of those years, to wonder whether Oswald's military experience might have been rather nor-mal, were it not all under such microscopic examination. Is it, a researcher must ask, like the case of some odd creature suddenly plucked from the ocean floor and examined—a creature perfectly normal on the ocean floor but grotesque when pulled out of its environment and placed under the magnifying glass of public atten-tion? No individual Marine career has ever been studied with the intensity brought to bear in Oswald's case, so the question of com-parison must remain academic. However, it certainly seems unlikely that there have been Marine careers *more* peculiar—or that have invited such a multitude of questions so rarely raised.

Lee Oswald possessed few, if any, of the personality features ordinarily associated with a typical Marine recruit. Nothing in his earlier life suggested that he would have the interest, stamina, or ability to acclimate himself to the strenuous physical requirements of the Marines. Reserved, bookish, somewhat puritanical, Lee Oswald had never demonstrated the temperament or the élan or the physical prowess normally associated with the dashing leatherneck— America's toughest and best recognized symbol of militaristic might. If anything, Lee Oswald had shown colors of a different hue.[18]

As early as high school, Oswald demonstrated his interest in Marxism, on occasion extolling the virtues of communism. Acquaintances recall hearing the young Oswald expound upon the evils of capitalism, once citing his own mother, who had a difficult time earning enough money to raise her three sons, as an example of the "oppressed."[19]

Given the duration and constancy of young Oswald's statements about communism and Marxism, it seems likely that they were true expressions of his personal political beliefs, at least during the early years. In light of his politics and demeanor, it is, under any circumstances, surprising to contemplate his urgent efforts to join the Marine Corps.[20]

After quitting high school just before he turned sixteen, Oswald lied to the Marine recruiting officer about his age, in an effort to join. He was caught in this lie and had to wait a year, during which time he largely idled about New Orleans, before moving with his family to Fort Worth. He continued his left-wing political interests by reading socialist literature, and even wrote to the Socialist Party.[21]

Finally, in October 1956, Oswald made it into the Marine Corps. The men who went through the ten weeks of boot camp with Oswald generally recall him as a quiet, easygoing fellow, who was particularly inept on the rifle range. Indeed, he was known as a "shitbird," the derisive term used to describe a recruit unable to pass his rifle-qualification test. Finally, after repeated efforts and much teasing from his colleagues, Oswald managed to pass his test by a single point. (Some of his fellow recruits recall that Oswald never really passed but was finally given a qualifying mark so that he could continue with his training.)[22]

Despite these problems, Oswald seems to have gotten along well enough with the other young men. However, a common feeling that most of his colleagues recall is that he never, by any stretch of events, fit into any normal mold for a young Marine recruit. One reason was that he continued to express his interest in Marxism and in the Soviet system. It seems reasonable to assume—given the reports of his genial demeanor—that he was not a firebrand in promoting his political beliefs. Still, his fellow Marines good-naturedly poked fun at him over his interests and came to call him Oswaldskowich. Lee encouraged this and would respond with simple phrases in Russian.[23]

By any measure, Oswald was an oddity for the Marine Corps. He was a young man with little physical coordination who could barely learn to shoot, a young man who openly persisted in his interests in Marxism, classical music, and the Russian language. Such wide-ranging interests, if mildly atypical of the average Marine, did reflect the "superior mental resources" noted by a child psychiatrist who examined Lee as a boy. It is surprising that Oswald was tolerated in remarkably amiable fashion by his barracks buddies. It is amazing that upon completion of his basic training, in May 1957, "Oswald-skowich" was promoted to private first class and given a security clearance of "confidential."[24]

It was just after earning his rank and security clearance that the first of Oswald's strange absences took place. He was at Keesler Air Force Base in southeast Mississippi, about ninety miles from New Orleans. He repeatedly secured weekend passes for the stated purpose of visiting relatives in New Orleans, yet his relatives barely recalled seeing him at all. Where he was really going on his weekend passes remains a mystery—a mystery that initiates the pattern that is seen repeatedly in Oswald's life until the weeks preceding his death.[25]

In June, Oswald qualified as an aviation electronics operator, a rating that allowed him to perform basic radar operations for air-traffic control. It was a duty reserved for men who had shown themselves to be of more than average intelligence. This must have been highly gratifying to Oswald after his miserable performance on the rifle range a few months earlier.[26]

Oswald was transferred to a Marine air control squadron known as MACS-1. By September Oswald had joined the other hundred or so men in MACS-1 assigned to the naval air station at Atsugi,

Japan. This was the home base of the CIA's Joint Technical Advisory Group (JTAG), as well as one of the major bases from which the CIA operated its secret reconnaissance flights over Russia. It was Oswald and his fellow radar operators who actually tracked the U-2 spy planes as they took off and returned, although these men officially had nothing further to do with the reconnaissance flights. Despite security regulations to the contrary, any of the radar operators could have stepped outside the radar hut near the end of the runway and photographed the U-2. Whether any did is not known, although it became clear years later that Oswald took pictures with his Minox camera of other military installations and aircraft while he was in the service.[27]

Oswald's pattern of strange absences continued in Japan. His fellow Marines recall that he took his weekend leaves—but they never knew where he went or what he did. Several years later, Oswald would tell a friend that during this period "he had some contacts with the Japanese Communists." Several of his Marine pals have recalled a beautiful Japanese woman in Oswald's company, a woman believed to have been working in a high-priced brothel called the Queen Bee. At a later stage of his Japanese tour, Oswald was reported to be in the company of a Eurasian woman said to speak Russian.[28]

In October, one month before MACS-1 was scheduled to ship out for maneuvers in the Philippines, Oswald shot himself in the fleshy part of his upper left arm with an unauthorized .22-caliber, two-shot derringer that he kept in his locker. The wound was superficial. The incident, which occurred while Oswald was near his locker in the barracks, was officially reported and accepted as an accident. As punishment for having the unauthorized weapon, Oswald lost his rank and was fined fifty dollars. (An additional sentence, twenty days at hard labor, was suspended.)[29]

The incident seemed so contrived—and the wound, according to Oswald's roommate, was "right where it would be if you were going to shoot yourself"—that there was a general assumption that Oswald had shot himself intentionally. The best speculation on his purpose seemed to be that he wanted to avoid going with his unit to the Philippines for maneuvers.[30]

If this is true, the important question is *why* Oswald wanted to remain in Japan. Whatever the answer, Oswald was released from the hospital—no doubt still nursing a sore arm—just in time to sail with his unit to the Philippines. During the maneuvers, which lasted from November until March, Oswald had an opportunity to watch the U-2 in operation at another base—this time at Cubi Point in the Philippines.[31]

In June, sometime after the MACS-1 returned to Japan, there occurred another strange incident involving Oswald. In an ostentatious, if uncharacteristic, display, Oswald sought out a sergeant in his unit whom he held accountable for the fact that he had been required to remain on mess duty for a greater period of time than usual. Oswald approached the sergeant in the Blue Bird Café and deliberately poured a drink over his head. For this, Oswald was sentenced to twenty-eight days in the brig with hard labor, fined fifty-five dollars, and forced to serve his earlier suspended sentence.[32]

The entire incident was so completely out of character for Oswald that some researchers have long speculated that this may have been a ploy on Oswald's part to remove himself from the mainstream— away from his fellow unit members. This could provide him with a suitable amount of time for some sort of espionage training. This presumption would hold if the recruitment was made by the American side. On the other hand, it could provide an opportunity to report to American handlers what he had gleaned in those earlier meetings with the Japanese Communists that he mentioned to a friend years later.[33]

These speculative points may never be clarified. However, the sure point is that while in Japan, Oswald engaged in highly uncharacteristic acts, back to back—once shooting himself and once engaging in an unprovoked assault on a man of superior rank. In each instance, Oswald was removed from the routine activities of his unit for several weeks. While military records show Oswald in the hospital and in the brig for the appropriate periods, such records are merely on paper. His fellow Marines who were familiar with Oswald were out of touch with him during these periods and cannot testify that he was actually confined.[34]

Such evidence of espionage activities is, of course, speculative and circumstantial. But it is indisputable that, just as in the cases of the mysterious weekend passes to New Orleans and to Tokyo, it is yet another example of Oswald's finding himself—either by design or circumstance—with the means and opportunity for espionage activity.

There are signs that when Oswald was released from the brig in August, he intensified his associations with his Japanese contacts. In September Oswald—according to accounts that are in some question—accompanied his unit to Taiwan. But, extending a familiar pattern, Oswald was separated from his unit and returned to Japan.[35]

Again, this removed Oswald from the familiar ranks of his unit and placed him in a position with nearly unlimited latitude for unusual meetings or activities. In this instance, after a brief stay at the hospital, Oswald was sent to the base at Iwakuni, where he was observed in the company of the beautiful Eurasian woman who spoke Russian.[36]

At Iwakuni Oswald encountered some Marines he had not seen since radar training—men who had been assigned to a unit different from Oswald's. One of them, Owen Dejanovich, noticed that a striking change had come over Oswald since he last saw him in radar school. Oswald had become hostile in expressing his bitterness about the American system, even to the point of speaking harshly and rudely to his comrades—a style far different from the basically polite disagreement that marked his earlier advocacy of Marxism and the Soviet system.[37]

Oswald left Japan for good in November. After briefly visiting his family in Texas, he reported to a new unit at Santa Ana, California. It was there that at least one of Oswald's skills apparently came to full bloom—his linguistic skill in Russian. In February he took a proficiency examination, which clearly showed that he had grasped the basics of Russian—indisputably one of the most difficult Indo-European languages for any Westerner. More than ever, Oswald spoke openly of his interest in Russia, and he made no secret of the fact that he received Communist and Socialist publications. He began openly studying books to help him in learning the Russian language. He became more outspoken in telling his colleagues of the defects in the American system, particularly when compared to the Soviet system.[38]

Part of this new outspokenness was Oswald's stated interest in Castro and Cuba. He made a trip to Mexico with one of his Marine pals—and while there disappeared for several hours. He also visited the Cuban consulate in Los Angeles and apparently carried on some correspondence with consulate officials. However, the particular area of his interest is not known.[39]

It is hard to judge the true importance of Oswald's showy display of interest in things Soviet. All signs are that the interest was genuine, but there will always be doubters who suggest that his ardor was feigned—that it was all part of a pattern of deception to make his subsequent defection to the Soviet Union seem the logical step of a known malcontent. Under this theory, Oswald would be continuing in an operation sponsored by some branch of U.S. intelligence.*

There was nothing speculative, however, about the fact that, by the summer of 1959, Lee Harvey Oswald had somehow become skilled and comfortable at speaking the Russian language. For the practical purpose of oral communication, he was able to converse for hours in a social setting with a woman who had taken linguistics courses aimed at developing such a skill.[40] This in itself would not seem all that unusual, were it not for the startling fact that there is no record of Oswald's ever having taken any formal course to learn Russian.

Though nothing in the known records indicates that Oswald received language training from the U.S. government, a peculiar reference was made by Warren Commission General Counsel J. Lee Rankin at an executive session in January 1964. Rankin told the commission members that the staff was trying "to find out what [Oswald] studied at Monterey School of the Army in the way of languages."[41] This famed school (now the Defense Language Institute) was then—and is now—the U.S. government's top language-training facility, primarily for its military personnel slated for overseas service. It is not clear why Rankin had the impression Oswald attended the school, but his comment was made following considerable study of Oswald's military background. The executive session was classified top secret until 1974.[42]

In any event, one thing is clear: somehow, somewhere, with someone, Lee Harvey Oswald had become fluent in Russian. And as with

---

*A former CIA finance officer, James B. Wilcott, testified to the HSCA that while stationed in Japan in the early sixties, he heard from other CIA personnel that Oswald was working for the agency in Japan while in the Marine Corps. Wilcott, who has been associated with CIA critic Philip Agee, was unable to provide the HSCA with any specific details. The committee concluded that Wilcott was "not worthy of belief."[43]

so many things in his life, it would serve him quite handily—and right away.

Soviet Sojourn

Bound for Moscow, the passenger train bearing Lee Harvey Oswald churned eastward from Finland, through Leningrad and across a vast sweep of Russia. Alone, Oswald had crossed eight borders. His papers were all in order—in supremely good order—as he glided out of the United States and through checkpoints at France, England, Finland and, finally, into the USSR. When he crossed into the Soviet Union on October 16, 1959, it was less than five weeks since he had signed papers severing him from active duty in the Marine Corps. On October 31, he walked into the U.S. embassy in Moscow, demanded to renounce his citizenship, and declared his intention to provide military secrets to the Soviet Union and to become a Soviet citizen. Former Marine Oswald's defection as an act of extraordinary defiance was shocking in 1959. In light of Oswald's destiny, the act was to become a primary ingredient for the most unfathomable mystery of this century.[44]

The implications of Oswald's defection cut in two directions, with each possibility holding promise for fearsome ramifications. Oswald's ease of passage can be cited as evidence that he had been recruited by the Soviets—probably while in Japan—and that KGB officials, expecting Oswald, made it possible for him to pick up the necessary papers on short notice during his five-day stay in Helsinki.[45]

The other argument goes that he was really working for some agency of the U.S. intelligence services and that the Soviet intelligence officials only *thought* they had recruited Oswald. In reality, this argument holds, Oswald was working for the United States and only pretending to defect to the Soviet Union. This supposedly would explain the ease of Oswald's passage out of the Marine Corps, from the United States, and into the Soviet Union.[46] Somewhere in this labyrinth, most people believe, the truth lies buried.

However, the only two official investigations of Oswald's defection—those of the Warren Commission and the House Select Committee—both apparently found neither of these possibilities likely. It was far more likely, the official versions suggest, that Oswald was acting purely on his own motivations and, perhaps even more surprising, acting purely on his own resources.[47] If that is the case, Oswald has still not been properly recognized as a man with exceptional capabilities. It would take a special ingenuity to orchestrate such a logistical performance *alone*—without experience, education, or ample money. Whatever Oswald's motive, his journey and defection were not undertaken in reckless haste.

Oswald's first known step toward defection occurred in March 1959, when he quietly applied for admission to the Albert Schweitzer College in Switzerland for the spring term of 1960. About five months later, Oswald applied for and received an early discharge from the Marine Corps, claiming he was needed at home to take care of his mother. Marguerite Oswald collaborated unwittingly with her son's false claim that she was suffering from physical hardships that required his presence and assistance.[48]

Seven days before Oswald was discharged from the Marines to care for his mother, he applied for a passport for the stated purpose of traveling through Europe and eventually attending school in Switzerland. On September 14 he arrived in Fort Worth, where he stayed with his mother for three days, gave her a hundred dollars, and bade her farewell. He told her he was going into some sort of export-import business. By September 17 Oswald had reached New Orleans and booked passage on the freighter SS *Marion Lykes*. He set sail for France on September 20.[49]

For the next sixteen days, Oswald was aboard the ship. There were only three other passengers—an older couple and Oswald's cabin mate, one Billy Joe Lord, a similarly bookish young Texan on his way to study in France. It would seem likely that Lord and Oswald had a good bit in common and that the two young men would have discussed their similar interests. Not so, according to Lord's published statements to investigators following the assassination. After spending a period of time teaching in Japan, Lord is now a schoolteacher in Texas. According to Lord's affidavit to the Warren Commission, the two young men hardly spoke to each other during the sixteen days. When they did it was about matters of no substance.[50]

It is, of course, extraordinary that no greater effort was made by officials to draw out Lord, since he probably spent more time with Oswald than any other person during the period just prior to Oswald's defection. However, Lord has insisted numerous times to this author and to other researchers that he will not elaborate on his original terse statement. At other times, Lord has said that he gleaned nothing from Oswald on their long voyage and for that reason he has nothing more to say.

Finally, in 1983, Lord consented to an interview with the author in which he offered additional details about his journey with Oswald. "He avoided me like the plague," Lord reports, even though their bunks were only five feet apart. Lord had the impression that Oswald had expected to be assigned to a private cabin and was sharply irritated over being placed with someone else.

At their first meeting, during which Oswald ridiculed Lord for having a Bible among his possessions, Oswald challenged Lord on religion: "How can you believe in God? Life is purely a material process." The ensuing debate, Lord insists, was their only substantive conversation. Even though Lord constantly prowled the ship, he never saw Oswald except for meals and in their cabin at night. He has no idea where Oswald spent his time.

The last mental picture Lord has of Oswald is perhaps the most appealing. Lord was in the cabin trying to press some pants and shirts. Oswald, whom Lord recalls as being very clean and neat about everything, came across the cabin and offered to help press Lord's clothes. "It was one of our brighter moments," Lord recalls.

As the ship was about to land in France, Oswald asked Lord to tell him how to say, in French, "I don't understand." Lord went over the phrase several times until Oswald could say it without difficulty. Given what Lord had seen of Oswald on the trip, he assumed the strange young man wanted to have the French phrase ready in case people tried to bother him.

Lord learned of Oswald's defection weeks later when his mother, back in Texas, mailed him a newspaper clipping. Mrs. Lord had recognized Oswald as being the person her son described in his letters home as his cabin mate aboard the ship. Lord had written that he would like to pitch Oswald overboard and that then his trip would have been perfect. Upon hearing the news of Oswald's defection, Lord says that he was "surprised but not shocked." By this time, Lord had become deeply involved in his studies and gave little additional thought to Oswald's defection.

Back in the United States, the Marine Corps instantly realized the security implications of Oswald's defection. Communication codes that Oswald would have known for tracking aircraft were changed for precautionary measures.[51] Some of Oswald's former Marine Corps colleagues later told of an investigation by civilians at Oswald's last Marine post in California.[52] Despite these moves by U.S. authorities to assess and minimize the potential damage of Oswald's defection, Billy Lord insists that he was never interrogated by anyone about his voyage with Oswald until after the assassination.

Had the authorities questioned Lord, they would have learned of the peculiar events that happened to him in France soon after Oswald's defection—events Lord has not made public until now.

A few weeks after getting settled in France at Tours, Lord was befriended by an older man who began to cultivate a rather intense friendship. Almost every day, for weeks on end, Lord was invited to the man's apartment to visit. The man was highly cultivated and seemed to have ample funds, though the source of his money was not clear to Lord. The two conversed on a great variety of subjects, ranging from philosophy to geopolitics.

Lord enjoyed the attention and the opportunity to converse with such a worldly fellow. However, he notes that he is not given to casual friendships and that, by nature, he has never devoted much of his time to socializing with others. Lord was struck then, as he is now, with the fact that this man singled him out from so many other students for these long visits almost every day.

Then, one evening at the height of this blossoming friendship, the man informed Lord that he once "had been honored in the Soviet Union for some work he had done as a young Communist." He said that in connection with receiving this honor, he had met Premier Khrushchev.

"This sudden revelation blew my mind," says Lord. "He was very serious as he told me this. It was almost as if he were confessing. It was an emotional thing for him, and he had tears in his eyes."

Lord later concluded that it was possible the man was a Soviet agent. Because he cannot be certain about such a serious charge, Lord refuses to identify the man beyond saying that he was not of Soviet, French, or American nationality. Lord *did* describe these events to an investigator from the Select Committee, but there is no hint in the published HSCA records that Lord was even interviewed, or that this matter was pursued.

The relationship with the man continued until Lord returned to the United States in June 1960. When Lord went back to France in 1961 for more schooling, he dropped in on his old acquaintance by surprise. The man was markedly less friendly toward Lord than in the past. He seemed preoccupied with cultivating the friendship of a young American Army officer stationed there.*

Lord states that he and the man never discussed his voyage with Lee Oswald. In retrospect, Lord wonders whether the man might have been assigned by Soviet intelligence to place himself in close contact with Lord to see what, if any, contact U.S. authorities would make with Lord to inquire about his knowledge of Oswald on his voyage to defection. In the event that Oswald was a genuine defector, it would stand to reason that the U.S. authorities would conduct such an inquiry of Lord. In the event that the Soviets were considering Oswald as a potential asset—or trying to judge whether he was a false defector on a mission—then it would be logical to try to learn whether U.S. officials contacted Lord, the person Oswald spent sixteen days with shortly before defection. If that was the purpose of the stranger's befriending Lord, it supports the old proposition that the KGB took a very keen interest in Oswald. Moreover, the absence of any debriefing of Lord by U.S. officials could have caused serious questions with the Soviets about whether Oswald was a genuine defector.

Oswald's ship docked at Le Havre on October 8, and the next day he traveled by boat train to Southampton. The Warren Commission states that Oswald flew to Helsinki on October 9, the same day he arrived in England. Oswald's passport, however, clearly shows that he did not leave England until the *next* day, October 10. These dates present quite a problem for the official version of events, for Oswald *also* checked into a Helsinki hotel on October 10—a practical impossibility given the timetable of the only direct flight from London to Helsinki.[53]

This contradiction in times and events was examined by the Select Committee, which finally gave up in its quest for a resolution.[54] There is no doubt that Oswald was moving very fast during that

---

*The inevitable question arises as to whether there was some homosexual aspect to the man's activities. Lord insists that he was never aware of any such interests on the man's part and that he seemed to have a very active social life with women. "He was sort of a playboy and always had girls around," Lord says.

period, but how he managed—according to the official version—to be in London and Helsinki at the same time seems downright supernatural.

Everything that is known about Oswald supports the proposition that he was exceedingly careful, even tightfisted, with his money. One reason, surely, was that he usually had so little of it. In practically all his movements, Oswald can be found at the cheapest hotel or rooming house. He nearly always used the cheapest form of transportation. However, on the occasion of his journey to the Soviet Union—traveling on funds that many observers feel were surely augmented by an unknown hand—Oswald broke his custom. Given the limitations of time, Oswald must have taken an airplane from London to Helsinki—one of only two times he was known to have spent personal money on such expensive transportation. Then, once in Helsinki, instead of finding the cheapest room available, he checked into one of the city's most expensive hotels. These movements alone have brought suspicions to the entire pattern of Oswald's strange journey.[55]

Soon after reaching Helsinki, Oswald took steps to make his way to the Soviet Union. He visited the Soviet consulate. His visa was approved and issued in what appears to be a near-record time—two days. (The Warren Commission determined that the shortest normal time was one week.) The HSCA examined the details of the procedure and found that such rapid issuance was at least *possible* under the prevailing circumstances and that the swift action "was not indicative of an American intelligence agency connection." The committee added: "If anything, Oswald's ability to receive a Soviet entry visa so quickly was more indicative of a Soviet interest in him."[56]

This, of course, again raised the question of *why* the Soviets might have an interest in Oswald—and whether the interest was stimulated by some counterintelligence concoction sponsored by U.S. intelligence. An observer is, again, brought back to the same maddening "wilderness of mirrors," a phrase once used by James Angleton, the dean of CIA counterintelligence, to describe such a maze of espionage.[57]

As if these events were not peculiar enough, one of the early acts by Oswald after reaching Moscow was to slash his wrist in what he claimed was a suicide attempt. Whatever the actual motive, the dramatic act created precisely the same effect as Oswald's earlier incident of shooting himself in the arm: he was removed from circulation and placed in a hospital for treatment and observation.[58]

Oswald's diary of his stay in the Soviet Union—which the Warren Commission declared not to be a bona fide contemporaneous account—states that the suicide was attempted out of Oswald's depression over his initial rejection by the Soviet officials. If the official account is accepted, Soviet officials told Oswald they did not want to talk to him or to hear about the military secrets he offered to give them. However, following the alleged suicide attempt and Oswald's stay in the hospital, Soviet officials decided to allow Oswald and his military secrets to remain in the Soviet Union.[59]

It was the last day of October when Oswald marched into the American embassy and rejected his U.S. citizenship. Soon after that, he gave an interview to an American reporter in which he outlined his philosophical reasons for defecting. He wrote to members of his family and included in one letter a ringing, rhetorical affirmation of communism.[60]

In December 1959 he dropped out of sight for more than a year. No friends or relatives in the United States heard from him.[61] Oswald's activities are known today only because of a reconstruction, following the Kennedy assassination, of events—a reconstruction based, often, on the most questionable of sources.

By these accounts, it was a year in which Oswald received extremely favorable treatment. In early January he was sent to Minsk and put to work as a metal worker in a radio and television factory. But he was no ordinary metal worker. While there was a Soviet policy of subsidizing defectors, it is still not fully understood why his economic circumstances were so exceptionally favorable. His factory salary was subsidized to the extent that he was receiving as much as the manager of the plant where he worked. In addition, he was given much better living quarters than his co-workers, a deviation from communism that brought no known objections from Oswald. "I'm living big and am very satisfied," Oswald wrote in his diary. Indeed, it seems to have been the only time in his life that he had an ample supply of money.[62]

However, Oswald's diary—which contains some anachronisms that prove it is not a purely contemporaneous account—chronicles a growing disillusionment with his life in the Soviet system. He even complains in the diary that there is no suitable place for him to spend his money. Even though the diary is *not* Oswald's spontaneous account, someone has developed a convincing progression of disillusionment over his years in the Soviet Union.[63]

The spring of 1961 brought Oswald what appears to have been a genuine bright spot—his introduction to Marina Prusakova, a lovely young woman with impressive credentials as the niece of a lieutenant colonel in the MVD, the domestic intelligence service of the Soviet Union. Oswald's introduction to this woman occurred a month after he had informed the American embassy of his desire to return to the United States. Trained as a pharmacist, Marina was heartily impressed by the unusual life-style Oswald enjoyed, especially the relatively spacious apartment that a young couple normally could not expect to acquire upon marriage. Marina was impressed with Oswald and, when she first met him, found his Russian so fluent that she simply believed he was from a different Russian-speaking region. She called him Alik. Their marriage took place in April 1961, less than two months after they met.[64]

Almost immediately Oswald began to intensify his efforts to return home with his new bride. (The American embassy in Moscow had received his first request for readmission to the United States in February.) Under normal circumstances during those years, it was very difficult for someone in Marina's position to leave the Soviet Union. In Oswald's case, he was in the supposedly peculiar position of now having to tell the Americans that *really* he wasn't all that keen on communism after all and that, more importantly, he was never even seriously debriefed by the Soviet secret police. He took the position that he never passed any military secrets. It is a tossup whether Lee or Marina had the more unorthodox situation.[65]

But as it turned out, this mattered very little. By the spring of 1962, all their papers had been approved. On June 1, Lee and Marina—their three-month-old daughter swaddled and in her mother's arms—began their journey to Oswald's homeland. On the surface, their passage seemed no more complicated than that of two vacationers returning from a European holiday. The young couple had managed to secure the full blessings of both governments. Marina later told the Warren Commission that the Soviet government never even asked her to give a reason for wanting to leave her native country.[66]

In reality, Oswald had spent over a year exchanging letters with

U.S. officials paving the way for his return—while seeking assurances that he would not be prosecuted. He presumably received everything he requested. Because of Oswald's shortage of funds, the U.S. State Department arranged a repatriation loan for him. Moreover, the State Department overruled strong objections by the Immigration and Naturalization Service to Marina's entry into the United States. Oswald's U.S. passport had been returned to him in Moscow a year before, with little fuss, by the same consular officer upon whose desk Oswald had slapped it down twenty months earlier.[67]

The Oswalds reached New York by ship on June 13, 1962. They were met by a Travelers' Aid Society representative, who helped them through Customs. The local welfare service found them a hotel for the night. There is no convincing indication that anyone from the FBI or the CIA made contact for the possible purpose of debriefing the Oswalds upon their arrival. (There is continuing speculation that Oswald may have been debriefed on his layover in Holland while en route to the United States, but there is no substantiation of this point.) The next day they flew to Love Field in Dallas, where they were met by Oswald's family. They drove to Fort Worth and moved in temporarily with his brother.[68]

The thirty-three months of Oswald's absence from Texas and from his family contained enough mystery for any one lifetime. Few believe that particular period will ever be understood. But for young Lee Oswald, assuming that *he* knew what was going on, the strands of the web were beginning to tangle.

When taken all together, the facts of Oswald's Soviet sojourn— and his smooth-sailing return—raise coincidence to a rare art form. The detailed truth of Oswald's time in the Soviet Union will probably never be known. It is possible that someday the answers will emerge with the coming of a new defector from the KGB. But it would seem that even truth—regardless of the purity of the wrapping—will be met with massive skepticism.

Indeed, a KGB officer named Yuri Nosenko defected to the West in early 1964 and claimed to have been in charge of the KGB file on Lee Oswald.* Nosenko assured his American CIA hosts of two

---

*Nosenko had made his first contact with U.S. officials much earlier—on June 3, 1962. That was two days after the Oswalds left the Soviet Union.

basic propositions. First, the KGB had not the slightest operational interest in Oswald and never even debriefed him. Second, when Oswald and his wife left the Soviet Union, Oswald had no intelligence connections with the KGB. The thrust of the second point was that since Oswald was not working for the KGB, that agency had nothing to do with the man officially believed to have pulled the trigger and, therefore, nothing to do with the murder of President Kennedy.[69]

As it happened, Yuri Nosenko's version of events was just what officials investigating Oswald wanted to hear. Nosenko's account was accepted by the FBI and the CIA. It was used to support the official conclusions pertaining to Oswald and the Soviet Union—that there had been no sinister relationship.[70]

But there was so much wrong with Nosenko as a defector that from the time of his arrival there were serious reservations about his legitimacy. The reservations spawned a debate that grew into a raging controversy which consumed the CIA for years. While Nosenko's supporters claimed he was telling the truth, his detractors insisted that, among many other complicated matters, he had been sent with a story tailored to exonerate the Soviet Union from any intelligence connection with Oswald. For over three years Nosenko was held under hostile detention while CIA officers worked to break his story.[71]

In the end, his image badly tarnished, Nosenko held on to his thin thread of acceptance. And his support, remarkably solid, seemed unweakened despite a House Select Committee conclusion that it was "certain Nosenko lied about Oswald."[72] Even Nosenko's greatest supporters would probably agree that no other defector has ever won acceptance after such bitter denunciation and suspicion. Any future defector from the KGB who comes bearing the "truth" about Oswald will doubtless encounter the harshest scrutiny by those on all sides of the question.

So, in the absence of the establishment of truth about Oswald's Soviet sojourn, there is the strange and great range of coincidence. The first investigators to perceive the difficulties were members of the Warren Commission staff—though, in the end, no genuine resolution of the contradictions was ever reached. General Counsel J. Lee Rankin summed up Oswald's year in Minsk when he made the following statement to the commission in executive session:

"That entire period is just full of possibilities for training, for working with the Soviet[s], and its agents."[73]

Indeed, Oswald's suspicious activities in the Soviet Union began almost upon his arrival in Moscow. The KGB would undoubtedly have had a great interest in Oswald's firsthand knowledge of the top secret U-2 flights—America's primary espionage tool against the Soviet Union.* The Soviets were aware of the overflights by the U-2, and they were known to be working hard to develop the capability to bring it down. It is extremely noteworthy that the second U-2 to fly over the USSR following Oswald's defection—piloted by Francis Gary Powers—was shot down in May 1960. The incident turned into an international humiliation for the United States when President Eisenhower was caught in public lying to the Soviets about the purpose of the spy flight.[74]

In view of this, it seems quite likely that Oswald was extensively debriefed after renouncing his American citizenship.[75] It is even logical that the debriefing could have begun at the time of Oswald's hospitalization for his alleged suicide attempt, during the days immediately before turning in his American passport. Support for this speculation appears in a December 1963 CIA memo, released many years later:

> First, there is no doubt that Oswald was debriefed by the secret police shortly after his arrival in Moscow. They were interested in him not only because he was a political defector, but also because he boasted publicly . . . that he intended to tell the Soviets "everything he knew" about Marine Corps radar installations. . . . This included the location of all radar units and their secret call signs, authentication codes and radio frequencies—all of which knowledge was grist for the Soviet intelligence mill.[76]

Whatever happened during the earliest period of Oswald's stay in the Soviet Union, it clearly appears to have paved the way for his extraordinary VIP treatment in Minsk. While there are a few

---

*An example of such interest is found in the testimony of Stanislav Levchenko, a KGB major who defected to the United States in 1979. He told the House Intelligence Committee of current Soviet policy to interrogate and debrief even the lowliest of American military personnel. Stated Levchenko: "We are talking about GIs who can provide low-level information, such as who his platoon commander is . . . and what kind of rifle he was using."

parallels between Oswald's treatment during that period and the treatment given other American defectors, the treatment was hardly comparable. To the Soviets, clearly, Oswald was a very special case. *Why* is not nearly so clear.

And the most pertinent question: Whose man was he anyway?

Nothing about Oswald's time in the Soviet Union is more peculiar and beguiling than his marriage to Marina, a woman whose recollections of events have, over the years, rolled around like quicksilver. Without much question, Marina was the most damning witness against Oswald produced by the Warren Commission. She was used to fill the gaps in Oswald's life and personality to make him into the cold-blooded assassin the commission was certain he was—a certainty on the commission's part unhampered by the absence of solid evidence to support the thesis.

But Marina—prodded by pressures that surely *were* irresistible to someone in her position—was conveniently facile in forgetting and recalling events as needed.*[77]

In the end, Marina's testimony was vital in establishing Oswald as the figure convicted by the Warren Commission. Specifically, she gave detailed accounts to suggest Oswald's capacity for violence— his supposed practice with the Mannlicher-Carcano rifle and photographs of Oswald with the official assassination weapon.†

There are manifold problems with taking Marina seriously, but the most basic trouble lies in the inconsistency of her testimony. Clearly, at first the Warren Commission pitied her and demonstrated compassion toward her. They viewed her as a young, terrified woman, the mother of small children, buffeted about in a strange and hostile country. They seemed to consider her an innocent and helpless creature tossed about in the wake of her husband's terrible acts.[78]

In the end, however, one characteristic of Marina's became well

*Today there is solid documentary evidence to support old suspicions that the Immigration and Naturalization Service pointedly—at the direction of the FBI—threatened Marina in 1963 with expulsion to the Soviet Union—no doubt a powerful impetus for her to recall events in a manner both supportive and convenient, if highly suspect.

†One of Marina's most elaborate tales for illustrating Oswald's capacity for violence concerned an occasion when Richard Nixon was supposed to be in Dallas. According to Marina's story, Oswald tried to leave the apartment with a pistol, the suggestion being that he was setting out to try to kill Nixon. Marina supposedly saved the day by shutting her husband in the bathroom. It was later learned, however, that Nixon was not even in Dallas on the date in question.[79]

established. Not only were her accounts often contradictory and inconsistent, but it was clear that, put simply, she was a natural (if not particularly skilled) liar. As early as February 1964, the Warren Commission staff was catching on to Marina as "cold, calculating, avaricious."[80]

A Warren Commission staff memo written in February 1964 states flatly that "Marina Oswald has repeatedly lied to the Secret Service, the FBI, and this Commission on matters which are of vital concern to the people of this country and the world."[81]

Ironically, the lies Marina was telling were the "facts" the Warren Commission wanted and needed. So, much of what Marina said was accepted and used to support the official version—just as the highly challenged tale of Yuri Nosenko was accepted in the same fashion, even if not quite in time for use in the Warren Report.

Today, Marina lives quietly in a Dallas suburb. Her two daughters by Lee Oswald are in college, the older one hoping to launch a career in journalism. Marina remarried many years ago and sought to build a new life. Still, she maintains a discreet interest in the events of 1963. She tells friends that she, like so many other Americans, believes that Lee Oswald was somehow a pawn in a conspiracy.[82] Given her record for honesty in these matters, however, it really doesn't matter what she has to say at this point; any truth would be indistinguishable from her past lies and contradictions.

Considering Marina's vital role in building the case for Lee Oswald as the lone assassin, it is worth considering several of the more astounding "facts" of her life as a Soviet citizen. Marina's own family origins—the identity of her father, for example—are in much dispute, due in large part to her own shifting accounts. However, it is certain that at the time of her marriage to Oswald she was living with an uncle who was a lieutenant colonel in the MVD and a member of the Communist Party. Even though she was trained as a pharmacist, she worked, immediately after graduating, only one day at her profession. Abruptly, she stopped her duties and went on a long "holiday." Toleration of such behavior reflected either a highly privileged position in Soviet society—or a key role in some purposeful intelligence operation.[83]

It is ironic, if not significant, that the period of Marina's several-month "holiday" happened to coincide almost precisely with Oswald's arrival in Moscow for the purpose of defection.[84] Marina's subsequent connection with Oswald—and the extraordinary haste with which they married—raises the question of whether Marina might have played some intelligence role in terms of Oswald. Indeed, during the early sixties, the KGB was known to be getting minor spies to marry outsiders and return with them to the West.[85]

These suspicions about Marina were heightened considerably by a CIA document released under legal pressure in 1976. In studying Marina's history, the CIA became aware of a "holiday" she took in the fall of 1960 at a government "rest home." In analyzing Marina's address book, the CIA located an acquaintance she had made at a certain address when she was on her 1960 "holiday." A computer analysis of the information yielded the disturbing fact that an American named Robert E. Webster lived at the time in the same building as Marina's acquaintance. Webster was a former U.S. Navy man who had renounced his citizenship in 1959 and defected to the Soviet Union; his defection to the USSR had occurred immediately after Oswald's, and Marina subsequently displayed indirect knowledge of Webster's defection.[86]

It could, of course, be mere coincidence that Marina Prusakova was on holiday and in the immediate vicinity of the two young American military men who had just defected. Or, it could mean that she was involved in some way with official Soviet interest in these Americans. Like her husband, Marina showed a striking ability to be in a particular place at a particular time that tended to compound suspicion and coincidence. There can be little wonder that, together, Lee and Marina generated the most substantial doubts about their real motives.

The official version of these events contains one proposition more surprising than any other: that when Oswald returned to the United States after thirty-one months of—at the very least—being integrated into Soviet society, the American intelligence services had so little interest in Oswald that he was never debriefed concerning his experiences and observations on the number-one intelligence target of the United States.[87] Also, according to the official version, Oswald was not linked operationally to any segment of U.S. or Soviet intelligence.

For twenty years, this official finding has been viewed with cynicism by nearly any objective observer of American and Soviet intelligence activities. Oswald's defection and return occurred at a time when the CIA was openly debriefing simple American visitors—to the tune of 25,000 annually—as they returned from the Soviet Union. Even tourists' snapshots were reviewed and those of CIA interest copied and filed. Through incredible coincidence, the CIA just happened to have a picture taken by a tourist of Oswald on a Minsk street.[88]

In view of the whole tangled web of prevarication in the assassination investigation, it is not surprising that so few observers accept the official claim that the Soviet sojourn of Lee Harvey Oswald was of no interest to the U.S. intelligence services.

Home

October 1962. The whole world watched tensely as the terrifying days of the Cuban Missile Crisis unfolded. The gut-wrenching standoff was between young, untested John F. Kennedy and wily, aging Soviet Premier Nikita S. Khrushchev. For the first time, the world tasted the reality of two nuclear powers puffed up into seemingly intractable stances. President Kennedy knew that the Soviets were constructing missile launch pads in Cuba that could wage a nuclear attack on the United States, ninety miles away. The President demanded that Khrushchev remove the launch facilities at once. Khrushchev refused, arguing that they were necessary for security.[89]

Rarely has top-grade intelligence been of greater importance to two leaders than in this volatile confrontation. Each side needed desperately to know what information the other possessed—and how sure the other could be of the information he had. In addition to excellent human intelligence sources, President Kennedy had access to frequent photographic surveillance from U-2 spy planes flying secret missions high above Cuba. Kennedy had pictures to authenticate what he was talking about.[90]

In the end, according to conventional versions of events, Khrushchev blinked. The standoff ended. The Soviets at least went through the motions of removing the missiles. Kennedy made a conditional promise not to invade Cuba—to cease official efforts to topple the Castro government with an invasion of exiles. Those critical days were to be the October of Khrushchev's long career. And to an extent still not known with certainty, they may have set the stage for the November of Kennedy's life.[91]

During those dark October days, with Kennedy and Khrushchev locked in a confrontation that could doom the world, Lee Harvey Oswald was working diligently at a Dallas graphic-arts company that was engaged in classified contract work for the Department of Defense, specifically the Army Map Service. Part of the work appears to have been related to the top secret U-2 missions, some of which were then making flights over Cuba. Oswald's employer, Jaggars-Chiles-Stovall (JCS), set the type for place names to go on maps. The actual maps were not in the Dallas shop, but the lists of names set in type could have provided evidence of what was being photographed by the U-2 spy planes. Many employees of JCS recall that during the period in question, Cuban place names were among those set in type.[92]

Despite his record as a defector to the Soviet Union—something presumably unknown to his employers—Oswald had full access to all this information. Personnel working with classified material were supposed to have security clearances, but there are persuasive indications that this formality was not observed. (One convicted bank robber was working with classified material, for example.) Moreover, the working area was so small that it was impossible in any practical sense to force employees to respect the "restricted" signs that were posted in certain areas to satisfy the occasional government security inspector. Indeed, anyone wanting to use the soft-drink machine had to pass through a "restricted" area to reach it. Security was so casual that one day, while walking by, Oswald overheard two employees as they tried to identify the Cyrillic type of Russian place names. Oswald, displaying his fluency in Russian, offered his help.[93]

In addition to his employment at the graphic-arts company doing classified military work, Oswald had in other ways resumed his pattern of murky associations with the world of espionage. It began soon after his return from the Soviet Union, when he went to work in Fort Worth at a small welding company. The shop was within walking distance of the small duplex he rented for his family. According to his supervisor, Oswald performed his job satisfactorily at Leslie Welding for nearly three months.[94]

It was during this period that Oswald became friendly with a Texas oil geologist named George DeMohrenschildt, certainly one of the most mysterious (if not bizarre) figures in the whole Oswald saga. Born of Russian nobility, the sophisticated DeMohrenschildt was a world traveler who had managed to marry into considerable wealth. In numerous ways, DeMohrenschildt veritably *oozed* the trappings of intelligence connections, and there is firm evidence that over his career he was formally associated with more than one intelligence service. His work and travels took him frequently to Europe, Central and South America, and the Caribbean.[95]

It is either ironic or significant that DeMohrenschildt became so involved with Oswald that on the evening of October 7, 1962, in the infancy of the Cuban Missile Crisis, he and his elegant wife and their daughter gathered at the Oswalds' modest duplex apartment in Fort Worth. Ostensibly, DeMohrenschildt had befriended the Oswalds because of ties Marina had established with the Russian community in the Dallas–Fort Worth area.[96]

Whatever the reason for the association, it is difficult to imagine the dashing, debonair DeMohrenschildt, a man who had moved in the highest business and social circles in the United States and Europe, spending time at the Oswald duplex, located near a cavernous Montgomery Ward warehouse. One account of the gathering suggests that Oswald sat quietly, as DeMohrenschildt dominated the group.[97]

It was, however, the very next day that Oswald abruptly quit his job at the welding company. He gave no notice and even failed to remain on the premises long enough to collect his final paycheck— a truly astonishing fact for anyone familiar with the parsimony of Lee Oswald. (He later requested in a letter that the check be mailed to him.) If the official account is accepted, Oswald quit this job with no known promise of other employment. The following day in Dallas, thirty miles away, he presented himself at the office of the Texas Employment Commission, where he was interviewed by Louise Latham, one of the placement officers.[98]

On October 12, 1962, Oswald reported for work at Jaggars-Chiles-Stovall. Coincidence or otherwise, he arrived two days before a U-2 flight ordered by President Kennedy was made over western Cuba. On October 15 the first U-2 photographs showed the launch pads and even one nuclear missile. It cannot be proved at this late date whether JCS was directly involved in support work by producing typeface for the U-2 surveillance photographs and maps of Cuba.

What *is* known with certainty is that the company was in the midst of doing classified work for the Army Map Service, and in performing these sensitive duties it was setting type for Cuban place names. Moreover, there was no physical barrier that prevented any employee from having the full run of the "restricted" area where the classified work was supposed to be done.[99]

What also is known is that, once again, Lee Harvey Oswald was in an enviable position for any self-respecting spy. The particulars of his operational role, if any, remain unknown.

The most obvious question is *how* Oswald managed to get such a job—one potentially much more sensitive than his earlier presence in the radar shacks during the flights of the U-2 from Japan. The answers are varying—and puzzling. Officially, Oswald got the job through normal channels.[100]

The only absolute point provided in the official record is that Oswald was sent to JCS by Louise Latham of the Texas Employment Commission. In an interview with the author, Mrs. Latham had clear recollections of Lee Oswald. She portrayed him as a very mannerly and intelligent young man whom she would readily send out for any promising position for which he was qualified. One would guess that an official investigator would be interested in talking to the person who sent Oswald to a company doing classified work for the United States government. This was not the case.[101]

In fact, the Warren Commission interviewed numerous witnesses aimed at illuminating this point. Mrs. Latham's name comes up at least eight times in testimony as the person who sent Oswald to JCS. Supervisors at JCS also recall that Mrs. Latham was normally the person at the Texas Employment Commission who sent them prospective employees.[102]

However, for reasons that remain obscure, Mrs. Latham was never questioned officially about her connection with Lee Oswald and her sending him to JCS. There is no record that she was among the thousands interviewed by the FBI. As the Warren Commission was busy interviewing her fellow workers about Oswald in March 1964, she abruptly resigned from her job. She and her husband, who as "an internal auditor for the post office" reviewed postal contracts, moved to a small town sixty-five miles south of Dallas. At a considerable cut in annual salary, Max Latham became the postmaster.[103]

In her interview with the author, Mrs. Latham was asked if George

DeMohrenschildt had anything to do with Oswald getting the job at JCS. "Don't believe it," she said. "I sent him [Oswald] over there."[104]

Then Mrs. Latham made several curious statements that seemed almost defensive. She said that she interviewed Oswald "five or six times" and that "I never sent him for a job he didn't get." There is no record that Louise Latham ever sent Oswald to any job other than the one at Jaggers-Chiles-Stovall. Mrs. Latham—a well-educated woman who had worked successfully in New York and Princeton, New Jersey, before going to Dallas—declined to elaborate. Mrs. Latham said that she had never been interviewed on this subject by anyone.[105]

Soon after Oswald went to work at JCS—and just as the Cuban Missile Crisis became public knowledge—another curious pattern resumed in Oswald's life: he vanished from sight. After work each day he would disappear and not be seen again until the next morning. Despite massive investigative efforts, there is no known record of where Oswald was living or what he was doing after work for most of the period from October 8 until November 3, 1962, when he moved with Marina into an apartment in Oak Cliff, across the Trinity River from where he worked in the downtown section of Dallas.[106] By early January 1963, Oswald had resumed another practice that had become distinctive to him in the Marine Corps—the ostentatious pursuit and study of left-wing political literature. He was in touch with the Communist Party in New York as well as the Socialist Workers Party. He offered to contribute to their publications.[107]

February 1963 found Oswald openly denouncing American imperialism to friends and speaking of his own advocacy of communism. Accounts from these witnesses to Oswald's monologues—including the sophisticated DeMohrenschildt—give the impression of a certain zealousness on the part of the former Soviet defector.[108]

As Lee and Marina scurried from one dingy apartment to another, Oswald maintained his closeness with DeMohrenschildt. The external contrast between Oswald and DeMohrenschildt was striking—even astounding. It is hard to imagine two more different men. On the other hand, beneath the diverse external features there may have been substantial common ground that, if ever known, could reveal important keys to the puzzle.[109]

By March, if the official findings are correct on these points,

Oswald's parlor politics entered a new phase. There is convincing circumstantial evidence that Oswald spied upon and photographed the Dallas home of General Edwin Walker, a right-wing extremist whose views had become a rallying point for ultra-conservatives. This also was the month that Oswald, using the alias A. Hidell, is believed to have ordered and received his Mannlicher-Carcano rifle. Separately, he also ordered a .38-caliber Smith & Wesson revolver through the mail, using a variation on the same alias: A. J. Hidell.[110]

On April 10, as he sat alone in his study, General Walker was fired upon. A fourteen-year-old eyewitness to the events outside Walker's house watched two men, after the shooting, get into separate cars and drive away. Police were unable to solve the case.[111]

Seven months later, after Oswald was charged with killing both President Kennedy and Officer Tippit, he was also blamed for the attempted murder of General Walker. This was used by the Warren Commission as a linchpin in its flimsy case aimed at demonstrating Oswald's capacity for violence. The Walker shooting was blamed on Oswald despite the lack of ballistics evidence linking Oswald's rifle to the slug found at the scene. The case against him was based on the dubious evidence supplied much later by Marina Oswald and the DeMohrenschildts. The intensely conflicting evidence used to pin the Walker shooting on Oswald seems even *more* peculiar than the testimony used to establish him as the killer of Officer Tippit.[112]

It was soon after the attempted shooting of Walker that George DeMohrenschildt left Dallas. Whether or not it was related to espionage activities, DeMohrenschildt's departure set off some activities within the CIA aimed at checking on the strange Russian. The Select Committee found that in May 1963, DeMohrenschildt met with the CIA in Washington, though the precise purpose of the meeting is unclear. Soon he and his wife were on their way to Haiti, ostensibly to engage in a business operation with the pro-American Duvalier government there. DeMohrenschildt and Oswald were never to see each other again.*[113]

---

*In 1977 Edward Jay Epstein interviewed DeMohrenschildt in connection with his book *Legend*. Shortly after the interview, which was one of a series that had been scheduled, DeMohrenschildt committed suicide. In 1983 Epstein reported in an article appearing in *The Wall Street Journal* that DeMohrenschildt had told him that the CIA had asked him "to keep tabs on Oswald."

The departure of DeMohrenschildt occurred shortly after Oswald lost his job at Jaggars-Chiles-Stovall for the stated reason that he had initially been hired as a trainee and that his performance had not been satisfactory.*[114] This turn of events set Oswald on yet a new course—again along a path that would take him into areas with even greater trappings of espionage. If ever there was a case of someone's behavior becoming more and more curious, it was Oswald's last odyssey—this time to New Orleans.

Less than a week after George DeMohrenschildt left Dallas, Lee Oswald was aboard a bus bound for New Orleans, the city of his birth. (On that same day, there was a front-page story in the *Dallas Times-Herald* reporting a statement by Vice-President Lyndon Johnson that President Kennedy would visit Dallas in coming months.) If later testimony from Marina is correct, Oswald had with him, disassembled and stashed in his luggage, his Mannlicher-Carcano rifle. He arrived in New Orleans on April 25, 1963, and—after several days that have never been accounted for—moved in temporarily with relatives he had not seen in nearly six years.[115]

The city was seething with perhaps the most heated political activity of its turbulent history. Thousands of exiles from Castro's Cuba filled certain quarters of the city, and the CIA and FBI maintained highly active operations to keep tabs on the exile community. Indeed, until the direct intervention of President Kennedy following the Cuban Missile Crisis, the CIA was operating training facilities near New Orleans to teach exiles paramilitary operations in preparation for a full-scale invasion. With the exception of Miami, it is unlikely that any other American city harbored such intense feelings.[116]

At the height of the United States's unofficial efforts to topple Castro, as many as 300 American intelligence officers and perhaps 2,000 intelligence agents were involved in what has come to be known as the secret war against Castro. Whatever the fine points of the arguments over the best way to destabilize Cuba, the most intense single passion was the hatred for Fidel Castro, the man who had led the fight to topple a corrupt dictatorship and had himself

---

*Actually, Oswald put in a significant amount of overtime work, which hardly suggests that his performance was unsatisfactory.

turned out to be something even worse, a murderous puppet whose strings ran to Moscow. Second in intensity was the hatred for John F. Kennedy, because of his perceived betrayal of the exile cause that led to the humiliating failure at the Bay of Pigs in April 1961.[117]

By May 10, Oswald had gotten a mundane job as an oiler of coffee-making machinery at the William B. Reily Company on Magazine Street, just off Canal Street and only a few blocks from the city's famed French Quarter. Next door was the Crescent City Garage, which held a contract with the U.S. government to service and maintain a portion of its huge fleet of vehicles. This, of course, meant that agents and operatives from government services were constantly dropping off vehicles and picking them up from the garage next door to Oswald's place of employment. Usually reticent, Oswald became quite friendly with Adrian T. Alba, an owner of the garage. Oswald also took an apartment in a residential area about a mile away. He sent for his wife and daughter.[118] (A full account of Oswald's activities in New Orleans appears in the following chapter.)

With these basics out of the way, Oswald settled into what appeared to be serious political activity. If it wasn't *genuinely* serious, it was certainly ostentatious and far-flung. He took firm positions espousing certain causes, and he made sure his statements got on the record. There, in the hotbed of anti-Castro passions, Oswald created a chapter of the pro-Castro Fair Play for Cuba Committee (FPCC). He established "A. J. Hidell" as its secretary.[119]

It was during this immediate period that the garage owner Adrian Alba made an interesting observation. He had just checked out a car to a government man he believed had shown him FBI credentials. Some time later he saw that same car stop alongside Oswald, who was walking nearby. A white envelope was handed out the window to Oswald, who leaned down, received it, and headed toward the coffee company where he worked.[120]

With the establishment of the FPCC chapter, one of Oswald's first moves was to send honorary membership cards to prominent figures in the Communist Party of the United States. As early as June, Oswald was handing out literature in the vicinity of a naval vessel docked at New Orleans. Around July, at Oswald's direction, Marina wrote her second letter to the Soviet embassy in Washington stating that she and her husband wanted to return to the Soviet Union.[121]

Oswald's activity during this period was addressed in the same CIA memorandum that reflected the official belief that the KGB probably *did* debrief Oswald upon his defection to the Soviet Union. The report states: "Long-standing KGB practice generally forbids agents serving outside the U.S.S.R. to have any contact with domestic communist parties or with Soviet embassies or consulates. [Deletion] . . . Yet Oswald blazed a trail to the Soviets which was a mile wide."[122]

If nothing else, this analysis—if accurate—suggests that the one bit of certainty in the confusion is that Oswald was *not* working for the Soviets.

Whatever his genuine motive for apparently throwing in with a pro-Castro group, Oswald could be certain of at least two accomplishments. First, he would become a lightning rod in attracting the most emotional and vocal disagreement with his position. Second, he would be well remembered, standing out as one of the only people in New Orleans willing to express such discordant minority views in public.

It was, therefore, predictable that by August Oswald found himself in a street brawl with some anti-Castro exiles angered by the pro-Castro leaflets he was openly distributing on Canal Street. Oswald was jailed overnight following the scuffle. About a week later, Oswald appeared on a local radio interview show where he expressed his unpopular views.[123]

Toward the end of August, Oswald engaged in a radio debate with one of the Cuban exile leaders with whom he had been in the street scuffle. Whatever Oswald was up to, he firmly established himself as a friend of Castro's Cuba.[124] The question persists: was Oswald really a friend of the Castro cause, or was he working for an element of the United States government that wanted him, for some operational purpose, to *appear* to be a Castro supporter—to ingratiate himself into the pro-Castro circles?

One reason for such enduring suspicions is that the office Oswald claimed for his FPCC activities was in the same relatively small building at 544 Camp Street as the headquarters of Guy Banister, a former FBI man who was deeply involved in managing and coordinating the Cuban exile activities—particularly in areas where the CIA and the FBI could not be officially involved. Banister's secretary insists today that on several occasions she witnessed Lee

Harvey Oswald talking in a friendly fashion to Guy Banister in the office. Her assumption then and now is that Oswald was involved in some of Banister's undercover *anti*-Castro activities.[125]

Previously housed in the same building were the offices of the Cuban Revolutionary Council, the primary group organized by the CIA to bring the various discordant leadership factions of anti-Castro exiles under one united front. (The building was less than a block from Oswald's job and Adrian Alba's garage.)[126]

Another person who frequented this building and worked in Guy Banister's office was a rabid anti-Communist and Castro-hater named David W. Ferrie. A New Orleans–style mad genius, memorable for many reasons, Ferrie was reportedly an associate of Clay Shaw, a prominent New Orleans businessman who was the only person ever brought to trial in the assassination of President Kennedy.[127] (Ferrie and Shaw—and the case against them made by New Orleans District Attorney Jim Garrison—will be examined in the next chapter.)

It is no minor irony that David Ferrie and Lee Oswald were quite possibly acquainted many years earlier, when Oswald attended Beauregard Junior High School in New Orleans. Ferrie was the head of a Civil Air Patrol unit, in which Oswald became a cadet. Although Ferrie and Oswald have never been absolutely linked in this connection, there is sure evidence that Ferrie sought out and befriended certain of Oswald's peers and friends during those years.[128]

Whatever their earlier association, Ferrie and Oswald are known with official certainty to have been in each other's company one day in the late summer of 1963. The scene was a black-voter-registration drive in Clinton, Louisiana, less than 100 miles northwest of New Orleans. The House Select Committee accepted the testimony of numerous respectable witnesses to the presence of Oswald and Ferrie in the area for most of the day, during which Oswald applied for a job at a state mental institution located in nearby Jackson. Many of the same witnesses whom the HSCA found to be credible insist also that Clay Shaw was present with Ferrie and Oswald, but the committee did not find the description of the man believed to be Shaw conclusive. The description of Ferrie, on the other hand, was indisputable.[129]

It is significant that at the height of Oswald's pro-Castro activity, he was found miles away from New Orleans and in the company of Ferrie, a virulent anti-Castro crusader and a man with strong ties to the CIA's efforts to overthrow the Cuban dictator. What Oswald and Ferrie—and possibly Shaw—were doing together remains unknown.

Whatever the truth about Oswald's allegiances, the stage was well arranged for him to pursue his quest for a passport allowing travel to Communist countries. In June Oswald applied at the New Orleans passport office and received his passport the following day. This promptness was odd, considering that Oswald's peculiar international travel habits—defection to an enemy country—might have been expected to cause his application to be considered with extra scrutiny. Among the countries Oswald listed to which he hoped to travel were France, England, Finland, and the Soviet Union—the very route he followed in his 1959 defection. [130]

On the day that Oswald was in the passport office, one of the most rabid anti-Castro Cuban exiles also was there. Orest Pena, the owner of the Habana Bar in New Orleans, appeared to apply for a passport. He would eventually use it to travel to East Germany. (Pena later made this trip, which lasted just one day, and has described it to the author as purely a sight-seeing holiday.) Pena, himself an FBI operative in New Orleans, has described in detail his own controversial evidence that Oswald was also working as an FBI informant. [131]

An obscure bit of published Warren Commission testimony supports the proposition that Oswald was seen once, in the dead of night, at the counter in Pena's Habana Bar. Oswald was in the company of a Latin—perhaps a Cuban—and the scene was memorable because Oswald ordered a lemonade, which the bartender had trouble making. Once served, Oswald regurgitated the drink all over a table in the bar. [132] In any event, Oswald's presence at the Habana Bar is further evidence of his association with the anti-Castro extremists in New Orleans.

While Pena today claims that he knew Oswald in other contexts—and knew him at the time they went to the passport office on the same day—Pena insists that it is purely coincidental that both he and Oswald appeared the same day to make plans for travel to Communist lands, destinations relatively uncommon in New Orleans. [133]

This was far from the weirdest coincidence to mark Oswald's efforts to make travel plans. On September 17 he walked into the Mexican consulate at New Orleans and requested a tourist card that would enable him to enter Mexico. He was issued a card bearing the number FM-824085, which he used later that month when he did go to Mexico.[134]

In its investigation, the Warren Commission deemed it useful to know of others who applied for such tourist cards at the same time as Oswald. (Indeed, it was just such an investigation that turned up the fact that Oswald and Orest Pena made passport applications the same day.) The Mexican government cooperated, but no one on the list of people had any perceivable connection with Oswald or the Kennedy assassination.[135]

However, the tourist card issued immediately prior to Oswald's—FM-824084—was not accounted for. The FBI, in its report, simply noted: "FM-824084—no record." That, it might seem, would close the case. For a long time, it did.[136]

For years critics and researchers expressed suspicion over the missing name for the tourist card issued just before Oswald's. This skepticism was dismissed by commission supporters as another example of the paranoia commonly charged to the community of researchers and critics.

Then, many years later, in an avalanche of released documents, there suddenly appeared a name to go with the tourist card prior to Oswald's. The release of this information was unintentional—a predictable blunder resulting from the massive bureaucratic duplication of documents.

The name, quite innocent in appearance, was that of one William G. Gaudet. There was a flurry of intense examination by critics of this disclosure. If Oswald possessed the fingerprints of intelligence, they found, Gaudet had whole hand prints covering his entire career. His association with the CIA on Latin American affairs went back to the agency's inception.[137]

As the publisher of the *Latin American Report*, Gaudet traveled frequently throughout the regions of keen CIA interest, and his reports to that agency were regular. And, indeed, Gaudet conceded that he traveled through Mexico at the time of Oswald's strange visit there.[138]

Upon the disclosure of Gaudet's name, researchers located him in South Mississippi, where he was living in retirement. They pounced on him with the disclosure that he was issued the Mexican tourist card just prior to Oswald's in sequential order. Gaudet, who did not deny his CIA connections, was angered by the manner in which his name had been disclosed. He stated that he had been aware of Oswald in New Orleans and that he had seen him on the street in New Orleans passing out his pro-Castro literature. He even volunteered that he had seen Oswald in the company of Guy Banister.[139]

Gaudet, who has since died, insisted, however, that he never actually met Oswald and did not know Oswald was in Mexico at the same time he was. Despite the fact that it is certain he and Oswald were at the Mexican consulate on the same day, Gaudet explained that the sequentially numbered tourist cards were a pure coincidence. He staunchly denied that his getting his tourist card had anything to do with a possible CIA assignment involving Oswald.[140]

Given the paucity of known facts, there can only be speculation about these oddities. However, it is possibly significant that, on the very day before Oswald and Gaudet were assigned their tourist cards for travel at the same time in Mexico, the CIA informed the FBI that it was "giving some thought to planting deceptive information which might embarrass the [Fair Play for Cuba] Committee."[141]

That committee, of course, was the pro-Castro group for which Oswald, alone in New Orleans, had been ostensibly working. In this capacity he made use of the alias A. J. Hidell, which was reserved for only the most significant of Oswald's dark movements.[142]

Oswald continued his dichotomous politics through most of September, before setting out for Mexico City. Exactly when and how Oswald left New Orleans has never been officially established. The Select Committee concluded that, given the intensive investigation on this point, it is not unreasonable to assume that Oswald departed by some form of private transportation, presumably in the company of one or more people.[143]

Sometime around September 26 or 27, Oswald made his way to Mexico. The Warren Commission concluded that the real Oswald was the person who boarded a bus in Houston on September 26 and created a prominent profile that would be recalled later by numerous passengers. Considering what is now known about the Oswald activities in Mexico City, it is far from certain who really was on the bus—or how Oswald reached Mexico.[144]

A man conventionally believed to be the real Lee Harvey Oswald crossed the border into Mexico on September 26. The point of crossing and means of travel remain in dispute, since debate persists about whether the Oswald on the bus was the real one or an imposter. Several witnesses—in convincingly corroborative testimony—describe details of a young man on the bus who, it appears rather persuasive, was Oswald. For whatever reason, he was maintaining a high profile—creating impressions that would be vividly recalled two months later, following his arrest for the assassination of the President. The Mexico visit was to last about a week—a period during which there was as much conflict and confusion as any other single period in Oswald's life.[145]

Once in Mexico City, Oswald checked into the Hotel del Comercio at $1.28 per night, a drastic departure from the style he had tasted in Helsinki as he headed for defection to the Soviet Union. Oswald's signature on the hotel-registration form is the only solid indication that he was actually in Mexico City, and even that finding is diluted by reservations noted by the handwriting expert who headed the HSCA panel that examined only a photo reproduction of the signature. Despite the expert's feeling that "there is always some possibility that there are some alterations," the panel concluded that the handwriting was Oswald's.[146]

(While a strong case can be made that the high-profile Oswald carrying on in Mexico City was an imposter, highly convincing evidence also supports the proposition that there was an imposter on the loose back in Texas. A later chapter will explore the evidence that there was an Oswald imposter at work in the United States.)

In Mexico City, the Soviet and Cuban embassies were very close to each other. A man claiming to be Oswald visited them both, his stated purpose being to obtain a visa that would allow him to return to the Soviet Union via Cuba. A large commotion occurred in the office of the Cuban embassy when this man attempted, over several increasingly frantic visits, to secure a Cuban transit visa.[147]

The man, bearing Oswald credentials, presented a veritable portfolio of material aimed at showing he was in sympathy with Communist Cuba. He cashed in all the evidence of his strange pro-Castro activities in New Orleans over the past six months, showing newspaper clippings as well as proof of his association with the Communist Party of the United States.[148]

The presentation was, in the end, too much for embassy officials. They recognized that something in the approach was suspicious. A person with such credentials would, logically, have secured his visa through Communist Party channels. The embassy officers refused to expedite the visa application, which the man insisted had to be done immediately.[149]

But Oswald—or whoever the person was—continued to return to the embassy, bringing new credentials and evidence supporting his argument that his application should be given priority treatment. There were three visits—each one more unpleasant than the last. Finally, officials simply ordered him to get out.[150]

However, by then the embassy personnel had an indelible memory of the persistent young man whose credentials identified him as Lee Harvey Oswald. Less than two months later, when Oswald was arrested for murdering the President, he was, of course, promptly recalled by the personnel at the Cuban embassy in Mexico City.[151]

The two main people who dealt with the Oswald at the Cuban embassy were Consul Eusebio Azcue and his secretary, a Mexican woman named Silvia Duran. Descriptions from both witnesses make it far from certain that the person dealt with in this matter was the real Oswald.[152]

Consul Azcue insisted to the House Select Committee that Oswald was not the man he dealt with that day. He told the committee that the obnoxious visitor was gaunt and blond, a description sharply different from the real Oswald.[153]

Silvia Duran has offered a similar demurral. In 1978 author Anthony Summers arranged to show Mrs. Duran film clips of Oswald during a New Orleans television interview to see if she could identify him as the man who caused the trouble at the Cuban embassy. According to Summers, Mrs. Duran, upon viewing the film of Oswald, stated: "The man on the film is not like the man I saw here in Mexico City. . . . The man on this film speaks strongly and carries himself with confidence. The man who came to my office in Mexico City was small and weak and spoke in a trembling voice."[154]

To add to the confusion, Mrs. Duran, in her description to the HSCA, stated that the man who came to the embassy was "short . . . about my size."[155]

Silvia Duran is about five feet, three inches tall—at least six inches shorter than the real Oswald. Like Consul Azcue, Mrs. Duran told the committee that the visitor bearing Oswald's credentials was gaunt and blond.[156]

At least one other witness to this particular Oswald—a man named

Oscar Contreras—was tracked down by Anthony Summers. Contreras, too, recalled that the Oswald he had seen was shorter than his own height of five feet, nine inches. Another former official at the embassy told the HSCA that, from the moment of the man's first appearance, he believed that his presence was a "provocation."[157]

Whatever was going on at the Cuban embassy, the confusion was far from over.

David Atlee Phillips, a former high CIA officer, has stated that the Cuban and Soviet embassies in Mexico City were under "thorough" surveillance by the CIA. The Cuban government confirmed this to the HSCA.[158] But this conceded surveillance by the CIA has clarified nothing. Indeed, the surveillance has only deepened the confusion.

The only photographs the CIA has ever made public of a person suggested to be Oswald are those of a large, brawny, heavyset man with a square jaw and a crew cut. No one, upon looking at these pictures, can argue that the man is Lee Harvey Oswald. But these were the photographs of "Oswald" dispatched to the FBI by the CIA from Mexico City soon after the assassination. Today, while the CIA agrees the man in the pictures is not Oswald, it has continued to insist that it does not know who the man is.[159]

However, the man appears to be the one described in a CIA memo of October 10, 1963, in which "Lee Henry [*sic*] Oswald" is reported to have "contacted the Soviet embassy in Mexico City."[160]

In the final analysis—and through some of the most complex explanations ever produced—all other surveillance failed also. The CIA has provided the lamest possible excuses for the fact that it has no evidence to support Oswald's presence at the Cuban or the Soviet embassy. Moreover, the Oswald who visited the embassies is said to have spoken very poor Russian; the real Oswald was fluent in that language.

To this day, the official version regarding Oswald's presence at the Cuban or Soviet embassy rests upon the murky recollection of the Cuban embassy staff, who disagree on whether the man bearing Oswald's credentials was actually Lee Harvey Oswald.[161]

In the case of the Soviet embassy, the CIA claims that its surveillance was suspended on weekends, explaining why Oswald's presence was not picked up. In the case of the Cuban embassy, the

CIA claims the systems happened not to be working during the period of Oswald's visit.

These lapses, if true, at a period of intense diplomatic strain between the United States and the Soviet Union, suggest an incompetence on the part of the CIA so convenient that it is very difficult to accept. If the CIA had a smidgen of hard evidence to show that the real Oswald was at either spot in Mexico City, such evidence would be the centerpiece of the case to settle once and for all that there was no Oswald imposter at work in Mexico City; the presence of an imposter, of course, no matter how shaded, spells conspiracy.

Many critics believe that if there is a single key to resolving the JFK assassination mystery, it lies in finding the truth about the murky events in Mexico City. The HSCA conducted an intense inquiry into this matter, and staff investigators produced a report of roughly 300 pages. In one of the most frustrating moves the committee made, the Mexico City report was withheld from the committee report and sealed away in the National Archives. The committee report explained that this was done in order to protect the "sensitive sources and methods" used by the CIA.[162]

In 1983, in a nationally broadcast radio program on the anniversary of the assassination, Anthony Summers stated that he had "had sight of that report." He stated that based on his knowledge of the classified report, photographs *were* taken during the supposed visits by Oswald to the Cuban and Soviet embassies and that they had "either been destroyed or were deliberately withheld from the committee." Summers added that the secret report indicated that the existence of these pictures was supported by five CIA officers named in the report.[163]

Summers also told the radio audience that the secret report included details about a "memoir" written by Winston Scott, who was the CIA station chief in Mexico City at the time of Kennedy's assassination. That secret account by Scott, along with the photograph of the real Oswald, was "preserved until [Scott's] death in the early seventies." Summers stated: "Both of these were removed from his Mexico City safe following his death by a senior and renowned counterintelligence chief, and that photograph [has] now, to all intents and purposes, vanished."[164]

If a surveillance photo of Oswald in Mexico City did exist, it is bewildering to imagine *why* the CIA did not promptly turn it over to the Warren Commission to shore up the tenuous official evidence that Oswald was the person who visited the Soviet and Cuban embassies. Possible reasons for withholding the picture would be that Oswald was in the company of another person, or that he was clearly at some surveillance point other than one of the embassies in question. As for the other pictures, it would be significant to know if any of them were of men who *looked* like Oswald, a situation tending to confirm the suspicions about an imposter. (However, given the testimony of the eyewitnesses, there is no reason to believe an imposter necessarily *looked* like Oswald.) Even more significant would be if any were of the "gaunt and blond-haired" man described by Silvia Duran and Consul Azcue. (The committee acknowledged that it "did obtain a photograph of a man whose description seemed to match that given by Azcue and Duran of the 'gaunt and blond-haired' visitor to the Cuban embassy. They each stated, however, that he was not the man they had described as the one who, in the name of Lee Harvey Oswald, had applied for a visa to Cuba.")[165]

The real Oswald was in Dallas on October 3 and about a month later wrote to the Soviet embassy in Washington. He stated that he had not been successful in getting a visa because he "could not take a chance on reqesting [*sic*] a new visa unless I used my real name, so I retured [*sic*] to the United States."[166] The reference to his visa is somewhat ambiguous, but the point is clearly made that Oswald was bashful about using his real identity. Why he should feel reluctant about this is not known—and certainly "Oswald's" behavior at the embassy made no pretense at concealing the identity of the real Oswald. The only logical possibility to explain Oswald's statement, if true, is that he might have been using a name other than his own in Mexico City—perhaps even A. J. Hidell.

Soon after his return to Dallas, Oswald got a job filling orders at the Texas School Book Depository. There have been exhaustive examinations into how he came to be working in a building overlooking Dealey Plaza. In the end, Oswald's getting the TSBD job appears far more routine than the strange events leading up to his acceptance at Jaggars-Chiles-Stovall a year earlier.[167]

Nothing during these days just before the assassination is more singular and teasing than the emergence in 1975 of a copy of a handwritten letter from Lee Oswald to "Mr. Hunt." Dated November 8, 1963, the copy was received by a Texas assassination researcher, after being mailed anonymously from Mexico City.[168]

In 1977 the *Dallas Morning News* obtained a copy of the letter and had it analyzed by three handwriting experts. They reached the unanimous conclusion that the writing was that of Lee Harvey Oswald. However, handwriting experts for the HSCA examined the document in 1978 and reported that "we were unable to come to any firm conclusion" as to whether the letter was written by Oswald. The experts noted that the document was not a sharp reproduction of the original.[169]

In any event, the November 8, 1963, letter to "Mr. Hunt" reads as follows:

> I would like information concerning [sic] my position.
> I am asking only for information. I am suggesting that we discuss the matter fully before any steps are taken by me or anyone else.
> Thank you.
> Lee Harvey Oswald[170]

Observers have adopted different lines of conjecture as to the identity of "Mr. Hunt." One often-mentioned possibility is the late Dallas oil billionaire, H. L. Hunt. Jack Ruby, of course, visited the offices of one of H. L. Hunt's sons the day before the assassination, though there is no solid evidence linking any member of the Hunt family to the Kennedy assassination.[171]

In 1983, however, FBI documents disclosed under the Freedom of Information Act revealed that the FBI had investigated the letter in terms of its being intended for a son of H. L. Hunt, Nelson Bunker Hunt. Results of this investigation are not known to the public.[172]

The truth about the note—and the identity of "Mr. Hunt"— remains a mystery.

Minutes after Oswald was arrested on the afternoon of November 22, police found a Selective Service card in his possession that identified him as Alek James Hidell. It did not matter at that early stage that the card was forged or that, most conveniently, it would neatly correspond with the name in which the suspected assassination rifle was ordered. For the moment, the name on this card—Hidell— was a peg upon which to launch the investigation into the man in custody. The name was fed into various circuits that transmitted it to government agencies to run checks that might yield pertinent information.[173]

In San Antonio, 270 miles south of Dallas, Lieutenant Colonel Robert E. Jones of the 112th Military Intelligence Group consulted his files to see if he had anything on Hidell. Immediately, Colonel Jones discovered that he *did* have a file on A. J. Hidell. In addition to certain other information, the file noted that Hidell was a name associated with one Lee Harvey Oswald.[174]

By 3:15 P.M. Colonel Jones had contacted the FBI and alerted that agency to the link between Oswald and Hidell. He also told the bureau that the complete military file on Hidell/Oswald was available to investigators. Apparently the FBI was not interested in the military intelligence file on Hidell/Oswald, for there is no known record that it was ever picked up. Apparently, the only part of the information that interested the investigators was that Hidell, who ordered the infamous Mannlicher-Carcano, was either actually Oswald or an Oswald associate.[175]

Fifteen years later, after a thorough examination, the HSCA concluded that Colonel Jones's account was credible. The committee stated: "His statements concerning the contents of the Oswald file were consistent with FBI communications that were generated as a result of the information he initially provided."[176]

Specifically, according to Colonel Jones's account, no government agency ever requested the Hidell/Oswald file, even though he told them of its existence on the afternoon of November 22. Colonel Jones himself was never questioned by any investigators until his interviews with the HSCA.[177]

Such dramatic and potentially significant information should, it seems, have been discussed at a higher level than Colonel Jones and the local FBI agents. Yet there is no indication that the Department of Defense ever tried to make these files available to the Warren Commission, despite the general orders from the President for all agencies to turn over all information of any possible relevance to the investigation. Moreover, it is now known that the Warren Commission made several requests of the Department of Defense for all pertinent information—and each time was assured that the request was fulfilled.[178]

It is unfortunate that the Hidell/Oswald file was not acquired by any investigative agency. In 1973, in one of the most outrageous official acts in the whole dismal debacle, the Department of Defense destroyed the Oswald/Hidell records. Five years later, the Department of the Army offered the following explanation to the Select Committee: "The Oswald file was destroyed routinely in accordance with normal files management procedures, as are thousands of intelligence files annually."[179]

No one, so far, has admitted to having a copy of this file, or even notes based on the file.

It is hard to say which is more maddening to historians and researchers—the routine destruction of an unexamined intelligence file on an alleged presidential assassin, or the fact that the Department of Defense defied the Warren Commission by not turning over the file in 1963. The HSCA found the destruction of the files "extremely troublesome" and offered the following observation: "Without access to this file, the question of Oswald's possible affiliation with military intelligence could not be fully resolved."[180]

In light of this, it is ironic that while the HSCA concluded, specifically, that government agencies—including the FBI, the CIA, the Secret Service—were *not* involved in the assassination, it did not offer any such specific exoneration to military intelligence agencies.[181]

In view of these puzzlements, it is worth considering the significant ways in which Oswald used the name Hidell. He is known to have used Hidell while in New Orleans, when he stamped it on his Fair Play for Cuba literature and when it appeared on his fabricated New Orleans FPCC membership card.*[182]

Oswald is also credited with using Hidell when he ordered his Smith & Wesson revolver from a mail-order gun house. He supposedly used the Hidell alias in ordering the Mannlicher-Carcano rifle. Then, of course, A. J. Hidell was the name that appeared on the Selective Service card in his wallet at the time of his arrest. (Incidentally, the forged Selective Service card also bore Oswald's photograph, although this was not a feature of a real card.)[183]

Without question, the name A. J. Hidell linked Oswald to the

---

*Colonel Jones believed that it might have been in this connection that his Military Intelligence Group received information on Oswald. In this instance, Hidell was not used as an alias. It was simply stamped on the literature, and Oswald continued to use his own name (or variations of it) prominently. In any event, since the file has been destroyed, Colonel Jones's observation is speculative at best.

foundation of the assassination case against him—and in so doing established a pattern of sorts. The name was readily connected to the pro-Castro activities of the Fair Play for Cuba Committee. The name was also on the order form for the murder weapon supposedly used to assassinate the President of the United States.[184]

The questions quickly present themselves. Did military intelligence have some special connection with A. J. Hidell? Was there an innocent reason for the presence of the name in the files and the ready cross-reference to Oswald? Given the destruction of the records, it is not likely the truth will ever be known.

There is but one sure point buried in this shifting confusion. If the Hidell evidence on that black Friday afternoon had led the United States to the conclusion that an agent of Fidel Castro had killed President Kennedy—and if there had been rash military retaliation against Cuba—certain elements of the military-intelligence establishment, long frustrated by the official toleration of Castro, would have been neatly satisfied.

Picking at the Puzzle

If the United States government is telling the truth, then none of its known intelligence services ever had any operational interest in Lee Harvey Oswald. Moreover, if the official account is accepted, no known intelligence service found Oswald's thirty-one-month defection to the Soviet Union of sufficient interest to ask him about it, even though other American citizens—simple tourists as well as defectors—were being closely questioned upon their return from the USSR.[185] Contradicting the official account, there is the veritable showcase of positive evidence suggesting a relationship between Oswald and *some* branch of the U.S. intelligence services.

The question of just *what* intelligence role Oswald might have played may never be settled with any wide acceptance. Even the possibilities of how he might have been used invite strenuous debate among experts. With this in mind, it is useful to consider some of the more conventional possibilities:

• *Marine Corps.* Recruited by U.S. intelligence to become a Russophile, to learn the Russian language, to infiltrate Communist groups in Japan and report information to American handlers.

• *Defection.* Part of a program of sending false defectors into the Soviet Union, perhaps to misinform the Soviets as well as to gather information.

• *Initial return.* Standard intelligence debriefing on all aspects of defection. Obliteration of these records after the assassination—records that would have shown Oswald's operational role—left *no* records of even normal interviews, such as those of American tourists returning from the Soviet Union.

• *Dallas.* Fully debriefed on his Soviet sojourn for CIA by DeMohrenschildt. Job at Jaggars-Chiles-Stovall a continuing exercise in operations techniques.

• *New Orleans.* Pro-Castro activities a cover for operational links with one or more elements of U.S. intelligence. Panorama of possible intelligence motives for this include sending him to Cuba or back to Soviet Union for additional duties.

• *Mexico City.* An extension of the New Orleans activities.

These possibilities are within the realm of theoretical connections with U.S. intelligence services. There is, of course, the scenario that calls for Oswald's recruitment by the KGB while a Marine in Japan and for his continuing his training as a Soviet agent during his defection. (This thesis is given full treatment in Edward J. Epstein's *Legend.*) While this thesis may be true, Oswald's continuing posture as a pro-Soviet, according to most respected critics as well as a CIA analyst, is certainly a peculiar adornment for a spy of that stripe. While every commonsense reason justifies the belief that the KGB *did* debrief Oswald upon his defection, Soviet denial of such a debriefing would not automatically suggest that he was their man. (Indeed, the KGB could have suspected Oswald as a false defector, just as so many CIA officers viewed Nosenko when he defected from East to West five years later.)

However the KGB viewed Oswald, there is no reason to believe that his suspected affiliations had a bearing on any operational designs the KGB had for Marina's future in the United States. U.S. intelligence experts on the KGB have long recognized the circumstantial evidence that strongly suggests Marina's role as a "sleeper agent," a KGB operative planted in the United States to be used at a later time. Such a role for Marina would not imply, necessarily, any operational connection between her husband and the KGB. But it seems likely that any role Marina was to play would have been forever quashed when her husband was blamed for the assassination.

Given the massive conflicting evidence on these matters, there is little promise in trying to sort out in precise detail the explanations for Oswald's odd activities. Paul L. Hoch, a veteran assassinations critic, is one of the most respected analysts in the area of Oswald's possible intelligence connections. In 1977 Hoch summed up the picture in a comment that has not lost its pertinence:

> Some of the theories . . . deal with facts which have a sub-
> stantial probability of meaning just the opposite of what they
> appear to mean. For example, if someone says that Oswald was
> working with a team of pro-Castro Cubans, someone else will
> say he was a CIA penetration agent. Ultimately, perhaps, if
> Oswald was working for the CIA, someone will say that the KGB
> had penetrated the CIA. In a mathematical analogy, [one] might
> find himself dealing with a non-convergent series; if you add one
> more term [one more piece of evidence], the whole direction of
> the result changes.[186]

Year after year researchers and critics have found themselves flummoxed by precisely this dilemma. In view of this, it seems far more useful to consider the thrust of general evidence rather than fine points. In fact, a powerful case can be made that the slow dribble of minutiae leaked from intelligence coffers over the past two decades has kept critics and researchers safely staring at the trees instead of the forest. Fitting the minutiae together, slowly and tediously, brings Oswald's possible intelligence activities into focus, but the overall picture is far from clear.

In weighing the possibilities of Oswald's intelligence connections, the candidate that surfaces the most frequently is military intelligence. It is that element, after all, that the Select Committee failed to exonerate—a shocking negative indictment that has received almost no public attention. Perhaps the best analysis of the pivotal importance of this possibility is found in an unpublished manuscript by four assassination critics. They write:

> If Oswald were involved in an unauthorized intelligence mis-
> sion, sponsored by a Defense agency but kept secret from the

rest of the intelligence community, many mysteries could be explained. Such an association would not implicate the U.S. military in the Kennedy assassination. On the contrary, any agency which decided to murder the President of the United States would presumably not choose an assassin who could ever be traced to its doorstep. But a super-secret link between Oswald and a covert military intelligence mission would explain the curious behavior of many agencies in the post-assassination investigation.[187]

The authors—all of them among the most diligent and respected of the critics—have suggested that military intelligence agencies, until about 1958, controlled U.S. agents, such as false defectors working in the Soviet Union. According to the authors:

> It remains a distinct possibility that the Department of Defense was reluctant to yield control of this crucial intelligence-gathering capacity to a rival agency. In short, it might have continued planting a few agents from time to time—without admitting to the CIA that it was ignoring the official bureaucratic guidelines delineating responsibilities and prerogatives.[188]

The fact that Oswald was believed by officials to be working for *some* agency is supported by an FBI memorandum explaining why the bureau failed to flag to the State Department Oswald's passport—making it possible for his application at New Orleans to breeze through the process in one day. Referring to Oswald, the FBI memorandum notes: "We did not know definitely whether or not he had any intelligence assignments at that time."[189]

This demonstrates, at the very *least*, that even if the FBI did not know Oswald was an operative, it recognized that he apparently had the full trappings of an agent.

Echoes of Oswald's possible connection to military intelligence were heard again in 1978, when Richard Helms, former Director of Central Intelligence, appeared before the HSCA. Helms was asked why it would not have been standard procedure for the CIA to debrief Oswald upon his return from the Soviet Union. Stated Helms: "Because he had been a member of the Marine Corps . . . the understandings were that military officers were handled by the intelligence organs of the Defense Establishment."[190]

While this falls far short of calling Oswald an agent of military intelligence, it does suggest that Helms considered that Oswald somehow retained an official connection with the Marine Corps. In the same testimony, Helms referred several times to the Navy's hypothetical responsibility for Oswald.[191]

There is at least one example of U.S. intelligence recruiting a Marine out of the service in order to work in Cuba—a Marine who served with Oswald in Japan. This man, who is credible on other points, told the author in interviews between 1977 and 1982 that the cover name of the group he worked for was Security Enforcement. He and his fellow mercenaries were never sure of the identity of the real organization, although he said they believed it to be the CIA. Certainly the organization's description sounds much like that of various CIA-sponsored groups now known to have been working for the overthrow of Castro during those years.

The recruit interviewed by the author is still in this kind of work and has acknowledged his recruitment on the condition his name not be disclosed. His account supports the proposition that U.S. intelligence did, at least in this one instance, recruit a Marine acquaintance of Oswald as he mustered out of the military service. While this illustration proves nothing about Oswald in particular, it does demonstrate that such recruitments were going on and were *possible* in the case of Oswald.

Additional support for the recruitment possibility is found in the experience of Marine Sergeant Gerry Patrick Hemming, a notorious figure in many CIA-backed exile activities. Hemming claims that he was assigned to radar operations at Atsugi shortly before Oswald and that he was recruited by naval intelligence as he mustered out of the Marines. He told Anthony Summers in 1978 that he met Oswald in California once in 1959 and, given the circumstances of the introduction, assumed Oswald had already been recruited.[192]

Furthermore, while interviewing naval intelligence personnel for a book about a defector from the Soviet navy, this author encountered a startling assertion from a high naval officer serving in an intelligence capacity. The officer, who served as an intelligence man in Moscow during the latter days of Oswald's defection, stated: "I felt that there was a CIA man under cover in the Naval attaché's office that I believe was sort of like a handler for Oswald. . . . There was more CIA connection to Oswald than has ever met the eye."[193]

This naval officer, who spoke only with the understanding that he not be named, stated that he never worked for the CIA—only for naval intelligence. [194] Although his statement concerning Oswald cannot be specifically corroborated, the officer proved reliable on other points unrelated to this particular area.

A peculiar incident possibly linking Oswald to the military intelligence was the mysterious telephone call involving Oswald in the Dallas County Jail following his arrest. The first account that emerged from intensely conflicting evidence was that Oswald tried to make an outgoing telephone call to one John Hurt in the 919 area code, which is eastern North Carolina. For years a debate continued about whether the call was really outgoing to North Carolina or incoming to the jail, since the best evidence was on a slip of paper written by a jail telephone operator and, according to one version, thrown into a trash can and later retrieved by a souvenir hunter. The evidence was tainted, to say the least, and the contradictory testimony of the telephone operators only added to the confusion. The speculation was that Oswald, if an agent, might have been trying to contact his control. [195]

When researchers finally found a John Hurt in Raleigh, North Carolina, he proclaimed complete ignorance about the matter. He said he had never known or heard of Oswald before the assassination and that he made no telephone call to Oswald and, of course, had no knowledge of Oswald's trying to telephone him. [196]

This claim was quickly tarnished, however, when researchers discovered that Hurt had a background in military intelligence as well as a law degree. Hurt insisted to researchers that he had no idea why Oswald might want to call him. That only fanned speculation that Hurt—who perhaps had some covert operations connection with Oswald—was keeping the cover. The mystery remained, even though arguments that the call was incoming were as strong as the arguments that Oswald made the call.*[197]

John Hurt died in 1981. A few months later, his wife told the author that Hurt had admitted the truth before he died. Terribly upset on the day of the assassination, he got extremely drunk—a

---

*The existence in North Carolina of training areas for CIA clandestine activities has been confirmed by Victor Marchetti, a former executive assistant to a CIA deputy director. Marchetti also feels there is a strong possibility that military intelligence, too, carried on activities in that area.

habitual problem with him—and telephoned the Dallas jail and asked to speak to Oswald. When denied access, he left his name and number. Mrs. Hurt said her husband told her he never had any earlier contact with Oswald and had been too embarrassed to admit that he got drunk and placed the call.[198] In view of the fact that Hurt's military-intelligence background appears innocent of any deep operational connections, the account by John Hurt's wife makes as much sense as anything else.

It is known that during the years in question the State Department was engaged in a study of U.S. defectors to the Soviet Union and other Communist countries. One of its aims, according to Otto Otepka, the official in charge of the study, was to determine which "defectors" were genuine and which were U.S. intelligence operatives on espionage missions.[199]

In June 1963 Otepka was ousted from his position at the State Department. He was barred from entering his safe or from access to the contents, which included the incomplete study of U.S. "defectors," one of whom was Lee Harvey Oswald.[200]

In 1971 Bernard Fensterwald, Jr., one of the original and most diligent of the assassination critics, interviewed Otepka and asked him what his study of Oswald had concluded. Otepka stated: "We had not made up our minds when . . . we were thrown out of the office."[201]

In view of the official obfuscation on the point of Oswald's possible intelligence links, it is useful to consider two pieces of evidence generated on the day of the assassination—presumably before there was time for any official participants in a cover-up to concoct a unified falsification. FBI Director Hoover told the Warren Commission that one of the bureau's aims in its initial interviews of Oswald was to obtain "information he might have been able to furnish of a security nature."[202] Such a reference suggests that at the earliest moment the bureau had some reason to believe Oswald might have intelligence links.

On the day of the assassination, the FBI asked the CIA for "any information" it had on Oswald. The CIA's official response, according to the FBI, was that "there is nothing in CIA file regarding Oswald other than material furnished to CIA by the FBI and the Department of State."[203]

This CIA statement of denial turned out to be false, as disclosed records readily indicate. The prevarication clearly suggests that there was something so important for the CIA to protect that it was worth lying to the FBI. What is suggested by the FBI's interest in Oswald's possible "information . . . of a security nature" and the CIA's denial of its own Oswald records is an initial assumption that Oswald was something more than a lone nut.

Ostensibly, the CIA first opened a file on Oswald in December 1960. The CIA told the House Select Committee that a file such as the one on Oswald, known as a 201 file, is "opened when a person is considered to be of potential intelligence or counterintelligence significance." Because Oswald was a defector, according to the CIA, he was "considered to be of continuing intelligence interest." Such files are maintained by the "black" side of the agency, the one "responsible for clandestine activities."[204]

The existence of the CIA's memorandum from Mexico City concerning Oswald is now known, of course. That report somehow changed his middle name from "Harvey" to "Henry." The CIA's 201 file on Oswald also used "Henry" for "Harvey," which has been explained only as a clerical error. The common mistake of using "Henry" for "Harvey" in both instances shows that the two must have been somehow keyed to each other. In any event, the Mexico City report is a solid example of an internal CIA report in the agency files on Oswald—despite the agency's specific assertion to the contrary on November 22.[205]

All things considered, the debate over documents actually *in hand* seems futile. Far more important would be knowledge of all the documents that have never come to public light.

One of the most shocking revelations of the HSCA was the disclosure of a February 1964 internal CIA memorandum concerning Oswald's 201 file. The memorandum notes that thirty-seven documents, including twenty-five cables, were missing from the Oswald file. This, added to such a well-established environment of manipulation and concealment, was seized on by assassination critics as hard evidence of the CIA's destruction of records. In the end, however, the HSCA accepted the CIA's claim that the thirty-seven documents were not really missing at all—that they just happened to be checked out of the file on the day the memorandum was prepared. Few critics were satisfied with this explanation, particularly since the thirty-seven documents were never produced for inspection. (It is not known how many were pre-assassination documents.)[206]

Perhaps the most substantive suspicion about Oswald's 201 file concerns the fact that it was not established until more than a year after his defection. This lapse of time has invited the speculation—discounted by the Select Committee—that Oswald's 201 file might be a cover file created to replace an operational file. Suspicions were heightened by the committee's disclosure of some handwritten notes made by the legendary William Harvey, a top CIA officer credited with some of the agency's more grandiose schemes and operations. Harvey's notes, in addressing the most effective way to create secure covers for agents, state: ". . . should have phoney 201 in (files) to backstop (cover), all documents therein forged and backdated."[207]

A persistent question is whether this was the real explanation for Oswald's perfectly innocent 201 file—opened more than a year *after* his defection.

Questions on this point intensified in 1976 with the forced disclosure of a CIA report that in 1960 the agency considered debriefing Oswald. (The author of the memo obviously was referring to activities in *1962*—not *1960* as he actually wrote.) This ran counter to everything the CIA had said on this point. Written three days after the assassination, the report notes that the CIA officers were "particularly interested in the [deletion] [information] Oswald might provide on the Minsk factory in which he had been employed." The report stated that there was interest in the city and in any Soviet citizens Oswald might have known. In every respect, the report suggested the perfectly logical interest critics and researchers for so long had insisted the CIA *must* have had in a person like Oswald—*if* he was not an intelligence agent.[208]

In a separate observation, the author of the CIA report notes that he was also interested in Oswald and Marina as a possible part of a pattern in which Soviet women were "marrying foreigners, being permitted to leave the U.S.S.R., then eventually divorcing their spouses and settling down abroad without returning 'home.'" The report states that eventually the CIA found that there were two dozen similar cases. Again, here was an indication of CIA interest that—though denied—seems completely logical.[209]

One former CIA man actually recalls reading a debriefing report based on a "re-defector" whom he believes to be Oswald. Donald E. Deneselya, who is no longer with the agency, was assigned to the Foreign Document Division, working in an area primarily concerned with the analysis of intelligence. Included in his area of coverage was electronics development in the Soviet Union. Deneselya specifically covered the Minsk Radio Factory, which was the factory where Oswald worked just before his return to the United States in June 1962. In the summer of 1962, Deneselya claims that a debriefing report from a re-defector came to him because the subject of the report had provided details on the place of his employment in the Soviet Union—the Minsk Radio Factory. He also recalls that the re-defector was a former Marine and had returned from the Soviet Union with his family.[210]

There is but one person who possesses these particular biographical characteristics: Lee Harvey Oswald. The CIA has specifically disclaimed Deneselya's recollection.[211]

In the end, it is really not possible even to make good guesses about what was going on with the CIA and Lee Harvey Oswald. Much of the evidence is conflicting and enigmatic. Other evidence is compelling—such as Oswald's close and peculiar association with shadowy George DeMohrenschildt, or his propinquity to William Gaudet on the matter of the Mexican tourist card. Then there is his known association with David Ferrie and other anti-Castro elements heavily sponsored by the CIA; these quiet associations were, of course, going on in concert with a prominent public profile showing just the opposite political inclinations. Though concrete evidence is scarce, the least that can be said is that there must be far more to the CIA's knowledge of Oswald than has yet been revealed.

Because Oswald did have routine dealings of record with the FBI, it is at once simpler yet more confusing to grasp the truth about that relationship. There is tempting, if inconclusive, evidence linking Oswald to the FBI as a possible informant during the time of his political activities in New Orleans.[212] Such evidence in Dallas is not nearly so tantalizing. It seems deliberately perverse that it is these proper contacts that have fueled the most intense speculation over a possible informant relationship between Oswald and the FBI.

The first high-level alarm over this possibility was expressed in an executive session of the Warren Commission. Details of the discussion were not known until 1965, when Gerald Ford breached the top secret security classification of the proceedings and exposed the debate. The revelations were made in an unofficial book in which Ford recounted his experiences. Until then, the public had not been privy to how the Warren Commission had handled the charges internally. Ford's account confirmed that the commission took to heart the allegations that had appeared in the press suggesting an Oswald-FBI link.[213]

In the end, the Warren Commission accepted FBI Director Hoover's assurances that Oswald was not an informant. However, the discussion of the issue included a revealing exchange concerning the general protocol of dealing with informants.[214] The point of how the FBI handled such a matter was under discussion by Senator Richard Russell and Allen Dulles, former Director of Central Intelligence. The exchange:

SENATOR RUSSELL: If Oswald never had assassinated the President or at least been charged with assassinating the President and had been in the employ of the FBI and somebody had gone to the FBI they would have denied he was an agent.

ALLEN DULLES: Oh, yes.

SENATOR RUSSELL: They would be the first to deny it. Your agents would have done exactly the same thing.

ALLEN DULLES: Exactly.[215]

In the absence of a similarly candid assessment by a former director of the FBI, the interpretation by Allen Dulles is surely next best.

On May 31, 1962, two weeks before Oswald's return from the Soviet Union, FBI headquarters informed its Dallas office that the ex-Marine was returning to Texas. Officials at headquarters told the Dallas office that the defector should be interviewed "to determine if Oswald had been recruited by a Soviet intelligence service." The bureau's position had been that it preferred to wait until Oswald was settled before interviewing him, rather than buttonholing him as he got off the boat at New York.[216]

The Dallas agents who interviewed Oswald on June 26 stated in their report that he became "impatient and arrogant" when asked why he had gone to the Soviet Union. Although the agents found Oswald generally uncooperative, they reported that he agreed to alert them in the event he was contacted by anyone from Soviet intelligence. The agents' report did not indicate that Oswald possessed any potential for violence.[217]

Less than two months later, FBI agents again interviewed Oswald. Two agents talked to him in their car on a Fort Worth street for more than an hour. The purpose, according to the FBI, was to impress upon Oswald the importance of reporting any contact from Soviet intelligence. Oswald agreed.*[218]

These early contacts appear completely routine. It was later that Oswald's contacts became peculiar—so peculiar that once again the observer finds himself wandering in the wilderness of mirrors. It is all but impossible to know if there was some mutual connection—or if, as it sometimes seems so clear, Oswald was using the FBI to help in his own image-making.

One of the strangest Oswald contacts with the FBI occurred at the New Orleans jail on August 10, 1963, the day after his arrest during the street scuffle over Cuban politics. Oswald allegedly requested that an FBI agent be sent to talk to him, and Agent John L. Quigley met with him for nearly an hour. Quigley's report, which contains false information provided by Oswald, is largely an account of Oswald's pro-Castro political stance. Reportedly, he even showed the FBI agent his membership card for the Fair Play for Cuba Committee.[219]

The possible significance of this contact runs in two directions: was Oswald actually reporting in to the bureau as an informant, or was this part of his far-flung efforts to establish himself as a pro-Castro figure in New Orleans? Or was he doing both? There is a familiar elusiveness to the answer.

Oswald had his most controversial contacts with the FBI in Dallas during the weeks preceding the assassination. On November 1, FBI Agent James P. Hosty, Jr., went to Ruth Paine's home, just outside Dallas, where Marina Oswald was staying. Hosty's aim was to interview Mrs. Oswald as "a Soviet immigrant in this country who could conceivably be here with [an] intelligence assignment."[220]

Hosty also hoped to glean some information about Oswald in an indirect way. There had been reports that Oswald had been in touch

---

*At no time during the FBI's official contacts with Oswald was there an indication that he possessed any potential for violence, according to the agents who interviewed him.

with a Communist publication. On that day, Agent Hosty spoke briefly to Marina Oswald and to Ruth Paine.[221]

Soon after the assassination, Hosty's name, license plate number, telephone number, and office address were found in Oswald's address book, a fact that—when finally revealed to the public—fired speculation that the notation indicated an informant relationship. The matter was confused further when the FBI initially concealed from the Warren Commission the presence of Hosty's name and other information in Oswald's notebook.[222]

There is testimony from Marina and others that Oswald was irritated that the FBI was contacting his family. Both the Warren Commission and the Select Committee concluded that there was nothing suggestive or sinister about Oswald's making notes concerning the FBI agent who interviewed his wife.[223]

It is unfortunate that Agent Hosty never talked to Oswald before the assassination, for his indirect contact caused the FBI man great difficulties—including official censure—that have followed him over the years. As the agent covering Oswald at the time, one of the things he has been criticized for is not placing Oswald's name in the Security Index, a file kept on individuals who posed a potential threat to the security of the United States.*[224]

Agent Hosty, other FBI men assigned to Dallas, and indeed the entire bureau have come under heavy fire over the years for the fact that Oswald's name was not on the Security Index. Years of intense official investigation have gone into examining this point. It

---

*In recent years, Agent Hosty has sought to exonerate himself on this point by explaining that he, as the FBI man handling the Oswald file before the assassination, was not fully informed about Oswald's supposed encounter in Mexico City with a high KGB officer named Valeri Kostikov. In charge of KGB espionage and counterintelligence in Mexico and the United States, Kostikov worked under cover as a "consular officer" at the Soviet embassy in Mexico City. It is widely believed that Kostikov is the man who dealt with Oswald on the question of his requested visa. Agent Hosty has told the author that if he had been informed about Kostikov's true role, he would have moved to place Oswald's name on the Security Index.

Hosty clearly views the Oswald-Kostikov contact far more seriously than most students of Oswald's role in the assassination. The general feeling about the supposed contact was summed up in 1978 by former Warren Commission Counsel W. David Slawson, who had concentrated on Oswald's relations with the Soviets. Slawson told the HSCA: "As far as I was able to ascertain . . . the fact that Kostikov was called down to see Oswald when Oswald showed up at the Russian embassy was probably not as significant as one might think because apparently he [Kostikov] would have been called down to see any out-of-the-ordinary person, anyone that might have intelligence significance, any secret significance to the Russians."

is noteworthy that according to released internal FBI memoranda, all FBI personnel involved in the official analysis—both field agents and headquarters brass—were "unanimous in the opinion that Oswald *did not* meet the criteria for the Security Index."[225]

The lone exception to this judgment was Director J. Edgar Hoover, who reacted to the internal report by scribbling across the page: "They [are] worse than mistaken. No one in full possession of all his faculties can claim Oswald didn't fall within this criteria." By the time the dust had settled, Hoover had punished seventeen agents over the handling of the Oswald case before the assassination.[226]

The ultimate irony in all of this is that even if Oswald's name had been placed on the Security Index, it probably would have changed nothing. Under the procedures then in effect, such a listing would not have led to Oswald's name being turned over to the Secret Service.[227]

There is an odd ring to the FBI claim that its information on Oswald gave no clue indicating he was a potential assassin. This determination, while exonerating men like Hosty and others who were censured, is also a strong card in the hand of those who do not believe Oswald ever shot at General Walker, Officer Tippit, or even President Kennedy.

The most explosive allegation involving Oswald and the Dallas FBI concerns a reportedly threatening note that Oswald supposedly delivered in person to the FBI office in Dallas two or three weeks before the assassination. All the evidence concerning the note— particularly the contents—is essentially contradictory and of questionable reliability. The only absolute certainty is that Agent Hosty, claiming that he was acting under orders, destroyed the note following the assassination.[228]

It is very difficult to discern from the conflicting evidence (including the contradictory accounts of the primary witnesses) exactly what happened. However, it appears that in early November a young man showed up at the desk of Nannie Lee Fenner, the receptionist at the Dallas FBI office. He asked to see Agent Hosty. When told Hosty was not in, the man left an unsealed envelope addressed to Hosty. The man departed. Mrs. Fenner opened the envelope and read the note. Twelve years later, Mrs. Fenner recalled that it said something like this:

Let this be a warning. I will blow up the FBI and the Dallas
Police Department if you don't stop bothering my wife.
Lee Harvey Oswald[229]

Mrs. Fenner believes that she showed the note to a superior and
then to several people in the office. Later that day, she gave it to
Hosty. The consensus among those who saw the note, according to
Mrs. Fenner, was that the writer must be a "nut." Mrs. Fenner has
stated that it was later, when she saw Oswald on television, that she
recognized him as the man who came to the office and his name as
the one signed to the note.[230]

Today, most of those to whom Mrs. Fenner says she showed the
note have been officially interviewed. Almost all have sworn they
never saw the note. However, several stated that at some point after
Oswald's death, they *heard* Mrs. Fenner talking about a note she
said Oswald left at the office.[231]

In any event, the incident involving the note was kept from the
public until 1975, when a top FBI official gave details of the allegations to a subcommittee of the House Judiciary Committee. In
later testimony, Agent Hosty swore that actually the note was anonymous—bearing no signature—and that it carried no specific threat
of violence. Hosty claims that he accepted the note at the time he
received it as having to do with another case—one in which he had
contacted the wife of a suspect completely unrelated to the Oswald
case.[232]

However, when Hosty interviewed Oswald at the Dallas jail on
November 22, Oswald—upon hearing Hosty's name—complained
that he was aware that Hosty had been "bothering" his wife. Since
this was the thrust of the anonymous note, Hosty believes that he
and others in the FBI office jumped to the conclusion that Oswald
sent it.[233]

Hosty swears that his superior, J. Gordon Shanklin, ordered him
to "get rid of it." Shanklin swears he recalls nothing about the note
and is certain he did not order its destruction. The HSCA investigated the entire matter and came up with no firm account of what
really happened. The committee did, however, regard the whole
incident as "a serious impeachment of Shanklin's and Hosty's credibility."[234]

The absence of the note itself for analysis—and the questionable credibility of the key witnesses—makes it impossible to know what the note said or who wrote it. The destruction of the note—if considered by *anyone* at the FBI to be a threatening message from Oswald—is reflective of the manner in which the whole case was handled. This, really, is the ultimate commentary.

Who was this contradiction named Oswald, this man webbed in intrigue who was sold to the public as a loner? This man who was a notoriously bad shot in the Marine Corps but was sold to the public as an expert marksman? This man so cool that he nipped in and out of Russia as he would his own front door, yet was sold to the public as a nut? This man who flaunted his Communist sympathies instead of concealing them as would any bona fide Soviet spy?

Oswald's life is as baffling as a Rubik's Cube: No sooner does a side start to take shape than another side becomes disordered. Now, more than twenty years after the fact, it may be unlikely that the truth about Oswald's intelligence connections will ever be known—at least with any certainty. Realistically, it is fairly hopeless to try to sort out precisely for whom Oswald was working or even what he was supposed to be doing. A strong case can be made that in the later stages, even Oswald did not know. Given Oswald's position, it is possible, even likely, that for him the wilderness of mirrors became a jungle of terror.

The U.S. intelligence community has created such relentless obfuscation that any firm resolution of Oswald, much less the assassination, seems virtually impossible. With the agencies' record of deceit, there is no reason to believe that the known lies are the *only* lies. There is no reason to believe that the known destruction of records is the *only* destruction of records. Most important, there is no reason to believe that the alluring clues that have inadvertently slipped (or been pried) out suggesting Oswald's intelligence connections are the *only* such clues. Others surely lie buried deep inside two decades of official mind-set proclaiming that Oswald was a lone nut.

Conversely, there is every temptation to accept the preponderance of commonsense evidence that veritably shouts Oswald's intelligence connections. Whether it be the revelation of the Defense Department's destruction of the Hidell/Oswald file—or the blunder that exposed the name of William Gaudet—the government seems always in this case to sink deeper into the quicksands of deceit.

One of the most remarkable aspects of the whole story is the patient tolerance of the critics and researchers who stand by attentively, awaiting the next scrap of information to be tossed out. At each tossing, the scraps hold less significance for fewer people. Finally, to be sure, the tiny new snippets of information will be meaningless. There may be no one left with the passion and persistence to pursue the clues. With the emotional juices drained away, the whole exercise will become as academic as today's parlor debate over who poisoned Napoleon. Then, from the government's standpoint, the truth can quietly and safely emerge. In the end, it seems sure, victory will belong to those agencies that hold the keys to the many mansions of U.S. intelligence.

10 · NEW ORLEANS, USA

Camelot and the New Frontier

The dawn of the sixties was accompanied by two powerful forces that surged through America, pulling and grinding at each other with a passion that can be seen much more clearly a quarter century later. One force was highly visible, the other not so clearly perceived but every bit as potent.

On the one hand, there was the palpable exuberance of that slim majority of American voters who had elected John F. Kennedy. They applauded his promise of a bold and unprecedented new direction for the country and the world. They believed that President Kennedy's vibrant espousal of new ideas would make the world community a better place for everyone—including multitudes of the hungry, ignorant, and sick. His election was seen as a signal that compassion and the sharing of material wealth with those less fortunate, both here and abroad, would be high priorities. There was the fervent belief that this new dimension would foster peace, justice, and equality around the world.

In his inaugural speech, President Kennedy exhorted Americans to "ask not what your country can do for you—ask what you can do for your country."[1] Such ringing phrases evoked wild enthusiasm from Kennedy's constituency, so many of whom were young, charmingly articulate, and wealthy. The men and women in the new Kennedy White House were described at the time as "the richest, prettiest, most interesting young people in the country."[2]

The tone was clearly set for what would come to be called Camelot. But not everyone across the land was pleased. Surging through America with equal intensity was a second force, one overshadowed by the glitter and self-adulation of the highly visible Kennedy supporters. This constituency represented a virtually total dissent from the frenzied loyalty of the Kennedy people. The dissent by some elements of this constituency was far more sinister than the traditional give-and-take in politics. Inevitably, the voices and tones of this dissent were viewed against the vibrant enthusiasm surrounding the new President. The very eagerness of Kennedy's supporters nourished the feeling that his accomplishments would take a terrible toll from those certain constituencies that were in fundamental opposition to all he stood for. To these opponents, there was a threatening ring in the privileged young President's exhortation that people should ask what they could do for their country. Many of them believed that they already did the maximum for their country, since it unhesitatingly helped itself and others to their wealth.

In an odd way, the enthusiasm for the new President was so ostentatious that it dominated the news here and abroad, as if he had won a mandate, ignoring completely the fact that he had barely squeaked in. Thus, the depth and breadth of his opposition was largely overlooked. So was its intensity, fed by the outrage of powerful adversaries who viewed the young President as having used them to get himself elected, then made political capital by turning against them. The feral intensity of the violent opposition to Kennedy blazed clear at Dealey Plaza. If Kennedy partisans saw in their President the dawn of a new age for America, so did the violent opposition. The question is whether the opponents determined that it was not to be.

In addition to the unsuspected virulence of Kennedy's domestic opposition, he faced opposition around the globe from Communist governments. The most immediate and explosive of these challenges was Fidel Castro, who had taken control of Cuba on January 1, 1959. When Kennedy took office in January 1961, he inherited the heated commitment of U.S. military and intelligence officials to rid the Western Hemisphere of Castro, whom they viewed as a Soviet puppet on the doorstep of the U.S. mainland. There were, of course, no more ardent allies of this official commitment than the thousands of fiery exiles who had sought refuge from Castro in the United States.[3]

The first major effort against Castro was launched in April 1961 with the U.S.-backed invasion by exiles at Cuba's Bay of Pigs. Coming only three months after President Kennedy took office, the invasion was a disaster that humiliated practically everyone connected with it. When the facts began to surface, President Kennedy faced the nearly hysterical wrath of the exiles, who accused him of betrayal by shortchanging them on military support, thus dooming their cause. Many of Kennedy's military and intelligence advisors were also angry at their commander-in-chief for the same reason. On the other side of the coin, Castro directly blamed the President for sponsoring the aborted invasion designed to topple him from power.[4]

Castro's anger toward Kennedy was menacingly intensified by his sure knowledge that official elements of the U.S. government—presumably with the sanction of President Kennedy—were repeatedly trying to assassinate him. Castro ultimately claimed that there were twenty-four U.S. attempts to murder him. In subsequent years a Congressional committee confirmed at least eight U.S. attempts to assassinate the Cuban premier.[5]

In its persistent efforts to murder Castro, the United States reached beyond its routine arsenal of military and intelligence resources. It is now officially conceded that the CIA recruited certain high-level figures from organized crime to carry out murder plots against Castro. As freakish as this collusion appears, both sides had important reasons for wanting to murder the Cuban leader. Not only had he established a hostile Communist government at the edge of the United States, but he had also closed down the narcotics, gambling, and prostitution operations run so lucratively by the U.S. mob. Perhaps it should not be too surprising that these unlikely conspirators had joined forces.[6]

There was an added reason for the mob's willingness to participate in the assassination plots—their desire to turn down the heat from the Justice Department. From the earliest days of the Kennedy administration, the Justice Department, under the direction of Attorney General Robert Kennedy, had exhibited an unparalleled commitment to fight organized crime in the United States. This commitment, taken with the full blessing of the President, particularly puzzled mob bosses, who felt they had virtually delivered the presidency to Kennedy when they brought in the state of Illinois by a whisker—giving him the twenty-seven electoral votes that guaranteed him his razor-thin margin of victory over Richard Nixon in the 1960 presidential election.[7]

In addition to his domestic opposition and that of the pro-Castro and anti-Castro forces, the oil industry had turned savagely against President Kennedy by 1963 because of his support for tax reform that threatened the oil-depletion allowance. This struck at one of the most lucrative tax loopholes ever enjoyed by the fabled oil millionaires of Texas, Louisiana, and other states with substantial oil interests.[8]

Added to this stew of Kennedy opposition were the right-wing extremists and racists, angry over the Kennedy brothers' promise to bring full desegregation to the South. Many feared that desegregation would virtually destroy hallowed traditions involving families, politics, and economics.[9]

All things considered, it is probable that a greater diversity of elements wanted President Kennedy out of office than had been at work during any previous presidency in American history. In simple terms, the most threatening forces boiled down to several darkly potent groups:

- Anti-Castro exiles.
- Pro-Castro elements, including perhaps Castro himself.
- Organized crime.
- Powerful oil interests.
- Right-wing and racist domestic factions.
- Elements of U.S. military and intelligence, enraged over Kennedy's denunciation of their efforts following the Bay of Pigs disaster.

Such forces possessed in abundance the classic ingredients for murder—motive, means, and opportunity. In fact, with such a rare confluence of threatening elements, a great range of shifting opportunities for assassination presented itself, as the President, with increasing frequency during 1963, moved about the country on political trips.

In retrospect, the possibility of a successful political assassination seems immense.

No place in America held a greater concentration of these diverse factions than steamy, seething New Orleans. As a whole, that city has traditionally tolerated, even welcomed, a tantalizing variety of races and creeds, political and social beliefs. The city took delight in its natural diversities, especially during the tumultuous years of the early sixties. This potpourri of diversity—and, by some lights, perversity—had fostered an atmosphere in which almost any extreme—political, philosophical, sexual, artistic, religious, or even criminal—was remarkably at ease. By 1961 the climate of laissez-faire was virtually absolute.

From the earliest days of Castro's power, the city was a major haven for displaced Cubans of all social and economic stripes. Included in the massive influx of hotheaded exiles were many professionals—doctors, lawyers, and bankers.[10] Given this strident Cuban population and an extensive presence of U.S. military and intelligence advisors working in and around New Orleans, it is not surprising that the city became one hub of the efforts by the United States government to stage either the overthrow or assassination of Fidel Castro.[11]

As the major city in one of the largest oil-producing states in the country, New Orleans, like much of Louisiana, was strongly influenced by the attitudes of the powerful companies and men who controlled these vast oil interests. Moreover, cosmopolitan, bohemian New Orleans only superficially escaped the racism and attendant hatred that was so virulent in the Deep South during the early sixties. Even the most prominent of the city's raucous Mardi Gras fêtes systematically excluded Negroes and Jews. Beneath a surface of tolerance, many residents harbored the same racist passions that infected so much of the rest of America.

One of the most important factors in any consideration of New Orleans is the powerful presence of Carlos Marcello, the kingpin of organized crime in the south central United States. Marcello, who once admitted to being merely a tomato salesman, had ubiquitous business interests that were intertwined with many aspects of the state's economy—including bars, restaurants, prostitution, transportation, real estate, and tourism. Hundreds of Louisianians worked for him either directly or indirectly, and even the legitimate business people granted him a certain respect, for the power that he represented. A convincing case can be made that for most of the decades of Marcello's power, local and state law-enforcement agencies in Louisiana have rarely taken punitive aim at his wide operations. What legal difficulty Marcello has experienced came from federal authorities, particularly during the Kennedy administration.[12]

Another addition to the volatile mix already described was that New Orleans produced the man the government insisted was the lone assassin of President Kennedy—Lee Harvey Oswald. Not only was Oswald born in New Orleans, he lived there for five months during 1963, until two months before the assassination.[13] In New Orleans, Oswald was associated in varying and confusing ways with elements that would ostensibly benefit from President Kennedy's death.

Finally, it is not surprising that a setting as flamboyant and tawdry as New Orleans should produce the only prosecution in which a man was brought to trial for conspiring to assassinate John F. Kennedy. The prosecution ultimately failed; but it introduced questions and evidence, at a national level, that leave almost any observer certain that *something* connected to the assassination was going on in New Orleans. Just *what* is as confusing a mystery as ever.

The Jolly Green Giant

On February 17, 1967, news began thundering around the world that, for the first time, a duly elected law-enforcement official in the United States was investigating the tangled leads left by the Warren Commission. A few days later, Jim Garrison, the boisterous district attorney of New Orleans, was already promising arrests and prosecution on charges of conspiracy to assassinate the President of the United States. The commission, of course, had found no evidence of a conspiracy. On the surface it appeared odd, if not preposterous, that such an investigation carried no imprimatur of federal sanction. However, there was the wide belief that those vested with the authority to follow the leads three years earlier had failed. Perhaps, it was reasoned, this was the only logical course for the pursuit of truth.[14]

Still, there could have been no more strange, even bizarre, setting for what was about to unfold. The case itself—the JFK assassination—may have been the only one in history that could withstand with even a modicum of seriousness such a sequence of events or so wild a cast of characters. Less than a week after the first confusing reports about the investigation, Jim Garrison confidently told the press that he had "positively solved the assassination of President John F. Kennedy."[15] With this, the bedlam turned into a public frenzy that dwarfed old New Orleans's legendary hysteria for Mardi Gras.[16]

In the beginning, press focus was chiefly on the prosecutor who made the sensational charges, a man of hulking physique, standing six and one-half feet tall and wearing size fourteen shoes. Jim Garrison, a man fond of Shakespeare and good living, was known to both friends and enemies as the Jolly Green Giant. Many years earlier, Garrison, who had worked briefly for the FBI, had shucked his real moniker of Earling Carothers for the simple first name of Jim. A decorated combat flier during World War II, Garrison later acquired a reputation as something of a crusader, for his vice raids on various Bourbon Street enterprises.[17]

While such activity generated considerable publicity, Garrison's critics point out that he customarily avoided any prosecution involving organized crime—a force he asserts did not exist in New Orleans during his years as district attorney. It is significant that in presenting his case, Garrison pointed to certain characters and evidence that even today seem pertinent, but he never once made the obvious connection between them and New Orleans mob boss Carlos Marcello.[18]

Perhaps the best illustration of Garrison's blindness concerning organized crime is seen in his comments on Oswald's killer Jack Ruby, whose organized-crime ties are solidly established. In *Contract on America*, one of the best analyses published on evidence of organized-crime participation in the JFK killing, author David E. Scheim points out: "Although Garrison made extravagant charges against an assortment of Cuban exiles, CIA agents, Minutemen, White Russians and Nazis, he conspicuously avoided any reference to one prime assassination suspect: the Mafia. . . . In discussing testimony concerning Ruby's anti-Castro activities . . . Garrison described Ruby as a 'CIA bagman' and an 'employee of the CIA.' But Garrison said nothing about Ruby's organized crime involvement."[19]

In this framework, Scheim writes: "It is logical to ask whether [Garrison's] probe was carried out with precisely [the] purpose . . . of deflecting attention from Carlos Marcello."[20]

Aaron Kohn, who for many years was the managing director of the respected private group called the Metropolitan Crime Commission of New Orleans, captured the more common perception when he observed: "Garrison never lets the responsibilities of being a prosecutor interfere with being a politician."[21] Whether or not Kohn's assessment is accurate, it is certain that legions of Garrison's critics agree with that description.

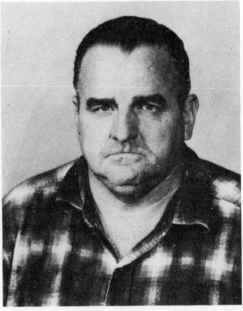

Robert W. Easterling is the only person ever to go on record with a detailed confession to participation in a conspiracy to assassinate President Kennedy (see chapter 12). The photographs (clockwise) were taken in 1969, 1976, and when the author first interviewed him in 1981.

One of Easterling's claims is that the real rifle used to kill President Kennedy was smuggled into the Book Depository in a wooden crate. The size described by Easterling seemed very peculiar and unlikely. Then, in 1983, during a tour of the sixth floor of the Book Depository, the author discovered several of the crates pictured here. Used to ship books, these are strikingly similar to the special crate described by Easterling. There is strong evidence, discussed in chapter 12, that the crates were in use on the sixth floor in 1963.

This Warren Commission exhibit (below), showing the three men who were on the fifth floor at the time of the shooting, also shows the presence of wooden book crates. They can be seen on the left, beside the stairwell leading down from the sixth floor.

Oswald handing out leaflets in New Orleans supporting the Fair Play for Cuba Committee. The man with the white shirt and tie, immediately to the right of Oswald, has never been identified. He appears to be working with Oswald. Given the strong evidence that Oswald was somehow manipulated in his peculiar activities in New Orleans, the identity of this man could provide a critical link to an understanding of what was going on. There has been no known official effort to make an identification.

HOTEL LA SALLE
NEW ORLEANS
GUEST INVOICE REGISTER

J. Gary Shaw

Thomas K. Noonan

Fir

Thomas Eli Davis (inset above left) is a logical candidate as one who may have impersonated Oswald (see chapter 13). The arrows in the photograph on the left point to a "T. E. Davis" who was registered at the La Salle Hotel in the heart of New Orleans on August 8 and 9, 1963. On August 9, Oswald was jailed after he provoked a street scuffle while handing out Fair Play for Cuba leaflets. However, there is no evidence to confirm that the Davis registered at the hotel is, in fact, Thomas Eli Davis.

One of Robert Easterling's most adamant claims is that he and a Cuban picked up Oswald on September 24 and drove him to Houston. Easterling claims that a diversionary fire was set across the street from the spot in New Orleans where Oswald, who Easterling says was under surveillance, was picked up. An exhaustive search of old New Orleans fire records shows that at the precise time of Easterling's claim (see entry at 9:22 A.M. below) a fire broke out in a wooden apartment building. This record shows that the fire was regarded as suspicious. Complete details are in chapter 12.

2ⁿᵈ Melpo… Fire Dis…

LOCATION	STORIES	Style of Building	CAUSE OF FIRE		BUILDING
elpomene + Magazine			False Alarm		
6 University Pl.			First Aid		
yodes + Howard Ave			Short Circuit		
716 Baronne			unnecessary		
211 Melpomene	2	Wood	under Investigation	nole	
hart + Union Station			Short Circuit	50 00	
Rampart + Canal			First Aid		
Magazine + Howard			First Aid		
Magazine + Howard			Wash down		
ythos + Claiborne			First Aid		
rol + La Salle			Wash down		

Thomas K. Noonan

Carlos Marcello (left), crime boss of New Orleans, was the subject of a vendetta by Attorney General Robert Kennedy in 1963. He has been accused of making threats against the Attorney General as well as the President.

Guy Williams Banister (right), former special agent in charge of the FBI's Chicago office, was a private investigator in New Orleans who employed David Ferrie. Banister's secretary claims that she saw Oswald in the office on several occasions. An unexplained fact is that one of Oswald's pro-Cuba leaflets, which he gave to an FBI agent, had Banister's office address stamped on the back. Banister was rabid in his hatred of Castro.

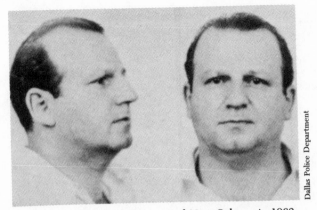

Jack Ruby, Oswald's killer, visited New Orleans in 1963 where he sought new girls in some of the mob-linked night clubs. Ruby made dozens of telephone calls to New Orleans with increasing frequency in the days before the assassination.

Antonio Veciana, one of the most prominent anti-Castro Cuban exiles, was highly active in the CIA's efforts to overthrow the Cuban premier. Veciana claims once to have seen his own CIA handler, a man he knew as Bishop, with Oswald in Dallas shortly before the assassination.

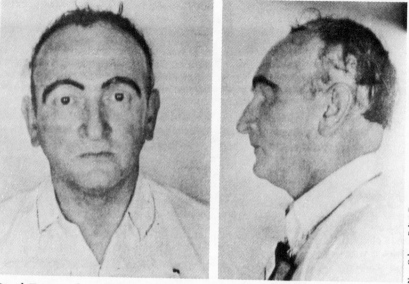

David Ferrie, who worked for both Guy Banister and Carlos Marcello, was the head of a Civil Air Patrol unit to which Oswald belonged as a youngster in New Orleans. Ferrie and Oswald have been convincingly linked by officials as having been together at a Louisiana town during the summer of 1963. Ferrie was found dead a few days before he was to be arrested by New Orleans District Attorney Jim Garrison in his investigation of the assassination.

Manuel Garcia Gonzales was an enigmatic figure sought by Garrison in his investigation. Believed to have been associated with Oswald, Gonzales' real identity remains unknown, although some private investigators believe he might actually have been a French mercenary.

Bolt-action 6.5 caliber Mannlicher-Carcano officially believed to be the assassination weapon used by Oswald. No one has ever officially duplicated Oswald's alleged shooting skills with this rifle under similar test circumstances.

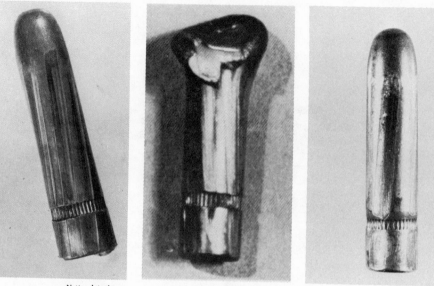

The Magic Bullet, left, officially designated as Warren Commission Exhibit 399, was found on a stretcher in a hallway at Parkland Hospital. The official version credits this bullet, in almost perfect condition, as having passed completely through the bodies of both Kennedy and Connally, shattering a rib as well as the large bone in Connally's wrist. A 6.5 mm test bullet, center, was shot through the wrist of a cadaver in an official test. Note the severe damage to the nose of the bullet, as compared to that of the Magic Bullet. On the right, a 6.5 mm Mannlicher-Carcano bullet fired into water by the author, in the fashion described by Easterling. Note that its condition is as virtually perfect as that of the Magic Bullet. See chapter 12 for full details.

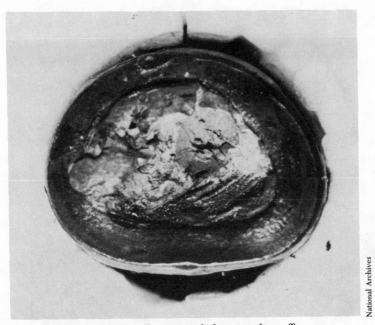

Base of the Magic Bullet, showing a slight crumpling effect.

Base of a similar bullet fired by the author into water. Note the similarities to the base of the Magic Bullet.

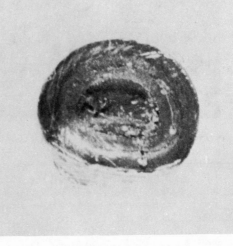

J. Gary Shaw

Jean Souetre, in photo above on left with circle around his head, was a known French terrorist who was once imprisoned after an assassination attempt against French President Charles de Gaulle. Souetre, or someone using his name, was in Dallas on the day of the JFK assassination. U.S. officials quietly expelled that person from the country, for reasons still unclear. In the picture opposite right, Oswald is seen with a man he identified to his wife only as "Alfred from Cuba." The photograph was found among Oswald's effects. There is an obvious similarity between Souetre and the man called "Alfred from Cuba."

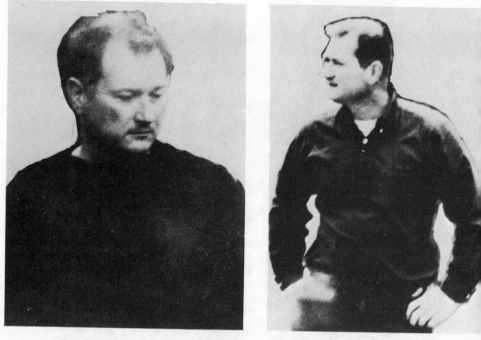

Unidentified man (above left and right) outside either the Soviet or Cuban embassy in Mexico City in the weeks prior to the assassination. This is the man the CIA originally reported as being Lee Harvey Oswald. When it became obvious that the man was not Oswald, the CIA refused to disclose his identity. The mystery remains.

But the world was interested not so much in Jim Garrison as in the evidence he was promising to deliver. In describing the atmosphere after the story broke, one reporter wrote: "A deluge of frantic incoming calls lighted up the telephone switchboard in the outer office of the district attorney of New Orleans, and for the next month it blazed like a pinball machine gone mad. Day after day, calls poured in from across the U.S., from London, Rome, Paris, Berlin, from South America, Mexico, Japan. At times, the trunk lines jammed completely."[22]

When the story first broke in the New Orleans States-Item, it was essentially void of names and details. Several enterprising reporters had pieced together certain facts of the investigation by examining vouchers that showed heavy travel expenses by the district attorney's office to places like Dallas, Houston, and Miami. On the day their story appeared, a man named David William Ferrie contacted the newspaper. He stated that he was a target of Garrison's investigation and that he wanted to talk about it. He said that Garrison's insinuations about him—that he was a getaway pilot for the assassins—were groundless.[23]

David Ferrie was, in nearly every sense, a New Orleans–style mad genius—a man to be seized upon by any red-blooded reporter. Rarely has such a wild figure emerged into the light for public scrutiny. Hairless from head to toe as the result of a rare disease, Ferrie compensated for this deficiency by gluing what looked like nothing so much as reddish orange monkey hair on the top of his head. More such hair was used to fashion eyebrows, grotesquely set off by sloppily applied mascara around the eyes. This visage was offset by a beaklike nose on an angular face. A big man of nearly six feet, Ferrie was widely known as an aggressive homosexual who had been arrested several times for molesting young boys. Ferrie, who constantly exhibited his proclivity for foul language, also had a knowledge of medicine. At one time he kept hundreds of mice in his filthy apartment, while working on a private cancer cure he had formulated.[24]

In addition, Ferrie was considered a master hypnotist as well as a student of philosophy, religion, and psychology. Three thousand volumes were crammed into his personal library. He claimed a Ph.D. in psychology and listed himself as a "doctor" in the telephone directory. He was active as a "bishop" in an obscure sect called the

Orthodox Old Catholic Church of North America. He made speeches to groups such as the Junior Chamber of Commerce. He was a violent anti-Communist, with prominent connections with the Cuban exile community of New Orleans. Many believe that he served as a CIA contract agent during the height of the Cuban exile activities.[25]

Ferrie was widely considered to be a brilliant pilot of various sorts of aircraft. Until September 1963 Ferrie was employed as a commercial pilot for Eastern Airlines. He was dismissed from Eastern following publicity over his arrest for sodomizing a minor boy. After this, Ferrie worked primarily as a private pilot and as an investigator. On the day of the assassination, he was in a federal courtroom in New Orleans with none other than Carlos Marcello, whose lawyer had retained Ferrie as an investigator.[26]

Ferrie told the newspaper that Garrison seemed to believe that his role in the JFK conspiracy was to be on hand to fly the Dallas assassins to safety outside the country. Ferrie's seemingly ironclad alibi did not deter Garrison, who, it would turn out, was concentrating his case on the act of *conspiracy* to assassinate, rather than actual participation in the murder. Ferrie's comments were the first substantive hint of what Garrison was up to. Investigation by reporters showed that within seventy-two hours of the assassination, Garrison had Ferrie and two friends brought in and then turned over to the FBI and Secret Service—which interviewed them and let them go, a fact duly reflected in the Warren Commission records. Now, three years later, reporters from around the world competed for interviews with the strange, bulbous-eyed man.[27]

One of the reporters who managed to follow Ferrie into his lair was George Lardner, Jr., of the *Washington Post*. He was admitted to Ferrie's apartment around midnight and talked to him for four hours. Lardner later told one of Garrison's investigators that he found Ferrie that night to be "[an] intelligent, well-versed guy [on] a broad range of subjects." Lardner reported that Ferrie was in good spirits when he left him at four o'clock that morning.[28]

Later that day Ferrie's nude, lifeless body was discovered in the apartment. The date was February 22, only five days after the story broke about Garrison's investigation. At the time of his death, Ferrie was forty-nine years old.[29] Two undated notes were found near Ferrie's body—one to a former lover named Al, the other to the world: "To leave this life is, for me, a sweet prospect. I find nothing in it that is desirable, and on the other hand everything that is loathe-some."[30]

Despite the note, the coroner ruled that the death was from natural causes, a brain hemorrhage. "There is no indication what-soever of suicide or murder," stated the coroner.[31] However, Jim Garrison argued that the death was a suicide, and solemnly told the press that David Ferrie was "one of history's most important indi-viduals."[32] Among the peculiar contents of Ferrie's home were three blank U.S. passports—seeming to need only photographs and bio-graphical information to appear valid. There were also a 100-pound bomb and numerous guns and military equipment.[33]

In Washington there was a clear measure of official concern over Garrison's activities. President Johnson telephoned Acting Attorney General Ramsey Clark to inform him of Ferrie's death. Years later an FBI report was disclosed that noted that President Johnson was "very concerned about this matter" and wanted full details about Ferrie's death.[34]

A few days later, when District Attorney Garrison assured re-porters that he had "solved" the assassination, he added: "We're working out details of evidence which probably will take months. We know that we're going to be able to arrest every person in-volved—at least every person who is still living. . . . The key to the whole case is through the looking glass. Black is white; white is black. I don't want to be cryptic, but that's the way it is."[35]

These comments were cryptic indeed. But, by this point, Garrison had a hammerlock on the attention of the Western world. Millions of people eagerly awaited the next development, the next pro-nouncement from Garrison. The wait was not long.

On March 1, the same day that David Ferrie was buried, Jim Garrison announced the arrest of Clay L. Shaw, a prominent New Orleans business and social figure. Only seventeen months earlier, the city of New Orleans had bestowed upon Shaw its highest honor, a medal for the International Order of Merit. At the time of the arrest, Garrison may have been short on evidence linking Shaw to the assassination, but he made certain the world was informed about some of the strange items his office had turned up in Shaw's home—one chain, five whips, one black hood and cape, and one black gown.[36]

People were outraged at this apparent invasion of Shaw's privacy.

He and his friends—and they were numerous and prominent—insisted that the kinky paraphernalia was part of Mardi Gras costumes. Others charged that this was a move on Garrison's part to somehow introduce Shaw's discreet homosexuality into the developing case. Whatever else Jim Garrison's capricious arrest of Shaw accomplished, it earned for Garrison widespread scorn about his motives and called into question the legitimacy of his whole prosecution. At the same time, many observers believed that the fact that Garrison, a man with high political ambitions, would go so far was a solid indication of the strength of the evidence he would present.[37]

The immediate result of Shaw's arrest was frenzied publicity. More than ever, the world's appetite was whetted for the next step—the presentation of evidence and the trial of Shaw and his as yet unarrested co-conspirators. Garrison loved the publicity and took to the limelight in a media blitz. He repeatedly asserted in forums all over the country that there would be more arrests and that he was confident of convictions. *Playboy* lent its pages for a full-length interview, and Garrison was invited to appear on Johnny Carson's "Tonight Show." Suddenly, the New Orleans prosecutor was a hot property everywhere.[38]

As Garrison talked, the world—and Clay Shaw—waited. This time, the wait would be a long one.

One of the most curious incidents attendant to Shaw's arrest occurred shortly afterward in Washington. Acting Attorney General Ramsey Clark made the startling statement that the FBI had investigated Shaw in the immediate wake of the assassination and found nothing to pursue. By the FBI's lights, Clark said, Clay Shaw was clean. Later that day, while the FBI officially refused to comment, usually well-informed government sources told *The New York Times* they had no knowledge of such an investigation of Clay Shaw.[39]

As if this were not confusing enough, a Justice Department official then tried to explain Clark's curious statements. In doing so, he managed to introduce a puzzling new name to the confusion. The official told *The New York Times* that the Justice Department "was convinced that Mr. [Clay] Bertrand and Mr. Shaw were the same man." The FBI *did* investigate Clay Bertrand—which probably was the source of the confusion.[40]

By June there was yet another story. The Justice Department, asserting again that Shaw had never been investigated, stated: "The

Attorney General has since determined that this was erroneous. Nothing arose indicating the need to investigate Mr. Shaw. . . . Clay Bertrand was not identified as a real person. No evidence was found that Clay Shaw was ever called Clay Bertrand."[41]

It is probably impossible to sift through this morass to find the truth. However, it is certain that, ultimately, a major thrust of Garrison's case against Shaw was predicated on Shaw's alleged use of the alias Clay Bertrand. The aim of the prosecution was to prove that Clay Bertrand *was* involved in the conspiracy—and then prove that Shaw and Bertrand were one and the same. Shaw, of course, absolutely denied ever using the alias Clay Bertrand.[42] Nonetheless, Shaw was not served well by the confusion raised by Attorney General Ramsey Clark.* Clark's motive, curiously enough, seemed to be to offer Shaw support, by saying the FBI investigated him earlier and found him clean.

But all this took place over a period of several months, following Shaw's arrest. Two weeks after the arrest, Garrison presented his charges against Shaw at a preliminary hearing. A three-judge panel was to determine whether there was "sufficient evidence" to go ahead with a trial. For the first time, the public got a glimpse of Garrison's chief witness, as well as the outlines of the case he intended to prove against Shaw.[43]

Perry Raymond Russo, a neatly attired young man of twenty-five who worked as an insurance salesman in Baton Rouge, told the panel of judges of his friendship with David Ferrie during the early sixties. He swore that in September 1963 he attended a party at Ferrie's home that included an older man called Clem Bertrand and Ferrie's roommate, a young man, with a scraggly beard, called Leon Oswald. Russo, a college graduate, testified that he believed the two were Clay Shaw and Lee Harvey Oswald.[44]

Russo swore that he heard the two men discussing with Ferrie the details of an assassination plot. He heard them use such terms as "diversionary tactics" and "triangulation of cross fire." Russo said that he had never told anyone about his knowledge of the plot until he came forward after hearing about Garrison's investigation.[45]

A second witness, a heroin addict, was used as a backup to link Shaw and Oswald. He testified that one day in 1963, while he was

---

*Clark was no longer merely the Acting Attorney General; his appointment was confirmed by the Senate in mid-March 1967.

administering drugs to himself at the lakefront, he observed Shaw and Oswald together talking. He said that he watched Shaw give some money to Oswald. He could not, he said, hear what they were talking about.[46]

Based on these witnesses and on Garrison's presentation, the judges ruled that there was sufficient evidence for a trial.[47]

James Phelan, a journalist who was to become significantly involved in the Garrison case, has described in his book *Scandals, Scamps and Scoundrels* what happened next:

> In the public's mind, the judicial ruling . . . was a clear-cut victory for Garrison and gave an aura of substance to his conspiracy solution. . . . No one but Garrison and a few of his top aides knew that he had played all of his evidentiary hole cards. He implied that there was much more to come, and then set out to discover what it was. . . .
>
> The preliminary hearing victory made him a national media celebrity, and while his staff was energetically seeking new evidence, [Garrison] embarked on a long series of speeches, talk-show appearances, television, radio and magazine interviews. He had a seemingly endless supply of "new disclosures," all revealed with the . . . confidence of a man who knew exactly what he was doing.[48]

It seems inevitable that in the media circus that followed, Garrison's claims became increasingly far-flung, in terms of the elements he believed to be involved in the assassination. As the months went by, Garrison came up with allusions to dozens of conspirators and numerous theories, including one in which the real killer concealed himself in a manhole in Dealey Plaza, fired a shot into the President's head, and then escaped through the sewer system. In nearly every case, some sort of obscure evidence could be found to support even Garrison's most outlandish assertions. In the end, Garrison settled on a villain that he was comfortable with. He placed the ultimate blame on this country's "military-industrial complex," citing elements of the CIA as being deeply involved in the assassination.[49]

It was becoming increasingly difficult to understand how the defendant, Clay Shaw, fit into such labyrinthine schemes. Garrison insisted that he had the evidence and was anxious to go to trial, where he could present it.[50] But it would be nearly two years before the trial got under way. Meanwhile, the media circus continued, unabated.

Most of what Garrison was saying—and he was spewing out thousands of words for public consumption, while coyly refusing to discuss his "evidence" against Shaw—was indisputably rooted in the gross deficiencies of the Warren Commission. This, of course, was a welcome development for many commission critics, who had been unable to attain a national forum for their findings and suspicions. Ironically, Garrison drew to his cause respectable support from men and women who were often glad for a chance to provide him with their expertise. Few, however, were able to help him with his case against Shaw.*[51]

It is impossible to know if Garrison's case would have self-destructed—or whether it was Garrison's clumsy effort to manipulate the press that exploded in his face and wrecked his prosecution. The stage was set when writer James Phelan was dispatched to New Orleans by the *Saturday Evening Post* for a magazine piece on the unfolding Garrison investigation. Phelan had a good relationship with Garrison, from an earlier article he had done about New Orleans, and hoped that he could cajole the district attorney into giving him some special treatment. This was during the two-week period between Shaw's arrest and the preliminary hearing, when no one knew what evidence Garrison had against Shaw.[52]

In his larger-than-life manner, Garrison acceded magnificently. He said he would like to see a major story explaining his case in the magazine. But, he said, things were too hectic in New Orleans for a proper interview; they needed to escape the hordes of reporters from around the world. Garrison told Phelan to pick him up the next day at the airport in Las Vegas, Nevada. They would spend a couple of days there, where, Garrison said, they could talk in peace.[53]

Phelan spent hours in a Las Vegas hotel listening to Garrison, who had agreed to outline "the whole fantastic story" and to reveal to Phelan his evidence against Shaw. It was a reporter's dream, a primary source pouring out exclusive information. But there was a

*Harold Weisberg is an excellent example of such a critic. Much of his highly respected, pioneering work on Oswald's ties to some of the figures in Garrison's case is found in his book *Oswald in New Orleans*. Some other critics, however, were more skeptical of Garrison's "evidence."

growing difficulty, as Phelan sensed it. The more he listened to Garrison talk, the more uncertain Phelan became that Garrison had much of a case at all. He finally told Garrison that it was clear he had "dug up a lot of odd things, but it comes across as just circumstances, speculation, theory."[54]

It was then that Garrison, with customary self-assurance, told Phelan that he was going to show him "something no one knows about but my top people." According to Phelan, Garrison handed him a packet of documents and stated, "I've got the witness who ties this whole case together. He's my case against Shaw. Here's the evidence my witness is going to present in the Shaw hearing next week."[55]

Back at his hotel Phelan read the papers. There were two documents. One was a 3,500-word memorandum of an interview with Perry Russo conducted by Andrew "Moo Moo" Sciambra, a former boxer and one of Garrison's top assistants. That interview took place on February 25, after Russo read of Ferrie's death and contacted Garrison's office. The second document in Phelan's hands was a stenographic record of what Russo had said when placed under hypnosis several days later.[56]

James Phelan stated: "I read the documents with a deepening sense of horror and disbelief. Russo had told two different stories a few days apart. On the essential issue—the Ferrie, Shaw, Oswald plot to kill Kennedy—they contradicted each other."[57]

The essential point was that in Sciambra's memo of his first interview with Russo, there was not a word about the party where Shaw, Ferrie, and Oswald were supposed to have hatched a plot to kill the President. It was a crucial omission, for that gathering represented the sum of Garrison's evidence tying Shaw to a conspiracy. The conspiracy surfaced in the second document, after Russo had been administered "truth serum," hypnotized, and shown a photograph of Shaw. The transcript showed that it was the hypnotist who introduced the concept that the people at the gathering "are talking about assassinating somebody," which was the first reference to such plans.[58]

After making photocopies of the papers, Phelan returned them to Garrison with as little comment as possible. He said nothing about the terrible gap he had noticed. It was Phelan's belief that Garrison had never bothered to actually read the documents, relying purely on his assistants, who had not warned him of the discrepancy.[59]

A few days after this, Russo appeared at the preliminary hearing and testified that he was at the conspiracy meeting involving Shaw, Ferrie, and Oswald. It was largely this testimony that bound Shaw over for trial. The next day Phelan went to Garrison's home to discuss what Phelan called "a big hole in Russo's testimony." Phelan was about to write his story for the *Saturday Evening Post* and needed Garrison's explanation. When informed, Phelan reports, Garrison became visibly upset and summoned Moo Moo Sciambra to explain it.[60]

Sciambra at first disputed that the conspiracy meeting was not mentioned in his memorandum of the initial interview. Then, when confronted with the fact that Phelan had a copy of it, Sciambra offered elaborate explanations about how he had simply overlooked putting it into the memorandum. He insisted that Russo *had* reported the conspiracy meeting in the first interview, even if Sciambra had forgotten to include it in his report to Garrison. He argued that he certainly had *told* Garrison about it, even if it was not in the report.[61]

In the end there was a single compelling point. If Russo actually told Sciambra of the conspiracy meeting with Shaw at their first interview, it is almost impossible to imagine that Sciambra would forget to include it, knowing that the report could well become the centerpiece of Garrison's case against Shaw. (In fact, the report *did* become extremely important, but not for reasons that suited Garrison's office.)[62]

Phelan then sought out Perry Russo and asked him when he first told the Garrison investigators about the actual conspiracy meeting. Without the slightest hesitation, according to Phelan, Russo stated that it was subsequent to his first meeting with Sciambra, *after* he had been placed under hypnosis.[63]

Phelan's article ran as the cover story in the *Saturday Evening Post*. Its revelations gave Clay Shaw his first glimpse of the real nature of Garrison's case against him. Phelan agreed to appear as a defense witness in Shaw's trial.[64]

The revelations of the two documents' damaging inconsistencies did little to diminish public enthusiasm for the case. Garrison by then was talking about even more titillating evidence, as people from around the country poured into his office and blitzed his telephone with claims to strengthen his case against Shaw. Most of the claims, it is now known, were wildly absurd. Still, Garrison had his pick to use as he saw best.[65]

Through this whole period, which was punctuated by intense national publicity, Garrison sought to force certain prospective witnesses to come to New Orleans to give evidence, including federal agents and the former director of the Central Intelligence Agency. By this time, Garrison was claiming that Shaw had, in fact, been an agent of the CIA—an allegation that turned out to have some merit, though of dubious relevance to the case as charged. It is not surprising that there was a general reluctance among federal agencies to cooperate.[66]

Garrison soon moved beyond assertions that the CIA had murdered JFK to claim he had evidence that federal agencies were deliberately executing elaborate machinations to undermine his case. They intended, he said, to abort the emergence of "truth." In the end, some evidence of this was indicated.[67] The reasons, however, may have been more in reaction to Garrison's tactics than anything else. In any event, Garrison managed to alienate himself and the Shaw case from nearly every level of government in the United States.

On January 21, 1969, almost two years after his arrest, Shaw's conspiracy trial opened in New Orleans. The selection of a jury was predictably difficult, in a case of such notoriety. The very first prospective juror examined—a man whose name had been drawn blindly in open court—was promptly excused. His name: John Kennedy.[68]

After nearly 1,200 prospects were examined, the jury was finally seated. Judge Edward A. Haggerty, Jr., told the press that the jurors could be photographed later at their motel, only after putting on dress shirts and ties. "I don't want them looking like the Scopes trial," Judge Haggerty explained. He then announced that he intended to recess court each day by 5:30 P.M. "so we can catch Huntley-Brinkley and Cronkite [to] see what they say about us." These announcements from the judge largely set the tone for the rest of the trial, which lasted thirty-nine days and was one of the best publicized in American history.[69]

Jim Garrison's strongest hand was played before Russo's testimony, on the opening day of the prosecution's presentation. The testimony came from six people who lived at Clinton, Louisiana, a small town about 130 miles from New Orleans. Remarkably diverse witnesses, they testified with impressive consistency that during the late summer of 1963, they had seen three strange men in their town. The three were identified as Lee Harvey Oswald, David Ferrie, and Clay Shaw. Oswald, accompanied by Ferrie and Shaw, seemed to be trying to secure a job. In doing so, he had visited a barber shop and later tried to register to vote. The testimony was a convincing boost to the basic prosecution assertion that Shaw, in contrast to his sworn denials, *did* know Ferrie and Oswald. The consensus among courtroom observers was that these witnesses were the most persuasive presented by the prosecution. This fresh evidence, never mentioned by the Warren Commission, was Garrison's most valuable contribution to an understanding of Oswald's activities. It was virtually lost in the circus atmosphere that characterized the rest of the trial.

From that point forward, everything was downhill for Garrison's case against Shaw.[70]

Perry Russo, Garrison's star witness, remained the centerpiece of his case to show that Shaw, Ferrie, and Oswald engaged in a conspiracy to assassinate the President. However, Russo's claims were devastated by the testimony of James Phelan. Even worse for Garrison, the defense presented a veteran New Orleans police officer, a lieutenant in the homicide division, who testified that Perry Russo told him that, in truth, Shaw probably was *not* the man he saw at Ferrie's apartment that night in 1963.*[71]

On the other hand, all Clay Shaw could do in his defense was to take the stand and deny that he ever knew Oswald or Ferrie, or that he ever used an alias. He asserted that he had never engaged in a conspiracy to murder the President of the United States. In trying to prove such a negative, there simply was nothing more of substance the defense could do, although witnesses—including Marina Oswald—were summoned to show the unlikely nature of some of the prosecution's basic points.[72]

Before it was all over, Garrison—who hardly ever appeared in the courtroom—struggled mightily to have his assistants put the

---

*The one likely explanation for Russo's erratic testimony is, as he told several people privately, that he never dreamed that he was the *only* witness Garrison had to make the conspiracy point. In agreeable innocence, Russo said that he *thought* he saw an older man at a gathering who *could* have been Shaw. At each step, Russo faced the wrath of Garrison's office if he retreated on a point he had been led to previously. Clear indications suggest that Russo was as shocked as anyone to find himself the star witness—the centerpiece around whom the rest of the case revolved.

Warren Commission on trial. Among some forty-five witnesses called by the prosecution, one was a JFK autopsy doctor, and several were FBI agents; numerous witnesses were presented who had been in Dealey Plaza at the time of the assassination. The real highlight of the trial was the showing of the Zapruder film, which the prosecution managed to screen ten times in an effort to show the "triangulation of cross fire" and the devastation to the President. Even Abraham Zapruder, retiring by nature, was on hand to testify that he made the famous home movie and to indicate where he was standing, using an elaborate chart of Dealey Plaza.[73]

The most amusing of the many unusual events at the trial was the prosecution's presentation of a surprise witness from New York City, one Charles I. Spiesel, who stated that he was an accountant. At first Spiesel was a marvelously impressive witness, whose presence sent chills through Shaw's defense. He dressed impeccably and spoke articulately and with calm authority. He testified that during the summer of 1963, while on a visit to see his daughter, who was in school in New Orleans, he attended a party with a man named David Ferrie, whom he had met at a bar. Spiesel then identified the host of the party as Clay Shaw. He calmly swore that he listened quietly as Ferrie and Shaw discussed plans to assassinate the President of the United States.[74]

Jim Garrison's heart must have leaped with joy to discover a witness who shored up the badly tarnished Perry Russo. Spiesel was the perfect witness—up until the moment the prosecution completed its examination.

By the time the defense lawyer concluded his long and gentle questioning of Spiesel, the dapper little man had enthusiastically revealed that, for years, he had been plagued by complete strangers who, at the flick of an eye, could hypnotize him and control his life. Spiesel guessed that as many as sixty different people had placed him under hypnosis—and that he could never be certain at any given moment whether he was under a hypnotic spell.[75]

Spiesel also acknowledged to the defense lawyer his life-long consuming fear that he was constantly followed by agents of various nefarious groups, among them the Communists seeking to disrupt his life. He stated that he had learned to be so careful that when his daughter visited, he fingerprinted her to make sure she actually was his daughter. He explained that, in this manner, he could be certain she was not some agent merely disguised as his daughter.[76]

Thus, Garrison's only witness to support Russo on the conspiracy point was demolished amid the muffled sniggers of the courtroom. If Garrison was desperate enough to use the pitiable Charles I. Spiesel, it leaves one breathless to consider the quality of witnesses he decided to turn away.[77]

Garrison's evidence on the matter of Shaw's alleged use of the name Clem or Clay Bertrand was a bit more persuasive. He produced a letter carrier who testified that he delivered mail to a Clem Bertrand at a location where Clay Shaw was temporarily receiving his mail. The postman said that none of the several letters he recalled delivering to Clem Bertrand at that address had ever been returned. Garrison also came up with a hostess from a VIP lounge at the New Orleans airport who testified that Clay Shaw was the man she saw sign her guest registry as Clay Bertrand. The guest registry book was produced, and each side presented a handwriting expert to counter the other on whether the writing was that of Clay Shaw.[78]

One of the most tantalizing aspects of the Clem Bertrand evidence concerned the original arrest sheet and fingerprint card, filled out when Shaw was booked following his arrest. The booking officer, a veteran New Orleans police officer named Aloysius J. Habighorst, stated that when he asked Shaw to list any aliases he used, Shaw gave the name Clay Bertrand. (This would have been prior to any wide publicity concerning the notoriety of the name Clem or Clay Bertrand.)[79]

Officer Habighorst claimed he dutifully typed that name onto the card. Clay denied that he provided anyone with that name at the time of his arrest, claiming that the fingerprint card was blank when he signed it. According to the testimony, the card with Shaw's fingerprints—which the judge deemed inadmissible as evidence—showed the name Clay Bertrand in the blank for any alias used by the person arrested. The name Clay Bertrand also appears in the space for aliases on the arrest sheet, which was supposedly filled out in Shaw's presence, but not signed by Shaw.[80]

However, in court, a technical legal debate erupted over whether Habighorst could testify that Shaw gave him the name Clay Bertrand as an alias.[81] Judge Haggerty refused to allow Habighorst to testify before the jury and stated, "Officer Habighorst did not forewarn

Shaw of his right to remain silent. Even if Officer Habighorst did question him—and from what I've heard I seriously doubt it—"

"Your honor!" shouted one of the assistant prosecutors. "Are you ruling on the credibility of Habighorst?"

"No jurors are present," answered Judge Haggerty.

"But you are passing on the credibility of a witness before the press and the world," said the prosecutor.

"I don't care," responded the judge. "The whole world can hear that I do not believe Officer Habighorst. I do not believe Officer Habighorst."[82]

The prosecutor then demanded a mistrial, which Judge Haggerty promptly denied. The jury thus never heard the testimony of Habighorst, a veteran policeman, who was prepared to swear that Clay Shaw told him that he used the alias Clay Bertrand.[83]

The dispute over the alias Clay Bertrand may have become academic at the trial, thanks to a lawyer named Dean Andrews. At the heart of an enormous amount of testimony and evidence—going back to what Andrews told the Warren Commission—is the clear fact that Andrews is the first person to introduce the name of Clay or Clem Bertrand into any consideration. Andrews linked Bertrand to Lee Harvey Oswald and several Latin Americans in New Orleans in 1963. Andrews claimed he had done some minor legal work for Oswald and that after the assassination, Clay Bertrand telephoned him and asked him if he would represent Oswald in Dallas.[84] Several years later, Garrison based much of his case on the proposition that Clay Bertrand and Clay Shaw were one and the same—despite the conflicting descriptions of "Bertrand" that Andrews gave at different times. After all, it complemented Perry Russo's allegations perfectly. However, the whole issue came apart at the seams when Andrews, testifying for Shaw's defense, said that the story he gave regarding Clay Bertrand and Oswald was purely a "figment of [his] imagination." (Garrison later charged Andrews with perjury and obtained a conviction.) Andrews's testimony must have had a powerful effect on the jury.[85]

Jim Garrison's performance proved to be disappointing, particularly after months of highly publicized promises of what he would present at the trial. He produced no witnesses to suggest CIA involvement in an assassination conspiracy. He produced nothing, really, that went beyond what had been presented at the preliminary hearing two years earlier. He did not even come to the courtroom to hear Clay Shaw's testimony. He also missed about half of the defense's closing statement.[86]

On the last day of the trial, Garrison appeared to offer the closing argument for the prosecution. In his carefully rehearsed address of twenty-five minutes, Garrison mentioned the name of Clay Shaw only once. His aim, obviously, was to address what he considered to be a larger and more significant point than the charges he had filed against Clay Shaw.[87]

Here are the closing paragraphs of Garrison's final statement to the jury:

> The murder of John Kennedy was probably the most terrible moment in the history of our country. Yet, circumstances have placed you in the position where not only have you seen the hidden evidence but you are actually going to have the opportunity to bring justice into the picture for the first time.
>
> Now, you are here sitting in judgment on Clay Shaw. Yet you, as men, represent more than jurors in an ordinary case because of the victim in this case. You represent, in a sense, the hope of humanity against government power. You represent humanity, which yet may triumph over excessive government power—if you will cause it to be so, in the course of doing your duty in this case.
>
> I suggest that you ask not what your country can do for you but what you can do for your country.
>
> What can you do for your country? You can cause justice to happen for the first time in this matter. You can help make our country better by showing that this is still a government of the people. And if you do that, as long as you live, nothing will ever be more important.[88]

It took the jury only one ballot to find Clay Shaw innocent of conspiracy to assassinate John F. Kennedy. His acquittal came on March 1, 1969, two years to the day after his arrest. Though his horrendous legal expenses had wiped out his personal resources, Shaw seemed to hold no bitterness. Obviously, things could have been worse.[89]

Two days later, Garrison charged Shaw with perjury, claiming he lied when he denied certain points in the trial. Such a move by a prosecutor toward an acquitted person was practically unheard of, raising the serious constitutional question of double jeopardy. Still, Shaw would not be goaded into making a negative comment about Garrison. Five years later, his legal entanglements with Garrison still in the courts, Clay Shaw died of cancer. He was sixty-one.[90]

Pearls in the Slime

The reaction to Jim Garrison's prosecution of Clay Shaw was howling outrage.[91] In a tone that was reflected across the country, the *New Orleans States-Item* demanded that Garrison resign, claiming that he had "perverted the law rather than prosecuted it." Railing against Garrison, the newspaper stated: "This travesty of justice is a reproach to the conscience of all good men. . . . Mr. Garrison stands revealed for what he is: A man without principle who would pervert the legal process to his own ends."[92]

The New York Times, accusing Garrison of the "persecution of an innocent man," called the whole episode "one of the most disgraceful chapters in the history of American jurisprudence."[93]

As Garrison was being vilified from every corner of America, Shaw was portrayed as one of the most noble victims in the history of capricious prosecutions.[94] The enumeration of shocking tactics began with Garrison's well-publicized seizure of Shaw's whips and chains on the day of his arrest. This ostentatious performance persisted through the long pretrial period and did not end even with the charge of perjury that followed Shaw's acquittal. To many observers, Jim Garrison seemed obsessed with the destruction of Clay Shaw.[95]

This international vilification never seemed to bother Jim Garrison or, for that matter, the majority of voters of New Orleans. Considering the attention Garrison had directed away from Carlos Marcello, it is not surprising that he continued to coexist peacefully with organized crime. Garrison was handily reelected to his office in 1970, and it is even possible that he was helped locally by the publicity he received over the Shaw trial. In 1973 he lost another bid for reelection.[96]

In 1971 Garrison experienced legal difficulties over federal charges of fraud and conspiracy. Garrison was acquitted of all charges— including an allegation that he accepted payoffs to allow illegal gambling operations—and rather proudly displays these difficulties as scars of his victories over the powers that be. Today, he serves as an appeals judge, an elected office in New Orleans.[97]

In 1981 Garrison reaffirmed to the author his belief that he conducted a just prosecution of Clay Shaw. He reiterated his feeling that the United States government has purposely allowed the JFK case to go unsolved. Garrison said, "The frustrating thing is that really there is no mystery about it at all." With that statement, Garrison launched into a harangue about the military-industrial-intelligence complex and how, he believed (and still believes), it somehow carried off the assassination of President Kennedy.[98]

None of this, however, goes to the heart of Garrison's prosecution of Clay Shaw. Today, in discussing the case, still with considerable enthusiasm, Garrison does not point to specific evidence that he found particularly persuasive against Shaw. Rather, he speaks of the much grander schemes to which he alluded in his closing statement at the trial. He mentions the witnesses he did *not* present—and from there he proceeds to explain his reasons for being certain he does know who killed JFK. He speaks of Clay Shaw's connections with a group that he claims was a CIA operation. He cites his evidence that Shaw *was* an agent for the CIA. He states his firm belief that Shaw *did* know Ferrie, and that the two of them associated with Oswald. He speaks of his certainty that Shaw used the alias Clay Bertrand. Garrison's fervor for his case has not diminished.[99]

The fundamental trouble with most of what Garrison says on this point is that it has absolutely *nothing* to do with the specific conspiracy charge of which Clay Shaw was acquitted. Lee Oswald associated fleetingly with hundreds of people during his short adulthood, and so far not a single one has been proved to have conspired with him to assassinate President Kennedy. It is worth keeping in mind that Shaw could have known Ferrie—and even Oswald, but that alone would not mean that he conspired with them to kill President Kennedy.[100] It could even be established that Shaw is the elusive Clay Bertrand, and that would not *prove* anything beyond his having a secret life and associations with dubious characters.

At every turn—then and now—Garrison seemed to be telling the world that since he was on to *something*, then it was only right that Shaw, who indeed may have known Oswald and Ferrie, should be convicted. The American judicial system, as the New Orleans jury quickly demonstrated, does not work that way.

But the questions persist. What did Jim Garrison have? Putting aside the matter of his proved innocence, who *was* Clay Shaw? Did he associate with Oswald and David Ferrie? Was he connected to the CIA? The great irony is that Jim Garrison was correct on several points that may well be related to the JFK assassination. He publicly raised questions that still cry out for resolution. Moreover, in one important area concerning Oswald's associations, Garrison today can claim complete vindication by the House Select Committee.

An event in Oswald's life that still challenges comprehension is his presence in Clinton, Louisiana, during the late summer of 1963, when he seemed to be seeking a job. It was perhaps Garrison's most important revelation. In 1978 the Select Committee examined the six Clinton witnesses, who included an elected state representative, a deputy sheriff, and a voting registrar.[101] In its final report, the committee states: "The Committee found that the Clinton witnesses were credible and significant. . . . Some of the witnesses said that Oswald was accompanied by two older men whom they identified as Ferrie and Shaw. If the witnesses were not only truthful but accurate as well in their accounts, they established an association of an undetermined nature between Ferrie, Shaw, and Oswald less than three months before the assassination."[102]

There is virtually no doubt that Oswald, or someone pretending to be Oswald, was in Clinton as described. Given Ferrie's outlandish appearance, it seems certain that the witnesses have properly identified him. As for the third man, cited as Clay Shaw, his identification falls short of the certainty evident in the identification of Oswald and Ferrie. (Oswald actually produced military identification.) The third man was seen only in an automobile, and the cited descriptions could just as well be that of Guy Banister, the former FBI agent and Ferrie associate who will be examined thoroughly in later pages. This possibility has been noted by other writers and critics, who have pointed out that both men were described as being tall and heavily built, with gray hair. As will be seen, it probably makes more sense to believe that the man was Banister rather than Shaw. A prime reason is that Ferrie and Banister are solidly linked in a variety of ways that are unrelated to this incident.[103]

Aside from Garrison's revelation about the Clinton visit, there are several aspects of interest about Shaw. Garrison intimated outside the courtroom that Shaw had been associated with the CIA, a point he did not bring up at the trial.[104] Indeed, Shaw's professional associations are, in this respect, extremely noteworthy. While they have no known connection to an assassination conspiracy, they do raise questions about just who Clay Shaw was and how sensitive the government might have felt about revelations stemming from his prosecution. And, while his sex life is irrelevant to the assassination conspiracy, it, at the same time, may explain misconceptions that have sprung up, some of which may have propelled Garrison along his disastrous course.

Following his distinguished service in Europe during World War II, including combat decorations, Clay Shaw returned to New Orleans. From 1946 until August 1965, he was the managing director of the International Trade Mart, an organization aimed at the development of international trade relations, especially for the Port of New Orleans. In the course of things, Shaw became quite wealthy through his private business dealings, particularly in real estate.[105]

Shaw seems to have done a masterful job for his employers, blending his work as a promoter into his personal life as a writer and patron of the arts. He was at ease in the cultivated social and artistic life of New Orleans and counted among his close friends the most prominent men and women of the city. Stories are told of Shaw's generosity toward friends and his willingness to make sacrifices for others.[106]

Shaw's homosexuality was not an open matter, but rather an aspect of his life that seems not to have interested the people who were his friends and business associates. Even in New Orleans, during those years, it is unlikely that flagrant homosexuality would have been acceptable for a man in Shaw's position. He was, after all, a leading promoter of New Orleans to the outside world. It is not surprising that Shaw's private sex life was not a subject of common knowledge or discussion.[107]

Nor should it be surprising that, indeed, there was a darker side to Shaw's life that he did not flaunt. Given what is known of Hoover's FBI during those years, it is fairly predictable that the sex life of a man of Shaw's stature would come under official scrutiny. As early as 1954, the FBI recorded in its files the report of a New Orleans informant who stated that he "had relations of a homosexual nature with Clay Shaw." The FBI report then notes the informant's report that Shaw was "given to sadism and masochism in his homosexual activities."[108]

In view of this—as well as other unseemly evidence of a similar nature turned up by Garrison's office—it is not outlandish that Shaw might have engaged in a sexual association with David Ferrie. By the same token, he could have been associated with a whole network of homosexual activity that existed in New Orleans's French Quarter, where Shaw lived. It could, indeed, be that Shaw, in a fairly discreet manner, maintained sexual relationships that he very much wanted to conceal—relationships having absolutely nothing to do with a conspiracy to assassinate the President. However, the mere act of concealment—particularly if he falsely denied a relationship in court—could be sufficient to stimulate dark suspicions. Such a hypothesis is enhanced by the fact that Shaw was apparently unhappy over the suggestions of his homosexuality that were bandied about during his two-year nightmare. [109]

In 1977 a CIA document was disclosed that confirmed that Shaw had a relationship with the CIA. The information was contained in a 1967 memorandum prepared by the CIA in response to queries from the Justice Department—queries stimulated by Garrison's investigation. It confirmed, at least in part, the connection Shaw had with the agency during his early years with the International Trade Mart. [110]

According to this document, reports from Shaw to the CIA were concerned with international trade as well as with political activities. The reports included various activities in East Germany, Czechoslovakia, Peru, Argentina, and Nicaragua. Between the years 1949 and 1956, according to the document, there were thirty occasions when the agency received information from Shaw. [111]

While the reported contacts stopped in 1956, Shaw apparently continued to enjoy a favorable relationship with the agency. It is not unreasonable to speculate that when the record of reports stopped in 1956, Shaw moved into a more significant role with the CIA—one that no longer went into an accounting in agency files. [112] Even Allen Dulles, the most prominent of the early directors of Central Intelligence, has stated that often no records are kept of the activities of agents. [113]

The apparently favorable relationship between Shaw and the CIA was made manifest in May 1961, when Shaw was asked to introduce the deputy director of the CIA, General Charles P. Cabell, who was in New Orleans to address the Foreign Policy Association. Shaw was program chairman of that group. General Cabell's speech in New Orleans came less than one month after he had personally supervised the disastrous Bay of Pigs invasion.*[114] But General Cabell, who later was replaced by President Kennedy, did not use the New Orleans occasion to castigate the President. (Instead, he spoke about how the Soviet system had applied science to further its ideological goals.) The point here is that the selection of Clay Shaw to introduce General Cabell, the second highest figure at the CIA, suggests—in the absence of any record of Shaw's continuing reports to the CIA after 1956—that Shaw continued to enjoy a good relationship with the agency.†[115]

Of the legitimate nuggets bandied about by Jim Garrison, none is more significant than the virtually solid evidence of Oswald's association with David W. Ferrie.[116] That link is a taproot from which Oswald's activities run in numerous directions. It is unlikely that the whole truth about Ferrie will ever emerge—or be widely accepted in the event that it does. He is, nonetheless, a significant subject for scrutiny.

Ferrie's known associations form a witch's brew of sinister elements. He can be solidly linked to the mobster Carlos Marcello, with whom he shared an intense hatred for President Kennedy. (See Chapter 8 for details about Marcello and the Kennedy administration.) For many years Ferrie was closely associated with Guy Banister, a rabid extremist and former FBI man who was deeply involved with government intelligence operations in New Orleans—particularly as they related to Cuban exiles and their plans to "liberate" Cuba. This close association makes it quite possible that it was Banister who was in Clinton, Louisiana, with Oswald and Ferrie in the summer of 1963.[117]

And there is the possibility of a more direct connection between Ferrie and U.S. intelligence—one that, not surprisingly, has never

---

*Today it is known that Cabell and his associates were vehement in their rage toward what they perceived as President Kennedy's "desertion" on the morning of the invasion—the President's refusal to send in military force sufficient to ensure victory. The dispute was so intense that President Kennedy was moved to make his famous comment about wanting to "splinter the CIA in a thousand pieces and scatter it to the winds" over his belief that they had so badly misinformed him about their invasion plans.

†It is one of history's odd coincidences that General Cabell's brother, Earle, was the mayor of Dallas in November 1963. He was riding in the motorcade several cars back from the President when Kennedy was struck.

been confirmed. The most likely role for Ferrie was as a pilot involved in the strategy leading up to the Bay of Pigs invasion.[118] While the HSCA could not confirm such a role, it seemed particularly impressed with the connections between Ferrie and Carlos Marcello. It found that it was likely Ferrie had been a private pilot for Marcello, and the committee even considered "an unconfirmed Border Patrol report" that Ferrie had secretly flown the mobster back to New Orleans from Guatemala following his sudden deportation by Robert Kennedy in April 1961. However, testifying in an executive session of the HSCA, Marcello denied this. Another interesting link between Ferrie and the New Orleans mob boss is that apparently following the JFK murder, Marcello set up Ferrie with a gas-station franchise—a fact ignored by Garrison in his investigation of Ferrie. If nothing else, the gesture suggested an obligation Marcello felt he owed Ferrie.[119]

Yet another oddity in Ferrie's activities examined by the Select Committee involved a fifteen-minute telephone call he appeared to have made to Jean West in Chicago two months prior to Kennedy's death. On the eve of the assassination, Miss West was in Dallas having drinks with Jack Ruby.[120] While none of this makes a conspiracy, it heightens the provocative interlocking connections that seem to link David Ferrie with various figures, including Marcello, Jack Ruby, and Lee Harvey Oswald.

David Ferrie's most important connection was one that he denied until his death—his suspected association with Oswald. Today the likelihood of that association is greater than ever. In addition to the sighting at Clinton in 1963, Oswald, as a teenager, belonged to Ferrie's unit of the Civil Air Patrol in New Orleans. Today, there are additional eyewitness reports that verify the association.[121]

Despite Ferrie's denial that he knew Oswald, he was plagued with the accusation from the first days of Oswald's notoriety. Even in 1963, the circumstantial evidence against Ferrie was so substantial that he was one of the earliest suspects questioned and released by the FBI.[122] It is worth considering Ferrie's activities—not because they prove anything, but because of the light they shed on this strange man. At the very least, Ferrie had a remarkable penchant for making himself *appear* to be involved, even if he was not.

During the fall of 1963, David W. Ferrie was supposedly occupied with his work on the immigration case involving Carlos Marcello.

Ferrie was employed as an investigator by Marcello's lawyer. During the two weekends prior to the JFK assassination in November, Ferrie was at Churchill Farms, Marcello's 3,000-acre estate just outside New Orleans. Ferrie was supposedly at Marcello's home to participate in strategy sessions for the trial.[123]

That trial ended on November 22, 1963, in a federal courtroom in New Orleans, when Marcello was acquitted. Ferrie was last seen by a reliable witness around midday that Friday, almost at the time word was received that Kennedy had been shot in Dallas.[124] Such a perfectly packaged alibi, it seems, was all too neat for the daring pilot with the orange monkey hair.

Around nine that evening, Ferrie set off on a trip to Texas. He later explained that he wanted to relax after the trial's conclusion; he claimed he first decided to depart New Orleans without firm plans, not really knowing if he was going off "hunting, drinking or driving."[125] This whim took Ferrie and two young male friends on a seven-hour drive through a storm from New Orleans to Houston, a distance of 364 miles.[126]

The sole purpose of this trip, according to Ferrie's later contradictory statements, was to look over an ice rink and to do some skating.[127]

When they reached Houston at 4:30 in the morning, Ferrie and his youthful companions checked into a motel. Telephone records show that while at the motel, Ferrie made four telephone calls to New Orleans—three of them seemingly innocuous. One of the calls, however, was to the headquarters of Carlos Marcello. The purpose of that call, Ferrie claimed, was an attempt to locate the lawyer for whom he worked.[128]

The following day, after getting some rest at the motel, Ferrie and his companions arrived at the Winterland Ice Skating Rink. (The rink's manager told investigators that Ferrie, whom he had never met, had called him from New Orleans to check on his hours of operation.) Upon arriving at the rink, Ferrie introduced himself and told the manager that he and his party would be in and out of the place during the weekend—a weekend that included, among other shattering events, the murder of Oswald by Jack Ruby.[129]

As if Ferrie's presence at the skating rink were not already odd enough, there is another twist. While there, Ferrie never put on a pair of ice skates. Instead, he stayed beside a public telephone for two hours, until he received a call. There is no record of the calls made over that telephone.[130]

When the strange trio left the rink, their first stop was another skating rink in Houston. They then decided to drive on to Galveston before heading back to Louisiana on Sunday night. During this final leg of the trip, Ferrie telephoned a friend in New Orleans who informed him that he was being sought in connection with the assassination of President Kennedy.[131]

In many ways, Ferrie was a predictable suspect. He readily admitted making violent comments suggesting the benefits to America if someone would shoot the President. He had bitterly denounced Kennedy following the Bay of Pigs debacle. On one occasion, Ferrie had to be removed from a speaker's podium at a men's civic club when his comments about Kennedy became violently offensive. Leaders of the group that had invited him to speak felt compelled to squelch his vitriolic and violent bombast.[132]

Much later, in a note apparently written hours before his death, Ferrie reaffirmed his political colors when he wrote that "an electorate cannot be depended on to pick the right man."[133] For all these reasons, it seems certain that Ferrie would not object to the fact or the manner of Kennedy's abrupt removal from office.

Ferrie's reputation as a Kennedy-hater no doubt contributed to the early reports in New Orleans that he had been involved in the assassination.[134] Many knew, too, of his close association with Carlos Marcello, a man with the most intense personal reasons for wanting to see an end to all Kennedy power in the United States.[135]

In any event, the day after his return from the skating escapade in Texas, Ferrie presented himself at the office of the New Orleans district attorney. He was questioned by Jim Garrison's staff and then turned over to the FBI and Secret Service for additional investigation.[136]

The specific reports that led to suspicions of Ferrie came from several sources. One report was that Oswald, when arrested, was carrying Ferrie's New Orleans library card. This apparently was not true. It was also alleged that Ferrie had taught Oswald how to shoot using a telescopic lens when Oswald was a cadet in Ferrie's unit of the Civil Air Patrol.[137]

Ferrie denied that he had ever even met Oswald. He was quickly sent on his way by the FBI and the Secret Service.[138] It was not until three years later that Garrison's office resurrected the whole matter of Ferrie's possible connection to the assassination.

What, though, could Ferrie have been doing at the ice-skating rink in Houston?

Garrison was convinced that the trip was part of the post-assassination phase of the conspiracy. He found that Jack Ruby placed a call to Galveston the night after the assassination, which was during the period of Ferrie's visit there.[139]

Despite intense efforts by Garrison to develop additional evidence to explain Ferrie's reasons for such behavior, the trip remains a mystery. Moreover, there is not the slightest indication that the young men with Ferrie—one of them a high school student—knew what was going on or knew the names of the people Ferrie was talking to on the telephone.[140]

Maybe the whole affair was nothing more than a romp through the rain. Maybe, too, it was something else.

From the moment of Ferrie's death and Clay Shaw's arrest, Jim Garrison saw sinister shadows dancing around (and even within) his prosecution. He believed that he and his office were under extensive surveillance, and he instigated an internal system of code words in an effort to thwart the perceived surveillance. He claimed that the intelligence powers in Washington were working to wreck his case. Garrison also saw evidence of collusion to disrupt his case in the fact that five states refused to extradite certain witnesses. There was the peculiar business of Attorney General Ramsey Clark's leaping into the New Orleans fray with his confused and contradictory statements about Clay Shaw's innocence. Clark's actions, if nothing else, demonstrated that the Justice Department was intent on doing its part to exonerate Shaw. Even President Johnson took a personal interest in the events surrounding the prosecution.[141]

If Garrison had offered a more persuasive case, perhaps some of his subsequent charges could be taken more seriously. Considering the mad atmosphere that marked the whole two-year episode, it is not surprising that five states declined to extradite their residents who did not want to become involved. Moreover, it seems predictable that officials in Washington would be reluctant to testify in such an extravaganza if they could avoid it. While there may have been some technical deficiencies in this lack of cooperation, it is, from a practical standpoint, easy to understand.

However, what is difficult to understand is a report that the CIA, at its highest level, was concerned on a regular basis with the progress of the Garrison case. Victor Marchetti, who resigned from the agency in 1969, served as an executive assistant to the CIA deputy director at the time of the case. Marchetti has told Warren Commission critic Bernard Fensterwald, Jr., that he heard agency officials, during their regular staff meeting one morning, discuss the need for providing help in the Garrison case. While Marchetti does not claim he heard specific discussion about ways to *wreck* Garrison's case, he says that the comments, even at the level of director, were in terms of questions like, "Are we giving them all the help they need?"[142]

It is likely that such comments did not refer to helping Garrison. However, what is not known are details of the "help," if any, Shaw may have been provided by the CIA. That was not discussed at the meeting attended by Marchetti. It was also on this occasion that Marchetti heard what would become public many years later—that Clay Shaw had been of service to the agency.[143]

In the final analysis, Jim Garrison never proved a single point in court against Clay Shaw—a fact that is largely responsible for the vilification of Garrison that continues to this day.[144] It will never be known what would have been proved if David Ferrie had lived. Garrison did, however, raise questions that go to the heart of the enduring mystery of the Kennedy assassination. Most of those questions were stimulated by the simple, logical belief of so many—that *something* was going on in New Orleans. Even today, no area of the incomplete investigation is richer than New Orleans in tantalizing irony and coincidence.

At the core of all the questions raised—about Oswald and Ferrie, Marcello, Guy Banister, various Cubans—is the persistent puzzle about the true nature of Oswald's activities in New Orleans. Two most obvious questions: Was he pretending to work for a pro-Castro group as a cover for true anti-Castro activities? Or was his behavior a normal extension of his lifelong flirtation with Marxist causes?

Any attempt to understand this must begin at a shabby building in the heart of New Orleans that, in light of what is known today, seems like a setting for a political farce—replete with false fronts, side exits, and dual addresses. The cast of characters within would rival David Ferrie himself. But what might have been comedy is darkened by the presence of shadowy figures involved in chilling counterintelligence games. Their interest ran to Cuban exiles, to the FBI, to the CIA, to organized crime. One of the more enigmatic of those shadowy figures was Lee Harvey Oswald.

The Camp Street Mysteries

The impassioned extremism of William Guy Banister burned with a rare intensity. His virulent racism was reflected in his open expression of bombastic segregationist views. A leading member of the John Birch Society, Banister was rabid in his opposition to communism. Such convictions easily fed his preoccupation with aiding Cuban exiles in their efforts to overthrow Fidel Castro. In addition to these searing emotional commitments, Banister was an alcoholic with a stormy temperament that made him a very dangerous character. In fact, there are reports of his using his pistol to beat the head of a man with whom he was angry. One can easily imagine this man's feelings about the Kennedy administration and its supporting cast—the New Frontier.[145]

But Banister was much more than just another right-wing fanatic. Before arriving in New Orleans in the 1950s, he had a long career with the FBI. By the time he retired in 1954, Banister had attained the coveted position of special agent in charge of the bureau's Chicago office, one of the most important in the country. Banister was eventually appointed by the mayor of New Orleans to be assistant superintendent of that city's police department. On paper, Guy Banister was eminently qualified for service in New Orleans—whether it be in law enforcement, intelligence work, private investigation, or plain old-fashioned rabble-rousing.*[146]

But Banister's bloom soon faded in New Orleans. He went into a bilious rage at a waiter in a Bourbon Street bar and pulled his gun. There was publicity. Banister was fired by the police department. This could only have added more bitterness to an already

---

* The HSCA determined that in September 1960 the CIA considered using Banister "for the collection of foreign intelligence but ultimately decided against it." Again, one is drawn to the authoritative comments cited earlier that indicate there might be no records of a covert relationship between the CIA and an agent.

embittered and dyspeptic psyche. Almost at once he formed something called Guy Banister Associates, a loosely organized private-detective agency dedicated to the zealous pursuit of Banister's personal political missions. One of his earliest recruits was the equally frenetic man for nearly any cause, that daring pilot, Communist hater, and religious zealot, David W. Ferrie.[147]

Also naturally drawn to Banister's group was a volatile mix of Cuban exiles—many of whom were also involved in carrying out missions for various segments of U.S. intelligence. Banister's office was filled with files and maps concerning Communist groups and Cuba. Observers who visited the office recall the vast assortment of weapons and military armaments, including grenades and ammunition, that was housed there. What lines ran to U.S. intelligence probably will never be firmly established, but there can be little doubt that the ties existed. While propinquity alone is hardly solid evidence, in this strange case it cannot be disregarded.*[148]

Banister's office was located in an old building in a drab and dingy part of central New Orleans bordered by two streets, Camp and Lafayette. The logistics of this location allowed the three-story building to have two legitimate addresses—531 Lafayette Street and 544 Camp Street.[149] This dual address would become the source of intense confusion regarding Banister and his associates.

Putting aside actual street numbers, the location of the Banister office was central to a variety of activities that no doubt interested him. He was close to the local headquarters of the CIA and the FBI. The Secret Service kept its fleet of automobiles less than a block from Banister at the Crescent City Garage. Close by was the post office, which reportedly housed drop sites for various agents.[150]

Given the presence of such facilities, it is far from surprising that the New Orleans chapter of the CIA-sponsored Cuban Revolutionary Council (CRC), headed by Sergio Arcacha Smith, took office space in Banister's building for several months, prior to Oswald's arrival in New Orleans. The CRC was an umbrella group formed to coordinate diverse exile activities. It was recognized as the CIA's primary front organization for intelligence and military activities against Cuba. Samuel Newman, the owner of the shabby old building, has stated that his tenant Banister urged him to lease space to

* In 1983, a CIA document was released that had been written in 1967. In that report, Banister is referred to as an "FBI Contact."

the Cuban exiles. At a glance, though, one would never suspect that the CRC had its headquarters in Banister's building; the address Banister used was 531 Lafayette Street, and the address for the CRC was 544 Camp Street. They were, of course, one and the same building.[151]

Less than one block from Banister's office was the William B. Reily Company, makers of Luzianne coffee. Only the most convoluted theories include the Reily company as a player in the possibly sinister New Orleans connections. However, during that period, the spring of 1963, the coffee company had among its employees one young man who, indeed, would become the prime player on center stage: Lee Harvey Oswald.[152]

In trying to grasp any possible significance in Oswald's proximity to Banister's operation, two factors become clear. First, there is no rational doubt that Guy Banister was sincere in his hatred for all that Fidel Castro stood for. No one can doubt Banister's commitment to aiding the overthrow of the Cuban government. No one has suggested that Banister's fanatical posture was a façade.[153] The second point that appears, on the surface, to be almost as certain is Oswald's pro-Castro position. From his youth, Oswald had shown such leanings, and his pro-Castro activities seemed perfectly in keeping with all that is known of his political persuasions.[154]

It therefore comes as a considerable surprise to look at the accumulation of convincing evidence showing Oswald's association with Guy Banister, David Ferrie, and the anti-Castro Cuban exiles. Oswald's connections to Ferrie have been established in earlier pages, and while he cannot be so firmly linked to Banister, some of the more impressive evidence is worth examination. It goes far beyond the certainty that Oswald frequented the small coffee shop, Mancuso's Restaurant, on the ground floor of Banister's building, along with Banister and his motley confederates. And it goes beyond the fact that William Gaudet, the CIA operative whose Mexican tourist card was issued immediately before Oswald's, has stated that he observed Oswald with Banister.[155]

Extraordinary testimony comes from Delphine Roberts, Banister's secretary and confidante for many years. She told the House Select Committee that she saw Oswald on numerous occasions, in Banister's office and even in Banister's presence, during the summer of 1963. Her belief is that Oswald worked for Banister.[156]

Prior to Mrs. Roberts's interview by committee investigators in 1978, she was interviewed by author Anthony Summers, to whom she first made her public statements about what she had seen as Guy Banister's personal secretary. According to Summers, Mrs. Roberts at first refused to talk to him and then denied knowing anything about Oswald before the assassination. However, Summers says that "after an upsetting confrontation with her own lawyer," Delphine Roberts began to relate in vivid detail what she remembered. In 1982 Mrs. Roberts told this author that Summers's published account was accurate. Mrs. Roberts's reason for talking was that she believed her information paralleled much of the material on Oswald's true activities in New Orleans that has emerged in recent years. She believed that what she was saying only confirmed these facts.[157]

Mrs. Roberts, who is as stridently right-wing as the late Guy Banister (who died of a heart attack in June 1964), claims that Oswald actually associated with people in Banister's office and carried on activities for Banister. She states that Oswald had a small room situated above Banister's Lafayette Street operation—one that could be reached either through Banister's office or by the entrance from 544 Camp Street—and that this room was filled with placards and literature connected with the *pro*-Castro Fair Play for Cuba Committee (FPCC). This, of course, was the group that Lee Oswald so oddly and ostentatiously represented, alone, in New Orleans.[158]

Moreover, Delphine Roberts's most striking claims are that she saw Oswald and Banister together on numerous occasions in the office. The two men were, she says, clearly in cahoots. She recalls that it was only under certain circumstances that Banister expressed any venomous feelings about the *pro*-Castro material housed in the building. That happened on several occasions when someone brought the material down from Oswald's cubicle into Banister's area. Banister objected only to the material's display in his own office; he did not object to its being in Oswald's area.[159]

In addition to Mrs. Roberts's startling account, the reliability of which the Select Committee said "could not be determined," there was confirmation of sorts from Allen and Daniel Campbell, young men who were working on Cuban matters for Banister in 1963. In separate ways, they both recalled Oswald's association with Banister.[160]

The culmination of these strange carryings-on seems to have come on August 9, 1963, when Lee Oswald was jailed as a result of his pro-Castro activities.[161] Viewed from any perspective, the events resist coming into clear focus.

A few days earlier, on August 5, Oswald had sought out Carlos Bringuier, a prominent and vocal figure in Cuban exile activities. Oswald told Bringuier that he wanted to aid in the overthrow of Castro and offered to help train exile guerrillas. Bringuier, who was suspicious of Oswald on sight, put him off, advising him to contact his group's headquarters in Miami if he was serious about wanting to join. The next day, as if to show his sincerity, Oswald returned to Bringuier's business place and left Bringuier his Marine training manual, a publication that describes various military training techniques.[162]

A few days later Bringuier and two friends heard that a man was on nearby Canal Street sporting a pro-Castro poster and handing out pro-Castro literature. Bringuier grabbed an anti-Castro sign and, with his friends, rushed to Canal Street to counter the message of the pro-Castroite. When Bringuier recognized Oswald, he began shouting and accusing him of trying to dupe him. A scuffle broke out, and the Cubans and Oswald were arrested. Oswald was jailed.[163]

In all accounts of the incident, there is the familiar pattern suggesting that perhaps Oswald set up the whole business. It is reminiscent of the times in his military service when he was placed in the brig for activities that seemed purely calculated to achieve that end.[164] The Canal Street incident—and two subsequent radio interviews—did spawn publicity about Oswald's purported pro-Castro position, publicity that later served to solidify the official finding that his true allegiance was to Castro and the Communists.[165] Delphine Roberts had once mentioned to her boss, Guy Banister, that she had seen Oswald passing out the pro-Castro leaflets. According to Mrs. Roberts, Banister told her, "Don't worry about him. . . . He's with us, he's associated with the office."[166]

Years after the event, when Anthony Summers asked Mrs. Roberts about the whole matter, she stated, "I knew that such things did take place. . . . I knew there were such things as counterspies, spies and counterspies. . . . I just didn't question them."[167]

Whatever Oswald was up to, once in jail he requested that an FBI agent be sent to interview him. Special Agent John L. Quigley went to the jail the next day, interviewed Oswald, and wrote a standard, detailed FBI report that included certain of Oswald's fabrications. Whatever else this incident accomplished, it absolutely established an official FBI record of the events. Oswald's true purpose, however, is today as murky as ever.[168]

At the end of his interview with Agent Quigley, Oswald turned over some examples of the FPCC literature he had been distributing. In describing this literature in his report, Agent Quigley noted that one was a pamphlet called "The Crime Against Cuba," by Corliss Lamont. In typically tedious fashion, the FBI agent noted various details of the literature given to him by Oswald, including the number of pages in the Lamont pamphlet. What Quigley failed to note is an electrifying bit of evidence that appears on page thirty-nine, which Quigley must have looked at in order to write in his report that there were thirty-nine pages in the pamphlet.[169] At the bottom of that page, in the black letters of an inked rubber stamp, is the following inscription:

FPCC
544 Camp St.
New Orleans, La.[170]

There, prominently stamped on the material Oswald purposely turned over to the FBI on August 10, 1963, is astounding evidence that places the origin of the *pro*-Castro literature in the very building that housed Guy Banister and his rabid band of *anti*-Castroites, and at the very address that had been used by the Cuban Revolutionary Council.[171] There can only be speculation about whether Oswald *meant* to provide such a powerfully suggestive lead to the FBI. What is certain, though, is that the FBI—either through calculated omission or pure ineptitude—later passed some of the information on to the Warren Commission without explaining or even noting the bewildering contradiction raised by the presence of the stamped address 544 Camp Street.[172] An understanding of this apparent contradiction could help unravel the persistent mystery of Oswald's strange activities in New Orleans. The foundation for such an understanding lies in grasping Oswald's association with Guy Banister and David Ferrie.

Soon after Oswald's arrest in August, the shadow of 544 Camp Street was cast over Clinton, Louisiana. That is the little town 130 miles northwest of New Orleans where numerous credible witnesses saw Oswald with David Ferrie and a man who, as discussed earlier, may have been Guy Banister. Piecing together the accounts of the various Clinton witnesses, it appears that Oswald was going through the motions of seeking employment in the area, or at least trying to register to vote. There is no conceivable reason why he would want to work in an unfamiliar town 130 miles from New Orleans. However, the time of this sighting by the Clinton witnesses does coincide with a time period—August 22 to September 17—for which Oswald's general whereabouts have never been established, despite intense efforts to do so by researchers as well as federal investigators.[173]

What, then, could have been the purpose of the visit to Clinton by Oswald, Ferrie, and possibly Banister? The most coherent analysis of the matter is found in critic Paul L. Hoch's newsletter, *Echoes of Conspiracy*. Hoch points out that during the summer of 1963 an intense voter-registration campaign was under way at the small Louisiana town. It was under the sponsorship of the Congress of Racial Equality (CORE). During the early sixties, CORE was one of the most potent and active of the civil-rights groups, and there were numerous confrontations between blacks and whites in the South as a result of CORE efforts. One of the most common charges made by segregationists against CORE—as well as against other civil-rights groups—was the claim that it was a Communist-front group. It was not unusual for an entire organization like CORE to be characterized and smeared because of the alleged pro-Communist associations of just one of its supporters.[174]

Given the well-established racist attitudes of Banister and Ferrie, it is not unreasonable, as Hoch suggests, to consider the possibility that an effort was under way to use Oswald "to link CORE to the pro-Castro FPCC."[175] If that were the case, anyone who participated in such a scheme would have good reason for wanting to conceal the story and their own participation. Such participants would, predictably, run for cover following the assassination, no matter how unrelated the two events might have been. However, proof of Oswald's manipulation in this fashion would open new doors in all directions, particularly in terms of Oswald's associates.

In *Conspiracy*, Anthony Summers reasons that such an effort could have been connected to the FBI's COINTELPRO exercise, a massive domestic spying operation going on during the sixties that only began to be exposed in 1972.[176] If true, that would involve the FBI—with its ex-agent Banister at the controls—in an effort to smear CORE with a purported pro-Communist like Oswald.[177] There is nothing necessarily farfetched about this scenario. Indeed, it represents a thoroughly rational, if speculative, explanation for the presence of Oswald, Banister, and Ferrie in Clinton.

If this is so, then where does it leave Oswald in terms of his true allegiance? In this murkiness, one can consider Oswald as either an active and cognizant agent of Banister and Ferrie or as a person who was not aware of what purpose he was serving. In light of other known factors, it seems more reasonable that Oswald really was not certain what he was doing. Conversely, it is just as likely that Banister and Ferrie—as well as the elements for whom they were acting—knew precisely what they were doing. And the truth about *that* remains locked in the mysteries of 544 Camp Street.

Browsing at the Crescent City Garage

Shortly after the death of President Kennedy, federal agents descended on Adrian Alba to question him about his knowledge of Lee Harvey Oswald. Alba partly owned and operated the Crescent City Garage, located at 618 Magazine Street, next to the William B. Reily Company, where Oswald worked during the spring and summer of 1963. Alba's garage, only a short distance from the office of Guy Banister, housed and serviced cars in a U.S. government motor pool. It was Alba who later reported seeing one of the government cars stopped near the entrance to the coffee company as the car's occupant handed an envelope through the window to Lee Harvey Oswald (see Chapter 9).[178]

But it was quite another matter that interested the Secret Service and the FBI almost immediately following the assassination. While working at the coffee company in 1963, Lee Oswald spent many hours hanging around next door at the Crescent City Garage. Oswald would come over to Alba's waiting room, where there was a coffeepot and a soda machine. The waiting room also contained dozens of magazines, many of them a reflection of Alba's own interest in guns and shooting.[179]

Oswald was talkative on this subject during these visits, and often probed Alba's knowledge of guns and questioned him about the relative merits of various weapons. Alba later testified that Oswald's special interest seemed to be in how one goes about ordering guns by mail and, in Alba's words, "how many guns had I ever ordered, and how long did it take to get them, and where had I ordered guns from."[180]

Alba recalls with certainty his impression of Oswald. It was the same as that of so many others who were familiar with him over a period of time. He found Oswald to be a mild-mannered fellow in whom Alba would not suspect a capacity for violence. Oswald seemed to enjoy browsing through Alba's gun magazines, occasionally asking permission to take one, to be returned a few days later.[181]

From the earliest hours of the investigation, both the FBI and the Secret Service shared a great interest in the gun magazines in Alba's garage. The day after the assassination, each agency removed several of the magazines.[182]

Ultimately, investigators found two mail-order coupons for the very rifle supposedly in Oswald's possession. In at least one case, the jagged edges of the coupon taken from Oswald's effects perfectly matched the space where a coupon had been ripped out of one of the magazines found in Adrian Alba's waiting room. It was an ad for, among other items, the infamous Mannlicher-Carcano, being offered by Klein's Sporting Goods in Chicago—the company identified as the supplier of the alleged assassination rifle.[183]

One of the remaining mysteries from those early days following the assassination concerns an unidentified man who showed up at the Crescent City Garage at nine o'clock on the very morning after the assassination. Adrian Alba was not there, but the stranger told an employee that he was one of Alba's "very best friends" and that he had come to borrow some of the magazines. The stranger was admitted without further questioning and spent a few minutes browsing over the magazines in the waiting room. The employee, thinking the man was his boss's friend, paid no more attention to him.[184]

If nothing else, the presence of this person tends to pollute the evidence gathered from Adrian Alba's waiting room, in terms of magazines discovered there as well as the condition of their contents. Whoever the stranger was, he had rummaged through the evidence even before the FBI got its hands on it.[185]

Inasmuch as there *was* evidence (an Oswald fingerprint) found in the magazines that linked Oswald to Klein's Sporting Goods and to the Mannlicher-Carcano, it seems doubtful that the stranger's mission—if there was anything sinister about it—was to remove or destroy evidence. Far more reasonable is the possibility that the stranger may have planted something to create a link between Oswald, Klein's Sporting Goods, and the Mannlicher-Carcano. During those early hours it was not clear that any evidence available in Dallas would be sufficiently solid in placing the weapon in Oswald's hands. Indeed, the only print from Oswald to be found on the rifle did not surface until several days later—after Oswald's death and after the rifle was returned to Dallas from the FBI laboratory in Washington. Discovery of the print at that late date raised suspicions in the minds of some Warren Commission members (see Chapter 5).[186]

In any event, no one has ever determined the identity of the stranger who arrived so promptly to inspect the magazines at the Crescent City Garage. It would have been simple enough for the Warren Commission, in its deposition of Adrian Alba, to ask him about the person who had claimed to be one of his "very best friends." There was, after all, a precise description of the stranger provided by Alba's employee. However, the Warren Commission never asked the question.[187]

Paul Hoch, who has made a careful if inconclusive study of this question, points out that, in the end, FBI laboratory examination of the June 1963 issue of the *American Rifleman* found in Alba's garage yielded Oswald's thumbprint. That same magazine had a Klein's ad coupon torn from it—a coupon that was found among Oswald's possessions.[188]

All this doubtlessly would have constituted prime evidence, except that records later produced by Klein's showed that, actually, Oswald ordered his rifle from the *February* issue of *American Rifleman*. With that conclusive discovery in Klein's records, interest in the solid evidence in the June issue of the magazine evaporated. However, the convenience and coincidence present in this development of evidence is so striking that, to observers seasoned by other FBI fact-fiddling, it is almost suspect.[189]

Given the astounding neatness with which a print could suddenly appear on the Mannlicher-Carcano in the frenzy of the Dallas investigation, an observer feels a certain doubt about the fortuity of the emergence of the New Orleans rifle evidence. The implication, of course, is that from the beginning—even in New Orleans—evidence was being manipulated to seal the case against Oswald. In this instance, ultimately, the evidence was not needed. At the very least, however, it is unfortunate that the Warren Commission did not inquire about the identity of the stranger, for it could have yielded additional light on the goings-on in New Orleans.

The implication in the official version of events is that Lee Oswald was seeking guidance from Adrian Alba on the best way to order guns—which tends to seal the proposition that Oswald was laying the groundwork for his later actions by learning how to order guns. However, by the time Oswald was browsing through the gun magazines at the Crescent City Garage, he had *already* ordered and supposedly received two guns, including the Mannlicher-Carcano from Klein's Sporting Goods in Chicago.[190] Thus, it seems odd that he would spend time questioning Adrian Alba about his gun-ordering experiences when Oswald himself had already ordered and received the two guns that would accompany him into the annals of momentous crimes.

The mere fact that Oswald chose to acquire his guns by mail order has never made much sense. Its only value is to the official version of events, in that the mail-order purchase created an absolute chain of documentary evidence to link Oswald to the weapons supposedly responsible for the murders of President Kennedy and Officer Tippit.[191] This oddness is heightened by the fact that the same make of rifle and revolver could have been purchased by Oswald at stores only a few blocks from where he worked in Dallas. Weapons from these stores would have been much simpler to acquire—and there would have been no record of his purchase and ownership.[192] However, for reasons unknown, Oswald took the precisely opposite course. He ordered his weapons in a fashion that absolutely tied the guns to him, despite his use of the flimsy and transparent alias Hidell.

All this inevitably suggests the possibility that some other motive was behind Oswald's browsing through gun magazines at the Crescent City Garage and his questioning of Adrian Alba about mail-order gun purchases. Given his limited experience with guns, and his presumed acquisition of two guns a few months earlier, Oswald's continued show of interest seems fishy—unless he had another motive.

One of the most interesting theories about what Oswald was *really* up to at the Crescent City Garage maintains that he believed he was working as an investigator or informant for a Senate subcommittee accumulating evidence of the frightening ease with which weapons could be ordered through the mails. According to this theory, the two weapons Oswald actually ordered by mail, before leaving Dallas in April, would have been a part of this activity, which he continued once he reached New Orleans.*[193]

In January 1963 hearings began in Washington before the Judiciary Committee's Subcommittee on Juvenile Delinquency, under the leadership of Senator Thomas J. Dodd. The proceedings came to be known as the Dodd Committee. Evidence was amassed to show that there was practically no control over the sale of firearms through the mails—sales that potentially could reach, in addition to children, the most maladjusted, criminal, and even crazed segments of American society.[194]

Part of the effort of the Dodd Committee was to show that absolutely anyone with a few dollars could successfully order weapons through the mails.[195] This potentially dangerous reservoir of American residents could include an ex-Marine who had defected to the Soviet Union and, after his return, had participated in pro-Castro (Communist) activities and been jailed for engaging in a street fight. Whether or not Oswald was a part of the Dodd Committee efforts, he certainly served to illustrate perfectly the point that the committee was trying to make.

The major gun houses under investigation by the Dodd Committee in 1963 included Seaport Traders of California. It was the company from which Oswald, it was officially determined, had ordered the pistol supposedly used in the Tippit murder. Inasmuch as Oswald ordered the rifle as well as the pistol under a false name, the point was demonstrated that there was virtually no control over even *that* aspect of mail-order guns.[196]

Despite all of Oswald's eccentricities, most students of his life

* Most of the work on this theory has been done by Fred Newcomb, an assassination researcher who made available his unpublished manuscript which covers this subject.

agree that in nearly everything he did, there was a purpose. His purpose in accumulating mail-order coupons for guns has never been clear—no more so than his reason for questioning Adrian Alba about ordering guns through the mail months after he had already done so.

One young Dodd Committee investigator—after getting into trouble with the police on the Mexican border, over a fight with a striptease dancer—was subsequently discovered by authorities trying to check two Thompson submachine guns, a pistol, and 5,000 rounds of ammunition through to Hyannis Port, Massachusetts, while President Kennedy was visiting there. Finally, the investigator was let go, after, according to one account, he "seized a Navy flare gun from the subcommittee's exhibits and brandished it menacingly during a temper tantrum."[197]

With an investigator like that on the payroll, it is difficult to argue that Lee Oswald would have made an unsuitable member of the team. Not only had Oswald been given a dishonorable discharge from the Marines on his defection to the Soviet Union, but he had gained notoriety by defecting. Back in New Orleans, he ostensibly continued his pro-Communist activities while also involving himself with anti-Communist fanatics and right-wing nuts.[198] Certainly, a record like Oswald's would lend itself effectively to the Dodd Committee's efforts to show that anyone, regardless of his background and current activities, could order guns through the mails.

In the event that Oswald did work for the Dodd Committee, even indirectly, his subsequent notoriety would ensure that the committee—as in the case of any other government agency Oswald may have been associated with—would try desperately to avoid having the relationship exposed. A Congressional investigating committee—no less so than the most obscure elements of U.S. intelligence, though for different reasons—could hardly afford to admit any link with a man officially established as a presidential assassin.

The other possibility put forward to explain Oswald's peculiar activities is that he *thought* he was working for the Dodd Committee, that someone pretending to represent the Dodd Committee had recruited him in an elaborate scheme to create a dossier for a dupe. If there is merit to the theory that Oswald was a patsy—a man duped, while others escaped—then the Dodd Committee angle becomes reasonable to consider. If Oswald were set up, this represents a convenient way to get him to order the weapons and leave a perfect paper trail linking himself to the guns. Moreover, it could even explain some of his peculiar posturing in New Orleans—associating with radical elements from extremes in the political spectrum, perhaps as a drug user or dealer. Such a role, conceivably, could even have developed to the point where Oswald was told to take his mail-order rifle into the building near the President's parade route in Dallas—again under some pretense of demonstrating an arcane point for the Congressional committee.

All things considered, it seems safe to assume that Oswald had no official connection with the Dodd Committee, although there has never been a known official inquiry into the matter. However, this does not in any sense negate the possibility that Oswald *believed*, rightly or wrongly, that he was working for this Congressional subcommittee. If Oswald believed this, for whatever reason, then his actions are better understood. The implications, however, point in only one sinister direction—conspiracy and manipulation.

Curiouser and Curiouser

In November 1963, after seeing pictures of Lee Harvey Oswald and hearing his recorded voice, Edward Gillin, then an assistant district attorney in New Orleans, contacted federal authorities with an extraordinary report. He told the FBI that during the preceding summer, a young man he believed to be Lee Oswald had come to his office to ask him about an exotic mind-altering drug. Oswald wanted to know if Gillin was aware of the drug and whether its use was legal. Gillin, thoroughly perplexed by this strange visit, finally advised the young man to take his questions to the City of New Orleans chemist, who, Gillin advised, might be able to help him. The assistant district attorney thought no more about the incident until a few months later, on the weekend of November 22, when he believed he recognized Oswald.[199]

Today a respected judge in New Orleans, Gillin recalls that the FBI was distinctly uninterested in his information. There are, indeed, FBI reports of Gillin's efforts to inform the authorities. The entire matter was lost to sight until 1983, when three respectable assassination critics presented the whole account in *Rolling Stone* magazine. The authors analyzed the Gillin report in terms of what is known today about the history of experimentation by U.S. intelligence with mind-altering drugs such as LSD.[200]

One of the aspects of Gillin's report in 1963 was that Oswald kept referring to a book by Aldous Huxley. The book apparently was *Brave New World*, which discusses a mind-altering drug. The FBI report of the matter reflects this, though the agents refer to the author as "Hucksley" and *Brave New World* as *This Great World*.[201]

While it seems highly unlikely that if Oswald were a drug user, it would have escaped the notice of the numerous people he was in contact with, it is not at all preposterous that he should make the visit described by Judge Gillin. Indeed, part of the story is supported by records of the New Orleans Public Library, which show that in September 1963 Lee Oswald checked out two books by Aldous Huxley.[202] But even if Judge Gillin's report is correct, the significance of the visit is as obscure as so many other aspects of Oswald's life.

It is only in recent years that much has been known about the CIA's aggressive experimentation with mind-altering drugs. Under the code name of MK ULTRA, the CIA, in the fifties and sixties, was involved in experimentation with a vast array of such drugs. The ultimate goals were to offset similar enemy efforts and to develop ways to control the minds of people. There is a massive amount of documentation showing hideously inhuman experiments conducted on people, often without their knowledge, much less their permission.[203]

Of the many different drugs tested and used, none is known to have held more initial promise than LSD. In recent years evidence has surfaced showing that the Atsugi Naval Air Station in Japan, the base where Oswald was assigned and from which the U-2 surveillance planes made their flights over the Soviet Union, might have been a center for testing LSD in the fifties and early sixties. The *Rolling Stone* article cites a report from a man in Oswald's unit who said that he was used in one of the LSD experiments. From that point, the authors proceed with heavy speculation about how Oswald might have been involved with CIA-sponsored LSD experiments in Japan. For many reasons this possibility seems unlikely.[204]

On the other hand, Judge Gillin's report of Oswald's visit makes good sense. It represents Oswald waltzing into the seat of New

Orleans authority and—in an ostentatious manner in keeping with his frequent posturing—staging a highly memorable visit. It seemed like a ploy, as when he summoned the FBI to inform agents about his Fair Play for Cuba Committee activities. The books checked out of the local library tend to support the whole story. What becomes clear is that Judge Gillin's report holds solid evidence of yet another example of Oswald's flagrant posturing. He had managed to link himself firmly with a pro-Castro, pro-Communist cause. He was also associated with right-wing fanatics like Banister and Ferrie. In the case of the Gillin visit, he was painting himself as a man possibly hooked on some heavy, mind-altering drugs. In fact, the only rational way the incident makes any sense is as another example of his posturing for the sake of creating an image. For what purpose remains as mysterious as ever.[205]

Repeatedly, the pieces of evidence in this case, taken alone, seem very solid. However, when an effort is made to fit them into a pattern, they spell contradiction and confusion. What does one make, for example, of the tantalizing fact that in 1960—more than three years before the assassination—a memo from FBI Director Hoover informed the State Department that an imposter might be posing as Lee Harvey Oswald, then a defector to the Soviet Union?[206] There is no question about the validity of the Hoover memo on Oswald, leading one to grasp futilely for reasons why the FBI would show such an interest in Oswald in 1960. One thing it clearly provides is a springboard for speculation.

The same is true as to the weird circumstances of Oswald's post-office box in New Orleans. About two weeks after he filed a change-of-address card, closed his box, and left that city in September 1963, someone filled out the exact same form again and mailed it in from New Orleans.[207] Who could have done this? Why was it done? The questions are merely typical of those that weave the fabric of the entire mystery.

Enormous attention has been given to the possibility that while in New Orleans Lee Oswald had some sort of informant relationship with a federal agency—either a known agency, such as the FBI, or some secret U.S. intelligence organization that, to this day, has not been revealed. Strident denials by officials must be considered in light of the obvious fact that if an intelligence entity is unknown to the public, then its principals cannot be examined for the record. If Oswald had been working for some branch of U.S. intelligence unknown to the public, officials could have testified just as they did and told the truth. Thus, there would be no revelation that Oswald was working for some branch of U.S. intelligence. There have been, of course, absolute denials by the FBI and the CIA that Oswald had any relationship with those agencies.[208] However, there have not been—and cannot be—denials from elements that have never been asked about Oswald because investigators and researchers never knew such organizations existed. As convoluted as this reasoning may seem, it is nourished by the frustrations felt by researchers who are certain, given the whole sweep of Oswald's activities, that he must have been working for someone, even a state or local agency. (See Chapter 9 for a full discussion of this point.)

In New Orleans, frenzied attention has been given to a possible relationship between Oswald and the FBI. That speculation has been fueled by a variety of factors—such as the 1960 Hoover memo— that are largely responsible for the persistence of the allegations. Finally, while loose ends proliferate into contradictions, there is no solid evidence that Oswald had a direct relationship of any sort with the FBI in New Orleans.

By the same token, there is little or no evidence to diminish the possibility that Oswald might have served as a "cut-out"—as a functionary operating in some capacity once removed from an official connection. Such a function might attach to the Guy Banister operation or to any work Oswald might have been doing for the Dodd Committee.

Still, there is a wide belief among critics that Oswald did have a relationship, even an indirect one, with the FBI in New Orleans. Most of the allegations of a direct Oswald-FBI link in New Orleans relate to Agent Warren deBrueys, who today is the managing director of the Metropolitan Crime Commission of New Orleans. Orest Pena, a prominent exile associated with the CIA-sponsored Cuban Revolutionary Council, also had a relationship with deBrueys and, on occasion, provided deBrueys and the FBI with information about Cuban exile activities. Pena and deBrueys are in agreement on these basic points, but the agreement stops there.[209]

As the owner and operator of the Habana Bar, which Lee Oswald is widely believed to have visited with a mysterious Latin, Orest

Pena makes the sensational claim that on a number of occasions, he observed deBrueys talking to Oswald. Pena also charges that de-Brueys threatened him with physical harm if he revealed this information to the Warren Commission.[210]

DeBrueys flatly denies both of Pena's allegations, claiming that he never met Oswald or knowingly spoke to him over the telephone.[211] The HSCA looked into these allegations and in light of Pena's evasiveness on other matters, declined to embrace him as a credible witness. The committee also found that official FBI records "served to corroborate relevant aspects of deBrueys' testimony."[212]

Another bothersome allegation that Oswald was an informant surfaced in 1975, when William S. Walter, who had worked as a security clerk for the FBI's New Orleans office in 1963, stepped forward to claim that he personally had seen an informant file on Oswald. He said that he was on duty the day Agent Quigley was sent to interrogate Oswald in the New Orleans jail, after his arrest for the street disturbance. Walter claimed that in connection with seeking information in local records on Oswald, he happened to see the informant file.[213]

The HSCA considered the whole matter and rejected it.*[214]

Even though there is not an inkling of solid evidence that Oswald worked directly as an operative for the FBI, the observation reported by Adrian Alba is suggestive of some sort of connection. It, too, was rejected by the HSCA, which found the report to be of "doubtful reliability."[215]

However, it is hard to dismiss the credibility of Adrian Alba, who still runs the Crescent City Garage. He has never sought publicity and has no conceivable gain in promulgating the story about seeing Oswald receiving an envelope from a man to whom Alba had checked out a car from the federal government's motor pool. Indisputably, Alba was acquainted with Oswald, and he knew the cars he garaged and serviced for the federal government. It seems unlikely that Alba, a man of good reputation, is simply amusing himself by offering a gratuitous prevarication.[216]

---

* The committee also examined a claim by Walter that he saw a teletype on November 17, 1963, sent by FBI headquarters, warning that there would be an assassination attempt against President Kennedy. Walter claimed the teletype had vanished a few days later, when he tried to locate it after the shooting in Dallas. Walter's prime witness, whom he believed could corroborate his story, has stated that she recalls nothing about it. Based on this, the Select Committee concluded that Walter was not a credible witness. Based on several contacts with Walter, the author concurs.

Even if one supposes that the car Alba saw was, by extraordinary coincidence, not the one he had checked out to the FBI agent, but one exactly like it, then who *was* that man handing Oswald an envelope? Could his identification shed some light on an operation still not understood? Could this be related to the Dodd Committee?

It is fairly clear that whatever was going on was a concoction of elements, none of which can be understood alone or without the benefit of new witnesses and evidence. There is no area that is thicker with coincidence or richer with undeveloped leads than the shifting shadows of New Orleans. It is not likely, at this late date, that those leads will ever be resurrected and pursued to fruition. The only certainty, really, is the strong feeling that raucous, indomitable New Orleans very likely is the graveyard for the most significant clues to the mystery of the JFK assassination.

11 · THE CUBAN QUESTION:

COINCIDENCE OR

CONSPIRACY?

> Kennedy was trying to get Castro, but Castro got him first. . . . It will all come out someday.[1]
> —President Lyndon B. Johnson

> Despite knowledge of Oswald's apparent interest in pro-Castro and anti-Castro activities and top-level awareness of certain CIA assassination plots, the FBI made no special investigative effort into questions of possible Cuban government or Cuban exile involvement in the assassination independent of the Oswald investigation. . . . [This] failure to follow significant leads in the Cuba area is surprising. These leads raise significant questions.[2]
> —The Schweiker Report

Castro and Camelot

One of the most compelling traditional theories about President Kennedy's assassination boils down to this: the Kennedy administration was engaged in a massive secret war to topple the government of Fidel Castro. This effort included the active, determined participation of the President and his brother, Attorney General Robert F. Kennedy. In addition, there were numerous extraordinary, ridiculously inept attempts by government officials to assassinate the Cuban premier—efforts that were surely sanctioned in some subtle form by the Kennedys. From a practical standpoint, none of this activity was a secret to those who needed to know—including, the evidence shows, Fidel Castro. The Cuban premier's knowledge of the schemes seems to have been in such intimate detail that he and his government managed to survive them all. Indeed, two decades later, it is clear that Castro has survived, in a political as well as a personal sense, all the sponsors of those schemes. He has managed to maintain his power as well as his life.[3]

Was a key element in Castro's successful survival the elimination of John F. Kennedy? Did he envision Kennedy's assassination as a final, desperate effort to save his own skin? From the moment of President Kennedy's death, there was an almost studied indifference to these questions by those empowered to investigate the assassination. While these chilling efforts to kill Castro were known to the CIA and the FBI—and one would imagine Warren Commission member Allen Dulles—all such information was excluded from the investigation.[4]

In the immediate wake of the assassination, it is now known, those who were privy to the secret operations against Castro wondered if retribution was not a logical possibility. One of those who wondered was Kennedy's successor, Lyndon B. Johnson. Another was Robert Kennedy.[5] Even Chief Justice Earl Warren referred privately to Cuba as "one of the principal suspects."[6] In classic terms, Castro possessed the motive, means, and opportunity. The last two elements were abundantly present in Castro's network of agents secreted among the thousands of Cubans who were operatives for U.S. intelligence in the effort to destroy the Cuban government.[7]

The most common dissent from this view holds that it is fatuous, if not preposterous, to suggest that Castro would risk retribution that could amount to his annihilation. Moreover, it is argued, Castro would have surely preferred the liberal and diplomacy-minded Kennedy as president over the alternative—a pragmatic Texan believed to be short on ideology and long on getting the job done. Johnson, that argument goes, represented a far greater potential threat to Castro.

It is true that, on the surface, President Kennedy was gesturing toward some sort of accommodation with Cuba in 1963. Today, his admirers claim that Kennedy had taken the initial steps toward the basic repair of the dangerous chasm between the United States and Castro. In evident reaction to the nightmare of the Cuban Missile Crisis some months earlier, Kennedy finally consummated the Nuclear Test Ban Treaty with the Soviet Union. But this laudable accomplishment really signified no substantive change in the President's actual position toward Cuba and Castro. The argument that Castro would have preferred Kennedy over Johnson also offers as evidence an agreement Kennedy made *not* to invade Cuba, in return for a promise from the Soviets that they would remove their nuclear missiles from the island. That agreement, however, never went into effect, inasmuch as Castro refused to meet the terms and allow an on-site inspection by the United Nations.[8]

The argument that Kennedy was making conciliatory gestures toward Cuba must be considered alongside the fact, well established today, that President Kennedy's plans to overthrow Castro—and the efforts to assassinate the Cuban leader—continued long after October 1962. Gestures aside, the important consideration is what Castro knew, and must have assumed Kennedy knew—that efforts by the U.S. government to overthrow the Cuban government and to murder Castro were continuing. Indeed, they were going full blast in November 1963, even as John F. Kennedy passed through Dealey Plaza in Dallas.[9]

If it is true that Castro would not have wanted President Kennedy replaced by Lyndon Johnson, there is particularly grim historical irony in what came to pass. With Kennedy's death and Johnson's succession, U.S. efforts against Castro and Cuba began at once to wind down, even though they continued in relatively "gentle" fashion for another year or so. President Johnson's interest in fighting communism focused immediately on a troubled land on the other side of the world, Vietnam. There, Johnson took his first steps toward the massive military and political disaster that ultimately drove him from office. At the same time, there is no evidence that President Johnson ever encouraged a single initiative against Castro or his country. Whether or not Castro had anything to do with Kennedy's death, a persuasive argument can be made that he was served supremely well by the change in administrations. In every practical sense, the events of Dealey Plaza vastly diminished the deadly difficulties Castro faced with the U.S. government.[10]

But would a leader as shrewd as Castro have risked the potent threat of an all-out invasion, which might have been precipitated by his killing of Kennedy? That question is purely academic: Kennedy was killed; Cuba was not invaded. But in any consideration of this point, one must ask whether Castro could reasonably expect to survive the continuing barrage of Kennedy efforts to destroy him. It is hard to imagine that, sooner or later, Castro's good fortune would not forsake him. Inevitably, one of the countless official efforts to overthrow his government would have succeeded, despite the humiliating failures that had become a hallmark of CIA foolishness and ineptitude during the sixties. If Castro took such a calculated risk as is suggested here, he once again demonstrated his uncanny shrewdness and ability to survive.

There are many popular variations on the thesis that Castro had something to do with the death of Kennedy, either through active plotting or through passive influence. One theory holds that Lee Harvey Oswald, a Castro admirer, was inflamed by press accounts, in September 1963, that Castro was threatening retaliation if the Kennedys did not cease their efforts to kill him. Supposedly motivated by a sense of protectiveness toward Castro, Oswald launched himself on a series of actions that culminated at Dealey Plaza. Another theory holds that some of the Kennedy agents sent to kill Castro were turned around by the Cuban premier and sent back on a successful mission to murder Kennedy. Or, one argument goes, Kennedy used the mob against Castro, and they turned against him of their own volition.[11]

Other proposed possibilities are that Castro knew of Oswald's supposed plans and did nothing to stop them, or that he sent his own agents to infiltrate the CIA-dominated exile groups in a successful plot against Kennedy.[12] There are also variations on each of these theories.

Another possibility in the hypothetical considerations is that Castro actively plotted the President's murder himself.[13] This position was flatly endorsed by former Senator Robert Morgan, a member of the Senate Intelligence Committee, which investigated these possibilities. "There is no doubt in my mind," Senator Morgan has stated, "that John Fitzgerald Kennedy was assassinated by Fidel Castro, or someone under his influence, in retaliation for our efforts to assassinate him."[14] However, Senator Morgan's committee did not reach such firm conclusions.[15]

On the other hand, it is possible that Castro had nothing at all to do with the Kennedy assassination, that he was the passive beneficiary of a change in the course of history that yielded him enormously favorable results.

Plans to destroy Castro and his regime began nearly a year before John F. Kennedy took office. The earliest known discussion of removing the Cuban premier from power took place in the spring of 1960, according to the subsequent Congressional testimony of officials who were involved. It was in September 1960 that the U.S. government first approached the Mafia with a lucrative offer to murder Castro. Thus, it is clear that the most extreme of the proposals concerning Castro were hatched during the Eisenhower administration. These early efforts certainly lacked the high priority that characterized subsequent attempts, following the disgrace of the Bay of Pigs invasion. Still, it was under President Eisenhower that the basic plans were conceived to secretly sponsor an invasion by Cuban exiles. The aim was to topple the Castro regime and restore Cuba as a country with interests compatible with those of the United States.[16]

Invasion plans were being made, and their sponsors were geared to go ahead with the invasion, when Kennedy was sworn in as president on January 20, 1961. Although the new President had been briefed about the plans by CIA Director Allen Dulles seven weeks before the inauguration, Kennedy had not offered specific approval. He had accepted the fact that the plans were progressing and, according to sympathetic biographers, viewed those plans as an option—something to be considered later.[17] The CIA director expedited the project.

In retrospect, it was virtually inevitable that the invasion plans would go forward that spring. Fourteen hundred zealous Cuban refugees were in training at a CIA camp in Guatemala. Meanwhile, in Cuba, Castro awaited delivery of new aircraft and arms from the Soviets. Cuban pilots were being trained in Czechoslovakia. In a few more months, the trained men and beefed-up arms would render a successful U.S.-mounted invasion impossible. Even worse, cancellation would mean unleashing the hundreds of trained Cuban exiles to act on their own—totally out of control. In addition, it would spread the angry word throughout Latin America that the will of the new administration was weak and even indifferent to the entrenchment of Soviet power just off the U.S. coast. The planned invasion had no realistic alternative.[18]

In this endeavor, President Kennedy set some very particular goals. While he wanted to orchestrate a victory, he felt strongly that his hand should not be seen behind that victory. While Kennedy wanted to be rid of the Castro regime, he did not want to be caught bringing about its overthrow. Such heavy-handed, unilateral military action was inimical to the world image he wished to create. Kennedy's dilemma was a blueprint for disaster.[19]

To this day there is disagreement about just what happened. However, it does seem clear that after agreeing to the plan, Kennedy's consequent decisions virtually assured its failure, although that could not be blamed entirely on him. There is little question that the President was handicapped by misleading advice from the CIA, as well as from his military advisors. The biggest difficulty, however, was that Kennedy continued to hope that he could achieve his goal without any notable sacrifice.[20]

Thomas Powers, in his analysis of this venture, writes: "Kennedy hoped to scale down the invasion sufficiently that it might pass relatively unnoticed. He was more alarmed, in short, by the possibility of noisy success than he was by the prospect of a quiet failure, failing to see that failure itself is the noisiest thing of all."[21]

Indeed, the invasion at the Bay of Pigs on April 17, 1961, was one of the most humiliating events in American history. No simple answers present themselves to explain why there was such an abysmal failure. It seems clear that the disaster was born of mixed signals, poor analysis, bad advice, and an absence of any firm resolve about what was needed to reach the ultimate goal. Castro's intelligence operation was so well oiled that just before the invasion, he rounded up 100,000 potential counterrevolutionaries, including nearly all CIA sources. However the blame should be placed, the Bay of Pigs calamity was without question the greatest debacle of the Kennedy administration. In addition, it was the seedbed for problems that would haunt President Kennedy for all his remaining days.[22]

Following the fiasco, the anti-Castro feelings harbored by the Kennedy brothers hardened into an absolute determination to do something about the Cuban premier.[23] Thomas Powers has written a cogent description: "The Bay of Pigs marked the beginning of Kennedy's determination to get rid of Castro, the moment when Fidel Castro ceased to be an enemy inherited from Eisenhower, and became his own."[24]

The entire administration and its supporters were stained with shame and failure. Setting aside the squabbles about what went wrong, officials had to face the fact that hundreds of brave and honorable men had been sent to that Cuban beach by the United States government and were now dead or in Castro's jails. President Kennedy was lectured on morality by Soviet Premier Khrushchev. Elements of Kennedy's own constituency denounced him not for what he failed to do, but for what he *tried* to do. Concurrently, those who despised the New Frontier added a new ingredient to their repertoire of criticism—ridicule.[25]

The House Select Committee on Assassinations summed it up this way: "While anti-Castro Cuban exiles in the United States believed they had been betrayed by Kennedy and accused him of being a weak leader who was soft on communism, the administration was criticized from the left as a reactionary return to barbarism."[26]

President Kennedy responded as subtly and as quietly and as strongly as he could. First, he accepted full blame for what had happened. Then he formed a special commission—which included his brother Robert—with stated orders to examine the entire Cuban debacle and to determine what went wrong.[27] It is clear today that, actually, the assignment went much further than simply to find out what happened. The assignment was to avenge the humiliation, to correct the terrible failure—in short, to get rid of Fidel Castro.

Operation Mongoose

Concurrent with the failure at the Bay of Pigs were a continuing series of harebrained schemes hatched by the Central Intelligence Agency to destroy the Castro regime. They go beyond anything found in satirical literature spoofing clandestine intelligence activities. While the goal of these efforts can still be debated, the efforts themselves have been almost universally denounced as idiocy of the highest order—made perceptively worse, perhaps, by their abject failure. Revelation, in 1975, of such schemes was surely the most devastating domestic assault the CIA has ever weathered. Some of its blackest secrets—including assassination plots against numerous foreign leaders—were extracted from the murk and soon exposed pitilessly to a derisive world.[28] Primary among those plots were the multiple efforts to kill Cuba's Fidel Castro.

Perhaps the most imaginative and ambitious of the dozens of plans to topple the Cuban regime was one to create a spontaneous, popular uprising. The CIA scheme called for nothing short of staging the

Second Coming of Christ. Cuba's deeply religious population was to be inculcated with the idea that Castro was the Antichrist and that the real Christ was about to appear in Cuba. When the people had been manipulated to the point of rising up against Castro, seen as the Antichrist, a manifestation of Christ's arrival was to appear. A U.S. submarine, out of sight off Cuba's shores, was to seal the scheme by launching a magnificent display of light and fire in the night that would convince the Cubans that Christ was indeed at their door. They, then, were to rise up to overthrow the Antichrist. The idea, dismissed at an early stage, was jocularly known as "elimination by illumination."[29]

While this particular CIA scheme did not proceed beyond the conceptual stage, others were pursued with more purpose. One plan called for spraying Castro's radio broadcasting studio with a hallucinogenic drug formulated to cause him to become irrational during a broadcast to the Cuban people. Another plan called for sprinkling the Cuban premier's shoes with chemicals concocted to make his beard fall out, on the supposition that a naked face would wreck his charismatic appeal. Poison cigars were created, so powerful that a person would die from placing one in his mouth. Inspired by Castro's fondness for skin diving, a diving suit, with deadly bacteria in it, was created as a gift to Castro. On the same underwater theme, a seashell, wired with explosives, would be placed in an area where it might be picked up by an unsuspecting Castro. He would then be killed in the detonation.[30]

Schemes such as these were littering intelligence files when the Kennedy administration settled down to its serious efforts to eliminate Castro. Subsequent plans were hardly better. In the wake of the Bay of Pigs disaster, the Kennedy people—including the President himself—allowed the seething exiles to believe that a new invasion was in the offing, one that would vindicate the rout at the Bay of Pigs. It is certain that administration officials promoted this feeling. According to one report, the President assured a top exile leader in May 1961 that he could be certain of another invasion, this one with enough military support to be successful. Throughout the summer of 1961, raids against Cuba by exile groups continued. The premier, while suffering some losses, managed to survive each of the exile assaults, which had usually been made under the sponsorship of the CIA.[31]

Frustration mounted among U.S. officials, and those charged with "doing something about Cuba" could sense the impatience from the White House. In early fall, Richard Bissell, the CIA officer in charge of resolving the Cuba problem, came face to face with wrath from the highest authority. According to later testimony before a Senate committee, Bissell was "chewed out in the Cabinet Room of the White House by both the President and the Attorney General for, as [Bissell] put it, sitting on his ass and not doing anything about getting rid of Castro and the Castro regime."[32] This urgency from on high was filtered down, and the natural result was the development of yet more plots and invasion plans. While there is continuing debate over whether the Kennedys subtly authorized the murder plots, there is no question about the brothers' zeal for ridding the Western Hemisphere of the Castro regime.[33]

A few months later, in November 1961, Operation Mongoose was launched. It set sail with the highest blessings of the Kennedy administration.[34] At a meeting in Robert Kennedy's office, the assembled leaders of Mongoose were told by the Attorney General that the overthrow of Castro "carried top priority in [the] U.S. Gov[ernmen]t. No time, money, effort—or manpower is to be spared." A memo of the meeting indicates that the assemblage was informed that President Kennedy, referring to Cuba, indicated "that the final chapter had not been written—it's got to be done and will be done."[35]

There could have been no more powerful official encouragement. The extraordinary array of activities thus set into motion had little to do with the laws of this country or the natural confines of morality.

Hot debate still exists over whether the Kennedys, in addition to authorizing all the other attempts to wreck Cuba and destroy Castro's government, also sanctioned the efforts to kill the Cuban premier. To a distant observer, the only issue seems to be one of semantics. Several of the defense and intelligence officers who were accustomed to dealing regularly with the White House believed that the orders were meant to include assassination. The counterargument is that these officers would claim to have understood the orders in that fashion in order to justify their actions. Partisans loyal to the Kennedys argue that the Kennedys would not have morally approved such a measure as murder. However, all sides seem to agree that under no protocol would it be acceptable for the subject of *assassination* to be broached at the highest levels.[36] "Nobody wants to embarrass a President of the United States by discussing the assassination of foreign leaders in his presence," Richard Helms told a Senate committee.[37]

On the other hand, what is certain is that most of the men in charge of operations interpreted their orders to mean assassination. Given the enormity of the question—and the fact that "getting rid of Castro" (and many variations on that language) was discussed at the highest levels—it seems sure that if assassination was *not* what the Kennedys had in mind, they obviously failed to make clear their position.[38]

The point is best illustrated by citing a graphic exchange President Kennedy once had in a private conversation with a reporter from *The New York Times*. Kennedy first asked the reporter how he personally would feel about the prospect of assassinating Castro. The reporter expressed a negative reaction as a matter of principle. President Kennedy agreed with the reporter, explaining that he had brought it up only because he was curious to see what the reporter would say. Then President Kennedy told the reporter that he "was under terrific pressure . . . to okay a Castro murder."[39]

This exchange, usually pointed to as evidence of Kennedy's disapproval of such measures, could actually be evidence that the President understood absolutely that his subordinates wanted to kill Castro.[40] In light of such certainty, it would seem, if the President really did oppose such an extreme measure, he needed to say so to his underlings—not just to speak to them in ambiguities to be debated later on semantic points.

In view of this, it is significant that there is no evidence that the President ever expressed any such firm counsel to his operatives. In fact, instead of prohibiting them from murdering Castro, President Kennedy ordered them to make getting rid of Castro and his regime the "top priority of the U.S. Government."[41]

The official launching of Operation Mongoose in late 1961 set into play the full force of United States intelligence and military facilities. While the ultimate goal may have been to make Castro's overthrow appear to be the work of the exiles alone, nothing was spared in the attempt to ensure its success. There was no room for a second Bay of Pigs.[42]

A special CIA operations station, code-named JM/WAVE, was set up in Miami for coordination and the training of soldiers. The station included 300 CIA officers and 2,000 Cuban contract officers. Exiled Cubans numbering into the thousands—many of them no doubt loyal Castro agents—were a part of the operation. Around the world, every major CIA station was ordered to designate an officer to work full-time on Cuban operations in the station's country. Those in South America were ordered to incite animosity toward Cuba. Elaborate plans were implemented to wreak havoc on Cuba's internal affairs, such as schemes to disrupt the sugar crops and other measures to wreck the economy. As a CIA station operating within the United States, JM/WAVE gave the appearance of operating against the strictures of the CIA's charter. It is ironic that this operation, with an annual budget of $50 million, quickly became the largest CIA station in the world.[43]

A prime function of JM/WAVE was to monitor the activities of the dozens of small bands of exiles. (In the earliest days after the Bay of Pigs, there were 700 anti-Castro groups.) Missions of varying descriptions were carried out almost constantly, including gunboat harassment, sabotage, and the dropping of propaganda leaflets, in addition to the planting of insurgents on the Cuban mainland. More than fifty commercial enterprises were set up as fronts, making the operation a significant economic influence on Miami.[44] Such size, however, inevitably had its drawbacks. One Army captain, on assignment to JM/WAVE, later wrote: "I had envisioned it as a highly responsive, uncluttered organization, but it . . . appeared to be a sprawling bureaucratic monster."[45]

With such a bureaucracy—and, no doubt, for many other reasons—the efforts to destroy Castro were not going well. A high proportion of the missions failed. While there were a few passing successes to pacify the Kennedy brothers, both hungry for news that Castro was weakening, they still were exceedingly unhappy about the failures. In fact, in early 1962, Attorney General Robert Kennedy, who was personally involved in the effort, spent three weekends in Florida, ostensibly to visit members of his family. However, Kennedy's presence in Florida at that time coincides with several unofficial reports that the Attorney General personally inspected the facilities at JM/WAVE. Indeed, the "secret war" against Castro was in full swing. To all concerned with the operation, the lines of authority clearly ran to the highest level—the President.[46]

No evidence suggests, during the early months of Operation Mongoose, a resurrection of the old idea to engage the Mafia to murder Castro. That scheme had been pursued much earlier without results. But in April 1962, with paltry success in the secret war against Castro, the CIA reactivated its plan to have the mob kill the Cuban premier. Key CIA officers met with a top U.S. mob figure. Soon enough—and for the second time around—the agency had placed one of its exotic murder weapons, pills, into the hands of mobster John Roselli for the purpose of murdering Castro. It seems certain that the revival of this particular scheme was done without the Kennedys' specific knowledge, since the Attorney General was then leading the Justice Department in its all-out fight to destroy the Mafia.[47]

When Robert Kennedy heard of the CIA's earlier recruitment of the mob to kill Castro, he was furious and stated that he expected in the future to be informed about any such initiative using the mob. However, despite Robert Kennedy's anger, it appears that the mob connection continued, under specific instructions from the CIA. It also is clear that the mob effort was highly ineffective. Castro was as skilled at avoiding mob plots as he was in escaping danger sent his way directly by the CIA.*[48]

By the fall of 1962, the secret war against Castro was still getting nowhere. Operation Mongoose was a continuing failure, and the Kennedys were exasperated as well as frustrated. On October 4, Robert Kennedy told the Mongoose sponsors that the President "feels that more priority should be given to trying to mount sabotage operations." On October 16, at the height of the Cuban Missile Crisis, the Attorney General assured the Cuba project group that he planned to devote more time to Operation Mongoose.[49]

That same day, according to papers released in November 1983,

---

*There is interesting speculation that perhaps the mob never tried to carry out any attempts to murder Castro—that it simply went through the motions. Such reasoning holds that the mob had made a secret agreement with Castro to use Cuba as a staging area for the importation of narcotics into the United States. They pretended to go along with the plots for two reasons: to curry favor with Castro by keeping him informed of the latest U.S. efforts to kill him through the mob and, second, to curry favor with U.S. officials in hopes of turning down the heat the mob was feeling from the Justice Department. Support for this proposition is offered by Jimmy Fratianno, the Mafia hit man who turned into a government witness. Fratianno quotes Johnny Roselli on the subject of the Mafia-CIA plots against Castro: "This whole thing has been a scam. . . . All these fucking wild schemes the CIA dreamed up never got further than Santos [Trafficante]. He just sat on it, conned everybody into thinking that guys were risking their lives sneaking into Cuba, having boats shot out from under them, all bullshit."

there was a meeting in the President's office to discuss the Missile Crisis. There, Robert Kennedy made it clear that he sensed possibilities that could solve the Cuba problem once and for all. He urged that rather than considering *just* taking the missiles out of Cuba, it might be better "if you're going to get into it at all . . . whether we should just get into it and get it over with." A few minutes later, the Attorney General asked the President and his advisors "whether there is some other way we can get involved in this . . . or whether there's some ship that, you know, sink the *Maine* again or something."[50]

Robert Kennedy's comments leave no question about the urgency that he, at least, felt over the continuing failure of Mongoose. While others at this Oval Office meeting were focused on the Soviets, Robert Kennedy was looking squarely at the Missile Crisis as an opportunity to do something about the Castro regime. In the light of events that came to pass, it is clear that the Attorney General had spotted what was probably the last real opportunity of the Kennedy administration to pull the country out of this political quagmire.[51]

The Cuban Missile Crisis was a watershed in the Kennedys' official view of Castro. Operation Mongoose was officially disbanded. An agreement was reached between Washington and Moscow that in return for the removal of nuclear missiles from Cuba, the United States would promise never to invade the island.[52] (Castro never permitted an inspection of the missile sites by the United Nations, a condition of the agreement. Thus, the agreement never really became operative.*[53]) There was a reshuffling of authority pertaining to Cuba, and at certain levels there appear to have been genuine efforts toward establishing some normalcy in relations between Washington and Havana.[54]

By the fall of 1963, William Attwood, then an advisor to the U.S. delegation to the United Nations, had developed a line of communication with Castro's regime that, at least on the surface, appeared to hold promise for better relations. Evidence shows that the President was directly involved in sponsoring this channel. Ambassador Attwood and others involved in the overtures felt opti-

---

*As a substitute for verification, the United States had to remain content with the postcrisis U-2 surveillance photographs. It is officially held that each missile known to have been in Cuba was removed.

mistic. It is difficult to know Castro's real reaction. He seemed to accept the overtures as genuine, and many years later insisted to the HSCA that he regarded them as genuine.[55]

Logic points another way. Castro had every reason to doubt the sincerity of any gesture by the United States, particularly in view of the events happening simultaneously with the overtures. It is difficult to grasp why Castro should have viewed Attwood's approach and other initiatives as anything more than what he had experienced previously. As for the President's dichotomous policy, it had already shown up plainly in his uncertainty over the Bay of Pigs. He had also urged a halt to the exile raids against Cuban facilities, while at the same time stepping up sabotage operations.[56] It is hard to imagine that Castro, as a wily skeptic, took a benevolent view toward any overtures from the Kennedy administration. At the same time, as a shrewd manipulator, Castro would certainly be expected to encourage any overture that might eventually permit him an advantage over the Americans—or over the Soviets, his economic and political sponsors, whom he was clearly beginning to resent.[57]

The possible signs of a budding rapprochement were first felt in some circles in the fall of 1962. The no-invasion agreement was believed to be in place, and Soviet missiles supposedly had been removed.[58] With this whiff of accommodation in the air, an agreement was made for the return of the men captured at the Bay of Pigs. The released prisoners were greeted in Miami by President Kennedy. He welcomed them not on a note of reconciliation toward Cuba but with a ringing denunciation of Castro.[59] The returning soldiers presented Kennedy with the flag of their fallen brigade. Kennedy began his rousing address with a promise to the exiles that the "flag will be returned to this brigade in a free Havana."[60]

President Kennedy went on to tell the world in his speech: "I can assure you that it is the strongest wish of the people of this country . . . that Cuba shall one day be free again."[61]

To anyone who was listening in Havana, particularly the premier, such strong language could only be interpreted as a call for the overthrow of the Castro regime. That absolutely was the interpretation made by the freed Cuban prisoners, who were as determined as ever to regain their homeland.[62]

Meanwhile, the CIA-trained exile groups were increasingly anxious to get down to the business of toppling Castro. JM/WAVE, the CIA station in Miami, was surging with activity. Training bases for Cubans in Miami were at maximum operation. CIA assassination plots against Castro entered a new phase, which included finally dropping the Mafia, after its notable lack of success. While historians are able to quibble over distinctions in American policy toward Cuba at this point, it is difficult to see any real change in policy following the Missile Crisis. Throughout that winter and into the spring of 1963, raids continued against Cuban installations. There were attacks on Soviet ships. Cuban exiles openly took credit for the attacks, but in view of all that had gone before, it certainly could not be assumed that all their actions were purely of their own volition. There were strident denials from Washington that any exile activities had the official sanction of the U.S. government.[63]

With all this, it seems unlikely that Castro really believed that 1963 brought anything from the United States but more double-talk and duplicity.

That spring, even after stern warnings from Moscow, President Kennedy continued to waffle in calls for an end to the exile forays against Cuba and the Soviets.[64] By this time, Castro had amassed 17,000 Soviet troops in Cuba, backed up by 500 anti-aircraft missiles.[65] However genuine Kennedy's pleas may have been at that late hour, few of the highly trained exiles were paying any attention to him. They continued to be encouraged by their CIA leaders, and it is feasible that in many cases exile leaders were told that Kennedy's statements were only window dressing to make it *appear* that he was trying to stop them. Those who chose to believe this could hark back to the President's rousing promise in Miami a few months earlier of a free Havana. Others had only to recall the double-talk earlier in the sixties, when Washington denied any hand in the exile raids while at the same time actually sponsoring them.

President Kennedy's familiar ambivalence in this area was seen most vividly at a press conference in May 1963, when he was asked if his government was aiding the exile activity against Castro. He stated: "We may well be. . . . Well, none that I am familiar with. . . . I don't think as of today that we are. But I wouldn't want to go into details, if we were."[66] Stirring the confusion, Kennedy had said in a speech a few weeks earlier: "Time will see Cuba free again. And . . . when that happens the record will show that the United

States has played a significant role."[67] These words certainly had an ominous ring—far from any sense of rapprochement.

Obviously, the retreat in the secret war seen in the spring of 1963 was short-lived. In June the National Security Council's Special Group decided "to increase covert activities against Cuba."[68] President Kennedy approved a sabotage program directed at "four major segments of the Cuban economy," including electric power, petroleum refineries, railroads, and highways. As late as October 1963, specific approval was given to more than a dozen major sabotage operations in Cuba.[69]

Whatever President Kennedy was saying publicly, it is clear that privately he wanted full efforts to destroy the Castro regime. Given Castro's impressive record in perceiving what the United States was *really* up to, the premier almost surely understood Kennedy's real intentions.

In spite of this evidence, there is today the wide belief that President Kennedy *was* trying to stop the exile raids against Castro and *was* trying to seek a genuine accommodation with Castro. Even if this is correct, it apparently was of little practical use. By that time, the exiles were too committed to their cause to consider pulling back. Nothing, at that point, could stop them completely. In addition, the CIA—in keeping with the official position of the National Security Council June dictum—was as active as ever in its own covert military initiatives against Cuba. By October Castro was openly denouncing Kennedy and the United States for encouraging the raids. Kennedy declined to comment on the charges. Shortly thereafter Castro produced several captured exile raiders on Havana television to give a public account of their work for the CIA.[70]

Today, it is established that Castro's versions of events in these matters were consistently correct. Whatever accommodations were attempted at diplomatic levels during this period, they surely could not have been viewed with total seriousness by Castro. Indeed, his highly vocal contempt seems completely understandable.

Fifteen years later and with access to classified information, the House Select Committee examined the turbulent year of 1963 and summed up the U.S.-Cuba relationship this way: "The United States had attempted in the period after the [October 1962] missile crisis to stem the anti-Castro raids by, at least publicly, refusing to sanction them. But covert action by the United States had neither ceased nor escaped Castro's notice, and the rhetoric indicated that the crisis could explode anew at any time."[71]

Among all the contradictions, there was one certainty: efforts to get rid of Castro and his regime had failed. Castro seemed as impervious and indestructible as the enduring hero of a cartoon in which, no matter how imaginative and villainous his adversaries, the hero always pops back. The Kennedy administration had committed the country's treasury of military and intelligence expertise to what would seem to be the simple goal of getting rid of Castro. There was a wholesale abandonment of morality. Murder was acceptable. Three years later, all those efforts had evaporated without a trace of lasting success. Castro and his country remained unscathed. Despite some reservations on his part, Castro was in the Soviet camp more solidly than ever.

In the war between Castro and Camelot, there was no question as to which side had prevailed.

The Exiles: Double Betrayal

When Castro began his march into Havana on January 1, 1959, to take control of the government, there was jubilation among the people of Cuba. It was believed that Castro's assumption of power would bring freedom and democracy to the island—qualities of life long denied by the dictatorial regime of Fulgencio Batista. Castro's ascension was a great political victory in Cuba as well as a military one. It was greeted as a substantial blow against corruption and repressiveness. In the beginning, Castro also enjoyed the blessings of the United States government.[72]

Soon enough it was clear that none of this optimism was warranted. By the end of Castro's first year, the honeymoon with the United States was long over. There was a general sense of horror at Castro's mass executions of former officials, and there were early signs that the new premier had no genuine interest in developing a good relationship with the United States. By the summer of 1960, Castro had seized more than $700 million in U.S. property and was openly dealing with the Soviets. During this metamorphosis, thousands of Cubans, increasingly disenchanted with Castro, were fleeing in waves to the United States. By the end of Castro's first year, 100,000 Cuban refugees were in the United States. They continued to pour in at the rate of 1,700 each week. Finally, on January 3, 1961—just two years after Castro came to power—the United States formally broke diplomatic relations with Cuba. That was the sorry state of affairs between the two countries when, less than three weeks later, John F. Kennedy was sworn in as president.[73]

Thousands of anti-Castro Cuban exiles had already begun forming small groups dedicated to reclaiming their homeland. Most sprang up to claim to be the *real* voice of the exiles, and the net result was an absence of any widely accepted single leader. The situation was improved with the CIA-backed creation in May 1960 of a powerful coalition of several of these exile groups. It was this coalition, eventually known as the Cuban Revolutionary Council (CRC) that was to coordinate with the CIA the fateful Bay of Pigs invasion. Despite that horrendous failure, the CRC remained a unifying force until the Cuban Missile Crisis, when there was an apparent reversal in the Kennedy administration's official policy toward the Cuban exiles. By 1963, an intense bitterness pervaded the community of anti-Castro Cubans toward the man they believed betrayed them, John F. Kennedy. That hatred was, at the least, as great as their hatred of Fidel Castro.[74]

On any list of suspects in the killing of President Kennedy, the exile community of anti-Castro Cubans is prominent. Examining the possibility of an exile role in the assassination, the HSCA stated that the anti-Castro Cubans "had the motive, based on what they considered President Kennedy's betrayal of their cause, the liberation of Cuba from the Castro regime; the means, since they were trained and practiced in violent acts . . . ; and the opportunity, whenever the President . . . appeared at public gatherings, as in Dallas on November 22, 1963."[75]

Such an official analysis of possible Cuban exile involvement was far from new. In 1964, in a report prepared by two Warren Commission staff lawyers, W. David Slawson and William T. Coleman, Jr., a similar suggestion was put forth. That assessment, withheld from the public until 1975, went even further and showed just how such exile involvement might have included the use of Lee Harvey Oswald. Slawson and Coleman, in urging the Warren Commission to pursue this angle, had this to say in their internal report about the possibility of anti-Castro Cubans' involvement in the Kennedy assassination:[76]

Oswald could have become known to the Cubans as being strongly pro-Castro. He made no secret of his sympathies, so the anti-Castro Cubans must have realized that the law-enforcement authorities were also aware of Oswald's feelings and that therefore, if he got into trouble, the public would also learn of them. . . . On these facts, it is possible that some sort of deception was used to encourage Oswald to kill the President when he came to Dallas. . . . The motive of this would, of course be the expectation that after the President was killed Oswald would be caught or at least his identity ascertained, the law-enforcement authorities and the public would then blame the assassination on the Castro government, and the call for its forceful overthrow would be irresistible.[77]

Most of the angry and vocal Cuban exile leaders posed no threat to Castro or Kennedy. Their organizations—dwindling from 700 to 100—became more dedicated to the preservation of history and culture than to the carrying out of raids, sabotage, and assassination attempts against Castro.[78]

On the other hand, there were anti-Castro groups organized and operated with military precision, capable of attempting nearly any hostile activity. Cuban leaders of these groups viewed official U.S. policy toward Cuba with a contemptuous indifference. Indeed, the highly delicate negotiations over the Missile Crisis in October 1962 were seriously threatened as some of the groups carried on successful attacks against Cuban and Soviet facilities and personnel—during the very hours when the White House was promising the Soviets that such attacks would stop.[79]

The House Select Committee considered the activities of several of the more violent groups and arrived at startling findings. A deeply disturbing revelation involves Homer S. Echevarria, a Cuban associated with one of the most violent exile groups—one that was reported to be receiving financial support from organized crime.[80]

Soon after President Kennedy's murder, the special agent in charge of the Chicago Secret Service office reported to his superiors that he had received reliable information about a Chicago group that "may have [had] a connection with the JFK assassination." The HSCA discovered that the Secret Service report "was based on a tip from an informant who reported a conversation on November 21, 1963, with a Cuban activist named Homer S. Echevarria."[81] Echevarria had come to the United States in 1960 and reportedly worked in Dallas for an oil-drilling company. He was quoted as saying on the day before the assassination that plans for an illegal arms transaction were in place and would go forward "as soon as we take care of Kennedy."[82]

An observer would expect—and the HSCA strongly believed— that the substance and timing of the Echevarria report should have been a prime target for a thorough investigation. *It was not.*[83] While the reasons for neglecting such a lead are familiar throughout this tale, it is worth examining this case because of the Cuban exile connection.

Just after the assassination, the Secret Service informed the FBI about the report and recommended further investigation. The FBI pitched the matter back to the Secret Service, explaining that the incident "was primarily a protection matter and . . . would be left to the U.S. Secret Service." Initially, the Secret Service considered refusing to accept this. Then the Warren Commission was estab- lished, with the FBI charged with primary investigative responsi- bility on the assassination. Soon after this, the FBI "made clear that it wanted the Secret Service to terminate its investigation" of the Echevarria report. The Secret Service halted its efforts and turned the records over to the FBI, which apparently never pursued the matter.[84] By that time, of course, orders had come from Hoover to work strictly toward building the case against Oswald.[85] The incident stands as a chilling example of the wholesale loss of promising leads generated by Hoover's command within hours of Kennedy's death to pursue *only* the case against Oswald.

The examination by the HSCA of the "most violent and frustrated" anti-Castro groups led the committee to one of the most violent, powerful and successful of all such groups, Alpha 66, and to its founder, Antonio Veciana.[86]

It was Alpha 66—which was actively spurred on by *Life* maga- zine—that conducted the most daring raids against Castro during the Cuban Missile Crisis. Later, when President Kennedy made a desperate appeal to the exiles to cease their capricious and highly personalized gunboat diplomacy, Tony Veciana publicly snubbed the President and said that Alpha 66 would continue. If anything, the activities of Alpha 66 were stepped up.[87]

Central to any consideration of Alpha 66's activities is whether renegade elements of the CIA were, even in the spring of 1963, guiding and encouraging Veciana's activities. Veciana, who in Castro's early days had been a well-known bank accountant, insists that at every step, including his own efforts to assassinate Castro, he was working for the CIA. With the exception of the official CIA denial, there is no serious doubt that Veciana and Alpha 66 were creatures of the CIA. Veciana has survived those years and has testified in detail about his contacts with the CIA—*and his encounter with Lee Harvey Oswald.* The Select Committee did not buy Veciana's full story, but its investigation unlatched enough leads to establish Veciana's importance, even if not fully understood.[88]

Veciana's basic story is this: over thirteen years, the mild-mannered, well-educated Cuban met with a man known to him as Maurice Bishop, whom he accepted as an officer of the Central Intelligence Agency. In more than 100 meetings, Veciana claims, Bishop advised him in detail concerning the organization and activities of Alpha 66. Bishop directed Veciana, who had had a close relationship with Castro, in attempts to kill the Cuban premier in Havana in 1961 and in Chile in 1971. Veciana reports that his relationship with the CIA did not end until 1973, when Maurice Bishop paid him $253,000 in cash for his thirteen years of service to the United States.[89]

This much of the story really comes as no surprise to anyone familiar with CIA activities during those years. What makes Veciana's account of compelling interest is what he claims happened in Dallas during late August or early September of 1963. Maurice Bishop had summoned Veciana to Dallas for a meeting. They were to meet at the ground-floor lobby of an office building in downtown Dallas. When Veciana arrived, he saw Maurice Bishop across the lobby, engaged in conversation with a pale young man unknown to Veciana. The Cuban waited without intruding. Soon, the man departed and Maurice Bishop greeted Veciana. No reference was made to the young man, but a few weeks later, Veciana recognized him when his picture was flashed around the world as the assassin of President Kennedy.[90]

The HSCA reported that it "devoted a significant portion of its anti-Castro Cuban investigation" to the Veciana allegations. In the end, the committee cited several reasons for finding Veciana to be "less than candid" and dismissed his claim to have seen Bishop with Oswald.[91]

However, in the course of reaching these conclusions, the HSCA did seem to unravel evidence that the CIA acted with an unusually high degree of duplicity in responding to most questions pertaining to Maurice Bishop and Veciana.[92] Still, the committee's report on Veciana is bland and dismissive.

Two years after the committee's final report was issued, an angry staff investigator from the committee broke his secrecy oath and went public with nearly every detail of the Veciana investigation. He claimed to do so because of his belief that the public should know the full story of the Veciana investigation.[93] Unfortunately, the net result is that while much fresh information was thrown into the public domain, each answer seems to spawn two or three additional questions. Still, it is worth examining what happened.

Gaeton Fonzi, the former investigator, is regarded by most colleagues as honorable, diligent, and intelligent. As a staff investigator, Fonzi brought to his tasks unflagging enthusiasm. Apparently, his chief fault, if it can be called that, was his disinclination to be corralled into the bureaucratic constraints necessitated by the committee's mandate. While Chief Counsel Robert Blakey was trying to close down the hatches and get the final report written, Gaeton Fonzi was busy pursuing the Veciana allegations. Fonzi fervently believed in the importance of that pursuit.[94] It could well be that he was correct.

To grasp the significance of the Veciana matter, it is necessary to review just how the information was developed by Fonzi. It is, in this case, the development of the information that enhances the probability of what might have happened to Veciana in the early sixties—and much later, as Fonzi began to draw out the story. Fonzi was then working as a staff investigator for Senator Richard Schweiker, a member of the Church Committee, which conducted the investigation that led to the shattering revelations about the CIA during the midseventies.[95] It is a story of obsession on the part of Fonzi, but obsessiveness is also apparent on the part of those officials who seemed determined to put the greatest possible distance between Veciana and the Central Intelligence Agency.

There seems to be little question that Antonio Veciana became a leading figure in the CIA's urgent efforts to get rid of Castro and his government. Veciana claims that he was recruited by Maurice Bishop in Havana sometime after Castro took over. For each mission,

Maurice Bishop was the man in charge, the man with the CIA connections, the man who brought the final decisions, the man who brought the huge amounts of cash, the weapons, the munitions, or whatever was needed to get the job done. According to Veciana, Bishop was a highly cultured man who was always well dressed. He was even handsome, with carefully arranged hair. Veciana was never given an exact location where he could reach his case officer, but he assumed Bishop lived in a southern climate because he usually had a tan. When Veciana needed to reach Bishop, he could leave a message with an intermediary at different places. Details for contact changed numerous times over the years.[96]

In the early years of their association, Bishop controlled Veciana directly in Havana. Later, when Veciana had openly defected from Castro and left Cuba and was staging the exile invasions from Florida, Bishop would meet him there. Veciana claims that all the trouble caused by Alpha 66 to disrupt JFK's diplomatic overtures was instigated by Maurice Bishop. At the height of the Missile Crisis, Veciana says, Bishop told him to step up his raids on Soviet and Cuban vessels. Other examples of such seeming insubordination are reported during this period when certain elements of the CIA appeared to be acting contrary to the policies of the government.[97]

During this time, Bishop was also bringing Veciana elaborate assassination plots aimed at Castro. In fact, to Veciana, Bishop also seemed to be the brains behind the overthrow of Salvador Allende in Chile, although Veciana claimed no direct involvement in that.[98]

In the late summer of 1963 Bishop told Veciana to meet him in the lobby of an office building in downtown Dallas—the occasion on which Veciana claims to have seen Oswald. Veciana states that in meetings with Bishop following the assassination he never asked about the connection with Oswald, sensing that this obviously would not be a suitable area for discussion.[99]

But it was not long after the assassination that Bishop had an odd assignment for Veciana. He pointed out that there had been much publicity about Oswald's having been seen in Mexico City with a Cuban couple; the reports were that the Cuban woman spoke excellent English. Bishop reminded Veciana that he (Veciana) had a cousin, a Cuban woman who spoke excellent English, in Mexico City. Bishop asked Veciana to get in touch with his cousin and her husband and offer them "a huge amount" of money to be willing to have themselves pinpointed as having had some casual encounter with Oswald, thus giving an explanation for the identity of the couple with whom Oswald was seen. Veciana got to work on this assignment, but Bishop stopped him soon after, explaining that it was no longer necessary.[100]

The compelling question, of course, is the real identity of Maurice Bishop. With that answered, other questions could be asked about Veciana's bizarre report concerning Oswald. While there is much debate about Bishop's real identity, there is no serious question that such an intelligence figure did exist and that he did control Tony Veciana.

The search for Maurice Bishop—officially dormant after the conclusion of the Church Committee—began anew in 1977, when the HSCA was cranking up. Fonzi was hired by the HSCA—*before* Robert Blakey became chief counsel.[101] Blakey, who later was angered by Fonzi's out-of-school revelations about the Select Committee, has stated that he would have never hired Fonzi because "he was so lacking in professional objectivity."[102] It was Fonzi who originally, in 1975, discovered Veciana and hauled him to Washington for the Church Committee hearings. Fonzi had arranged for a top police artist, after many days of work with Veciana, to complete a drawing that Veciana felt looked like Maurice Bishop. When Fonzi showed the drawing to Senator Schweiker, the senator immediately said that he recognized the man as someone who had been testifying in executive session before the Church Committee. But he could not recall which of the dozens of witnesses from the intelligence community it was. Schweiker's effort to recall was complicated by the fact that the committee occasionally permitted CIA covert personnel to use aliases during secret testimony, or not give any name at all.[103]

Finally, Senator Schweiker believed that he could pinpoint where he had seen the man depicted in the artist's drawing of Maurice Bishop. Schweiker stated that he was thinking of David Atlee Phillips, who indeed had testified before the committee.[104] Phillips—who had been a key CIA officer in Cuba, Mexico, Guatemala, Brazil, the Dominican Republic, Venezuela, and even Lebanon—went on to become the chief of the Western Hemisphere Division of the CIA.[105] He was in charge of covert action for the CIA's Mexico City station during the time of Oswald's supposed visit there in September 1963.[106] Much of Phillips's work involved anti-Castro propaganda operations. Phillips has published a CIA-cleared book, *The Night Watch*, that chronicles his adventures in all those places, including his contacts with fledgling anti-Castro movements in Havana after Castro took over.

With Schweiker's impression, Fonzi was anxious for a reaction from Veciana. He got a picture of Phillips and presented it to Veciana. Moments passed as Veciana studied the photograph. "It is close, but it is not him," he finally said. "But I would like to talk with him."[107]

At this point, Fonzi and Schweiker had held their information about Maurice Bishop very closely. No queries had been made to the CIA. David Phillips was not contacted.[108] In fact, Phillips was by then retired and busy organizing an association of retired intelligence officers. Fonzi hatched a plan with one of Schweiker's assistants to get themselves and Veciana into a luncheon meeting of Phillips's association. At the luncheon, Phillips greeted the trio and said that he was delighted Senator Schweiker's office was showing an interest in his new organization. According to Fonzi, David Phillips never changed his expression as he was introduced to Veciana. After shaking the Cuban's hand, Phillips ignored him.[109]

During the luncheon, Veciana managed to sit directly across from Phillips. They never spoke. Veciana rather ostentatiously put on eyeglasses, folded his arms, and stared directly at Phillips throughout lunch. Veciana continued to stare at Phillips, who continued to ignore him, throughout an address by General Sam V. Wilson.[110]

After the speech, as the crowd milled about, Fonzi caught up with Phillips and suggested that perhaps Phillips could be of some use to Senator Schweiker. Phillips asked Fonzi what Senator Schweiker was working on that would involve him. Fonzi told Phillips that Schweiker was working on the Kennedy assassination. Phillips smiled and said, "I'll be glad to talk with any Congressman, or with any representative of Congress—in Congress." These were words that Phillips would recite many times as Fonzi tried to pursue his inquiry.[111]

Veciana was standing nearby as Phillips spoke to Fonzi. Speaking in Spanish, Veciana asked Phillips if he was in Havana in 1960. Phillips said that he was. Veciana asked him about various names, and in each case Phillips stated that he had some recollection of the name or person mentioned. (They were names very well known to almost anyone who had ever been involved in Cuban affairs.) Then Phillips looked at Veciana and asked him for his own name. Veciana, known throughout the hierarchy of Cuban affairs at CIA as the leader of Alpha 66, told Phillips his name.[112]

Innocently, Phillips asked Fonzi, "Is he with Schweiker's staff?"[113] His manner suggested that he had never heard of Veciana—a claim he clung to throughout subsequent testimony. Ironically, it was this very claim that influenced the Select Committee to doubt Phillips's testimony on this and other points.[114] Dozens of news articles of the period cited Veciana prominently, and in 1983 a CIA document was released that noted: "Alpha 66 and Veciana were synonymous to most people."[115]

Fonzi claims that at the luncheon, when Phillips was sitting near Veciana, he appeared nervous. During their later conversation, still smiling, but becoming testy, Phillips recited several times his lines about talking to Congress. Finally, his smile disappearing altogether, Phillips abruptly walked away. Fonzi and Veciana departed. They rode in silence to the airfield. Fonzi asked Veciana if Phillips was the man he had known as Maurice Bishop. Veciana said nothing. Fonzi waited in silence. Finally, he asked again, but Veciana said nothing. Then, Fonzi said to Veciana, "He's not Bishop?"[116]

"No, he's not him," said Veciana. There was another long silence before Veciana spoke the rest of his thought: "But he knows."[117]

That was the end of it. The Senate investigation had closed down several months earlier, and Senator Schweiker decided they had carried on this particular investigation as far as they could on their own. The one good lead on the identity of Maurice Bishop had evaporated with Veciana's statement that Phillips was not Bishop. Fonzi would have to await a new Congressional investigation, the HSCA, in order to pursue Maurice Bishop.[118]

At the time of Kennedy's death, David Phillips was in charge of covert action for the CIA station in Mexico City. As such, he was actively involved in anti-Castro propaganda operations and was consequently kept informed of activities at the Cuban embassy. He was apparently the agent charged with collecting intelligence about visits such as the one Oswald supposedly made to the Cuban embassy a few weeks before Kennedy's death. Phillips is the chief architect of the nearly incomprehensible explanations of how the CIA failed to garner evidence that could have proved beyond a doubt that it was Oswald who visited the Soviet and Cuban embassies.[119]

When David Phillips testified in 1978 about Mexico City at an executive session of the Select Committee, he was asked about the Veciana matter. According to Fonzi, Phillips became testy with the committee and gave an account of the luncheon meeting that was at variance with what happened. Among other things, according to Fonzi, Phillips began waffling and stated that he was told by Fonzi that Veciana was merely a driver for the other two; Phillips said that no matters of substance were discussed. In any event, Phillips told the committee that he had never heard of Tony Veciana.[120]

Even though Veciana has stated that Phillips is not Maurice Bishop, fascinating evidence suggests the possibility that he is—a point that both Phillips and Veciana find it convenient to deny. The most interesting revelations come from a comparison of details from Phillips's book, *The Night Watch*, with information Fonzi garnered from Veciana long before Phillips's book was published. For example, Maurice Bishop had casually taken Veciana to a restaurant in Havana—the same restaurant that Phillips cites in his book as a favorite of his. Also, Veciana believed Bishop to have grown up in Texas, which is where Phillips grew up. It is important to keep in mind that Bishop and Veciana knew each other fairly well over a dozen or so years, and it is equally important that none of this information about Phillips was widely available when Veciana first talked with Fonzi about Bishop.[121]

As the HSCA investigation got under way, Fonzi began to try to locate case officers who had worked out of the CIA's JM/WAVE station in Miami. He discovered at least one who was able, on his own and without specific prompting, to recall that it was David Phillips, who was prominently involved in the Miami CIA station, who used the operational name of Bishop. The man told the committee investigators that the name he recalled being used by David Phillips was none other than Maurice Bishop. Another JM/WAVE officer reluctantly offered some support for this.[122]

The Select Committee requested that the CIA search its records to determine whether any Maurice Bishop turned up in its files. The CIA reported that an exhaustive search showed that the agency had *never* used the name Maurice Bishop in any of its operations covers. Moreover, the CIA was able to report that David Phillips in particular had never used that name.[123]

Later, in a separate area of the investigation by the HSCA, the CIA produced a deep-cover agent who had worked for many years with David Phillips on Cuban operations. The HSCA interest in this agent was completely unrelated to the issue of Maurice Bishop. Fonzi heard that this man was going to be interrogated and asked the staff person assigned to the job to slip in an unscheduled question—namely, whether this agent had ever heard of Maurice Bishop. His answer was far from simple.[124]

When asked, the deep-cover agent became effusive and said that, indeed, he did recall Maurice Bishop. He was then asked to elaborate, which led him to volunteer that he knew both Bishop *and* David Phillips. He emphasized that he was acquainted with them both—a situation that, if true, certainly established that Phillips was not Bishop. In fact, the deep-cover agent seemed to go out of his way, almost artificially, to say several times that he had known both men.[125]

Then he was asked how he came to be acquainted with Maurice Bishop. He stated that he was not sure, but that he believed someone had probably pointed Bishop out as he was walking down a corridor at CIA headquarters—about as improbable an explanation as one can imagine. The main trouble with all this, obviously, is that the CIA had already told the HSCA that no one in its records had ever used the name Maurice Bishop. The incident created the impression that the deep-cover agent was acting under some confused instructions clumsily aimed at showing that Phillips was not Bishop.[126]

A week later, an HSCA investigator took a deposition from former CIA Director John McCone. When asked about Maurice Bishop, McCone stated that indeed *he* had known a Maurice Bishop and believed him to be an employee of the CIA. The HSCA informed the CIA of this oddity and asked for an explanation. Two months later, a reply came back from the CIA that reaffirmed its earlier statement that nothing could be found in the files. This was followed by a message, conveyed by the CIA, from former Director McCone, in which he stated that he had been mistaken in his assertion that he recalled Maurice Bishop, and he wished to make a retraction.[127]

The Select Committee concluded that David Phillips was probably lying when he denied under oath that he had ever heard of Veciana and his connection to Alpha 66, given Veciana's prominence during those years. The HSCA also concluded that Veciana was probably lying when he stated that David Phillips was not Maurice Bishop.[128] The sense of all this is that David Phillips was probably Veciana's case officer Maurice Bishop—and that both Veciana and Phillips knew this and, for reasons that can only be speculated upon, decided to lie about their knowledge of each other.

In a long magazine article describing what he sees as the shabbiness of the HSCA investigation, Fonzi explains how he and Veciana later became friends. Fonzi clearly has a tremendous admiration for Veciana and feels he is both courageous and honorable.[129] Fonzi writes, in the first person, of a conversation he had with Veciana:

> "You know that I believe what you have told me," I went on. "I believe you about everything. Except when you told me that David Phillips is not Maurice Bishop."
> His eyes never moved, his expression never changed.
> "Now," I said. "I would like you to tell me this one time very truthfully: Would you have told me if I found Maurice Bishop?"
> A slow smile crossed Veciana's face as he let out his breath. He put his head down and scratched his forehead, taking time to think carefully. Then he looked up with a half-smile still on his face.
> "Well, you know," he said. "I would like to talk with him first."
> I looked at him for a moment, then laughed. Veciana laughed with me.[130]

Soon after it became public knowledge that he had testified before the Select Committee, Veciana was gunned down while driving to his home in Miami. His assailant fired four times. Only a bullet fragment hit its mark, entering near Veciana's temple and, almost miraculously, lodging in the skull without entering the brain. Veciana completely recovered. The case has never been solved.[131]

In 1982 Veciana conceded in an interview with the author that even if he were certain that David Phillips *was* the man he had known as Maurice Bishop, he would not betray him by identifying him.[132] For practical purposes, in view of this, Veciana's statements on David Phillips are useless.

Assuming for the sake of this discussion that David Phillips is Maurice Bishop, it does not necessarily follow that there is any truth in Veciana's story about seeing Bishop in Dallas a few weeks before the assassination with a man he believes was Oswald. However, it is the extraordinary air of official deception in this matter—as strong today as ever—that encourages the feeling that, somehow, the secrets of Tony Veciana and David Phillips, if known, could unlock many mysteries. The discouraging irony is that those answers would probably spawn puzzles even more complex.

While Miami was the center for the most frantic CIA-sponsored exile operations, similar activities were also going on in New Orleans.[133] As early as 1961, Sergio Arcacha Smith, one of the exile leaders, was dispatched from Miami to set up a chapter of the Cuban Revolutionary Council (CRC), the primary CIA-backed exile group. In New Orleans, Arcacha got in touch with a man who was to become a close friend, Guy Banister, the former FBI agent who maintained his ties with the bureau. Banister arranged for Arcacha and his group to obtain space in the building where he kept his offices, 544 Camp Street. That, of course, is where witnesses have often placed Lee Harvey Oswald.[134]

It also is the address that, so curiously, was stamped on the pamphlets that Oswald distributed in the name of the Fair Play for Cuba Committee, a group diametrically opposed to the interests of Arcacha and the CRC. David F. Lewis, Jr., who worked for Banister as a private detective, has stated that he once met Oswald in the late summer of 1963 in a restaurant in the Camp Street building. With Oswald was Sergio Arcacha Smith, says Lewis. Arcacha has denied that he ever met Oswald.[135]

Another figure closely attached to Banister was David W. Ferrie. In addition, countless Cuban exiles frequented the building in connection with various activities aimed at Castro. It seems likely that some of the exiles were actually agents working *for* Castro, reporting back to the Cuban premier. How Oswald fit into all this is not known with any certainty. What *is* known, however, is that Oswald did have a variety of connections with the exile community and its sympathizers. He almost certainly had some role in their activities that may never be understood.[136] (A full discussion of Oswald's Cuban connections is found in Chapters 9 and 10.)

The Cuban connection of the JFK case is as filled with bizarre coincidences as any other part of the saga. One rather stunning coincidence worth a brief examination involves David Ferrie, with whom Oswald was convincingly associated in the late summer of 1963. One of Ferrie's closest associates in the CIA's secret war against Castro was Eladio del Valle, formerly a prominent and wealthy Cuban official. As stated earlier, David Ferrie was a prime target in the investigation of Jim Garrison, the New Orleans district attorney. Only hours before Garrison planned to arrest David Ferrie in New Orleans, Ferrie was found dead under very strange circumstances. A few hours later, 860 miles away in Miami, del Valle was found dead in a parking lot. He had been tortured and then shot through the heart at point-blank range. His head was split open, apparently by an ax. The murder of del Valle remains unsolved. [137]

The incident is but one of many such chilling coincidences that have contributed to the speculation and paranoia that characterize the whole case—particularly in terms of the possible role of the anti-Castro Cubans.

There was Cuban exile activity going on in New Orleans during the summer of Oswald's last stay there—a period during which Oswald's own whereabouts for considerable lengths of time are officially unknown. Training activities were under way for exile terrorists, and there was an exchange of exile soldiers and leaders between New Orleans and Miami. At the same time, the FBI carried out some of the threats from Washington to quash exile activities. There were FBI raids on training facilities and munitions dumps, for example, which were publicized. This was part of an effort to refocus anti-Castro efforts *away* from U.S.-based activity and to place a new emphasis on the aim of fomenting increased covert sabotage within the island of Cuba. Despite the gaps in Oswald's chronology during this period, it is well established that he was in contact with some of the very men engaged in these activities; there is, however, virtually no hope of ever sorting out just what was going on. Too much of the pertinent information is lost to sight, almost purely because of the tremendous pressures following the JFK assassination to conclude the investigation, to follow only those leads that could not be ignored. [138]

For example, one of the most mysterious and possibly important of Oswald's connections is the dark-haired man who can be seen in the photographs showing Oswald distributing Fair Play for Cuba Committee leaflets in New Orleans in the summer of 1963. There was not another member of that pro-Castro group in all of New

Orleans, no one other than Oswald. One can only speculate about the identity and role of this mystery man—whether he was truly pro-Castro, or whether he was engaged somehow in the creation and manipulation of Oswald's image.[139]

There are several simplistic certainties about Cuban exile activity in New Orleans during the summer of 1963. The exiles and their leaders hated Premier Castro and President Kennedy with almost equal intensity. The CIA and the FBI had well-established channels into exile activities, and probably had access to much high-grade intelligence. By the same token, the exile movement was so skillfully infiltrated by Castro's intelligence agents that the evidence suggests that Castro was much better served than Kennedy. The other relative certainty is that right in the middle of all of this was a strange young man of historic destiny: Lee Harvey Oswald.[140]

Countdown to Death

During the early sixties in the United States, political assassination became an acceptable last option in the effort to wield influence and control over foreign countries. In nearly every instance, it was justified as a means of fighting what was seen as the menace of spreading communism. The assassination program, operated under the sponsorship of the CIA, was called by the cryptonym ZR/RIFLE. The CIA expended considerable energy trying to perfect the ways and means of successful assassination. In doing so, it placed itself in the position of deciding, as a matter of political practicality, who should live and who should die. A well-greased concept known as "plausible deniability" protected the top political officers of the United States from technically knowing what was going on in these intelligence and military operations, which included assassination. There was, of course, a great deal of debate among even the intelligence operatives over the morality of the whole business, but there is no doubt that as a last alternative, assassination became acceptable.[141]

Despite all the planning and expertise that went into the concept of assassination of foreign leaders, all available records—and an investigation by a U.S. Senate Select Committee—seem to indicate that the United States never once carried off a successful assassination attempt against a foreign leader.[142] In spite of this record, there was a strikingly high mortality rate among those very leaders

U.S. officials planned to kill and then, for various reasons, decided *not* to assassinate.

However, in the case of Fidel Castro, the decision to assassinate was not rescinded. Despite active efforts that went on for many years, Castro is one of the few leaders ever targeted by the CIA for assassination who has survived. In a perverse way, Castro should be thankful that U.S. officials never gave the order to *stop* trying to kill him.[143]

This irony is enriched by the spectacular plans that were formulated to kill Premier Castro. In addition to the various plots described earlier, perhaps the most forthright effort was made through the direct dealings with an agent given the cryptonym AM/LASH.[144] The activities of this assassin become even eerier when considered in the larger context of Castro's personal friendship with him, and some of the striking coincidences about what Castro seems to have known and when he knew it. Was AM/LASH an agent who pretended to work for the United States, while his real allegiance was to Castro? Despite some reservations, the CIA proceeded as though he were genuine.

The CIA's first contact with AM/LASH, whose real name is Rolando Cubela, came in March 1961. Cubela, who had acted as an assassin for Castro during the revolution, had become an official in Castro's government. He was personally close to Castro and—seemingly because he believed or pretended to believe Castro had betrayed the cause—was willing to carry out a plot to kill him and overthrow his government. Of all the schemes afoot to assassinate Castro, this one, it would seem, had the most promise. AM/LASH possessed an ideological motive and ample opportunity. All he needed was the means, and the U.S. government was willing to provide whatever was required. It was a marriage of considerable convenience. Why it never worked is a far greater puzzle than the failure of several of the other, crazy plots.[145]

In the spring of 1961, Cubela contacted the CIA and expressed an interest in defecting. The CIA urged him to remain in Cuba and to maintain his position in the Castro government, and his close relationship with the premier.[146] Considering Cubela's willingness as an assassin, it is somewhat surprising that the agency waited so long—more than a year—before activating him for what would certainly have been the most important assassination in the Western Hemisphere.

There was CIA contact with Cubela in August 1962, when he proposed an elaborate scheme for overthrowing the Cuban government. The first step in the coup was to be the murder of Castro and other high officials, including the Soviet ambassador to Cuba. The CIA was apparently not inclined, at that time, to become involved in so elaborate a scheme, particularly, one would guess, a plot that called for killing the Soviet ambassador. But the CIA let Cubela know that this was something he might want to pursue on his own. It is now known that the CIA had other schemes of its own in the works, which is perhaps why Cubela's plan was not embraced wholeheartedly. Nothing more was heard from Cubela for more than a year.[147]

It was not until September 1963, with friction high between Castro and the United States, that Cubela emerged from Cuba and made contact with his CIA case officer in Brazil. That contact initiated several meetings. Cubela was told that American interest in getting rid of Castro and his government remained high. Cubela wanted assurances of U.S. interest and stated that he was prepared to move against Castro once he had that assurance. He also wanted a plan of action.[148]

The date of the first Cubela-CIA contact in 1963 was September 7. In this jungle of coincidences, something else very remarkable happened on that day. In Havana that evening, Fidel Castro buttonholed Daniel Harker, a reporter for the Associated Press, and gave him a highly unusual, three-hour interview. Castro's purpose? It was an angry message to "United States leaders" that he would "answer in kind" any attempt to murder Cuban leaders.[149]

As for claims that tensions were easing at that time between Castro and Kennedy, it is notable that on this occasion Castro publicly denounced Kennedy as a "cheap and crooked" politician. Castro also stated that he could envision no difference in U.S. policy toward Cuba, regardless of who was president—even if Kennedy lost to a Republican challenger in the next election.[150]

But the crux of Castro's voluntary comments was a bitter denunciation of the raids on Cuban territory and his warning of the danger U.S. officials faced. "We are prepared to fight them and answer in kind," Castro said. "United States leaders should think that if they are aiding terrorist plans to eliminate Cuban leaders, they themselves will not be safe."[151]

Rolando Cubela should have found his leader's words chilling, since it was that same day that Cubela had discussed assassination plans with the CIA. If Cubela was not terrified, there is the inevitable suggestion that perhaps his heart was closer to Castro than to the CIA. The Senate investigation into these matters concluded that this sequence suggested that Castro "was aware of some activity attributable to the U.S. Government." More specific conclusions were not drawn.[152]

It is difficult to judge the security of the CIA's contacts with Cubela, or whether in truth Cubela was reporting everything to Castro. However, it became known many years later, with the disclosure of certain documents, that one month after the September 7 CIA contact with Cubela, the FBI learned of that meeting from one of its Cuban informants in Miami. The FBI information actually included AM/LASH's real name, Rolando Cubela, and identified him as a Cuban official.[153]

But the FBI did not inform the CIA of this clear evidence of an important security breach. Thus, the operation continued in spite of a security problem that might have been self-defeating to the whole operation. In any event, the CIA officers involved in the AM/LASH operation have testified that they had serious doubts about its security even while it was running, so there is no particular reason to believe that revelation of the FBI intelligence would have changed anything.[154]

Contact continued between the CIA and Cubela to discuss measures to destroy Castro and his government. Cubela was persistent in demanding assurances that the plans considered had the blessings of top U.S. officials. He was told by his CIA case officers that the plans—which, at least from Cubela's supposed standpoint, included the assassination of Castro and other top leaders—were being considered at the "highest levels."[155]

Either sensing some doubt or wanting to establish with certainty who in the U.S. government was behind the plans, Cubela requested a personal meeting with Robert Kennedy. Cubela wanted to be certain of top U.S. support. A decision was made—apparently without specific knowledge of the Kennedys—to send Desmond FitzGerald, a senior CIA officer and social friend of the Kennedys, to meet with Cubela. Pretending to be the "personal representative" of Robert Kennedy, FitzGerald, using an alias, met with Cubela in Paris on October 29, 1963. While there has been much debate over just what FitzGerald told Cubela at that meeting, subsequent events make it appear almost certain that Cubela felt assured that the highest levels of the U.S. government—with the cachet of a personal representative of Robert Kennedy—would support his plan, which included the murder of Fidel Castro.[156]

A couple of weeks later, in mid-November, final approval was given to Cubela's requests for technical assistance from the CIA. The case officer in charge of Cubela was informed by Desmond FitzGerald that the CIA would provide the requested munitions, including rifles with telescopic sights that Cubela said were needed to kill Castro from a distance. There was a slight delay at CIA headquarters, as technical experts took more time than expected to complete their work on a poison pen that Cubela might use to murder Castro. It had a hypodermic needle so thin that the victim could not feel its insertion. In Paris, Cubela agreed to await the arrival of Desmond FitzGerald, who was coming from Washington and bringing the poison pen, as well as the final official approval for U.S. support of Cubela's plans for the assassination of Castro and the overthrow of the Cuban government.[157]

It was November 18, 1963.[158]

On that day, President Kennedy was in Miami. In a speech to the Inter-American Press Association, he denounced Castro and his government as "a small band of conspirators [that] has stripped the Cuban people of their freedom and handed over the independence and sovereignty of the Cuban nation to forces beyond this hemisphere."[159] The Associated Press called the speech "an appeal to the Cuban people to overthrow the Castro regime." At least one newspaper bannered the story across the top of page one: "KENNEDY URGES OVERTHROW OF CASTRO."[160]

Four days later, on November 22, 1963, Desmond FitzGerald met in Paris with Cubela to convey officially what Cubela had been told to expect: assurance of the full support of the U.S. government in the overthrow of the Castro regime, which included the murder of the highest officials. FitzGerald presented Cubela with the deadly pen, which, when filled with poison, could be used as a murder weapon to assassinate Fidel Castro.[161]

"It is likely," states a subsequent CIA analysis, "that at the very moment President Kennedy was shot, a CIA officer was meeting with a Cuban agent and giving him an assassination device for use against Castro."[162]

In the wake of the assassination, Desmond FitzGerald moved up the hierarchy of the CIA. By March 1964 he had become the chief of the CIA's Western Hemisphere Division. With the new Johnson administration, the earlier enthusiasm regarding the overthrow of Fidel Castro had largely evaporated.[163]

In Buenos Aires that March, four months after the assassination, FitzGerald told a group of his men: "If Jack Kennedy had lived, I can assure you we would have gotten rid of Castro by last Christmas. Unfortunately, the new President isn't as gung-ho on fighting Castro as Kennedy was."[164]

Any description of Cubela is incomplete without noting his erratic personality, bordering on instability. This was complicated by a severe drinking problem.[165] It is difficult to imagine that such a man, as one of Castro's confidants, was not watched by Cuban and Soviet intelligence agents when he was outside of Cuba. There is, however, no confirmation that he was under the observation or control of those intelligence agencies. Despite all the bizarre appearances and coincidences, there is nothing in the record to suggest that Cubela is officially believed to have been anything other than a genuine U.S. agent.[166]

Following President Kennedy's death, Cubela left Paris and returned to Havana. He says that he did not take the poison-pen device, though his CIA case officer does not recall Cubela's giving it back to him. Until June 1965 Cubela continued as an agent for the CIA, still engaged in plotting the overthrow of Castro. Eight months after that, in February 1966, Cubela was arrested and charged with treason, including conspiracy to murder Premier Castro.[167]

Cubela's trial was simple. Not only did he readily confess his treachery, but he shouted to the court that he deserved to die, that he should be taken "to the wall" and promptly executed. An interesting aspect of the trial was that the bill of charges against Cubela all started in 1964, *after* the JFK assassination. Cubela was never asked—nor did he testify to—any plot against Castro prior to 1964. The proceedings were all based on Cubela's alleged activities against Castro beginning in 1964.[168]

Despite Cubela's dramatic appeal for execution, Premier Castro stepped in to ensure clemency. As a dictator who executed more than 500 government officials, Castro argued that no laudable purpose was served by putting Cubela to death. Cubela was sentenced to twenty-five years in prison.[169] In recent years Cubela has been interviewed by at least one journalist who asked him about the pre-1964 plot to assassinate Castro. Cubela did not deny the plot, but he said it was instigated purely by the CIA, an answer that is not surprising or necessarily credible.[170]

The basic question is whether during the early sixties, Cubela was reporting his CIA contacts to Castro. Was it Castro who made Cubela repeatedly ask for assurances that the plots to kill the Cuban premier were being authorized at the highest levels? Did Castro order Cubela to demand to hear the authorization from Robert Kennedy? It appears more logical to believe that Castro was in control of Cubela than not. Even if he were, that does not yield a clear answer to the ultimate question of whether Castro, as a desperate act of self-preservation, brought about the assassination. Today, all that can be said is that whatever his connection, if any, Castro was better served than any other leader in the world by the death of President John F. Kennedy.

12 · THE CONFESSION
OF ROBERT EASTERLING

> The Committee believes . . . that President John F. Kennedy was probably assassinated as a result of a conspiracy. The Committee is unable to identify the . . . extent of the conspiracy.[1]
>
> —House Select Committee
> on Assassinations, 1978

Robert Wilfred Easterling is a multiple felon, an ex-convict, a raging alcoholic, a diagnosed psychotic and schizophrenic. He is a physically powerful man of bellicose personality and violent temperament whose family members have so feared him that on several occasions they obtained court orders to commit him to mental institutions. He has been charged with assault and convicted for burglary and bootlegging.[2]

In addition to these matters of record, Easterling is a self-confessed multiple murderer. He claims to have conspired, in 1953, in an insurance fraud scheme in which he and another man placed a bomb in a National Airlines plane with forty-six aboard. The DC-6 airliner was lost in the Gulf of Mexico and, to this day, there is no certain official explanation for that crash. (The official report suggests that extreme weather conditions probably caused the crash.) All lives were lost.[3] One witness to the purported bombing conspiracy was an eighteen-year-old boy, whom Easterling claims he made dig a grave and then executed by shooting him through the back of the head.

346 ·

Equally gruesome is the horrific account, related by a close member of Easterling's family, of a time when Easterling teased his wife and daughter by tossing flaming papers onto a bed where they were reading and then threatened to butcher them with a large knife if they tried to escape. At the last moment, he relented and they survived without serious physical injury. He once tried to drown his wife in a bathtub and then left her for dead. There is a reliable report that Easterling has been involved in child prostitution, and Easterling himself admits to additional crimes ranging from sophisticated safecracking to running an interstate car-theft operation in the Deep South during the fifties. He also claims to have been involved with the Communist Party in Milwaukee as an informant for the FBI.[4]

It is this man who, on September 29, 1981, picked up the telephone and called the author to describe his connection to still another crime: the assassination of John F. Kennedy.

In vivid detail, Easterling portrayed himself as a low-level conspirator intimately involved in certain plans that led to President Kennedy's death in Dallas on November 22, 1963. His stated motive for coming forward with a confession was that he believed he was dying, that he wanted to clear his conscience. He blamed the private hell he had lived in—the belief that he could have prevented the assassination—for the fact that he has been committed to several mental institutions.[5]

The confession of Robert Easterling was approached with enormous skepticism. Some of Easterling's stories about matters unrelated to the assassination ranged from the fanciful to the absurd—one example being his claim to have had a warm personal relationship with FBI Director J. Edgar Hoover. Easterling states the friendship was so close that Hoover would slip away from Washington, fly to New Orleans alone, hire a car and travel eighty miles to Baton Rouge, where he would confer with Easterling, who slyly suggests that Hoover was smitten with his wife. Anyone with the slightest knowledge of Hoover knows that such a story is preposterous.

Claims such as this make it easy to understand the comments in psychiatric reports noting Easterling's grandiose delusions—comments echoed by many people who have known the man since the assassination.[6]

Seventy-five hours have been spent by the author in face-to-face interviews with Robert Easterling, including trips with him to areas where he declares events took place that are related to the assassination. Dozens more hours have been spent in telephone conversations with Easterling.

Born at Hattiesburg, Mississippi, on June 30, 1926, Easterling dropped out of high school to travel with a rodeo and thus earned the nickname Cowboy. Later, he learned to work on engines, and his most frequent legitimate occupation has been as a diesel mechanic, working for oil-drilling companies and construction contractors, primarily in Texas, Ohio, Louisiana, and Mississippi. At times he operated a bulldozer, and it was this sort of work that earned him his best-known sobriquet, Hardhat. He has lived under several false names. His most commonly used alias during the years following the assassination was George Taylor.[7]

Pieced together, Easterling's life is that of a quintessential loser. The partially redeeming feature—noted by friends, enemies, family, and employers—is that Easterling possesses a bright and inventive mind, although one terribly ravaged by alcohol. It was this very characteristic of brightness that caused the most concern in trying to verify the confession of Robert Easterling. Was it all a fabrication, one so masterfully and subtly tuned that there were just enough enticing elements to lure one on? Under the best of circumstances, only the periphery of his story could be checked. From the start it was clear there would be no tidy package of confirmation, no chance of a claim that the confession checked out beyond a reasonable doubt.

Despite all these negative factors, Easterling's account of his participation in an assassination conspiracy was verified in ways that— even if peripheral—simply could not be ignored.

Soon after Easterling's telephone call, the author sent a registered letter to FBI Director William Webster describing the circumstances of Easterling's confession. The letter also informed Webster that Easterling claimed knowledge of other grimly serious crimes. The author's position with Easterling from the beginning was that any information he had concerning illegal activities would be promptly turned over to the proper authorities.[8]

In response to the letter, FBI agents were sent to talk to the author, who provided Easterling's address. At the request of the FBI, the author also turned over current photographs of Easterling.[9]

In the 25,000 released FBI and Secret Service interviews of people claiming information about the assassination, there is not a single known example of an individual's stepping forward to offer a confession of his own participation.*[10] The uniqueness of Easterling's confession is remarkable, given the notoriety of the case. Far more baffling is the fact that the FBI—citing massive evidence of Robert Easterling's alcoholism, erratic personality, and general unreliability in reporting other criminal activities—has continued to show a determined lack of interest in his confession. While claiming to have investigated Easterling's allegations in the past, the FBI concedes that it never talked to the alleged conspirators named by Easterling because "they could not be identified or located."[11]

In their official contacts with the author, FBI officials were clearly unimpressed with the striking fact that Robert Easterling, the only person ever known to offer such a confession for the crime of the century, is a man who possessed, at the very least, the mercenary motive, the means, and the opportunity to have done just what he has admitted in his statements. Moreover, it would seem that what is known of his violent character should give chilling support to the whole proposition of his involvement.

It is fatuous for the FBI to claim it could not locate the conspirators named by Easterling. Of those still living, one is a prominent figure, and another was located and interviewed by the author. Moreover, it is downright myopic that the official indifference to Easterling's confession and allegations persists even *after* the House Select Committee reached a conclusion of probable conspiracy and made an

---

*In the 25,000 reports, there are a number of examples of citizens offering tips to authorities about individuals whom they suspected of being involved in the murder of President Kennedy. There is at least one anonymous confession void of details. Several books have been published in which an author reports a claim by an anonymous person to have participated in the assassination. In 1980 Charles Harrelson, a mob assassin serving a life sentence for murdering a federal judge, reportedly stated that he was involved in killing President Kennedy. Arresting police officers who heard the statement suspected Harrelson of being under the influence of drugs at the time. Harrelson's brother, a respected former police detective in Houston and now a private investigator, has determined to the author's satisfaction that Charles Harrelson's claim is probably false. In addition, Harrelson seemed to back off from his claim in a subsequent public statement. However, it is known that he had underworld links to some of the mobsters suspected of having a role in the JFK assassination. But beyond those tenuous links, no other evidence is even suggestive of Harrelson's participation. In 1984, a man with whom the author had been in contact during the course of this project, made allusions to having participated in a conspiracy, but his specific claims were in sharp contradiction to his earlier assertions. Moreover, this man would not allow his claims to be scrutinized. As far as this investigation can determine, Easterling is the only person who has ever stepped forward to offer a full, detailed confession to direct participation in a conspiracy to assassinate President Kennedy.

official plea for help from the Justice Department and FBI in developing the case.[12] Ironically, the FBI's pointed lack of attention is in keeping with the widely held belief that the government has never *wanted* to know any new information about the JFK case that would distort the long-standing official version. It is not unreasonable to view the bureau's refusal to pay attention to Easterling as persuasive evidence that the FBI will never abandon the twenty-year-old conclusions embraced by J. Edgar Hoover within hours of the President's death.

Robert Easterling was first committed to a mental institution in 1974, more than ten years after the assassination. There is not a hint in the hospital records that he mentioned anything about the JFK case at that time. However, in subsequent commitments, notably after the assassination attempts against President Gerald Ford in 1975, Easterling got in touch with the FBI. Shortly afterward, he was interviewed by a Secret Service agent, whom Easterling says he tried to persuade of the veracity of his account. He claimed the man he knew as the rifle marksman who killed Kennedy had said he hoped to kill a second United States president in his lifetime. The attempt on Ford was seen by Easterling as possible evidence of this, which is what he says first compelled him to turn to the authorities.[13]

However, indications are that each time Easterling has tried to provide his account to the FBI, he has been sent to the Secret Service, which is charged with the protection of the president. As late as 1982, the Secret Service again listened to Easterling's story, presumably as it might pertain to the safety of the current president. While little is known about how the Secret Service responded to Easterling, it is fairly clear that the FBI never took his assertions seriously. According to members of Easterling's family, the FBI interviews concerning his allegations were perfunctory, even dismissive, in tone. Easterling's sister recalls that an FBI agent who interviewed her really said no more than to suggest that her brother was a lunatic and should be placed in an asylum.[14]

Following Easterling's release from his initial confinement to a mental institution, it appears that he attempted several times to relate his story in a forum where it might attract official attention. He knew that the Secret Service officials had nothing to do with investigating the murder of President Kennedy, yet that was the direction in which he was always sent. He told the story to drinking companions and family members and even attempted to interest various publications. For a host of reasons—a prominent one being Easterling's character and demeanor—no one would take him seriously.

One of the points that seemed to favor Easterling's credibility was that when he contacted the author, he did not ask for payment in return for his story. No commitment was made to him as his account was assessed. During those months he occasionally complained that he was broke, and small amounts of money were given to him, since he was destitute and disabled. For his time spent in interviews, the amount was about half his hourly rate as a diesel mechanic. Eighteen months after the original telephone call from Easterling, he was offered a standard financial agreement for all the rights to his story. Easterling accepted.

From the beginning, there has been the obvious possibility that Easterling's story is a delusion or his own fabrication—or an elaborate hoax with antecedents so obscure that they could never be identified. But if his confession is a hoax—and, to be sure, Easterling would have no compunction about committing any deception—then there is a fascinating story to be told about such an extraordinary scheme.*

While it is not possible to verify Easterling's story in traditional fashion, a number of points have been confirmed. In the end, they lead to a single compelling certainty: Easterling's confession, with all its ragged edges, provides a persuasive version of events that fills the void of uncertainty created by the tendentious conclusions of the Warren Commission in 1964 and the tentative findings of the House Select Committee on Assassinations in 1978. The Warren

---

*Aspects of Easterling's account that are flagrantly preposterous have been omitted from this presentation. In an obvious delusion, for example, Easterling claims that the real assassin departed from the TSBD Building, following the assassination, by descending from a window by means of a rope ladder. Easterling also claims that the conspirators he was working with were planning in early 1963 to shoot the President from that building—even though there were no known plans in the works at that time for Kennedy to go to Dallas. Easterling provides elaborate details about his asserted informant relationship with the CIA and the FBI. He claims hearsay knowledge that the same people involved in the conspiracy to kill JFK were also involved in the murder of Robert Kennedy, and that the tragic scandal at Chappaquiddick involving Senator Edward Kennedy was actually a botched assassination attempt by the same conspirators. There is much more. The aim in these pages is to follow the basic threads of Easterling's story as he claims they relate to the JFK assassination, focusing on those aspects of his story that have remained consistent during numerous interviews with the author conducted from September 1981 on into 1984.

Commission found no credible evidence of conspiracy and blamed the entire crime on a solitary assassin: Lee Harvey Oswald.[15] The HSCA concluded that there probably was a conspiracy behind the assassination, but it found the clues too old and sketchy to permit identification of anyone involved, other than Oswald. However, the committee broadly hinted at elements from organized crime and/or elements from the violent Cuban exile community—the Cubans who believed their interests were betrayed by President Kennedy at the disastrous Bay of Pigs invasion in April 1961.[16] In several respects, Easterling's story complements and supplements these official versions in unpredictable ways that lend support to his credibility.

The Habana Bar

In early 1963, Robert Easterling was living in a trailer at the Windmill Trailer Court in Marrero, Louisiana, just across the Mississippi River from New Orleans. He was working for one of the dozens of oil companies located on the river's west side. Easterling's job at the company was primarily working on diesel engines, a trade at which he is an acknowledged expert. Even the company owner, who today claims Easterling was stealing from him, concedes that Easterling was a good mechanic.[17]

Easterling's job often took him across the river into New Orleans, where, using one of the company trucks, he picked up the parts that were needed for his work. It was in this capacity that Easterling began stopping regularly to drink at the Habana Bar, located at 117 Decatur Street.[18]

The Habana Bar did not cater to tourists from the heart of New Orleans's famed French Quarter a few blocks away. Open twenty-four hours a day, its chief customers were exiled Cubans, sailors in port, and some businessmen who worked in the large office buildings on Canal Street, less than a block away. Directly across the narrow street from the Habana Bar was one side of the huge granite U.S. Customs building. Within blocks was the center of U.S. intelligence operations then going on around New Orleans. These operations related primarily to the official efforts of the U.S. government to instigate, through the Cuban exile community, the overthrow of the Castro regime.[19]

There is little question about the prominence of the Habana Bar as a haven for Cuban exile activities in the early sixties. Orest Pena, the bar's owner, was a leading member of the Cuban Revolutionary Council. In this connection, Pena served as a source for the FBI. In 1982 Pena told the author that he had a similar relationship with the CIA. Indeed, such a dual relationship was not uncommon during those stormy days in New Orleans. Such government connections enhanced Pena's prominence—as well as the prominence of the Habana Bar—in the Cuban exile cause.[20]

From the time of Castro's seizure of power in Cuba in January 1959, New Orleans was a haven for displaced Cubans. First, there were the established professionals and government officials who had fled. Then came the wave of Cubans who had decided that Castro was as undesirable as the dictator they had helped him overthrow.[21]

Robert Easterling, naturally loquacious and a generous drinking companion, knew a smattering of Spanish. He fit easily into the camaraderie and intrigue that swirled through the Habana Bar, and he understood the disenchantment of the Cuban exiles. Invariably, President Kennedy was the focus of attention during heated arguments over what should be done about Castro.[22]

To some extent, all the diverse forces threatening Kennedy were present at the Habana Bar, creating in that establishment almost a microcosm of the city itself. It was in that bar, on a Friday afternoon in February 1963, that Robert Easterling encountered an acquaintance who, he declares, enlisted him in the conspiracy that led to the death of John F. Kennedy.[23]

A Man Named Manuel

As he walked into the Habana Bar that afternoon, Easterling was wearing the white hard hat that had earned him his nickname. A Cuban who was across the room called out to him, "Hey, Hardhat!" Easterling, who is blind in one eye from an accident, peered through the dimness and, to his surprise, recognized the man. It was Manuel Rivera, an acquaintance he had last seen in 1961. Since it was crowded around the bar, Easterling waved acknowledgment, took a seat at a nearby table, and ordered a drink.[24]

Spanish music blared from a jukebox. Men bantered with the girls who worked the bar as well as with the prostitutes who hung around the establishment. Occasionally, Easterling overheard a discussion at the bar. Apparently, Manuel had just arrived in a small plane from Cuba bringing rum and cigars that were displayed behind the bar.[25]

Easterling had first met Manuel Rivera in November 1960.* The Cuban was then twenty-five. Easterling describes him as being five feet, six inches tall, stockily built, with an oval face, a receding hairline, a black mustache, and hairy arms. He also had a noticeable gold tooth and a brown birthmark on the right side of his neck. Easterling had been immediately impressed by Rivera's self-assurance and ingenuity in various illegal activities, such as lock-picking, safecracking, and the procurement of young girls.

At that time, Rivera was involved with organized crime in New Orleans as a numbers runner. Cubans with whom Easterling worked placed their weekly bets with Rivera in the mob's numbers racket. Easterling had occasionally asked Manuel to send him a prostitute at the Tamanaca Motel on Tulane Avenue, not far from the main business district of New Orleans. He had been given a telephone number where he was able to reach Rivera on occasions when he wanted such services.

He had last seen Rivera at a bar on Airline Highway outside New Orleans. There, Easterling says, Rivera, Easterling, and several Cubans were in the company of a prominent U.S. military figure with whom they were discussing Cuban invasion plans. At the end of the conversation, Rivera told Easterling that they might not see each other again. Indeed, Easterling had not seen Manuel Rivera until this Friday afternoon.

Where had Rivera been?

As he was later to tell Easterling, Rivera had lived through extraordinary adventures in the past two years. They were adventures, as he related them, which leave a dispassionate observer dazed in trying to comprehend Manuel's true allegiances. He was to tell Easterling at various times that he was working for the CIA *against* Castro—only later to claim that in truth he was working all along *for* Castro as a double agent. He said that he had been one of the Cubans recruited by the CIA to kill Castro but that he had tipped off the Cuban leader so that Castro was safe when the explosives

---

*Manuel Rivera is not the actual name reported by Easterling. The real name has been changed here, because complete verification of Easterling's story is not possible.

intended to kill him were detonated. Manuel claimed to have warned Castro about the invasion planned at the Bay of Pigs. Rivera also told Easterling that since he last saw him in 1961, he had been "captured" by Castro during the Bay of Pigs invasion and then sent to the Soviet Union, where he received training in the Russian language as well as in techniques of sabotage and assassination.

But Easterling knew none of these things as he sat in the Habana Bar that Friday afternoon. He was glad to see Rivera chiefly because he knew that Rivera possessed attributes that Easterling found useful in his own illegal activities. He was happy Rivera was back at the Habana Bar.

As Easterling sat there, he noticed standing at the bar with Manuel one of the strangest-looking men he had ever seen. The man had prominent dark eyes, but more notably was completely hairless—without eyebrows, facial hair, or hair on his head. This was David W. Ferrie, the man who had just flown Manuel to New Orleans from Cuba.[26]

From his seat, Easterling could see that the men had a rifle they were passing back and forth. Also present at the bar was a New Orleans businessman whom Easterling believes was Clay Shaw, along with a Cuban called Joe, whom Easterling has not been able to identify.*

When Ferrie and his companions left, Easterling got up and approached Manuel Rivera, who had begun tending the bar. Rivera served Easterling a drink, and the two men began to renew their acquaintance. It was during this conversation, Easterling states, that Rivera told him that he and the men who had just left the bar were hatching a plot to kill President Kennedy. Easterling recalls that Manuel looked at him and said, "I want you to help us, and I'll pay you well."

Easterling agreed: "Let's kill the bastard. He betrayed us at the Bay of Pigs!"

---

*Orest Pena, the owner of the Habana Bar, has told the author that Ferrie and Shaw were customers at his bar. Shaw's office at the International Trade Mart was only a few blocks from the bar, and Pena claims that it was not unusual for both Shaw and Ferrie to stop in for a drink in the late afternoon. However, Easterling has viewed photographs of a prominent figure in Cuban exile activities, Guy Banister, and feels that the man he believed to be Shaw could have been Banister, a far more logical possibility. There is persuasive evidence that Shaw and Banister were confused with each other on at least one other occasion, as described fully in Chapter 10.[27]

It was not all that unusual to hear such wild talk in New Orleans during that period. What was extraordinary, in Easterling's recollection, was that Rivera was actually recruiting him to help kill the President.

It was then that Rivera showed Easterling a magnificent Czech-made automatic rifle. He explained that he had personally supervised its design and construction at a gun factory in Czechoslovakia. He pointed out a unique feature of the rifle—a catch box on the side designed so that ejected shells would not be scattered and lost when fired. They would be caught in the cuplike box attached to the side of the rifle. Easterling examined the rifle. He noticed that the only imprint stated, "7 mm," which he assumed meant that it used seven-millimeter cartridges.

Shortly after this, Easterling went with Rivera out of the bar and watched as he placed the Czech rifle in the back seat of his gray Volkswagen. There was another rifle already on the car's seat, which Easterling declares was a Mannlicher-Carcano—the make allegedly used by Oswald to kill President Kennedy.

Back inside the Habana Bar, Rivera explained to Easterling that he needed a barrel of water into which he could fire the Mannlicher-Carcano rifle. He wanted to retrieve the bullets. Manuel said he needed to shoot from the tailgate of a truck so that he could collect the ejected shells from the back of the truck. He also wanted a place where he could fire the Czech automatic he had just brought in from Cuba. Easterling assured Rivera that he could accommodate him in the spacious, open field behind the trailer park where he lived, across the river from New Orleans.[28]

The following afternoon, around four o'clock, Manuel Rivera arrived at Easterling's trailer. Easterling drove his pickup truck down into a large field behind the trailer park. He backed the truck up until it was just beside a large barrel of water that was in the field. Manuel loaded the Mannlicher-Carcano, stood on the tailgate of the truck, and fired downward into the water.[29]

Then the two men searched the back of the truck and found the ejected cartridge shells. Manuel dropped them into his pocket. After that, the men dumped over the barrel of water and retrieved the slugs. Manuel held one of them up in front of Easterling and told him that someday the slug would be famous.

After Manuel pocketed the slugs, Easterling saw three men arrive in a large car. The first two were David Ferrie and the man he believed to be Clay Shaw. The third man was the Cuban who had been with them at the Habana Bar—the man called Joe, who had a slightly deformed hand. Manuel removed three traffic cones from his Volkswagen and placed them in staggered positions, several feet apart, about 250 feet from where the men were standing. Upon each cone, Manuel placed a coconut. Then he walked to the spot where the other men had gathered.

Manuel removed the Czech-made automatic rifle from his car and loaded it. The Cuban known as Joe held a stopwatch. Manuel fired quickly, drilling each of the coconuts. The time was a little over five seconds.

"Scratch one Kennedy," said the Cuban with the stopwatch.

"That'll get the job done," was the comment from the man Easterling thought was Clay Shaw.

David Ferrie didn't say anything, according to Easterling—"he just smiled."

Meanwhile, Easterling's wife was in their trailer in sight of the field where the men were shooting.*[30] She has told the author that while she recalls some men coming to the trailer park, she has no idea who they were. Although it was not unusual for men to target practice in the field on Saturday afternoons, there were several unusual details that have caused the event to stick in her mind.

Before any of the shooting started, she has recalled, Easterling came to the trailer and demanded that she give him some dishcloths. It happened that she had several dishcloths that she had just bought, and it was with some irritation that she let him have them.[31]

Twenty years later, Easterling was asked what he remembered about using dishcloths that day. At first, he recalled nothing about it. Then, after a few minutes, he remembered that indeed he and Manuel had tried unsuccessfully to suspend the dishcloths about halfway down in the barrel of water in order to catch the bullets in the cloth and thus avoid dumping out all the water, and risk losing the bullets.

However, Easterling said, they realized the idea would not work and abandoned it. Easterling was surprised that his former wife recalled the dishcloths.

---

*Today she is remarried and spoke only with an agreement of anonymity.

Among other things, this incident is a measure of Mrs. Easterling's credibility—as well as that of her husband. Her most vivid recollection of that afternoon, however, is after the target practice was over and the other men had gone. Easterling brought her three coconuts in varying states of destruction. The one common condition was that each had been shot with a bullet. Mrs. Easterling cleaned them off, shredded the meat and made coconut pies for her husband and children. Easterling says that when he gave her the coconuts, he told her that his friends were thinking of going bear hunting and had used the coconuts for practice.[32]

For his services that afternoon, Robert Easterling claims he was paid $500. That was easy money, even easier than cracking a safe. He eagerly awaited the next chance to do some work for Manuel Rivera.

The following Friday evening, in late February, in another incident verified by both Mrs. Easterling and one of her neighbors, a large white car stopped near their trailer. It remained there for more than two hours before Easterling got home. The several men in the car appeared to be Cubans. Mrs. Easterling was terrified when she saw the strangers watching her trailer. When Easterling arrived at the trailer and saw the car and heard his wife's report, he telephoned Rivera, who told him he was aware of the car. The men inside, he said, had guns with silencers and cans of gas.[33]

"They want to kill you and your wife and burn your trailer," Rivera said. He explained that the Cubans feared that the Easterlings would talk about the events they observed the preceding Saturday in the field behind the trailer court. Manuel said he would be there in a few minutes. Waiting for Manuel, Mrs. Easterling recalls the terror she felt as she crouched on the floor of the trailer with the lights off, keeping her crying children from going to a window. Moments later, the fear passed. Manuel arrived and ordered the men away.[34]

About six weeks later, perhaps in early April, Easterling stopped to drink at the Habana Bar. He was driving his new 1963 Ford XL, painted yellow and black. It was a car he is still very proud of. Easterling states that he was in the bar drinking and talking to Rivera and that they were discussing, in general terms, the murder of President Kennedy. It was then that Manuel stated, to Easterling's surprise, that he wanted a photograph of Hardhat, that he needed a permanent record of all the men who were involved in such historically significant business.

Two men, one a Cuban and the other an American, accompanied them to Easterling's car, where Manuel got behind the wheel. Hardhat got into the back seat. Balls of cotton were placed over Easterling's eyes and held in place by a large bandanna, so that he could see nothing. Manuel drove for about thirty minutes, perhaps going in circles.

At the destination, which Manuel referred to only as "headquarters," the blindfold was removed. Easterling, wearing his white hard hat, was photographed with a studio-type camera. Then his fingerprints were taken. Easterling noticed that the lettering on the fingerprint cards was in Spanish. A photocopy was made of his driver's license, which bore his real name. It was a moment Easterling would never forget. Until that time, Easterling believes, Manuel and the others—who had only called him Hardhat—had not known his true identity.

Afterward, Manuel showed Easterling a heavily constructed, rectangular wooden box, which he said he had built himself. Odd in its dimensions, the box was about five feet long, three feet wide, and four feet high. In the floor of the box was a false bottom, concealing a compartment that housed a spring-tension cradle, designed to hold a rifle securely.

Manuel then picked up the Czech-made automatic rifle, secured it in the cradle, and replaced the false floor. According to Easterling, no one would suspect that the heavy box contained anything. It appeared empty.

Easterling and Rivera returned to the Habana Bar. Again, Manuel drove while Hardhat, blindfolded, sat in the back with the Cuban. At one point, the Cuban became agitated, pulled out a pistol, and pressed it against Easterling's head. He accused him of being an FBI agent. Easterling denied it, and Manuel ordered the man to put away the pistol, explaining that Hardhat was part of the team.

Once back at the Habana Bar, huddled together so others would not overhear them, Manuel explained the details of the assassination plan to Easterling. It called for the rifle and box to be in place at an assassination site and for the rifle to be concealed in the box following the shooting. There would be someone with a different rifle, a bolt-action Mannlicher-Carcano, who would unwittingly be on hand to take the blame. The real assassin's rifle would be so well concealed that it could be smuggled out much later.

Shells fired from the Mannlicher-Carcano would be placed at the scene. A bullet fired from the Mannlicher-Carcano would be planted in an area where it would be discovered and become prime evidence to seal the case against the Mannlicher-Carcano—and its owner. The bullets for the 7-mm Czech-made automatic were designed to practically disintegrate into untraceable fragments upon impact; the bullets Easterling saw had slits cut in the sides.

After relating all this, Manuel Rivera told Easterling that he was going to need his continuing help. He gave him $750.

Easterling's next assignment from Manuel Rivera was in May. The Cuban came to Easterling's trailer around eight one morning and said that he needed to borrow his car to transport the box and rifle to Texas. The plan was to hook a U-Haul trailer to the car to carry the large box. Easterling gave Rivera the keys to his car, and Manuel departed, saying he would return the car in a few days.

Easterling claims nothing further to do with the transport of the box. (Mrs. Easterling recalls her surprise over her husband's lending his new car to the Cubans, although she was told only that they used it to make a trip "up north.") His next contact was a few days later when Manuel returned the car. Along with the car keys, Rivera gave Easterling a *Time* magazine that had $850 tucked in the pages.[35]

Enter Lee Harvey Oswald

It was deep into a muggy New Orleans night in 1963 when the odd pair entered the Habana Bar. One of the men was a stockily built fellow of Latin appearance, possibly a Cuban, about twenty-eight, with a receding hairline. He ordered a tequila. The Latin's companion was an American who seemed to be drunk. It was this young man who made the postmidnight visit memorable. He ordered lemonade, the first time that drink was ever ordered in the Habana Bar. The bartender did not know how to fix it. Orest Pena, the owner of the bar, was asked to give directions on how to make the lemonade.[36]

Once the drink was served, the American's companion made a caustic remark about the price of twenty-five cents set by Pena. He considered this exorbitant and muttered something about Cuban capitalists. Then the American vomited all over the table at which he and his Latin friend were seated. It was only then that they left.[37]

Months later, following the assassination of President John F. Kennedy, this incident was vividly recalled with unanimity by those who witnessed it. The identity of the Cuban in the bar that night remains a mystery—although the description of him in Warren Commission records is virtually identical to Easterling's description of Manuel Rivera.[38]

But there is little question about the identity of the American: he was Lee Harvey Oswald.

Robert Easterling was not among the witnesses in the Habana Bar that night. Easterling claims he first encountered Oswald during the spring or summer of 1963. While he is not sure of the date, Easterling insists that he witnessed an incident involving Oswald and the Habana Bar that is unrecorded in standard accounts of Oswald's New Orleans activities. Easterling claims he came upon a sidewalk fracas on Decatur Street near the doorway to the Habana Bar. Several Cubans were kicking and stomping a young man Easterling came to know as Oswald. As Easterling stood watching, Rivera rushed out of the bar with a broken beer bottle and forced the men to stop beating Oswald. Police officers arrived about the time the scuffle ended. Easterling claims that Oswald got up and, without any comment, walked away. Easterling did not learn what the altercation was about.*

Easterling also saw Oswald on several other occasions that spring. When Rivera and Oswald were together, according to Easterling, they spoke to each other in Russian. Manuel told Easterling that he first met Oswald in Czechoslovakia when the automatic rifle was built. He said that Oswald fired the rifle and was a terrible marksman.†

At some point after Hardhat met Oswald, Rivera confided that Oswald was going to take the rap for the assassination of President Kennedy. Easterling instantly realized this was the man the conspirators had chosen as their dupe and who would have a Mannlicher-Carcano rifle. Manuel explained that it would be nec-

---

*Another well-known street brawl involving Oswald and several Cuban exiles occurred August 9. That fight erupted after Oswald pretended to want to help an exile group in its efforts to overthrow Castro, only to be discovered blatantly handing out pro-Castro leaflets on busy Canal Street. The leaflets were for the Fair Play for Cuba Committee.[39]
†The account ascribed to Rivera concerning Oswald's presence in Czechoslovakia coincides with that period during Oswald's Soviet defection when his whereabouts and activities remain a virtual mystery.[40]

essary to kill Oswald after the assassination. While this did little to clarify in Easterling's mind just what was going on, one chilling fact came into focus: if Oswald was so expendable, then there was little reason to believe the conspirators would want Easterling around after it was all over.

At first, Easterling believed that the ballistics evidence generated during the practice firing at the Windmill Trailer Court would be used to cinch the case against Oswald. However, it is a matter of record that Oswald did not order his Mannlicher-Carcano until March, while he was still in Dallas. So, if Easterling's account is true, the rifle-firing at the trailer park in February was simply a dry run for later doing the same thing with Oswald's rifle.[41]

By April, Oswald was in New Orleans and apparently had his rifle with him. The setup of the trailer court was such that it would be quite simple for Manuel and his colleagues to return there and conduct additional firings. While Easterling never witnessed such activity—he had moved out of the trailer court by the end of June—other witnesses have told the author that it was not uncommon to find people target shooting in that particular field.[42]

For many years Easterling had been casually acquainted with a wealthy businessman, who has acknowledged to the author his association with Easterling, whom he calls Hardhat. Easterling's acquaintance had built an extensive business that valued among its customers some of the most powerful oil companies in America. The businessman owned various Louisiana companies, operating under different names.[43]

The businessman's association with Easterling was never a close one. Nevertheless, Easterling says, during June 1963 the businessman summoned Easterling to his office, across the Mississippi River from New Orleans. He gave him fifty dollars and told him to go out and buy a large suitcase. Back in New Orleans on Canal Street, Easterling found a green Samsonite two-suiter that had been damaged in a fire. He paid $22.50 for it and pocketed the change. He returned to the businessman's office and gave him the suitcase.

On the following morning, a Sunday, according to Easterling, he parked in the lot beside the office building of the businessman. Inside the building, Easterling saw that the businessman had packed

$100,000 into the suitcase. He explained to Easterling that he was expecting some men who were coming to pick up the cash.

According to what Easterling says the businessman told him— and what Easterling learned from company employees—the $100,000 in clean, untraceable cash had been raised for a wealthy Dallas oil man with whom the company did business. The funds were presumably transferred by checks through normal billing procedures; they represented overcharges and overpayments, supposedly spaced over enough time for illicit billings to escape routine audits. The actual cash came from a supermarket whose manager was cooperative about furnishing soiled currency.

About ten o'clock that Sunday morning, two men arrived at the businessman's office. One was the person Easterling believed to be Clay Shaw, who in reality might have been Guy Banister. The second was a man from Dallas named Jack Ruby.

The men checked the cash in the suitcase. Ruby then went to the telephone and placed a call to a man in Dallas. After some perfunctory conversation, Ruby handed the telephone to his companion, who spoke for several minutes. He then hung up.

At one point, the businessman asked Ruby if he was going to be able to take care of so much cash. According to Easterling, Ruby pulled back his suit jacket, pointed to a pistol, and said, "Yeah. I got my little heater."

As Ruby and his companion left, Easterling looked out at their car and saw two men sitting inside. He believes they were Manuel Rivera and the Cuban known to Easterling as Joe.

It was after the men drove away that the businessman told Easterling that although he was not certain, he suspected that this was all part of a plot to kill President Kennedy. He pulled from his desk a small tape recorder that was attached to his telephone line. He indicated that he had taped the telephone call Jack Ruby had made to Dallas. Now, he played the tape so that he and Easterling could hear the entire conversation. What stuck most vividly in Easterling's mind was one comment made by the Dallas oil man: "Don't pay the bastards too much, because it will run up the price on Bobby and the rest of them."

"Hardhat," the businessman said with finality, "they're going to kill the Kennedys." He then burned the tape in an ashtray.

As far as Easterling could determine, the businessman's only connection with the plot was in laundering the cash, as a personal favor for his business associate in Dallas. Easterling did not reveal to the businessman that he had any independent knowledge of an assassination conspiracy. The New Orleans businessman told Easterling that the Dallas oil man had paid him $10,000 to launder the $100,000 in cash. He gave Easterling $500 and told him never to repeat what he had seen or heard. With this, Easterling realized that he had become involved with more than one faction that appeared seriously committed to murdering the President. While it was not clear that the plans of each group were coordinated, there was one central figure whose presence seemed to span more than one camp: Manuel Rivera.

"I was getting scared," Easterling concedes. And the more he thought about it, the more frightened he became. In addition, the IRS was threatening him for his failure to pay income taxes, and he believed his employer had caught him stealing parts and reselling them.

A few days after the meeting at the businessman's office to transfer the cash, Easterling quit his job. According to his wife of that period, he urged her to move into an apartment and to sell the trailer, since the Cubans knew where it was. Hardhat abruptly left Louisiana and did not stop until he reached Ohio, where he got a job with a construction company.

Fearful or not, Easterling knew it would be a mistake to completely sever his relationship with Manuel Rivera. Not long after he reached Ohio, he telephoned Manuel to let him know where he was in case Manuel had additional work. Easterling was greatly attracted to the easy money he had been paid. He called Manuel several more times over the summer to say that he was available.

Toward the end of September Easterling got a message to telephone Manuel, who told him, "It's time to get Oswald out of town." Manuel told him to return to New Orleans and to meet him at the Habana Bar. He instructed him to have his fast XL Ford gassed up and ready to travel.

During the third week of September, early in the morning, Easterling arrived at the Habana Bar. Manuel Rivera was there, along with the Cuban called Joe. The first thing Easterling did was to begin drinking. The fear that had propelled him from New Orleans to Ohio had not moderated upon his return to Decatur Street.

Easterling noticed that Manuel had with him the green suitcase with the burn mark. It was the one Hardhat had bought to pack the $100,000 in cash for Jack Ruby and the man who may have been Clay Shaw. Easterling observed to Manuel that he recognized the suitcase and assumed that it meant that Manuel had gotten the money. Manuel nodded and smiled. "I like to be paid both ways," he said. To Easterling, these words confirmed that Manuel's activities were serving the interests of both Cuban and domestic conspirators.

It was then that Manuel Rivera picked up the telephone, dialed a number and said, "Hardhat is here, and we are ready. Start the fire."

Manuel told Easterling they would wait about fifteen minutes and then pick up Lee Oswald and drive him to Houston. Easterling gulped down several more drinks, and Manuel ordered a full bottle of whiskey for them to drink during their long drive.

Rivera and Easterling bade farewell to Joe and walked out of the Habana Bar onto Decatur Street. They removed the license plate from Easterling's car, got in, and headed across Canal Street, where Decatur becomes Magazine Street. Manuel gave Easterling precise directions about each turn to make, and today Easterling admits his disorientation concerning how they reached the scene of a fire large enough to require several fire trucks and hoses pulled across the street.

On the way to the fire, Manuel told Easterling that he knew that Oswald had been under surveillance recently because of his pro-Castro activities with the Fair Play for Cuba Committee.[44] Manuel said that it was necessary to set the fire as a diversionary tactic in order to pick up Oswald surreptitiously, in the confusion, to get him out of town and on his way to Mexico.*

Manuel said that he had wanted Easterling to drive Oswald all the way to Mexico, but Oswald insisted on taking the bus. However, when Oswald realized how tight the surveillance on him was, according to Manuel, he agreed to be spirited out of New Orleans so he could catch the bus in Houston.

Less than sober by the time they reached the fire, Easterling

*Confirmation of such surveillance came years later from an odd source—a CIA report that had been withheld for reasons of national security. That report states: "As a redefector from the USSR [Oswald] would immediately be suspect and thus under surveillance by the FBI."[45]

remembers the fire engines and sirens and, most vividly, the fact that several times he had to run his car over the fire hoses when after passing the fire on the right, Manuel ordered him to double back and cross the hoses again. His fuzzy recollection is that the fire was at a church in a black neighborhood.

Easterling finally stopped across from the fire and waited while Manuel ran into a building that had some small steps in front. Easterling noticed, as he looked across the street, that the smoke was coming from the rear of a wooden building. Manuel promptly returned with Oswald in tow. With his head ducked down as he darted from the building, Oswald got into the back seat of the car and stretched out with a blanket over him. Easterling gunned the engine of his powerful car, and they sped away.

According to Easterling, men in an unmarked car who could have been FBI agents gave chase. There was a wild ride along the broad New Orleans streets as Easterling, at speeds up to 100 miles an hour, headed out of the city. At one point, on the outskirts of the city, Manuel directed him into a residential section where they pulled into someone's carport and parked, hoping to evade their pursuers. They remained there until the owner of the carport returned home and noticed them. They put the license plate back on and departed. By then they had eluded their pursuers.

On the trip to Houston, Oswald said virtually nothing. Most of the way he was lying down in the back seat, and during other times he quietly looked out the window. They made one stop during the 360-mile drive, and Oswald got out to use the rest room and to buy some food and drink. Easterling reports no substantive conversation between Oswald and Manuel Rivera.

In Houston the trio went to the bus station. Easterling and Rivera waited in the car while Oswald went in alone. In a few minutes Oswald returned with a young man who looked strikingly like himself. Manuel introduced the young man as Carlo. Easterling's impression was that Carlo was able to speak very little English. In fact, the only words of English Easterling heard him utter were, in stilted fashion, "Good luck to you."

Easterling claims that Carlo, Manuel, and Oswald all spoke in Russian. Then, a few minutes after their arrival, Manuel asked Easterling to take a photograph of the three of them standing together. Carlo stood on Manuel's left and Oswald stood on the right. Easterling took the picture with Manuel's camera. Easterling recalls that Carlo was no more than an inch taller than Oswald and a little heavier.

Soon after taking the picture, Easterling said farewell to the three men and drove away. Manuel had paid him $1,500 and given him his next assignment: to drive to Monterrey, Mexico. He was to wait at a motel there for Oswald to arrive a few days later. Easterling was then to drive Oswald to Fort Worth.

An Interim Assessment

There is much more to the story of Robert Easterling, but at this point it is useful to consider the credibility of the foregoing. In general terms, nothing Easterling relates here is rendered in error by any known facts. Oswald was in New Orleans at the right times. Easterling's employment as he described it is verified. His ex-wife is able to corroborate much of his account of the shooting at Windmill Trailer Court. Even a neighbor, twenty years later, recalled the incident of the Cubans' threatening to burn the trailer. Easterling has returned to the trailer park with the author, and the conditions are just as he described them. [46]

On the other hand, Orest Pena, owner of the Habana Bar, has told the author that he does not remember a man called Hardhat. Nor does Pena recall a man called Joe who had a deformed hand and hung around his establishment, often tending bar. Pena certainly does not recall an assassination plot against President Kennedy being hatched there, although he concedes he heard people in his bar talking about killing the President. Pena confirms that David Ferrie and Clay Shaw were patrons of the bar. [47]

Could Pena recall a Manuel Rivera? He looked at the author and said, "So many people ask me about Manuel Rivera." He would not explain what this meant. [48]

While only Easterling places David Ferrie with Manuel Rivera and the Czech rifle in the Habana Bar, there is other evidence that Ferrie did frequent the establishment. Moreover, Ferrie can be officially linked with Oswald on two occasions. [49] (There is a full examination of these matters in Chapter 10.)

For various reasons unrelated to his now *known* Oswald connections, David Ferrie was an immediate suspect when President Kennedy was killed. Ferrie's ironclad alibi illustrated not only the remarkable diversity of his associations but his connections with another of the prime elements interested in eliminating Kennedy: organized crime. As we have seen, at the hour of the assassination, Ferrie was in a federal courtroom in New Orleans with organized crime boss Carlos Marcello, whose lawyer employed Ferrie as an investigator. Federal investigators have found that Marcello himself, a number-one target of Robert Kennedy's Justice Department, had made at least one threat against President Kennedy.[50]

As for the June meeting with Jack Ruby, the New Orleans businessman, and possibly Shaw or Banister, there are some significant points of confirmation. According to official records, Ruby did visit New Orleans in June 1963. Moreover, it is known that while there Ruby spent most of his time in association with club operators whose ties, even if informal and associative, ran to the organized-crime family of Carlos Marcello. One of the club operators, Harold Tannenbaum, was listed by the Select Committee as deceased. Quite alive, Tannenbaum has confirmed to the author his own contact with Ruby in New Orleans at this time—though he denies the mob links attributed to him by the HSCA.[51]

As for Easterling's claim that he encountered Oswald in a street scuffle unreported in the official record, there is tempting confirmation from an extremely obscure aspect of Oswald's murky biography. On August 1, 1963, Oswald wrote a letter to the head of the Fair Play for Cuba Committee in New York and reported that during his efforts to distribute FPCC handbills, he had been "attacked" by some Cuban exiles and that the incident "robbed me of what support I had, leaving me alone." Oswald also wrote that he was "officialy [sic] cautioned by police."[52]

The trouble with this account has always been that it was written more than a week *prior* to the date Oswald was arrested in the street scuffle. This anachronism has been cited by researchers as evidence that Oswald already was planning to stage an event that would lead to his arrest when he wrote to FPCC on August 1. It is just as possible that the incident is the very one reported by Easterling, who also noted that the police showed up briefly.

Another confirming detail is Easterling's acquaintance and association with the wealthy businessman whom he claims he met with that Sunday morning to transfer the cash. That man, while denouncing Easterling as a drunken liar and "the scum of the earth," concedes that he knew Hardhat over a number of years. He insists that he never engaged in any discussion of politics with him. He claims he has no particular political interests beyond casting his ballot.[53]

The businessman strenuously denies ever having a meeting such as the one described by Easterling. However, he concedes his business connection to the Dallas oil man in question but insists he never met him or talked to him, even on the telephone. In a telephone call from Easterling to the New Orleans businessman in May 1983, the businessman told Hardhat, "If a word of this is printed, I guarantee you one thing, you will regret it the last day you live!"[54]

There is a fascinating array of purely circumstantial evidence indicating the businessman's preoccupation with the JFK assassination—details completely unknown to Easterling. However, inasmuch as it is entirely possible that the businessman is telling the truth in his denials, the author has not identified him.*

Perhaps the most significant point of confirmation for Easterling's story has to do with his claim to have driven Oswald from New Orleans to Houston. There has never been any official explanation as to how Oswald got from New Orleans to Houston toward the end of September, despite a strenuous investigation aimed at discovering how Oswald made the trip. It seems nearly certain that he did not use any public transportation for the trip. But there has never, until now, been any rational conjecture about the details of the private transportation.[55]

In addition to this mystery is the question of the precise date of Oswald's departure from New Orleans. It has been established that Oswald's wife, Marina, packed a friend's station wagon and left New Orleans with the baby and a friend on September 23 to return to Dallas. The last certain sighting of Oswald in New Orleans also occurred on that date.[56]

*Not far from the location of the businessman's office is a large military compound officially called the Naval Support Activity. During the years of U.S. efforts to topple Castro, this facility served as a base for military and intelligence activities. In yet another confounding irony, the businessman's *exact name*, plus the rank of captain, appears in the 1963 telephone directory with an address located at the naval facility. The name is not a particularly common one, and there were no others by that name listed in the New Orleans area that year. Most astonishing of all is that the telephone number listed for the Navy man is one digit different from that of the businessman. When asked about this, the businessman claimed complete ignorance and volunteered that the only time he ever went to the naval facility was to watch a performance of the Blue Angels.[57]

As to events following that sighting—Oswald's boarding a bus near his apartment on the evening of September 23—a highly ambiguous paper trail suggests that Oswald remained in New Orleans as late as September 25. Among the bits of evidence are the cashing of a check and the completion of a change-of-address card. However, if one is going to posit a conspiracy, as did the HSCA, these transactions were conceivably carried out by someone other than Oswald.[58]

In any event, not a single witness in the official records could recall seeing Oswald in New Orleans after September 23.*

In Robert Easterling's account of driving Oswald to Houston, he never claimed to know the specific date that Manuel ordered the diversionary fire set so that they could pick up Oswald. Given Easterling's drunkenness that morning, it is not surprising that he has been confused and mistaken about precisely where they picked up Oswald. What Easterling has been absolutely adamant about—in the face of denunciations by the author that he was lying—is that there *was* a fire, that he *did* run over hoses, that there *was* a church nearby, that it *did* happen in the area bordered by Canal and Magazine streets, south of Claiborne Avenue.

Initially, the investigation into this appeared hopeless. The New Orleans Fire Department claimed that the central fire records for those years could not be found. Newspapers reported no fires that could conceivably be the one described by Easterling. Arson records showed no cases pursued on fires that occurred around that time.

---

*It is widely assumed in the literature on Oswald that he was last seen in New Orleans leaving his apartment building on the evening of September 24, the day *after* his wife Marina departed for Dallas. However, careful scrutiny of the pertinent testimony from the Warren Commission records shows that actually Oswald was last seen on the evening of September 23, the *same* day that his wife departed. The source of confusion on this point is the hopelessly ambiguous testimony of one Eric Rogers, an Oswald neighbor who used words in a fashion that seems to have confused his Warren Commission interrogator.

For example:

INTERROGATOR: Now, did Oswald leave . . . on the same day that the station wagon [bearing Marina] left, or on the next day?

ERIC ROGERS: . . . yes; they left on the same day, the following evening.

The confusion seems to have stemmed from Eric Rogers's use of the word "following." In the context of his complete testimony, his use of the word in several instances suggests that he was referring to the very evening following the day in question. Whatever, in three specific instances Rogers states that he saw Oswald depart for the last time on the same day as Marina's departure—September 23. Moreover, two other Warren Commission witnesses who were neighbors of the Oswalds provided testimony suggesting Oswald was not seen after Marina's departure.[59]

Despite the author's strenuous assertions that he was lying, Easterling could not be shaken from his claim about the fire.[60]

It was then that Tom Noonan, a private researcher working with the author, made a startling discovery in the basement of the New Orleans Public Library: many of the original fire-report ledgers that had been kept at each firehouse in the city. They existed, even though the central records, which were based on these originals, could not be found.

There, on a long ledger sheet and in the clear handwriting of a New Orleans fireman, was an entry for September 24, 1963—the morning *after* the last known sighting of Oswald. The report of a fire was received at 9:22 A.M. The structure involved was an old, two-story wooden apartment building, located in a black section of town, diagonally across from a church. The address, 2011 Melpomene, was no more than a couple of minutes' drive from where Easterling originally believed that he and Manuel picked up Oswald. It was about two miles from where Oswald had been last spotted the previous evening.[61]

Perhaps most significant of all was that the cause of the fire apparently was suspicious, for the fireman noted that it was "under investigation."[62]

The fire report itself was unusual. For all of September 1963, in the Second Fire District, there were 119 reports of fires listed in the ledgers. Of those, only 3 were reported to be under investigation.[63]

A key question was whether hoses might have been pulled across the street to reach the blaze at 2011 Melpomene. Inspection of that scene shows that the closest fire hydrant to the address was diagonally across the street and in front of the Israelite Baptist Church. It would have been necessary to pull the hoses across the street if the pumper on the scene did not have sufficient water—a point of fact now uncheckable.*[64]

At the time of the 1963 fire, the address in question was in the heart of a run-down neighborhood primarily consisting of black families. (In 1978 part of the street was renamed Martin Luther King Boulevard.) Across from 2011 Melpomene were small apartment

---

*New Orleans, like most cities, has a law that prohibits driving across fire hoses. However, conversations with veteran New Orleans firemen indicate that it was a law rarely enforced twenty-two years ago.

buildings and two-family houses of similar construction, as well as a larger building that housed the Tennessee Furniture Company. That building, it would appear, is the most likely one for Oswald to have emerged from. Residents of the street recall that it had a few steps leading up to a narrow stoop in the front. Other steps were on the side that led to small apartments.[65]

Today, the entire block across from 2011 Melpomene has been torn down. In place of the old buildings stands a modern fire station.

An effort was made to trace the people who either worked at the Tennessee Furniture Company or lived in nearby apartments. The several people located had no conceivable connection to the events at hand and could recall nothing of relevance. The building owners, a family that owned many buildings in the area, could scarcely remember the fire.*[66]

An exhaustive effort was made to locate the woman who was listed in the fire report as the occupant of the apartment. The city directory indicated that she lived there with a man listed as a laborer in the New Orleans shipyards. As it turned out, the woman is reportedly dead, but the dockworker was located in Mississippi.[67]

With the help of his wife of thirty-four years, he explained to the author that he had never been married to the woman who claimed his last name. In fact, he added, her last name had never been the same as his, even though she assumed it. He told the author that the chief reason he moved out of the Melpomene apartment—and he said he did so before the fire—was that his companion was in the habit of letting a great number of casual acquaintances hang around the apartment.[68]

While proving nothing, such a situation allows for the possibility of an atmosphere that would permit the sort of staged fire described in the Easterling account.

One of the most intriguing aspects of Easterling's report is how it might relate to a strange but credible story of a young and well-educated Cuban woman named Silvia Odio. From a prominent Cuban family, Mrs. Odio was living in Dallas in 1963. Her father and mother remained in Castro's jails in Cuba. On either September 26 or 27, Mrs. Odio had a visit from three men that has never been explained satisfactorily.[69]

*Interested researchers can find all the names of neighbors in the New Orleans City Directory.

The three men arrived unannounced around nine o'clock in the evening to ask Mrs. Odio's help in preparing a fund-raising letter for a Cuban exile group in which her family had been active. Two of the men appeared to be Cubans and the third an American. He was introduced as Leon Oswald. One of the Cubans explained that they had just arrived from New Orleans and wanted to discuss with Mrs. Odio certain activities for the exile group. During the conversation, they mentioned several times that they were about to leave on a trip. Mrs. Odio spoke to them only from her doorway. After about twenty minutes, the men left.[70]

The following day, Mrs. Odio received a telephone call from one of the Cubans. She judged from his initial comments that he was simply being "fresh." Then the Cuban volunteered that the American she had met, "Leon," was "kind of nuts," that he had been in the Marine Corps and was an expert rifle shot. The Cuban strongly insinuated that "Leon" was prepared to kill President Kennedy over his perceived betrayal of the exile cause at the Bay of Pigs. Mrs. Odio hung up the telephone.[71]

The phone call was quite upsetting to Mrs. Odio, and she subsequently told others about the whole incident, including her doctor. However, she did not report it to authorities. Less than two months later, when President Kennedy was assassinated, Mrs. Odio instantly recognized the man who was taken into custody. She was sure he was the "Leon Oswald" who had come with the Cubans to her house. She was too terrified to go to the authorities.[72]

Later, however, a friend who had heard the story reported it to the FBI, which went through the motions of an investigation. The Warren Commission published its report before the FBI investigation was complete. Nonetheless, it concluded with certainty that Oswald did not visit Mrs. Odio's home. Years later, the House Select Committee reviewed the entire matter and, in sharp contrast to the Warren Report, concluded that it was "inclined to believe Silvia Odio."[73]

It is practically impossible to reach substantive conclusions by comparing visual descriptions of people observed under casual conditions. Still, it is interesting to consider the Odio account in view of Easterling's claim that he left Manuel Rivera, Lee Oswald, and an Oswald look-alike called Carlo at a bus station in Houston on September 24, two days or so before the Odio incident.

In this consideration, it is a given that no determination can be made about whether Mrs. Odio saw the real Oswald or an impersonator.

Questions also remain about the dominant figure in the trio that visited Mrs. Odio. He was a Cuban who called himself Leopoldo. Described as tall, slim, and wearing glasses, his appearance is starkly different from Easterling's description of Manuel Rivera.[74]

However, the third man, who was called something like Angelo, was described by Mrs. Odio in terms that are strikingly similar to Easterling's description of Manuel. She recalled him as a man of medium height, stocky build, and with heavy body hair. She recalled dark markings on his skin, which could possibly be related to the birthmark Easterling claims was visible on Manuel's neck. Mrs. Odio also recalled that one of the Cubans—she was uncertain which—had sort of a bald spot in the front, which coincides with Easterling's claim that Manuel had a receding hairline.[75]

In addition, Mrs. Odio's description of Angelo also parallels that of the man who appeared with Oswald in the Habana Bar—a man who might have been Manuel Rivera.[76]

While no sure conclusions can be drawn from the parallels between the Easterling and Odio descriptions, one thing is inescapable: if there is truth to the Easterling story, the man he knew as Manuel Rivera probably was not the dominant figure in the conspiracy. That figure would not be shooting into water barrels and dealing with the likes of Robert Easterling. That figure would, logically, be Manuel's superior.

In this context, it is not unreasonable to speculate that there was a third man in Houston, one who joined Manuel and Carlo after Easterling left for Mexico. Perhaps that man—Manuel's boss—was the "Leopoldo" who appeared at the Odio home to create one of the numerous memorable events that, later, would spring up to seal the guilt of Lee Harvey Oswald.

Countdown to Dallas

For ten days, Robert Easterling waited at the motel in Monterrey for Lee Harvey Oswald. When he realized Oswald was not going to show up, he left and drove to several spots in Mexico. Then he drove back to Baton Rouge and went to work operating a bulldozer on a construction project in St. Francisville, Louisiana. It was mid-October.

Easterling's days alone in Mexico had given him time to realize that, as he puts it, "My life wasn't worth a plug nickel." Never a stupid man, Easterling understood that he—and perhaps others— were every bit as expendable as Lee Harvey Oswald. He was glad that Oswald had stood him up in Mexico and half hoped that he was finished with carrying out assignments for Rivera.

Then, one rainy day in early November when he could not work, Easterling began drinking. He telephoned Manuel Rivera at his number in New Orleans. In the course of the conversation he mentioned the name of the motel where he was staying at Baton Rouge. Manuel said that he was going to have a new assignment for him soon. Easterling accepted this with mixed feelings.

A few days after that, several Cubans arrived at the motel and told Easterling that Manuel had sent them to make certain Easterling had not wavered in his readiness to follow Manuel's orders. Easterling assured them of his steady loyalty to the cause. The Cubans told him when to telephone Manuel for his next assignment. They threatened to return if he failed to call.

On Tuesday, November 19, Easterling telephoned the number in New Orleans where he always reached Manuel. This time, instead, David Ferrie answered the phone. Manuel had gone to Dallas. Easterling's assignment, Ferrie said, was to be at a bus station in Dallas around 10:30 the coming Friday morning. Ferrie said that he would find Oswald waiting for him there. Easterling was to drive Oswald to Mexico City, where Manuel would meet them.

Easterling promised Ferrie he would be in Dallas on November 22 to pick up Lee Harvey Oswald.

The next two days, Easterling says, were among the most terrible in his life. If he went through with his assignment—picking up Oswald in Dallas—he was sure he would be killed along with Lee once they reached Mexico. On the other hand, Manuel's henchmen had repeatedly threatened Easterling, and at any moment they could appear as they had in the past. If he actually skipped out on an assignment, he knew they would not hesitate to kill him.

Robert Easterling is hard put to salvage much honor from his role in these matters, but he is without shame when it comes to making the attempt. He asserts that through this entire time, he was working as an informant for the FBI, at the behest of the CIA, though he admits he never tried to report the developing conspiracy. But on Thursday, November 21, he claims with frantic sincerity, the pressures of fear, confusion, and drunkenness conspired to drive him to drastic measures.

That evening, about 9:30, he went to a public telephone booth at a service station just outside Baton Rouge. He dialed the operator and asked to be put through to J. Edgar Hoover, the director of the FBI. "They're going to kill the President!" he shouted to the operator.*

Soon enough, Easterling says, he was speaking to someone at FBI headquarters in Washington. The man asked if Easterling owned a yellow and black Ford XL. Easterling assured him that he did. "You're in too deep," Easterling says the FBI man told him. "You're going to get killed. We have lines open to Dallas now."

"But they're going to kill the President!" Easterling shouted. "They have an automatic rifle with a catch box on the side."

"We know all about it," said the FBI man, according to Easterling. "We're going to catch them red-handed. You're in too deep. Whatever you do, don't go to Dallas."

Easterling hung up.

The FBI denies that it ever had any sort of informant relationship with Easterling, and according to an official bureau statement, there is "nothing in FBI files to substantiate Mr. Easterling's claim that he called the FBI on the night of November 21, 1963." Indeed, it is preposterous to think that anyone at the bureau would have made the statements Easterling claims were made to him that night.[77]

However, much of what Easterling claims happened in the next few hours has been confirmed. Before long, it was past midnight. The calendar had slipped to November 22, 1963. There was but one rational course of action for Easterling. He would commit a burglary that, if ever needed, could provide a solid alibi if anyone tried to link him to the assassination. And at any time he felt in danger from his co-conspirators, he could find safety by confessing to the break-in and being jailed.

---

*Despite a thorough investigation, including interviews with operators working in Baton Rouge in 1963, no operator was located who ever heard of such a message. Considering the prophetic nature of the statement, it is hard to believe that someone could hear such a message and never tell anyone else about it.[78]

On Airline Highway outside Baton Rouge, there was a Gibson's Discount Center, a place Easterling had cased many times as he cashed his paychecks there. About 1:30 A.M. he parked his car a block from the store and walked to it with a sledgehammer. He hammered his way through concrete blocks and entered the building.[79]

Once inside, he immediately encountered a night watchman. Easterling fled to his car and took off at a high speed. Almost at once—perhaps even before the break-in was reported—a police car gave hot pursuit. After a high-speed chase, Easterling crashed his car into a ditch. He jumped out and ran. For the rest of the night he walked and hid as he made his way toward the construction job where, soon after daybreak that Friday morning, he could collect a paycheck.

After cashing his check, Easterling caught a ride to a town where he could get a bus to Jackson, Mississippi. As he got off the bus in Jackson, he heard the first radio reports of the shooting of the President. He checked into the Heidelberg Hotel, Jackson's finest, and ordered up a supply of whiskey. He spent the next three days watching the events of Dallas unfold on television. Those events sealed forever any doubt in Easterling's mind about his fate if he had gone to Dallas.

By Monday, Oswald had been murdered and Ruby was being held as his killer. Now using an assumed name, Easterling left the hotel and traveled to his mother's home near Hattiesburg to tell her he would have to go away—perhaps for a long time. The next day he caught a bus out of Mississippi. He cracked a safe in a small supermarket in Hagerstown, Maryland, and stole about $3,000, which enabled him to continue his travels.

As those funds ran low, Easterling headed south and stopped in Durham, North Carolina, where he broke into a Chevrolet dealership. He cracked a safe and stole several thousand dollars and made a clean getaway. (Twenty years later, Durham police confirmed such a break-in at Carpenter's Chevrolet on December 17, 1963. The police also confirmed Easterling's claim that the safe was on the second floor. The Durham authorities said the crime has never been solved.)[80]

By early 1964 Easterling was back in Hattiesburg and hiding out with relatives. On February 22, the FBI picked him up on a fugitive warrant and returned him to Baton Rouge to face charges for the break-in there on November 22, 1963. When the time came in his trial to offer a defense for his activities, Easterling pleaded guilty without comment. His lawyer, today a judge in Louisiana, remembers that Easterling seemed resigned to plead guilty and be sentenced with as little protest as possible. Court records show that for the November 22 break-in, Easterling was sentenced to five years in the Louisiana State Penitentiary at Angola.[81]

In the FBI's official comment concerning Easterling's confession, a statement was offered that lent curious support to one of Easterling's claims—that the FBI has never listened seriously to him. In a letter to the author, the FBI stated:

> The following information, which appears in our files, tends to indicate that Mr. Easterling's allegations regarding the assassination of President Kennedy are unsupported by facts: Mr. Easterling was not in Dallas, Texas, on November 22, 1963, with Lee Harvey Oswald's clone as Mr. Easterling claims. He was fleeing the local authorities in East Baton Rouge, Louisiana, who had interrupted his burglary of Gibson's Discount Center on November 22, 1963. Mr. Easterling outdistanced his pursuers.[82]

In its haste to discredit Easterling's allegations, the bureau demonstrates that despite its claim to the contrary, it never took Easterling's confession seriously enough to realize that he does not claim to have been "in Dallas with Lee Harvey Oswald's clone." If the FBI *is* in possession of a prior statement from Easterling to this effect, it has never disclosed it, despite repeated efforts by the author to secure all of its information about Easterling.

Easterling claims to have been doing precisely what the FBI investigation finds that he was doing during the early hours of November 22. If nothing else, this demonstrates that as late as September 1983, the FBI continued to pay no serious attention to Easterling's claims—the familiar indifference that Easterling asserts met all of his earlier efforts to inform the authorities.

It is a crowning irony that Easterling's position should receive convincing FBI corroboration on the critical point of whether the bureau has *ever* paid serious attention to Easterling's account. Clearly, the FBI in reality has given only perfunctory attention to these allegations—allegations with potentially awesome significance.

The Years After Dallas

For nearly three years Easterling quietly did his time.[83] If he talked during those years, when the topic was fresh, about his role in the assassination, there is no available evidence that he ever mentioned it to officials. He says that he did not. Easterling's claim is persuasive that during this period he was terrified for his life.

When he got out of prison in February 1967, Hardhat found the Garrison investigation in full swing. He stayed away from New Orleans and his old haunts. His fear over being dragged into any investigation propelled him toward one of the most stable periods of his life—three good years of steady employment at a skilled job in Baton Rouge.[84]

By then he was divorced, and in 1969 he married a young Mexican woman. By 1970 that union was on the skids, and his wife returned to Mexico City. Easterling had lost his job because of an injury, and he worked at odd jobs for cash to avoid risking a cutoff of his disability income.[85]

In 1972 Hardhat went to Mexico City to see his estranged wife and the child she had borne by another man. While there, Easterling claims that he barely escaped a trap by several Cubans he believes were sent to kill him. They appeared at his hotel and tried to trick him into going for a drive, but he says he outwitted them. He returned to Louisiana thankful to be alive. Despite this incident, Easterling found that by 1972 the fear was wearing off, that he was becoming more open in his activities around New Orleans.

In December 1973 two New Orleans businessmen familiar with Easterling's skills as a diesel mechanic hired him to travel to Belize (formerly British Honduras), on his own, to try to repair the engines on an old boat they had bought and hoped to refurbish for profit. The entrepreneurs wanted Easterling to put the engines into shape so that the boat could make it to the States under its own steam, to save the expense of towing. They gave Easterling a couple of thousand dollars and told him to handle the matter. Not since the days of Manuel Rivera had Hardhat been given such a choice assignment.[86]

Eight years after the incident, the businessmen offered the author vivid confirmation of the manner in which Easterling disappeared with the money. Easterling's passport supports the fact that he traveled to Honduras on the dates in question. However, Easterling—perhaps in a rationalization that is instructive on other points—tells the story in a manner that makes him appear somewhat justified in skipping town with the money. He claims that he went to Belize, where he inspected the boat. It was in such terrible condition that its engines were beyond repair. He says he informed the owners of his recommendation that the vessel be towed to Miami.[87]

Considering his affairs with the New Orleans businessmen settled, Easterling, wearing his white hard hat, set off for Honduras to do some sightseeing. His first stop was at Tegucigalpa, and after that he traveled on to San Pedro Sula. There, still sporting the hard hat he had worn for years, he settled in for some serious drinking at the bar of the Gran Sula Hotel. It was January 1974. A young man approached him, slapped him on the back, and said, "I would know you anywhere with that damn hard hat on." As Easterling looked around, the young man added, "You were in on the Kennedy assassination, weren't you?"

"Who told you *that*?" Easterling said.

"Manuel Rivera told me," said the young man. "I am Francisco, his younger brother." With a chill of fear, Easterling tried to maintain his composure. He invited Francisco to sit down. Francisco asked if Easterling were armed, and then the two men patted each other down. No weapons were found.

For the next several hours, Easterling and Francisco talked. The Cuban explained that he recognized Easterling because of his white hard hat. He said he had seen a photograph of Easterling, wearing the hard hat, on the wall in a den of Raul Castro's home in Cuba. (As the brother of Fidel, Raul Castro is widely considered to be the premier's most powerful and influential military and intelligence advisor.[88]) Easterling challenged the Cuban, saying that he found this very hard to believe—even though he distinctly remembered the day in 1963 when he was driven blindfolded by Manuel to have his photograph taken.

Then, right at the bar, Francisco pulled from his inside breast pocket a small portfolio of photographs. They were Polaroid pictures of items and photographs that apparently were exhibited in Raul

Castro's den. There was a gallery of pictures of men who had been involved in the assassination. Easterling recognized Ruby, Oswald, and Ferrie. There were others whom he had never seen, as well as the man who may have been either Shaw or Banister. In nearly every case, the person's face had an X marked over it. Then, above the picture of Easterling in his hard hat, there was a question mark. The chill of fear turned to terror.

Another photograph showed Manuel Rivera standing beside the box, which was turned on its end to show the rifle securely placed in its cradle. In another picture, the Czech-made automatic rifle, with the catch box visible on the side, was attached to a handsome wooden board and mounted on the wall. A mahogany plaque hung from the board on a brass chain. The inscription on the plaque said: "Kennedy 1963."

Francisco and Easterling parted ways amicably, and Easterling spent the rest of the evening at the Cricket, a whorehouse in San Pedro Sula. Easterling felt, however, that he had come to the end of the line, that there was little chance of his getting back to the United States alive. The next morning, there was a knock on Easterling's door. It was Francisco saying that he had a Lear jet leaving very shortly for Houston and that he would like to give Hardhat a ride back to the States. Easterling sensed a plot—one that could change the question mark over his picture into an X.

He denounced Francisco as a Cuban intelligence agent and then fled from the hotel. He went to the airfield and got on the first plane to Belize and then a flight into New Orleans.

It was after his return from the encounter with Francisco that he was first sent to a mental institution. His drinking had become constant. From that time forward, Robert Easterling's course through life was one of manic highs and crashing alcoholic lows. In retrospect, it seems clear that the dissolution of Robert Easterling's sanity was inevitable.

Until his encounter with Francisco, Easterling had not known what happened in Dallas the day Kennedy was killed. In Honduras, Francisco gave him a full report that was based, he said, on what Manuel told him.

Shortly before the motorcade was due to arrive in Dealey Plaza, Manuel took advantage of the gathering crowd to slip into the Book

Depository. Presumably it was not his first visit. He made his way to the sixth floor, overlooking the spacious plaza area below. He located his special box, even though there were dozens of other boxes of varying descriptions in the cavernous, warehouselike room.[89]

Carlo, the Oswald look-alike, was already in the building. Numerous people saw him and later remembered him. Like the real Oswald, he kept to himself and said little.[90] Since midmorning, the real Lee Harvey Oswald had been at the bus station a few blocks away, waiting to be picked up by Robert Easterling.

During the minutes before the arrival of the motorcade, Manuel and Carlo made their preparations. They made sure the Mannlicher-Carcano—the Oswald rifle—was stashed between some boxes at the other end of the room. Francisco claimed that they then took three empty cartridge shells that had been fired earlier from the Oswald rifle and placed them on the floor beside the assassin's window. Manuel removed the Czech rifle from the special box and checked it over. All was ready.

Manuel stood back from the window as he watched the presidential motorcade approaching his position. He could see the tanned and smiling face of John F. Kennedy, the President of the United States, as he waved to the cheering crowds. As the President's limousine made the turn from Houston onto Elm Street, just below him, Manuel stepped to the window and crouched.

The head of President Kennedy filled the rifle scope. Manuel took a deep breath, expelled it slowly, then squeezed the trigger. With stunning speed and accuracy, he fired three times in 5.6 seconds to strike his moving target. His firing time had been even better on the coconuts, but this got the job done. Manuel waited a fraction of a second after the last shot to see if another was needed. But he could see that it was not necessary. He had blown apart the President's head.

Moving quickly, Manuel returned the Czech rifle to its hiding place beneath the false bottom of the special box. At that moment, Carlo was dawdling about at the soda machine four floors below. He was challenged by a police officer who was rushing past him to reach the upper floors of the building. But Carlo remained calm and said nothing. A man who worked in the building told the policeman that Carlo—whom he believed to be Oswald—also worked there. Carlo then slowly made his way out of the building and melted into the hysterical crowds.

Within minutes, Manuel Rivera had left the building. At the parking lot, he and Carlo got into a car and were on their way home. At some point, a little later, the nearly perfect bullet that had been fired from the Oswald rifle into a water barrel was placed on an unattended stretcher in a public corridor at Parkland Hospital, where the dying President had been taken.

There was much Francisco did not tell Easterling. He did not say how it was arranged for Jack Ruby to kill Oswald once Hardhat failed to pick him up and take him to Mexico. He did not say what Oswald believed his role to be. However, he did explain that it was necessary to wait seven months before finding the opportunity to retrieve the special box and Czech rifle from the Book Depository and return them to Cuba.

A Final Assessment

It is not possible to prove the accuracy of this account of events in Dallas. The chance for the positive establishment of truth has evaporated with the passage of time and the destruction of evidence since the findings of the Warren Commission. What remains is a massive public skepticism over the official account that Lee Harvey Oswald, alone, was responsible for the assassination of John F. Kennedy.

By any standard, Robert Easterling is a terribly sullied witness. While aspects of his story are obviously preposterous, the underlying account is compelling in certain respects. In the absence of a full revelation of facts by government agencies, it would be irresponsible not to present Easterling's story—the only known confession in which an individual has gone on record to chronicle his participation in a conspiracy to murder the President. As an answer to the overwhelming public skepticism, the account of Robert Easterling— given the telescoping of his participation as a bit player who backed out—fills the enduring void left by the Warren Commission and the HSCA. Keeping in mind Easterling's story, consider the following established facts, most of which are fully examined in other sections of this book.

In sharp contrast to the Warren Commission findings, the House Select Committee firmly established Jack Ruby's heavy association with organized crime. He had connections with the mob in New Orleans as well as in Dallas. He is officially placed in New Orleans around the time of the meeting described by Easterling. Every indication is that he murdered Oswald on someone's orders. When the Warren Commission interviewed Ruby at the Dallas jail, he begged to be taken to Washington, where, he said, he could speak freely. The Warren Commission refused his request, even though he repeated it several times.[91]

In summary, the HSCA had this to say about possible connections between Ruby and Oswald: "The committee's investigation of Oswald and Ruby showed a variety of relationships that may have matured into an assassination conspiracy. Neither Oswald nor Ruby turned out to be 'loners,' as they had been painted [by the Warren Commission]."[92]

One of the enduring oddities of the evidence found in the assassin's lair is the discovery of the three cartridge shells ballistically linked to the Oswald rifle. Those shells were not scattered widely as one would expect them to be if ejected from a rifle in the normal fashion. Moreover, two of them were only inches apart.

Another curious point is the failure by investigators to find a single Mannlicher-Carcano cartridge other than those, including a live round still in the rifle, discovered at the scene. No extra cartridge was ever found on Oswald or in his possessions. No evidence was found that he ever purchased ammunition at all. If he was the assassin, his only ammunition was at the scene—the cartridge shells lined up as evidence in the assassin's lair. There is no official explanation as to where Oswald supposedly got his four cartridges.[93]

As for the Mannlicher-Carcano that was officially established as the Oswald assassination rifle, the ancient, bolt-action weapon was one of the *worst possible* selections for such skilled shooting. There is no indication that Oswald knew much about guns, and he was never regarded as a superlative marksman while he was in the Marine Corps. Yet he is credited with a combination of shooting skills on November 22 that has *never* been matched in repeated government tests by the most proficient riflemen in the United States.[94]

Moreover, there is no evidence that the Mannlicher-Carcano was even fired on the day of the assassination.[95]

The primary official ballistics evidence linking the Mannlicher-Carcano with the murder of President Kennedy was a lone bullet found on an unattended stretcher at Parkland Hospital. The stretcher was in a busy corridor, parked opposite an elevator. (While the Warren Report declared false the reports of Jack Ruby's presence at Parkland Hospital, the HSCA later confirmed those reports.) That bullet, scorned by critics as the Magic Bullet, has become the cornerstone of the official version of the assassination. In nearly perfect condition when found, the Magic Bullet is credited with passing through seven layers of skin and shattering two bones in the attack on Kennedy and Texas Governor John Connally.[96]

The appealing and compelling fact about this bullet—the one that caused the government to leap to embrace it—is the absolute ballistics finding that it was fired from the Mannlicher-Carcano linked to Oswald. That position prevails, despite the failure of government experts over the years to fire a similar bullet into *anything* more solid than cotton and have it emerge virtually undamaged.[97]

To this day, the feat of the Magic Bullet has never been duplicated in any test conducted by the government. There is no indication in the records that any government test ever included firing the Mannlicher-Carcano into water. In the course of this investigation the author acquired a vintage Mannlicher-Carcano and old ammunition similar to that used in government tests. Firing these bullets into water consistently produced nearly pristine slugs, strikingly similar to the Magic Bullet.

Much has been made of the fact that finally, in 1977, a highly sophisticated neutron testing technique was applied to the Magic Bullet and certain fragments believed to have come from the wrist of John Connally, who in the official version was hit by the same bullet that passed through Kennedy. The test, which in effect measures metallic composition, indicated that the fragments came from the Magic Bullet. The trouble with the test results is that the basic evidence is so severely sullied. There is, for example, uncertainty about the origins of both the Magic Bullet *and* the wrist fragments; there are disturbing lapses in the chain of possession of the evidence; there is even the mysterious disappearance of certain bits of this evidence while in the official custody of the National Archives. The same test suggested that fragments found in the presidential limousine came from Mannlicher-Carcano ammunition, but in that case there are the same problems with the basic evidence. It is difficult, at best, to accept the test results with much enthusiasm. To do so requires a wholesale suspension of the sort of discernment one expects to prevail in a case of this magnitude.[98]

On the other hand, if there is a basic validity to Easterling's account, there is no particular reason to believe that he knows precisely what was going on in Dallas on that day, when he wasn't even there. Consider the hypothesis that there was a shooter in the place of Oswald—an expert marksman using an automatic rifle capable of firing at a speed faster than that of the sluggish Mannlicher-Carcano. In that scenario, the real death bullets would have been frangible slugs that, on impact, were destroyed beyond ballistics identification, leaving only fragments. Such fragments could come from bullets that were molded from the lead of the Mannlicher-Carcano cartridges. In such a case, under any sort of testing of metallic composition, the fragments would be linked to the bullet found on the stretcher, if indeed it was planted there. That bullet, the Magic Bullet, could be linked absolutely to the Mannlicher-Carcano.

On the day of the assassination, when police officers swarmed through the Book Depository, the Mannlicher-Carcano was discovered at 1:22 P.M., less than one hour after the shooting. There is no evidence that after the discovery of the Oswald rifle, there was any further search of the building or its contents. Indeed, according to the Warren Report, ten days passed before Lee Harvey Oswald's clipboard was discovered on the sixth floor. His jacket was not found until late November. Clearly, there was no systematic search of the building once the Mannlicher-Carcano rifle was discovered.[99]

From the beginning, one of the most troubling aspects of Easterling's allegation was his insistence that he saw an odd-sized wooden box with a false bottom in which the real assassination rifle was to be concealed. The dimensions of the box, as described by Easterling, do not correspond to any boxes that are normally familiar. One would expect such a box to be prominently out of place among the hundreds of small cardboard cartons that official accounts report filled the sixth floor. Moreover, in the dozens of official photographs of the sixth floor, none shows any wooden boxes of this description, though many of the pictures show a jumble of cardboard cartons that are filled with textbooks. Conversely, there are no photographs that exclude the possibility that such a wooden crate was there.*

On October 21, 1983, the author was shown through the sixth floor of the building by a member of the Dallas County Historical Commission, which is preserving the site as an educational and historical exhibit. The restoration work was far from complete, and a variety of debris was scattered about. The cavernous sixth floor had been emptied of most of its contents a few years after the assassination, when the Book Depository was moved to a new location and the building closed. The floor had been used for nothing since then.[100]

Among the items on the sixth floor that day were a few small cardboard cartons, now empty. The most prominent items on the floor were at least seven heavy wooden boxes. While not all the same size, the empty boxes were generally of odd dimensions strikingly similar to the box described by Easterling. The boxes were stamped with the names of publishing companies, such as Bobbs-Merrill, and addressed to the Texas School Book Depository. One of the boxes, for example, bore a stamp which indicated it had once been used to ship 500 copies of *The Red Pony*.

Judson Shook, a former Dallas official who played an important role in the preservation of the building, is regarded as an expert on the building and its usage since 1963. He explained to the author that at one point, everything on the sixth floor was moved to another floor. Later, some of the things were returned to the sixth floor. Shook stated that there had been no reason to keep track of what was moved where. While no one can confirm that the boxes were on the sixth floor in 1963, it also is impossible to state that they were *not* there. In any case, it is virtually indisputable that such boxes were somewhere in the building, quite possibly on the sixth floor.[101]

---

*Only days before the Warren Commission issued its report, someone apparently became concerned that the "cardboard cartons" piled around the sniper's window to ensure seclusion might have been too heavy to be moved by one man. Such a fact would, of course, indicate the presence of more than one man, suggesting a conspiracy. On September 11, 1964, the FBI hastily interviewed the superintendent of the Book Depository and reported that none of the cartons around the window was too heavy to be handled by one man. The report also contains the statement that "there were no cartons on the sixth floor . . . which could not have been handled by one man." The cover sheet on the FBI report indicates that it is concerned with "cardboard cartons." It seems certain that the cardboard cartons are distinctly different from—and could not possibly be confused with—a large and heavy wooden box, such as the one described by Easterling.[102]

The most stunning evidence that wooden boxes such as these were at least in proximity to the sixth floor is found in a photograph taken on the *fifth* floor soon after the assassination. It appears in the Warren Commission exhibits but is not published in the Warren Report. The purpose of the photograph is to show the three men who were on the fifth floor at the time of the assassination. There, at the edge of the photograph, are at least two of the wooden boxes, apparently being used as storage bins. They are located right beside the stairwell, the only one leading down from the sixth floor.[103]

There are credible reports of a man believed to be a Cuban who was seen in Dealey Plaza just after the assassination. He was seen in a light-colored car. There is even a photograph of a light-colored Rambler station wagon as it passes in front of the TSBD Building. A police officer has sworn that he saw a man who looked like Oswald get into it. He watched as the car was driven away, heading out of town.[104]

G. Robert Blakey, chief counsel of the House Select Committee, once told the author in an informal discussion that based on his own studies, he theorizes that an assassin in addition to Oswald would be a Latin man between the ages of twenty-five and thirty-five and from either Miami or New Orleans. There is no indication that Blakey knows anything about Manuel Rivera.[105]

The case against Lee Harvey Oswald has always been circumstantial at best. No reliable witness ever placed him in the assassin's lair. The FBI laboratory could not find Oswald's fingerprints on the rifle. There is only the most tenuous evidence to indicate that Oswald took the Mannlicher-Carcano into the building—evidence that would be severely challenged in court.[106]

Scrutiny of Warren Commission testimony shows highly disputed evidence concerning Oswald's movements immediately after he presumably left the building. There is only the official *presumption* that he walked seven blocks away from the scene and then caught a bus headed back toward Dealey Plaza. The first certainty of Oswald's whereabouts following the shooting is at 12:48 P.M., when he got into a taxicab that was parked in front of the Greyhound bus station about five blocks from Dealey Plaza. There is no credible testimony about whether Oswald walked along the street until he came to the cab—or whether he walked out of the bus station and got into it.[107] In either case, the bus station is the spot where Easterling claims he was supposed to pick up Oswald.

Even the United States government has never come up with a motive for Oswald to want to assassinate the President. There is but the flimsiest evidence that he had the means to commit the act— or that he was even in the official assassin's lair. During his interrogation, Oswald stoutly denied his guilt. "I didn't shoot anyone," he stated in a corridor encounter with the press.[108]

What, then, *was* Oswald's role?

He was silenced, of course, before he could give his version of events. However, in one of his last statements on record, Oswald shouted to reporters:

"I'm just a patsy! I'm just a patsy!"[109]

In the final analysis it is not possible to prove that the Easterling confession is true. However, it is possible to show that there is, at least, every reason for the FBI to investigate Easterling's leads vigorously. The evidence provided to the author by the FBI shows persuasively that a shocking indifference, even a sloppiness, continues to mark the FBI's position on Easterling. It is also astonishing that the FBI's official position is that Easterling was "not in Dallas . . . with . . . Oswald's clone as Mr. Easterling claims." This shows that the bureau has never really listened to what Easterling is saying.*[110]

Another example of this official indifference concerns Easterling's claim to have participated in the bombing of a commercial airliner en route to New Orleans from Tampa. "No such bombing ever occurred," states the FBI in commenting on this. The bureau statement goes on to describe the crash of an airliner flying from *Miami* to New Orleans on the date in question—a plane that did crash and for which there is no certain official explanation.[111]

If the FBI had taken Easterling's allegation seriously, it would

---

*The author has made vigorous efforts to acquire the investigative reports on Easterling under the Freedom of Information Act. The bureau initially accepted a release from Easterling to provide the documents and then, two months later, stated that the release was not satisfactory. As this book goes to press, efforts are continuing to acquire the documents. If it should develop that the FBI claims it was responding to an earlier, different assertion from Easterling, then it must account for the years it maintained its myopic position after being alerted in 1981 to Easterling's confession.

have investigated the case sufficiently to learn that the flight it refers to from Miami to New Orleans made a stop in *Tampa*, prior to the fatal crash. That, according to Easterling, is where he helped place the explosives on board. The crash occurred after the plane took off from Tampa. The point here is not whether Easterling really bombed the plane but that the FBI has not taken what he says with enough seriousness to make even the simplest investigation.[112]

A careful reading of Easterling's account cannot lead to any certain conclusion as to who killed John F. Kennedy. It is perhaps significant, however, that when one considers those who may have wanted Kennedy dead—Cuban exiles, Fidel Castro, fanatical right-wing oil men, renegade elements of the intelligence services, the mob— they all play roles in this remarkable story.

During the months of his contact with the author, Robert Easterling lived with his elderly mother in a small house in the quiet countryside of Rawls Springs, Mississippi. His alcoholism and mental condition grew obviously worse throughout the last months of 1982. During the spring of 1983, he was jailed for drunken driving and hospitalized for various medical problems, including a heart attack.[113]

Then, on July 31, 1983, Robert Easterling went berserk at his home. His mother fled the house. Easterling terrorized his family by threatening to burn down the home. For more than twelve hours he systematically went through the house with a hammer, smashing every piece of glass, including dozens of family treasures. He used razors to slash the furniture.[114]

During the worst hours, the author was in telephone contact with Easterling, trying unsuccessfully to convince him to stop the rampage. At one point, as the author was telling him how desperately he needed psychiatric help, Easterling bellowed, "Well, you just can't blow up goddamn airplanes and kill presidents and all that, and when you get as close to dying as I am, hell, it worries you!"

Soon after that sheriff's deputies crashed into the house and seized Easterling. He was held for a lunacy hearing and committed to a state mental hospital for an indefinite period.[115] He remained confined as this book went to press. In October 1983 the author visited Easterling at the hospital and found him considerably subdued. During that conversation, Easterling was asked again how he felt about his role in the assassination of President Kennedy. His reply: "I'm just as guilty as if I pulled the trigger."

13 · THE ENDURING PUZZLE

Twenty-two years after the JFK assassination, a festering reservoir of indisputable, disjointed facts has made its way into the public domain. Some of these facts raise the most ominous questions. Nearly all the information was known by some officials at the time of Kennedy's death. For the most part, the leads went unpursued, primarily because they pointed *away* from Lee Harvey Oswald as a lone, demented assassin. It is believed today, without any serious question, that in those early days President Johnson, Attorney General Robert Kennedy, FBI Director Hoover, as well as the Warren Commission were all anxious to have the matter resolved with deliberate speed. This establishment powerhouse was fueled by a multitude of motives—some of which are known, while others are as elusive as ever. One motive was preeminent. The only quick settlement of the JFK assassination was for Lee Harvey Oswald to be firmly, swiftly, and unanimously adjudged the lone assassin.[1]

At this point, nearly a quarter-century after the fact, it is unlikely that the full truth about the Kennedy assassination will ever be known. It is impossible, even now, to be sure how much faith or credence can be placed in any particular piece of evidence, no matter how suggestive. While the purity and integrity of certain evidence might be established, what cannot be satisfactorily known is just *how* that evidence fits into a larger pattern, much less how these patterns are interlocked.

The preceding chapters have included detailed examinations of those aspects of the case that possess enough discernible interlocking characteristics to fit into a cohesive pattern, even if the context of that pattern remains out of kilter. It is established, for example, that the FBI never vigorously investigated the assassination beyond building a case against Oswald. It is known that the Warren Commission ignored leads of intriguing promise, often because essential information—such as the FBI files on Ruby—was withheld from it.

Thousands of tantalizing documents were entombed with the belief that they were fit only to be seen by distant generations. The President's autopsy, without question, was a forensic disaster of such magnitude that the integrity of that evidence is lost forever. Extremely important questions may never be resolved. It is clear that the Tippit murder was never given even a remotely adequate investigation, and that persuasive evidence that Oswald did not shoot him was pointedly ignored. It is officially established that Jack Ruby was a creature of organized crime who clearly stalked Oswald from the day of his arrest. It is established that various Cuban elements, as well as organized crime, possessed sufficient motive and means to murder the President—and that from the earliest hours these possibilities were swept aside in favor of evidence against Oswald.

Such stark certainties are the basis for the overwhelming skepticism that is so deeply engrained in the American psyche. It is a skepticism that has swollen into a mountain of reasonable doubt. In addition to the larger patterns that create this doubt, there is a grab bag of evidence that possibly is every bit as important but far more difficult to corral into a cohesive package. That grab bag is worth examining.

The Other Oswald

Of all the mysteries in the JFK case, none is greater than Lee Harvey Oswald's murky alliances and contradictory behavior. Yet from the moment of his arrest, given the official mind-set, it was virtually inevitable that he would shoulder the complete responsibility for the crime of the century.

With a character like quicksilver, Oswald was certainly the most elusive, slippery person imaginable to attempt to squeeze into any mold—particularly one that called for a simplicity in character and personal history. By any standard, Lee Oswald was a formidably complex young man. To turn the screw of contradictions to the breaking point for the authorities, strong evidence suggests that at least one person was impersonating Oswald prior to the assassination. This grating note is in addition to the persuasive evidence that the real Oswald had some sort of connection to the intelligence operations of the United States.

Over the years, no evidence has been more pointedly ignored or dismissed by officials than the suggestion of a second Oswald. This hypothesis holds that in the period preceding the assassination, there was at least one Oswald look-alike who behaved in ways that, after Kennedy's murder, provided evidence convenient to seal the case against the real Oswald. In certain cases, examination of that very evidence suggests clearly that an impersonator was at work. Once such impersonation is accepted, on this basis alone the fact of conspiracy becomes absolutely established.

However, in official versions the issue is commonly ducked with the assertion that, in a given instance, such a person could not have been the real Oswald since Oswald was known to be in a particular place, or that he could not drive a car, or that he did not own the sort of rifle the witness saw in the man's possession. This sort of dismissive analysis does not go to the issue. It pointedly overlooks the possibility of imposture. The HSCA report indicated fleeting attention to the possibility, which was dismissed for insufficient evidence.[2]

Any consideration of the double-Oswald concept becomes immediately entangled with the even more complicated question of Oswald's possible connections with U.S. intelligence. That is an area so mired in deceit and obfuscation that examination of anything attaching to it quickly brings on blurred double images.

Peter Dale Scott, one of the most respected critics, believes that the genesis of the false Oswald evidence lies in what has been glimpsed of CIA records, going back to 1960. Scott observes in his concise book *Crime and Cover-up* that in November 1960 the CIA prepared what was called the American Defectors List, which was sent to the White House. States Scott: "In that list of fourteen names, the life history of one defector, 'Lee Henry Oswald,' had been so altered (even in a secret memo) as to make him untraceable."[3]

That single instance could, of course, be a bureaucratic blunder, except that it was consistent—continuing in various intelligence records right up until the time of the assassination. Such apparent fooling with the facts—wittingly or unwittingly—has fueled the speculation that the intelligence services were seeking, long before the assassination, to obscure the emergence of any real picture of one of its own agents. It remains a mystery that probably will never be resolved, but one that must be considered as a basis for the other bizarre reports suggesting either a second Oswald or one so altered as to be rendered in double image.[4]

In the weeks before the assassination, numerous credible witnesses were aware of a man they were certain was Lee Harvey Oswald. These accounts were lost among the hundreds of such reported sightings that poured into the authorities after November 22, most of which were clearly without merit. The prevailing technique by officials has been to lump *all* such reports into the crank category, overlooking numerous incidents in which the witnesses and corroborative circumstances go well beyond the criteria for reasonable credibility.[5]

On September 25, the day Oswald was supposed to be somewhere between New Orleans and Mexico on a bus, a person claiming to be Harvey Oswald presented himself at the Selective Service office in Austin, Texas. He was there for thirty minutes discussing what he might do about his dishonorable discharge from the Marine Corps. He wanted to have it amended. Two other people in Austin recalled seeing Oswald in town around that date. The report was dismissed because of the official version that Oswald was on a bus headed for Mexico, and never anywhere near Austin.[6]

At about that time, possibly even the same day, "Leon Oswald" showed up in Dallas with two Latins at the home of Silvia Odio, a young woman whose Cuban family was prominent in anti-Castro activities. The whole Odio visit, which is discussed in detail in Chapter 12, is powerful evidence of Oswald's connection to anti-Castro Cubans—or evidence of the existence of an Oswald imposter.[7]

Soon after the strange visit, one of the Latin men telephoned Mrs. Odio and mentioned that "Leon Oswald," an ex-Marine sharpshooter, had expressed an interest in killing President Kennedy. Two months later, Mrs. Odio had to be hospitalized when she (and her sister) recognized "Leon Oswald" as the accused assassin of President Kennedy. While the Warren Commission and FBI officials considered Mrs. Odio's report to be erroneous, the HSCA reviewed all of the evidence and found her account to be credible.[8]

The strange events of Mexico City are treated fully in Chapter 9. Much has been made in the official version about Lee Oswald's activities there in terms of visits to the Soviet and Cuban diplomatic facilities. However, the only known CIA photographs of that "Oswald" were clearly someone else who has never been identified. The wire-tapped tapes of that "Oswald" speaking were "routinely destroyed or recycled" before a comparison could be made with the voice of the Oswald arrested in Dallas. (One report from FBI Director Hoover stated that FBI agents who knew Oswald's voice had listened to the tape and were convinced the voice was not that of Oswald. Later, there was an FBI denial of the validity of the Hoover message about the tapes—a denial subsequently supported by the HSCA.)[9]

Out of all this confusion arises the strong possibility that while the real Oswald may have been in Mexico City, the person who presented himself at the Cuban consulate and at the Soviet embassy was someone else bearing the real Oswald's papers and passport. Of all the evidence of imposture, this certainly is the most significant. It suggests an ominous and purposeful control of the man who was soon to be blamed for assassinating the President.

Other evidence was, perhaps, less significant but every bit as important in trying to stitch together a pattern of activity for an imposter.

Six weeks before the assassination, Mrs. Lovell Penn heard the blasts from a high-powered rifle being fired out in her cow pasture. A high school teacher, Mrs. Penn lived about fifteen miles southwest of downtown Dallas. She confronted three men, one of whom had the rifle, and stated that she was afraid they might shoot one of her cows. One of the men, whom she later believed could have been Lee Oswald, became angry. Mrs. Penn threatened to call the police, and the men left. Another of the trio may have been a Latin, according to Mrs. Penn's description.[10]

After the assassination, when Mrs. Penn thought she recognized Oswald's picture, she turned over a cartridge case, which she had picked up in her pasture, that had been ejected from the rifle the men were firing. An FBI examination showed that the cartridge case was for a 6.5-caliber Mannlicher-Carcano. The examination also showed the case could not have been fired from Oswald's rifle. That finding marked the end of any official interest in Mrs. Penn's report.[11]

Shortly after the assassination, at a gun shop in the Dallas suburb where Oswald's family was staying, a rifle-repair tag bearing the name Oswald was found. The tag indicated that three holes had been drilled and a telescopic sight had been mounted. After a subsequent FBI investigation, which included an intense but unsuccessful search for any Oswald in the Dallas–Fort Worth area who might have had a rifle repaired at that gun shop, the Warren Commission dismissed the significance of the repair tag for lack of evidence connecting the real Oswald to the repair at that shop.[12]

Numerous reliable witnesses reported several corroborated instances in November of seeing Oswald target-shooting at a firing range with a foreign rifle. Indeed, this man called attention to himself by requesting assistance from a stranger to help him adjust the scope on his rifle. Witnesses reported that the man was an excellent marksman. He was particularly well remembered because he angered others by cross-shooting—firing out of his prescribed lane and hitting someone else's target, abominable and highly unusual conduct on a shooting range. Such behavior would be vividly recalled.[13]

The Warren Commission, which must have been sorely tempted to use such testimony as evidence that Oswald was a good marksman, dismissed the numerous credible reports. The commission cited its reasoning that the man could not have been Oswald because he was known to be elsewhere.[14]

Certainly one of the most vivid recollections of an out-of-place Oswald involves an incident that occurred early in November. Introducing himself as Lee Oswald, a young man who looked like the real Oswald walked into an automobile dealership in downtown Dallas, a few blocks from Dealey Plaza. He asked to try out a car. A salesman went for a drive with "Oswald," who created an indelible impression in the salesman's mind by racing along a city freeway at speeds up to eighty-five miles an hour.[15]

Back at the showroom, a discussion ensued regarding Oswald's credit rating. He claimed he expected to come into a large amount of money very soon. At a certain point, according to one report, "Oswald" loudly stated that he would go back to Russia if he needed to buy a car. The matter was officially discounted, largely on the grounds that Oswald could not drive a car.[16]

This aspect of possible imposture is enhanced by evidence that a Texas driver's license may have been issued to a Lee Harvey Oswald. There are reports from individuals at the Texas Department of Public Safety that such a license was seen in the files, although there is no official certification of this.[17]

Another convincing report in this category comes from Ed Brand, a Dallas businessman who was selling automobile insurance in 1963. Brand told the author that his insurance business was located across the street from Oswald's rooming house. In the early part of November, a young man, whom Brand had noticed on several occasions at the bus stop across the street, came into his office to inquire about insurance for a car he was considering buying. Brand asked the man for his driver's license in order to use the vital data to calculate the cost of the insurance. The name on the license, Brand says, was O. H. Lee. The young man said he planned to buy the car in the next couple of weeks and that he would pay cash for it. Oswald, who was living across the street under the name of O. H. Lee, never returned. After the assassination, Brand called the telephone number printed in the newspapers for people with information. He was never contacted in person, although there is an FBI report on Brand's call that contains his information.[18]

Certainly one of the most intriguing reported sightings of Oswald comes from a U.S. Customs officer working in Montreal. Soon after the assassination, the Secret Service was informed that Customs Investigator Jean Paul Tremblay reported that he had seen Lee Harvey Oswald handing out Fair Play for Cuba Committee pamphlets on a Montreal street in August 1963. Tremblay, who was working on cases involving Cuba at that time, took one of the handbills from the man he believes was Oswald. Two men and a woman were with Oswald at the time, according to Tremblay.[19]

The FBI investigated Tremblay's report and concluded that it was in error, in view of the official belief that Oswald was in New Orleans at the time. Additional FBI documents on the matter were released in 1975 and 1978, both containing large areas of deletions—omissions that provoke questions, in view of the FBI position that the Tremblay report deserves no credence. To some extent, this sensitivity on the part of the FBI could be over fear of compromising certain foreign intelligence sources.[20]

This whole mystery is heightened by the fact that photographs were taken of the person Tremblay believes was Oswald. As late as 1984, the FBI was still firm in its refusal to release the photographs, sought through lawsuits under the Freedom of Information Act. If the photographs show a man clearly *not* Oswald, they would support the FBI's version. On the other hand, a picture of the real Oswald— or a man who looked very much like him—in company with the pro-Castro activists would raise the sorts of questions the government has sought to quash.[21]

Some of the strongest evidence of an Oswald imposter is found in official FBI records. It was none other than J. Edgar Hoover who raised the first high-level alarm in June 1960, while Oswald was in the Soviet Union. In a memorandum to the State Department, Hoover wrote: "Since there is a possibility that an imposter is using Oswald's birth certificate, any current information the Department of State might have concerning subject will be appreciated." Another FBI memorandum, ten months later, seems to hark back to Hoover's alert to the State Department when it refers to the report "that there is an imposter using Oswald's identification data."[22]

What this means is as ambiguous as anything else in the puzzle. However, it clearly shows an interest in Oswald and/or an interest in an imposter pretending to be Oswald. Hoover's memorandum was written more than three years before Oswald was vaulted to infamy.

Seven months after the Hoover memorandum, in January 1961, while Oswald was still in the Soviet Union, two men opened negotiations with a Ford dealership in New Orleans for the purchase of ten trucks. The pair told the manager they represented a group called Friends of Democratic Cuba. The manager of the Ford dealership noted that the purchase order should be made out to "Oswald," the name of one of the men. It was indicated that he would be paying for the trucks. The manager also noted the name of "Oswald's" group on the order form: "Friends of Democratic Cuba." That was the group sponsored by FBI contact Guy Banister and his investigator, David W. Ferrie.*[23]

Such imposture can be interpreted in many ways and can lead in several directions. The basic significance is that certain anti-Castro Cubans, nearly three years before the JFK assassination, had reason to use the name Oswald in connection with the Banister-linked exile group, Friends of Democratic Cuba.[24]

This evidence is highly suggestive of the existence of an ongoing manipulation of Oswald's name and reputation. (It is separate from the evidence showing that Oswald himself was manipulated.) Toward what end remains speculative.

In any accounting of these possibilities, one cannot overlook per-

---

*Another incident occurred in early 1963 in New Orleans, prior to the established date of Oswald's arrival in that city. An inspector for the Immigration and Naturalization Service (INS), Ronald L. Smith, disclosed to the Senate Intelligence Committee that he interviewed a man who was being held in jail whom he is certain was Oswald. The man was claiming to be a Cuban. At that time, the real Oswald was still in Dallas. In keeping with INS procedures, once Smith determined that "Oswald" was not a Cuban, no report was filed and the matter was dropped.

haps the most persuasive of all "other Oswald" sightings. It happened about fifteen minutes after the assassination, well after the official version insists that Lee Harvey Oswald left Dealey Plaza. As discussed earlier, Roger Craig, a highly respected police officer, saw a man come running toward the street from the direction of the Texas School Book Depository and get into a car driven by a man of Latin appearance. They drove away. This was perfectly corroborated by an independent witness. Later that afternoon, the policeman swore that the man he had seen running from the Book Depository and jumping into the car was now in custody—Lee Harvey Oswald.[25]

Thomas Eli Davis III

Once the possibility of a second Oswald is permitted, the potential avenues for conspiracy run in many directions. One writer has postulated his whole case on the presumption that Jack Ruby did murder Oswald—but not in plain view of the world in 1963. Rather, the execution was carried off quietly and efficiently in New Orleans in 1959 during a brief overlap of New Orleans visits by Oswald and Ruby. Thus, the Oswald who departed for the Soviet Union was even then an imposter—an imposter whose training was continued by the Soviets, who later sent him to murder President Kennedy and then be murdered himself by Jack Ruby.[26] Nonsense such as this provokes almost universal scorn over the prospect of a second Oswald. But such scorn, when applied sweepingly, is misdirected.

As demonstrated in earlier pages, the evidence of a second Oswald is highly persuasive. Because of the official contempt for the possibility, researchers have had to piece together the evidence not from the results of positive investigation, but from the rubble heap of unpursued leads—possibilities cast off by a government determined to find a different answer. It is not surprising that the emerging picture is clouded by shadows of contradiction, yielding only the faintest pattern of the *manner* of possible imposture.

What makes the most likely sense is that an imposture was not a highly tuned part of a grand conspiracy but a function of convenience, carried out at different times, by different people, for different specific reasons. Whatever prompted the FBI to be concerned that someone might be using Oswald's identification papers in 1960 was not necessarily the same set of circumstances that led to the reports of Oswald's activities around Dallas in the fall of 1963—activities ruled out as impossible by official investigators. On the other hand, such a connection is *possible*, even if mightily difficult to fathom.[27]

Of all the conjecture and speculation about a second Oswald, the activities of one man more than any other make him appear to be the most logical candidate for an imposter. His activities qualify him in at least some of the known instances where the "Oswald" in question could not have been the one accused of assassinating the President. The accumulation of the slender threads of evidence is largely the work of Seth Kantor, the acknowledged expert on Jack Ruby, and Gary Shaw, one of the most tireless investigators and critics of the JFK case. Both Shaw and Bernard Fensterwald, Jr., another prominent assassination investigator, believe that this man is the most likely candidate for one of the second Oswalds.[28]

Thomas Eli Davis III was born in McKinney, Texas, on August 27, 1936. He came from a respectable family and was an easy-talking young man fond of pretty women and good living. He served in the United States Army. Numerous people who knew him say he had a brilliant mind. There were, however, flaws. In 1958, at the age of twenty-one, Davis was convicted for attempted bank robbery in Detroit and placed on probation for five years. He was returned to Texas, where he remained under probationary supervision until early 1962. During those four years, he could have been almost anywhere in the southern United States between his periodic meetings with probation officers.[29]

In January 1963 Davis was in New Orleans, where he applied for a passport. Always on the move, according to the people who knew him, he headed for California. There, in May 1963, he placed an advertisement in a Los Angeles newspaper to recruit mercenaries to invade Haiti and overthrow President Duvalier. When the FBI investigated this, Davis claimed he was a free-lance writer trying to glean information for an article on soldier-of-fortune activities.[30]

Later that year, according to a State Department telegram, Davis was arrested in Tangiers for trying to sell guns. At that time, Davis's wife told the consulate general in Tangiers that her husband had worked as a soldier of fortune in Indochina, Indonesia, Algeria, and Cuba. Just prior to Davis's arrest, she said, they had traveled through London, Paris, and Madrid.[31]

This biographical information comes largely from the official files of the FBI and the State Department. These are but the bare bones of the short, messy life of Thomas Eli Davis III. With his fluent Spanish, Davis was deeply involved in anti-Castro Cuban exile activities, including gunrunning operations. Davis's most ominous alleged connection is to one of the CIA's more sinister operatives— a man code-named QJ/WIN, who worked under the auspices of the agency's ZR/RIFLE assassination program and served as one of its "principal agent[s]."[32]

What is of particular interest is that Davis clearly possessed a resemblance to Lee Harvey Oswald—in general stature, age, coloration, and facial features. The two would not be mistaken for each other under close examination, but the general similarities were there, especially for people whose later recall was based on their studying photographs. Prior to any attention that was given to the possibility of a second Oswald, Davis admitted to having used the name Oswald in his activities. Those activities clearly are worth a closer look.[33]

In 1963, as Jack Ruby wrestled with his lawyers over the best strategy on the Oswald murder charge, he was asked if any names might come up that could cause trouble to his defense. Ruby told his lawyers about his gunrunning activities with Davis, adding that he hoped to go back into that business with Davis if he could beat the rap for murdering Oswald. (Ruby's first contact with Tommy Davis was even more shoddy. Davis approached Ruby about making a pornographic movie using some of Ruby's exotic dancers.) Both Davis and Ruby had been involved with Robert Ray McKeown, who was prominently identified as a supplier of munitions to Castro before the revolution. One of the confirming points of this association was that it occurred during the time that Tommy Davis was on probation and working around Beaumont, Texas, not far from where McKeown had his headquarters. While McKeown told the FBI that he recalled that Ruby was associated with someone called Davis, he claimed he did not remember that man's first name.[34]

According to Seth Kantor, this was a period when Tommy Davis had become involved with anti-Castro Cubans—a point confirmed by members of Davis's family. Kantor writes that Davis "carried out his work with the skill of an underwater commando. He was a professional deep-sea diver who operated on the Gulf of Mexico. He had become involved in training anti-Castro units at a hidden encampment in Florida and at another site in South America."[35]

Kantor, a well-respected Washington journalist, asserts that his own confidential sources have convinced him that during this period Davis was working with the CIA. It is now established by FBI documents that during this identical period, Jack Ruby was an official contact for the FBI. (See Chapter 8 for a full examination of Ruby's activities.)[36]

Davis was busy in 1963 with his mercenary activities. His wife of that period has confirmed that he maintained his contacts with anti-Castro Cubans until early 1963. Official records establish that during 1963 Davis was in California and Louisiana. There were several possible times during this period when Davis may have been posing as Oswald.[37]

Perhaps the most intriguing possibility for imposture occurred toward the end of September when the three men—two Latins and "Leon Oswald"—showed up at the home of Silvia Odio in Dallas, an incident examined elsewhere in these pages. Mrs. Odio's description of "Leon Oswald" is very similar to the real Oswald, except for one difference that, despite the official acceptance today of the Odio account, has never been reconciled. She stated that "Leon Oswald" had a faint mustache. That, it turns out, was a prime difference between Davis and Oswald: Davis *did* have a mustache, according to an FBI report describing Davis's appearance during an investigation four months earlier.[38]

Another provocative parallel emerged in 1983 with the discovery of old guest ledgers from the Hotel LaSalle in New Orleans. On August 8, 1963, "T. E. Davis" registered as a guest at the hotel. He checked out August 10. Lee Oswald was arrested in New Orleans on August 9 for engaging in the street scuffle over his pro-Castro demonstration. It is not provable whether Thomas Eli Davis was or was not in New Orleans at that time.[39]

On November 2, 1963, Davis and his wife left the United States. After traveling to London, Paris, and Madrid, they arrived in Tangiers on November 28. Ten days later, Davis was arrested in Morocco for trying to sell guns. What concerned Moroccan officials more than the gun-dealing was a letter they discovered on Davis, in his handwriting, dealing with "Oswald" and the assassination. The letter was addressed to a lawyer in New York called Thomas G. Proctor, who has never been found. In the letter, according to an official paraphrasing, Davis suggests that Proctor should donate money to newly succeeded President Lyndon Johnson for his campaign, a reference so odd that it suggests the possibility of a coded message.[40]

In a State Department telegram about the matter, the document was described as a "rambling, somewhat cryptic, unsigned letter in Davis' handwriting which refers in passing to 'Oswald' and to Kennedy assassination." The actual letter is not in the public record.[41]

In these exotic travels, where was Thomas Eli Davis III on November 22, 1963?

His wife of that period has indicated that she was never sure of Davis's whereabouts—that Davis was difficult to keep up with. For part of their travels they stayed in Madrid with friends of hers. Seth Kantor, however, writes that on November 22 Tommy Davis was in jail in Algiers for gun-dealing with anti-Algerian terrorists. According to Kantor, who reiterated his assertions to the author in 1984, Tommy Davis was released almost immediately from the Algerian prison through the efforts of the CIA assassination figure code-named QJ/WIN. That sensational report cannot be confirmed beyond Kantor's assertion that he has full confidence in the credibility of his intelligence source. The arrest itself, however, has other support.[42]

About a year after the assassination, Tommy Davis was interviewed by veteran Dallas newspaperman George W. Carter, who had covered the JFK assassination. Carter enjoyed a reputation as an excellent reporter. Years before Kantor's published account, Davis told Carter that he *was* in Algiers on the day of the assassination and that he was arrested. Davis also told Carter that while in Algeria, he was using the name Oswald.[43]

Davis stated to Carter that he was worried that someone might try to link him to the assassination because of these connections. He told Carter that his passport had been canceled but that he was leaving the country anyway.[44]

Carter had first heard about Tommy Davis from one of Jack Ruby's lawyers, Tom Howard, who evidently remained intrigued by the Ruby-Davis connection, which went unexamined by the Warren Commission. Carter's interview with Tommy Davis, whom he described as having "a tremendous mind," came about after Carter started asking questions of people in the town where Davis lived. Carter believed that Davis talked to him in an effort to find out how much was known about his Algerian activities—and whether there was any evidence of official interest. There was, of course, no official interest at all. George Carter, who has since died, never wrote about Davis. However, he did share the details of his interview with fellow Dallas reporter Earl Golz, who made them available to researchers several years later.[45]

The Warren Commission pointedly ignored all the Ruby-Davis leads, despite urgings by two staff members to have Ruby questioned about the matter. In 1978 the House Select Committee on Assassinations considered the Ruby-Davis-Oswald connection and reviewed the evidence at hand. The committee then arrived at a statement that was all too familiar: "Due to the limitations of time and resources, the committee did not thoroughly investigate Ruby's possible connection with Davis. It did not interview his wife or other relatives, nor did it determine exactly what Davis said about the assassination."[46]

The mystery of Thomas Eli Davis III will probably never be resolved. His third and last wife, whom he married after the events surrounding the assassination, has said that Davis once told her that he knew who killed President Kennedy. Whatever Davis knew, he took it with him when he died in 1973 at a remote rock quarry in Wise County, Texas. He was thirty-seven. Officials, who conducted no autopsy, said that Davis was electrocuted when he cut into a power line while trying to steal copper wiring from the quarry.[47]

The only hope for resolution of the Tommy Davis question lies in the restricted government files. The CIA states that it cannot find any records on Davis. The FBI still has documents on Davis, more than 200 pages at the least, that the bureau claims cannot be released for reasons of national security. As for State Department passport files, they are officially reported as lost. The only other hope might have been the military intelligence file on Davis. However, in 1980, the Army stated that it believed that the file had been routinely destroyed.[48]

Oswald's Finances

Parsimony was one of the most consistent characteristics of Lee Oswald's personality. He never had much money, and he scrupulously accounted for every cent that came his way, or that he spent. Because of this fact, a great deal of attention has been given by investigators and researchers to the examination of his finances. The aim has been to discover some source of funds that cannot be explained—evidence that would suggest Oswald's connection to someone not supposed to be in the picture. It can be demonstrated that at times around the period of his departure for the Soviet Union and his return, Oswald had extra money—money that has never been explained.[49]

Where did this extra money come from?

Any examination of Oswald's finances over the years has been complicated by the government's refusal to release Oswald's 1962 tax return. The issue of privacy has been raised to keep the return under wraps. This is particularly ludicrous when even a picture of Oswald's pubic hairs is in the record and available for inspection by the public. This secretiveness is in blazing contrast with the fact that the government readily released seven years of Jack Ruby's tax returns, even while Ruby was still alive.[50]

Researchers have long believed that Oswald's 1962 tax return would contain information revealing sources of income that are incompatible with the official version of events. There was no other conceivable reason for such compulsive secrecy about what should be so simple an issue.[51]

As late as 1984, the National Archives continued to honor the seal placed on the release of Oswald's 1962 tax return. However, in 1981 Oswald's widow, who had signed the joint return, asked the IRS and the National Archives for a copy. The IRS informed her that such returns are kept for a limited time only and that Oswald's return had been routinely destroyed. She eventually received a copy of the 1962 tax return from the National Archives. While she has not released it to the public, she did give a copy to Mary Ferrell, the indefatigable Dallas researcher.[52]

The most startling aspect of the return is that, on its surface, it appears to give complete support to the proposition that Oswald had no unexplained sources of income. The return appears to be in Oswald's handwriting, although the copy is barely legible. The amounts of income from his jobs are generally correct, showing his annual earnings at a little more than $1,350. Why the Warren Commission and subsequent officials have been so fussy about disclosure of the return remains unfathomable.[53]

There was but one oddity, which was plucked out by Mary Ferrell. Under the 1962 tax laws, Oswald, considering his dependents and income, should not have had to pay any income tax. Oswald should have been returned *all* the money withheld from him in his jobs that year. On this point, there is a discrepancy.[54]

Oswald did not note on his return the taxes withheld by one of his two employers, Leslie Welding Company. He thus missed out on about forty dollars in refunds, to which he was entitled. There is no explanation for this highly uncharacteristic incident, a mystery further compounded by a note Oswald sent along with his return. He wrote to the IRS: "I believe if you check your records to substaniate [sic] these figures you will find I should get a substantial refund."[55]

What all this means, beyond the obvious, remains a mystery.

Early Warnings

During the early hours of November 24, the sheriff's office and FBI officials in Dallas received almost identical warnings that suspected assassin Lee Harvey Oswald would be murdered as he was transferred to the county jail. The person who made the call stated that he was doing so with the hope there would be no gun battle, in which innocent police officers could be injured or killed. The FBI took the warning seriously and made sure that the Dallas police were informed. Consequently, there were some minor adjustments made regarding the transfer. But nonetheless, Oswald was shot to death, right on target, during the transfer. There was something eerily routine about the whole business, the manner of the warning as well as the execution. It is impossible to say if this is just another coincidence, but it becomes far more interesting in light of the strong official findings in recent years that Jack Ruby, Oswald's executioner, was a mob creature probably acting under orders.[56]

It has never made any sense that a group planning the murder of Oswald should telephone the police with an advance warning, even one including the specifics that are found in this instance. In 1984 a possible explanation for this oddity emerged.

Dallas Police Lieutenant Billy R. Grammer, then a rookie policeman, was working in the communications section of the police department in 1963. Lieutenant Grammer, who is highly respected among his colleagues, was on duty in the communications room on the Saturday night prior to Oswald's murder the next morning.

"Calls were coming in from all over the country," Grammer told the author in an interview, explaining that extra personnel from other departments had to be brought in to help man the switchboard. There were numerous crank calls from people threatening Oswald, as well as from people who wanted to offer information.

Late in the evening, one of the women on the switchboard received a call from a man who asked her to look around the room and to name the police officers who were there. He explained to her that he wanted to talk to someone that he knew. The woman began telling the caller the names of different men in the communications room. When she named Billy Grammer, the caller stated that he knew Grammer and that he wanted to speak to him.

Grammer, who had taken about fifty calls that evening, immediately felt that he recognized the voice that he heard, but he could not put a face or name with the voice. When Grammer asked the caller's identity, the man said, "I can't tell you that, but you know me." Grammer did not press the caller for his identity.

It was then that the caller stated, "We are going to kill Lee Harvey Oswald in the basement tomorrow." Even though Grammer had fielded all sorts of threats to Oswald earlier in the evening, he perked up when he heard this. The caller began speaking of details of the transfer plans that were not known even to Grammer. He motioned for one of his superiors to listen in on the call. Lieutenant Henry Putnam came in on the line and listened.

The caller described precise details of the transfer plans. As the man spoke, Grammer did not know whether or not the details were correct. The caller described the decoy vehicle that would be sent out with red lights and sirens and police escorts, only to be followed a little later with the real car containing Oswald. Grammer then pressed the man to say who he was, but the man insisted that it made no difference. "You're going to have to make some other plans," he warned, "or we're going to kill Oswald right there in the basement."

When the caller hung up, Grammer told Lieutenant Putnam, "I know I know who that is, but I cannot recall his name." Lieutenant Putnam told Grammer that, indeed, the caller did have solid inside information on the secret police plans for moving Oswald. He told Grammer to type up a report of the call for Dallas Police Chief Jesse Curry. Grammer did so, and he and Putnam together went to Curry's office, which was swarming with reporters, and handed the report to Curry. The FBI and sheriff's office were notified about the call.

After working most of the night, Billy Grammer went home and to bed. When his wife and children returned from church the next morning, Mrs. Grammer shook her husband awake to tell him that she had just heard on the radio that a man named Jack Ruby had murdered Oswald in the basement of the Dallas jail.

Grammer was stunned. He told his wife that he suddenly realized that it was Jack Ruby who had called the night before. The voice was familiar because he had met and talked to Ruby only a week or so earlier. The execution had come off just as the caller had said it would.

Grammer rushed to his television set and watched the replays of Ruby's execution of Oswald. He thought of the incident about a week earlier when he and another policeman were having a meal about 2:00 A.M. at an all-night restaurant not far from police headquarters. Ruby had come into the restaurant, spotted the two policemen, introduced himself, and sat down. In his typical fashion, he insisted on paying for the meal. Before that, Grammer had seen Ruby around town and usually spoke to him, but that occasion was the only time he ever sat down and talked to him.

A cautious, conservative man, Grammer could not be certain that the voice on the telephone had been that of Jack Ruby. When he got to the police station that day, he consulted with Lieutenant Putnam, who also had heard Ruby's voice in the past. While Putnam would not rule out that the voice was Ruby's, according to Grammer, he said that he simply did not have enough familiarity to be certain. That, too, was Grammer's opinion. Even today, he says that while he still is not absolutely certain, he tends to believe the caller was Ruby. (Lieutenant Putnam has since died.)[57]

It was some time later that two inspectors from the Dallas Police Department asked Grammer about the call. He described it, adding that he had submitted a report to Chief Curry. Even though Lieutenant Putnam supported Grammer's version of events, the report of the incident has never surfaced. The reported warnings that are in the record—the ones the police concede were ignored—did not include knowledge of secret inside plans for the transfer.[58]

Lieutenant Grammer points out that in view of the Warren Commission version of events, it never made any sense that Ruby would have made such a call.[59] Today, however, in view of what is known of Ruby—including the House Select Committee's strong feeling that he may have been acting under orders—it perhaps *does* make sense.[60] If Ruby were under the control of powers that ordered him to murder Oswald—powerful enough to make him do so—then there was but one way for Ruby to escape his duty. He would have to be thwarted in his effort.

The everlasting irony is that if the Dallas police had paid attention to this warning and others, Ruby's mission would have been thwarted— and Oswald might have lived. A thwarted Ruby could tell his masters that he did the best he could, and surely that would be better for him than what was inevitable if he were successful, or if he refused to try.

In retrospect, the warnings of Oswald's execution—particularly the one reported by Grammer that contained clear evidence of inside knowledge of police plans—must be taken seriously. If those warnings were as genuine as they appear, they are firm evidence of a conspiracy to silence Oswald. Such a conspiracy obviously suggests a wider conspiracy involving the manipulation of Oswald himself.

On November 9, 1963, in Miami, a wealthy right-wing extremist named Joseph A. Milteer informed a "friend" that the assassination of JFK was in the works. Milteer explained that Kennedy would be killed "from an office building with a high-powered rifle." He stated that "they will pick up somebody . . . within hours afterwards . . . just to throw the public off."[61]

As for *when* such an assassination would take place, Milteer stated, "It's in the works. . . . There ain't any countdown to it. We have just got to be sitting on go. Countdown, they can move in on you, and on go they can't. Countdown is all right for a slow, prepared operation. But in an emergency operation, you have got to be sitting on go."[62]

Milteer's "friend" was actually a police informant who was secretly taping the conversation. The chilling comments from Milteer were turned over by the Miami police to the Secret Service. There was a flurry of inquiries. The case was closed later that month. The information was not relayed to the Secret Service agents in charge of the President's Dallas trip. However, when the President visited

Miami a week after Milteer's statements, on November 18, his motorcade was canceled and he was transported by helicopter from the airfield to the site of his address. No official reason was ever given for this last-minute switch in plans.[63]

On November 22, Milteer telephoned his "friend," the informant, and told him he was in Dallas.*[64] Prior to the midday events, Milteer told the informant that Kennedy was expected in Dallas that day and would probably never again visit Miami.

Back in Florida the next day, Milteer again spoke to the informant. "Everything ran true to form," Milteer said. "I guess you thought I was kidding you when I said he would be killed from a window with a high-powered rifle." As for the arrest of a suspect, Milteer later told the informant not to worry about Lee Harvey Oswald's getting caught because he "doesn't know anything."[65]

On November 27 FBI agents asked Milteer about all these statements. He denied he had made any threats against the President. The matter was dropped. In the closing days of the Warren Commission, the FBI passed on the documents about Milteer. The matter is ignored in the Warren Report and its twenty-six volumes of published evidence.† Milteer died a few years later.[66]

Many other reports have been interpreted as early warnings, although none is quite as pointed as the Milteer matter.

One of the most haunting incidents concerns a prostitute called Rose Cheramie. Her life as a drug addict and an alcoholic would certainly render anything she said highly suspect, except for what happened to her on the night of November 20, 1963. She was found lying injured on a road near Eunice, Louisiana. Bruised and disoriented, she told state police that she had been traveling to Texas with two Latin men when, during a stop, they quarreled, and she was left stranded behind.[67]

What made her story of chilling significance, however, was her claim to police—two days *before* the assassination—to have listened as the two men discussed a plot, in which they were involved, to kill JFK in Dallas. Because of her condition, no attention was paid to what she said about a pending assassination. A few days later,

---

*Years later, the HSCA was not able to confirm that Milteer actually was in Dallas. It also failed to show that he was elsewhere.
†The story finally began to trickle out in 1967 in a Miami newspaper.

after President Kennedy was killed, the police lieutenant who first heard Miss Cheramie's story notified Dallas police about it. The police in Dallas stated that they were not interested, presumably because Oswald was already in custody and considered to be the lone gunman. Miss Cheramie's story became much more elaborate following the events in Dallas—involving associations with Ruby and Oswald—but it is her pre-assassination statements that are significant.[68]

There has been much speculation about the identity of the Latin men Miss Cheramie overheard discussing the plot. However, there has never been any concrete resolution of the matter. Miss Cheramie was killed two years later when she was run over while lying in the road near Big Sandy, Texas.[69]

In each of these cases—and there are others—there is nothing absolutely conclusive about the early warning. Each *could* be coincidence. But one must always return to this: police in any city in the United States, receiving a tip that a bank would be robbed under particular circumstances, would act on that tip. Why such indifference to tips about the death of a President? Or, in the case of Rose Cheramie, why was there no subsequent FBI investigation to find out the identities of the men she overheard?

Those are questions that, in this particular case, will probably never be answered.

Mysterious Deaths

Nothing has excited more attention from the public than the notion that an inordinate number of witnesses to various aspects of the assassination have died mysteriously. *Executive Action*, perhaps the most popular movie about the assassination, fueled this excitement with the following promotional hype:

> In the three-year period which followed the murder of President Kennedy and Lee Harvey Oswald, eighteen material witnesses died—six by gunfire, three in motor accidents, two by suicide, one from a cut throat, one from a karate chop to the neck, three from heart attacks, and two from natural causes.
> An actuary engaged by the London *Sunday Times* concluded

that on November 22, 1963, the odds against these witnesses being dead by February, 1967, were one hundred thousand trillion to one.[70]

There is no question that there have been deaths that are, indisputably, suspicious. Many have been chronicled in these pages, including those of David Ferrie, John Roselli, Roger Craig. However, there is quite a difference between an isolated mysterious death and what might be considered a pattern of such deaths.

The House Select Committee investigated the proposition and found it to have no merit. The HSCA case is convincing, particularly in that it traces the origin of the wide belief back to the actuarial findings of the distinguished *Sunday Times*. Indeed, that newspaper *did* report in its U.S. edition the astounding figures cited in *Executive Action* and in dozens of books and articles.[71]

The first step in the HSCA investigation was to ask the editors of *The Sunday Times* to provide the committee with the actuarial study upon which the findings were based. The response was sobering:

> Our piece about the odds against the deaths of the Kennedy witnesses was . . . based on a careless journalistic mistake and should not have been published. . . . There was no question of our actuary having got his answer wrong: It was simply that we asked him the wrong question. He was asked what were the odds against 15 named people out of the population of the United States dying within a short period of time, to which he replied—correctly—that they were very high. However, if one asks what are the odds against 15 of those included in the Warren Commission index dying within a given period, the answer is, of course, that they are much lower. Our mistake was to treat the reply to the former question as if it dealt with the latter—hence the fundamental error.[72]

The newspaper reported that the error was only in the edition that reached the United States. Subsequent editions of that date did not carry the error. The basic point, of course, is that the originator of the sensational report is on record as explaining why it is entirely without merit.[73]

The committee, however, attempted to make a valid actuarial study of the deaths. The first step was to establish a universe of individuals to which the individuals who died could be compared. Such an effort involved thousands of people in dozens of categories, and in the end it was impossible in any given category to be certain that all possibilities were included. The committee staff became convinced that the task was impossible.[74]

Nonetheless, these findings do not rule out the possibility of sinister deaths in specific cases relating to the assassination. However, the committee's work does put to rest the wide misperception that as an actuarial matter, there is any demonstrable pattern of an extraordinary increase in mortality among those with some connection to the assassination events or to the subsequent investigation.[75]

The French Connection

In early 1977 Mary Ferrell, the renowned Dallas archivist of assassination material, was making her way through a new carton of documents forced from the Central Intelligence Agency by a suit brought under the Freedom of Information Act. Thousands of pages faced her, many of them so apparently illegible that a casual observer would consider them hopeless to decipher. In addition to the acutely poor copies, many of the documents were so heavily obliterated with deletions that the few remaining words made little sense. In her twenty years of work on the JFK case, Mrs. Ferrell has never discarded a single document. On this occasion she was using bright lights and a huge magnifying glass as she pored over the papers. With these tools she could illuminate the passages. With a tiny ruler she measured the spaces in blacked-out areas, counting spaces, working toward filling in deleted words.[76]

One of the hundreds of pages she studied that afternoon was CIA Document 632–796. "It looked like a Xerox of a Xerox of a Xerox of a faint carbon copy," Mrs. Ferrell declares. "It was possibly the worst document I've ever seen in terms of legibility." As she began to make out the words, Mrs. Ferrell sensed nothing extraordinary about the document. It appeared to be a simple request from the French government to the U.S. government inquiring about the whereabouts of an individual. Mrs. Ferrell perked up as she coaxed the words from the page.[77]

The document, dated April 1, 1964, reported that the French intelligence service wanted help in locating one Jean Souetre, a French OAS terrorist considered a threat to the safety of French

President Charles de Gaulle. In fact, Souetre had been convicted in one instance for participation in an assassination attempt. The document noted that de Gaulle planned to visit Mexico. The French had approached the FBI's legal attaché in Paris to ascertain from U.S. authorities the last known whereabouts of Souetre, in order to ensure the safety of de Gaulle. Subsequent released documents would show that Souetre had allegedly been a suspect in an earlier assassination attempt on de Gaulle.[78]

But why should the French believe that U.S. intelligence would know the whereabouts of Souetre? The answer to that question is absolutely astounding.

The document asserted that Jean Souetre was in Fort Worth, Texas, on the morning of November 22, 1963. That morning President Kennedy also was in Fort Worth, where he made his first speech of the day in a parking lot outside his hotel. A few hours later, John F. Kennedy was in Dallas, where, at 12:30 P.M., he was assassinated. Also in Dallas that afternoon was Jean Souetre.[79]

Within forty-eight hours of Kennedy's death, according to the query from the French, Jean Souetre was picked up by U.S. authorities in Texas. He was immediately expelled from the United States. French intelligence wanted to ascertain whether he was expelled to Canada or to Mexico. The French also wanted to know why the U.S. authorities had expelled Souetre. The simple purpose was to ensure the safety of President de Gaulle on his pending trip to Mexico.[80]

One would expect that the U.S. officials who reportedly picked up Souetre in Dallas following the assassination might have an interest in a man of his reputation. A court document later described Souetre as "a trained and experienced terrorist and perfectly capable of murder." Evidently there *was* considerable interest by certain officials, but it was carefully concealed from the Warren Commission and, of course, from the public. There is no reason to believe the matter would have ever come to light were it not for the routine query from French intelligence. It seems highly unlikely that the CIA officer charged with deciding the release of secret papers in 1976 had even an inkling of the revelations contained in this particular document. The contents possibly would have never been known if the document had not fallen under the sharp eyes of Mary Ferrell.[81]

The precise manner of U.S. response to the presence of a French

416 • REASONABLE DOUBT

assassin in Dallas on November 22 is officially unknown. The CIA document asserts that the FBI told the CIA that it had nothing in its files on the subject. The accuracy of that assertion seems questionable. Some of the facts have been pieced together by Bernard Fensterwald, Jr., and Gary Shaw, who have been in hot pursuit of the French connection since learning of the document. Among their findings is that Souetre had developed contacts with radical right-wing fanatics in Dallas and New Orleans and that he was in touch with the anti-Castro Cubans in this country.[82]

The original document asserted that Jean Souetre also used the names Michel Roux and Michel Mertz. These were not ordinary aliases for, as it soon became clear, Roux and Mertz were themselves individuals quite separate from Souetre—and every bit as intriguing in their own connections.[83]

As researchers puzzled over which of the three might be the real man who was in the Dallas area on November 22, another wild card was shuffled into the game. It turned out that the real Michel Roux had been in Fort Worth visiting social acquaintances on November 22, 1963. The subsequent release of documents has shown that the FBI did know Roux was visiting Fort Worth, looked into it, and dismissed its significance. Records show that Roux entered the United States at New York on November 19, 1963, and left this country on December 6, 1963, at Laredo, Texas, on the Mexican border. Since Roux clearly was not expelled, this seemed to rule him out, at least in terms of being the Souetre mentioned in the CIA document.[84]

Nothing official is known about why U.S. authorities were prompted to pick up Jean Souetre following the assassination. It is known, however, that at least two inspectors for the INS were given urgent orders to pick up specific foreign nationals in Dallas in the immediate aftermath of the assassination. INS Inspector Virgil Bailey, responding to a request of top priority, picked up a Frenchman in Dallas whose name he does not remember. Another INS inspector, Hal Norwood, received two urgent telephone calls from Washington ordering him to pick up another foreigner. Before Norwood could respond, he learned that the foreigner in question had already been picked up. Norwood does not remember the man's name. No files on this matter ever reached the public or the Warren Commission. It has been pieced together by private researchers.[85]

In a brief filed in connection with a Freedom of Information Act suit for documents in this matter, Fensterwald and Shaw point to the reasons why French OAS terrorists would be logical suspects in the assassination of President Kennedy:

> The Algerian civil war . . . ended in 1962 when President de Gaulle granted independence to Algeria. This independence had been granted over the most violent terrorist opposition of the OAS, which consisted in large measure of French military deserters . . . who were violently opposed to de Gaulle's "giving away Algeria." The OAS were trained in all sorts of mayhem and killed thousands of French and Moslem Algerians. They made more than thirty attempts on the life of de Gaulle. . . . As they were *persona non grata* in France, they settled primarily in Spain, Portugal, Italy and South America. These were 2,000–3,000 well-trained and available-for-hire killers. In 1963, they were the pool from which one would hire a competent assassin.[86]

From his earliest days as a United States Senator, John F. Kennedy was publicly and passionately in favor of Algerian independence. Kennedy was vocal in his opposition to all OAS activities, and there was even a belief that Kennedy had been influential in de Gaulle's change of course from keeping French Algeria to granting its independence.[87]

Next to de Gaulle, Shaw and Fensterwald's legal brief asserts, the OAS hated Kennedy the most.[88]

Clearly, the OAS—like various other groups—possessed the classic ingredients necessary for murder. If more than thirty attempts could be made against de Gaulle, the argument goes, why not one against Kennedy?

The point is that Jean Souetre, or someone using his name, was in Fort Worth and Dallas at the times when Kennedy was in those cities on the day of the assassination. Michel Roux, another French army deserter—like Souetre—was paying a social visit on the fateful day, twenty-eight miles from Dallas in Fort Worth. Indications are that the United States picked up the man believed to be Souetre in Dallas that day and kicked him out of the country. No government agency has admitted to having dealt with Souetre on the given day. The FBI, however, does say that it interviewed Roux's hosts soon after that and became confident of Roux's innocence.[89]

There was one additional clue in the original CIA document: a reference to possible contact between Souetre and "a dentist named Alderson" in Houston, Texas. When researcher Gary Shaw tracked down Alderson, the story he heard was quite different from the official version—that the FBI knew nothing of the Souetre matter until the French query cited in the CIA documents of April 1, 1964.[90]

Dr. Lawrence Alderson, a respected dentist and longtime resident of Houston, insists that the FBI began tailing him immediately after the assassination and followed him incessantly for several weeks. Finally, the agents approached him for an interview. The subject was his relationship with Jean Souetre. Dr. Alderson is certain this took place no later than the end of December, and he cooperated fully.[91]

As a first lieutenant in the U.S. Army, Dr. Alderson was stationed in France in 1953. He met Jean Souetre, then a captain in the French Air Force. Dr. Alderson recalls Souetre as a political activist of the neo-Nazi persuasion. Dr. Alderson found Souetre to be an interesting, engaging man. They became friends. They did not see each other again after Alderson left France. For the next ten years they corresponded around Christmastime.[92]

Dr. Alderson insists that he told all this to the FBI, making clear that he had never seen Souetre in the United States. Dr. Alderson also asserts that the FBI agents told him that the bureau "had traced Souetre to Dallas a day before the assassination and then lost him." Alderson adds, "The FBI felt Souetre had either killed JFK or knew who had done it." He also recalls that an agent told him the bureau was trying to find out who had Souetre picked up that day and flown out of Dallas. The impression of the agent was that orders had come from Washington.[93]

There is no known evidence that the FBI contacted Alderson until *after* the receipt of the query from the French. Given Dr. Alderson's good reputation and the fact that he has no known motive for dissembling, his position cannot be automatically discounted.

Jean Souetre today is the public relations director of an elegant gambling casino in France, reportedly operated by the Mafia. In 1983 Souetre denied to a reporter that he was in Dallas in 1963 or that he had any special knowledge of JFK's death. He also denied that he knew Dr. Alderson. Though Dr. Alderson has not retained his correspondence with Souetre, he did produce a snapshot that he took of Souetre when they were together in France.[94]

Souetre, however, had one tip for the reporter. He suggested that a man he had not seen in many years, Michel Mertz, may have been using his name, that they were old enemies. Souetre claimed to have been informed that Mertz on occasion did use Souetre's name.[95]

This, of course, turned things quite upside down. Could it be that, really, Michel Mertz was the man expelled from Dallas and that *he* was using Souetre's name? In such a quagmire, it would not be surprising for French intelligence to have confused just who was using whose name that day.

Michel Mertz was different from the other two possibilities—Souetre and Roux. Mertz had longtime connections with French intelligence, working once as an infiltrator into the OAS. This connection sealed his enmity with the likes of Souetre. Mertz is even credited with once saving the life of President de Gaulle in an OAS terrorist attack. Meanwhile, he had already become involved in international narcotics dealing. In fact, Mertz is reputed to be a legend of sorts in the black world of espionage and narcotics smuggling. There is interesting speculation that Mertz could have had a connection with the CIA in some of its more nefarious activities.[96]

Which or how many of these three Frenchmen were in the Dallas area on November 22 is not nearly as important as the fact that U.S. authorities knew at least one was there and concealed the information from the Warren Commission. One of the few certainties supported by documents is that both the CIA and the FBI were aware of the French presence long before the commission wrapped up its work.[97]

Even more startling to contemplate is that someone, representing some authority in Washington, apparently authorized the pickup and deportation of a known French terrorist on the day of the assassination. Those agencies that could have been involved include the CIA, the FBI, the State Department, and the Immigration and Naturalization Service. Given all that is known, Dr. Alderson's version of events seems credible—suggesting a frantic investigation immediately after the assassination. Whatever documentation might prove this has never surfaced. All these years later, with a few slender exceptions, it is likely that that information remains entombed in the vaults of U.S. intelligence.[98]

Cubans on the Move

In 1960 Gilberto Policarpo Lopez, a young Cuban-American, moved from Havana to Florida. He claimed American citizenship through his mother and was an unusual refugee in one important respect. Unlike so many of those leaving Cuba, Policarpo was pro-Castro in his political beliefs. He even once got into a fistfight in Florida over his pro-Castro stance. He also became involved in the Fair Play for Cuba Committee. Back in Cuba, according to a Secret Service document disclosed under a Freedom of Information Act procedure in 1983, Policarpo's brother was active in Castro's military apparatus. That brother also had been sent to the Soviet Union for training.[99]

On November 17, 1963, Policarpo, then twenty-three, attended a meeting in Tampa at the home of a member of the local chapter of the Fair Play for Cuba Committee. President Kennedy was in Florida at the time of the meeting. Policarpo reportedly stated that he was awaiting a "go-ahead order" which would enable him to leave the United States and return to Cuba. He explained that he had been having difficulties acquiring permission to return to Cuba.[100]

The following facts are known about Policarpo's next moves:

On November 20, 1963, he was issued a Mexican tourist card in Tampa. Three days later, on the day after the Kennedy assassination, Policarpo crossed into Mexico from Texas at Nuevo Laredo. It was only hours after this border was reopened following its closure in the wake of the assassination. Policarpo's activities during the previous three days are not known.[101]

On November 25 Policarpo checked into the Roosevelt Hotel in Mexico City. On November 27 he flew to Havana. He was traveling on a Cuban "courtesy visa" and an expired U.S. passport. The flight carried a crew of nine. Policarpo was the only passenger.[102]

By March 1964 Policarpo's name had been put forward by a CIA source as having been "involved" in the Kennedy assassination. Still, the CIA never informed the Warren Commission of Policarpo's activities, which, at the heart, had rather striking parallels to what was eventually known of Lee Harvey Oswald's activities regarding Cuban politics.[103]

In 1976 the Senate Select Committee on intelligence activities suggested that Oswald may have been in contact with Policarpo's Tampa chapter of the Fair Play for Cuba Committee. The HSCA could find no supportive evidence for this allegation. In the end the HSCA called the Policarpo matter "a troublesome circumstance that the committee was unable to resolve with confidence."[104]

One of the most striking reports of odd activities around the time of the assassination concerns another flight from Mexico City to Havana. The Senate Select Committee first examined this in the midseventies and reported that on November 22 a Cubana Airlines flight from Mexico City to Cuba was delayed for five hours, awaiting a passenger. The airfield at Mexico City was particularly clogged that afternoon with Cuban diplomatic personnel.[105]

Finally, the passenger for whom the flight was being held arrived, aboard a private twin-engine plane, at 10:30 P.M. The passenger got onto the Cubana flight directly, without going through Customs, where he would have been identified. Once aboard, the mystery passenger entered the cockpit of the aircraft and remained there during the entire flight to Havana. No other passengers saw him well enough to be able later to identify him.[106]

The Senate Select Committee was understandably astonished that there evidently was no investigation into this matter, particularly since the information seemed to come from CIA sources. When asked about this oddity, the CIA informed the committee that there was "no information indicating that a follow-up investigation was conducted to determine the identity of the passenger and [there was] no further information on the passenger, and no explanation for why a follow-up investigation was not conducted."[107]

The HSCA looked into this incident two years later. Its investigation seemed to stop upon the discovery of discrepancies in the timing of the Cubana Airlines departure and the arrival of the private plane. This was information the earlier Senate committee had found to be unavailable. The HSCA concluded that because of these discrepancies, "the transfer did not occur." Official interest ended there.[108]

Today, the identity of the mystery passenger seems to have been established by documents disclosed under procedures of the Freedom of Information Act. The information in the documents, dated late 1963, is somewhat contradictory on several points, but the basic identification and other factors seem certain.[109]

The mystery passenger is believed to have been one Miguel Casas Saez. He was described by CIA sources cited in the documents as having been born in Cuba and as having been either twenty-one or twenty-seven at the time of the assassination. He was described as being of stocky build and short to medium height.[110]

According to a CIA document disclosed in 1983, Casas spoke the Russian language and was an ardent admirer of Raul Castro, the brother of the Cuban premier. He also was believed to be part of the Cuban intelligence service. The CIA document is based on two reports from its sources—one dated November 5, 1963, and the other November 15, 1963. Those reports on Casas were made prior to JFK's death. The document also shows that the CIA reviewed the reports on Casas soon after the assassination.[111]

Using the fictitious name of Angel Dominiguez Martinez, Casas was believed to have entered the United States at Miami in early November 1963. One source cited in the CIA documents reported that Casas was on a "sabotage and espionage mission" in the United States. That source described Casas in 1963 as "about 5' 5" tall, about 155 pounds, and about 26 to 28 years of age."[112]

The documents disclosed are somewhat confusing, with their contradictions and with the deletions made by the CIA prior to public release. However, it is clear that CIA sources in Cuba confirmed that Casas was in Dallas with two friends on November 22, 1963. He then returned to Cuba that day.[113]

One of the CIA's sources—described as "a responsible and serious person"—reported information from Casas's aunt. She apparently knew Casas as "Miguelito." According to the document, the aunt told the CIA source, "Miguelito has just arrived from the U.S., he was in Dallas, Texas, on the day of the assassination of Kennedy, but he managed to leave through the frontier of Laredo; already in Mexico a . . . plane brought him to Cuba. . . . You know that he is one of Raul's men . . . ; Miguelito is very brave, very brave!"[114]

One of the CIA documents, disclosed to researchers on November 21, 1983, reports that the CIA's Cuban source learned that "Casas had firing practice in militias and [is] capable of doing anything." That report, dated December 9, 1963, also states that the CIA source assigned two of his best men to investigate the Casas matter in Cuba. The CIA source states: "Investigation by two men confirms that Casas [was] indigent [and] poorly dressed prior [to] disappearing . . . for several weeks. [He] now dresses well, has much money, owns large amount [of] T-shirts, jackets and shoes, all American made."[115]

In these documents, with maddening finality, the information stops. One is left to guess *why* Casas was in Dallas, *how* he acquired his money, for what reason he was spirited back to Cuba from Dallas on November 22 with speed and efficiency that would be the envy of a head of state.

The Casas report is complemented by information from another CIA document, disclosed in 1983. It is conceivable that this report, if true, could explain how the two men who were reported to be with Casas got back to Cuba from Dallas. In late 1964 the CIA informed the FBI that it had received information from "an untested source." That source was reporting information received from "a well-known Cuban scientist," who was at the Havana airfield late on the afternoon of November 22, 1963. He observed an airplane with Mexican markings that landed and stopped on the far side of the field. The scientist saw two men "whom he recognized as Cuban gangsters" emerge from the plane and go into the back doors of the airfield's administration building, thus avoiding routine customs procedures. Curious, the scientist made inquiries about the flight and was informed that it had originated in Dallas.[116]

On the routing sheet that accompanies this document, someone at the CIA has scrawled, "I'd let this die its natural death, as the Bureau is doing." It was just as well, perhaps, because even by then—December 1964—the CIA source in Cuba who made the report was dead. That fact is noted in the report with no additional details.[117]

All these reported movements by Cubans around Dallas at the time of the assassination could be matters of coincidence. There are, of course, stranger instances of coincidence. What is unfortunate is that federal agencies and official investigators never followed these leads beyond the first convenient point where the pursuit could be abandoned. Areas such as this are practically impossible for private researchers to pursue. Thus the tantalizing trails stop, their promise eroded by official obfuscation and the passage of time.

The Lifton Thesis: Alteration of JFK's Body

The most sensational serious theory on the JFK case to emerge in recent years is that of David S. Lifton, whose book, *Best Evidence*, was published in 1980. It is a massive and intricate dissection of the events surrounding the removal of the President's body from the Dallas hospital and the subsequent autopsy at Bethesda Naval Hospital. Lifton posits that sometime between leaving Dallas and reaching Bethesda, the body was secretly altered in order to eliminate medical evidence of a shooter in front of the President. The purpose of the secret surgery asserted by Lifton was to make it appear that the bullets that killed the President all came from a common source, a gunman firing from behind the motorcade.

Lifton's book, which he worked on for fifteen years, was greeted with enormous skepticism and ridicule. But, as serious reviewers soon discovered, much of the evidence upon which Lifton built his case was indisputably correct. His basic research was solid, and the new factual information that he presented has stood up remarkably well. In the end, even though *Best Evidence* won few converts from the side of the official version, the book sold more than 100,000 copies in its hardcover edition and thus became the most successful of all recent books on the assassination.

Lifton's overall thesis is extremely difficult to accept, partly because it calls for the sort of grand conspiracy that would seem impossible to ever work. But there is no question that he has brought into sharp focus a number of critical discrepancies that cry out for official explanation. In the absence of explanations, one must consider those suggested by Lifton.

One of the most powerful aspects of Lifton's findings is that his witnesses, all reputable people who in some cases are, today, employed as they were in 1963, stand solidly behind their observations. In several cases, those witnesses had no idea that what they were saying conflicted with the official version of events. The simple fact is that Lifton was the first person to seek out certain people in Dallas and Bethesda, get their observations, and then compare those observations. Lifton has an impressive videotape of some of these witnesses in which the direct contradictions are graphically presented in a highly convincing manner.

For instance, a great deal of evidence is in the public record about the sort of coffin the President's body was placed in at the Dallas hospital before it was shipped to Washington. It was a heavy, bronze ceremonial coffin, said to be the best the local mortuary could provide on short notice. Numerous photographs show that coffin being lifted aboard Air Force One in Dallas and being removed from the plane at Andrews Air Force Base in Washington.[118]

At Bethesda Naval Hospital, however, men who unloaded the coffin from the ambulance at the rear of the hospital swear that the coffin was a cheap, standard military coffin, similar to the ones used to ship bodies back from Vietnam. Lifton presents other witnesses, perfectly credible, who state that the coffin from which the President's body was removed was a simple shipping casket.[119]

Just as puzzling are the contradictory accounts of how the President's body was wrapped. The standard version of events in Dallas, according to doctors and nurses who were present, is that the body was wrapped in sheets before being placed in the ceremonial coffin. Some recall that a plastic liner was placed under the body. Not a person in Dallas has said that the body was placed in a body bag.[120]

However, Lifton has come up with a witness at Bethesda who declares that he unzipped a standard military body bag when he removed the body from the shipping casket. Others at Bethesda insist that the President's remains were in a body bag. These witnesses are as vivid in their recollections as the Dallas witnesses who say the body was wrapped in sheets.[121]

In addition to these amazing discrepancies, some of Lifton's witnesses who removed the simple shipping coffin from an ambulance at the hospital's rear loading dock later saw the large ceremonial coffin being brought to the front door of the hospital moments after the arrival of Robert Kennedy and the President's widow. An X-ray technician, who was carrying X rays he had already taken of the President's body, was walking through the hospital lobby when he saw the arrival of the Kennedy entourage. One witness recalls asking about this and being told it was for security purposes.[122]

Lifton believes that actually the President's body was in the simple shipping casket and that it was removed from Air Force One from the front right side and taken away by helicopter. However, no particular attention was being paid to anything other than the removal of the ceremonial coffin from the left rear of the plane. Mrs. Kennedy was with that coffin, and she and Robert Kennedy rode with it in the ambulance to Bethesda.[123]

The first question to come to mind is *when* could the body have been removed from the ceremonial coffin? Part of the lore of the events surrounding the assassination is that Jacqueline Kennedy never left the side of the coffin from the time her husband's body was placed in it at Parkland Hospital until it was delivered to Bethesda Naval Hospital. However, Lifton points out that Mrs. Kennedy *did* leave the rear of the plane on one known occasion: the swearing in of Lyndon Johnson as president. Lifton's theory is that during those few minutes, the body was removed from the ceremonial coffin and placed in a body bag. It was quickly stowed in another part of the plane. Later, the body bag was transferred to the helicopter. (Indeed, the autopsy photographs show numerous scratches on the President's back that conceivably could be explained by hastily moving the body around in this fashion.)[124]

Lifton does not have a concrete theory about where the body bag containing JFK's corpse was taken, but he believes it was during that period that the surgical alterations were made. He figures there was a period of about thirty minutes when such work could be done, and he believes Walter Reed Army Hospital is the most logical place for the body to have been taken.[125]

Lifton's theory is buttressed by a comparison of what the autopsy doctors noted as compared to what the Dallas doctors have said they saw a few hours earlier. (Some of these differences are described in Chapter 3.) On the surface, those differences appear as striking as the ones concerning the coffins and the manner in which the body was wrapped.[126]

Lifton's clearest piece of documentary evidence is the report written by two FBI agents who were present at the autopsy. Their job was to record what transpired, and Lifton posits that there is no evidence in their report of their making their own interpretations of events. He believes that the agents simply recorded what they heard the doctors say, and what they watched the doctors do.[127]

That FBI account, known as the Sibert-O'Neill report, described the condition of the President's head at the beginning of the autopsy. The report states that it was "apparent" that there had been "surgery of the head area, namely, in the top of the skull." This assertion is in stark contradiction with the undisputed fact that no surgery whatsoever was done on the President's head at the Dallas hospital.[128]

Lifton acknowledges that the statement could be in error—a possibility that he concedes would deserve more serious consideration if that were the *only* suggestion of surgery. But, he contends, it must be viewed as a complementary element that is supportive of all the other evidence that he believes suggests surgical alteration. That FBI statement on "surgery" is a cornerstone of Lifton's case.[129]

There is wide support today, from a variety of legitimate sources, that enormous discrepancies exist between the wounds the Dallas doctors and nurses saw and the official descriptions put into the record by the autopsy doctors. In 1981, for example, the *Boston Globe*, in the course of investigating these discrepancies, interviewed fourteen of the doctors and nurses who saw the President's body at Parkland Hospital. The *Globe* found that five of the doctors and three of the nurses were certain in their recall of a large wound in the right rear of the President's head. No such wound is visible in the autopsy photographs, which show a massive wound in the right side of the President's head. The presence of *that* wound finds virtually no support among the Dallas hospital personnel.[130]

In terms of actual measurements, the head wound was reported in Dallas to be about 35 square centimeters in size, while the autopsy diagram done by the autopsy doctors shows it to be 170 square centimeters—about five times larger. In Dallas, the brain was reported to be protruding from the head wound, but the condition was quite different when the body reached Bethesda. Two hospital technicians at Bethesda—one of whom actually opened the coffin—assert that at that point the opening in the head was massive and that the cranium was empty. The brain was gone. This condition, Lifton points out, suggests a standard postmortem surgical procedure that could explain the FBI's report of "surgery of the head area, namely, in the top of the skull." Under normal conditions, removal of the roof of the head to get to the brain would be a routine autopsy procedure.[131]

It is not surprising that Lifton's theory has been vehemently denounced by various officials who were involved in the events surrounding the JFK autopsy. Dr. James J. Humes, the chief autopsy doctor, told this author in 1984: "[Lifton's] book is so ridiculous that it's incredible." However, Dr. Humes refused to discuss details of issues raised in the book.[132]

Brigadier General Godfrey McHugh, an Air Force aide to President Kennedy who was with the casket for much of its journey, told the *Boston Globe* that Lifton's book is "absolutely absurd. It's full of lies and false implications."[133]

Notwithstanding these official denunciations, Lifton builds a powerful case that the President's body was taken somewhere else while the Kennedy family participated in a ceremonial entourage to Bethesda Naval Hospital. Lifton's evidence is equally strong on the point that *something* happened to the wounds on the body between Dallas and Bethesda. However, his sinister interpretation of what might have happened does not have the strong supportive evidence found for his basic points.

It does not seem unreasonable that the Secret Service and other powerful elements in the government might have felt an overwhelming necessity to examine the body for evidence at the soonest possible moment. At that early hour, many high government officials feared that the assassination could have been the result of an international plot that, perhaps, would not stop with the killing of President Kennedy. It does not seem unreasonable that these circumstances could have coalesced into an overriding concern for national security that demanded the President's body be placed on an autopsy table as soon as humanly possible—without awaiting the folderol of transporting the body through the streets with the family and public at hand. Moreover, it does not seem unreasonable that certain security people in the government were appalled that the official autopsy was going to be conducted at the whim of the family and by Navy brass with pitifully little experience in forensic pathology.

Lifton builds a powerful case for the possibility of some sort of postmortem work *prior* to the blue-ribbon autopsy. Whether the motive behind that work was necessarily sinister is quite a different question. Sure answers to that question will not be known until people who possess the truth decide to divulge more of their secrets.

14· AFTERMATH AND PERSPECTIVE

The seeds of neglected evidence sown across the landscape in the wake of the assassination have matured into a jungle of powerful contradictions. Nourished by solid information, each promising theme contends with other themes. This entanglement has become so impenetrable that no single theory, no final answer, can break free to stand unchallenged as a solution to modern America's most momentous crime. There is too much that is not known, too many facts that remain hidden, for a clear answer to emerge.

More than two decades later, this jungle continues to grow, drawing its nourishment from the slivers of new information tossed to the public by the custodians of the country's treasury of secrets. Millions of Americans, coolly cynical about the official version, believe that concealed somewhere in those vaults of U.S. intelligence is evidence that might finally reveal the truth.[1] However, the prospect for the emergence of that truth is not promising. The most dismaying irony of all is that if the truth were to be laid bare in the heart of the jungle, few would recognize it or accept it. The deep doubt felt by millions around the world may have locked even the most receptive minds into a skepticism that is beyond fracture.

The assassination of a president is, of course, a numbing tragedy. In the JFK case, the tragedy spawned a scandal of remarkable endurance. While the truth of the matter remains elusive, a great historical lesson is evident. Through this doubt and skepticism, nurtured in the relative innocence of the early sixties, Americans may have learned that their institutions—all of them—are subject to the precise weaknesses of the individuals who make them up. All the individual deceits—the denial of a valid witness's credibility, the failure to pursue a legitimate lead, the shading of facts to fit a mold, the false classification of a document, the destruction of even the tiniest piece of evidence—compound to form what must be called, in this case, a national disgrace.

Of all the gross deficiencies on the part of the government agencies and the Warren Commission, one ingredient is common at each juncture: a flagrant disregard for the truth. This fundamental flaw is at the core of every major debacle in the investigation of the JFK assassination. That flaw, with all its black ramifications, is the foundation upon which rests the current historical impasse.

Evidence is overwhelming that Lee Harvey Oswald was someone's tool in a conspiracy to murder the President of the United States. Regardless of the origin of the conspiracy, it was a political act of such magnitude that it changed the course of history. A number of nefarious elements, both domestic and foreign, benefited from the destruction of the Kennedy administration. In this case it is important to understand that the greatest beneficiaries of this political change are not necessarily the prime suspects in bringing it about. Above all, it is useless, if not foolish, to attempt to argue conclusively in favor of a particular theory. While some theoretical answers may appear more promising than others, such speculation is purely an academic exercise. Too much pertinent evidence is either missing, destroyed, or languishing under seals of national security. Hope for a final answer must be held in abeyance until the day when there is full access to those secrets.

One judgmental observation is offered to anyone considering the events described in these pages. The existence of a conspiracy to murder President Kennedy does not automatically mean that the subsequent investigative debacle was a part of that conspiracy. It *may* have been, of course, and many critics believe that it was. It seems eminently more reasonable to believe that once the gunfire was over in Dealey Plaza, the natural forces of bureaucratic ineptitude instantly came into play. As officials scurried either to demonstrate their efficiency or to conceal the deficiencies of their own agencies, they perhaps set the first threads in the cover-up that led to the tangled web. The intensity of these natural forces would have been greatly heightened if, as so much evidence suggests, Lee Oswald had *any* sort of operational connection to a branch of U.S. intelligence. However, that connection, if it existed, would not necessarily mean complicity of the government in the murder of its

President—the denouement so favored by some of the theorists.[2]

These natural tendencies were enhanced markedly by an over-whelming concern, apparently genuinely felt in most cases, that it was for the good of the country to get the whole awful business into the past as quickly as possible. In addition, the family of the slain President—including his powerfully influential brother, the Attorney General—accepted the Warren Commission version without a public hint of dissent, even though it is known today that Robert Kennedy and so many others in power had agonizing doubts.[3]

What, then, should be done now?

Another official investigation into the JFK assassination is unpromising for the very reasons the others have failed. There have been eight official inquiries into various aspects of the assassination—the Warren Commission, the original Texas inquiry, the Garrison investigation, the Rockefeller Commission, the Senate Intelligence Committee, as well as public hearings conducted by Congressman Don Edwards and, later, by Congresswoman Bella Abzug. The last investigation, that of the House Select Committee on Assassinations in 1978, arrived at a conclusion of probable conspiracy. Some of its leads—in addition to the quirky acoustics evidence—were turned over to the Justice Department and FBI with a request that they be developed. The Justice Department examined the acoustics evidence and dismissed its significance. A long promised report on the investigation of other leads still had not been released as this book went to press.[4]

There is little reason to believe that the Justice Department would respond any more positively to another, similar finding reached after yet another Congressional investigation. Anyone who speaks to high FBI officials about these matters will quickly sense an attitude of loyalty toward the original findings. Rather than any expression of interest in new leads on the part of the FBI, there appears to be the firm pride that nothing so far has succeeded in shaking the bureau's original conclusions, those embraced a few hours after the death of the President. Any hope that this attitude would change under FBI Director William Webster has long since evaporated. Webster has stated that he considers the bureau's JFK investigation to be "very intensive and thorough." He knows of no evidence that would cast doubt on the original conclusions.[5]

Some have suggested that the appointment of a Special Prosecutor to pursue the case might be an answer. Again, the whole political process would be involved—a process that carries pointed deficiencies when attempting to examine secret workings within government agencies.

One suggestion, advanced to this author by James H. Lesar, seems more reasonable. A lawyer who has devoted much of his career to the pursuit of answers in the JFK case, Lesar suggests the creation of a special unit of the Justice Department with specific funding from Congress. It would be fashioned after the office of Special Investigations, created in 1979 to expedite the handling of reports on Nazi war crimes. That unit serves as a repository for information on Nazi criminals. Despite some internal bickering, it has operated with relative efficiency and notable achievement. Funded directly by Congress, the unit's very autonomy from the political process has allowed it to move with relative expediency in its pursuits to bring about fresh revelations and specific recommendations—in its case, the identification and deportation of Nazi war criminals living in the United States.[6]

If such a unit were established, its function would include the continuing collection and analysis of information on the JFK case, as well as the pursuit of leads considered insignificant by the FBI and the Justice Department. The unit would have authority to examine classified documents and to subpoena and question officials and other witnesses about the case. It could recommend specific prosecutions. The best JFK files and indexes in the country are today in the private hands that created them. Those owners have begun to consider how they might bequeath their priceless stores of information, and the possibilities are that the material will be scattered and maintained under perilously unreliable circumstances. Such a unit, established properly, would be the natural repository for such information—a function that somehow has been abrogated by a government smugly satisfied with its sealed case.

There is no dearth of highly competent citizens who could serve on such a unit—people whose long years of dedication to the case are proof of their commitment to finding the truth. Of the various possibilities for specific action, none makes more sense than this relatively modest proposal.

In the beginning, as the Warren Commission closed down business, it preserved its files for future generations. The mass of material was to be housed at the National Archives, under seal, for seventy-five years. The material was so disorganized and ungainly that it was not measured by pieces of paper but by volume: 357 cubic feet. That stockpile did not include physical evidence in the case, such as clothing and weapons. That material, initially, remained in the custody of the FBI.[7]

There was nothing unusual or nefarious about these procedures. The seventy-five-year seal was a general policy often applied to material emanating from an investigative body. There was nothing unreasonable about the Warren Commission's statement on the matter, which appeared in the final paragraph of the foreword of the report: "The Commission is committing all of its reports and working papers to the National Archives, where they can be permanently preserved under the rules and regulations of the National Archives and applicable Federal law."[8]

Soon, however, there was a public clamor for access to the material, a clamor that was rather promptly heeded in high places. Chief Justice Earl Warren, by whose name the presidential commission was known, was explicit in his stated position that the intent of the commission was to make "the fullest possible disclosure" to the public. He approved a plan by which the material could be partially released before the end of the seventy-five-year embargo.[9]

In a letter to the Attorney General, Nicholas deB. Katzenbach, in April 1965, Chief Justice Warren set out the commission's feeling that it would be necessary for the agency that originated a particular document to decide when it could be released without damaging innocent people or national security. The White House approved this recommendation, which had the concurrence of all pertinent agencies with the exception of one: the CIA. That agency not only urged the continuation of the seventy-five-year seal but recommended "that at the end of the seventy-five year period another security appraisal be made before such documents are disclosed."[10]

Thus began the odyssey by critics and researchers to the keepers of the secrets, trying to wrench their way into these materials. It is a misconception that the National Archives has capriciously withheld large numbers of documents. Most decisions on the release of material have rested with the agencies that originated the documents in question. In fact, Marion Johnson, the archivist who has been in charge of the Warren Commission materials practically from the start, and his former assistants, Michael Leahy and Mike Simmons, who is now deceased, earned general praise from researchers, who found them unfailingly helpful and courteous.[11]

It is impossible to give a precise report on what has been released from the National Archives. Of the original 357 cubic feet of sealed material, all but 12 cubic feet have been released to the public. Obviously, the most sensitive and important information in the entire case could be in that small remaining portion of material. On the other hand, a large percentage of that remaining material possibly is information with little relevance to the case—information that could be embarrassing to individuals, or actually could compromise a sensitive intelligence source.[12]

The figures, however, are virtually irrelevant because of the extensive amount of "sanitizing" done by the agencies to the documents that have been released. Even though a document with heavy deletions may be officially "released," most of the information in that document is no more in the public domain than it ever was because of the deletions. Thus, it is impossible to offer a relevant assessment on how much Warren Commission material—including pertinent documents from the CIA, FBI, and other agencies—has reached the public.

An unknown factor of far greater significance is the sure knowledge that the CIA and the FBI withheld thousands of pages of pertinent information from the Warren Commission in the first place. The most flagrant example of this was the complete withholding of all information regarding the efforts by President Kennedy's administration to assassinate Fidel Castro and to overthrow the Cuban government, thus hiding a powerful possible motive. Other good examples of this withholding of information are the documents on Thomas Eli Davis III and Jean Souetre, to cite only those cases examined a few pages earlier. Other concealed information included the FBI's complete files on Jack Ruby, as well as the Army file on Oswald that was finally destroyed. Such information, denied to the Warren Commission, is therefore completely separate from the rules governing disclosure of documents held at the Archives. For years there was no way for the public to pursue documents in this category, and there was little to go on but the mere suspicion that they existed.[13]

In 1966 Congress enacted the Freedom of Information legislation. With this tool researchers were armed with the potential ability to pry out new information pertaining to the JFK case, under certain reasonable restrictions. In practice it didn't work quite that way. Through almost sheer obstinacy on the part of the agencies, practically nothing was released under this law until Congress strengthened it in 1974. Following that, the only releases beyond absurdly classified documents, such as newspaper clippings, were the results of costly lawsuits brought against the agencies.[14]

As the different agencies began to go through the motions of compliance, the censors' deletions became so pervasive that the released documents were often of little practical use. The copies provided were so nearly impossible to read that in one early case U.S. District Judge John Sirica rejected an offering of illegible documents from the CIA and ordered the agency to produce copies that could be read.[15]

It is difficult to escape the suspicion that such impediments were the purposeful manipulation by the various agencies as the material was prepared for release. There was even a mocking quality about the "release" of documents in which every word was deleted, or the continuing release of newspaper articles that some agency had seen fit to withhold from the public. (A favorite example of this among researchers is a newspaper article in which the name of an FBI agent has been deleted from the text.[16])

Ostensibly, most deletions pertained to sensitive sources, innocent people, or national security. No one doubts that in some cases these exclusions were fair and proper, even though it is difficult to imagine how very much twenty-year-old material could fall into that category. Few have confidence that there were not numerous cases in which these lofty banners were flown to conceal information that would either demonstrate some impropriety or foolishness on the part of the agency involved, or reveal something about the case that would throw new kinks into the official version.

One of the most frustrating aspects of the struggle for informative documents is the discovery that much material pertinent to the JFK case is filed in ways unconnected to the assassination. In the instance of the Cubans Policarpo and Casas, or Thomas Eli Davis III, most of the documents would never have been produced if researchers had not been meticulous in the tedious process of requesting files on individual names.[17]

It was not until 1978 that researchers confirmed that the material filed at FBI headquarters on the JFK case did not include all the information that originated in FBI field offices around the country. (In an unrelated case, a federal judge found that an FBI field office had four to five times more material on any particular subject than is sent to Washington. In the words of the judge, the field-office material is "the stuff of primary research.") Thus, all investigative records in the JFK case handled by the FBI in New Orleans or Dallas would not necessarily have been sent to FBI headquarters in Washington. In 1983 a letter written by FBI Director William Webster was made public in a Freedom of Information lawsuit. Webster noted that the Dallas and New Orleans field offices alone generated 170,000 pages of documents.[18]

The net result of this practice was that thousands of documents of potential relevance to researchers were still buried in the FBI field offices—not at FBI headquarters, where most research efforts had been focused.

Finally, in 1978, this field-office material began to become available under Freedom of Information disclosures. Somewhat later it was discovered that FBI field offices "routinely" purge their files. One of the more blatant examples to surface so far—an instance in 1983—is the destruction of records in the New Orleans field office pertaining to the activities of David W. Ferrie.[19]

The great hope of researchers and critics in terms of the release of documents was the House Select Committee on Assassinations. Hundreds of thousands of pages of investigative records were turned over to the committee by various agencies. Thousands of pages of investigative material were also generated by the committee itself. One of the most grating ironies in the whole case is what happened to that treasure trove of documents. In the end, the Select Committee sealed them in the National Archives, not to be released for fifty years. The only documents to reach the public were those routine few included in the committee's published material. Thus, the great hope of the critics for getting these massive CIA and FBI files into the public record was lost.*[20]

Veteran critic Paul L. Hoch has written: "The irony of the situation . . . is clear: the Congressional investigators who broke the JFK case wide open and reversed the official government verdict have left us with more material withheld than ever before."[21]

---

*Some of those documents, heavily censored, have been pried loose in a lawsuit against the FBI brought under the Freedom of Information Act. Mark Allen, a young Washington lawyer, has been in the forefront of this effort.

G. Robert Blakey, chief counsel to the HSCA, has stated that his committee received everything of significance pertaining to the JFK case that could be found in the records of the CIA and the FBI. During the course of a 1981 Freedom of Information lawsuit, an internal CIA memorandum was placed in the public record. It is an account of a 1979 visit made to CIA headquarters by Blakey to review the final plans for the handling of the CIA's JFK material. The memorandum contains astounding revelations.[22]

According to the internal memorandum, Blakey was at the agency for an hour. The memorandum conveys the following information, illustrating what must be key deletions: "Mr. Blakey examined only that material held [deletion]. He apparently did not go elsewhere within the Agency, [deletion], to examine their holdings." This clearly suggests that Blakey did not inspect holdings that were housed at some other place in the building. One presumes that Blakey was not made aware of these other holdings, but the wording on this point is ambiguous.[23]

In all, according to the memorandum, Blakey "spent only twenty or thirty minutes discussing and examining the contents of some fifteen safes of Agency materials." The contents of nine four-drawer safes had been examined earlier by HSCA staff members.[24]

Of this material, it is likely that the most significant information was contained in the eight drawers of these safes, which housed the 201 file of Lee Harvey Oswald. The CIA memorandum flatly states: "Oswald's 201 file was not completely reviewed by HSCA staff members."[25]

In summary, the CIA memorandum states that sixteen file drawers of material were *not* reviewed by the HSCA.[26] If this CIA account is true, public cynicism about a "genuine" investigation of the JFK case is more than warranted when so many CIA documents—certainly tens of thousands of pages—went unexamined by those charged with carrying out the investigation.

As for the assertion that the committee failed to review the complete 201 file on Oswald, Blakey told the author in 1984, "My memory is that we did it. If the CIA says we did not, its records are incomplete."[27]

Whatever the actual facts are about the 201 file, the prime significance is that the CIA has placed itself flatly on record as claiming it has sixteen file drawers of material on the JFK case that have never been seen outside of the agency. The CIA specifies that this mass of material includes information on Oswald, the man so many suspect had some operational connection with a branch of U.S. intelligence. The presence of these tens of thousands of secret pages, unexamined by anyone other than the agency that originated them, must stand as a monument to the appalling obdurateness of the CIA.[28]

Since 1978 some documents have been pried out of the CIA by Freedom of Information procedures and by litigation. In 1982 the agency stated that it had released 1,655 documents in part and in whole. A spokesman stated that 513 documents remained classified.[29] Each document could contain anywhere from one page to hundreds of pages, so the significance of these figures is unknown. Moreover, it is highly likely that a considerable divergence of opinion would exist over just which documents of the CIA pertain to the JFK case and which do not.

In spite of these figures, it is impossible to be precise about the numbers of documents pertaining to the Kennedy assassination that are still withheld by various agencies. In addition to the FBI and the CIA, the Secret Service, the State Department, and the Immigration and Naturalization Service have documents that have not been released. The Defense Intelligence Agency claims it has released everything it has on the case, but certain Oswald records are known to have been destroyed by Army intelligence. Indications are that upward of one-half million pages remain under wraps.[30]

Hardly a piece of useful evidence has come willingly from the government coffers. Almost all of it has been fought for by researchers and lawyers who refused to accept the government's simplistic explanations for withholding documents. Their greatest weapon has been the Freedom of Information Act—passed into law for the very purpose it has served in these matters.

In view of the extraordinary success of this law, it should not come as a surprise that serious moves are under way to change those parts of the law that have yielded the most significant results.[31] If the government succeeds in gutting the Freedom of Information Act by getting the rules changed to fit its purposes, any hope of closing in on the truth about the Kennedy assassination will be seriously impeded.

Decades from now, when the subject has become an esoteric matter for parlor debate, the truth may emerge. However awful that truth may be, there will be no sense of passionate public outrage.

Many people will probably recall that their grandparents, long since gone, used to talk about the Kennedy assassination, and more often than not said they were sure the official version was wrong. The only logical hope for keeping the case alive is, perhaps, in the creation of a special unit modeled after the one designed to expose Nazi war crimes. It would be ironic to deny creation of such a body for a case so widely controversial as the JFK murder while funds are committed to seek justice for crimes of a war that was fought forty years ago and squarely won.

Four out of five Americans do not believe the government version of the JFK assassination.[32] Implicit in this skepticism is a feeling that the public has been deceived by those vested with the special trust to conduct national affairs out of the sight and reach of the ordinary citizenry. Perhaps the ultimate deceit is found in the words that greet any citizen who is permitted to enter the main lobby of the Central Intelligence Agency. Etched on the south wall are words put there while Warren Commission member Allen Dulles was director of Central Intelligence. Drawn from the Bible, the passage is a familiar one:

"And ye shall know the truth and the truth shall make you free."[33]

It is grossly sanctimonious for officials to lash out at the researchers and critics who have fought for the truth in this tangled case. Those citizens, after all, are the ones who have kept alive this passionate quest for facts about the assassination of one of America's most popular presidents. If a responsible effort in this direction had been made two decades ago, there would not today be such a corruption of historical integrity, nor such a resonance of reasonable doubt.

Notes

Abbreviations

CD   Warren Commission Document. To be found in the National Archives.

HSCA   House Select Committee on Assassinations volumes. Listed in bibliography as U.S. House. Select Committee on Assassination. *Investigation of the Assassination of President John F. Kennedy: Appendix to Hearings Before the Select Committee on Assassinations*, and *Investigation of the Assassination of President John F. Kennedy.*

HSCR   House Select Committee on Assassination report. Listed in bibliography as U.S. House. Select Committee on Assassination. *Report of the Select Committee on Assassinations: Findings and Recommendations.*

WC   Warren Commission volumes. Listed in bibliography as U.S. President's Commission on the Assassination of President John F. Kennedy. *Investigation of the Assassination of President John F. Kennedy.*

WR   Warren Report. Listed in bibliography as U.S. President's Commission on the Assassination of President John F. Kennedy. *Report of the President's Commission on the Assassination of President John F. Kennedy.*

Complete facts of publication for all books cited in the notes can be found in the selected bibliography beginning on page 524.

Introduction

1. HSCR, pp. 230–31.
2. Ibid., p. 232.
3. *Washington Post*, November 21, 1983.
4. Ibid., November 20, 1983.
5. *The New York Times*, November 14, 1983.
6. Ibid., November 23, 1983.
7. Ibid., December 27, 1983.

8. Herbert S. Parmet, *JFK*, p. 238; Arthur M. Schlesinger, Jr., *A Thousand Days*, p. 244.
9. Harris Survey, April 2, 1985; *Washington Post*, November 20, 1983.
10. Gaeton Fonzi, "Who Killed JFK?", *The Washingtonian*, November 1980.
11. *Public Papers of the Presidents of the United States*, 1962, pp. 162–63.
12. Ibid., p. 163.

1: The Stage

1. WR, pp. 19, 48–49, 108–12; Abraham Zapruder film; XXI WC, p. 548; XVIII WC, p. 758.
2. WR, pp. 49–50, 52; Sylvia Meagher, *Accessories After the Fact*, pp. 3–5; Carl Oglesby, *The Yankee and Cowboy War*, pp. 93–94; Anthony Summers, *Conspiracy*, pp. 37, 47; VI WC, p. 309; "The Day Kennedy Died," *Newsweek*, December 2, 1963; HSCR, p. 41; XVIII WC, p. 759; Zapruder film; interview with Doris Nelson, director of emergency room, Parkland Memorial Hospital, November 1982.
3. Interview with Nelson, November 1982; WR, pp. 53–55; John K. Lattimer, *Kennedy and Lincoln*, p. 148; Stephen Goode, *Assassination!*, p. 15.
4. WR, pp. 49, 53–57; interview with Nelson, November 1982; Jim Bishop, *The Day Kennedy Was Shot*, pp. 196, 220; United Press International and *American Heritage* Magazine, comps., *Four Days*, p. 25; *The New York Times*, November 23, 1963.
5. WR, p. 4; Bishop, *The Day Kennedy Was Shot*, pp. 222–24; Lattimer, *Kennedy and Lincoln*, p. 153; Kitty Kelley, *Jackie Oh!*, pp. 215–16.
6. XVIII WC, pp. 798–800; Michael Kurtz, *Crime of the Century*, pp. 11, 76; VI WC, p. 130; WR, pp. 79, 81; David W. Belin, *November 22, 1963: You Are the Jury*, pp. 209–10; David S. Lifton, *Best Evidence*, p. 360.
7. WR, pp. 58–59, 484–85; *Congressional Quarterly Almanac, 1965*, 89th Cong., 1st sess., vol. 21, p. 582; spokesman for Attorney General's Office, Austin, Texas; William Manchester, *The Death of a President*, pp. 298–99, 325; Lattimer, *Kennedy and Lincoln*, pp. 154–55; Summers, *Conspiracy*, p. 42; Peter Dale Scott, Paul L. Hoch, and Russell Stetler, eds., *The Assassinations: Dallas and Beyond*, p. 19.
8. WR, pp. 46, 60; Scott, Hoch, and Stetler, *The Assassinations*, p. 17; "President Kennedy Is Laid to Rest," *Life*, December 6, 1963; UPI and *American Heritage*, *Four Days*, pp. 45, 99.

9. J. Gary Shaw with Larry R. Harris, *Cover-up*, p. 8; Mark Lane, *Rush to Judgment*, p. 399; HSCR, pp. 41–42, 87; Meagher, *Accessories*, pp. 9, 27; Harold Feldman, "Fifty-one Witnesses: The Grassy Knoll," *The Minority of One*, March 1965; Scott, Hoch, and Stetler, *The Assassinations*, p. 187; WR, p. 61; XXI WC, p. 548; XVIII WC, pp. 758–59; Summers, *Conspiracy*, pp. 53, 56; Jesse Curry, *J.F.K. Assassination File*, p. 105.

10. Shaw with Harris, *Cover-up*, pp. 5, 14; Josiah Thompson, *Six Seconds in Dallas*, p. 27; WR, pp. 71, 72, 76; *Dallas Morning News*, April 5, 1981; Meagher, *Accessories*, pp. 9, 16; HSCR, pp. 88–89.

11. WR, p. 70; Meagher, *Accessories*, p. 11; II WC, p. 234; VI WC, pp. 328–29, 338, 371; XXII WC, pp. 642, 683.

12. Shaw with Harris, *Cover-up*, p. 82.

13. WR, pp. 143–44, 155; XXIII WC, pp. 843–44; Summers, *Conspiracy*, p. 83; Meagher, *Accessories*, p. 10.

14. WR, pp. 156, 166–67; XXIII WC, pp. 857, 860–61; Summers, *Conspiracy*, p. 83.

15. WR, pp. 176, 178; Summers, *Conspiracy*, p. 84.

16. WR, p. 178; Summers, *Conspiracy*, p. 84; Oglesby, *Yankee and Cowboy War*, p. 82; XXIII WC, pp. 873–74.

17. WR, pp. 178–80; XXIII WC, p. 875; XXIV WC, p. 820; VII WC, p. 59; Summers, *Conspiracy*, p. 84; "President Kennedy Is Laid to Rest."

18. WR, p. 198; FBI memo, Hoover to Tolson, Belmont, et al., November 22, 1963; *Dallas Morning News*, November 24, 1963; interview with William F. Alexander, former Dallas assistant district attorney, 1983; Howard Roffman, *Presumed Guilty*.

19. WR, pp. 180, 198–99; Oglesby, *Yankee and Cowboy War*, p. 82; Summers, *Conspiracy*, p. 85; XXIV WC, p. 822; Scott, Hoch, and Stetler, *The Assassinations*, p. 34.

20. WR, pp. 17, 199, 210, 216; Lattimer, *Kennedy and Lincoln*, p. 317; interview with Nelson, November 1982; Scott, Hoch, and Stetler, *The Assassinations*, p. 36.

21. WR, p. 180; XXIV WC, p. 822; Summers, *Conspiracy*, p. 85; Scott, Hoch, and Stetler, *The Assassinations*, p. 34; Oglesby, *Yankee and Cowboy War*, p. 82; *Miami News*, February 2, 1967; HSCA, p. 461.

22. Senate Select Committee to Study Governmental Operations with Respect to Intelligence Activities, *Final Report, Book Five, The Investigation of the Assassination of President John F. Kennedy*, Book V, 94th Cong., 2d sess., 1976, pp. 32–33.

23. XXIV WC, p. 823.

24. WR, p. ix; Scott, Hoch, and Stetler, *The Assassinations*, pp. 10–13.

2: Blue-Ribbon Whitewash

1. WR, p. vii; A. L. Goodhart, "The Mysteries of the Kennedy Assassination and the English Press," *Law Quarterly Review*, London (January 1967), p. 123.
2. WR; David S. Lifton, *Best Evidence*, p. 19; Sylvia Meagher, *Accessories After the Fact*, pp. xiv, xxiii, xxvii; Harold Weisberg, *Whitewash IV*, p. 5; Peter Dale Scott, Paul L. Hoch, and Russell Stetler, eds., *The Assassinations: Dallas and Beyond*, p. 5.
3. WR, pp. 19, 350.
4. Ibid., p. 20.
5. Ibid., pp. 21, 350.
6. Ibid., p. 21.
7. Ibid., p. 18.
8. Ibid., pp. 19, 88.
9. Ibid., p. 1; Ovid Demaris, *The Director*, p. 282; G. Robert Blakey and Richard N. Billings, *The Plot to Kill the President*, p. 26; Carl Oglesby, *The Yankee and Cowboy War*, p. 144; Edward J. Epstein, *Inquest*, pp. 32–33; Oscar Handlin, "Reader's Choice: The Warren Commission," *The Atlantic*, August 1966.
10. Scott, Hoch, and Stetler, *The Assassinations*, p. 264; Howard Roffman, *Presumed Guilty*, p. 278; "The Untold Stories," *U.S. News & World Report*, October 12, 1964; Herbert L. Packer, "A Measure of the Achievement," *The Nation*, November 2, 1964; Kenneth Crawford, "The Warren Impeachers," *Newsweek*, October 19, 1964; Loudon Wainwright, "The Book for All to Read," *Life*, October 16, 1964; "Reporting the Report," *Newsweek*, October 12, 1964; "Again, the Assassination," *Newsweek*, August 15, 1966; Lord Devlin, "Death of a President: The Established Facts," *The Atlantic*, March 1965; "Warren Report in Mass Production," *Saturday Review*, November 7, 1964.
11. *Washington Post*, October 19, 1964; *New York Herald Tribune*, European Edition, September 29, 1964.
12. Louis Nizer, "An Analysis and Commentary," introduction, *The Official Warren Commission Report on the Assassination of President John F. Kennedy* (New York: Doubleday, 1964).
13. Arthur M. Schlesinger, Jr., *Robert Kennedy and His Times*, p. 643.
14. "Again, the Assassination"; Alexander M. Bickel, "The Failure of the Warren Report," *Commentary*, October 1966; Scott, Hoch, and Stetler, *The Assassinations*, p. 7; Epstein, *Inquest*, p. 154; "Warren's Secret," *National Review*, April 7, 1964.
15. Meagher, *Accessories*, pp. xxxi–xxxii; Scott, Hoch, and Stetler, *The Assassinations*.

16. Harold Weisberg, *Oswald in New Orleans*, pp. 106, 143. See also Meagher, *Accessories*; Epstein, *Inquest*; "Again, the Assassination"; Loudon Wainwright, "Warren Report Is Not Enough," *Life*, October 7, 1966; "Autopsy on the Warren Commission," *Time*, September 16, 1966.

17. Meagher, *Accessories*; Anthony Summers, *Conspiracy*; Scott, Hoch, and Stetler, *The Assassinations*; Roffman, *Presumed Guilty*; Epstein, *Inquest*; M. Stanton Evans, "A Sober Assessment," *National Review*, January 11, 1966; Alex Campbell, "What Did Happen in Dallas?", *New Republic*, June 25, 1966; "Again, the Assassination"; "Autopsy on the Warren Commission"; Richard J. Whalen, "The Kennedy Assassination," *Saturday Evening Post*, January 14, 1967.

18. "Again, the Assassination"; "Letters to the Editor," *Commentary*, April 1967; David W. Belin, *November 22, 1963: You Are the Jury*; "Overwhelming Evidence Oswald Was Assassin," *U.S. News & World Report*, October 10, 1966; letter, Gerald R. Ford to Henry Hurt, August 6, 1982; interview with Arlen Specter, October 1982.

19. Handlin, "Reader's Choice"; "Autopsy on the Warren Commission"; *New York Herald Tribune*, European Edition, September 29, 1964; DeLloyd J. Guth and David R. Wrone, comps., *The Assassination of John F. Kennedy: A Comprehensive Historical and Legal Bibliography, 1963–1979*, p. xxv.

20. "Food for the Suspicious," *Time*, July 8, 1966; Devlin, "Death of a President"; Scott, Hoch, and Stetler, *The Assassinations*, pp. 4, 264; Meagher, *Accessories*, pp. xxxii, 459–60; Norman Podhoretz, "The Warren Commission: An Editorial," *Commentary*, January 1964.

21. Meagher, *Accessories*, p. 461; Donald Jackson, "The Evolution of an Assassin," *Life*, February 21, 1964; "Assassination: The Trail to a Verdict," *Life*, October 2, 1964; "A Matter of Reasonable Doubt," *Life*, November 25, 1966; Wainwright, "Warren Report Is Not Enough"; Whalen, "The Kennedy Assassination"; *Washington Post*, October 19, 1964, October 3, 1966.

22. HSCR, p. 41; Whalen, "The Kennedy Assassination"; George O'Toole, *The Assassination Tapes*, p. 118.

23. Epstein, *Inquest*, p. 26; O'Toole, *The Assassination Tapes*, p. 118; Blakey and Billings, *Plot to Kill*, p. 72; "Again, the Assassination"; Whalen, "The Kennedy Assassination."

24. Epstein, *Inquest*, p. 150; O'Toole, *The Assassination Tapes*, p. 8; Packer, "A Measure of the Achievement"; Whalen, "The Kennedy Assassination"; WR, pp. xii, 18, 22; HSCR, p. 241; Senate Select Committee to Study Governmental Operations with Respect to Intelligence Activities, *Final Report, Book Five, The Investigation of the Assassination of President John F. Kennedy*, Book V, 94th Cong., 2d sess., 1976, p. 45; Paul Hoch and Jonathan Marshall, "JFK: The

Unsolved Murder," *Inquiry*, December 25, 1978; Handlin, "Reader's Choice."

25. Senate Select Committee, *Investigation of the Assassination*, pp. 25, 95–97; HSCR, pp. 195–96, 244, 253.
26. V WC, pp. 178, 180; original transcript of Mrs. John F. Kennedy's testimony.
27. Roffman, *Presumed Guilty*, p. 77; Harold Weisberg, *Post Mortem*, pp. 467–72; Senate Select Committee, *Investigation of the Assassination*, pp. 5, 45–46; Demaris, *The Director*, p. 282; Blakey and Billings, *Plot to Kill*, p. 26; WR, pp. 6–7; Epstein, *Inquest*, pp. xv, 157; Guth and Wrone, *Assassination of John F. Kennedy*, p. xv; *The New York Times*, January 19, 1978.
28. HSCR, p. 128.
29. *The New York Times*, April 5, 1977; Demaris, *The Director*, p. 282; Meagher, *Accessories*, p. 317; Blakey and Billings, *Plot to Kill*, p. 26.
30. Schlesinger, *Robert Kennedy and His Times*, p. 642.
31. Senate Select Committee, *Investigation of the Assassination*, pp. 4, 51–53; *Philadelphia Inquirer*, September 21, 1978; HSCR, p. 243; interview with James Hosty, December 1982.
32. Blakey and Billings, *Plot to Kill*, pp. 27–28; Roffman, *Presumed Guilty*, pp. 256–62; Weisberg, *Post Mortem*, pp. 467–72.
33. WR, pp. v, xiii; Meagher, *Accessories*, pp. xxx–xxxi; Epstein, *Inquest*, p. 109; Guth and Wrone, *The Assassination of John F. Kennedy*, p. xvi; *The New York Times*, January 19, 1978; Blakey and Billings, *Plot to Kill*, p. 77; Jonathan Steele, "Ford Kept FBI Briefed on Kennedy Inquiry," *The Guardian* (London), January 20, 1978; Committee to Investigate Assassinations, *Coincidence or Conspiracy?*, p. 133.
34. Interview with Robert Tienken, Congressional Research Service, Library of Congress, October 1982; interview with H. Douglas Price, professor of government, Harvard University, October 1982.
35. Ibid. (both).
36. WR, p. xiii; Epstein, *Inquest*, pp. 21, 105.
37. Alexander M. Bickel, "Return to Dallas," *New Republic*, December 23, 1967; Devlin, "Death of a President"; Roffman, *Presumed Guilty*, p. 27; Bickel, "The Failure of the Warren Report"; Whalen, "The Kennedy Assassination."
38. Interview with Richard B. Russell, WSB-TV, Atlanta, February 2, 1970.
39. Ibid.
40. Interview with Lyndon B. Johnson, "CBS Evening News with Walter Cronkite," April 25, 1975; "The American Assassins," CBS Reports Inquiry with Dan Rather, November 26, 1975; FBI memo, DeLoach to Tolson, April 4, 1967; *The New York Times*, June 25, 1976; Oglesby, *Yankee and Cowboy War*, p. 145; Leo Janos, "The Last Days of the

President," *The Atlantic*, July 1973; O'Toole, *The Assassination Tapes*, p. 8.

41. Letter, Lewis F. Powell, Jr., to Henry Hurt, April 6, 1982; WR, p. xiv; Epstein, *Inquest*, p. 19.
42. Letter, Powell to Hurt, April 6, 1982.
43. Letter, Ford to Hurt, August 6, 1982.
44. Weisberg, *Whitewash IV*, p. 11; "Gerald Ford's Little White Lie," *Rolling Stone*, April 24, 1975; Committee to Investigate Assassinations, *Coincidence or Conspiracy?*, p. 135; *U.S. Code Annotated*, Title 13, #798; Senate Committee on Rules and Administration, *Hearings on the Nomination of Gerald R. Ford of Michigan to Be Vice President of the U.S.*, 93rd Cong., 1st sess., 1973, pp. 89–90, 92; *Congress and the Nation* 4, 1973–1976, p. 927.
45. The President's Commission on the Assassination of President John F. Kennedy, *Report of Proceedings*, January 27, 1964, pp. 127–212; Gerald R. Ford with John R. Stiles, *Portrait of the Assassin*; Weisberg, *Whitewash IV*, pp. 11, 12, 124–130.
46. III HSCA, pp. 594–95.
47. Ibid., pp. 577, 586.
48. Letter, Ford to Hurt, August 6, 1982.
49. Hoch and Marshall, "JFK: The Unsolved Murder"; HSCA; *The New York Times*, December 23, 1978; "A Fourth Shot?" *Time*, January 1, 1979.
50. HSCR, p. 1.
51. Ibid.
52. Ibid.
53. *The New York Times*, January 27, 1979, July 15, 1979, December 2, 1980, May 15, 1982; *Washington Post*, May 15, 1982; press release, Department of Justice, December 1, 1980.
54. Guth and Wrone, *The Assassination of John F. Kennedy*, pp. xxvii–xxxiv; Hoch and Marshall, "JFK: The Unsolved Murder."
55. Hoch and Marshall, "JFK: The Unsolved Murder"; Harris Survey, December 4, 1978.
56. Harris Survey, April 2, 1981.

3: Autopsy of the Century

1. Marshall Houts, *Where Death Delights*, p. 55.
2. "Overwhelming Evidence Oswald Was Assassin," *U.S. News & World Report*, October 10, 1966.
3. VII HSCA, pp. 17, 37, 257; Houts, *Where Death Delights*, pp. 25–30, 32; Tracy Kidder, "Washington: The Assassination Tangle," *At-*

lantic Monthly, March 1979; "JFK: Settling Some Doubts," *Newsweek,* September 18, 1978.

4. "JFK: Settling Some Doubts"; VII HSCA, pp. 9, 13–15, 181, 191, 257; David S. Lifton, *Best Evidence,* p. 475.
5. VII HSCA, pp. 17, 182, 190; Houts, *Where Death Delights,* pp. 29, 56.
6. II WC, p. 348.
7. Ibid., pp. 347–76.
8. VII HSCA, pp. 8, 182; II WC, pp. 349, 378; Josiah Thompson, *Six Seconds in Dallas,* p. 198.
9. VII HSCA, pp. 188–89; Kidder, "Washington: The Assassination Tangle."
10. VII HSCA, pp. 10, 11, 39, 348; I HSCA, p. 324; II WC, pp. 349–50.
11. VII HSCA, pp. 10–12, 46, 216, 348; II WC, pp. 349, 372; Harold Weisberg, *Whitewash IV,* pp. 167, 271, 536.
12. Interview with Marion Johnson, National Archives.
13. II WC, p. 378; VII HSCA, pp. 81–83, 192; interviews with medical examiners in New York, Chicago, Los Angeles, San Francisco, 1982; VI WC, pp. 58–59.
14. VII HSCA, pp. 11–13, 24, 305; II WC, pp. 351, 361; Houts, *Where Death Delights,* pp. 38, 64; Michael Kurtz, *Crime of the Century,* p. 18; XVII WC, p. 2; I HSCA, p. 143.
15. VII HSCA, pp. 2, 263; I HSCA, p. 143; II WC, pp. 349–50.
16. WR, p. 60.
17. Ibid.
18. The President's Commission on the Assassination of President John F. Kennedy, *Report of Proceedings,* January 27, 1964, p. 193; Thompson, *Six Seconds in Dallas.*
19. II WC, p. 127; VII HSCA, p. 12.
20. Thompson, *Six Seconds in Dallas,* pp. 43, 45; Harold Weisberg, *Post Mortem,* p. 535; VII HSCA, p. 7.
21. Thompson, *Six Seconds in Dallas,* pp. 43–44, 58.
22. II WC, p. 93.
23. Ibid., p. 378; VII HSCA, p. 182.
24. II WC, p. 361.
25. VII HSCA, p. 12.
26. Ibid., p. 13; Weisberg, *Post Mortem,* pp. 535–36.
27. VII HSCA, p. 17; Thompson, *Six Seconds in Dallas,* p. 279; Houts, *Where Death Delights,* p. 41.
28. VII HSCA, p. 13.
29. Ibid., pp. 13, 16, 94; I HSCA, p. 330.
30. VII HSCA, pp. 16, 193; II WC, pp. 361–62; Weisberg, *Post Mortem,* p. 588; United Press International and *American Heritage* Magazine,

comps., *Four Days*, p. 45; Thompson, *Six Seconds in Dallas*, pp. 197, 279.
31. VII HSCA, pp. 16, 257.
32. Ibid.; I HSCA, p. 330.
33. VII HSCA, p. 12.
34. WR, p. 543; VII HSCA, p. 94.
35. I HSCA, p. 330; VII HSCA, p. 257; XVII WC, p. 48; II WC, p. 373.
36. Interviews with medical examiners, 1982; interview with Paul Hoch; interview with Bernard Fensterwald, Jr.
37. VII HSCA, pp. 191–92, 258.
38. Ibid., p. 258; Weisberg, *Post Mortem*, p. 209.
39. VII HSCA, pp. 16, 181.
40. VI WC, pp. 22, 35, 37, 42, 55, 71, 141; VII HSCA, pp. 12–13, 101; Harold Feldman, "Fifty-one Witnesses: The Grassy Knoll," *The Minority of One*, March 1965, pp. 12, 101.
41. Transcript of Warren Commission meeting, December 16, 1963 (executive session).
42. The President's Commission on the Assassination of President John F. Kennedy, *Report of Proceedings*, January 27, 1964, pp. 193–94.
43. VII HSCA, p. 257; I HSCA, p. 358; Houts, *Where Death Delights*, pp. 62–65.
44. Cyril Wecht, M.D., "JFK Assassination," *Modern Medicine*, October 28, 1974; The President's Commission on the Assassination of President John F. Kennedy, *Report of Proceedings*, January 27, 1964, p. 193. Reference for information in footnote is interview with Hoch.
45. Transcript of Warren Commission meeting, December 5, 1963, p. 37.
46. WR, p. 60.
47. David W. Belin, *November 22, 1963: You Are the Jury*, pp. 345–46; VII HSCA, p. 2; I HSCA, p. 143; "Overwhelming Evidence Oswald Was Assassin"; Kurtz, *Crime of the Century*, pp. 144–45.
48. VII HSCA, p. 193; XVII WC, pp. 30–44; Kurtz, *Crime of the Century*, p. 145.
49. Kurtz, *Crime of the Century*, p. 18; VII HSCA, p. 12; Thompson, *Six Seconds in Dallas*, p. 43.
50. XVI WC, p. 981.
51. Weisberg, *Post Mortem*, p. 303; VII HSCA, pp. 6, 17, 46, 102, 177, 180, 191, 193, 311.
52. VII HSCA, pp. 3, 136–37, 191, 259; John Nichols, M.D., "President Kennedy's Adrenals," *Journal of the American Medical Association* 201, no. 2 (July 10, 1967); "Fit for the Presidency?", *Time*, November 3, 1980.
53. VII HSCA, p. 243.
54. Ibid., pp. 137, 243, 279.

55. Ibid., pp. 14–15, 17.
56. *Dallas Morning News,* January 11, 1981.
57. I HSCA, p. 323.
58. WR, pp. 18–19; President's Commission on the Assassination of President John F. Kennedy, *Report of Proceedings,* January 27, 1964, p. 193; Thompson, *Six Seconds in Dallas,* p. 281.
59. Weisberg, *Post Mortem,* p. 535; XVIII WC, p. 744.
60. XVIII WC, p. 744.
61. WR, pp. 87, 541.
62. VII HSCA, pp. 17, 87; Thompson, *Six Seconds in Dallas,* pp. 279, 281.
63. VII HSCA, p. 88; Thompson, *Six Seconds in Dallas,* p. 281; *Baltimore Sun,* November 25, 1966; *Washington Star,* November 24, 1966.
64. *Baltimore Sun,* November 25, 1966; *Washington Star,* November 24, 1966; XVII WC, p. 45.
65. XVII WC, p. 45; Weisberg, *Post Mortem,* pp. 262, 533; interview with Harold Weisberg; VII HSCA, p. 88.
66. Weisberg, *Post Mortem,* p. 533; Kurtz, *Crime of the Century,* p. 69.
67. Interview with Admiral George Burkley, 1982.
68. Oral History Interview Transcript with Admiral George G. Burkley, October 17, 1967, p. 18, Kennedy Library, Boston. References for information in footnote are interview with Burkley, 1982; letter, Henry Hurt to Burkley, October 6, 1982; letter, Burkley to Hurt, October 14, 1982; interview with Burkley, January 1983.
69. VII HSCA, pp. 81, 83, 192–93; V WC, pp. 59–60; XVIII WC, p. 744; Weisberg, *Post Mortem,* p. 262; Thompson, *Six Seconds in Dallas,* pp. 47–48.
70. WR, p. 91.
71. Marshall Houts, "1. The Warren Commission Botched the Kennedy Autopsy; 2. Warren Commission One-Bullet Theory Exploded," *Argosy,* July 1967; Houts, *Where Death Delights,* p. 13; interview with Dr. Elliot Gross, chief medical examiner, New York City, 1982.
72. Houts, *Where Death Delights,* pp. 14, 60.
73. VII HSCA, pp. 3, 260, 263; Weisberg, *Post Mortem,* pp. 22, 141.
74. VII HSCA, pp. 3–4.
75. Ibid., p. 4.
76. Ibid., pp. 1, 4, 5; HSCR, p. 42; I HSCA, p. 298.
77. VII HSCA, pp. 6, 17, 46, 102, 177, 180, 193, 311.
78. VII HSCA, pp. 199–203, 215; Thompson, *Six Seconds in Dallas,* pp. 278–84; I HSCA, p. 367.
79. I HSCA, p. 358.
80. Ibid., p. 310.
81. Ibid., pp. 250, 256, 301; VII HSCA, pp. 254–61.
82. *Dallas Morning News,* January 11, 1981; VII HSCA, pp. 254–61.

83. Lifton, *Best Evidence*, pp. 318–19.
84. WR, p. 521; VI WC, pp. 6, 33, 54, 65, 71.
85. VI WC, p. 33.
86. WR, pp. 521, 540–41; VI WC, pp. 6, 54, 65, 71.
87. XVII WC, p. 48; VII HSCA, pp. 3, 25, 257.
88. VII HSCA, pp. 114–15.
89. Ibid., p. 254.
90. Ibid., p. 255.
91. Ibid., pp. 79, 115.
92. Ibid., p. 175; I HSCA, pp. 233, 325, 330; WR, p. 87; HSCR, p. 43; Lifton, *Best Evidence*, p. 548; I HSCA, pp. 146–48, 186, 215, 234.
93. News conference #1, Dallas, November 22, 1963, Lyndon B. Johnson Library, Austin; VII HSCA, pp. 37–38, 101, 175; Houts, *Where Death Delights*, p. 58; Lifton, *Best Evidence*, pp. 57–59.
94. VII HSCA, p. 175; HSCR, p. 43.
95. VII HSCA, p. 17; I HSCA, p. 317.
96. HSCR, p. 44; VII HSCA, pp. 194, 199–203, 210; I HSCA, p. 332; VI HSCA, pp. 43–56.
97. I HSCA, p. 322; Weisberg, *Post Mortem*, p. 51; Weisberg, *Whitewash—The Report on the Warren Report*, pp. 165–66; Mark Lane, *Rush to Judgment*, pp. 69–80.
98. VII HSCA, pp. 3, 25; Cyril Wecht, M.D., "Pathologist's View of JFK Autopsy," *Modern Medicine*, November 27, 1972; Kurtz, *Crime of the Century*, pp. 75, 100; II WC, p. 363; Weisberg, *Post Mortem*, pp. 358–59.
99. Kurtz, *Crime of the Century*, pp. 91, 100; Wecht, "Pathologist's View of JFK Autopsy"; Weisberg, *Post Mortem*, p. 587; VII HSCA, p. 17.
100. I HSCA, p. 333; Thompson, *Six Seconds in Dallas*, pp. 278–84; VII HSCA, pp. 23–33, 201.
101. VII HSCA, pp. 2, 26; I HSCA, pp. 145, 367.
102. VII HSCA, pp. 3, 23–33; I HSCA, pp. 145, 368.
103. VII HSCA, pp. 23, 28, 33; I HSCA, pp. 146, 368.
104. VII HSCA, p. 33.
105. Kurtz, *Crime of the Century*, pp. 75, 100; Weisberg, *Post Mortem*, pp. 358–59.
106. Interview with Marion Johnson; XVII WC, pp. 23–26.
107. VII HSCA, pp. 17, 24, 134, 201; Wecht, "Pathologist's View of JFK Autopsy"; interviews with medical examiners, 1982; II WC, p. 355; I HSCA, pp. 230, 348; WR, p. 544.
108. I HSCA, p. 333; interviews with medical examiners, 1982.
109. Wecht, "Pathologist's View of JFK Autopsy."
110. Harris Survey, April 2, 1981; VII HSCA, pp. 135, 199, 243–44.
111. VII HSCA, p. 175; Edward J. Epstein, *Inquest*, pp. 43, 126; I HSCA, p. 377; Kidder, "Washington: The Assassination Tangle"; Thompson,

Six Seconds in Dallas, pp. 203–4; Wecht, "Pathologist's View of JFK Autopsy"; Kurtz, *Crime of the Century*, p. 173; Summers, *Conspiracy*, pp. 66–67; Houts, *Where Death Delights*, pp. 45–46; WR, p. 88.

112. Kurtz, *Crime of the Century*, pp. 143–56, 172–87; VII HSCA, p. 262; Harold Weisberg v. U.S. Dept. of Justice, DCCA 82-1073, U.S. Court of Appeals for the District of Columbia; Weisberg v. U.S. Dept. of Justice, DCCA 75-226, affidavit of John W. Kilty, June 23, 1975; interview with Weisberg, 1982.

113. Kurtz, *Crime of the Century*, p. 67; XVII WC, p. 45; VII HSCA, pp. 80, 175; WR, p. 539.

114. News conference #1, November 22, 1963, Lyndon B. Johnson Library; Lifton, *Best Evidence*, pp. 56–62; Kurtz, *Crime of the Century*, pp. 70, 83; WR, p. 92; VII HSCA, pp. 90–91.

115. V WC, pp. 61–62; VII HSCA, p. 89; Weisberg, *Post Mortem*, pp. 209, 313, 318, 353; Kurtz, *Crime of the Century*, p. 75; Thompson, *Six Seconds in Dallas*, p. 281.

116. VI WC, pp. 58–59, 82; III WC, pp. 359, 362; interview with Weisberg.

117. Weisberg, *Post Mortem*, pp. 323, 330–34, 347, 356; VI WC, p. 136; *Baltimore Sun*, November 25, 1966; *Washington Star*, November 24, 1966; interview with Weisberg.

4: The Mystery of the Magic Bullet

1. XI HSCA, p. 125; Marshall Houts, *Where Death Delights*, pp. 62–63, 70; Josiah Thompson, *Six Seconds in Dallas*, pp. 146–47, 149, 157; *Philadelphia Inquirer*, November 25, 1966; Earl Golz, "Confidential: The FBI's File on JFK," *Gallery*, November 1982; I HSCA, p. 332; Edward J. Epstein, *Inquest*, pp. 43, 126, 149; HSCR, pp. 65–93.

2. Howard Roffman, *Presumed Guilty*, pp. 131–48; Houts, *Where Death Delights*, pp. 62–63; XVII WC, p. 49; Anthony Summers, *Conspiracy*, p. 67; *Dallas Morning News*, August 12, 1979; Sylvia Meagher, *Accessories After the Fact*, pp. 94, 106–10, 165–77; Harold Weisberg, *Whitewash—The Report on the Warren Report*, p. 165; Thompson, *Six Seconds in Dallas*, pp. 146–47, 152; Michael Kurtz, *Crime of the Century*, p. 185; I HSCA, pp. 309, 492; John Nichols, M.D., "The Wounding of Governor John Connally of Texas, November 22, 1963," *Maryland State Medical Journal*, October 1977.

3. WR, pp. 96, 110; Kurtz, *Crime of the Century*, p. 50; Summers, *Conspiracy*, p. 51; VII WC, p. 346.

4. HSCR, p. 81.

5. Epstein, *Inquest*, p. 113; WR, p. 97; Thompson, *Six Seconds in Dallas*, p. 31; Kurtz, *Crime of the Century*, p. 30.

6. WR, pp. 111–12, 115, 117; Nichols, "Wounding of Connally"; Golz, "Confidential"; Epstein, *Inquest*, p. 117; Kurtz, *Crime of the Century*, pp. 33–34.

7. Kurtz, *Crime of the Century*, p. 48; WR, pp. 18, 60, 76, 557; XXIV WC, p. 413; V WC, pp. 67–68; Thompson, *Six Seconds in Dallas*, p. 147.

8. WR, pp. 77, 79, 558; VII HSCA, p. 368; III WC, p. 429; VI WC, pp. 129–30.

9. Epstein, *Inquest*, pp. 43–45, 141, 149; HSCR, p. 44; WR, pp. 81, 193–94; Kurtz, *Crime of the Century*, pp. 30–32.

10. WR, pp. 105–6; HSCR, p. 44.

11. Epstein, *Inquest*, p. 43. Reference for information in footnote is interview with Norman Redlich, April 1983.

12. Epstein, *Inquest*, pp. 119–22; *Philadelphia Inquirer*, November 25, 1966; Golz, "Confidential"; III WC, p. 430; Summers, *Conspiracy*, p. 67.

13. I HSCA, pp. 342, 377; VI WC, p. 111; WR, p. 114; XVIII WC, p. 744; II WC, p. 143; V WC, p. 59; Thompson, *Six Seconds in Dallas*, p. 43; Harold Weisberg, *Post Mortem*, p. 535; VII HSCA, pp. 92, 257; Kurtz, *Crime of the Century*, pp. 56, 173.

14. WR, pp. 88, 91, 104; I HSCA, pp. 377, 339–41, 344–45; VII HSCA, p. 143; Nichols, "Wounding of Connally"; VI WC, p. 101; XVII WC, p. 16; IV WC, pp. 104–5.

15. VII HSCA, p. 199; XVII WC, pp. 18, 20, 49; I HSCA, p. 308; WR, pp. 19, 95; Nichols, "Wounding of Connally"; III WC, pp. 428–29.

16. WR, pp. 87–93, 105–09; HSCR, p. 44; I HSCA, p. 344.

17. Houts, *Where Death Delights*, p. 65; Weisberg, *Whitewash II*, p. 168; Thompson, *Six Seconds in Dallas*, pp. 63–64; Kurtz, *Crime of the Century*, pp. 33–34, 58. References for information in footnote are IV WC, pp. 132–33; letter, John B. Connally to Henry Hurt, April 17, 1982.

18. Interview with William F. Alexander, 1983.

19. I HSCA, pp. 333, 487; III WC, pp. 428, 430; V WC, p. 68; VII HSCA, pp. 365, 372; Nichols, "Wounding of Connally"; Thompson, *Six Seconds in Dallas*, pp. 146–47, 151; Kurtz, *Crime of the Century*, pp. 76, 80, 82.

20. IV WC, pp. 113–14; VII HSCA, p. 328; Weisberg, *Whitewash*, p. 165.

21. IV WC, pp. 117, 119–20, 123; VI WC, p. 111.

22. Interview with Charles Harbison, 1983; David S. Lifton, *Best Evidence*, p. 558; *Dallas Morning News*, April 1, 1977.

23. III WC, p. 430.

24. HSCR, p. 44; XVII WC, p. 18; IV WC, pp. 117, 123; WR, pp. 19, 56; II WC, p. 375.
25. WR, pp. 115, 193; Meagher, *Accessories*, pp. 107–9; Nichols, "Wounding of Connally"; Roffman, *Presumed Guilty*, p. 228; Epstein, *Inquest*, pp. 142–44; III WC, pp. 402–5, 443–47.
26. VII HSCA, pp. 342, 357; Kurtz, *Crime of the Century*, p. 56; Epstein, *Inquest*, pp. 43–45.
27. "A Matter of Reasonable Doubt," *Life*, November 25, 1966; Thompson, *Six Seconds in Dallas*, pp. 71–76; WR, pp. 105–9.
28. IV WC, pp. 132–33.
29. Ibid., pp. 132–33, 136, 147; letter, Connally to Hurt, April 17, 1982.
30. "A Matter of Reasonable Doubt."
31. I HSCA, p. 43. Reference for information in footnote is interview with J. Doyle Williams, February 1983.
32. II WC, p. 78.
33. Epstein, *Inquest*, p. 119; Thompson, *Six Seconds in Dallas*, pp. 69, 203; I HSCA, pp. 321–22.
34. Houts, *Where Death Delights*, pp. 62–63.
35. HSCR, p. 50; WR, pp. 19, 79; XVIII WC, pp. 799–800; XXIV WC, p. 412; III WC, p. 429; VI WC, p. 130; Kurtz, *Crime of the Century*, pp. 48, 143–56.
36. I HSCA, pp. 491–567.
37. WR, p. 79; VI WC, pp. 129–34.
38. XVIII WC, p. 800; VI WC, pp. 132–33; Thompson, *Six Seconds in Dallas*, p. 156; Kurtz, *Crime of the Century*, pp. 46–47; IV WC, p. 118; Lifton, *Best Evidence*, p. 94; Jesse Curry, *J.F.K. Assassination File*, p. 34.
39. WR, p. 79; Meagher, *Accessories*, p. 174; Thompson, *Six Seconds in Dallas*, pp. 154–65; Epstein, *Inquest*, pp. 77, 117.
40. XXIV WC, p. 412; III WC, p. 428; Meagher, *Accessories*, p. 176.
41. Thompson, *Six Seconds in Dallas*, p. 175; Kurtz, *Crime of the Century*, p. 47; III WC, p. 428.
42. III WC, p. 429.
43. President's Commission on the Assassination of President John F. Kennedy, *Report of Proceedings*, January 27, 1964, pp. 127–212; transcripts of Warren Commission meetings, December 5 and December 16, 1963 (executive sessions); I HSCA, p. 336.
44. CD 1095t; CD 1095v; Kurtz, *Crime of the Century*, p. 49; Thompson, *Six Seconds in Dallas*, p. 165.
45. FBI memos, J. Doyle Williams to SAC Dallas, November 22, 1963, and February 12, 1964; FBI memo, Sullivan to Brennan, February 13, 1964 (HQ 62–109060–2437); interview with Williams, February 1983.
46. Interview with Williams, February 1983.

47. Ibid.
48. Ibid.
49. Ibid.
50. Ibid.
51. XXV WC, pp. 216–17; XV WC, pp. 72, 80; WR, pp. 335–36; HSCR, pp. 158–59.
52. WR, p. 19; HSCR, p. 1; Epstein, *Inquest*, p. 43.
53. WR, p. 580; Epstein, *Inquest*, pp. 119–20; Thompson, *Six Seconds in Dallas*, p. 152; Kurtz, *Crime of the Century*, p. 78.
54. Houts, *Where Death Delights*, pp. 62–63; III WC, p. 430; Thompson, *Six Seconds in Dallas*, pp. 146–47; I HSCA, p. 487.
55. V WC, pp. 76–77; Houts, *Where Death Delights*, p. 71; Epstein, *Inquest*, pp. 119–20; Robert Sam Anson, *"They've Killed the President!"*, p. 50; Kurtz, *Crime of the Century*, p. 78.
56. I HSCA, pp. 335–36.
57. Ibid., pp. 336, 400.
58. Ibid., pp. 335–36, 400.
59. Ibid.
60. Ibid., pp. 335–36.
61. Ibid., pp. 307–9, 400; WR, pp. 107–9, 584; Epstein, *Inquest*, pp. 120–21.
62. WR, pp. 584–85; I HSCA, p. 400; V WC, pp. 85–86; VI WC, p. 106; II WC, p. 376; Kurtz, *Crime of the Century*, pp. 79, 177.
63. I HSCA, p. 307.
64. Ibid.
65. Ibid., pp. 307–8.
66. Ibid., pp. 382–83.
67. Ibid., p. 337.
68. VII HSCA, p. 200.
69. *Philadelphia Inquirer*, November 25, 1966; Epstein, *Inquest*, p. 115; Thompson, *Six Seconds in Dallas*, pp. 146, 202.
70. Interview with Arlen Specter, October 1982.
71. WR, p. 584.
72. VII HSCA, p. 368; Thompson, *Six Seconds in Dallas*, pp. 146–47; HSCR, p. 50; III WC, p. 429; WR, pp. 19, 79; VI WC, p. 130.
73. III WC, pp. 402–5, 428, 445; Meagher, *Accessories*, pp. 107–8; VII HSCA, p. 558.
74. Meagher, *Accessories*, p. 172; interview with Dr. Perry Morton, physics department, Samford University, Birmingham, Alabama, 1983; interview with Dr. Ben Chastain, professor of chemistry, Samford University, 1983; interview with Dr. Lou Henry, director, Nuclear Science and Technology Facility, Buffalo, New York, 1983.
75. V WC, pp. 58, 67, 69; Roffman, *Presumed Guilty*, p. 101; XV WC, pp. 746–52; Weisberg, *Whitewash*, p. 164.

76. WR, p. 85; Meagher, *Accessories,* p. 172.
77. Weisberg, *Whitewash* IV, p. 171; interview with Harold Weisberg; interview with James H. Lesar, 1983.
78. Interview with Weisberg; interview with Lesar, 1983; Weisberg, *Whitewash* IV, pp. 174–75; DeLloyd J. Guth and David R. Wrone, comps., *The Assassination of John F. Kennedy: A Comprehensive Historical and Legal Bibliography, 1963–1979,* p. 50.
79. Interview with Weisberg.
80. Cyril Wecht, M.D., "JFK Assassination," *Modern Medicine,* October 28, 1974; interview with Weisberg.
81. Wecht, "JFK Assassination"; interview with Weisberg; I HSCA, p. 558.
82. I HSCA, pp. 490, 493, 558; Wecht, "JFK Assassination"; *Washington Post,* September 9, 1978; XV WC, p. 747; Werner Wahl and Henry Kramer, "Neutron–Activation Analysis," *Scientific American,* April 1967.
83. I HSCA, p. 558; Wecht, "JFK Assassination."
84. Ibid. (both).
85. Harold Weisberg v. U.S. Dept. of Justice, DCCA 82-1072, U.S. Court of Appeals for the District of Columbia; interview with Weisberg.
86. Ibid. (both).
87. Interview with Weisberg.
88. *Dallas Morning News,* April 6, 1983; interview with Weisberg; interview with Lesar, 1983.
89. I HSCA, pp. 490, 556; interview with Vincent P. Guinn, March 1983.
90. I HSCA, pp. 490–567; *Washington Post,* September 9, 1978.
91. HSCR, p. 45.
92. I HSCA, p. 562; *Washington Post,* September 9, 1978.
93. I HSCA, p. 562.
94. Partial transcript of Guinn interview made by David Lifton.
95. III WC, pp. 432, 435.
96. FBI memo, Jevons to Conrad, March 20, 1964 (HQ 62–109060–2874).
97. III WC, pp. 432, 435; XXIV WC, p. 413; Curry, *J.F.K. Assassination File,* p. 34; V WC, pp. 67–68. Reference for information in footnote is Doris F. Kinney et al., "Four Days That Stopped America," *Life,* November 1983.
98. XXIV WC, p. 413.
99. I HSCA, p. 497; II WC, p. 354.
100. I HSCA, p. 494.
101. Ibid.
102. Meagher, *Accessories,* p. 113; XXVI WC, p. 62.
103. HSCR, p. 45.

5: Oswald and the Sniper's Perch

1. III WC, pp. 249–52; WR, pp. 149–56.
2. WR, p. 152.
3. IV WC, p. 307; FBI memo, Jevons to Conrad, November 23, 1963 (HQ 62–109060); CD 7, pp. 378–79; FBI memo, Handley to Rosen, November 29, 1963; WR, pp. 79–80, 122, 134, 555, 599; VII WC, pp. 46, 107, 109; IV WC, pp. 266–68; III WC, pp. 284–86, 290, 293; XVII WC, p. 221; FBI memo, Jevons to Conrad, November 23, 1963 (HQ 62–109060–434).
4. WR, pp. 118–21, 181; XVII WC, p. 635; VII WC, p. 420.
5. FBI memo, Jevons to Conrad, November 23, 1963 (HQ 62–109060); FBI memo, Jevons to Conrad, November 23, 1963 (HQ 62–109060–434); WR, pp. 120, 124; IV WC, pp. 82, 85; Sylvia Meagher, *Accessories*, p. 120; interview with Carl Day, 1983.
6. WR, pp. 122–23; FBI memo, Jevons to Conrad, November 23, 1963 (HQ 62–109060); Meagher, *Accessories*, pp. 120–21; IV WC, pp. 260–61.
7. IV WC, pp. 31, 260, 269; WR, pp. 123–24, 140, 866; FBI memo, Ponder to Trotter, November 29, 1963 (HQ 109060–989); XXIV WC, p. 823; CD 5, p. 166.
8. WR, pp. 63, 145; III WC, pp. 141–43, 148, 154–55, 157; XXII WC, p. 847.
9. III WC, pp. 147–48; Meagher, *Accessories*, p. 372; Howard Roffman, *Presumed Guilty*, pp. 190–97; WR, pp. 145–46.
10. WR, pp. 152–53.
11. WR, pp. 64–65, 80, 152, 178; II WC, p. 159; III WC, pp. 251–52, 293; Harold Weisberg, *Whitewash*, p. 37; Meagher, *Accessories*, p. 226; J. Gary Shaw with Larry R. Harris, *Cover-up*, p. 679.
12. WR, p. 143; Meagher, *Accessories*, p. 65; III WC, p. 167; Roffman, *Presumed Guilty*, pp. 180–88; VI WC, pp. 328, 383.
13. Meagher, *Accessories*, p. 68; III WC, pp. 169–71, 173, 288; WR, pp. 156, 250.
14. *Dallas Morning News*, November 26, 27, 1978, December 19, 1978; CD 5, p. 41.
15. Anthony Summers, *Conspiracy*, p. 108; *Dallas Morning News*, November 26, 1978.
16. Ibid. (both).
17. Roffman, *Presumed Guilty*, pp. 180–88; WR, pp. 182, 600, 613; III WC, pp. 169–70.
18. VI WC, p. 307; WR, pp. 80, 135; Roffman, *Presumed Guilty*, pp. 211–14; III WC, p. 293.
19. WR, pp. 19, 600; HSCR, p. 1.
20. VI WC, pp. 157, 194, 203; VII WC, p. 486; II WC, pp. 159, 194, 209; III WC, p. 145.

21. VI WC, p. 181; II WC, pp. 167–69, 171–74; II WR, p. 250.

22. XXV WC, pp. 903–8; WR, pp. 145, 251; Roffman, *Presumed Guilty*, pp. 189, 192–97; Meagher, *Accessories*, p. 372; III WC, p. 148.

23. *Dallas Morning News*, December 19, 1978; XXV WC, p. 908; VI WC, pp. 189–90; WR, pp. 251–52.

24. Meagher, *Accessories*, p. 372; Roffman, *Presumed Guilty*, pp. 190–97; WR, p. 252.

25. WR, p. 251; XXIV WC, p. 522; *Dallas Morning News*, November 26, 1978, December 19, 1978.

26. XXIV WC, p. 522; *Dallas Morning News*, November 26, 1978.

27. XXIV WC, p. 524; *Dallas Morning News*, December 19, 1978; FBI lead sheet, November 28, 1963 (DL 89–43–1010).

28. *Dallas Morning News*, December 19, 1978; Meagher, *Accessories*, p. 15.

29. *Dallas Morning News*, December 19, 1978.

30. Summers, *Conspiracy*, p. 75; *Dallas Morning News*, December 19, 1978.

31. *Dallas Morning News*, November 27, 1978; FBI memo on the assassination of President Kennedy, January 18, 1980 (DL 89–43–10510); FBI memo, Newson to SAC Dallas, November 25, 1963 (DL 89–43–493).

32. *Dallas Morning News*, November 26, 1978; Summers, *Conspiracy*, p. 75.

33. VI HSCA, p. 120; I HSCA, p. 61; Summers, *Conspiracy*, p. 75.

34. VI HSCA, pp. 308–9.

35. Ibid.

36. Michael Kurtz, *Crime of the Century*, pp. 36–37, 112; XXVI WC, p. 455; Summers, *Conspiracy*, p. 102; WR, pp. 131, 133–34, 590–92; Meagher, *Accessories*, pp. 59, 62.

37. WR, p. 137.

38. II WC, pp. 212–13, 222, 226, 245, 248; WR, pp. 131–32; FBI memo, Handley to Rosen, November 29, 1963 (HQ 62–109060–1111); I WC, p. 28.

39. WR, p. 133; II WC, pp. 228–29; Roffman, *Presumed Guilty*, pp. 173–74; VI WC, pp. 376–77.

40. WR, pp. 135, 1357; IV WC, p. 93; Weisberg, *Whitewash*, p. 20; II WC, p. 222.

41. Meagher, *Accessories*, pp. 54–55; II WC, pp. 226, 248–51; WR, pp. 131–34, 605.

42. II WC, p. 239; WR, p. 133; Kurtz, *Crime of the Century*, pp. 36, 114; Meagher, *Accessories*, pp. 55–57.

43. WR, p. 134; Meagher, *Accessories*, pp. 54–55; Roffman, *Presumed Guilty*, p. 170; Weisberg, *Whitewash*, pp. 15, 19.

44. Richard Popkin, *The Second Oswald*, pp. 61–62.

45. CD 205, p. 148; Meagher, *Accessories*, pp. 63–64.

46. Interview with Gary Shaw; interview with Mary Ferrell; CD 5, p. 129, obtained in 1968; WR, pp. 135–37.
47. Interview with Shaw; CD 5, p. 129, obtained in 1980.
48. CD 5, p. 129, obtained in 1980.
49. Interview with Shaw; interview with Ferrell; interview with Vincent Drain, May 1984.
50. HSCR, p. 1; WR, p. 19.
51. WR, p. 191; Roffman, *Presumed Guilty*, p. 229.
52. WR, pp. 191–93, 687–88; XIX WC, pp. 17–18; Meagher, *Accessories*, pp. 111, 376; Weisberg, *Whitewash*, pp. 24–25.
53. VIII WC, p. 235; WR, pp. 385, 687.
54. Edward J. Epstein, *Legend*, p. xiv; interviews with Marines, 1977.
55. Interview with Sherman Cooley, January 20, 1977.
56. Interviews with Marines, 1977; Meagher, *Accessories*, p. 370.
57. Kurtz, *Crime of the Century*, p. 110; WR, p. 81; Meagher, *Accessories*, pp. 131–32; Ken Warner, "Big Bargains in Rifles," *Mechanix Illustrated*, October 1964; Frederick Myatt, *An Illustrated Guide to Rifles and Automatic Weapons*, p. 53.
58. Warner, "Big Bargains in Rifles"; WR, p. 194; III WC, pp. 406–7; Meagher, *Accessories*, p. 102.
59. Meagher, *Accessories*, pp. 107–8; III WC, pp. 407, 441–51; V WC, pp. 152–53; WR, pp. 49, 189.
60. Memo, Dulles to Rankin, July 27, 1964 (CIA 1647–452B); WR, p. 195.
61. VIII HSCA, pp. 183–84.
62. Ibid., p. 183.
63. Ibid.; HSCR, p. 483.
64. VIII HSCA, p. 185.
65. HSCR, p. 484; VIII HSCA, pp. 184–85.
66. HSCR, p. 1; WR, p. 19.
67. HSCR, p. 484.
68. Warner, "Big Bargains in Rifles"; V WC, p. 560; VII WC, p. 108; XXIV WC, p. 228.
69. VII WC, pp. 105, 107–8.
70. III WC, p. 295; XIX WC, pp. 507–9; Robert Sam Anson, *"They've Killed the President!"*, p. 77.
71. XXIV WC, pp. 829, 831; CIA report on Oswald, November 25, 1963 (CIA 104–40).
72. VII HSCA, p. 372.
73. WR, pp. 118–19.
74. XXV WC, p. 808; WR, p. 119.
75. Meagher, *Accessories*, p. 116.
76. Ibid., pp. 116–20; WR, p. 555.
77. Meagher, *Accessories*, pp. 116–20.

78. Ibid., p. 118; WR, p. 555.
79. Meagher, *Accessories*, p. 120.
80. Ibid., pp. 112–16.
81. Ibid., p. 112; *The New York Times*, November 24, 1963.
82. Meagher, *Accessories*, pp. 113–14.
83. Ibid., pp. 112–13; WR, pp. 555, 646.
84. Meagher, *Accessories*, p. 113; XXVI WC, p. 62.
85. XXVI WC, pp. 62–63.
86. FBI memo, Jevons to Conrad, December 2, 1963 (unrecorded).
87. Edgar F. Tatro, "Where Have All the Bullets Gone?", *The Continuing Inquiry*, January 22, 1983.
88. WR, p. 124.
89. IV WC, pp. 258–61; WR, p. 123.
90. IV WC, p. 261; NBC News, *Seventy Hours and Thirty Minutes*, p. 58; interview with Drain, February 1983; David S. Lifton, *Best Evidence*, p. 356.
91. WR, pp. 123, 216; IV WC, p. 262; *Fort Worth Press*, November 25, 1963.
92. *Fort Worth Press*, November 25, 1963.
93. Ibid.; Lifton, *Best Evidence*, p. 356.
94. Interview with Drain, February 1983.
95. XXIV WC, p. 821.
96. Ibid.
97. WR, p. 123; Meagher, *Accessories*, p. 121; CD 7, pp. 378–79.
98. WR, pp. 122–24.
99. FBI memo, Rosen to Belmont, August 28, 1964 (FBI 105–82555–4814). Reference for information in footnote is XXVI WC, p. 829.
100. Interview with Drain, May 1984; interview with Day, April 1984.
101. XXVI WC, p. 455.

6: The Puzzles of Dealey Plaza

1. XXII WC, pp. 596, 600; VII WC, pp. 533, 535.
2. XXII WC, p. 600; VII WC, p. 535.
3. VII WC, p. 535; Anthony Summers, *Conspiracy*, p. 81; Sylvia Meagher, *Accessories After the Fact*, p. 26; *Dallas Morning News*, December 31, 1978, August 27, 1978.
4. *Dallas Morning News*, August 27, 1978; Meagher, *Accessories*, p. 26; VI WC, pp. 311–12.
5. VII WC, pp. 532, 535; VI WC, p. 308.
6. V HSCA, p. 589; WR, pp. 52, 446; *Dallas Morning News*, December 22, 31, 1978, August 27, 1978; Meagher, *Accessories*, p. 25.
7. Josiah Thompson, *Six Seconds in Dallas*, p. 25; Meagher, *Accessories*.

p. 9; III WC, pp. 282–83; VII WC, pp. 106, 546, 567; XIX WC, pp. 457, 502, 514, 524, 530, 540, 541, 543; IV WC, p. 165; XXIII WC, pp. 910, 913; *Dallas Times Herald*, November 22, 1963; Harold Feldman, "Fifty-one Witnesses: The Grassy Knoll," *The Minority of One*, March 1965.

8. VII WC, p. 508; II WC, p. 234; VI WC, pp. 329, 338, 365, 371, 388; XXII WC, pp. 638, 642, 648, 685; III WC, p. 227.

9. III WC, pp. 175, 191–92; Meagher, *Accessories*, pp. 11–12.

10. VII WC, p. 572; XIX WC, pp. 481, 486; XXIV WC, pp. 219, 525; *Dallas Morning News*, November 23, 1963; interview with Gordon Arnold, May 1982.

11. *San Diego Star News*, November 20, 1983.

12. *Dallas Morning News*, August 27, 1978; interview with Arnold, May 1982.

13. *Dallas Morning News*, August 27, 1978, December 22, 31, 1978; Summers, *Conspiracy*, pp. 58–59; interview with Arnold, May 1982.

14. Summers, *Conspiracy*, p. 58; *Dallas Morning News*, August 27, 1978, December 22, 31, 1978; interview with Arnold, May 1982.

15. *Dallas Morning News*, August 27, 1978, December 22, 31, 1978; interview with Arnold, May 1982; Summers, *Conspiracy*, p. 48.

16. Ibid. (all).

17. Interview with Arnold, May 1982.

18. Ibid.; *Dallas Morning News*, August 27, 1978; Summers, *Conspiracy*, p. 59.

19. Interview with Arnold, May 1982.

20. Ibid.; *Dallas Morning News*, August 27, 1978, December 31, 1978; interview with Earl Golz, 1983.

21. VII WC, p. 439; *Dallas Morning News*, December 31, 1978.

22. XIII HSCA, p. 16.

23. Interview with Julia Ann Mercer, 1983; XIII HSCA, p. 16; Jim Garrison, *A Heritage of Stone*, pp. 17, 170; XIX WC, p. 483.

24. Garrison, *A Heritage of Stone*, p. 170; interview with Mercer, 1983; VII WC, p. 352; XIX WC, p. 483; XIII HSCA, p. 16.

25. XIX WC, p. 483; XIII HSCA, p. 17; Garrison, *A Heritage of Stone*, p. 171; interview with Mercer, 1983.

26. CD 205, p. 320.

27. Interview with Mercer, 1983.

28. Ibid.

29. Ibid.

30. Ibid.; XIII HSCA, p. 17; Garrison, *A Heritage of Stone*, p. 171.

31. Garrison, *A Heritage of Stone*, p. 172; interview with Mercer, 1983.

32. I WC, pp. 153–54, 238.

33. Interview with Mercer, 1983; CD 205, pp. 313–14; Garrison, *A Heritage of Stone*, p. 172; XIII HSCA, pp. 16–17; XIX WC, p. 483; CD 205, pp. 315–16; analysis of Warren Commission volumes by critic (unnamed).
34. CD 5, p. 129, obtained in 1968; CD 5, p. 129, obtained in 1980; FBI memo on the assassination of President Kennedy, January 18, 1980 (DL 89–43–10510); FBI memo, Newson to SAC Dallas, November 25, 1963 (DL 89–43–493).
35. *Dallas Morning News*, August 27, 1978.
36. Thompson, *Six Seconds in Dallas*, pp. 115–16, 118; Meagher, *Accessories*, p. 18; Robert Sam Anson, *"They've Killed the President!"*, p. 21; VI WC, pp. 284–87; Summers, *Conspiracy*, p. 61.
37. XXIV WC, p. 201; VI WC, pp. 285–86; Thompson, *Six Seconds in Dallas*, p. 116; Anson, *"They've Killed the President!"*, p. 21.
38. Anson, *"They've Killed the President!"*, pp. 21–22; Thompson, *Six Seconds in Dallas*, pp. 116–17; VI WC, p. 286; XXIV WC, p. 201.
39. VI WC, pp. 287–88; Meagher, *Accessories*, p. 18; Thompson, *Six Seconds in Dallas*, p. 118; Summers, *Conspiracy*, p. 61.
40. Thompson, *Six Seconds in Dallas*, p. 118.
41. XIII HSCA, pp. 23–24.
42. Meagher, *Accessories*, p. 19; XIII HSCA, pp. 24–25.
43. Summers, *Conspiracy*, p. 62; Thompson, *Six Seconds in Dallas*, pp. 124, 254–55, 257, 261; VII WC, pp. 486–87; VI WC, p. 165; XX WC, p. 351; Feldman, "Fifty-one Witnesses," *The Minority of One*, March 1965.
44. Meagher, *Accessories*, pp. 16–17; Summers, *Conspiracy*, p. 58; Thompson, *Six Seconds in Dallas*, pp. 125, 158; XIX WC, p. 481; interview with Arnold, May 1982.
45. J. Gary Shaw with Larry R. Harris, *Cover-up*, p. 155; Thompson, *Six Seconds in Dallas*, p. 103.
46. Thompson, *Six Seconds in Dallas*, p. 126.
47. *Dallas Morning News*, November 23, 1963; interview with Arnold, May 1982; VII WC, p. 572; XIX WC, pp. 481, 486; XXIV WC, p. 525; Howard Roffman, *Presumed Guilty*, pp. 254–70; Feldman, "Fifty-one Witnesses," *The Minority of One*, March 1965.
48. Feldman, "Fifty-one Witnesses," *The Minority of One*, March 1965; Shaw with Harris, *Cover-up*, p. 134; VI WC, p. 298.
49. XX WC, p. 163; VI WC, pp. 240–44; Summers, *Conspiracy*, p. 60; Anson, *"They've Killed the President!"*, p. 28; Thompson, *Six Seconds in Dallas*, pp. 121–22.
50. VII WC, pp. 106–7; XIX WC, pp. 516, 518; Anson, *"They've Killed the President!"*, p. 28.
51. Thompson, *Six Seconds in Dallas*, p. 122; VII WC, p. 107.

52. Thompson, *Six Seconds in Dallas*, p. 122.
53. XIX WC, p. 479; VI WC, pp. 206, 209–13; *Dallas Morning News*, August 27, 1978, December 31, 1978, June 10, 1979; XIII HSCA, p. 11; Summers, *Conspiracy*, pp. 81–82.
54. XIX WC, p. 492; Thompson, *Six Seconds in Dallas*, pp. 123, 253; Summers, *Conspiracy*, p. 80; Meagher, *Accessories*, pp. 19–20; VI WC, p. 211.
55. CD 385, pp. 24–27; CD 5, p. 70; VI WC, pp. 266–67; XIX WC, p. 524; Shaw with Harris, *Cover-up*, pp. 16–17.
56. Anson, *"They've Killed the President!"*, p. 32; XIII HSCA, pp. 8–9; CD 385, pp. 24–27; Thompson, *Six Seconds in Dallas*, p. 241.
57. Shaw with Harris, *Cover-up*, p. 13; XIII HSCA, pp. 8–9.
58. CD 5, p. 70; XIII HSCA, p. 18; Shaw with Harris, *Cover-up*, p. 14; Anson, *"They've Killed the President!"*, p. 32.
59. Shaw with Harris, *Cover-up*, p. 14.
60. Award of Merit for Roger Dean Craig, Dallas County Sheriff's Department, 1960; CD 205, p. 47.
61. XIX WC, p. 524; XIII HSCA, p. 17.
62. XIII HSCA, p. 18; XIX WC, p. 524.
63. WR, pp. 52, 446; Shaw with Harris, *Cover-up*, pp. 15–17.
64. XIX WC, p. 524; XIII HSCA, p. 18; CD 205, p. 47.
65. Interview with Roger Craig, Jr., 1983.
66. NBC News, *Seventy Hours and Thirty Minutes*.
67. Shaw with Harris, *Cover-up*, pp. 82–90. Reference for information in footnote is Committee to Investigate Assassinations, *Coincidence or Conspiracy?*, p. 289.
68. XIX WC, p. 540; VI WC, p. 312; I HSCA, pp. 120–21; Shaw with Harris, *Cover-up*, p. 84.
69. I HSCA, pp. 119–21; HSCR, pp. 91–92; interview with Ferrell; Shaw with Harris, *Cover-up*, pp. 83–84.
70. *Dallas Times Herald*, December 8, 1963; Shaw with Harris, *Cover-up*, p. 87.
71. Ibid. (both).
72. *Dallas Times Herald*, November 22, 1963.
73. Ibid.
74. Shaw with Harris, *Cover-up*, p. 88; *Dallas Times Herald*, November 2, 1967.
75. Shaw with Harris, *Cover-up*, p. 88.
76. XIX WC, pp. 476, 517; Shaw with Harris, *Cover-up*, pp. 84–85.
77. Thompson, *Six Seconds in Dallas*, pp. 132, 139; Shaw with Harris, *Cover-up*, p. 84; XX WC, p. 499.
78. Seth Kantor, *Who Was Jack Ruby?*, p. 35; Peter Noyes, *Legacy of Doubt*; FBI Criminal Record #799431; Summers, *Conspiracy*, p. 476;

Anson, *"They've Killed the President!"*, p. 31; Shaw with Harris, *Cover-up*, p. 85; XXIV WC, p. 202; IX HSCA, p. 424.

79. FBI Criminal Record #799431; Shaw with Harris, *Cover-up*, pp. 85–86; David Scheim, *Contract on America*, p. 255; Noyes, *Legacy of Doubt*, p. 81; IX HSCA, p. 397; Committee to Investigate Assassinations, *Coincidence or Conspiracy?*, p. 288; FBI memo to SAC Dallas, February 7, 1977 (DL 89–43–9998).

80. XXIV WC, p. 202; Summers, *Conspiracy*, p. 476.

81. XXIV WC, p. 202; Summers, *Conspiracy*, pp. 476–77; Noyes, *Legacy of Doubt*, pp. 81–82, 85; Committee to Investigate Assassinations, *Coincidence or Conspiracy?*, p. 287; IX HSCA, p. 424; FBI Criminal Record #799431.

82. Committee to Investigate Assassinations, *Coincidence or Conspiracy?*, p. 287; Anson, *"They've Killed the President!"*, p. 31.

83. Interview with Shaw.

84. Award of Merit for Roger Dean Craig, Dallas County Sheriff's Department, 1960; Committee to Investigate Assassinations, *Coincidence or Conspiracy?*, p. 442; Noyes, *Legacy of Doubt*, p. 84; *Dallas Morning News*, May 16, 1975; interview with Craig, Jr., 1983; CD 205, p. 47; XIX WC, p. 524; VI WC, pp. 266–67, 270; VII WC, p. 535; CD 5, p. 70; WR, pp. 160, 252–53.

85. VI WC, p. 270; Michael Kurtz, *Crime of the Century*, p. 131; interview with Craig, Jr., 1983; Mark Lane, *Rush to Judgment*, pp. 173–74; WR, p. 598; interview with Captain J. Will Fritz, January 1983.

86. Interview with Craig, Jr., 1983; Kurtz, *Crime of the Century*, p. 131; IV WC, p. 245.

87. Interview with Craig, Jr., 1983; Jesse Curry, *J.F.K. Assassination File*, p. 72; Kurtz, *Crime of the Century*, p. 132.

88. *Dallas Times Herald*, November 2, 1967, May 16, 1975; interview with Craig, Jr., 1983; FBI memo, SAC Dallas to Director, February 9, 1976 (HQ 62–109060–7500); Anson, *"They've Killed the President!"*, p. 217; Noyes, *Legacy of Doubt*, p. 95.

89. Interview with Craig, Jr., 1983; Anson, *"They've Killed the President!"*, p. 217; *Dallas Morning News*, May 16, 1975; *Dallas Times Herald*, May 16, 1975; XIII HSCA, p. 18.

90. *Dallas Morning News*, August 20, 1978; Shaw with Harris, *Cover-up*, p. 88; XIX WC, p. 523; CD 301, pp. 111–12.

91. Ibid. (all).

92. Shaw with Harris, *Cover-up*, p. 88; XIX WC, p. 523.

93. Senate Select Committee to Study Governmental Operations with Respect to Intelligence Activities, *Final Report, Book Five, The Investigation of the Assassination of President John F. Kennedy*, Book V, 94th Cong., 2d sess., 1976, pp. 884–85; Shaw with Harris, *Cover-up*, p. 88.

94. Interview with Ferrell; interview with Shaw; Shaw with Harris, *Cover-up*, pp. 88–89; Meagher, *Accessories*, p. 10; Kurtz, *Crime of the Century*, p. 42.
95. Fred J. Cook, "The Irregulars Take the Field," *The Nation*, July 19, 1971; interview with Bernard Fensterwald, Jr.
96. Cook, "The Irregulars Take the Field"; interview with Fensterwald; Shaw with Harris, *Cover-up*, p. 90.
97. Ibid. (all).
98. Ibid. (all).
99. I HSCA, p. 115; IV HSCA, pp. 379–81; Shaw with Harris, *Cover-up*, pp. 89, 169; Peter Dale Scott, Paul L. Hoch, and Russell Stetler, eds., *The Assassinations: Dallas and Beyond*, pp. 117, 124, 127; FBI memo, FBI Director to SACs Miami, Atlanta, Knoxville, November 29, 1963 (HQ 62–109060–1245); memo of conversation between Bernard Fensterwald, Jr., and Bill Somersett, Miami, June 5, 1968; HSCR, pp. 91, 234.
100. Abraham Zapruder film; "President Kennedy Is Laid to Rest," *Life*, December 6, 1963.
101. Zapruder film.
102. Richard B. Stolley, "What Happened Next . . . ," *Esquire*, November 1973; WR, pp. 96–97; XVIII WC, pp. 1–85.
103. VI HSCA, p. 175; Senate Select Committee, *Investigation of the Assassination*, p. 23.
104. "President Kennedy Is Laid to Rest."
105. WR, p. 88; *The New York Times*, December 20, 1965.
106. Zapruder film; VI WC, p. 294; David S. Lifton, *Best Evidence*, p. 316.
107. Zapruder film.
108. Meagher, *Accessories*, p. 22; I HSCA, p. 100.
109. I HSCA, pp. 414–27; HSCR, p. 44.
110. VII HSCA, p. 174.
111. HSCR, p. 44.
112. VII WC, pp. 552–53; XXI WC, p. 483.
113. VII WC, p. 553; WR, p. 116.
114. VII WC, p. 547; WR, p. 116; CD 205, p. 31; FBI memo, Rosen to Belmont, June 8, 1964; XX WC, pp. 1–2; FBI laboratory report by L. Shaneyfelt, August 6, 1964 (HQ 105–82555–4668X); XXI WC, p. 475; XV WC, p. 700.
115. XXIII WC, p. 914.
116. FBI memo, FBI Director to SAC Dallas, July 13, 1964 (HQ 62–109060–3659); FBI airtel, SAC Dallas to FBI Director, June 16, 1964 (HQ 105–82555–4295); FBI report, SAC Dallas to FBI Director, attention FBI Laboratory, July 24, 1964 (HQ 62–109060–4199 EBF Pt. 2); *Dallas Morning News*, November 24, 1963.

117. CD 1.
118. *Washington Evening Star*, December 10, 1963.
119. XXI WC, p. 391.
120. FBI airtel, SAC Dallas to FBI Director, June 16, 1964 (HQ 105–82555–4295); *Dallas Morning News*, November 24, 1963.
121. CD 1, p. 1; CD 87, SS235, p. 1; Thompson, *Six Seconds in Dallas*, p. 64.
122. Affidavit of James T. Tague, August 23, 1977, Civil Action no. 75–226, U.S. District Court for the District of Columbia; CD 1245, pp. 32–33.
123. Meagher, *Accessories*, p. 5; VI WC, pp. 162, 167; FBI report, SAC Dallas to FBI Director, attention FBI Laboratory, July 24, 1964 (HQ 62–109060–4199 EBF Pt. 2).
124. VI WC, p. 166; Meagher, *Accessories*, p. 5; CD 5, p. 16.
125. VI WC, pp. 298–99; Meagher, *Accessories*, p. 6.
126. VI WC, p. 299.
127. Meagher, *Accessories*, p. 6.
128. CD 1, p. 1; CD 87, SS235, p. 1; Thompson, *Six Seconds in Dallas*, p. 64.
129. VII WC, pp. 553, 555; Meagher, *Accessories*, p. 6.
130. VII WC, p. 556.
131. Warren Commission memo, Specter to Rankin, June 11, 1964.
132. Interview with Tom Dillard, April 1984; letter, Rankin to Hoover, July 7, 1964 (HQ 62–109060–36); FBI memo, FBI Director to SAC Dallas, July 13, 1964 (HQ 62–109060–3659); XXI WC, p. 472; Meagher, *Accessories*, p. 6; XV WC, p. 697.
133. XXI WC, pp. 473–74; interview with Tom Dillard, April 1984; XV WC, p. 698.
134. XXI WC, pp. 472–74.
135. Meagher, *Accessories*, p. 6; VII WC, p. 552; XV WC, p. 698.
136. Meagher, *Accessories*, p. 6; VII WC, pp. 552–58; Edward J. Epstein, *Inquest*, p. 23.
137. VII WC, pp. 545, 550; Meagher, *Accessories*, p. 6.
138. VII WC, p. 555.
139. VII WC, pp. 555–56; affidavit of Tague, August 23, 1977.
140. XV WC, pp. 698–700; Meagher, *Accessories*, p. 6; *The New York Times*, August 6, 1964; XXI WC, p. 476.
141. CD 1395, p. 1.
142. Ibid.; XXI WC, p. 476.
143. FBI laboratory report by Shaneyfelt, August 6, 1964 (HQ–105–82555–4668x); XXI WC, pp. 475–77; WR, p. 116.
144. XXI WC, p. 476.
145. Ibid.
146. XX WC, p. 1.

147. *Dallas Morning News*, April 6, 1983; interview with James H. Lesar, attorney to Harold Weisberg, 1983; interview with Harold Weisberg.
148. Interview with Lesar, 1983; DeLloyd J. Guth and David R. Wrone, comps., *The Assassination of John F. Kennedy: A Comprehensive Historical and Legal Bibliography, 1963–1979*, p. 53.
149. Interview with Weisberg.
150. Ibid.
151. Harold Weisberg, *Post Mortem*, p. 425.
152. Interview with Lesar, 1983; interview with Weisberg.
153. FBI memo, Stack to Cochran, June 20, 1975; *Federal Supplement*, vol. 438, pp. 492, 502.
154. Brief for Plaintiff-Appellant, Harold Weisberg v. U.S. Dept. of Justice, U.S. Court of Appeals for the DCCA 82-1072, U.S. Court of Appeals for the District of Columbia.
155. Interview with Weisberg.
156. Deposition of FBI Laboratory SA John W. Kilty, June 16, 1981.
157. Interview with Weisberg.
158. Report by Construction Environment, Inc., March 17, 1983.

7: Tippit's Murder: Rosetta Stone or Red Herring?

1. David W. Belin, *November 22, 1963: You Are the Jury*, p. 466.
2. VI WC, pp. 438–39.
3. Ibid., pp. 440, 443–44.
4. Ibid., pp. 439–40; XXII WC, p. 93; XXIV WC, p. 882.
5. XXIV WC, p. 882; VI WC, p. 441.
6. WR, pp. 156–58; Harold Weisberg, *Whitewash*, p. 111.
7. WR, pp. 158, 161–62; Michael Kurtz, *Crime of the Century*, pp. 128–29; CD 87, SS447.
8. WR, pp. 158, 162; CD 87, SS447; Kurtz, *Crime of the Century*, pp. 13–14.
9. Kurtz, *Crime of the Century*, p. 127; WR, pp. 157–58, 161–62.
10. VI WC, pp. 443–44; Kurtz, *Crime of the Century*, p. 134; XXV WC, pp. 909–15; WR, pp. 158, 166.
11. Weisberg, *Whitewash II*, p. 27; Kurtz, *Crime of the Century*, p. 199; Sylvia Meagher, *Accessories After the Fact*, p. 254.
12. WR, pp. 165, 176; III HSCA, p. 588.
13. WR, pp. 158, 165; Meagher, *Accessories*, p. 267; Kurtz, *Crime of the Century*, pp. 137–38.
14. WR, p. 165.
15. VI WC, pp. 448–49; WR, p. 165; Gaeton Fonzi, "Loose Ends," *Greater Philadelphia Magazine*, January 1967; XXIII WC, p. 857; XXIV WC, p. 202.
16. Meagher, *Accessories*, pp. 283–92; WR, pp. 183–87.

17. WR, p. 16; Committee to Investigate Assassinations, *Coincidence or Conspiracy?*, p. 424.
18. I HSCA, p. 443; VI WC, p. 448; III WC, p. 466; WR, p. 559. References for information in footnote are WR, pp. 558–59; report by Dr. William J. Bruchey, Jr., May 8, 1984.
19. WR, pp. 6, 158, 163; VI WC, p. 438; XXIII WC, p. 857; XXIV WC, p. 882; Kurtz, *Crime of the Century*, p. 134.
20. III WC, p. 306; George Nash and Patricia Nash, "The Other Witnesses," *The New Leader*, October 12, 1964.
21. Kurtz, *Crime of the Century*, p. 135; Meagher, *Accessories*, pp. 254–55; III WC, p. 306; XXIV WC, p. 202.
22. WR, p. 6; Meagher, *Accessories*, pp. 254–55.
23. Interview with William F. Alexander, former Dallas assistant district attorney, 1983.
24. WR, pp. 166–71; Meagher, *Accessories*, pp. 255–56; VI WC, p. 447. Reference for information in footnote is Kurtz, *Crime of the Century*, p. 138.
25. III WC, pp. 310–11; XX WC, p. 500.
26. III WC, p. 304.
27. Ibid., pp. 310–11.
28. Ibid., p. 319.
29. Anthony Summers, *Conspiracy*, pp. 116–17; WR, p. 166; Nash and Nash, "The Other Witnesses."
30. VII WC, pp. 234, 238, 241, 246; Meagher, *Accessories*, pp. 257–58; Nash and Nash, "The Other Witnesses."
31. WR, pp. 166–69, 171; Meagher, *Accessories*, p. 258.
32. XI WC, pp. 434–36; XXV WC, p. 731.
33. XI WC, p. 436; XXV WC, p. 731.
34. XI WC, p. 435; XXV WC, p. 731.
35. XXV WC, p. 731.
36. XI WC, pp. 434–35, 437–38; XXV WC, p. 870.
37. Kurtz, *Crime of the Century*, p. 137; Meagher, *Accessories*, p. 256; XXIII WC, p. 858; XXIV WC, p. 202; Nash and Nash, "The Other Witnesses"; Fonzi, "Loose Ends."
38. Belin, *November 22, 1963*, p. 112.
39. Nash and Nash, "The Other Witnesses"; Fonzi, "Loose Ends"; Summers, *Conspiracy*, p. 121; Mark Lane, *Rush to Judgment*, p. 194.
40. Nash and Nash, "The Other Witnesses."
41. Ibid.; Lane, *Rush to Judgment*, p. 194.
42. Lane, *Rush to Judgment*, p. 194; Summers, *Conspiracy*, pp. 120, 123; Robert Sam Anson, *"They've Killed the President!"*, p. 35; Nash and Nash, "The Other Witnesses"; Fonzi, "Loose Ends."
43. III WC, p. 325; XXIV WC, p. 225; CD 87, SS447; Jesse Curry, *J.F.K. Assassination File*, p. 84; WR, p. 6.
44. Summers, *Conspiracy*, p. 124; VI WC, p. 447.

45. VII WC, p. 274; XIX WC, p. 113.
46. VII WC, p. 274.
47. Fonzi, "Loose Ends"; Lane, *Rush to Judgment*, p. 203; Meagher, *Accessories*, pp. 274–75; XVII WC, p. 471.
48. Josiah Thompson, *Six Seconds in Dallas*, p. 229; Weisberg, *Whitewash* II, p. 27; Weisberg, *Whitewash*, p. 59; Fonzi, "Loose Ends."
49. Thompson, *Six Seconds in Dallas*, pp. 228–29; CD 868; CD 1066i; CD 993; CD 1245.
50. Fonzi, "Loose Ends"; Thompson, *Six Seconds in Dallas*, pp. 228–30; XXIII WC, p. 521; Meagher, *Accessories*, p. 279.
51. Weisberg, *Whitewash*, p. 59.
52. Fonzi, "Loose Ends."
53. VII HSCA, pp. 357, 376; III WC, pp. 466, 475–76.
54. I HSCA, p. 442; III WC, pp. 465, 475.
55. III WC, pp. 465, 475; VII HSCA, p. 375.
56. III WC, pp. 473, 476, 478–79; VII HSCA, p. 378; CD 87, SS447; Weisberg, *Whitewash*, p. 57.
57. XXIV WC, p. 415; interview with J. M. Poe, March 1984.
58. VII WC, pp. 68–69.
59. Interview with Poe, March 1984.
60. Ibid.
61. Interview with Gerald Hill, April 1984.
62. XXIV WC, pp. 253, 260, 332; Summers, *Conspiracy*, p. 119.
63. III WC, pp. 474, 477; Meagher, *Accessories*, p. 281.
64. XXIII WC, pp. 868, 870; Meagher, *Accessories*, p. 273.
65. J. Gary Shaw with Larry R. Harris, *Cover-up*, p. 95.
66. VII WC, pp. 1–4.
67. Ibid., pp. 4, 9, 11.
68. Ibid., pp. 5–6, 11; CD 87, SS447; XXIII WC, p. 873.
69. CD 87, SS447; Weisberg, *Whitewash*, p. 61; WR, p. 174; VII WC, pp. 25, 54.
70. Meagher, *Accessories*, pp. 253–82; interview with Gary Shaw; interview with Alexander, 1983.
71. Interview with Alexander, 1983.
72. Ibid.
73. Ibid.; Meagher, *Accessories*, pp. 253–82; WR, pp. 156–57.
74. XXVI WC, p. 487; WR, p. 6; Earl Golz, "Confidential: The FBI's File on JFK—Part Two," *Gallery*, December 1982; "A Story of Generosity," *U.S. News & World Report*, January 20, 1964; Meagher, *Accessories*, pp. 253–54.
75. "A Story of Generosity"; Frank X. Tolbert, "The Odd Fate of Oswald's Other Victims," *Saturday Evening Post*, August 29, 1964.
76. XXVI WC, p. 487; XIII HSCA, pp. 36–37; Meagher, *Accessories*, p. 260.

77. XXVI WC, p. 487; Meagher, *Accessories*, p. 260.
78. XXI WC, pp. 388–400; Meagher, *Accessories*, pp. 260–66.
79. Meagher, *Accessories*, pp. 260–61; VII WC, pp. 75–82.
80. Meagher, *Accessories*, p. 261; XVII WC, pp. 390–485.
81. Meagher, *Accessories*, p. 261; XVII WC, p. 397; XXIII WC, p. 844.
82. Ibid. (all).
83. Meagher, *Accessories*, p. 262.
84. Ibid.; Kurtz, *Crime of the Century*, p. 198.
85. XXI WC, p. 393; XXIII WC, pp. 844, 850; XVII WC, pp. 397, 401.
86. XXIII WC, p. 844; XVII WC, pp. 397, 410; Meagher, *Accessories*, p. 263.
87. Interview with R. C. Nelson, April 1984.
88. Interview with Murray Jackson, April 1984.
89. Meagher, *Accessories*, p. 262.
90. Letter, Hoover to Rankin, January 14, 1964; Weisberg, *Whitewash*, p. 56; XXIII WC, pp. 842–44.
91. XXIII WC, pp. 843–44; CD 87, SS447; Curry, *J.F.K. Assassination File*, p. 115.
92. Golz, "Confidential: The FBI's File on JFK—Part Two."
93. Ibid.
94. XXVI WC, p. 516; "In the Shadow of Dallas," *Ramparts*, November 1966; XIII HSCA, p. 35; Meagher, *Accessories*, p. 269.
95. Golz, "Confidential: The FBI's File on JFK—Part Two"; Committee to Investigate Assassinations, *Coincidence or Conspiracy?*, pp. 426–27; Anson, *"They've Killed the President!"*, p. 352.
96. Committee to Investigate Assassinations, *Coincidence or Conspiracy?*, pp. 417, 430; IX HSCA, p. 130; XIV WC, pp. 628–29, 634; Golz, "Confidential: The FBI's File on JFK—Part Two"; III HSCA, p. 496; Nash and Nash, "The Other Witnesses"; Weisberg, *Whitewash*, p. 55.
97. XIII HSCA, p. 41; Golz, "Confidential: The FBI's File on JFK—Part Two"; XXVI WC, p. 487.
98. XIII HSCA, p. 41; XXVI WC, pp. 486, 488.
99. XIII HSCA, p. 37.
100. Interview with Shaw.
101. Anonymous letter to Jim Garrison, February 5, 1968.
102. Ibid.
103. Interview with Larry Harris, 1983.
104. Ibid.; birth certificate for child, June 17, 1964.
105. Original petition for divorce, case #68–8294–DR2, District Clerk, Dallas; birth certificate for child.
106. "A Story of Generosity"; Tolbert, "The Odd Fate of Oswald's Other Victims."
107. Original petition for divorce, #68–8294–DR2, Dallas; interview with Harris, 1983; interview with Tippit's lover.

108. Golz, "Confidential: The FBI's File on JFK—Part Two"; XXVI WC, p. 487; "A Story of Generosity."
109. Original petition for divorce, #68–8294–DR2; interview with Tippit's lover.
110. Ibid. (both).
111. Interview with retired Dallas police officer, March 1984.
112. Ibid.

8: Jack Ruby: Pimp for All Seasons

1. WR, p. 22.
2. G. Robert Blakey and Richard Billings, *The Plot to Kill the President,* p. 339.
3. Interviews with Jim Garrison, 1981, 1984.
4. *National Observer,* December 2, 1963; Blakey and Billings, *Plot to Kill,* p. 373.
5. WR, pp. 21–22.
6. HSCR, pp. 148–80.
7. WR, pp. 22, 370, 801; HSCR, pp. 148–49.
8. V WC, pp. 197–98; XX WC, pp. 42–43; HSCR, pp. 148, 158.
9. HSCR, p. 180.
10. Blakey and Billings, *Plot to Kill,* p. xiv.
11. *The New York Times,* January 4, 1967.
12. WR, pp. 779–81, 784–85; Blakey and Billings, *Plot to Kill,* pp. 280–83; *National Observer,* December 2, 1963; FBI report, "Investigation of Killing of Lee Harvey Oswald, Dallas, Texas, November 24, 1963," Dallas, December 13, 1963; CD 4, pp. 13–18, 160–63; CD 223, pp. 2–17.
13. WR, p. 786; Blakey and Billings, *Plot to Kill,* pp. 185, 283; XXII WC, pp. 311, 356, 423; Saul Pett et al., *The Torch Is Passed,* p. 59; IX HSCA, p. 199; FBI Telex, SAC San Francisco to SAC Dallas and Las Vegas, November 26, 1963; *Las Vegas Sun,* October 9, 1978; CD 4, pp. 13–18, 160–63; Seth Kantor, *Who Was Jack Ruby?,* pp. 65, 98; Editors of Time-Life Books, *This Fabulous Century,* pp. 174–75.
14. WR, pp. 786, 788; Kantor, *Who Was Jack Ruby?,* pp. 98–99, 102; Blakey and Billings, *Plot to Kill,* pp. 283–84; XXII WC, p. 433; XXVI WC, pp. 467, 469; *National Observer,* December 2, 1963; CD 4, pp. 13–18, 160–63; CD 223, pp. 2–17; FBI report, "Investigation of Killing of Oswald," Dallas, December 13, 1963.
15. I WC, p. 468; Blakey and Billings, *Plot to Kill,* pp. 285–86, 290; CD 4, pp. 13–18, 160–63; CD 223, pp. 2–17; WR, p. 790; XXV WC, p. 710; IV HSCA, p. 549; XXVI WC, p. 470; FBI report, "Investigation of Killing of Oswald," Dallas, December 13, 1963.

16. IX HSCA, pp. 149, 151, 152, 514, 516–18; Kantor, *Who Was Jack Ruby?*, pp. 102–6; XXII WC, p. 360; David Scheim, *Contract on America*, p. 74.

17. IX HSCA, pp. 152–53; XXII WC, p. 360; Blakey and Billings, *Plot to Kill*, p. 285.

18. IX HSCA, pp. 152–53; Blakey and Billings, *Plot to Kill*, pp. 286, 290; CD 4, pp. 13–18, 160–63; WR, p. 792.

19. Blakey and Billings, *Plot to Kill*, p. 290; XXVI WC, p. 468; IX HSCA, p. 1080.

20. Blakey and Billings, *Plot to Kill*, p. 291; IX HSCA, p. 1080; WR, p. 794.

21. WR, p. 794; IX HSCA, p. 1080; CD 4, pp. 13–18, 160–63; Blakey and Billings, *Plot to Kill*, p. 291.

22. XXIII WC, p. 374.

23. Ibid., pp. 335, 922; XXV WC, p. 709.

24. XXII WC, p. 920.

25. XIV WC, pp. 135, 137–44; IX HSCA, p. 978; Kantor, *Who Was Jack Ruby?*, p. 107; Blakey and Billings, *Plot to Kill*, p. 291; CD 4, pp. 13–18, 160–63; FBI report, "Investigation of Killing of Oswald," Dallas, December 13, 1963.

26. WR, pp. 794–95; CD 4, pp. 13–18, 160–63; CD 223, pp. 2–17; Kantor, *Who Was Jack Ruby?*, pp. 108–9.

27. WR, p. 805.

28. Kantor, *Who Was Jack Ruby?*, p. 109.

29. WR, p. 800; XXIII WC, pp. 17–18.

30. WR, p. 796; XXIII WC, pp. 1, 4, 7; Blakey and Billings, *Plot to Kill*, p. 291; XV WC, pp. 210, 662–63; XXV WC, p. 385.

31. Kantor, *Who Was Jack Ruby?*, p. 110; XXIII WC, p. 369.

32. Kantor, *Who Was Jack Ruby?*, pp. 110–11; CD 732e.

33. Kantor, *Who Was Jack Ruby?*, p. 111; XXIII WC, p. 363; IX HSCA, p. 428.

34. CD 732j; XI HSCA, p. 282; XXVI WC, p. 469; IX HSCA, p. 1080; WR, p. 796; CD 4, pp. 13–18, 160–63.

35. XXVI WC, p. 469; Blakey and Billings, *Plot to Kill*, p. 39; XXIII WC, p. 110; XXII WC, pp. 880, 917; IX HSCA, p. 984; FBI document DL 89–43, 44–1639; FBI Telex, SAC Albuquerque to SAC Dallas, December 23, 1963.

36. XXII WC, p. 327; XXVI WC, p. 469; FBI memo, Switzer to SAC Dallas, June 29, 1964; *Dallas Morning News*, March 12, 1964; Kantor, *Who Was Jack Ruby?*, pp. 173–74; XXV WC, p. 394; WR, p. 804.

37. Kantor, *Who Was Jack Ruby?*, p. 114.

38. Interview with G. Robert Blakey, 1983; *The New York Times*, December 21, 1975; Kantor, *Who Was Jack Ruby?*, pp. 25–26; Blakey and Billings, *Plot to Kill*, pp. 380, 389; Judith Exner, *My Story.*

39. Exner, *My Story*, p. 6; *The New York Times*, December 18, 21, 1975, August 14, 1976; Blakey and Billings, *Plot to Kill*, pp. 379–81.

40. Senate Select Committee to Study Governmental Operations with Respect to Intelligence Activities, *Alleged Assassination Plots Involving Foreign Leaders: Interim Report*, Book V, 94th Cong., 1st sess., November 20, 1975, pp. 74–85; *Las Vegas Sun*, October 9, 1978; *The New York Times*, August 14, 1976; *Miami News*, April 8, 1977; *The New York Times*, February 25, 1977; *Washington Post*, August 27, 1976; interview with Blakey, 1983.

41. Exner, *My Story*, p. 205; Blakey and Billings, *Plot to Kill*, pp. 380–81.

42. Scheim, *Contract on America*, p. 85; XXII WC, p. 335; Blakey and Billings, *Plot to Kill*, p. 292; *Dallas Times Herald*, June 5, 1982.

43. Scheim, *Contract on America*, p. 160; Blakey and Billings, *Plot to Kill*, pp. 79, 229–30, 294; Anthony Summers, *Conspiracy*, p. 267; Kantor, *Who Was Jack Ruby?*, p. 135.

44. IX HSCA, pp. 178–79; *Dallas Morning News*, April 6, 1978; Kantor, *Who Was Jack Ruby?*, pp. 15, 128–29; Blakey and Billings, *Plot to Kill*, pp. 294–95.

45. *Life*, March 10, 1958; IX HSCA, p. 169.

46. CD 732, pp. 1–3; CD 1052; FBI Potential Criminal Informant File of Jack Ruby (HQ 44–24016–1138); Blakey and Billings, *Plot to Kill*, pp. 295–96; Kantor, *Who Was Jack Ruby?*, p. 128.

47. Blakey and Billings, *Plot to Kill*, p. 296; Kantor, *Who Was Jack Ruby?*, p. 128; V HSCA, p. 204; IX HSCA, p. 1082; XXIII WC, p. 61.

48. Blakey and Billings, *Plot to Kill*, pp. 82, 293, 299; V WC, pp. 201, 205; IX HSCA, pp. 159, 164; XXII WC, p. 302; FBI Telex, SAC San Francisco to SAC Dallas and Las Vegas, November 26, 1963; CD 223, pp. 2–17; XXIII WC, p. 170.

49. XXIII WC, pp. 170–71; IX HSCA, p. 161. Reference for information in footnote is IX HSCA, pp. 164–65.

50. CD 686d; Blakey and Billings, *Plot to Kill*, pp. 299–301; V HSCA, pp. 161, 351; IX HSCA, pp. 165, 169; HSCR, pp. 152–54; XXIII WC, p. 170.

51. Blakey and Billings, *Plot to Kill*, pp. 298–99; CD 686d.

52. Interview with Bernard Fensterwald, Jr.; interview with Gary Shaw; interview with Mary Ferrell.

53. IX HSCA, pp. 162–74.

54. III HSCA, pp. 197–281.

55. IX HSCA, p. 173; Blakey and Billings, *Plot to Kill*, pp. 301–2; interview with Blakey, 1983.

56. IV HSCA, p. 552; Blakey and Billings, *Plot to Kill*, p. 293.

57. Blakey and Billings, *Plot to Kill*, p. 302.

58. IX HSCA, p. 162; *The New York Times*, March 15, 1964.

59. Blakey and Billings, *Plot to Kill*, pp. 186, 292, 303; XXIII WC, p.

49; XIV WC, p. 149; IV HSCA, p. 498; IX HSCA, p. 1086. References for information in footnote are IV HSCA, p. 498; HSCR, p. 171.

60. IX HSCA, pp. 1086–87; FBI Telex, Director to Dallas, December 3, 1963 (FBI 44–24106–316); FBI Telex, SAC New Orleans to Dallas, November 26, 1963 (FBI 44–24016–322); FBI Telex, SAC New York to Dallas, December 4, 1963 (FBI 44–24016–463); CD 223, pp. 2–17; FBI Telex, SAC New Orleans to Dallas, November 27, 1963 (FBI 44–24016–52); FBI Teletype, SAC New Orleans to Director and SAC Dallas, November 28, 1963 (FBI 44–24016–530); XXIII WC, pp. 13, 49.

61. XIV WC, p. 149; IX HSCA, pp. 243, 1087; FBI Telex report, Director to Dallas, December 3, 1963 (FBI 44–24016–316); CD 223, pp. 2–17; FBI Telex, SAC New Orleans to Dallas, November 27, 1963 (FBI 44–24016–52); XXII WC, pp. 517–18, 520; XV WC, pp. 210–11; XXI WC, p. 412.

62. XXV WC, pp. 252–54; interview with Blakey, 1983; IX HSCA, pp. 1088–90, 1098.

63. IX HSCA, pp. 191, 196; Kantor, *Who Was Jack Ruby?*, pp. 21–22; Blakey and Billings, *Plot to Kill*, pp. 303, 306, 308.

64. Kantor, *Who Was Jack Ruby?*, p. 10; Blakey and Billings, *Plot to Kill*, p. 307; WR, p. 798.

65. IV HSCA, pp. 496, 561; IX HSCA, pp. 190–91.

66. Kantor, *Who Was Jack Ruby?*, p. 22; Blakey and Billings, *Plot to Kill*, pp. 304–5; XXV WC, p. 244; Robert F. Kennedy, *The Enemy Within*, p. 60; IX HSCA, pp. 194–95.

67. XXV WC, p. 242; IX HSCA, pp. 193, 1040, 1042; Blakey and Billings, *Plot to Kill*, pp. 206, 304; Kantor, *Who Was Jack Ruby?*, p. 30; *The New York Times*, January 22, 1983; *Wall Street Journal*, January 21, 1983.

68. XXV WC, p. 242; IX HSCA, p. 194; HSCR, p. 155; Blakey and Billings, *Plot to Kill*, p. 306.

69. Summers, *Conspiracy*, p. 472.

70. IX HSCA, p. 194.

71. Ibid.; IV HSCA, p. 498; interview with Aaron Kohn, 1983.

72. Kantor, *Who Was Jack Ruby?*, p. 27; IX HSCA, pp. 61, 74; Blakey and Billings, *Plot to Kill*, pp. 243–44.

73. IX HSCA, pp. 75, 77.

74. HSCR, p. 171; IX HSCA, pp. 76–77, 82–83; Blakey and Billings, *Plot to Kill*, pp. 244–45.

75. Blakey and Billings, *Plot to Kill*, p. 245.

76. IX HSCA, p. 84.

77. HSCR, p. 174.

78. CD 4, p. 672; CD 223, pp. 2–17; Blakey and Billings, *Plot to Kill*, p. 315.

79. CD 4, p. 672.

80. Ibid.; CD 223, pp. 2–17; *National Observer*, December 2, 1963; CD 4, pp. 13–18, 160–63; Blakey and Billings, *Plot to Kill*, p. 315; V WC, p. 183. References for information in footnote are V WC, pp. 184, 188; CD 223, pp. 2–17; XX WC, p. 254.

81. XV WC, pp. 578, 583; Kantor, *Who Was Jack Ruby?*, p. 189; Blakey and Billings, *Plot to Kill*, p. 315; interview with Shaw.

82. IX HSCA, pp. 1100, 1103; Kantor, *Who Was Jack Ruby?*, pp. 40–41; XV WC, pp. 72–73, 80.

83. IX HSCA, p. 1103; V WC, p. 207; CD 223, pp. 2–17; WR, pp. 336–37; XV WC, p. 80; XXV WC, pp. 216–17; HSCR, p. 158; Blakey and Billings, *Plot to Kill*, p. 315.

84. V WC, p. 199; *National Observer*, December 2, 1963.

85. WR, pp. 17–18; HSCR, p. 157.

86. V WC, p. 183; CD 223, pp. 2–17; IX HSCA, pp. 335, 343, 363–64, 1099, 1146; *Dallas Morning News*, March 11, 1978; XXV WC, p. 184; Scheim, *Contract on America*, p. 41; Blakey and Billings, *Plot to Kill*, pp. 291, 313–14.

87. IX HSCA, p. 396; Blakey and Billings, *Plot to Kill*, p. 314.

88. WR, pp. 198, 200–204.

89. IX HSCA, pp. 1100, 1106; XIX WC, p. 645; XIII WC, p. 187; XXV WC, pp. 154, 240; XX WC, p. 254; XV WC, pp. 350–52; Blakey and Billings, *Plot to Kill*, pp. 317–18; CD 4, pp. 13–18, 160–63; WR, p. 340.

90. CD 4, pp. 13–18, 160–63; CD 223, pp. 2–17; V WC, pp. 187–88; IX HSCA, p. 1107; WR, p. 208; Blakey and Billings, *Plot to Kill*, p. 318; Kantor, *Who Was Jack Ruby?*, p. 47; XXV WC, p. 554; FBI report, "Investigation of Killing of Oswald," Dallas, December 13, 1963.

91. CD 223, pp. 2–17; V WC, p. 205; Blakey and Billings, *Plot to Kill*, p. 318; Kantor, *Who Was Jack Ruby?*, pp. 11, 47.

92. XXIV WC, pp. 830–31; IX HSCA, p. 187; V WC, p. 189; IV HSCA, p. 550; Kantor, *Who Was Jack Ruby?*, p. 47.

93. IX HSCA, pp. 1113–14; WR, p. 346; XV WC, pp. 434, 587–88; XXV WC, pp. 201, 286–87; Kantor, *Who Was Jack Ruby?*, p. 54.

94. XV WC, pp. 434, 491, 355–57; Scheim, *Contract on America*, p. 123; Blakey and Billings, *Plot to Kill*, p. 319; Kantor, *Who Was Jack Ruby?*, p. 55.

95. XXII WC, pp. 291, 498, 717; XX WC, p. 175.

96. WR, pp. 213, 216. References for information in footnote are XXII WC, p. 870; XV WC, p. 217.

97. *National Observer*, December 2, 1963; CD 4, pp. 13–18, 160–63; Kantor, *Who Was Jack Ruby?*, p. 73; WR, pp. 536–37; *Las Vegas Sun*, October 9, 1978.

98. XX WC, pp. 43–44, 558; XXIV WC, pp. 73, 88; HSCR, pp. 156–57; IX HSCA, pp. 132, 134–39; WR, pp. 221–22.

99. Summers,*Conspiracy*, pp. 487–88; Sylvia Meagher, *Accessories After the Fact*, p. 403; IX HSCA, p. 132. References for information in footnote are IX HSCA, p. 139; copy of Warren Report autographed by Jack Ruby; interview with Patrick Dean, 1983.
100. WR, pp. 340–42.
101. Blakey and Billings, *Plot to Kill*, p. 323.
102. *The New York Times*, February 18, 1964, March 4, 15, 1964, January 4, 1967; *Washington Post*, October 6, 1966; Kantor, *Who Was Jack Ruby?*, pp. 8, 118; Blakey and Billings, *Plot to Kill*, pp. 324, 333.
103. V WC, p. 181; Kantor, *Who Was Jack Ruby?*, p. 7; Blakey and Billings, *Plot to Kill*, p. 334.
104. Kantor, *Who Was Jack Ruby?*, pp. 3, 89; Blakey and Billings, *Plot to Kill*, p. 333; Gerald Ford's description of interview with Ruby, June 7, 1964, Gerald R. Ford Library, Ann Arbor, Michigan.
105. V WC, p. 198; CD 4, pp. 13–18, 160–63; Ford's description of interview with Ruby, June 7, 1964.
106. Melvin Belli with Maurice Carroll, *Dallas Justice*, p. 41.
107. HSCR, p. 148.
108. Ford's description of interview with Ruby, June 7, 1964.
109. V WC, p. 194.
110. V WC, pp. 190–92, 194, 210–11; Ford's description of interview with Ruby, June 7, 1964.
111. V WC, p. 195.
112. WR, p. xiii; examination of Warren Commission volumes.
113. Press conference with Jack Ruby, KTVT-TV, Fort Worth, 1964.
114. Psychiatric examination of Jack Ruby by Dr. Werner Tutour, July 12–15, 1965.
115. Ibid.
116. Blakey and Billings, *Plot to Kill*, pp. 338–39.
117. HSCR, pp. 1, 180.
118. Ibid., pp. 43–44.
119. Ibid., p. 171; IV HSCA, p. 498.
120. HSCR, pp. 161–69; IX HSCA, pp. 60, 76; Blakey and Billings, *Plot to Kill*, pp. 193, 243–44.

9: Fingerprints of Intelligence

1. Anthony Summers, *Conspiracy*, p. 296.
2. WR, pp. 262, 265.
3. Letter, McNamara to Warren, September 22, 1964 (HQ 105–82555–5060); HSCR, p. 207; WR, pp. 327, 659–60; XVII WC, p. 814.
4. The President's Commission on the Assassination of President John F. Kennedy, *Report of Proceedings*, January 27, 1964, pp. 127–212.

5. Ibid., p. 139.
6. Ibid., pp. 152–53.
7. Interview with Gary Shaw; interview with Mary Ferrell; interview with Paul Hoch.
8. FBI memo, DeLoach to Tolson, April 4, 1967 (HQ 44–24016).
9. Preliminary biographical study on Lee Harvey Oswald, December 6, 1963 (CIA 339–136); WR, pp. 377–78; HSCR, p. 170; IX HSCA, p. 95; David Scheim, *Contract on America,* pp. 52–53.
10. WR, pp. 262, 381, 383, 385–86, 680; XXII WC 812; preliminary biographical study on Oswald, December 6, 1963 (CIA 339–136); interviews with Marines, 1977.
11. Preliminary biographical study on Oswald, December 6, 1963 (CIA 339–136); WR, pp. 683–84; Powers and Gentry, *Operation Overflight,* pp. 23, 68, 357; XIX WC, pp. 658, 662; interviews with Marines, 1977; Victor Marchetti and John D. Marks, *The CIA and the Cult of Intelligence,* pp. 356, 388.
12. Preliminary biographical study on Oswald, December 6, 1963 (CIA 339–136); WR, pp. 257–58, 260, 262, 386, 689, 690, 711, 713; XIX WC, pp. 678–79; I WC, p. 202; XI HSCA, p. 117; XVIII WC, p. 419; Marchetti and Marks, *The CIA and the Cult of Intelligence,* pp. 356, 388; Powers and Gentry, *Operation Overflight,* pp. 23, 357; XXII WC, p. 745; interviews with Marines, 1977.
13. WR, pp. 713–14; Sylvia Meagher, *Accessories After the Fact,* p. 328; I WC, p. 135; XXII WC, p. 789; XXIV WC, pp. 866–67; interview with Dennis Ofstein, July 1977; interview with Jack Bowen, July 1977; interview with Terry Savage, July 16, 1977; letter, Hoover to Rankin, March 1964 (HQ 105–82555–2860); interview with Robert Stovall, 1983.
14. CD 7, p. 122; X WC, p. 189; WR, pp. 377, 403, 724–26; Senate Select Committee to Study Governmental Operations with Respect to Intelligence Activities, *Final Report, Book Five, The Investigation of the Assassination of President John F. Kennedy: Performance of the Intelligence Agencies,* 94th Cong., 2d sess., 1976, pp. 11–13; VIII WC, pp. 133, 137, 139; X HSCA, pp. 8–12.
15. HSCR, pp. 140–41; WR, pp. 290, 407, 728; XXIV WC, p. 822.
16. WR, pp. 299–301, 734–36; III HSCA, pp. 25–26, 47.
17. WR, pp. 2–3, 13–14, 216, 377, 736, 738; III WC, p. 214; House Committee on the Judiciary, *Circumstances Surrounding Destruction of the Lee Harvey Oswald Note,* 94th Cong., 1st sess., October 21, December 11, 12, 1975, pp. 126–27.
18. Interviews with Marines, 1977; spokesman for public relations office, Marine Corps Headquarters, Washington, D.C.
19. XXII WC, p. 703; WR, pp. 383–84; XI WC, pp. 117–18.
20. WR, pp. 376, 384, 388–90.
21. WR, pp. 384, 680–81; I WC, p. 200.

22. XIX WC, p. 665; WR, p. 681; interviews with Marines, 1977; Edward J. Epstein, *Legend*, p. 63.
23. Interviews with Marines, 1977; Summers, *Conspiracy*, pp. 143, 147; WR, pp. 315, 388; VIII WC, pp. 299, 315, 319–20, 323.
24. Interviews with Marines, 1977; VIII WC, p. 315; WR, p. 380; XX WC, pp. 89–90; XIX WC, pp. 660, 665; Epstein, *Legend*, p. 64.
25. WR, pp. 682–83; XIX WC, pp. 755–56; Epstein, *Legend*, p. 65; Summers, *Conspiracy*, p. 143; VIII WC, p. 126.
26. XIX WC, pp. 658, 662, 753–54; WR, p. 683; spokesman for the public relations office, Marine Corps Headquarters, Washington, D.C.
27. WR, p. 683; XIX WC, p. 658; interviews with Marines, 1977; Marchetti and Marks, *The CIA and the Cult of Intelligence*, pp. 25, 208; Powers and Gentry, *Operation Overflight*, pp. 61, 357; CD 931; Summers, *Conspiracy*, pp. 231–32; XXIV WC, p. 340.
28. CD 654; interviews with Marines, 1977; Summers, *Conspiracy*, pp. 145–47; IX WC, p. 242; Epstein, *Legend*, pp. 71, 82–83; CD 36, p. 8; VIII WC, p. 316.
29. WR, pp. 663–64; Office of Naval Intelligence, document #163; XXIII WC, p. 796; Summers, *Conspiracy*, p. 146; VIII WC, p. 320; interviews with Marines, 1977; XIX WC, p. 663.
30. Interviews with Marines, 1977; CD 36, p. 8; Summers, *Conspiracy*, p. 146.
31. XXIII WC, p. 796; WR, pp. 683–84; Summers, *Conspiracy*, p. 146; Powers and Gentry, *Operation Overflight*, p. 68; CD 36, p. 8.
32. Interviews with Miguel Rodriguez, January 1977; XXIII WC, p. 796; WR, pp. 386, 684; CD 324, p. 1; CD 75, p. 395; XIX WC, p. 664.
33. IX WC, p. 242; Epstein, *Legend*, p. 71.
34. VIII WC, p. 309; XXIII WC, p. 796; interviews with Marines, 1977.
35. VIII WC, p. 309; Summers, *Conspiracy*, p. 146; Epstein, *Legend*, p. 79; XXIII WC, p. 797; HSCR, p. 220; WR, p. 684.
36. Summers, *Conspiracy*, p. 147; Epstein, *Legend*, pp. 82–83; XXIII WC, p. 797.
37. Epstein, *Legend*, p. 82.
38. WR, pp. 255, 257, 684–85; XIX WC, pp. 658, 662; XVI WC, p. 337; XXII WC, p. 180; Epstein, *Legend*, pp. 85–86; Summers, *Conspiracy*, pp. 147–48.
39. Summers, *Conspiracy*, p. 148; VIII WC, pp. 241, 250, 253; Epstein, *Legend*, p. 88.
40. CD 129, p. 1; XXIV WC, p. 430; WR, p. 685; VIII WC, p. 321.
41. The President's Commission on the Assassination of President John F. Kennedy, *Report of Proceedings*, January 27, 1964, p. 192.
42. Spokesman for the Defense Language Institute, Arlington, Va.; The President's Commission on the Assassination of President John F. Kennedy, *Report of Proceedings*, January 27, 1964.

43. Summers, *Conspiracy*, pp. 159–60; HSCR, pp. 198–99; *The New York Times*, March 27, 1978; *Washington Post*, August 3, 1978.

44. XVI WC, p. 94; WR, pp. 260, 262, 265, 690; XVIII WC, pp. 98, 101, 419; XIX WC, p. 734; *The New York Times*, November 1, 3, 1959. Reference for information in footnote is VIII WC, pp. 297–98.

45. XVIII WC, p. 162; WR, p. 690.

46. HSCR, p. 219.

47. WR, pp. 655–57; HSCR, pp. 219–21.

48. XVI WC, p. 621; WR, p. 688; preliminary biographical study on Oswald, December 6, 1963 (CIA 339–136); XIX WC, pp. 725, 732–33, 735–36.

49. WR, pp. 257–58, 688–89; I WC, p. 202; preliminary biographical study on Oswald, December 6, 1963 (CIA 339–136); XI WC, p. 117.

50. WR, p. 690; XI WC, pp. 117–18; FBI report, SAC El Paso to Director, March 15, 1977 (HQ 62–109060–7675); interviews with Billy Joe Lord. (Unless otherwise noted, all information in the following section comes from these interviews.)

51. Interviews with Marines, 1977; VIII WC, pp. 297–98.

52. Epstein, *Legend*, p. 101.

53. WR, p. 690; XVIII WC, p. 162; Meagher, *Accessories*, p. 331; XXVI WC, p. 32; HSCR, p. 211.

54. HSCR, p. 211.

55. WR, pp. 257, 713, 741–45; Meagher, *Accessories*, p. 330; XXVI WC, p. 32.

56. WR, pp. 258, 690; XXVI WC, p. 88; HSCR, pp. 211–12.

57. David C. Martin, *Wilderness of Mirrors*, p. 10.

58. Marchetti and Marks, *The CIA and the Cult of Intelligence*, p. 472; WR, pp. 260, 392, 692; XVIII WC, pp. 466–73; XVI WC, p. 94.

59. XVI WC, pp. 94–105; WR, pp. 259–60.

60. XVIII WC, pp. 97–102; WR, pp. 260, 695; XXII WC, p. 703; I WC, p. 128; XVI WC, pp. 815–22.

61. WR, pp. 274–75; Summers, *Conspiracy*, p. 208.

62. XXII WC, p. 120; XVIII WC, pp. 404–5, 430; WR, pp. 267, 269, 393, 697–98; XVI WC, p. 99.

63. WR, pp. 259, 394–95; XVI WC, pp. 100–105.

64. WR, pp. 274, 416, 657, 702–3; XVI WC, pp. 99, 102; I WC, p. 2; Summers, *Conspiracy*, pp. 189–90, 743, 745; XXII WC, p. 119; V WC, p. 407; XVIII WC, pp. 600, 605; IX WC, p. 229.

65. XVI WC, pp. 102–3; WR, pp. 274, 278, 704–6; V WC, p. 410; XXII WC, pp. 119–21; William J. Gill, *The Ordeal of Otto Otepka*, p. 325.

66. WR, pp. 711, 712; XXII WC, p. 48; VIII WC, p. 169; IX WC, p. 248; V WC, pp. 415, 592; Meagher, *Accessories*, pp. 328–29.

67. WR, pp. 277, 325–26, 704–6, 712; XVI WC, p. 705; Meagher, *Accessories*, pp. 327, 343–45; V WC, p. 417.

68. WR, pp. 712–14; I WC, pp. 3–4, 318, 331; Summers, *Conspiracy,* p. 216.
69. HSCR, p. 101; Thomas Powers, *The Man Who Kept the Secrets,* p. 54; II HSCA, pp. 436, 443–44, 449, 464; Summers, *Conspiracy,* pp. 195–96; IV HSCA, p. 21. References for information in footnote are Henry Hurt, *Shadrin,* p. 272; WR, p. 712.
70. II HSCA, p. 497; Summers, *Conspiracy,* pp. 199–200.
71. Powers, *The Man Who Kept the Secrets,* pp. 54, 284; HSCR, pp. 101–2; Summers, *Conspiracy,* pp. 199–202; II HSCA, pp. 436, 444–48, 495.
72. II HSCA, pp. 437, 452; Summers, *Conspiracy,* p. 200; HSCR, p. 102.
73. The President's Commission on the Assassination of President John F. Kennedy, *Report of Proceedings,* January 27, 1964, pp. 202–3.
74. Powers and Gentry, *Operation Overflight,* pp. 58, 60, 69, 141, 354, 358; Harold Berman, introduction, *The Trial of the U-2,* pp. iii, vii, xiv; David Wise and Thomas Ross, *The U-2 Affair,* pp. 16–17, 74, 82, 108. Reference for information in footnote is House Permanent Select Committee on Intelligence, *Soviet Active Measures,* 97th Cong., 2d sess., July 13–14, 1982, pp. 137, 151–52.
75. Summers, *Conspiracy,* p. 185.
76. CIA memo, "Additional Notes and Comments on the Oswald Case," December 11, 1963 (CIA 376–154).
77. Meagher, *Accessories,* p. 113; XXVI WC, p. 59. References for information in footnote are FBI memo, Malley to SAC Dallas, November 23, 1963 (DL 89–43–1295); FBI memo, Heitman to SAC (89–43), November 30, 1963; FBI memo, Shanklin to File (89–43), November 29, 1963 (DL 89–43–1297).
78. I WC, pp. 2, 11, 13, 16.
79. V WC, pp. 387–88; 393; WR, p. 188; Meagher, *Accessories,* p. 241; XXII WC, p. 786.
80. XI HSCA, pp. 126–27; Summers, *Conspiracy,* pp. 188–89.
81. XI HSCA, p. 126.
82. Interview with Ferrell.
83. WR, pp. 657, 702–3; I WC, p. 84; Priscilla Johnson McMillan, *Marina and Lee,* pp. 13–26; Summers, *Conspiracy,* pp. 189–90; XXII WC, pp. 743–45; XVI WC, p. 80.
84. XVI WC, p. 80; Summers, *Conspiracy,* pp. 190–91.
85. CIA memo, November 25, 1963 (CIA 435–173A).
86. XII HSCA, pp. 437, 449–50; Summers, *Conspiracy,* p. 191.
87. HSCR, p. 208.
88. Ibid., pp. 204–5, 218; XX WC, pp. 474–75; Summers, *Conspiracy,* p. 210.
89. Lance Morrow, "J.F.K.," *Time,* November 14, 1983; Adam B. Olam, "Lost Frontier," *New Republic,* November 21, 1983; "Foreign Re-

lations: The Backdown," *Time*, Special Anniversary Issue, November 1983; Steve Neal, "Reconsidering Kennedy," *Philadelphia*, November 1983; *The New York Times*, October 23, 24, 1962; David Wise and Thomas Ross, *The Invisible Government*, p. 295; Arthur M. Schlesinger, Jr., *A Thousand Days*, pp. 729, 733, 737; I HSCA, p. 157.

90. Herbert S. Parmet, *JFK*, p. 284; Powers and Gentry, *Operation Overflight*, p. 342; David A. Phillips, *The Night Watch*, p. 125; Schlesinger, *A Thousand Days*, pp. 731–33; Marchetti and Marks, *The CIA and the Cult of Intelligence*, pp. 179, 310; "Foreign Relations: The Backdown"; *The New York Times*, October 24, 29, 1962.

91. Morrow, "J.F.K."; "Foreign Relations: The Backdown"; Neal, "Reconsidering Kennedy"; *The New York Times*, October 29, 1962; Wise and Ross, *The Invisible Government*, pp. 299–300; HSCR, pp. 106, 132; I HSCA, p. 7; X HSCA, p. 12.

92. Interview with Charles Calverly, June 18, 1977; interview with Ofstein, July 1977; interviews with Bowen, July 1977; interview with Savage, July 1977; *Dallas Morning News*, June 15, 1978; Powers and Gentry, *Operation Overflight*, p. 342; Marchetti and Marks, *The CIA and the Cult of Intelligence*, p. 308; Summers, *Conspiracy*, p. 231; interview with Stovall, 1983; interviews with Leonard Calverly, June and July 1977.

93. Summers, *Conspiracy*, pp. 230–31; interview with Charles Calverly, June 1977; interviews with Leonard Calverly, June and July 1977; interviews with Bowen, July 1977; interview with Savage, July 1977; letter, Hurt to Epstein, July 25, 1977; XXV WC, pp. 65–66; CD 205, p. 471.

94. X WC, pp. 163–66, 230; letter, Hoover to Rankin, March 31, 1964 (HQ 105–82555–2860); CD 385, pp. 224, 226; CD 5, pp. 283–84; XXIV WC, pp. 866–67.

95. IX WC, pp. 168–69, 173, 190, 236; XIII HSCA, pp. 50, 55, 63; Summers, *Conspiracy*, pp. 222–28.

96. XXIV WC, p. 867; Summers, *Conspiracy*, pp. 229–30; WR, pp. 281–82, 716–17; IX WC, pp. 222–26, 236.

97. Epstein, *Legend*, p. 189.

98. XXII WC, p. 789; X WC, pp. 150, 166; CD 385, pp. 224–26; CD 5, pp. 283–84; WR, p. 402.

99. Letter, Hoover to Rankin, March 31, 1964; Schlesinger, *A Thousand Days*, pp. 732–33; interview with Charles Calverly, June 1977; interviews with Leonard Calverly, June and July 1977; interview with Ofstein, July 1977; interviews with Bowen, July 1977; interview with Savage, July 1977; interview with Stovall, 1983.

100. Powers and Gentry, *Operation Overflight*, p. 357; interview with Stovall, 1983; WR, pp. 402–3.

101. X WC, p. 179; interview with Louise Latham, June 1977.
102. X WC, pp. 117, 136, 143, 174–79; interviews with Leonard Calverly, June and July 1977; interviews with Bowen, July 1977; CD 7, pp. 123–24.
103. Interview with Latham, June 1977; X WC, pp. 117, 130, 138.
104. Interview with Latham, June 1977.
105. Ibid.
106. CD 897, pp. 445–47; CD 735, pp. 329–37; letter, Rankin to Hoover, January 23, 1964 (105–82555–1730); WR, p. 720; XI WC, pp. 121, 133, 137, 138; VIII WC, p. 395; I WC, p. 8; interview with Ferrell.
107. XXII WC, p. 272; WR, pp. 287–89, 309; XIX WC, pp. 576–80; XX WC, pp. 261–68.
108. Epstein, *Legend,* pp. 204–6.
109. XX WC, pp. 155–61; Summers, *Conspiracy,* p. 228.
110. FBI airtel, Director to SAC Dallas, February 14, 1964 (HQ 105–82555–2010); FBI memo, Branigan to Sullivan, February 3, 1964 (HQ-82555–1699); FBI memo, Griffith to Conrad, February 11, 1964; XXII WC, p. 735; XVI WC, pp. 3, 5, 7; WR, pp. 119, 174, 185.
111. WR, p. 183; XI WC, p. 405; XVI WC, pp. 437–38, 440–41.
112. WR, pp. 183–87, 198, 562; XXIII WC, p. 757; IX WC, pp. 249, 317.
113. IX WC, pp. 248, 276–81, 299; WR, pp. 282–83; XIII HSCA, p. 57. References for information in footnote are *Wall Street Journal,* November 22, 1983; Epstein, *Legend,* p. xiv.
114. X WC, p. 187; WR, pp. 403, 724; CD 7, p. 122. References for information in footnote are Summers, *Conspiracy,* p. 237; interview with Ferrell.
115. Summers, *Conspiracy,* p. 292; *Dallas Times Herald,* April 24, 1963; I WC, p. 21; IV HSCA, p. 480; VIII WC, pp. 133, 184.
116. Senate Select Committee to Study Governmental Operations with Respect to Intelligence Activities, *Final Report, Book Five, The Investigation of the Assassination of President John F. Kennedy,* pp. 11–13, 65; spokesman for the Cuban American Foundation, Washington, D.C.
117. X HSCA, pp. 6–7, 9, 11; Arthur M. Schlesinger, Jr., *Robert Kennedy and His Times,* p. 478; Schlesinger, *A Thousand Days,* pp. 204–5; HSCR, p. 115.
118. VIII WC, pp. 59, 72, 137, 139, 186; WR, pp. 403, 726; HSCR, p. 193; Summers, *Conspiracy,* pp. 311–12; X WC, pp. 220–28; IV HSCA, p. 480.
119. WR, pp. 290–92, 407; XIX WC, p. 175; IV HSCA, p. 482; XXI WC, p. 621; XVI WC, p. 33.
120. HSCR, p. 193; Summers, *Conspiracy,* p. 312.
121. WR, pp. 407, 410, 412, 727; XX WC, pp. 257–58; XXII WC, pp. 803–8; I WC, pp. 20, 40.

122. CIA memo, "Additional Notes and Comments on the Oswald Case," December 11, 1963 (CIA 376–154).
123. WR, pp. 407, 728; XXII WC, p. 820; XI WC, pp. 163–65; XXI WC, p. 621.
124. XX WC, p. 528; XIX WC, p. 175; XI WC, p. 165; WR, p. 291.
125. XXII WC, p. 828; X HSCA, pp. 123–27; HSCR, pp. 143–46, 170; Summers, *Conspiracy*, pp. 315–16, 324.
126. X HSCA, pp. 15, 57, 123; HSCR, pp. 141, 144, 146.
127. FBI report, interview of Carroll S. Thomas, New Orleans, March 21, 1967 (NO 89–69–1781; HQ 62–109060–4864); X HSCA, p. 127; HSCR, pp. 143–44; James Kirkwood, *American Grotesque.*
128. VIII WC, p. 14; X HSCA, pp. 108, 115, 132; I WC, p. 199; Summers, *Conspiracy*, pp. 330–31.
129. HSCR, pp. 142–43, 145.
130. WR, p. 727; XVII WC, pp. 666–67; Meagher, *Accessories*, p. 336.
131. XXI WC, pp. 43–44; XI WC, p. 350.
132. XI WC, pp. 341–42, 350–51.
133. WR, p. 727; interview with Orest Pena, 1981.
134. WR, p. 730; XXV WC, pp. 674, 677; HSCR, p. 218.
135. XXIV WC, p. 685; XXV WC, p. 18; XI WC, p. 360; CD 75, p. 364; CD 21, p. 25.
136. WR, p. 730; FBI file on William George Gaudet (82–1602); HSCR, p. 218; Summers, *Conspiracy*, p. 363; CD 21, p. 25.
137. FBI file on Gaudet (82–1602); letter, Ferrell to Fensterwald, May 5, 1975; memo of conversation between Gaudet and Fensterwald, May 13, 1975; CD 75, p. 588; CIA reports (CIA F82–0381/7–8); Foreign Service of the U.S. memo, Bragonier to State Dept., February 2, 1951 (State Dept. 920.6211/2–1251); State Dept. memo to certain American Diplomatic Officers in the other American Republics, February 2, 1951 (State Dept. 920.6211/2–251).
138. FBI file on Gaudet (82–1602); memo of conversation between Gaudet and Fensterwald, May 13, 1975; letter, Ferrell to Fensterwald, May 5, 1975; CD 75, p. 588; Peter Dale Scott, *Crime and Cover-up*, p. 15; Summers, *Conspiracy*, p. 363.
139. Memo of conversation between Gaudet and Fensterwald, May 13, 1975; Scott, *Crime and Cover-up*, p. 15; HSCR, p. 219; Summers, *Conspiracy*, pp. 363–64.
140. HSCR, p. 219; CD 75, p. 588; memo of conversation between Gaudet and Fensterwald, May 13, 1975; Summers, *Conspiracy*, pp. 363–66; FBI file on Gaudet (82–1602).
141. HSCR, p. 218; Senate Select Committee, *Investigation of the Assassination*, p. 65.
142. WR, pp. 119, 174, 185, 292, 407.
143. X HSCA, p. 21; HSCR, pp. 138–39.

144. WR, pp. 299, 732–33; XI WC, pp. 214, 217.
145. Ibid. (both).
146. WR, pp. 331, 733; FBI memo, Handley to Rosen, November 29, 1963 (HQ 62–109060–1111); IV HSCA, pp. 257, 326, 352.
147. WR, pp. 299–301, 306, 734–35; III HSCA, p. 25–26, 47.
148. III HSCA, pp. 33–34, 130–31, 142; WR, pp. 288, 301, 734.
149. III HSCA, pp. 34–35, 141; WR, pp. 301, 734–35.
150. III HSCA, pp. 25, 48, 133, 154.
151. Ibid., pp. 78, 136.
152. Ibid., p. 130; Summers, *Conspiracy*, pp. 371–72; HSCR, p. 124.
153. HSCR, p. 124; III HSCA, p. 136.
154. Summers, *Conspiracy*, p. 376.
155. III HSCA, p. 103.
156. Ibid., pp. 103–5; XXIV WC, p. 7.
157. Summers, *Conspiracy*, pp. 377–78; III HSCA, p. 177.
158. Interview with David A. Phillips, 1984; HSCR, p. 251; Phillips, *The Night Watch*, p. 114; Summers, *Conspiracy*, pp. 379–80.
159. HSCR, pp. 249–50; Phillips, *The Night Watch*, p. 141; XX WC, p. 691; XVI WC, p. 638.
160. IV HSCA, p. 219; CD 347, p. 1.
161. HSCR, p. 251; XXII WC, p. 745.
162. HSCR, pp. 248, 641.
163. John F. Kennedy Special, WBAI, November 22, 1983.
164. Ibid.
165. HSCR, p. 125.
166. WR, pp. 309, 735; XVI WC, p. 33.
167. CD 5, pp. 196–97; III WC, p. 214; WR, p. 738.
168. *Dallas Morning News*, February 6, 1977, April 2, 1977; anonymous letter to Penn Jones, Jr., August 18, 1975; IV HSCA, p. 337.
169. *Dallas Morning News*, February 6, 1977, April 2, 6, 1977, September 26, 1978; IV HSCA, pp. 358–59.
170. IV HSCA, p. 337.
171. *Dallas Morning News*, February 6, 1977, March 7, 1977, April 2, 1977; Scheim, *Contract on America*, p. 255; XXVI WC, p. 473; XXV WC, p. 194.
172. FBI memo, Legal Counsel to Associate Director, February 9, 1977 (HQ 62–117290–161).
173. XVII WC, p. 681; Meagher, *Accessories*, p. 182; WR, pp. 180–81.
174. *Dallas Morning News*, March 19, 1978; HSCR, pp. 221–22.
175. HSCR, pp. 222–23; *Dallas Morning News*, March 19, 1978.
176. HSCR, p. 223.
177. *Dallas Morning News*, March 19, 1978; HSCR, p. 223.
178. WR, pp. x-xi, xiii; HSCR, p. 223; Warren Commission memo, Slawson to Stern, March 31, 1964; letters, Rankin to McNaughton, February

18, 1964, March 11, 1964; letter, McNaughton to Rankin, received March 5, 1964; letter, Bartino to Rankin, March 16, 1964.
179. HSCR, pp. 223–24.
180. Ibid., p. 224.
181. Ibid., p. 2.
182. XVIII WC, pp. 52–54. Reference for information in footnote is HSCR, p. 222.
183. WR, pp. 118–19, 174, 182, 571–72; XVII WC, p. 681.
184. WR, pp. 118–19, 409.
185. HSCR, pp. 205, 208–9.
186. Letter, Paul Hoch to Donovan Gay, October 8, 1977.
187. Peter Dale Scott et al., "Beyond Conspiracy" (unpublished).
188. Ibid.
189. Senate Select Committee, *Investigation of the Assassination,* p. 54.
190. IV HSCA, p. 184.
191. Ibid., pp. 178, 184, 186.
192. Summers, *Conspiracy,* pp. 171–72.
193. Interview with naval officer, March 24, 1981.
194. Ibid.
195. Record of John Hurt's telephone call to Oswald, November 23, 1963; *Raleigh Spectator,* July 17, 24, 1980; *The News and Observer* (Raleigh), July 17, 1980; Surell Brady, HSCA Book 3, vol. VIII, E7 (unpublished).
196. *Raleigh Spectator,* July 17, 1980; interview with Mrs. John Hurt, March 1982; *The News and Observer,* July 17, 1980; Brady, HSCA Book 3, vol. VIII, E7.
197. Interview with Mrs. Hurt, March 1982; *Raleigh Spectator,* July 17, 1980; *The News and Observer,* July 17, 1980; Brady, HSCA Book 3, vol. VIII, E7; Summers, *Conspiracy,* p. 176. Reference for information in footnote is interview with Victor Marchetti, 1983.
198. Interview with Mrs. Hurt, March 1982.
199. Gill, *The Ordeal of Otto Otepka,* p. 324; Committee to Investigate Assassinations, *Coincidence or Conspiracy?,* p. 231; Summers, *Conspiracy,* p. 180; interview with Otto Otepka, 1983.
200. Charles Stevenson and William J. Gill, "The Ordeal of Otto Otepka," *Reader's Digest,* August 1965; Committee to Investigate Assassinations, *Coincidence or Conspiracy?,* pp. 230–31; interview with Otepka, 1983.
201. Committee to Investigate Assassinations, *Coincidence or Conspiracy?,* p. 231.
202. XVII WC, p. 816.
203. CD 49, p. 22.
204. HSCR, p. 200; CD 692, p. 111.
205. HSCR, p. 202; CD 692, p. 111.

206. Memo, Mark Allen to Interested Researchers, March 14, 1979; CIA memo on documents available in Oswald's 201 file, February 20, 1964 (CIA 568–810); IV HSCA, p. 208; HSCR, pp. 203–4.
207. HSCR, pp. 200, 202; IV HSCA, pp. 197–201, 209; Summers, *Conspiracy*, pp. 166–68.
208. CIA memo, November 25, 1963 (CIA 435–173A).
209. Ibid.
210. Interview with Donald Deneselya, 1982; HSCR, p. 208.
211. Interview with Deneselya, 1982; HSCR, p. 209.
212. Interview with Pena, 1981.
213. Gerald R. Ford with John R. Stiles, *Portrait of the Assassin*, pp. 21–25; The President's Commission on the Assassination of President John F. Kennedy, *Report of Proceedings*, January 27, 1964, pp. 127–212.
214. *Dallas Morning News*, February 20, 1978; FBI memo, Jones to DeLoach, February 10, 1964 (HQ 105–82555–2638); President's Commission on the Assassination of President John F. Kennedy, *Report of Proceedings*, January 27, 1964, pp. 143–47.
215. President's Commission on the Assassination of President John F. Kennedy, *Report of Proceedings*, January 27, 1964, p. 143.
216. XXVI WC, p. 92; Epstein, *Legend*, p. 163.
217. XVII WC, pp. 728, 730; House Committee on the Judiciary, *Circumstances Surrounding Destruction*, p. 224.
218. I WC, p. 20; HSCR, p. 190; XVII WC, p. 738; WR, p. 716. Reference for information in footnote is Senate Select Committee, *Investigation of the Assassination*, p. 51.
219. HSCR, p. 191; XVII WC, pp. 758–60; House Committee on the Judiciary, *Circumstances Surrounding Destruction*, p. 225.
220. WR, p. 420; House Committee on the Judiciary, *Circumstances Surrounding Destruction*, p. 125; FBI memo, Jones to DeLoach, March 30, 1964; FBI report by Hosty, December 6, 1963; CE 833; FBI memo—DL 57–5593–15; interview with James Hosty, 1983.
221. House Committee on the Judiciary, *Circumstances Surrounding Destruction*, pp. 126–27; interview with Hosty, 1983; I WC, p. 57; IX WC, p. 341.
222. XVI WC, p. 64; HSCR, pp. 186, 244; Meagher, *Accessories*, pp. 210–11; House Committee on the Judiciary, *Circumstances Surrounding Destruction*, pp. 19, 32; FBI memo, Jones to DeLoach, March 30, 1964.
223. I WC, p. 49; House Committee on the Judiciary, *Circumstances Surrounding Destruction*, p. 132; XIII HSCA, pp. 157, 328; III WC, pp. 18, 102; WR, p. 327; HSCR, p. 185.
224. House Committee on the Judiciary, *Circumstances Surrounding Destruction*, pp. 125, 137, 168–69; FBI report by Hosty, December 6,

1963; interview with Hosty, 1983; FBI memo, Bassett to Callahan, December 31, 1975 (HQ 62–109060–7462x). References for information in footnote are interview with Hosty, 1983; WR, pp. 309–10; FBI memo—DL 57–5593–15; CD 347, p. 1; XI HSCA, pp. 173, 175.
225. Senate Select Committee, *Investigation of the Assassination*, p. 51.
226. Ibid.
227. Ibid., p. 51; interview with Hosty, 1983.
228. Interview with Hosty, 1983; House Committee on the Judiciary, *Circumstances Surrounding Destruction*; FBI memo, Director to Attorney General, July 29, 1975 (HQ 62–109060–7229x).
229. House Committee on the Judiciary, *Circumstances Surrounding Destruction*, pp. 4, 37; FBI memo, Director to Attorney General, July 29, 1975 (HQ 62–109060–7229x).
230. House Committee on the Judiciary, *Circumstances Surrounding Destruction*, pp. 4, 42; FBI memo, Director to Attorney General, July 29, 1975 (HQ 62–109060–7229x); FBI memo, Bassett to Callahan, December 31, 1975 (HQ 62–109060–7462x).
231. House Committee on the Judiciary, *Circumstances Surrounding Destruction*, p. 4; FBI memo, Director to Attorney General, July 29, 1975 (HQ 62–109060–7229x).
232. House Committee on the Judiciary, *Circumstances Surrounding Destruction*, pp. 2–33, 129–30; FBI memo, Director to Attorney General, July 29, 1975 (HQ 62–109060–7229x); *Washington Post*, October 22, 1975.
233. House Committee on the Judiciary, *Circumstances Surrounding Destruction*, pp. 132, 160; FBI memo, Director to Attorney General, July 29, 1975 (HQ 62–109060–7229x); HSCR, p. 195.
234. HSCR, pp. 195–96; FBI memo, Director to Attorney General, July 29, 1975 (HQ 62–109060–7229x); FBI memo, Bassett to Callahan, December 31, 1975 (HQ 62–109060–7462x); *Washington Post*, October 22, 1975; House Committee on the Judiciary, *Circumstances Surrounding Destruction*, pp. 5, 62, 134; HSCR, p. 196.

10: New Orleans, USA

1. Inaugural speech, January 20, 1961, John F. Kennedy Library.
2. Ralph G. Martin, *A Hero for Our Time*, p. 262.
3. X HSCA, p. 6; HSCR, p. 24; Richard M. Nixon, "Cuba, Castro, and John F. Kennedy," *Reader's Digest*, November 1964; Warren Hinckle and William Turner, *The Fish Is Red*, pp. 20–21; Taylor Branch and George Crile III, "The Kennedy Vendetta," *Harper's*, August 1975.
4. HSCR, p. 25; Hinckle and Turner, *The Fish Is Red*, pp. 17, 99, 200; IV HSCA, p. 471; David Scheim, *Contract on America*, p. 156; in-

terview with Dr. Jorge Dominguez, specialist on Cuban affairs, Harvard University, 1984; interview with William Attwood, 1983.

5. ABC-TV News, "Fidel Castro Speaks," Barbara Walters interview, June 9, 1977; Daniel Schorr, *Clearing the Air*, p. 175; X HSCA, pp. 181–82; Senate Select Committee to Study Governmental Operations with Respect to Intelligence Activities, *Alleged Assassination Plots Involving Foreign Leaders: An Interim Report*, 94th Cong., 1st sess., November 20, 1975, p. 71.

6. IX HSCA, p. 14; Scheim, *Contract on America*, p. 160; Senate Select Committee, *Alleged Assassination Plots*, pp. 74–85, 100; G. Robert Blakey and Richard Billings, *Plot to Kill*, pp. 229–30; Hinckle and Turner, *The Fish Is Red*, pp. 25, 78; Ovid Demaris, *The Last Mafioso*, p. 108.

7. Senate Select Committee, *Alleged Assassination Plots*, p. 85; HSCR, pp. 33–34, 114; IX HSCA, p. 60; Scheim, *Contract on America*, pp. 3, 38–39; Harris Wofford, *Of Kennedys and Kings*, pp. 401, 403; Hinckle and Turner, *The Fish Is Red*, p. 215; Herbert S. Parmet, *JFK*, p. 60; Nixon, "Cuba, Castro, and John F. Kennedy."

8. Robert Sam Anson, *"They've Killed the President!"*, p. 16; Scheim, *Contract on America*, pp. 57–158; "How Tax Changes Split Policy-Makers," *Nation's Business*, November 1962; "Depletion Allowance: Loophole or Merited Relief?", *Business Week*, April 1, 1961; "Kennedy's Latest Word on Tax Cuts," *U.S. News & World Report*, December 24, 1962; spokesman for the Texas Independent Producers and Royalty Owners Association, Austin.

9. Louis Lomax, "The Kennedys Move in on Dixie," *Harper's*, May 1962; "The South: Crisis in Civil Rights," *Time*, June 2, 1961; Simeon Booker, "What Negroes Can Expect from Kennedy," *Ebony*, January 1961; HSCR, p. 31; Hinckle and Turner, *The Fish Is Red*, p. 199.

10. Spokesman for the Cuban American Foundation, Washington, D.C.

11. Interview with Aaron Kohn, 1983.

12. Ibid.; Warren Rogers, "The Persecution of Clay Shaw," *Look*, August 26, 1969; "Carlos Marcello: King Thug of Louisiana," *Life*, September 8, 1967.

13. WR, pp. 670, 725–31.

14. *New Orleans States-Item*, February 17, 23, and 24, 1967; Rosemary James and Jack Wardlaw, *Plot or Politics?*, pp. 16, 26; "A Taste for Conspiracy," *Newsweek*, March 20, 1967; Joachim Joesten, *The Garrison Enquiry*, p. 10; Eric Norden, "Playboy Interview: Jim Garrison," *Playboy*, October 1967; Committee to Investigate Assassinations, *Coincidence or Conspiracy?*, p. 459; WR, p. 21; Edward J. Epstein, *Counterplot*, p. 21.

15. *New Orleans States-Item*, February 24, 1967.

16. "Clay Shaw," *Penthouse*, November 1969; *Washington Post*, March 4, 1969; *New York Post*, March 1, 1969.

17. James and Wardlaw, *Plot or Politics?*, pp. 16–18, 21–22, 29, 72; *The New York Times*, February 25, 1967, March 2, 1969; Rogers, "The Persecution of Clay Shaw"; interview with Kohn, 1983; *Washington Post*, February 23, 1969; James Phelan, "Rush to Judgment in New Orleans," *Saturday Evening Post*, May 6, 1967; *New Orleans States-Item*, February 23, 1967; Jim Garrison, *A Heritage of Stone*; interview with Jim Garrison; Joesten, *The Garrison Enquiry*, pp. 18–19; FBI memo on assassination of John Kennedy, February 20, 1967 (HQ 105–82555); Epstein, *Counterplot*, p. 24; James Kirkwood, *American Grotesque*, p. 78; Walter Sheridan, *The Fall and Rise of Jimmy Hoffa*, p. 78; Bernard Fensterwald, "Jim Garrison, District Attorney Orleans Parish vs. the Federal Government," *Computers and Automation*, August 1971.

18. Epstein, *Counterplot*, p. 25; Sheridan, *The Fall and Rise of Jimmy Hoffa*; Rogers, "The Persecution of Clay Shaw"; Blakey and Billings, *Plot to Kill*, p. 50; *Wall Street Journal*, February 9, 1968; Anson, *"They've Killed the President!"*, pp. 126–27; interview with Kohn, 1983; Kirkwood, *American Grotesque*, p. 529; James and Wardlaw, *Plot or Politics?*, p. 26.

19. Scheim, *Contract on America*, p. 57.

20. Ibid., p. 59.

21. Interview with Kohn, 1983.

22. Phelan, "Rush to Judgment in New Orleans."

23. *New Orleans States-Item*, February 17, 23, 1967; Norden, "Playboy Interview: Jim Garrison"; Phelan, "Rush to Judgment in New Orleans"; James and Wardlaw, *Plot or Politics?*, pp. 33–34, 39; Kirkwood, *American Grotesque*, p. 141; Joesten, *The Garrison Enquiry*, pp. 10, 12; *Dallas Times Herald*, February 19, 1967; FBI memo (HQ 105–82555); statement of George Lardner, Jr., to New Orleans district attorney's office, February 22, 1967.

24. Kirkwood, *American Grotesque*, pp. 123–26; X HSCA, pp. 106, 110; Blakey and Billings, *Plot to Kill*, p. 167; James and Wardlaw, *Plot or Politics?*, pp. 42–43; Joesten, *The Garrison Enquiry*, p. 11; Harold Weisberg, *Oswald in New Orleans*, pp. 165–66; FBI memo, DeLoach to Tolson, February 23, 1967 (HQ 62–109060–4582); CD 87; interview with Harold Weisberg; Garrison, *A Heritage of Stone*, p. 121; *The New York Times*, February 23, 1967.

25. Kirkwood, *American Grotesque*, p. 124; Blakey and Billings, *Plot to Kill*, p. 167; Phelan, "Rush to Judgment in New Orleans"; James and Wardlaw, *Plot or Politics?*, p. 43; X HSCA, pp. 106–7, 109; Weisberg, *Oswald in New Orleans*, p. 163; Joesten, *The Garrison Enquiry*, pp. 11–12; CD 75, pp. 285–97; *New Orleans States-Item*, February 23, 1967; *Chicago Sun-Times*, March 29, 1967; interview by Bernard Fensterwald of Victor Marchetti, April 22, 1975; Garrison, *A Heritage of Stone*, p. 122; Committee to Investigate Assassinations, *Coinci-*

dence or Conspiracy?, pp. 298–99; Hinckle and Turner, *The Fish Is Red*, p. 204; Peter Boyles, "Fear and Loathing on the Assassination Trail," *Denver Magazine*, November 1980.

26. Blakey and Billings, *Plot to Kill*, p. 168; X HSCA, pp. 108, 110; Joesten, *The Garrison Enquiry*, p. 11; Kirkwood, *American Grotesque*, pp. 123–25; James and Wardlaw, *Plot or Politics?*, p. 42; *The New York Times*, February 23, 1967; X HSCA, p. 112; HSCR, p. 142.

27. *Dallas Times Herald*, February 19, 1967; Kirkwood, *American Grotesque*, p. 142; James and Wardlaw, *Plot or Politics?*, p. 39; *The New York Times*, February 23, 1967; X HSCA, p. 105; *Chicago Tribune*, February 23, 1967; Joesten, *The Garrison Enquiry*, p. 29; HSCR, p. 39; Phelan, "Rush to Judgment in New Orleans"; *New Orleans States-Item*, February 23, 1967; CD 87; FBI memo, Rosen to Belmont, November 29, 1963; IX HSCA, p. 103.

28. *Washington Post*, February 23, 1967, March 1, 1967; statement of Lardner to New Orleans district attorney's office, February 22, 1967; *Chicago Tribune*, February 23, 1967; Kirkwood, *American Grotesque*, p. 142; James and Wardlaw, *Plot or Politics?*, p. 40; *New York World Journal Tribune*, February 23, 1967; *Washington Post*, February 23, 1967.

29. FBI memo (HQ 62–109060–4582); Weisberg, *Oswald in New Orleans*, p. 163; *The New York Times*, February 23, 1967; Kirkwood, *American Grotesque*, p. 142; James and Wardlaw, *Plot or Politics?*, p. 40; CD 75, pp. 285–97; FBI teletype, SAC New Orleans to Director, et al. (HQ 62–109060–482).

30. *Chicago Tribune*, February 23, 1967; *New York World Journal Tribune*, February 23, 1967; *Washington Post*, March 1, 1967; FBI airtel, SAC New Orleans to Director, February 28, 1967 (HQ 62–109060–4579).

31. *New York World Journal Tribune*, February 23, 24, 1967; Kirkwood, *American Grotesque*, p. 124; *Washington Post*, March 1, 1967; *Chicago Tribune*, February 23, 1967.

32. *New York World Journal Tribune*, February 23, 1967; *New Orleans States-Item*, February 23, 1967, January 13, 1979; *The New York Times*, February 23, 1967; *Chicago Tribune*, February 23, 1967; Kirkwood, *American Grotesque*, p. 143.

33. Weisberg, *Oswald in New Orleans*, p. 163; *New York World Journal Tribune*, February 28, 1967.

34. FBI memo (HQ 62–109060–4582).

35. *New Orleans States-Item*, February 24, 1967.

36. Kirkwood, *American Grotesque*, pp. 19, 26–27, 145; "Clay Shaw"; Rogers, "The Persecution of Clay Shaw"; FBI memo, Branigan to Sullivan, March 2, 1967 (HQ 105–82555); *The New York Times*, March 2, 3, 1967; Epstein, *Counterplot*, p. 65; Phelan, "Rush to

Judgment in New Orleans"; James and Wardlaw, *Plot or Politics?*, p. 53.

37. James and Wardlaw, *Plot or Politics?*, pp. 16–30, 54, 59; *The New York Times*, August 16, 1974; Rogers, "The Persecution of Clay Shaw"; "Clay Shaw"; Kirkwood, *American Grotesque*, pp. 27, 80; interview with Kohn, 1983; Anson, *"They've Killed the President!"*, p. 119.

38. "Clay Shaw"; Rogers, "The Persecution of Clay Shaw"; Blakey and Billings, *Plot to Kill*, p. 51; Kirkwood, *American Grotesque*, p. 154; James and Wardlaw, *Plot or Politics?*, p. 68; *The New York Times*, March 2, 3, 1967, March 2, 1969; Norden, "Playboy Interview: Jim Garrison"; *Los Angeles Free Press*, February 9–15, 1968; Epstein, *Counterplot*, p. 74.

39. *The New York Times*, March 3, 1967; James and Wardlaw, *Plot or Politics?*, p. 58.

40. *The New York Times*, March 3, 1967.

41. Phelan, "Rush to Judgment in New Orleans"; James and Wardlaw, *Plot or Politics?*, p. 59.

42. Norden, "Playboy Interview: Jim Garrison."

43. "Clay Shaw"; *Chicago Sun-Times*, March 29, 1967; *The New York Times*, March 18, 1967; Kirkwood, *American Grotesque*, pp. 60, 64–65.

44. *The New York Times*, March 18, 1967; Rogers, "The Persecution of Clay Shaw"; James and Wardlaw, *Plot or Politics?*, pp. 14, 22, 74, 76–78; Kirkwood, *American Grotesque*, p. 144; *The New York Times*, March 16, 1967; Phelan, "Rush to Judgment in New Orleans"; *Dallas Morning News*, March 15, 1967.

45. "Clay Shaw"; James and Wardlaw, *Plot or Politics?*, p. 78; *Dallas Morning News*, March 15, 1967; Epstein, *Counterplot*, p. 55; *The New York Times*, March 16, 1967.

46. Kirkwood, *American Grotesque*, pp. 157, 225; James and Wardlaw, *Plot or Politics?*, pp. 81, 136; *The New York Times*, March 18, 1967; Phelan, "Rush to Judgment in New Orleans"; "Clay Shaw."

47. *The New York Times*, March 18, 1967; Phelan, "Rush to Judgment in New Orleans"; Kirkwood, *American Grotesque*, p. 157; James and Wardlaw, *Plot or Politics?*, p. 81.

48. James Phelan, *Scandals, Scamps and Scoundrels*, pp. 166–67.

49. Epstein, *Counterplot*, pp. 70–71; *Washington Post*, February 23, 1969; *New York Post*, February 12, 1968; *The New York Times*, September 22, 1967, March 2, 1969; *Cincinnati Enquirer*, September 11, 1967; *Daily Oklahoman*, December 10, 1967; interview with Kohn, 1983; interview with Mary Ferrell; Norden, "Playboy Interview: Jim Garrison"; interview with Jim Garrison; Blakey and Billings, *Plot to Kill*, p. 50; *Washington Post*, July 13, 1968; Kirkwood, *American Grotesque*, p. 492.

50. Anson, *"They've Killed the President!"*, pp. 113–14; interview with Kohn, 1983; *Cincinnati Enquirer*, September 11, 1967.

51. *The New York Times*, July 12, 1968; Norden, "Playboy Interview: Jim Garrison"; Rogers, "The Persecution of Clay Shaw"; James and Wardlaw, *Plot or Politics?*, pp. 122, 133; Blakey and Billings, *Plot to Kill*, pp. 45, 51; Anson, *"They've Killed the President!"*, p. 110; Kirkwood, *American Grotesque*, pp. 178–79; interview with Weisberg; interview with Ferrell. References for information in footnote are interview with Weisberg; interview with Ferrell; interview with Sylvia Meagher; Weisberg, *Oswald in New Orleans*.

52. Phelan, "Rush to Judgment in New Orleans"; *New Orleans Times-Picayune*, February 27, 1969; Phelan, *Scandals, Scamps and Scoundrels*, pp. 139, 143–45.

53. Phelan, *Scandals, Scamps and Scoundrels*, pp. 139–45; *New Orleans Times-Picayune*, February 27, 1969; Phelan, "Rush to Judgment in New Orleans."

54. Phelan, *Scandals, Scamps and Scoundrels*, pp. 142, 145–51; Phelan, "Rush to Judgment in New Orleans."

55. Phelan, *Scandals, Scamps and Scoundrels*, p. 151; Phelan, "Rush to Judgment in New Orleans."

56. *New Orleans Times-Picayune*, February 27, 1969; Phelan, "Rush to Judgment in New Orleans"; Phelan, *Scandals, Scamps and Scoundrels*, pp. 151–52; FBI memo, Branigan to Sullivan, February 13, 1969; *The New York Times*, February 20, 1969; Kirkwood, *American Grotesque*.

57. Phelan, *Scandals, Scamps and Scoundrels*, p. 152.

58. *Washington Post*, February 23, 1969; Phelan, "Rush to Judgment in New Orleans"; James and Wardlaw, *Plot or Politics?*, p. 29; *New Orleans Times-Picayune*, February 27, 1969; FBI memo, Branigan to Sullivan, February 13, 1969; Phelan, *Scandals, Scamps and Scoundrels*, pp. 152–54; "Clay Shaw"; Kirkwood, *American Grotesque*, p. 150.

59. Phelan, *Scandals, Scamps and Scoundrels*, pp. 154–55; *New Orleans Times-Picayune*, February 27, 1969.

60. *New Orleans Times-Picayune*, February 27, 1969; Phelan, *Scandals, Scamps and Scoundrels*, pp. 156–58; James and Wardlaw, *Plot or Politics?*, pp. 78, 81; "Clay Shaw"; Kirkwood, *American Grotesque*, p. 157; *The New York Times*, March 18, 1967; Phelan, "Rush to Judgment in New Orleans."

61. *New Orleans Times-Picayune*, February 27, 1969; Phelan, *Scandals, Scamps and Scoundrels*, p. 158; Phelan, "Rush to Judgment in New Orleans"; FBI memo, Branigan to Sullivan, February 13, 1969.

62. Kirkwood, *American Grotesque*, pp. 211, 399; Phelan, *Scandals, Scamps and Scoundrels*, p. 159; Phelan, "Rush to Judgment in New Orleans"; FBI memo, Branigan to Sullivan, February 13, 1969.

63. Phelan, *Scandals, Scamps and Scoundrels*, p. 159; *New Orleans Times-Picayune*, February 27, 1969.

64. Phelan, "Rush to Judgment in New Orleans"; "Clay Shaw"; Phelan, *Scandals, Scamps and Scoundrels*, pp. 159–60; James and Wardlaw, *Plot or Politics?*, pp. 79–80; *The New York Times*, February 27, 1969; *New Orleans Times-Picayune*, February 27, 1969.

65. Epstein, *Counterplot*, pp. 75–80; interview with Tom Bethell, researcher for Garrison during Shaw case, 1983; *Dallas Times Herald*, November 21, 1982; interview with Ferrell.

66. *The New York Times*, April 19, 1967, January 27, 1968, November 9, 1968; James and Wardlaw, *Plot or Politics?*, pp. 81, 114; *Atlanta Journal*, May 10, 1967; "Clay Shaw"; interview with Garrison; Epstein, *Counterplot*, pp. 96, 118, 133; *Washington Post*, February 17, 1968; Anson, *"They've Killed the President!"*, p. 122; FBI memo, Branigan to Sullivan, May 8, 1968 (HQ 62–109060–6404); CIA memo, "Garrison Investigation; Queries from Justice Dept.," September 28, 1967 (CIA 1326–1042); FBI memo, Branigan to Sullivan, May 14, 1968; FBI memo, Branigan to Sullivan, May 13, 1968 (HQ 62–109060–6405).

67. James and Wardlaw, *Plot or Politics?*, p. 114; Blakey and Billings, *Plot to Kill*, p. 50; *Washington Post*, July 13, 1968; *The New York Times*, May 10, 1967, June 25, 1967, March 2, 1969; Kirkwood, *American Grotesque*, pp. 492, 535; interview with G. Robert Blakey; *Washington Post*, February 23, 1969; *National Observer*, March 1969; FBI memo, Branigan to Sullivan, May 8, 1968 (HQ 62–109060–6404); Epstein, *Counterplot*, p. 133; interview with Kohn, 1983; "Clay Shaw."

68. *Washington Post*, January 21, 1969; *The New York Times*, January 21, 22, 1969; "Clay Shaw"; Kirkwood, *American Grotesque*, pp. 62–63.

69. *Dallas Morning News*, February 2, 1969; "Clay Shaw"; Kirkwood, *American Grotesque*, pp. 62, 187.

70. *Washington Post*, February 7, 1969; *New Orleans Times-Picayune*, February 22, 1969; HSCR, p. 142; IV HSCA, p. 485; Kirkwood, *American Grotesque*, pp. 213–23; Blakey and Billings, *Plot to Kill*, p. 170; interview with Ferrell.

71. Kirkwood, *American Grotesque*, pp. 249–50, 290, 399–401, 479; "Clay Shaw"; *Chicago Sun-Times*, March 29, 1967; *The New York Times*, February 27, 1969; Rogers, "The Persecution of Clay Shaw"; *New Orleans Times-Picayune*, February 27, 1969. References for information in footnote are Kirkwood, *American Grotesque*, pp. 442, 612; *The New York Times*, February 12, 1969; *New Orleans Times-Picayune*, February 27, 1969; *Dallas Times Herald*, November 21, 1982; *Washington Post*, February 27, 1969.

72. Kirkwood, *American Grotesque*, pp. 368, 404–7, 410; *New York News*, February 28, 1969; "Clay Shaw"; *New Orleans Times-Picayune*, February 22, 1969; *National Observer*, February 24, 1969.

73. *Washington Post*, February 14, 1969, March 4, 1969; *National Observer*, February 24, 1969, March 1969; Kirkwood, *American Grotesque*, pp. 97, 311–14, 315, 320–21, 324, 332, 361, 374; *The New York Times*, February 16, 25, and 26, 1969, March 2, 1969; "Clay Shaw"; interview with Garrison; *New Orleans States-Item*, February 19, 20, 1969; *New Orleans Times-Picayune*, February 26, 1969.

74. *Washington Post*, February 8, 1969; *The New York Times*, February 8, 1969, March 2, 1969; Kirkwood, *American Grotesque*, pp. 231–32; Rogers, "The Persecution of Clay Shaw"; interview with Ferrell.

75. *The New York Times*, February 8, 10, 1969; *Washington Post*, February 8, 1969; Kirkwood, *American Grotesque*, pp. 232, 239; Rogers, "The Persecution of Clay Shaw."

76. *New Orleans States-Item*, February 20, 1969; *The New York Times*, February 8, 1969, March 2, 1969, August 16, 1974; Rogers, "The Persecution of Clay Shaw"; Kirkwood, *American Grotesque*, pp. 235–36.

77. Kirkwood, *American Grotesque*, pp. 240, 242; interview with Ferrell; Rogers, "The Persecution of Clay Shaw."

78. Kirkwood, *American Grotesque*, pp. 207, 306–7, 348, 397–98, 423–25; *New Orleans States-Item*, February 19, 20, and 26, 1969; *The New York Times*, February 20, 26, 1969; *New Orleans Times-Picayune*, February 27, 1969.

79. Arrest record for Clay Shaw, New Orleans; *New Orleans States-Item*, February 20, 1969; Kirkwood, *American Grotesque*, p. 353; spokesman for New Orleans Police Department; *The New York Times*, February 20, 1969.

80. Interview with Ferrell; *New Orleans States-Item*, February 20, 1969; *The New York Times*, February 20, 1969; Kirkwood, *American Grotesque*, p. 353.

81. Kirkwood, *American Grotesque*, p. 358; *New Orleans States-Item*, February 20, 1969.

82. *New Orleans States-Item*, February 20, 1969.

83. Ibid.; *The New York Times*, February 20, 1969; Kirkwood, *American Grotesque*, pp. 353–59; spokesman for New Orleans Police Department.

84. XI WC, pp. 325–39; XXVI WC, p. 771; FBI memo, Branigan to Sullivan, March 2, 1967 (HQ 105–82555); *The New York Times*, March 3, 11, 1967; XXIII WC, p. 726; Kirkwood, *American Grotesque*, p. 130; *New Orleans Times-Picayune*, February 26, 1969; "Clay Shaw"; James and Wardlaw, *Plot or Politics?*, pp. 14, 53.

85. *New Orleans Times-Picayune*, February 26, 1969; Kirkwood, *American Grotesque*, pp. 139–40, 159–60, 385–95; James and Wardlaw, *Plot or Politics?*, p. 140; interview with Garrison.
86. *New York Post*, February 24, 1969; Kirkwood, *American Grotesque*, pp. 404–5, 491; interview with Ferrell; "Clay Shaw."
87. Interview with Garrison; Kirkwood, *American Grotesque*, pp. 454–60; *Washington Post*, March 2, 1969.
88. Kirkwood, *American Grotesque*, pp. 459–60.
89. *National Observer*, March 1969; *Dallas Times Herald*, November 21, 1982; "Clay Shaw"; *Washington Post*, March 2, 1969; Kirkwood, *American Grotesque*, pp. 461, 466, 472–73; *The New York Times*, March 4, 1969; *New York News*, March 2, 1969; Rogers, "The Persecution of Clay Shaw."
90. *The New York Times*, March 4, 1969, August 16, 1974; *Washington Post*, March 4, 1969; Kirkwood, *American Grotesque*, p. 478; "Clay Shaw"; *Dallas Times Herald*, November 21, 1982; *New York Post*, March 7, 1969; interview with Kathryn Kuss, cousin of Clay Shaw, 1983.
91. *The New York Times*, March 4, 1969, November 30, 1969; Kirkwood, *American Grotesque*, pp. 471, 477; *Christian Science Monitor*, March 5, 1969; *Washington Post*, March 4, 1969; *National Observer*, March 1969; *New York Post*, March 1, 3, and 7, 1969; *New York News*, March 2, 1969.
92. *New Orleans States-Item*, March 1, 1969.
93. *The New York Times*, March 2, 1969.
94. Rogers, "The Persecution of Clay Shaw"; *The New York Times*, November 30, 1969; *Christian Science Monitor*, March 5, 1969; *Washington Post*, March 4, 1969; Kirkwood, *American Grotesque*, pp. 471, 477; *New York Post*, March 1, 3, and 7, 1969.
95. Rogers, "The Persecution of Clay Shaw"; *The New York Times*, March 3, 1969; Kirkwood, *American Grotesque*, pp. 26–27, 471, 477, 603; Phelan, "Rush to Judgment in New Orleans"; interview with Kohn, 1983.
96. Rogers, "The Persecution of Clay Shaw"; interview with Kohn, 1983; *The New York Times*, November 10, 1969, February 22, 1970, December 17, 1973, March 27, 1974, August 16, 1974; *New Orleans Times-Picayune*, December 19, 1973; Kirkwood, *American Grotesque*, p. 648.
97. *Christian Science Monitor*, July 3, 1971; *The New York Times*, July 2, 1971; *Wall Street Journal*, May 30, 1972; indictment, U.S. v. Jim Garrison, et al., U.S. District Court, Eastern District of Louisiana (CA 71–542); indictment, U.S. v. Jim Garrison, U.S. District Court, Eastern District of Louisiana, New Orleans Division (CA 71–541); judgment, U.S. v. Jim Garrison, U.S. District Court, Eastern District

of Louisiana (CA 71–542); judgment, U.S. v. Jim Garrison, U.S. District Court, Eastern District of Louisiana (CA 71–541); interview with Garrison; *The New York Times*, March 27, 31, 1974, May 29, 1978.
98. Interview with Garrison.
99. Ibid.
100. FBI report, interview of Carroll S. Thomas, New Orleans, March 21, 1967 (N.O. 89–69–1781; HQ 62–109060–4864).
101. HSCR, p. 142; Blakey and Billings, *Plot to Kill*, p. 170; Kirkwood, *American Grotesque*, pp. 213–15.
102. HSCR, pp. 142–43.
103. HSCR, pp. 143, 145–46; Blakey and Billings, *Plot to Kill*, p. 170; Kirkwood, *American Grotesque*, pp. 129, 214–16; Anson, *"They've Killed the President!"*, p. 121; Summers, *Conspiracy*, p. 335; *New Orleans Times-Picayune*, February 27, 1969; "Clay Shaw"; X HSCA, pp. 110, 126.
104. Interview with Garrison; Kirkwood, *American Grotesque*, p. 574; "Clay Shaw."
105. *The New York Times*, March 2, 3, 1967; Kirkwood, *American Grotesque*, pp. 18–19; James and Wardlaw, *Plot or Politics?*, pp. 55, 63–64, 67; FBI memo, Branigan to Sullivan, March 2, 1967 (HQ 105–82555); "Clay Shaw"; Norden, "Playboy Interview: Jim Garrison"; Committee to Investigate Assassinations, *Coincidence or Conspiracy?*, p. 451; *New Orleans Times-Picayune*, February 27, 1969.
106. Norden, "Playboy Interview: Jim Garrison"; interview with Kuss, 1983; Kirkwood, *American Grotesque;* Anson, *"They've Killed the President!"*, p. 114; interview with Kohn, 1983.
107. Committee to Investigate Assassinations, *Coincidence or Conspiracy?*, p. 454; Rogers, "The Persecution of Clay Shaw"; James and Wardlaw, *Plot or Politics?*, p. 59; interview with Kohn, 1983; interview with Kuss, 1983.
108. FBI memo, Branigan to Sullivan, March 2, 1967 (HQ 105–82555).
109. Spokesman for New Orleans Police Department; interview with Kuss, 1983; Rogers, "The Persecution of Clay Shaw."
110. CIA memo, "Garrison Investigation: Queries from Justice Department," September 28, 1967.
111. Ibid.
112. Ibid.
113. The President's Commission on the Assassination of President John F. Kennedy, *Report of Proceedings*, January 27, 1964, p. 152.
114. Senate Select Committee, *Alleged Assassination Plots*, p. 91; CIA memo, "Garrison Investigation," September 28, 1967 (CIA 1326–1042); Hinckle and Turner, *The Fish Is Red*, p. 87. References for

information in footnote are Martin, *A Hero for Our Time*, pp. 329–30; Charles Murphy, "Cuba: The Record Set Straight," *Fortune*, September 1961; Herbert S. Parmet, *JFK*, pp. 158–59, 169; Hinckle and Turner, *The Fish Is Red*, pp. 92, 100; Arthur M. Schlesinger, Jr., *A Thousand Days*, p. 256; *The New York Times*, April 25, 1966.

115. Interview with Ferrell; interview with Paul Hoch. References for information in footnote are WR, p. 65; Committee to Investigate Assassinations, *Coincidence or Conspiracy?*, p. 237; David A. Phillips, *The Night Watch*, p. 86.

116. HSCR, p. 170.

117. HSCR, pp. 144, 170–71; X HSCA, pp. 107, 126; Rogers, "The Persecution of Clay Shaw"; CD 75, p. 287; Anson, *"They've Killed the President!"*, p. 121; Kirkwood, *American Grotesque*, pp. 129, 216.

118. Summers, *Conspiracy*, p. 329; interview by Fensterwald of Marchetti, April 22, 1975; Committee to Investigate Assassinations, *Coincidence or Conspiracy?*, p. 302; Hinckle and Turner, *The Fish Is Red*, p. 204; interview with Marchetti, 1983.

119. X HSCA, pp. 109, 111–12; HSCR, pp. 143, 147, 169–70; Rogers, "The Persecution of Clay Shaw"; Anson, *"They've Killed the President!"*, p. 123; Blakey and Billings, *Plot to Kill*, p. 50.

120. Garrison, *A Heritage of Stone*, p. 124; Summers, *Conspiracy*, p. 477; IV HSCA, p. 499; *New Orleans States-Item*, January 3, 1979; XXV WC, p. 190; IX HSCA, p. 807.

121. CD 75, pp. 285–97; James and Wardlaw, *Plot or Politics?*, p. 12; *New York World Journal Tribune*, February 23, 1967; *Chicago Tribune*, February 23, 1967; IX HSCA, pp. 103–15; HSCR, p. 145; XXII WC, p. 826.

122. James and Wardlaw, *Plot or Politics?*, pp. 12, 43; *New York World Journal Tribune*, February 23, 1967; IX HSCA, pp. 103–5; CD 75, pp. 285–97; *Chicago Tribune*, February 23, 1967.

123. X HSCA, pp. 110–12; CD 75, pp. 285–97; James and Wardlaw, *Plot or Politics?*, p. 44; Blakey and Billings, *Plot to Kill*, pp. 168–69; IX HSCA, p. 75.

124. Blakey and Billings, *Plot to Kill*, p. 169; James and Wardlaw, *Plot or Politics?*, p. 44; CD 75, pp. 219–20, 287; *The New York Times*, February 25, 1967; *Chicago Tribune*, February 23, 1967; X HSCA, pp. 105, 113.

125. CD 75, pp. 285–97; Scheim, *Contract on America*, p. 51; X HSCA, p. 113; *The New York Times*, February 25, 1967.

126. *The New York Times*, February 25, 1967; William W. Turner, "The Garrison Commission on the Assassination of President Kennedy," *Ramparts*, January 1968; Hinckle and Turner, *The Fish Is Red*, p. 218; CD 87; CD 75, pp. 285–97; FBI memo, Branigan to Sullivan,

February 13, 1969; statement of Alvin R. Beaubouef, Office of the District Attorney, New Orleans, December 15, 1966.

127. Statement of Beaubouef, December 15, 1966; FBI memo, Branigan to Sullivan, February 13, 1969; CD 75, p. 287; FBI teletype, SAC New Orleans to Director et al. (HQ 62–109060–482).

128. CD 75, pp. 285–97; *The New York Times*, February 25, 1967; CD 301, pp. 85–87; X HSCA, p. 113; Blakey and Billings, *Plot to Kill*, p. 169; FBI teletype, SAC New Orleans to Director et al. (HQ 62–109060–482).

129. CD 75, pp. 285–97; CD 301, pp. 85–87; X HSCA, p. 113; Hinckle and Turner, *The Fish Is Red*, p. 221; WR, p. 216.

130. Turner, "The Garrison Commission"; Hinckle and Turner, *The Fish Is Red*, p. 221; Kirkwood, *American Grotesque*, p. 304.

131. CD 75, pp. 285–97; X HSCA, p. 113; CD 301, pp. 85–87; *The New York Times*, February 25, 1967; HSCR, p. 144.

132. CD 75, pp. 285–97; Hinckle and Turner, *The Fish Is Red*, pp. 206, 223; HSCR, p. 170; Blakey and Billings, *Plot to Kill*, p. 168; Rogers, "The Persecution of Clay Shaw"; X HSCA, p. 107; Weisberg, *Oswald in New Orleans*, p. 65.

133. FBI airtel from SAC New Orleans to Director, February 28, 1967 (HQ 62–109060–4579).

134. X HSCA, p. 112; CD 75, pp. 309–11.

135. HSCR, p. 171; Rogers, "The Persecution of Clay Shaw."

136. X HSCA, p. 113; HSCR, p. 144.

137. CD 75, pp. 285–97, 309; FBI airtel, SAC New Orleans to Director, February 24, 1967 (HQ 105–82555–5555); Weisberg, *Oswald in New Orleans*, pp. 176, 183–84; Anson, *"They've Killed the President!"*, p. 107; HSCR, p. 144; Hinckle and Turner, *The Fish Is Red*, p. 221; X HSCA, p. 105.

138. X HSCA, p. 105; HSCR, pp. 144–45; *The New York Times*, February 23, 1967.

139. X HSCA, p. 113; XXV WC, p. 251; Garrison, *A Heritage of Stone*, p. 125; letter, Garrison to Sissi Maleki (researcher), February 19, 1984.

140. X HSCA, p. 105; interview with Garrison; interview with Ferrell; CD 75, pp. 307–8.

141. Interview with Garrison; Kirkwood, *American Grotesque*, pp. 114, 534; *Dallas Times Herald*, November 21, 1982; interview with Ferrell; James and Wardlaw, *Plot or Politics?*, p. 114; *The New York Times*, March 3, 1967, May 10, 1967, June 3, 1967, June 25, 1967; *Washington Post*, February 23, 1969; Committee to Investigate Assassinations, *Coincidence or Conspiracy?*, p. 452; FBI memo, DeLoach to Tolson, February 23, 1967 (HQ 62–109060–4582).

142. Interview with Marchetti, 1983; Anson, *"They've Killed the Presi-*

dent!", p. 122; interview by Fensterwald of Marchetti, April 22, 1975; Committee to Investigate Assassinations, *Coincidence or Conspiracy?*, pp. 299, 452.

143. Anson, *"They've Killed the President!"*, p. 122; Committee to Investigate Assassinations, *Coincidence or Conspiracy?*, pp. 298–99.

144. Phelan, *Scandals, Scamps and Scoundrels*, pp. 138–76; interview with Ferrell; interview with Kohn, 1983.

145. X HSCA, pp. 126, 129; Anson, *"They've Killed the President!"*, p. 124; Hinckle and Turner, *The Fish Is Red*, pp. 204–5; Summers, *Conspiracy*, pp. 319–20; interview with Ferrell; HSCR, p. 144; Blakey and Billings, *Plot to Kill*, pp. 165–66.

146. Hinckle and Turner, *The Fish Is Red*, p. 203; Summers, *Conspiracy*, p. 319; Blakey and Billings, *Plot to Kill*, p. 165; X HSCA, p. 126; information from FBI Research Unit; James and Wardlaw, *Plot or Politics?*, p. 110; spokesman for New Orleans Police Department; *The New York Times*, January 22, 1983. Reference for information in footnote is X HSCA, p. 126.

147. Spokesman for New Orleans Police Department; *Baton Rouge State Times*, March 7, 1957; Weisberg, *Oswald in New Orleans*, p. 328; Hinckle and Turner, *The Fish Is Red*, pp. 203, 206; Summers, *Conspiracy*, pp. 319–20; Blakey and Billings, *Plot to Kill*, p. 166; X HSCA, pp. 110, 126; memo, Ward to Garrison, January 31, 1967; memo, Gurvich to Garrison, February 14, 1967; HSCR, p. 144.

148. Blakey and Billings, *Plot to Kill*, pp. 165–66; HSCR, p. 144; James and Wardlaw, *Plot or Politics?*, pp. 110–11; memo, Ward to Garrison, January 31, 1967; Hinckle and Turner, *The Fish Is Red*, p. 204; X HSCA, pp. 127, 131; Summers, *Conspiracy*, pp. 320–21. Reference for information in footnote is CIA report on Sergio Arcacha Smith, October 26, 1967 (CIA 1363–501).

149. Hinckle and Turner, *The Fish Is Red*, p. 203; Garrison, *A Heritage of Stone*, pp. 107–8; X HSCA, p. 110; Blakey and Billings, *Plot to Kill*, p. 165; James and Wardlaw, *Plot or Politics?*, p. 110.

150. Press office, FBI, New Orleans; interview with Weisberg; HSCR, p. 146; Weisberg, *Oswald in New Orleans*, p. 103; Garrison, *A Heritage of Stone*, p. 107.

151. Blakey and Billings, *Plot to Kill*, p. 165; X HSCA, pp. 57, 61, 110, 123–24, 127; Anson, *"They've Killed the President!"*, p. 123; Schlesinger, *A Thousand Days*, p. 243; Weisberg, *Oswald in New Orleans*, pp. 51, 339; Hinckle and Turner, *The Fish Is Red*, pp. 205–6.

152. HSCR, p. 146; Garrison, *A Heritage of Stone*, pp. 149–54; WR, p. 403.

153. Hinckle and Turner, *The Fish Is Red*, pp. 204–5; X HSCA, pp. 123–29.

154. WR, pp. 383–84.

155. Ibid., p. 728; HSCR, p. 146; Hinckle and Turner, *The Fish Is Red*, pp. 204–9; Blakey and Billings, *Plot to Kill*, p. 167; Weisberg, *Oswald in New Orleans*, p. 343; Summers, *Conspiracy*, p. 365.

156. X HSCA, pp. 128–29; HSCR, p. 145; Hinckle and Turner, *The Fish Is Red*, p. 208; Summers, *Conspiracy*, p. 324.

157. X HSCA, p. 135; Summers, *Conspiracy*, pp. 323–25; interview with Delphine Roberts, 1982.

158. Summers, *Conspiracy*, pp. 323–24; Norden, "Playboy Interview: Jim Garrison"; James and Wardlaw, *Plot or Politics?*, p. 111; Weisberg, *Oswald in New Orleans*, p. 328; memo, Sgt. Fenner Sedgebeer to Garrison, January 10, 1967; WR, pp. 406–12.

159. X HSCA, p. 129; HSCR, p. 145; Summers, *Conspiracy*, p. 324.

160. Summers, *Conspiracy*, p. 322; interviews of Allen and Daniel Campbell by Andrew Sciambra, 1969.

161. XXIV WC, p. 822; WR, p. 728; HSCR, p. 141.

162. X WC, pp. 34–37; HSCR, p. 141; WR, p. 728; Hinckle and Turner, *The Fish Is Red*, p. 207.

163. X WC, pp. 37–38; HSCR, p. 141; Hinckle and Turner, *The Fish Is Red*, p. 207; WR, p. 728.

164. Hinckle and Turner, *The Fish Is Red*, p. 207; VIII WC, p. 309; XIX WC, p. 664.

165. WR, p. 291; Hinckle and Turner, *The Fish Is Red*, p. 206; XIX WC, p. 175; XXI WC, p. 621; XI WC, p. 165.

166. Summers, *Conspiracy*, p. 324.

167. Ibid., pp. 324–25.

168. HSCR, p. 191; WR, pp. 436–37; XVII WC, pp. 758–62.

169. XVII WC, pp. 760–61; XXVI WC, p. 783; analysis by Paul L. Hoch, "FBI Investigation of Oswald's Use of the Address 544 Camp Street," December 26, 1968.

170. XXVI WC, p. 783; Hoch analysis, December 26, 1968.

171. Ibid.; X HSCA, pp. 61, 124; Hinckle and Turner, *The Fish Is Red*, pp. 205–6; XVII WC, p. 758.

172. Interview with Hoch; interview with Ferrell; Hoch analysis, December 26, 1968.

173. WR, p. 728; HSCR, p. 142; IV HSCA, p. 485; Blakey and Billings, *Plot to Kill*, p. 170; Anson, *"They've Killed the President!"*, p. 121; Kirkwood, *American Grotesque*, pp. 129, 213–16; interview with Ferrell; Gaeton Fonzi, "Who Killed JFK?", *The Washingtonian*, November 1980, p. 180.

174. Paul L. Hoch, *Echoes of Conspiracy* 3, no. 7; spokesman for Harlem Congress of Racial Equality, New York.

175. Hoch, *Echoes of Conspiracy* 3, no. 7.

176. Summers, *Conspiracy*, p. 336; *The New York Times*, January 4, 1974, January 29, 1975; HSCR, pp. 432–33.

177. Summers, *Conspiracy*, p. 336.

178. XXIII WC, p. 727; XXVI WC, p. 764; X WC, p. 220; WR, pp. 403–4; HSCR, p. 193.
179. XXIII WC, pp. 727–28; XXVI WC, p. 764; X WC, pp. 220, 227.
180. X WC, pp. 220–22; XXIII WC, pp. 727–29.
181. Gerald R. Ford with John R. Stiles, *Portrait of the Assassin*, p. 226; Sylvia Meagher, *Accessories After the Fact*, pp. 244–46; X WC, p. 225, 227–28; XXIII WC, p. 727.
182. XXVI WC, p. 764; XXIII WC, p. 728; memos, Hoch to critics, 1970; CD 75, pp. 455–56.
183. Memos, Hoch to critics, 1970.
184. Ibid.; CD 75, p. 262.
185. Memos, Hoch to critics, 1970.
186. Ibid.; WR, p. 123; FBI memo, Rosen to Belmont, August 28, 1964 (FBI 105–82555–4814).
187. Memos, Hoch to critics, 1970; CD 75, p. 262.
188. Memos, Hoch to critics, 1970; CD 75, pp. 455–56; FBI airtel, SAC New Orleans to Director, November 23, 1963.
189. Memos, Hoch to critics, 1970; WR, p. 119; VII WC, p. 367.
190. WR, pp. 723, 726.
191. Meagher, *Accessories*, p. 193; WR, pp. 119, 174.
192. Meagher, *Accessories*, p. 193.
193. Fred Newcomb and Perry Adams, *Murder from Within*, pp. 269–73; *Christian Science Monitor*, October 26, 1963; *Congressional Record-Senate*, August 2, 1963, p. 13945, November 27, 1963, pp. 22868–69; *Washington Post*, January 27, 1963; WR, p. 725. Reference for information in footnote is Newcomb and Adams, *Murder from Within*.
194. *Washington Post*, January 27, 1963; *Congress and the Nation*, vol. II, 1965–1968, p. 324; Newcomb and Adams, *Murder from Within*, pp. 269–73; *Congressional Record-Senate*, August 2, 1963, November 27, 1963.
195. *Congressional Record-Senate*, August 2, 1963, p. 13945, November 27, 1963, pp. 22868–69; *Washington Post*, January 27, 1963; *Congress and the Nation*, vol. II, 1965–1968, p. 324.
196. Newcomb and Adams, *Murder from Within*, p. 272; WR, p. 174; Meagher, *Accessories*, p. 194.
197. Drew Pearson and Jack Anderson, *The Case Against Congress*, pp. 67–68.
198. XIX WC, p. 665; WR, pp. 390, 728; HSCR, p. 142.
199. Martin A. Lee, Robert Ranftel, and Jeff Cohen, "Did Lee Harvey Oswald Drop Acid?", *Rolling Stone*, March 3, 1983; CD 194, pp. 37, 38; FBI memo, SAC to file, November 25, 1963 (NO 89–69–80).
200. Interview with Judge Edward Gillin, 1983; Lee, Ranftel, and Cohen, "Did Lee Harvey Oswald Drop Acid?"; CD 194, pp. 37, 38; FBI

memo, SAC to file, November 25, 1963 (NO 89–69–80); *The New York Times*, September 20, 1977.

201. CD 194, pp. 37, 38; Lee, Ranftel, and Cohen, "Did Lee Harvey Oswald Drop Acid?"
202. XXII WC, p. 82.
203. *The New York Times*, July 17, 21, 1977, September 20, 1977; Lee, Ranftel, and Cohen, "Did Lee Harvey Oswald Drop Acid?"; "Science Under the Cloak," *Science*, June 27, 1975; Tad Szulc, "The CIA's Electric Kool-Aid Acid Test," *Psychology Today*, November 1977; "Mind-Bending Disclosure," *Time*, August 15, 1977; "Mind Bending—Latest CIA Scandal," *U.S. News & World Report*, August 15, 1977; *Washington Post*, August 4, 1977.
204. Lee, Ranftel, and Cohen, "Did Lee Harvey Oswald Drop Acid?"; Szulc, "The CIA's Electric Kool-Aid Acid Test."
205. WR, pp. 406–12; HSCR, pp. 142, 146; XXII WC, p. 82; Summers, *Conspiracy*, pp. 324–25.
206. FBI airtel, SAC New York to Director, May 23, 1960 (HQ 105–82555); *The New York Times*, February 23, 1975.
207. WR, p. 132; VII WC, pp. 529–30; Harold Weisberg, *Whitewash*, p. 139.
208. HSCR, pp. 181–225.
209. Interview with Warren deBrueys, 1983; HSCR, p. 193; XI WC, p. 361; interview with Orest Pena, 1981.
210. Interview with deBrueys, 1983; interview with James H. Lesar, 1983; HSCR, pp. 192–93; CD 1203a, pp. 1–3.
211. Interview with deBrueys, 1983; HSCR, p. 193.
212. HSCR, p. 193.
213. Ibid., p. 191.
214. Ibid. References for information in footnote are FBI Director to Attorney General, October 7, 1975 (HQ 62–109060–7335); *Morgan City Review*, October 1, 1975; letter, FBI Director to Attorney General, April 4, 1968 (HQ 62–109060–6313); HSCR, pp. 191–92; *Washington Post*, October 1, 1975.
215. HSCR, pp. 191–94.
216. Ibid., pp. 193–94; Summers, *Conspiracy*, p. 312.

11: The Cuban Question: Coincidence or Conspiracy?

1. *Daily Telegraph* (London), June 26, 1976; interview with Howard K. Smith, February 1984.
2. U.S. Senate Select Committee to Study Governmental Operations with Respect to Intelligence Activities, *Final Report, Book Five, The Investigation of the Assassination of President John F. Kennedy: Per-*

formance of the Intelligence Agencies, 94th Cong., 2d sess., 1976, pp. 4, 60.

3. Interview with Dr. Ray Cline, February 1984; Taylor Branch and George Crile III, "The Kennedy Vendetta," *Harper's*, August 1975; ABC-TV News, "Fidel Castro Speaks," Barbara Walters interview, June 9, 1977; Herbert S. Parmet, *JFK*, p. 221; Senate Select Committee to Study Governmental Operations with Respect to Intelligence Activities, *Alleged Assassination Plots Involving Foreign Leaders: An Interim Report*, 94th Cong., 1st sess., November 20, 1975, pp. 71–180; III HSCA, pp. 216–17; interview with Dr. Jorge Dominguez, specialist on Cuban affairs, Harvard University, 1984; interview with Gaeton Fonzi, 1984; *Washington Post*, May 2, 1976; interview with Herbert Parmet, 1984; *Wall Street Journal*, December 30, 1983; *Time*, January 16, 1984.

4. HSCR, p. 117; Arthur M. Schlesinger, Jr., *Robert Kennedy and His Times*, p. 615; Senate Select Committee, *Alleged Assassination Plots*, pp. 79, 94–95; Senate Select Committee, *Investigation of the Assassination*, pp. 4–5.

5. Harris Wofford, *Of Kennedys and Kings*, p. 418; Daniel Schorr, *Clearing the Air*; *News American* (Baltimore), April 22, 1975; Schlesinger, *Robert Kennedy and His Times*, p. 616.

6. G. Robert Blakey and Richard N. Billings, *Plot to Kill*, p. 140.

7. *Washington Post*, November 25, 1983; interview with Dominguez, 1984; HSCR, p. 115; interview with Cline, February 1984; Blakey and Billings, *Plot to Kill*, pp. 137, 176.

8. Interview with Dominguez, 1984; interview with Cline, February 1984; Wofford, *Of Kennedys and Kings*, p. 397; Schlesinger, *Robert Kennedy and His Times*, pp. 525, 551; interview with Parmet, 1984; Parmet, *JFK*, p. 300; Blakey and Billings, *Plot to Kill*, p. 144; ABC-TV News, "Fidel Castro Speaks"; interview with William Attwood, 1983; Warren Hinckle and William Turner, *The Fish Is Red*, p. 135; X HSCA, p. 12; *Dallas Morning News*, May 10, 1979; Richard M. Nixon, "Cuba, Castro, and John F. Kennedy," *Reader's Digest*, November 1964; *Public Papers of the Presidents*, 1963, p. 609; Arthur M. Schlesinger, Jr., *A Thousand Days*, p. 332.

9. ABC-TV News, "Fidel Castro Speaks"; Hinckle and Turner, *The Fish Is Red*, p. 144; Parmet, *JFK*, p. 300; interview with Cline, February 1984; interview with Dominguez, 1984; Blakey and Billings, *Plot to Kill*, p. 137; Senate Select Committee, *Alleged Assassination Plots*, p. 89; *Washington Post*, May 2, 1976; Wofford, *Of Kennedys and Kings*, p. 397.

10. Interview with Dominguez, 1984; interview with Parmet, 1984; interview with Cline, February 1984; Bradley Earl Ayers, *The War That Never Was*, pp. 186, 188–89, 203, 215; Hinckle and Turner,

The Fish Is Red, p. 238; X HSCA, p. 68; Merle Miller, *Lyndon: An Oral Biography*; Senate Select Committee, *Alleged Assassination Plots*, p. 264.

11. Schorr, *Clearing the Air*; *New Orleans Times-Picayune*, September 9, 1963; *Washington Post*, September 7, 1976, November 25, 1983; *News American* (Baltimore), April 22, 1975; HSCR, pp. 114–15.

12. *Washington Post*, November 25, 1983; *National Enquirer*, October 15, 1967; interview with Dominguez, 1984.

13. ABC-TV News, "Fidel Castro Speaks"; CIA memo on Jack Anderson broadcast (CIA #1329–484–c); M. Stanton Evans, "Coverup Proved in JFK Murder Probe," *Human Events*, July 24, 1976; *Washington Post*, May 2, 1976.

14. *Washington Post*, May 2, 1976.

15. Senate Select Committee, *Investigation of the Assassination*, p. 79.

16. Schlesinger, *A Thousand Days*, p. 213; X HSCA, p. 7; Charles Murphy, "Cuba: The Record Set Straight," *Fortune*, September 1961; Senate Select Committee, *Alleged Assassination Plots*, pp. 75, 110–11, 114; HSCR, p. 25; interview with Parmet, 1984; ABC-TV News, "Fidel Castro Speaks"; Nixon, "Cuba, Castro, and John F. Kennedy"; interview with Cline, February 1984.

17. Interview with Parmet, 1984; interview with Cline, February 1984; Ralph G. Martin, *A Hero for Our Time*, p. 327; Murphy, "Cuba"; Schlesinger, *A Thousand Days*, p. 219; Senate Select Committee, *Alleged Assassination Plots*, p. 120; Nixon, "Cuba, Castro, and John F. Kennedy."

18. Schlesinger, *A Thousand Days*, pp. 225, 227, 250; Murphy, "Cuba"; interview with Parmet, 1984; interview with Cline, February 1984; X HSCA, p. 15.

19. Interview with Dominguez, 1984; interview with Parmet, 1984; Murphy, "Cuba"; Branch and Crile, "The Kennedy Vendetta"; Schlesinger, *A Thousand Days*, p. 220; Martin, *A Hero for Our Time*, p. 330; interview with Cline, February 1984.

20. David A. Phillips, *The Night Watch*, pp. 107, 110, 232–56; interview with Dominguez, 1984; interview with Cline, February 1984; Murphy, "Cuba"; Nixon, "Cuba, Castro, and John F. Kennedy"; Martin, *A Hero for Our Time*, p. 33; Hinckle and Turner, *The Fish Is Red*, p. 100; interview with Parmet, 1984.

21. Thomas Powers, *The Man Who Kept the Secrets*, p. 113.

22. Interview with Dominguez, 1984; interview with Attwood, 1984; interview with Cline, February 1984; interview with Parmet, 1984; Hinckle and Turner, *The Fish Is Red*, p. 100; Schlesinger, *A Thousand Days*, pp. 232–42, 256, 278; Martin, *A Hero for Our Time*, p. 332; Murphy, "Cuba"; Powers, *The Man Who Kept the Secrets*, pp. 110–12.

23. Interview with Cline, February 1984; Hinckle and Turner, *The Fish Is Red*, p. 99; interview with Dominguez, 1984; Branch and Crile, "The Kennedy Vendetta."
24. Powers, *The Man Who Kept the Secrets*, p. 133.
25. Senate Select Committee, *Alleged Assassination Plots*, p. 135; Powers, *The Man Who Kept the Secrets*, pp. 111–12; Murphy, "Cuba"; *Public Papers of the Presidents*, 1961, p. 305; Schlesinger, *A Thousand Days*, pp. 259, 268; X HSCA, p. 66; *The New York Times*, April 23, 1961; HSCR, p. 26; interview with Cline, February 1984; interview with Parmet, 1984; Branch and Crile, "The Kennedy Vendetta"; Martin, *A Hero for Our Time*, pp. 334–35.
26. HSCR, p. 26.
27. Schlesinger, *A Thousand Days*, pp. 268, 270–71; Martin, *A Hero for Our Time*, pp. 331–32; Murphy, "Cuba"; HSCR, p. 131; X HSCA, p. 9; Powers, *The Man Who Kept the Secrets*, p. 112; Senate Select Committee, *Alleged Assassination Plots*, p. 135; Branch and Crile, "The Kennedy Vendetta."
28. Senate Select Committee, *Alleged Assassination Plots*.
29. Ibid., p. 142.
30. Ibid., pp. 72–73, 85–86.
31. Hinckle and Turner, *The Fish Is Red*, p. 102; X HSCA, pp. 10–11; interview with Fonzi, 1984; "Another Cuban Fiasco?", *U.S. News & World Report*, April 29, 1963; HSCR, p. 105; Branch and Crile, "The Kennedy Vendetta"; Senate Select Committee, *Alleged Assassination Plots*, p. 140; interview with Cline, February 1984.
32. Senate Select Committee, *Alleged Assassination Plots*, pp. 117, 140–41.
33. Ibid., pp. 116–35, 139, 159; X HSCA, pp. 10–11; Lawrence R. Houston, letter to the editor, *Atlantic*, March 1980; ABC-TV News, "Fidel Castro Speaks"; Branch and Crile, "The Kennedy Vendetta"; letters to the editor, *Atlantic*, December 1979; Wofford, *Of Kennedys and Kings*, pp. 395, 398–99.
34. Senate Select Committee, *Alleged Assassination Plots*, pp. 139, 144; X HSCA, pp. 10–11.
35. Senate Select Committee, *Alleged Assassination Plots*, p. 141.
36. Martin, *A Hero for Our Time*, p. 508; ABC-TV News, "Fidel Castro Speaks"; Houston, letter to the editor; Branch and Crile, "The Kennedy Vendetta"; letters to the editor, *Atlantic*, December 1979; Wofford, *Of Kennedys and Kings*, pp. 393, 395–96, 399; Senate Select Committee, *Alleged Assassination Plots*, pp. 11–12, 95, 116–35, 149, 157; interview with Parmet, 1984.
37. Senate Select Committee, *Alleged Assassination Plots*, p. 150.
38. Ibid., pp. 114, 135, 141–43, 149, 154, 158.
39. Ibid., p. 138.

40. Ibid., p. 139.
41. Ibid., pp. 141, 149; Martin, *A Hero for Our Time*, p. 508.
42. Senate Select Committee, *Alleged Assassination Plots*, pp. 139–40; X HSCA, pp. 10–11; interview with Fonzi, 1984.
43. Branch and Crile, "The Kennedy Vendetta"; interview with Fonzi, 1984; interview with Cline, February 1984; Gaeton Fonzi, "Who Killed JFK?", *The Washingtonian*, November 1980, pp. 165–66; X HSCA, p. 11; *Washington Post*, May 2, 1976, November 25, 1983; Schlesinger, *Robert Kennedy and His Times*, p. 478; Blakey and Billings, *Plot to Kill*, p. 137; HSCR, p. 115; Hinckle and Turner, *The Fish Is Red*, pp. 18, 113, 115.
44. Interview with Fonzi, 1984; interview with Parmet, 1984; Fonzi, "Who Killed JFK?", pp. 163, 165; Senate Select Committee, *Alleged Assassination Plots*, p. 146; X HSCA, pp. 11, 42; Branch and Crile, "The Kennedy Vendetta"; Hinckle and Turner, *The Fish Is Red*, p. 115.
45. Ayers, *The War That Never Was*, p. 27.
46. Interview with Parmet, 1984; Branch and Crile, "The Kennedy Vendetta"; Hinckle and Turner, *The Fish Is Red*, p. 122; Schlesinger, *Robert Kennedy and His Times*, p. 544; Powers, *The Man Who Kept the Secrets*, pp. 141, 338; Ayers, *The War That Never Was*, pp. 76, 147; HSCR, p. 132; interview with Cline, February 1984.
47. Senate Select Committee, *Alleged Assassination Plots*, pp. 74–85, 128, 132–33; Powers, *The Man Who Kept the Secrets*, p. 148; *Washington Post*, September 7, 1976; Wofford, *Of Kennedys and Kings*, p. 399.
48. Houston, letter to the editor; Senate Select Committee, *Alleged Assassination Plots*, pp. 84–85, 132–33, 259; Wofford, *Of Kennedys and Kings*, p. 401. References for information in footnote are interview with Cline, February 1984; interview with G. Robert Blakey; Blakey and Billings, *Plot to Kill*, p. 152; HSCR, p. 114; *Washington Post*, May 16, 1976; Peter Dale Scott, *Crime and Cover-up*, p. 20; V HSCA, p. 432; IX HSCA, p. 44; David Scheim, *Contract on America*, p. 55; Ovid Demaris, *The Last Mafioso*, p. 193.
49. Senate Select Committee, *Alleged Assassination Plots*, pp. 146–47.
50. Off-the-record meeting on Cuba with JFK and RFK, October 16, 1962.
51. Ibid.
52. Schlesinger, *Robert Kennedy and His Times*, p. 533; Senate Select Committee, *Alleged Assassination Plots*, p. 170; HSCR, p. 106; X HSCA, p. 12; "Another Cuban Fiasco?"; Nixon, "Cuba, Castro, and John F. Kennedy."
53. "Another Cuban Fiasco?"; Schlesinger, *Robert Kennedy and His Times*,

p. 525; HSCR, pp. 106, 132. Reference for information in footnote is Schlesinger, *A Thousand Days*, p. 762.

54. Senate Select Committee, *Alleged Assassination Plots*, pp. 170, 173–74; interview with Parmet, 1984; interview with Attwood, 1984.
55. Interview with Attwood, 1984; Schlesinger, *Robert Kennedy and His Times*, pp. 551–54; Senate Select Committee, *Alleged Assassination Plots*, pp. 173–74; III HSCA, pp. 222–24; HSCR, p. 127.
56. Senate Select Committee, *Alleged Assassination Plots*, p. 173; *The New York Times*, March 3, 1963, April 1, 6, 1963; Branch and Crile, "The Kennedy Vendetta."
57. Interview with Dominguez, 1984; interview with Attwood, 1984; interview with Cline, February 1984.
58. Interview with Parmet, 1984; X HSCA, p. 12; Schlesinger, *A Thousand Days*, p. 762.
59. Schlesinger, *Robert Kennedy and His Times*, pp. 534–38; Branch and Crile, "The Kennedy Vendetta"; *Public Papers of the Presidents*, 1962, pp. 911–12; X HSCA, p. 67.
60. *Public Papers of the Presidents*, 1962, pp. 911–12.
61. Ibid., p. 912.
62. "Another Cuban Fiasco?"; Schlesinger, *Robert Kennedy and His Times*, p. 538; X HSCA, p. 67; Hinckle and Turner, *The Fish Is Red*, p. 152; Branch and Crile, "The Kennedy Vendetta."
63. Ayers, *The War That Never Was*; Branch and Crile, "The Kennedy Vendetta"; Senate Select Committee, *Alleged Assassination Plots*, p. 85; *DC News*, February 19, 1963; *The New York Times*, December 6, 1962, March 20, 1963, April 1, 6, 1963; Hinckle and Turner, *The Fish Is Red*, pp. 156–57; interview with Fonzi, 1984; *Public Papers of the Presidents*, 1963, p. 277.
64. *Public Papers of the Presidents*, 1963, pp. 277–78, 305–6.
65. HSCR, p. 20.
66. *Public Papers of the Presidents*, 1963, p. 421.
67. Ibid., p. 330.
68. Senate Select Committee, *Investigation of the Assassination*, p. 3.
69. Senate Select Committee, *Alleged Assassination Plots*, p. 173.
70. Ibid.; *The New York Times*, October 31, 1963, November 1, 3, 1963.
71. HSCR, p. 106.
72. Interview with Dominguez, 1984; X HSCA, p. 6; Phillips, *The Night Watch*, p. 63; HSCR, pp. 104, 130; Schlesinger, *A Thousand Days*, pp. 204–5, 207; *Public Papers of the Presidents*, 1963, p. 876.
73. HSCR, pp. 104, 130; X HSCA, pp. 6–8; interview with Dominguez, 1984; Phillips, *The Night Watch*, p. 63; Schlesinger, *A Thousand Days*, pp. 204–5, 207; *Public Papers of the Presidents*, 1963, p. 876; Murphy, "Cuba"; *The New York Times*, January 4, 1961.
74. "Cuba: Every Exile Is an Island," *Newsweek*, October 29, 1962; HSCR,

p. 115; X HSCA, pp. 7–15, 57–59; Schlesinger, *A Thousand Days,* p. 229; Blakey and Billings, *Plot to Kill,* p. 171; Hinckle and Turner, *The Fish Is Red,* p. 158.
75. HSCR, p. 129.
76. Interview with Marion Johnson, National Archives; William Coleman, Jr., and David Slawson, "Oswald's Foreign Activities: Summary of Evidence Which Might Be Said to Show That There Was Foreign Involvement in the Assassination of President Kennedy" (report), pp. 110–11.
77. Coleman and Slawson, "Oswald's Foreign Activities," pp. 110–11.
78. Interview with Dominguez, 1984; HSCR, p. 133; Schlesinger, *Robert Kennedy and His Times,* p. 539; X HSCA, p. 15.
79. Interview with Dominguez, 1984; X HSCA, pp. 14–15, 65.
80. HSCR, p. 133; X HSCA; III HSCA, pp. 377–78.
81. HSCR, p. 133; III HSCA, p. 372.
82. III HSCA, pp. 372–74; CD 87 (SS477); HSCR, pp. 133–34.
83. HSCR, p. 133.
84. Ibid., p. 134.
85. Senate Select Committee, *Investigation of the Assassination,* pp. 32–33.
86. CIA to FBI et al., November 12, 1962 (CIA #F82–0430/106); Hinckle and Turner, *The Fish Is Red,* p. 107; X HSCA, p. 37; HSCR, pp. 133, 135.
87. CIA to FBI et al., November 12, 1962 (CIA #F82–0430/106); *Sunday Star,* October 14, 1962; *Washington Post,* October 30, 1962; HSCR, pp. 134–35; *Dallas Morning News,* May 10, 1979; Hinckle and Turner, *The Fish Is Red,* pp. 164–67; Fonzi, "Who Killed JFK?"
88. Fonzi, "Who Killed JFK?"; HSCR, pp. 135–37.
89. X HSCA, pp. 37–40; HSCR, p. 135.
90. HSCR, p. 135; X HSCA, p. 41; Fonzi, "Who Killed JFK?", pp. 180–81.
91. HSCR, p. 137.
92. X HSCA, pp. 47–51.
93. Fonzi, "Who Killed JFK?"; interview with Fonzi, 1984.
94. Interview with Fonzi, 1984.
95. Schorr, *Clearing the Air;* Senate Select Committee, *Alleged Assassination Plots;* Senate Select Committee, *Investigation of the Assassination;* Fonzi, "Who Killed JFK?"
96. Fonzi, "Who Killed JFK?", pp. 176–78, 184; X HSCA, pp. 37, 39, 46; interview with Fonzi, 1984.
97. X HSCA, pp. 38–39; Fonzi, "Who Killed JFK?", pp. 176–78.
98. Hinckle and Turner, *The Fish Is Red,* p. 293; Fonzi, "Who Killed JFK?", pp. 178–79, 224; interview with Fonzi, 1984.
99. X HSCA, p. 41; Fonzi, "Who Killed JFK?", pp. 176, 180–81.

100. X HSCA, p. 41; Fonzi, "Who Killed JFK?", p. 182; HSCR, p. 135.
101. Interview with Fonzi, 1984; Fonzi, "Who Killed JFK?", p. 197; G. Robert Blakey letter to the editor, *The Washingtonian*, February 1981.
102. Blakey, letter to the editor, *The Washingtonian*, February 1981.
103. Fonzi, "Who Killed JFK?", pp. 183, 185–86; X HSCA, p. 46; interview with Fonzi, 1984.
104. X HSCA, p. 46; Fonzi, "Who Killed JFK?", p. 186.
105. Phillips, *The Night Watch*; X HSCA, p. 46; Fonzi, "Who Killed JFK?", p. 223.
106. Phillips, *The Night Watch*, p. 114; Fonzi, "Who Killed JFK?", p. 114.
107. Fonzi, "Who Killed JFK?", pp. 190–91; X HSCA, p. 46.
108. Interview with Fonzi, 1984; Fonzi, "Who Killed JFK?", pp. 191, 196.
109. X HSCA, pp. 46–47; Fonzi, "Who Killed JFK?", pp. 190, 194.
110. Fonzi, "Who Killed JFK?", pp. 194–95.
111. Ibid., p. 195; X HSCA, p. 47; interview with Fonzi, 1984.
112. Interview with Fonzi, 1984; Fonzi, "Who Killed JFK?", p. 195; X HSCA, p. 47.
113. X HSCA, p. 47; Fonzi, "Who Killed JFK?", p. 195.
114. Interview with Fonzi, 1984; HSCR, p. 136.
115. CIA report on Alpha 66 and Veciana (CIA #F82–0430/163).
116. Fonzi, "Who Killed JFK?", p. 195.
117. Ibid.
118. Interview with Fonzi, 1984; Fonzi, "Who Killed JFK?", pp. 195–97.
119. Phillips, *The Night Watch*, pp. 113–15; X HSCA, p. 47; Fonzi, "Who Killed JFK?", p. 204.
120. Fonzi, "Who Killed JFK?", p. 224; X HSCA, pp. 48–49; interview with Fonzi, 1984.
121. Fonzi, "Who Killed JFK?", pp. 176, 222–24; Phillips, *The Night Watch*, pp. 4, 65; interview with Fonzi, 1984.
122. Interview with Fonzi, 1984; Fonzi, "Who Killed JFK?", pp. 226–27; X HSCA, pp. 47–48.
123. Fonzi, "Who Killed JFK?", p. 226; X HSCA, pp. 49–50.
124. Fonzi, "Who Killed JFK?", p. 230; X HSCA, p. 49.
125. Ibid. (both).
126. Ibid. (both).
127. Fonzi, "Who Killed JFK?", pp. 230–31; X HSCA, pp. 49–50.
128. HSCR, p. 136; Fonzi, "Who Killed JFK?", p. 233.
129. Fonzi, "Who Killed JFK?"; interview with Fonzi, 1984.
130. Fonzi, "Who Killed JFK?", p. 235.
131. Ibid., p. 234; *Miami Herald*, June 19, 1983; interview with Ana Veciana-Suarez, 1984.
132. Interview with Antonio Veciana, May 1982.
133. Senate Select Committee, *Investigation of the Assassination*, pp. 11–

13, 65; Branch and Crile, "The Kennedy Vendetta"; Schlesinger, *Robert Kennedy and His Times*, p. 478; Hinckle and Turner, *The Fish Is Red*, pp. 18, 113.

134. HSCR, pp. 26, 146; X HSCA, pp. 61, 127; CIA report on Sergio Arcacha Smith, October 26, 1967 (CIA #1363–501).

135. XXVI WC, p. 783; Robert Sam Anson, *"They've Killed the President!"*, p. 124; Anthony Summers, *Conspiracy*, p. 326; statement by David F. Lewis, December 15, 1966.

136. X HSCA, pp. 61, 110; Blakey and Billings, *Plot to Kill*, pp. 137, 176; HSCR, pp. 115, 142; Anson, *"They've Killed the President!"*, p. 124.

137. HSCR, p. 142; William W. Turner, "The Inquest," *Ramparts*, June 1967; Rosemary James and Jack Wardlaw, *Plot or Politics?*, p. 46; James Kirkwood, *American Grotesque*, p. 143; *The New York Times*, February 23, 1967; Committee to Investigate Assassinations, *Coincidence or Conspiracy?*, pp. 303–4; Anson, *"They've Killed the President!"*, p. 104.

138. Summers, *Conspiracy*, p. 292; Fonzi, "Who Killed JFK?", p. 180; Senate Select Committee, *Investigation of the Assassination*, pp. 11–13, 65; Anson, *"They've Killed the President!"*, p. 124; HSCR, p. 142.

139. Photograph in U.S. House of Representatives, *The Final Assassinations Report, Report of the Select Committee on Assassinations* (New York: Bantam, 1979). XXI WC, p. 139; Anson, *"They've Killed the President!"*, p. 103; WR, p. 407; Summers, *Conspiracy*, p. 299.

140. HSCR, p. 115; Blakey and Billings, *Plot to Kill*, p. 171; CD 1085; CIA documents on Alpha 66, July 14, 1983 (CIA #F82–0430); interview with Cline, February 1984.

141. Senate Select Committee, *Alleged Assassination Plots*, pp. xiii, 11–12, 83, 181.

142. Ibid., p. 256; Melvin R. Laird, "Let's Stop Undermining the CIA," *Reader's Digest*, May 1976.

143. Senate Select Committee, *Alleged Assassination Plots*.

144. Ibid., p. 86; *Washington Post*, May 2, 1976.

145. HSCR, p. 107; *Washington Post*, May 2, 1976; *The New York Times*, March 6, 1966; Senate Select Committee, *Alleged Assassination Plots*, pp. 86, 175; III HSCA, p. 240.

146. Senate Select Committee, *Alleged Assassination Plots*, p. 86; *Washington Post*, May 2, 1976.

147. HSCR, pp. 111–12; Senate Select Committee, *Alleged Assassination Plots*, p. 85.

148. HSCR, p. 112; Schlesinger, *Robert Kennedy and His Times*, p. 547; Hinckle and Turner, *The Fish Is Red*, p. 191; *Washington Post*, May 2, 1976; Senate Select Committee, *Investigation of the Assassination*, pp. 14–17; Senate Select Committee, *Alleged Assassination Plots*, p. 87.

149. Senate Select Committee, *Investigation of the Assassination*, p. 14;

New Orleans Times-Picayune, September 9, 1963; HSCR, p. 106; *Washington Post*, September 7, 1963, May 2, 1976.

150. *New Orleans Times-Picayune*, September 9, 1963.
151. Ibid.
152. Schlesinger, *Robert Kennedy and His Times*, p. 547; Hinckle and Turner, *The Fish Is Red*, p. 191; Senate Select Committee, *Investigation of the Assassination*, p. 15.
153. Senate Select Committee, *Investigation of the Assassination*, p. 17; Hinckle and Turner, *The Fish Is Red*, p. 192.
154. Senate Select Committee, *Investigation of the Assassination*, pp. 3, 17; Hinckle and Turner, *The Fish Is Red*, p. 192.
155. Senate Select Committee, *Investigation of the Assassination*, pp. 14, 17; Senate Select Committee, *Alleged Assassination Plots*, p. 87; *Washington Post*, May 2, 1976.
156. *Washington Post*, May 2, 1976; Senate Select Committee, *Alleged Assassination Plots*, pp. 87–88, 174–75; Senate Select Committee, *Investigation of the Assassination*, pp. 3, 18–19; HSCR, p. 112.
157. Senate Select Committee, *Investigation of the Assassination*, pp. 19–20; Senate Select Committee, *Alleged Assassination Plots*, pp. 88–89; *Washington Post*, May 2, 1976.
158. *Public Papers of the Presidents*, 1963, p. 876; Senate Select Committee, *Investigation of the Assassination*, p. 19; HSCR, p. 106.
159. *Public Papers of the Presidents*, 1963, pp. 872, 876.
160. *Ithaca Journal*, November 19, 1963.
161. Senate Select Committee, *Alleged Assassination Plots*, p. 89; *Washington Post*, May 2, 1976; Hinckle and Turner, *The Fish Is Red*, p. 219.
162. Senate Select Committee, *Alleged Assassination Plots*, p. 89.
163. Joseph P. Smith, *Portrait of a Cold Warrior*, p. 384; Senate Select Committee, *Alleged Assassination Plots*, p. 177; Hinckle and Turner, *The Fish Is Red*, p. 238.
164. Smith, *Portrait of a Cold Warrior*, p. 384.
165. Hinckle and Turner, *The Fish Is Red*, p. 192; Schorr, *Clearing the Air*; *Washington Post*, May 2, 1976; *The New York Times*, March 15, 1966; Schlesinger, *Robert Kennedy and His Times*, p. 546; Senate Select Committee, *Alleged Assassination Plots*, p. 87.
166. *Washington Post*, May 2, 1976; IV HSCA, p. 176.
167. *Washington Post*, May 2, 1976; Summers, *Conspiracy*, p. 351; Senate Select Committee, *Investigation of the Assassination*, p. 20; Senate Select Committee, *Alleged Assassination Plots*, pp. 89–90; *The New York Times*, March 6, 1966.
168. *Washington Post*, May 2, 1976; *The New York Times*, March 6, 8, 1966; III HSCA, pp. 243–44; Summers, *Conspiracy*, p. 436; HSCR, p. 113.

169. III HSCA, p. 244; *The New York Times*, March 9, 11, 1966; *Washington Post*, May 1, 1976; X HSCA, p. 6.
170. Summers, *Conspiracy*, pp. 350–51.

12: The Confession of Robert Easterling

1. HSCR, p. 1.
2. Interview with Easterling's first wife, 1983; information on Easterling's commitment to Mississippi State Hospital, Whitfield, August 1983; interview with Easterling's former neighbor, December 2, 1981; social evaluation of Easterling, Southeast Louisiana Hospital, March 6, 1974; case notes on Easterling, Mississippi State Hospital, June 9–August 4, 1980; social and medical history of Easterling, February 10, 1977; clinical notes on Easterling, East Mississippi State Hospital, September 15, 1976; information, State of Louisiana v. Robert Easterling, case #49,588, 19th Judicial District Court, East Baton Rouge, March 6, 1964; FBI file #88–29044 (on Easterling).
3. Civil Aeronautics Board, *Accident Investigation Report*, file #1–0013, May 27, 1954.
4. Interviews with Easterling's first wife, 1981, 1983.
5. Interview with Easterling's first wife, 1983.
6. Social evaluation, Southeast Louisiana Hospital, March 6, 1974; case notes, Mississippi State Hospital, June 9–August 4, 1980; clinical notes, East Mississippi State Hospital, September 15, 1976.
7. Social evaluation, Southeast Louisiana Hospital, March 6, 1974; case notes, Mississippi State Hospital, June 9–August 4, 1980; clinical notes, East Mississippi State Hospital, September 15, 1976; interview with Easterling's former employer, 1983; FBI file #88–29044.
8. Letter, Henry Hurt to William Webster, December 3, 1981.
9. Author's file memo, December 30, 1981.
10. WR, p. xii; interview with Marion Johnson, National Archives; interview with Harold Weisberg; interview with Mary Ferrell. References for information in footnote are judgment and probation/commitment order, Charles Voyde Harrelson, U.S. District Court, docket #SA82CR57(2), March 18, 1983; interviews with Harrelson's brother, 1983; *Dallas Morning News*, March 20, 1981.
11. Letter, Robert S. Young, assistant director in charge, Office of Congressional and Public Affairs, FBI, to Henry Hurt, September 27, 1983.
12. HSCR, pp. 1, 6–7.
13. Social evaluation, Southeast Louisiana Hospital, March 6, 1974; case notes, Mississippi State Hospital, June 9–August 4, 1980; interviews

with official of Sheriff's Department, Hattiesburg, Mississippi, January 1983; Joseph M. Kane, *Facts About the Presidents*, p. 293.

14. Interview with Easterling's sister, November 1983.
15. WR, p. 21.
16. HSCR, pp. 1, 19, 25–26.
17. Interview with company owner, June 1982.
18. XI WC, p. 347.
19. Interviews with Orest Pena; Senate Select Committee to Study Governmental Operations with Respect to Intelligence Activities, *Alleged Assassination Plots Involving Foreign Leaders*, 94th Cong., 1st sess., November 20, 1975, pp. 67–180.
20. Interviews with Pena; Anthony Summers, *Conspiracy*, pp. 311–12; HSCR, p. 193.
21. Spokesman for Cuban American Foundation, Washington, D.C.; interview with Dr. Jorge Dominguez, specialist on Cuban affairs, Harvard University, 1983.
22. Interview with Easterling's first wife, May 1983; interview with Pena.
23. Interview with Pena.
24. Social and medical history, February 10, 1977; FBI file #88–29044; interview with Easterling's first wife, 1983.
25. Interview with Easterling's first wife, 1983.
26. X HSCA, p. 106.
27. Interview with Pena.
28. Interview with Easterling's first wife, 1981.
29. Ibid.
30. Ibid. References for information in footnote are interviews with Easterling's first wife, 1981, 1983.
31. Interviews with Easterling's first wife, 1981, 1983.
32. Ibid.
33. Interview with Easterling's former neighbor, December 2, 1981; interviews with Easterling's first wife, 1981, 1983.
34. Interviews with Easterling's first wife, 1981, 1983.
35. Interview with Easterling's first wife, 1983.
36. XI WC, pp. 341–42, 350.
37. Ibid., pp. 342, 350–51.
38. Ibid., pp. 341–42, 350–51.
39. X WC, pp. 36–38; WR, p. 728.
40. Summers, *Conspiracy*, p. 183.
41. WR, p. 119.
42. Interview with Easterling's former neighbor, December 11, 1981; WR, p. 403.
43. Interview with businessman, June 1982.
44. WR, p. 290.
45. CIA report, "Additional Notes and Comments on the Oswald Case," December 11, 1963, CIA 376–154.

46. WR, pp. 403–4; interviews with former employers, June 1982, June 1983; interviews with Easterling's first wife, 1981.
47. Interview with Pena; XI WC, p. 347.
48. Interview with Pena.
49. Ibid.; HSCR, pp. 142–43.
50. X HSCA, pp. 112–13; G. Robert Blakey and Richard N. Billings, *The Plot to Kill the President*, p. 46; HSCR, pp. 143, 169, 171.
51. WR, p. 802; IX HSCA, p. 1087; XXIII WC, p. 49; IV HSCA, p. 498; David Scheim, *Contract on America*, pp. 212–16; HSCR, p. 171; interview with Harold Tannenbaum, 1983.
52. WR, pp. 407–8; XX WC, pp. 524–25.
53. Interview with businessman, June 1982.
54. Ibid.
55. Interview with Weisberg; interview with Ferrell; FBI report, SAC New Orleans to Director, December 1, 1963; WR, p. 323; XXIV WC, pp. 716–27; X HSCA, pp. 21, 31–32.
56. XXII WC, p. 191; WR, p. 730; XXIV WC, pp. 693, 696, 697; XI WC, p. 463.
57. Interview with businessman, June 1982; *Polk's New Orleans City Directory*, 1964, 1971, 1977; New Orleans Telephone Directory, 1963.
58. WR, p. 731; XXIV WC, p. 716; XI WC, pp. 462–63.
59. WR, p. 730; XI WC, pp. 462–63; X HSCA, p. 21; X WC, pp. 272, 276.
60. Interview with director of public information, New Orleans Fire Department, 1983; research by Tom Noonan.
61. XI WC, p. 463; fire report ledger, New Orleans, November 1963; research by Noonan; X WC, p. 276.
62. Fire report ledger, New Orleans, November 1963.
63. Ibid.
64. Interview with director of public information, New Orleans Fire Department, 1983. References for information in footnote are ibid.; interview with director of public information, New Orleans Police Department, 1983; research by Noonan.
65. Interview with information officer, New Orleans Housing Authority, 1983; interview with Councilman Jim Singleton, New Orleans, 1983; interview with director of public information, New Orleans Fire Department, 1983.
66. Research by Noonan; interview with building owner, New Orleans, 1983. Reference for information in footnote is *Polk's New Orleans City Directory*, 1964.
67. *Polk's New Orleans City Directory*, 1964; interview with dockworker, June 9, 1982.
68. Interview with dockworker, June 9, 1982.
69. XI WC, pp. 367–70, 373; X HSCA, pp. 23–25, 31; HSCR, pp. 137–39.

70. XI WC, pp. 369–73; X HSCA, pp. 25–26; HSCR, p. 137.
71. XI WC, pp. 372–73, 377; X HSCA, p. 27; HSCR, p. 137.
72. XI WC, pp. 371–73, 380; X HSCA, pp. 27–28; HSCR, p. 137.
73. XI WC, pp. 379–80; HSCR, pp. 137–39; WR, p. 322; X HSCA, p. 30.
74. XI WC, pp. 370, 383, 387.
75. Ibid., pp. 370, 377, 383, 387.
76. WR, p. 325.
77. Letter, Young to Hurt, September 27, 1983.
78. Interviews with telephone operators, March 1983.
79. Letter, Young to Hurt, September 27, 1983; Information, State of Louisiana v. Robert Easterling, East Baton Rouge, March 6, 1964.
80. Research by Noonan; interview with Carpenter's Chevrolet employee, December 1983.
81. FBI file #88–29044; information, State of Louisiana v. Robert Easterling, East Baton Rouge, March 6, 1964; interview with Judge Daniel Le Blanc, May 12, 1983.
82. Letter, Young to Hurt, September 27, 1983.
83. Interview with warden's assistant, Louisiana State Penitentiary, Angola, Louisiana, 1983.
84. Ibid.; social evaluation, Southeast Louisiana Hospital, March 6, 1974; case notes, Mississippi State Hospital, June 9–August 4, 1980.
85. Social evaluation, Southeast Louisiana Hospital, March 6, 1974; case notes, Mississippi State Hospital, June 9–August 4, 1980; interview with Easterling's first wife, 1983; clinical notes, East Mississippi State Hospital, September 15, 1976; social and medical history, February 10, 1977.
86. Interviews with businessman, February 1982.
87. Ibid.; Easterling's passport.
88. Interview with Dominguez, 1983.
89. WR, pp. 80, 142.
90. VI WC, p. 328; *Dallas Morning News*, November 26, 1978; CD 5, p. 41; Howard Roffman, *Presumed Guilty*, pp. 180–88.
91. WR, p. 801; HSCR, pp. 149, 155, 157; V WC, pp. 190–92, 194–95, 210; Scheim, *Contract on America*, pp. 111–12, 212–16.
92. HSCR, p. 180.
93. WR, p. 79; Sylvia Meagher, *Accessories After the Fact*, pp. 114–15.
94. VIII HSCA, p. 185; Meagher, *Accessories*, pp. 101, 107–10; WR, pp. 79, 191; Frederick Myatt, *An Illustrated Guide to Rifles and Automatic Weapons*, p. 53; Ken Warner, "Big Bargains in Rifles," *Mechanix Illustrated*, October 1964.
95. Interview with Carl Day, 1983; HSCR, p. 485.
96. Marshall Houts, *Where Death Delights*, pp. 62–63; Roffman, *Presumed Guilty*, p. 144; Summers, *Conspiracy*, p. 67; *Philadelphia*

Inquirer, November 25, 1966; WR, pp. 79–81, 95, 336–37; VI WC, p. 133; XV WC, p. 80; XXV WC, pp. 216–17; HSCR, p. 158; I HSCA, p. 332; III WC, p. 430.

97. I HSCA, pp. 335–36; WR, pp. 95, 118–19.
98. I HSCA, pp. 490–567; partial transcript of Guinn tape made by David Lifton (undated).
99. WR, pp. 48, 79, 143, 163.
100. "The Story of an Historic Site, the Former Texas School Book Depository," brochure, Dallas County Administration Building.
101. Interview with Judson Shook, 1984.
102. CD 1546, pp. 35–37.
103. XVII WC, p. 206.
104. XIX WC, p. 524; XIII HSCA, p. 8; VI WC, pp. 266–67.
105. Interview with G. Robert Blakey.
106. FBI memo, Jevons to Conrad, November 23, 1963 (HQ 62–109060); WR, p. 123; Meagher, *Accessories*, p. 121.
107. WR, pp. 158, 161.
108. WR, pp. 180, 423; records of Mary Ferrell.
109. Records of Ferrell.
110. Letter, Young to Hurt, September 27, 1983. Reference for information in footnote is letter, Hurt to Young, August 19, 1983.
111. Civil Aeronautics Board, *Accident Investigation Report*, file #1–0013, May 27, 1954; letter, Young to Hurt, September 27, 1983.
112. Civil Aeronautics Board, *Accident Investigation Report*, file #1–0013, May 27, 1954.
113. Interview with Easterling's first wife, 1983; interview with file clerk, Forrest General Hospital, Hattiesburg, Mississippi, 1983.
114. Information on Easterling's commitment to Mississippi State Hospital, Whitfield, August 1983.
115. Ibid.

13: The Enduring Puzzle

1. Senate Select Committee to Study Governmental Operations with Respect to Intelligence Activities, *Final Report, Book Five, The Investigation of the Assassination of President John F. Kennedy: Performance of the Intelligence Agencies*, 94th Cong., 2d sess., 1976, pp. 32–33.
2. WR, pp. 317, 319–21, 324; HSCR, pp. 250–51.
3. Peter Dale Scott, *Crime and Cover-up*, p. 12.
4. Ibid., pp. 12–13; interview with Peter Dale Scott, March 1984.
5. XXIV WC, p. 736; WR, pp. 316, 317, 320–24; CD 23.

6. XXIV WC, pp. 731–33, 736; J. Gary Shaw with Larry R. Harris, *Cover-up*, p. 107; WR, pp. 731–33.

7. HSCR, p. 137; X HSCA, pp. 23–26; XI WC, pp. 370–71.

8. XI WC, pp. 371–72, 377; X HSCA, p. 27; HSCR, pp. 137, 139; WR, p. 322.

9. HSCR, pp. 249–50; XVI WC, p. 638; Gaeton Fonzi, "Who Killed JFK?", *The Washingtonian*, November 1980, p. 204; interview with David A. Phillips, 1984.

10. Shaw with Harris, *Cover-up*, p. 111; XXVI WC, p. 406; CD 1, pp. 267–68.

11. Shaw with Harris, *Cover-up*, p. 111; CD 205, p. 182; XXV WC, p. 588.

12. XXII WC, pp. 523, 526; WR, pp. 316, 737.

13. X WC, pp. 358–60, 362, 370–71, 380, 385–87, 391–93; WR, p. 318.

14. WR, pp. 119–20, 319.

15. XXVI WC, p. 664; FBI memo, Branigan to Sullivan, January 14, 1964 (HQ 105–82555–1379); CD 205, pp. 218–21; CD 329, pp. 75, 77–80; *Dallas Morning News*, May 8, 1977; Shaw with Harris, *Cover-up*, p. 110.

16. XXVI WC, pp. 453, 664, 685; WR, pp. 320–21; *Dallas Morning News*, May 8, 1977; interview with Eugene Wilson, car salesman, May 1977.

17. Investigation of Oswald's driver's license by Ace R. Hayes in November 1982 (contacted Texas Department of Public Safety); Garrison file memo on statement of Aletha Frair, February 15, 1968 (subject: Oswald's driver's license).

18. Interview with Ed Brand, May 1977; Garrison file memo on Oswald's driver's license, December 12, 1967; CD 7, p. 169; WR, p. 737.

19. CD 729; notice of appeal, Shaw v. FBI, U.S. District Court for the District of Columbia, CA 82–0756; complaint for declaratory and injunctive relief, Shaw v. FBI, CA 82–0756.

20. CD 729; interview with Gary Shaw.

21. CD 729; complaint for declaratory and injunctive relief, Shaw v. FBI; CD 1, pp. 267–68.

22. FBI airtel, SAC New York to Director, May 23, 1960 (HQ 105–82555 unrecorded); FBI memo, Hickey to White, March 31, 1961; III HSCA, p. 573.

23. X HSCA, pp. 110, 126; FBI memo, Alker to SAC New Orleans, November 25, 1963 (NO 89–69–94); Harold Weisberg, *Oswald in New Orleans*, pp. 101–2; WR, p. 701. References for information in footnote are INS memo, Smith to Assistant Commissioner of Investigations, December 11, 1975; INS memo, Roach to Commissioner, USINS Central Office, Washington, D.C., December 11, 1975; Senate Select Committee, *Investigation of the Assassination*, p. 91; WR, pp. 723–24.

24. X HSCA, pp. 110, 126.

25. WR, pp. 156–57, 160; XIX WC, p. 524; XIII HSCA, p. 8; CD 5, p. 70; Fred J. Cook, "The Irregulars Take the Field," *The Nation*, July 19, 1971.
26. Confirmed by Mary Ferrell.
27. III HSCA, p. 573; FBI airtel, SAC New York to Director, May 23, 1960 (HQ 105–82555 unrecorded); HSCR, p. 137; WR, pp. 318–21.
28. Interview with Bernard Fensterwald, Jr.; interview with Shaw; Seth Kantor, *Who Was Jack Ruby?*, pp. 15–16.
29. Kantor, *Who Was Jack Ruby?*, p. 15; IX HSCA, p. 183; notice of filing, Shaw v. Dept. of State et al., CA 80–1056, p. 35; FBI file on Thomas Eli Davis III (HQ 105–120907, LA 105–14523); interview with supervisor, U.S. Probation Office, U.S. Courthouse, Fort Worth, 1984.
30. FBI file on Davis (HQ 105–120907, LA 105–14523); interview with Shaw; IX HSCA, pp. 183–84.
31. State Department telegram from Tangiers, December 10, 1963 (HQ 105–120907–14); memo of interview by Gary Shaw of Carolyn Davis, November 1, 1979; IX HSCA, p. 184.
32. IX HSCA, pp. 1137–38; memo from Earl Golz on conversation with George Carter concerning Thomas E. Davis III, May 31, 1979; interview with Shaw; FBI file on Davis (HQ 105–120907, LA 105–14523); Kantor, *Who Was Jack Ruby?*, pp. 15–16; IV HSCA, p. 198.
33. Interview with Fensterwald; interview with Shaw; memo from Golz, May 31, 1979.
34. Kantor, *Who Was Jack Ruby?*, pp. 15, 138; IX HSCA, p. 183; XXIII WC, pp. 157–59.
35. Kantor, *Who Was Jack Ruby?*, p. 15; interview with Shaw; memo of interview by Shaw of Carolyn Davis, November 1, 1979.
36. Interviews with Seth Kantor, 1983, 1984; G. Robert Blakey and Richard N. Billings, *The Plot to Kill the President*, p. 295; CD 1052; FBI Potential Criminal Informant file of Jack Ruby (HQ 44–24016–1138).
37. IX HSCA, pp. 183–84; State Department telegram from Tangiers, December 10, 1963 (HQ 105–120907–14); FBI file on Davis (HQ 105–120907, LA 105–14523).
38. HSCR, pp. 137–39; XI WC, pp. 371, 385; FBI file on Davis (HQ 105–120907, LA 105–14523).
39. Guest invoice register, Hotel LaSalle, New Orleans, August 7–10, 1963; WR, p. 728.
40. State Department telegram from Tangiers, December 10, 1963 (HQ 105–120907–14); IX HSCA, p. 184.
41. State Department telegram from Tangiers, December 10, 1963 (HQ 105–120907–14).
42. Memo of interview by Shaw of Carolyn Davis, November 1, 1979; interview with Kantor, 1984; Kantor, *Who Was Jack Ruby?*, p. 16.

43. *Dallas Morning News,* October 9, 1980; *Dallas Times Herald,* December 1, 10, 1963; memo from Golz, May 31, 1979.
44. Memo from Golz, May 31, 1979.
45. *Dallas Morning News,* October 9, 1980; memo from Golz, May 31, 1979.
46. Kantor, *Who Was Jack Ruby?,* pp. 15–16; IX HSCA, pp. 184–85.
47. Certificate of death for Thomas Eli Davis III; notes of interview by Shaw of Sheriff Eldon Moyers, Decatur, Texas, June 19, 1979; Kantor, *Who Was Jack Ruby?,* p. 16; notice of filing, Shaw v. Dept. of State et al., CA 80–1056, p. 36.
48. Letter, Thomas F. Conley, chief, Freedom of Information Office, Department of the Army, to Gary Shaw, August 12, 1980; notice of filing, Shaw v. Dept. of State et al., CA 80–1056, p. 35; letter, William Wharton, director, Office of Citizenship Appeals and Legal Assistance, Department of State, to Gary Shaw, September 13, 1982; motion of defendant Central Intelligence Agency for summary judgment, Shaw v. Dept. of State et al., U.S. District Court for the District of Columbia, CA 80–1056; interview with Shaw.
49. Interview with Ferrell; WR, p. 732; Sylvia Meagher, *Accessories After the Fact,* p. 329; Anthony Summers, *Conspiracy,* pp. 157–58.
50. Interview with Ferrell; interview with Marion Johnson, National Archives; XXI WC, p. 593; XXIII WC, pp. 208–69; Mary Ferrell, "Lee Harvey Oswald's 1962 Income Tax Return—CD 90a," *Continuing Inquiry,* September 22, 1977.
51. Summers, *Conspiracy,* p. 158; interview with Ferrell.
52. Interview with Ferrell; letter, Marina Oswald Porter to Robert Warner, National Archives, November 9, 1981; letter, Marina Oswald Porter to Roscoe Egger, IRS, November 9, 1981; letter, Clarence Lyons, Jr., Civil Archives Division, National Archives, to Marina Oswald Porter, May 18, 1982; letter, Joseph Sommers, Public Services Branch, IRS, to Marina Oswald Porter, June 2, 1982.
53. Interview with Ferrell.
54. Ibid.
55. Ibid.; Ferrell, "Lee Harvey Oswald's 1962 Income Tax Return—CD 90a."
56. XXIV WC, pp. 429, 434, 436; WR, p. 216; HSCR, pp. 156, 180; XV WC, pp. 116–17, 125.
57. Interview with Billy Grammer, May 1984.
58. Ibid.; XXIV WC, pp. 429, 434, 436.
59. Interview with Grammer, May 1984.
60. HSCR, pp. 156, 180.
61. I HSCA, p. 115; III HSCA, pp. 448, 450; HSCR, p. 232; CD 1347, pp. 120–21, 123; information received by electronic device by Intelligence Unit, Miami Police Department, November 9, 1963.

62. Information received by Intelligence Unit, Miami Police Department, November 9, 1963.
63. HSCR, pp. 232–33; III HSCA, p. 363; *Public Papers of the Presidents*, 1963, pp. 871–72, 877; Summers, *Conspiracy*, p. 430; Blakey and Billings, *Plot to Kill*, p. 9.
64. HSCR, p. 234; memo of conversation between Bernard Fensterwald and Bill Somersett, Miami, June 5, 1968. References for information in footnote are HSCR, p. 234; memo of conversation between Fensterwald and Somersett, June 5, 1968; Shaw with Harris, *Cover-up*, p. 169.
65. Peter Dale Scott, Paul L. Hoch, and Russell Stetler, eds., *The Assassinations: Dallas and Beyond*, p. 129; CD 1347, pp. 120–21, 123.
66. CD 20, p. 24; Scott, Hoch, and Stetler, eds., *The Assassinations*, p. 118; Summers, *Conspiracy*, p. 607; HSCR, p. 234. Reference for information in footnote is *Miami News*, February 2, 1967.
67. X HSCA, pp. 199–202.
68. Ibid.
69. Ibid., pp. 199, 202–3.
70. IV HSCA, p. 462.
71. Ibid., pp. 453–68.
72. Ibid., pp. 464–65.
73. Ibid.
74. Ibid., p. 465.
75. Ibid., p. 467.
76. Interview with Ferrell.
77. Ibid.; CIA document on Jean Souetre's expulsion from U.S., April 1, 1964 (CIA 632–796).
78. Notice of filing, Shaw v. Dept. of State et al., CA 80–1056; CIA document on Souetre's expulsion, April 1, 1964 (CIA 632–796); CIA report on OAS, Deputy Director (Plans) to Deputy Director for Coordination, Bureau of Intelligence and Research, Department of State (CIA CSCI–3/776, 742); CIA report on alleged plans of secret army organization for post–de Gaulle takeover in France, June 25, 1963 (CIA CSDB–3/655, 207); CIA report on Souetre, June 25, 1963 (CIA CSDB–3/655, 207); interview with Shaw.
79. CIA document on Souetre's expulsion, April 1, 1964 (CIA 632–796); notice of filing, Shaw v. Dept. of State et al., CA 80–1056, p. 12; *Public Papers of the Presidents*, 1963, p. 887; Blakey and Billings, *Plot to Kill*, p. 10; WR, pp. 1, 3.
80. CIA document on Souetre's expulsion, April 1, 1964 (CIA 632–796); notice of filing, Shaw v. Dept. of State et al., p. 37.
81. Notice of filing, Shaw v. Dept. of State et al., pp. 37–38; CIA document on Souetre's expulsion, April 1, 1964 (CIA 632–796); interview with Shaw.

82. Interview with Shaw; notice of filing, Shaw v. Dept. of State et al., p. 12; letter from French investigator to Bernard Fensterwald, Jr., December 7, 1981.
83. CIA document on Souetre's expulsion, April 1, 1964 (CIA 632–796).
84. Notice of filing, Shaw v. Dept. of State et al., pp. 18–20; FBI memo, ASAC Brooking to SAC San Antonio, March 6, 1964 (SA 105–2975–4); interview with Shaw; FBI teletype, Dallas to Director and Houston and New York, March 11, 1964 (HQ 105–1–8529–3).
85. Interview with Shaw; notice of filing, Shaw v. Dept. of State et al., p. 5.
86. Notice of filing, Shaw v. Dept. of State et al., p. 6.
87. Geoffrey Bocca, *The Secret Army*, p. 37; Arthur M. Schlesinger, Jr., *A Thousand Days*, p. 510; notice of filing, Shaw v. Dept. of State et al., p. 6; Alistair Horne, *A Savage War of Peace*, p. 463; John Talbott, *The War Without a Name*, p. 36.
88. Notice of filing, Shaw v. Dept. of State et al., p. 6.
89. Ibid., pp. 9, 18; interview with Shaw; FBI teletype, Dallas to Director and Houston and New York, March 11, 1964 (HQ 105–1–8529–3); FBI teletype, Houston to Director, March 12, 1964 (HQ 105–128529–11).
90. Notice of filing, Shaw v. Dept. of State et al., p. 14; CIA document on Souetre's expulsion, April 1, 1964 (CIA 632–796); interview with Shaw.
91. Interview with Shaw; notice of filing, Shaw v. Dept. of State et al., pp. 14–15; Gary Shaw and Larry Harris, "Is the FBI Shielding a JFK Assassin?", *Continuing Inquiry*, November 22, 1977.
92. Notice of filing, Shaw v. Dept. of State et al., pp. 8–9, 14; interview with Shaw; Shaw and Harris, "Is the FBI Shielding a JFK Assassin?"; FBI report on Souetre, Houston, March 6, 1964.
93. Notice of filing, Shaw v. Dept. of State et al., pp. 14–15; interview with Shaw; Shaw and Harris, "Is the FBI Shielding a JFK Assassin?"; FBI report on Souetre, Houston, March 6, 1964.
94. Interview with Shaw; notice of filing, Shaw v. Dept. of State et al., p. 13; Jacques Chambaz, "Ce 'french terrorist' accuse du meurtre de Kennedy," *Le Quotidien de Paris*, January 1, 1984.
95. Chambaz, "Ce 'french terrorist' accuse du meurtre de Kennedy."
96. Ibid.; Staff and Editors of *Newsday, The Heroin Trail*, pp. 109, 113; notice of filing, Shaw v. Dept. of State et al., pp. 15–16; interview with Shaw.
97. CIA document on Souetre's expulsion, April 1, 1964 (CIA 632–796); notice of filing, Shaw v. Dept. of State et al., p. 38.
98. Interview with Shaw; notice of filing, Shaw v. Dept. of State et al., p. 5; CIA document on Souetre's expulsion, April 1, 1964 (CIA 632–796).

99. HSCR, pp. 118–20; Office of the Secretary of the Treasury memo, McBrien to Burke, June 9, 1976 (SS 157–76–100); abstracted notes, Senate Select Committee on Intelligence draft report, June 15, 1976, pp. 111–17; Senate Select Committee, *Investigation of the Assassination*, pp. 61–62.

100. HSCR, pp. 118, 120; Senate Select Committee, *Investigation of the Assassination*, p. 62; abstracted notes, Senate Select Committee on Intelligence draft report, June 15, 1976, pp. 111–17; *President's Appointment Book*, John F. Kennedy Library.

101. HSCR, pp. 118, 120; Senate Select Committee, *Investigation of the Assassination*, pp. 61–62; U.S. Secret Service, abstracted notes of pp. 111–17 of SSC draft report, June 15, 1976.

102. Senate Select Committee, *Investigation of the Assassination*, p. 61; McBrien to Burke, June 9, 1976 (SS 157–76–100); HSCR, p. 118.

103. HSCR, pp. 119–20; Senate Select Committee, *Investigation of the Assassination*, pp. 61–63; U.S. Secret Service, abstracted notes of pp. 111–17 of SSC draft report, June 15, 1976.

104. Senate Select Committee, *Investigation of the Assassination*, p. 63; HSCR, p. 121.

105. Senate Select Committee, *Investigation of the Assassination*, p. 60.

106. Ibid., pp. 60–61.

107. Ibid., p. 61.

108. Ibid., p. 30; HSCR, pp. 117–18.

109. CIA dispatch on Miguel Casas Saez, January 27, 1964 (CIA 510–199); CIA report on Casas, January 25, 1964 (CIA 491–201).

110. Ibid. (both).

111. CIA dispatch on Casas, January 27, 1964 (CIA 510–199).

112. Ibid.; CIA report on Casas, January 25, 1964 (CIA 491–201).

113. CIA dispatch on Casas, January 27, 1964 (CIA 510–199).

114. Ibid.

115. CIA report on Casas, January 25, 1964 (CIA 491–201).

116. CIA dispatch, "Information Possibly Connected with the Assassination," November 2, 1964 (CIA 979–929 AX); CIA routing and record sheet for CIA 979–929 AX.

117. Ibid. (both).

118. David S. Lifton, *Best Evidence*, pp. 205, 579, 598, 674.

119. Ibid., p. 598; videotape of interviews by David Lifton.

120. Lifton, *Best Evidence*, p. 595.

121. Ibid., pp. 595, 599; videotape of interviews by Lifton.

122. Lifton, *Best Evidence*, pp. 571–82, 620–21.

123. Ibid., pp. 390, 682–90; letter, David Lifton to Henry Hurt, December 6, 1983.

124. Lifton, *Best Evidence*, pp. 677, 680–81.

125. Ibid., pp. 679–90; letter, Lifton to Hurt, December 6, 1983.

126. Lifton, *Best Evidence*, pp. 271–94, 308–37.
127. Ibid., p. 296.
128. Ibid., p. 172; WR, p. 518.
129. Interviews with Lifton, 1982, 1983; letter, Lifton to Hurt, December 6, 1983.
130. *Boston Globe*, June 21, 1981.
131. Lifton, *Best Evidence*, pp. 172, 318–19, 439, 602; WR, p. 518; videotape of interviews by Lifton.
132. Interview with James J. Humes, 1984.
133. *Boston Globe*, June 21, 1981.

14: Aftermath and Perspective

1. *Washington Post*, November 20, 1983.
2. Jim Garrison, *A Heritage of Stone*; Michael Canfield and Alan J. Weberman, *Coup d'Etat in America*.
3. Senate Select Committee to Study Governmental Operations with Respect to Intelligence Activities, *Final Report, Book Five, The Investigation of the Assassination of John F. Kennedy: Performance of the Intelligence Agencies*, 94th Cong., 2d sess., 1976, p. 23; Leo Janos, "The Last Days of the President," *Atlantic Monthly*, July 1973; letter, Lewis F. Powell, Jr., to Henry Hurt, April 6, 1982; interview with Richard B. Russell on WSB-TV, Atlanta, February 2, 1970; Arthur M. Schlesinger, Jr., *Robert Kennedy and His Times*, p. 616.
4. WR; HSCR, pp. 1, 7; Senate Select Committee, *Investigation of the Assassination*, p. 45; James Kirkwood, *American Grotesque*; Commission on CIA Activities Within the U.S., *Report to the President by the Commission on CIA Activities Within the U.S.*, June 1975; DeLloyd J. Guth and David R. Wrone, comps., *The Assassination of John F. Kennedy: A Comprehensive Historical and Legal Bibliography, 1963–1979*, pp. 12–13; *The New York Times*, May 15, 1982.
5. *Washington Post*, January 8, 1979; spokesman for press office, FBI, Washington, D.C.
6. Interview with James H. Lesar, 1984.
7. Interview with Marion Johnson, National Archives.
8. WR, p. xv.
9. Letter, Robert M. L. Johnson, mayor, Cedar Rapids, Iowa, to President Lyndon B. Johnson, January 4, 1965; memo, McGeorge Bundy to Acting Attorney General Nicholas deB. Katzenbach, January 18, 1965; letter, Earl Warren to Katzenbach, April 5, 1965 (DOJ 129–11).
10. Letter, Warren to Katzenbach, April 5, 1965; memo, Bundy to Attorney General, April 19, 1965; "Summary of Views of Interested Federal Agencies Concerning the Disclosure to the Public of Mate-

rials Delivered to the National Archives by the President's Commission on the Assassination of President Kennedy" (National Archives).
11. Guth and Wrone, *The Assassination of John F. Kennedy*, pp. 45–67; interview with Marion Johnson; David S. Lifton, *Best Evidence*, p. xiii; Anthony Summers, *Conspiracy*, p. 10.
12. Interview with Marion Johnson.
13. Ibid.; HSCR, pp. 223, 244–46, 252.
14. Guth and Wrone, *The Assassination of John F. Kennedy*, pp. viii, 45–67; interview with Harold Weisberg; interview with Lesar, 1984; *Congress and the Nation* 4, 1973–1976, pp. 805–6.
15. Interview with Bernard Fensterwald, Jr.
16. Article attached to FBI memo, McDaniel to Trotter (re: Murkin), October 28, 1968.
17. Interview with Lesar, 1983; interview with Gary Shaw.
18. Interview with Lesar, 1984; interview with Weisberg; American Friends Service Committee v. William H. Webster, 485 Fed. Supp. 222 (D.D.C. 1980); letter, Webster to Assistant Attorney General of Criminal Division, June 7, 1978 (HQ 62–117290–958).
19. Interview with Lesar, 1984; interview with Weisberg; Harold Weisberg v. William H. Webster et al., U.S. District Court for District of Columbia, CA 78–0322.
20. Interview with George Perros, Legislative and Diplomatic Branch, National Archives, 1984. Reference for information in footnote is interview with Mark Allen, 1983.
21. Paul Hoch, "Access to HSC Records," *Echoes of Conspiracy* 4, no. 5 (October 5, 1982).
22. Interview with G. Robert Blakey; interview with Lesar, 1984; CIA memo for the record, on Blakey's visit to CIA headquarters on April 27, 1979, dated April 27, 1979.
23. CIA memo for the record, April 27, 1979.
24. Ibid.
25. Ibid.
26. Ibid.
27. Interview with Blakey.
28. CIA memo for the record, April 27, 1979.
29. Interview with public information officer, CIA, August 1982.
30. Interview with Lesar, 1984; HSCR, pp. 223–24; interviews with critics.
31. Senate Select Committee on Intelligence, *Intelligence Information Act of 1983*, 98th Cong., 1st sess., 1983, S. Rpt. 98–305; "Locking the Files," *The Nation*, April 14, 1984; Angus Mackenzie, "The Operational Files Exemption," *The Nation*, September 24, 1983; interview with press officer, Senate Intelligence Committee, June 1984.
32. *Washington Post*, November 20, 1983.
33. John 9:32.

Selected Bibliography

Agee, Philip. *Inside the Company: CIA Diary*. New York: Bantam, 1976.

Anson, Robert Sam. *"They've Killed the President!": The Search for the Murderers of John F. Kennedy*. New York: Bantam, 1976.

Ayers, Bradley Earl. *The War That Never Was*. New York: Bobbs-Merrill, 1976.

Bakal, Carl. *The Right To Bear Arms*. New York: McGraw-Hill, 1966.

Bamford, James. *The Puzzle Palace: A Report on NSA, America's Most Secret Agency*. Boston: Houghton Mifflin, 1982.

Barron, John. *KGB*. New York: Reader's Digest Press, 1974.

Belin, David W. *November 22, 1963: You Are the Jury*. New York: Quadrangle, 1973.

Belli, Melvin, with Maurice Carroll. *Dallas Justice*. New York: David McKay, 1964.

Berman, Harold. *The Trial of the U2*. Chicago: Translation World Publisher, 1960.

Bishop, Jim. *The Day Kennedy Was Shot*. New York: Funk & Wagnalls, 1968.

Blakey, G. Robert, and Richard N. Billings. *The Plot to Kill the President*. New York: Times Books, 1981.

Bloomgarden, Henry S. *The Gun: A "Biography" of the Gun That Killed John F. Kennedy*. New York: Grossman Publishers, 1975.

Bocca, Geoffrey. *The Secret Army*. Englewood, N.J.: Prentice-Hall, 1968.

Bonner, Judy Whitson. *Investigation of a Homicide: The Murder of John F. Kennedy*. Anderson, S.C.: Droke House, 1969.

Brener, Milton E. *The Garrison Case: A Study in the Abuse of Power*. New York: Clarkson N. Potter, 1969.

Bringuier, Carlos. *Red Friday: November 22, 1963*. Chicago: Charles Hallberg, 1969.

Buchanan, Thomas C. *Who Killed Kennedy?* New York: G. P. Putnam's Sons, 1964.

Canfield, Michael, and Alan J. Weberman. *Coup d'Etat in America: The CIA and the Assassination of John F. Kennedy*. New York: The Third Press, 1975.

Clark, James W. *American Assassins: The Darker Side of Politics*. Princeton, N.J.: Princeton University Press, 1982.

Colby, William, and Peter Forbath. *Honorable Men: My Life in the CIA*. New York: Simon & Schuster, 1978.

Committee to Investigate Assassinations. *Coincidence or Conspiracy?* New York: Zebra Books, 1977.

Congressional Quarterly Almanac, 1965. 89th Cong., 1st sess., vol. 21. Washington, D.C.: Congressional Quarterly Service, 1966.

Curry, Jesse. *JFK Assassination File: Retired Dallas Police Chief Jesse Curry Reveals His Personal File.* American Poster and Publishing, 1969.

Dallas, Tita, with Jeanira Ratcliffe. *The Kennedy Case.* New York: Popular Library, 1973.

Davison, Jean. *Oswald's Game.* New York: W. W. Norton, 1983.

Demaris, Ovid. *The Director.* New York: Harper's Magazine Press, 1975.

———. *The Last Mafioso.* New York: Times Books, 1981.

De Vosjoli, P.L. Thyraud. *Lamia.* Boston: Little, Brown, 1970.

Dulles, Allen. *The Craft of Intelligence.* New York: Harper & Row, 1963.

Eddowes, Michael. *The Oswald File.* New York: Clarkson N. Potter, 1977.

Epstein, Edward J. *Counterplot.* New York: Viking Press, 1969.

———. *Inquest: The Warren Commission and the Establishment of Truth.* New York: Viking Press, 1966.

———. *Legend: The Secret World of Lee Harvey Oswald.* New York: Reader's Digest Press/McGraw-Hill, 1978.

Evica, George Michael. *And We Are Still All Mortal: New Evidence and Analysis in the Assassination of John F. Kennedy.* West Hartford, Conn.: University of Hartford, 1978.

Exner, Judith. *My Story: As Told to Ovid Demaris.* New York: Grove Press, 1977.

Feldman, Harold. *Fifty-one Witnesses: The Grassy Knoll.* San Francisco: Idlewild Publishing, 1965.

Ford, Gerald R., with John R. Stiles. *Portrait of the Assassin.* New York: Simon & Schuster, 1965.

Fox, Sylvan. *The Unanswered Questions About President Kennedy's Assassination.* New York: Award Books, 1975.

Garrison, Jim. *A Heritage of Stone.* New York: G. P. Putnam's Sons, 1970.

Gershenson, Alvin H. *Kennedy and Big Business.* Beverly Hills, Calif.: Book Company of America, 1964.

Gertz, Elmer. *Moment of Madness: The People vs. Jack Ruby.* Chicago: Follett Publishing, 1968.

Gill, William J. *The Ordeal of Otto Otepka.* New York: Arlington House, 1969.

Goode, Stephen. *Assassination!* New York: Franklin Watts, 1979.

Guth, DeLloyd J., and Wrone, David R., comps. *The Assassination of John F. Kennedy: A Comprehensive Historical and Legal Bibliography, 1963–1979.* Westport, Conn.: Greenwood Press, 1980.

Haley, J. Evetts. *A Texan Looks at Lyndon: A Study in Illegitimate Power.* Canyon, Texas: Palo Duro Press, 1964.

Hannibal, Edward, with Robert Boris. *Blood Feud.* New York: Ballantine, 1979.

Hepburn, James. *Farewell America*. Vaduz, Liechtenstein: Frontiers, 1968.

Hinckle, Warren, and William Turner. *The Fish Is Red: The Story of the Secret War Against Castro*. New York: Harper & Row, 1981.

Horne, Alistair. *A Savage War of Peace: Algeria 1954–1962*. New York: Penguin Books, 1979.

Hougan, Jim. *Spooks*. New York: William Morrow, 1978.

Houts, Marshall. *Where Death Delights*. New York: Coward-McCann, 1967.

Hunt, E. Howard. *Give Us This Day*. New York: Arlington House, 1973.

Hunter, Diana, and Alice Anderson. *Jack Ruby's Girls*. Atlanta: Hallux, 1970.

Hurt, Harry, III. *Texas Rich: The Hunt Dynasty from the Early Oil Days Through the Silver Crash*. New York: W. W. Norton, 1981.

Hurt, Henry. *Shadrin: The Spy Who Never Came Back*. New York: Reader's Digest Press/McGraw-Hill, 1981.

In the Shadow of Dallas: A Primer on the Assassination of President Kennedy. San Francisco: Ramparts Magazine, 1967.

Israel, Lee. *Kilgallen*. New York: Dell, 1979.

James, Rosemary, and Jack Wardlaw. *Plot or Politics?: The Garrison Case and Its Cast*. New Orleans: Pelican Publishing House, 1967.

Joesten, Joachim. *The Biggest Lie Ever Told: The Kennedy Murder Fraud and How I Helped Expose It*. New York: Joachim Joesten, 1968.

———. *The Garrison Enquiry: Truth & Consequences*. London: Peter Dawnay, 1967.

———. *Onassis*. New York: Tower Publications, 1963.

Johnson, Haynes. *The Bay of Pigs: The Leaders Story of Brigade 2506*. New York: W. W. Norton, 1964.

Johnson, Lyndon Baines. *The Vantage Point: Perspectives of the Presidency, 1963–1969*. New York: Holt, Rinehart and Winston, 1971.

Jones, Penn, Jr. *Forgive My Grief: A Critical Review of the Warren Commission Report on the Assassination of President John F. Kennedy*. Midlothian, Texas: Midlothian Mirror, 1966.

———. *Forgive My Grief, Volume II: A Further Critical Review of the Warren Commission Report on the Assassination of President John F. Kennedy*. Midlothian, Texas: Midlothian Mirror, 1967.

———. *Forgive My Grief III*. Rev. ed. Midlothian, Texas: Penn Jones, Jr., 1976.

———. *Forgive My Grief IV*. Midlothian, Texas: Penn Jones, Jr., 1974.

Kane, Joseph M. *Facts About the Presidents*. New York: H. W. Wilson, 1981.

Kantor, Seth. *Who Was Jack Ruby?* New York: Everest House, 1978.

Kaplan, John, with Jon R. Waltz. *The Trial of Jack Ruby: A Classic Study of Courtroom Strategies*. New York: Macmillan, 1965.

Kelley, Kitty. *Jackie Oh!* Secaucus, N.J.: Lyle Stuart, 1978.

Kennedy, John F. *Public Papers of the Presidents of the United States*. Washington, D.C.: U.S. Government Printing Office, 1962–1964.

Kennedy, Robert F. *The Enemy Within*. New York: Harper & Row, 1960.

———. *Thirteen Days: A Memoir of the Cuban Missile Crisis*. New York: W. W. Norton, 1969.

Kirkpatrick, Lyman B. *The Real CIA*. New York: Macmillan, 1968.

Kirkwood, James. *American Grotesque: An Account of the Clay Shaw–Jim Garrison Affair in the City of New Orleans*. New York: Simon & Schuster, 1970.

Kurtz, Michael. *Crime of the Century*. Knoxville, Tenn.: University of Tennessee Press, 1982.

Lane, Mark. *A Citizen's Dissent: Mark Lane Replies*. New York: Holt, Rinehart and Winston, 1966.

———. *Rush to Judgment: A Critique of the Warren Commission's Inquiry into the Murder of President John F. Kennedy, Officer J. D. Tippit, and Lee Harvey Oswald*. New York: Holt, Rinehart and Winston, 1966.

Lasky, Victor. *It Didn't Start with Watergate*. New York: Dell, 1978.

Lattimer, John K. *Kennedy and Lincoln: Medical and Ballistic Comparisons of Their Assassinations*. New York: Harcourt Brace Jovanovich, 1980.

Leek, Sybil, and Bert R. Sugar. *The Assassination Chain*. New York: Corwin Books, 1976.

Lesberg, Sandy. *Assassination in Our Time*. New York: Peebles Press International, 1976.

Leslie, Warren. *Dallas, Public and Private: Aspects of an American City*. New York: Grossman, 1964.

Lewis, Richard Warren. *The Scavengers and Critics of the Warren Report: The Endless Paradox*. New York: Dell, 1967.

Lifton, David S. *Best Evidence: Disguise and Deception in the Assassination of John F. Kennedy*. New York: Macmillan, 1980.

Lincoln, Lawrence. *Were We Controlled?* New Hyde Park, N.Y.: University Books, 1967.

McDonald, Hugh C., as told to Geoffrey Bocca. *Appointment in Dallas: The Final Solution to the Assassination of JFK*. New York: Zebra Books, 1975.

McDonald, Hugh C., with Robin Moore. *L.B.J. and the J.F.K. Conspiracy*. Westport, Conn.: Condor, 1978.

McGarvey, Patrick J. *CIA: The Myth and the Madness*. Baltimore: Penguin, 1973.

McKinley, James. *Assassination in America*. New York: Harper & Row, 1977.

McMillan, Priscilla Johnson. *Marina and Lee*. New York: Harper & Row, 1977.

Manchester, William Raymond. *The Death of a President, November 20–November 25, 1963*. New York: Harper & Row, 1967.

Mankiewicz, Frank, and Kirby Jones. *With Fidel: A Portrait of Castro and Cuba.* New York: Ballantine, 1975.

Marchetti, Victor, and John D. Marks. *The CIA and the Cult of Intelligence.* New York: Alfred A. Knopf, 1974.

Martin, David C. *Wilderness of Mirrors.* New York: Harper & Row, 1980.

Martin, Ralph G. *A Hero for Our Time.* New York: Macmillan, 1983.

Matthews, James P. *Four Dark Days in History: A Photo History of President Kennedy's Assassination.* Los Angeles: Associated Professional Services, 1963.

Meagher, Sylvia. *Accessories After the Fact: The Warren Commission, the Authorities, and the Report.* New York: Bobbs-Merrill, 1967.

―――. *Subject Index to the Warren Report and Hearings and Exhibits.* New York: Scarecrow Press, 1966.

Meagher, Sylvia, and Gary Owens. *Master Index to the JFK Assassination Investigations.* Metuchen, N.J.: Scarecrow Press, 1980.

Miller, Merle. *Lyndon: An Oral Biography.* New York: Ballantine, 1980.

Miller, Tom. *The Assassination Please Almanac.* Chicago: Henry Regnery, 1977.

Model, Peter, with Robert J. Groden. *JFK: The Case for Conspiracy.* New York: Manor Books, 1976.

Moldea, Dan E. *The Hoffa Wars.* New York: Paddington Press, 1978.

Morin, Relman. *Assassination: The Death of President John F. Kennedy.* New York: New American Library, 1968.

Morrow, Robert D. *Betrayal: A Reconstruction of Certain Clandestine Events from the Bay of Pigs to the Assassination of John F. Kennedy.* Chicago: Henry Regnery, 1976.

Murr, Gary. "The Murder of Police Officer J. D. Tippit." Unpublished. 1971.

Myatt, Frederick. *An Illustrated Guide to Rifles and Automatic Weapons.* Arco Publishing, 1981.

Nash, H. C. *Citizens' Arrest: The Dissent of Penn Jones, Jr., in the Assassination of JFK.* Austin, Texas: Latitudes Press, 1977.

NBC News. *Memo to JFK.* New York: G. P. Putnam's Sons, 1961.

―――. *Seventy Hours and Thirty Minutes.* New York: Random House, 1966.

Newcomb, Fred, and Perry Adams. *Murder from Within.* Santa Barbara, Calif.: Probe, 1974.

Newman, Albert H. *The Assassination of John F. Kennedy: The Reasons Why.* New York: Clarkson N. Potter, 1970.

Newsday, Editors of. *The Heroin Trail.* New York: Holt, Rinehart and Winston, 1975.

Noyes, Peter. *Legacy of Doubt.* New York: Pinnacle Books, 1973.

Oglesby, Carl. *The Yankee and Cowboy War.* Kansas City: Sheed Andrews & McMeel, 1976.

Oswald, Robert L., with Myrick and Barbara Land. *Lee: A Portrait of Lee Harvey Oswald by His Brother.* New York: Coward-McCann, 1967.

O'Toole, George. *The Assassination Tapes: An Electronic Probe into the Murder of John F. Kennedy and the Dallas Cover-up.* New York: Penthouse Press, 1975.

Parmet, Herbert S. *JFK: The Presidency of John F. Kennedy.* New York: Dial Press, 1983.

Pearson, Drew, and Jack Anderson. *The Case Against Congress.* New York: Simon & Schuster, 1968.

Pett, Saul, et al. *The Torch Is Passed.* New York: Associated Press, 1963.

Phelan, James. *Scandals, Scamps and Scoundrels: The Casebook of an Investigative Reporter.* New York: Random House, 1982.

Phillips, David A. *The Night Watch.* New York: Atheneum, 1977.

Popkin, Richard. *The Second Oswald.* New York: Avon, 1966.

Powers, Francis G., and Curt Gentry. *Operation Overflight.* New York: Holt, Rinehart and Winston, 1970.

Powers, Thomas. *The Man Who Kept the Secrets: Richard Helms and the CIA.* New York: Alfred A. Knopf, 1979.

Prouty, Leroy Fletcher. *The Secret Team: The CIA and Its Allies in Control of the United States and the World.* Englewood Cliffs, N.J.: Prentice-Hall, 1973.

Rather, Dan, with Mickey Herskowitz. *The Camera Never Blinks: Adventures of a TV Journalist.* New York: William Morrow, 1977.

Reid, Ed, and Ovid Demaris. *The Green Felt Jungle.* New York: Trident Press, 1963.

Roffman, Howard. *Presumed Guilty.* Cranbury, N.J.: Associated University Presses, 1975.

Rositzke, Harry. *The CIA's Secret Operations.* New York: Reader's Digest Press, 1977.

Sauvage, Leo. *The Oswald Affair: An Examination of the Contradictions and Omissions of the Warren Report.* Cleveland: World Publishing, 1966.

Scheim, David. *Contract on America.* Silver Spring, Md.: Argyle Press, 1983.

Schlesinger, Arthur M., Jr. *Robert Kennedy and His Times.* Boston: Houghton Mifflin, 1978.

————. *A Thousand Days: John F. Kennedy in the White House.* Greenwich, Conn.: Fawcett, 1965.

Schorr, Daniel. *Clearing the Air.* Boston: Houghton Mifflin, 1977.

Scott, Peter Dale. *Crime and Cover-up: The CIA, the Mafia, and the Dallas-Watergate Connection.* Berkeley, Calif.: Westworks, 1977.

————. "The Dallas Conspiracy." Unpublished.

————. *The War Conspiracy.* New York: Bobbs-Merrill, 1972.

Scott, Peter Dale, Paul L. Hoch, and Russell Stetler, eds. *The Assassi-*

nations: Dallas and Beyond: A Guide to Cover-ups and Investigations. New York: Random House, 1978.

Shaw, J. Gary, with Larry R. Harris. *Cover-up: The Governmental Conspiracy to Conceal the Facts About the Public Execution of John Kennedy.* Cleburne, Texas: Shaw, 1976.

Sheridan, Walter. *The Fall and Rise of Jimmy Hoffa.* New York: Saturday Review Press, 1973.

Smith, Joseph B. *Portrait of a Cold Warrior.* New York: G. P. Putnam's Sons, 1976.

Sorensen, Theodore. *The Kennedy Legacy.* New York: New American Library, 1970.

Sparrow, John. *After the Assassination.* New York: Chilmark Press, 1967.

Stafford, Jean. *A Mother in History: Mrs. Marguerite Oswald.* New York: Farrar Straus Giroux, 1966.

Steiner, Paul. *175 Little Known Facts About J.F.K.* New York: Citadel Press, 1964.

Sullivan, William C., with Bill Brown. *The Bureau: My Thirty Years in Hoover's FBI.* New York: W. W. Norton, 1979.

Summers, Anthony. *Conspiracy.* New York: McGraw-Hill, 1981.

Talbott, John. *The War Without a Name.* New York: Alfred A. Knopf, 1980.

Talese, Gay. *Honor Thy Father.* New York: World Publishing, 1971.

Teresa, Vincent, with Thomas C. Renner. *My Life in the Mafia.* London: Hart-Davis, McGibbon, 1973.

Thompson, Josiah. *Six Seconds in Dallas: A Microstudy of the Kennedy Assassination.* New York: Bernard Geis Associates/Random House, 1967.

Thompson, Nelson. *The Dark Side of Camelot.* Chicago: Playboy Press, 1976.

Thompson, Robert E. *The Trial of Lee Harvey Oswald.* New York: Ace Books, 1977.

Thornley, Kerry. *Oswald.* Chicago: New Classics House, 1965.

Time-Life Books, Editors of. *This Fabulous Century, Volume 3.* New York: Time-Life Books, 1969.

Tully, Andrew. *CIA: The Inside Story.* Greenwich, Conn.: Fawcett Crest, 1962.

United Press International and *American Heritage* Magazine, comps. *Four Days.* New York: American Heritage Publishing, 1964.

U.S. Congress. *Congress and the Nation, Volume 2, 1965–1968.* Washington, D.C.: Government Printing Office, 1968.

U.S. House. Committee on the Judiciary. *Circumstances Surrounding Destruction of the Lee Harvey Oswald Note.* 94th Cong., 1st sess., 1975.

———. Committee on the Judiciary. *Hearings Before the Subcommittee on Civil and Constitutional Rights of the Committee on the Judiciary.* 94th Cong., 1st sess., 1975.

———. Select Committee on Assassinations. *Investigation of the Assassination of President John F. Kennedy: Appendix to Hearings Before the*

Select Committee on Assassinations. 95th Cong., 2d sess., 7 vols., March 1979. (Abbreviated in notes as HSCA.)

———. Select Committee on Assassinations. *Hearings Before the Select Committee: Investigation of the Assassination of President John F. Kennedy.* 95th Cong., 2d sess., 5 vols., 1978. (Abbreviated in notes as HSCA.)

———. Select Committee on Assassinations. *Report of the Select Committee on Assassinations: Findings and Recommendations.* 95th Cong., 2d sess. H. Rpt. 95–1828, part 2. (Abbreviated in notes as HSCR.)

U.S. President's Commission on the Assassination of President John F. Kennedy. *Investigation of the Assassination of President John F. Kennedy: Hearings.* 26 vols. Washington, D.C.: U.S. Government Printing Office, 1964. (Abbreviated in notes as WC.)

———. *Report of the President's Commission on the Assassination of President John F. Kennedy.* Washington, D.C.: U.S. Government Printing Office, 1964. (Abbreviated in notes as WR.)

U.S. Senate. Select Committee to Study Governmental Operations with Respect to Intelligence Activities. *Alleged Assassination Plots Involving Foreign Leaders: An Interim Report.* 94th Cong., 1st sess., November 20, 1975. S. Rpt. 94–465.

———. *Final Report, Book Five, The Investigation of the Assassination of President John F. Kennedy: Performance of the Intelligence Agencies.* 94th Cong., 2d sess., 1976. S. Rpt. 94–755.

———. Committee on Rules and Administration. *Hearings on the Nomination of Gerald R. Ford of Michigan to Be Vice President of the U.S.* 93rd Cong., 1st sess., 1973.

Weisberg, Harold. *Oswald in New Orleans—Case for Conspiracy with the CIA.* New York: Canyon Books, 1967.

———. *Photographic Whitewash—Suppressed Kennedy Assassination Pictures.* Frederick, Md.: H. Weisberg, 1976.

———. *Post Mortem: JFK Assassination Cover-up Smashed!* Frederick, Md.: H. Weisberg, 1975.

———. *Whitewash.* Vols. I–IV. Hyattstown, Md.: H. Weisberg, 1965, 1966, 1967, 1974.

White, Theodore H. *The Making of the President, 1964.* New York: Atheneum, 1965.

Wilber, Charles G. *Medicolegal Investigation of the President John F. Kennedy Murder.* Springfield, Ill.: Charles C. Thomas, 1978.

Wills, Gary, and Ovid Demaris. *Jack Ruby: The Man Who Killed the Man Who Killed Kennedy.* New York: New American Library, 1967.

Wise, David, and Thomas B. Ross. *The Espionage Establishment.* New York: Random House, 1964.

———. *The Invisible Government.* New York: Random House, 1967.

———. *The U-2 Affair.* New York: Random House, 1962.

Wofford, Harris. *Of Kennedys and Kings.* New York: Farrar Straus Giroux, 1980.

Index